The Clinical Psychologist

The Clinical Psychologist

BACKGROUND, ROLES, AND FUNCTIONS

Bernard Lubin and Eugene E. Levitt

editors

ALDINETRANSACTION
A Division of Transaction Publishers
New Brunswick (U.S.A.) and London (U.K.)

First paperback printing 2009
Copyright © 1967 by Bernard Lubin and Eugene E. Levitt.

This book is printed on acid-free paper that meets the American National Standard for Permanence of Paper for Printed Library Materials.

Library of Congress Catalog Number: 2009016213
ISBN: 978-0-202-36270-0
Printed in the United States of America

Library of Congress Cataloging-in-Publication Data

The clinical psychologist : background, roles, and functions / Bernard Lubin and Eugene E. Levitt, editors.
      p. cm.
Originally published: Chicago : Aldine Pub., 1967.
Includes bibliographical references and index.
ISBN 978-0-202-36270-0
    1. Clinical psychologists. I. Lubin, Bernard, 1923- II. Levitt, Eugene E.

RC467.C578 2009
616.89--dc22

2009016213

Contents

PART IV: INTERPROFESSIONAL RELATIONS AND COMMUNICATION

PART V: INTERNATIONAL ASPECTS OF CLINICAL PSYCHOLOGY

PART VI: GENERAL INFORMATION

As a professional specialty and behavioral science, clinical psychology has grown so rapidly in the past two decades that even instructors and practitioners have a difficult time keeping up with current trends and developments. Accompanying this phenomenal growth are several recurring dilemmas and controversies over the nature of clinical psychology. Is it limited to the practice of psychology in a mental health setting? How does it differ from psychiatry, social work, or other professions in the mental health field? What is the scientific basis for clinical psychology? If the role of the clinical psychologist in our society is changing and his techniques are being modified, how can the interested student select wisely from among the many variations in graduate training programs to prepare himself as the clinical psychologist of the future?

These and many other questions are constantly asked by graduate students, academicians, concerned citizens, and even clinical psychologists themselves. The comprehensive, timely articles chosen for this book of readings focus on these important issues in a way that will appeal to professional and layman alike. Graduate instructors and practicum supervisors will find this collection of papers ideally suited for student seminars. Psychologists and other behavioral scientists will recognize many familiar issues that still remain unresolved as well as some new ones highlighted here for the first time. Formerly widely scattered and relatively inaccessible, most of these articles will prove invaluable to the seasoned professional and neophyte alike for some time to come. And for the growing number of laymen who serve on agency boards, who deal with legislation or program development, or who merely wish to be well informed about the background, roles, and functions of clinical psychologists, this set of articles will provide a welcome introduction to the subject.

At the time of the Boulder Conference in 1949, there was an urgent need to define the role of the clinical psychologist and to establish definite standards for graduate education and practicum training. Subsequent accreditation and support of graduate programs by the APA Education and Training Board, the Veterans Administration, and the National Institute of Mental Health proved to be a determining factor in crystallizing a definite pattern for the newly emerged profession. Establishing high standards for clinical psychology has invigorated all of the behavioral sciences while at the same time producing severe strains within psychology. Achieving an appropriate integration of academic and practicum experiences for students, finding a satisfactory balance between private practice and public health activities, coming to grips with the new emphasis upon community mental health, education, and social welfare, promoting new subspecialties and nondoctoral programs to meet the increased social demands, and establishing responsible standards of conduct and social control for psychologists are all major objectives of the profession that have yet to be fully attained.

Clinical psychologists have shown a high degree of adaptability in the past, but the real challenges are in the immediate future. With the momentous social forces currently at work in our society no one can predict, even for the next five years, what specific direction clinical psychology will take as it attempts to meet these challenges. It is to these challenging opportunities and risks that this book is so cogently addressed.

WAYNE H. HOLTZMAN
University of Texas

SPECIALIZATION within psychology has never been well understood by the public. This should not be too surprising; it is not clear within psychology itself. Psychologists whose specialties are announced by such modifiers as "educational," "social," "experimental," and so forth, do not make up homogenous groups either with respect to training or occupation. The sole specialty whose outlines are reasonably clear is clinical psychology. The entitlements, training, and pursuits of the clinical psychologist have become established with relative firmness over the past twenty years. The superior delineation is a result of greater need. Clinical psychology is the subarea of the field that deals most directly and frequently with public health and welfare. It is also the largest one within American psychology. About 37 per cent of the nearly 27,000 members of the American Psychological Association regard themselves as clinical psychologists.[1] This is about three times as great a number as the next ranking specialty, experimental psychology. Furthermore, clinical psychology's plurality is on the increase. The trend is irregular from year to year, but the proportion of clinical psychologists in APA has increased more than 4 per cent since 1957.

The growth of clinical psychology reflects a national demand, but it is not keeping pace with it. About two-thirds of the job openings advertised through employment facilities of the American Psychological Association in recent years called for clinical psychologists. About three positions are usually available for every registered job applicant. One explanation of the growing shortage is that it takes a substantial length of time to accumulate the educational requirements necessary for the practice of clinical psychology. All but a small fraction of clinical psychologists currently in practice possess graduate degrees. About 60 per

cent hold the doctorate, usually a Ph.D., and another 37 per cent have a master's degree. It requires an average of more than nine years of graduate education and training to obtain the clinical doctorate, while other specialty groups, such as experimental psychologists, require less than six years on the average.

Government has been the heaviest contributor to the increased demand for clinical psychologists. A plurality of clinical psychologists—about 39 per cent—are now employed by governmental agencies. The next largest subgroup is the university, which employs almost 20 per cent. Thirteen per cent are self-employed, and 12 per cent work for non-profit hospitals and clinics. The remaining 7 per cent are employed by private industry and a variety of organizations.

Despite variations in employment setting, a majority of clinical psychologists—about 55 per cent—are engaged primarily in clinical practice. This usually consists of diagnostic evaluation and psychotherapy or other treatment procedures, in approximately equal proportions. It is not surprising to find that two-thirds of clinical psychologists regard clinical practice as the area of their greatest professional competence. A growing number of clinicians, however, are employed primarily as researchers. At present, this includes 8 per cent in general research endeavors and another 13 per cent in test development. About 11 per cent regard themselves primarily as teachers and about 9 per cent as administrators. The latter figure is probably also growing.

As clinical psychology proliferates, it spreads into more and more avenues of our society. This advance is accompanied by a need in many circles to know something about the clinical psychologist, his background and training, and the nature of his functioning in various settings. Such information would be valuable to potential employers, members of other disciplines and occupations with whom the clinical psychologist interacts or works in a multidisciplinary structure, and students interested in the profession as a career. This volume of readings is addressed to all these groups and

---

[1] Most of the normative data in this introduction are taken from "Information about Psychologists," by R. F. Lockman and F. M. Throne, in *Preconference Materials Prepared for the Conference on the Professional Preparation of Clinical Psychologists* (Washington, D.C.: American Psychological Association, 1965).

especially to the student. We believe that it can be of substantial value in undergraduate and graduate courses in clinical and counseling psychology, in medical psychology, and in seminars in professional problems in psychology. It can contribute to appropriate courses for students preparing for careers in medicine, psychiatry, psychiatric social work, psychiatric nursing, and other disciplines. It may also serve to acquaint the general public with this largest specialty of American psychology.

The substantive material of this book is contained in the 51 articles and reports which compose Sections I through VI. The history of clinical psychology is summarized in Section I. Section II deals with the training of the clinical psychologist, viewed from a number of different angles; the first four papers in the section derive from a conference held prior to the American Psychological Association convention in 1965, and represent the most current thinking.

Section III details the broad range of roles and functions that characterize the science and profession of clinical psychology, while the critically important area of interprofessional relations and communication is taken up in Section IV. Section V surveys the practice of clinical psychology in other countries. Section VI contains three articles that are clearly of consequence to clinical psychology but that do not logically fit into any of the previous sections.

We are grateful to the various authors and publishers who permitted us to reproduce the contents of this book. We are especially indebted to Joseph D. Matarazzo and Alexander J. Morin for their perceptive assistance in the final selection of articles to be included. We also wish to thank Alice W. Lubin for the compilation of the index which contributes to the usefulness of the book.

BERNARD LUBIN
EUGENE E. LEVITT

THE CLINICAL
PSYCHOLOGIST

I
HISTORICAL PERSPECTIVES

Historians are fond of saying that the study of history sharpens the perspective of the current scene. To understand what has gone before improves the comprehension of what is now. We trust that the historians are correct in their conjecture and have hence included in this compendium a section on the history of clinical psychology.

It has been said that psychology in general has a long history but a brief existence as yet. This is true of clinical psychology in 1967. Its history dates back identifiably to the nineteenth century, but the actual establishment of the specialty was a consequence of World War II, as Watson and Rotter clearly show. The former presents broad trends up to the immediate postwar decade. Rotter's account adds the developments of the succeeding ten years and treats the subject matter more specifically in terms of the major functions of the clinical psychologist as they are presented in Part III.

The 1947 report of the Shakow Committee on clinical training is included here because of its great influence on contemporary clinical psychology. The so-called Shakow Plan, which is the substance of the 1947 report, has been the basis of formal training of the clinical psychologist for the past two decades. It deserves an eminent place of its own in any historical account of clinical psychology.

1. *A Brief History of Clinical Psychology*

ROBERT I. WATSON

CLINICAL psychologists have been surprisingly ahistorical. Very little thought has been given to, and less written about, the origin and development of clinical psychology. In the literature there are articles and books which interpret historically various special aspects or evaluate related fields, some of which have been of considerable help in preparing this paper. Nevertheless, whatever the reasons, there is no available general account of the history of clinical psychology from the perspective of today.

In part, this neglect is due to the upsurge of interest in clinical psychological activity during and following the second World War. Since then, clinical psychologists have had little time to spend inquiring into their origins. Then, too, their day-to-day activities impress them as so new and vital that they are hardly to blame for tacitly accepting that they are pioneers and that somewhere in the chaos of war and its aftermath was born a new profession having little or no relation to what went before. The state of affairs today is curiously reminiscent of the situation found by Kimball Young in 1923 in tracing the history of mental testing. He remarked, "Making history on every hand as we are, we have a notion that we somehow have escaped history" (*121, p. 1*).

To capture in full measure the sweep and continuity of the history of clinical psychology is beyond the competence of the reviewer, to say nothing of space limitations. In order to do justice to all aspects of the subject one would have to deal with the complex history of the psychology of motivation and dynamic psychology. Similarly, all the ramifications of the relation of clinical psychology to the rest of the field of psychology, of which it is an integral part, as well as an account

Reprinted from *The Psychological Bulletin*, 1953, 50, 321–346, by permission of the American Psychological Association and the author. Dr. Watson is Professor of Psychology and Director of the Graduate Training Program in Clinical Psychology at Northwestern University.

of the history of test development would have to be considered.

The present account, perforce, presents an examination of men and ideas influential in shaping clinical psychology. But, since psychology is now a profession, attention must also be devoted to those internal and external controls which characterize a profession and to the settings in which the professional practice is conducted.

In presenting a historical account the question arises concerning the most appropriate date at which to begin. With some justification it was decided that since clinical psychology, as we know it, arose at about the turn of the present century it would be appropriate to begin with the immediate forerunners of this first generation of clinical psychologists. The origins of clinical psychology, the first major section of this account, are to be found in the psychometric and dynamic traditions in psychology; the psychologist in the settings of the psychological clinic, child guidance, mental hospitals, institutions for the mentally defective; and the beginnings of psychology as a profession. Somewhat arbitrarily this early pioneer work is considered to come to a close with the end of the second decade of this century. This is followed by a section concerned with clinical psychology in the twenties and thirties. The same topics just mentioned, e.g., the dynamic tradition and psychology as a profession, are again considered. The work of psychologists in the armed services during the second World War and its effect upon psychology in the postwar period are next evaluated. A brief overview of clinical psychology today closes the account.

THE ORIGINS OF CLINICAL PSYCHOLOGY: THE PSYCHOMETRIC TRADITION

This tradition, one of the headwaters from which clinical psychology sprang, was, in turn, a part of the scientific tradition of the nineteenth century. With all the limitations with which it is charged today, it is to this movement that the clinical psychologist owes much of his scientific standing and tradition. Whenever a clinical psychologist insists upon objectivity and the need for further research, he is, wittingly or otherwise, showing the influence of this tradition. Moving with Galton through Binet and Terman, this tradition met the demand that psychology, if it was to become a science, must share with other sciences the respect for quantitative measurement.

Psychometrics as a tool for clinical psychology owes its beginnings to Francis Galton (53) in England. Grappling as he was with the problem of individual differences, he and his followers did much to lay the groundwork for the investigation of ability by using observations of an individual's performance for information on individual differences. He thus founded mental tests.

In 1890 Cattell (29) introduced the term "mental tests" in an article describing tests which he had used at the University of Pennsylvania. Even at that date he was pleading for standardization of procedure and the establishment of norms. From the time of his days as a student of Wundt's, Cattell was interested in the problem of individual differences and did much to stimulate further investigation. Along with Thorndike and Woodworth, he also stressed dealing with individual differences by means of statistical analysis—a really new approach at this time. Some of these investigations, both from Cattell's laboratory and from others in various parts of the country, made positive contributions to various facets of the problem of psychometric measurement. For example, Norsworthy (82) in 1906 compared normal and defective children by means of tests and found the latter not a "species apart," pointing out that the more intelligent of the feebleminded were practically indistinguishable from the least intelligent of the normal.

Most of the investigations of the time were concerned with simple sensorimotor and associative functions and were based on the assumption that intelligence could be reduced to sensations and motor speed, an attempt which, as is now known, was doomed to failure. Furthermore, although more suitable verbal material was used, the studies of college students at Cornell, such as Sharp's (95), and the Wissler study (113) at Columbia, were found to be essentially nonpredictive. What the workers failed to take into account was that the college students are a highly selected group having a considerably restricted range. The negative finding of these studies effec-

tively blocked further investigation at the college level for years. When one stops to consider that the dominant systematic position of the day was the structuralism of Titchener, who had banished tests as nonscientific, it is no wonder that "tests" were viewed with at least a touch of condescension.

In the meantime Binet had been working in France developing his tests based on a wider sampling of behavior than had yet been used. His success in dealing with the intellectual classification of Paris school children is well known and needs no amplification at this point. The translation of his tests and their use in this country followed shortly after the turn of the century. It was Goddard (simultaneously with Healy), a student of G. Stanley Hall, who introduced the Binet tests to this country. Through a visit abroad and contact with Decroly, he became acquainted with Binet's work (121). In 1910 he began publishing findings with the test and in 1911 published his revision of the 1908 Binet Scale. This revision, along with Kuhlmann's, also published in 1911, gained some popularity among clinicians, but the subsequent development by Terman far overshadowed their work.

Probably the test that had the most influence upon trends in clinical psychology was the Terman Revision of the Binet Scale (83). In fact, for years the major task of the clinical psychologist was to administer the Stanford-Binet. In view of the importance of this test it is desirable to present in some detail the background of its development.

Lewis M. Terman (101) received his graduate training at Clark just after the turn of the century under Hall, Sanford, and Burnham. As Terman put it, "For me, Clark University meant briefly three things: freedom to work as I pleased, unlimited library facilities and Hall's Monday evening seminar. Any one of these outweighed all the lectures I attended" (101, p. 315). This influence of Hall's was more from the enthusiasm he inspired and the wide scope of his interests than from his scientific caution and objectivity. Sanford was his doctoral adviser, but Terman chose his own problem in the area of differentiation of "bright" and "dull" groups by means of tests and worked it through more or less independently.

By a severely limited survey such as this it would be easy to give the impression that little or nothing else was being done along the lines under discussion except that reported. Terman was not alone in his interest in the development and standardization of tests by any manner of means. In his autobiography Terman (101) mentions as known to him in 1904 the work of Binet,

Galton, Bourdon, Oehrn, Ebbinghaus, Kraepelin, Aschaffenburg, Stern, Cattell, Wissler, Thorndike, Gilbert, Jastrow, Bolton, Thompson, Spearman, Sharp, and Kuhlmann.

At the suggestion of Huey, who had been working in Adolf Meyer's clinic at Johns Hopkins, Terman, undeterred by the prevailing hostile attitude of most psychologists, began work with the 1908 Binet Scale and in 1916 published the Stanford Revision of the Binet-Simon tests. Terman's interest in both the test and results from it continued unabated, resulting in still another revision in 1937.

Performance tests, so necessary for work with the linguistically handicapped, actually antedated the Stanford-Binet. The Seguin, Witmer, and Healy form boards and other performance tests were already in clinical use. Norms, although not lacking, were undeveloped, and the directions placed a high premium on language. What seemed to be needed was a battery of performance tests sampling a variety of functions and not as dependent upon language. Among the earliest to appear and to come into fairly common use was the Pintner-Paterson Scale of Performance Tests (*85*), published in 1917. Included in this scale were several form boards, a manikin and a feature-profile construction test, a picture completion test, a substitution test, and a cube-tapping test.

Another major step was the development of group tests under the impetus of the need for large scale testing of recruits in World War I. This testing program is described with a wealth of detail by Yerkes (*120*). Although group tests were not unknown before the war, as witness those described in Whipple's *Manual of Mental and Physical Tests* (*110*), the need for quick appraisal of the basic intelligence of a large number of men provided the impetus for extensive development. The *Alpha* scale for literate English-speaking recruits and the *Beta* scale for illiterates and non-English-speaking recruits were developed rapidly under this demand. The Woodworth Personal Data Sheet (*118*), the first of a long line of psychoneurotic inventories, also was a product of military needs. So successful were these tests in overcoming the prejudices against testing both within the field of psychology and in the general public that after the war a veritable flood of group tests appeared. Many extensive surveys in the public schools were made for classificatory purposes. Further developments in this tradition during the twenties and thirties will be appraised after examination of other aspects of the origin of clinical psychology.

A major source of influence contributing to the growth of clinical psychology was the thinking and writing of the "Boston group" who promulgated "the new psychology"—William James, G. Stanley Hall, and their associates. Although in no way could they be labeled clinical psychologists, their thinking was much closer to the heart of the clinical psychology movement and to progressive psychiatry than was the structural point of view of Titchener. Heresy though it may be, it cannot be denied that at that time academic psychology had relatively little to contribute to clinical psychology. Psychology, to be sure, had been placed by Fechner, Helmholtz, Wundt, Kraepelin, and others upon a scientific, quantitative foundation instead of being permitted to remain an indistinguishable cohort of philosophy. This was an essential step without which there could have been no clinical psychology; nevertheless, a sensationalistic approach to conscious intellectual experience offered relatively little for the clinical method and the profession with which it was to be associated.

The psychiatry of the day was in the main concerned with pathology and the search for an explanation of mental disturbances in disease processes. Kraepelin (*68*) had introduced clarity through his classification of mental disease, but at the expense of deeper understanding. Based upon symptoms and primarily descriptive in character, his classification served to diminish—even to discourage—in its users any urge toward understanding the psychological dynamics.

French psychiatric thinking and research profoundly influenced James (*80*). The work of Janet and Charcot was particularly important in this connection. With Morton Prince, he did much to stimulate interest in the phenomena of dissociation, feeling as he did that it was a fruitful method of investigation of personality functioning. Early in his career he recognized the value of a clinical approach which led him "whenever possible to approach the mind by way of its pathology" (*77*, *p. 20*).

The influence of James was expressed primarily through his *Principles of Psychology* (*65*), published in 1890, and to a lesser degree by his *Varieties of Religious Experience* (*66*), published in 1902. Both of these works were sufficiently removed from the otherwise prevailing psychological thinking of his day to be considered major pre-Freudian, dynamic influences. The choice of the term *dynamic* in this context is neither idle nor wishful thinking. James himself used the term to distinguish his point of view from the structural approach of Titchener (*86*).

Concerning the influence of the *Principles*, Morris had this to say:

> Great books are either reservoirs or watersheds. They sum up and transmit the antecedent past, or they initiate the flow of the future. Sixty years after its publication, the *Principles* appears to be one of the major watersheds of twentieth-century thought. Directly or indirectly, its influence had penetrated politics, jurisprudence, sociology, education and the arts. In the domain of psychology, it had foreshadowed nearly all subsequent developments of primary importance. Viewed introspectively, the permanent significance of the *Principles* was incentive. It explored possibilities and indicated directions. These led, eventually, into social, applied and experimental psychology; into the study of exceptional mental states, subliminal consciousness and psychopathology. Because of its extreme fertility in the materials for hypothesis, most of the competitive schools of psychological theory that arose during the first half of the century could claim common ancestry in the *Principles* for at some point it implied their basic assumptions (*77, p. 15*).

This aptly catches James's influence on clinical psychology, not through work directly in the field or with the method, but through the fertile (and contradictory) character of his thinking.

In addition to the stimulation of his writings, James did take specific action of direct relevance to clinical psychology in his support of Clifford W. Beers, whose book, *A Mind that Found Itself* (*19*), did so much to further the mental hygiene movement. This he did through an endorsing letter which appeared in the first edition and, according to Henry James, his son, by departing from his fixed policy of "keeping out of Committees and Societies" (*64, p. 273*). In addition, he was interested in psychical research and in the efforts of Freud and Jung, although dubious about both of these trends (*64*).

Obviously it is impossible to capture the full flavor of William James in a paragraph or two, but this "defender of unregimented ideas" is at the least the eccentric brilliant uncle of the men in clinical psychology who followed after.

Another of the pioneers of this time and place was G. Stanley Hall. He was more influenced by the evolutionary concept stemming from Darwin than by French psychopathological thinking. Shakow, in considering Hall's influence on psychiatry, so well summarizes his contributions that they may be seen as contributions to clinical psychology as well. He writes that it was:

> Hall, the propagandist, who gave Freud his first academic hearing, who gave courses in Freudian psychology beginning in 1908 and whose pressure for its consideration remained life-long; Hall, who influenced Cowles in establishing the psychological

laboratory at McLean Hospital which had as directors following Hoch, Franz, Wells and Lundholm; Hall, who stimulated Adolf Meyer, by his early interest in child study, to write his first paper on a psychiatric topic—*Mental Abnormalities in Children during Primary Education . . .* —and who did so much to make the country child-conscious; Hall, whose students Goddard and Huey (also Meyer's students at the Worcester State Hospital) did the early pioneer work on feeblemindedness . . . ; Hall, whose bravery in handling the problem of sex did so much to break down the first barriers, thus greatly facilitating the later child guidance handling of this and related problems; Hall, whose student Terman achieved so much in the development of the Binet method in the United States and whose student Gesell did so much for other aspects of developmental psychology; Hall, whose journals regularly published material of psychopathological interest; Hall, the ramifications of whose psychological influence are most pervasive in fields related to psychopathology. . . (*92, p. 430*).

Certain other factors might also be mentioned. Before his period as president of Clark University, Hall, while at Johns Hopkins, held weekly clinics at Bay View Hospital and, until its medical staff was organized under his direction, served as lay superintendent. For a period of years he taught and demonstrated for psychiatrists at Worcester State Hospital, handing over the actual instruction in 1895 to Adolf Meyer, but continuing his interest in the field (*74*). Other students of this period who made substantial contributions to clinical psychology included Blanchard, Conkin, Kuhlmann, and Mateer.

Something of the spirit and activity of the associates of these men may be captured by an examination of the journal that was begun early in the century. *The Journal of Abnormal Psychology*, later called *The Journal of Abnormal and Social Psychology*, was a major source publication of the more enlightened efforts of its time. Until 1913, when the *Psychoanalytic Review* was founded, it was the only journal in which psychoanalytic papers were published (*32*). Founded in 1906 for the express purpose of serving both medicine and psychology, it had as its editor Morton Prince, later professor of psychology at Harvard University, and numbered among its associate editors Hugo Münsterberg, James Putnam, August Hoch, Boris Sidis, Charles L. Dana, and Adolf Meyer. The papers in the first issue aptly catch the various influences at work in the psychology and psychiatry of the day. The first is a paper by Janet and thus represents the French psychopathological school; the second concerns hypnosis; the third, a critique of Freud by Putnam (the first article in English calling attention to Freud's work); and the fourth, a paper by Morton Prince concerning his most famous case of multiple personality, Miss Beauchamps. The first book review in this new journal was that of Freud's *Psychopathology of Everyday Life*, which had been published in Germany in 1904. So far as this writer is aware, the first critical article concerning psychoanalysis by an American psychologist appeared in the February 1909 issue of this journal. It was entitled "An Interpretation of the Psychoanalytic Method in Psychotherapy with a Report of a Case so Treated" (*90*). This is apparently the second instance of a report of personal psychotherapeutic experience by a psychologist. Its author, known for endeavors in fields far removed from this, was Walter Dill Scott, the psychologist, later president of Northwestern University.

The situation in the official psychiatric journal may be used for contrast. The first psychoanalytic paper to appear in the *American Journal of Insanity* was in the October 1909 issue. This paper was by Ernest Jones of Toronto and deplored the fact that Freud's methods had been neglected. None of Freud's books was reviewed in this journal for some years and, indeed, the first review to appear was that of Brill's *Psychoanalysis* in July 1914.

Isador Coriat (*32*), in presenting some reminiscences of psychoanalysis in Boston, attributes the interest in psychotherapy there to stimulation of William James. Although A. A. Brill began psychoanalytic practice in New York in 1908, he was the only psychiatrist in the United States at that time engaging in such practice. He, Putnam, and Ernest Jones, then of Toronto, were the first in America to do active work with psychoanalytic methods. The first English translation of a work by Freud, *Selected Papers on Hysteria*, appeared in 1909 according to Coriat (*32*). It was in this same year that G. Stanley Hall, as president of Clark University, invited both Freud and Jung to come to the United States to lecture on the occasion of the twentieth anniversary of Clark University. Both by attendance and by the subsequent publication of these lectures in the *American Journal of Psychology* (*51*) psychologists became more familiar with their work. In the meantime, Brill (*23*) was translating Freud's works, and other psychoanalysts began practice. By 1911 there was enough interest that the first psychoanalytic association, the New York Psychoanalytic Society, was founded.

In view of these factors in the history of clinical psychology, it is possible to offer the interpretation that actually it was partly the psychologists and not psychiatrists alone, as is commonly supposed, who offered the first support to psychoanalysis in the United States. To be sure, in the twenties the psychiatrists in increasing numbers became interested and during the following twenty years became so firmly identified with the field that it is only today that psychologists, as psychologists, are again beginning to assume any prominence in psychoanalytic thinking and practice.

THE PSYCHOLOGIST AND THE PSYCHOLOGICAL CLINIC

It has been accepted by psychologists quite generally that the case leading to the founding of the first psychological clinic was treated by Lightner Witmer (*114*) at the University of Pennsylvania in March 1896. Witmer was the first to speak of the "psychological clinic," of "clinical psychology," and the "clinical method in psychology" (*26*). The history of his clinic has been discussed elsewhere (*26, 27, 93, 107, 114*) and is quite well known. It is, therefore, unnecessary to dwell upon it. Instead, after very briefly examining its functioning, attention will be given to the extent of its influence upon the history of clinical psychology.

Even a cursory examination of the early issues of the *Psychological Clinic*, a journal founded and edited by Witmer, will show that the work attempted in this clinic included referral to medical sources, the presence of social workers, and many other "modern" innovations discussed by the writer elsewhere (*107*). On the other hand, although the juvenile court and social agencies referred cases to Witmer's clinic, the great majority came from the school system. Much attention was paid to the relation of physical defects and neurological conditions to behavior problems. Cooperation with special teachers of the blind and deaf and the mentally defective was stressed. In general, intellectual aspects of children's problems was emphasized, using a biographical approach. Relatively few psychologists published in the *Psychological Clinic* in the early years. Educators, either teachers, principals, or professors, wrote the majority of the articles during this period. In later years the publications of psychologists predominated. The articles are chiefly of antiquarian interest today.

The clinic founded by Seashore (*91*) at the University of Iowa about 1910 was modeled after Witmer's clinic, and others, such as that founded by J. E. W. Wallin of the University of Pittsburgh in 1912, undoubtedly owe part of their impetus to it, but many other psychological clinics and activities seemed to grow up independently and with little knowledge of the development of this first clinic (97). For example, Seashore (91) speaks of his as the "second" psychological clinic. And yet in 1914 Wallin (105) found about 20 psychological clinics to be in existence, of which some at least must have developed under a different tradition except in the rather unlikely event that the great majority were founded after 1910, but before 1914. Although the Witmer clinic has been functioning continuously since its inception, it is quite difficult to find evidence of its effects upon clinical psychology today. This has not been due to lack of local support; rather it is because its influence did not spread beyond Philadelphia to any considerable degree. The reasons for this relative lack of influence will be discussed after considering a related development: the child guidance movement.

THE PSYCHOLOGISTS IN CHILD GUIDANCE

Still another stream which merged into the torrent that is clinical psychology today came from the so-called child guidance movement. In this effort William Healy (59), a psychiatrist, was the most important early figure. The beginnings of this movement arose from the conviction that antisocial behavior was treatable by psychiatric means. A subsequently discarded tenet which went hand in hand with this conviction was an emphasis upon pathology. Hence the first "child guidance" clinic, at the time of its founding in Chicago in 1909, was called "The Juvenile Psychopathic Institute." It is perhaps prophetic that the selection of Healy for the position of director was "as a pupil of James and a free lance in competition with a more rigid Wundtian and experimentally and statistically minded psychologist" (76, p. 242). Its first staff was very small, consisting of Dr. Healy, as psychiatrist, Dr. Grace M. Fernald, as psychologist, and one secretary. It is important to note that no social worker was a paid member of the staff, but Healy indicates that social workers from cooperating agencies worked with them from the very beginning. Only later did the specialty of psychiatric social worker, as such, emerge. Mental testing by Fernald, and later by Augusta F. Bronner, emphasized performance testing and other instruments of local origin. In 1910, however, Healy introduced the Binet-Simon tests into the United States (as did Goddard at Vineland simultaneously and independently). A direct out-

growth of the use of this and other instruments was the publication in 1927 of a *Manual of Individual Tests and Testing* (25) by Bronner, Healy, and their co-workers. Both Healy and Bronner had migrated eastward, organizing in 1917 a clinic in Boston under the name of Judge Baker Foundation, later changed to the Judge Baker Guidance Center. This venture was enormously successful and resulted in still further important work in the field of delinquency. Many publications, including several books upon problems of the delinquent, had considerable influence upon patterns in this field.

In contrasting the relative success of Healy's venture and its continuity with the present with the relative lack of influence of Witmer's clinic, Shakow (92) presents a thoughtfully detailed statement, one or two points of which can be mentioned. The psychologist Witmer was concerned with intellectual aspects of the functioning individual, worked primarily with mental defectives or school retardation problems, when concerned with medical aspects focused more on the physical or neurological, and, most important of all, identified himself with the Wundt-Kraepelin point of view. On the other hand, the psychiatrist Healy was concerned with affective aspects of the personality, worked primarily with behavior problems and delinquency, when concerned with medical problems stressed the psychiatric, and, again most important of all, was profoundly influenced by James and Freud. Although a pioneer, Witmer turned has back on almost all that was to predominate in the later days of clinical psychology and became of historical significance only. Healy is still a contemporary.

THE PSYCHOLOGIST IN MENTAL HOSPITALS

The importance of McLean Hospital in Waverly, Massachusetts, has never been fully appreciated in the history of psychiatry and psychology. Founded in 1818, its superintendent at the turn of the century was Dr. Edward Cowles, a former surgeon in the Union Army. Years later he took some incidental training in psychology at Johns Hopkins (57). In many ways he was a man ahead of his time. He encouraged research and brought to this hospital biochemists, pathologists, physiologists, and psychologists. One could date the beginnings of conjoint medicine as taking place at McLean Hospital since these approaches were used in its laboratory some time before 1894.

In that year Hall described the laboratory as follows: "The work of this laboratory was begun in 1889, for the clinical purposes of the hospital. It is sought to combine neurological studies in the departments of psychiatry and physiological psychology, and their relations with anatomical and chemical pathology, etc." (*57, p. 358*). Only a quotation from Cowles will bring out the contemporary ring of his words:

> The purpose of establishing and developing the laboratory has been carried on under much difficulty, naturally due to the newness of the attempt to combine with psychiatry the other departments of scientific medical research. The pathology of the terminal stages of insanity must be studied as heretofore, and it is necessary to add that of the initial conditions which lead to mental disorder. Such studies must therefore be combined with physiological psychology in the attempt to determine the exact nature and causes of departures from normal mental function. Also, in the dependence of these changes upon general physiological processes, and in order to take into account all the elements of vital activity involved, it is supremely necessary to study both physiological and pathological chemistry in their direct and indirect relations to mental changes (*57, p. 363*).

Research effort along these lines apparently first emerged from this laboratory. In presenting the history of psychiatric research, Whitehorn (*111*) recognized this contribution and first described McLean Hospital and its work before dealing with any other developments.

Cowles, in a review of the progress in psychiatry at the time of the fiftieth anniversary of the American Psychiatric Association in 1894, emphasized the importance of what he referred to as the systems of "new psychology" as one of the "most hopeful signs of progress" to bring about advancement in the understanding of mental diseases (*34*). Either as frequent visitors from nearby Boston or as members of the staff of McLean Hospital at this time were Morton Prince, August Hoch, Boris Sidis, and Adolf Meyer. Interest in psychology is shown by the fact that Cowles and William Noyes, of the same hospital, were among the approximately 13 to 18 individuals who were present at the founding of the American Psychological Association at Clark University in 1892 (*36*).

In 1893 August Hoch (*75*) was selected by Cowles to be psychologist and pathologist at McLean. The use of the term *psychologist* was neither idle nor esoteric. Having previously received a medical education, he now was sent abroad for further training, and it would appear that much of his training was in psychology with Wundt, Külpe,

Marbe, and Kiesow. He also worked with Kraepelin. On assuming his post at McLean he turned to work with the ergograph in clinical problems and in the first volume of the *Psychological Bulletin* (*62*) summed up experimentation in this field. Subsequently, as professor of psychiatry at Cornell and director of the Psychiatric Institute, he turned to more narrowly psychiatric problems, but there would appear to be little doubt that during this period at McLean he functioned, in part at least, as a psychologist.

It was in this atmosphere that a psychological laboratory was founded. This laboratory was begun in 1904 at McLean Hospital by Shepard Ivory Franz (*50*). It was influential in the *rapprochement* of psychology and psychopathology, although often interested in matters more physiological than psychological. The laboratory became established under the direction of Franz, and on his leaving for what is now St. Elizabeth's Hospital of Washington, E. Lyman Wells was appointed his successor and remained there until 1921.

Franz continued his interest while in Washington, not only writing such articles with a modern ring, although published in 1912, as "The Present Status of Psychology in Medical Education and Practice" (*25*), but also introducing in 1907 a routine clinical psychological examination of all new patients in a mental hospital setting. This was probably the first instance of routine psychological testing of psychiatric hospital patients. Among Franz's associates during the early period were Grace H. Kent and Edwin G. Boring, both of whom published on learning in dementia praecox. Although Boring, as is well known, returned to other fields, he nevertheless felt that the summer he spent in the hospital was a very valuable, broadening experience (*22*). From 1906 to 1921 Grace H. Kent was psychologist at Philadelphia Hospital, Kings' Park State Hospital, and St. Elizabeths, respectively. In 1922 she went to Worcester State Hospital, remaining there until 1926 (*79*). Thereafter, for many years she was at Danvers State Hospital.

THE PSYCHOLOGIST AND INSTITUTIONS FOR THE MENTALLY DEFECTIVE

It was Goddard's laboratory at the Vineland Training School that was the second center to be devoted to the psychological study of the feeble-minded. Henry H. Goddard became director of psychological research at this institution in 1906 and was influential in the establishment of the psychologist as a person working with the mentally defective. As mentioned earlier, he first translated and used the Binet in this country. For practical purposes, the use of the Binet was at this time almost exclusively restricted to the feebleminded. It was from this center that the Binet spread to other institutions (84). His directorship continued until almost the twenties.

PSYCHOLOGY AS A PROFESSION

It was as early as 1904 that Cattell (30) made the prediction that there would eventually be a profession as well as a science of psychology. Actually professional action preceded this pronouncement.

For purposes of this presentation the relevant characteristics of a profession include establishment of commonly agreed-upon practices concerning relationship with colleagues and with the public served. The questions of competency and the means of controlling competency immediately arise. Traditionally, a profession controls competency among its own members. Thus, self-determined control of its members is the hallmark of a profession.

The first stirrings of attempts at control arose in the American Psychological Association and took the form of considering control of clinical procedure through evaluation of test data. In 1895, only three years after the founding of the Association, J. Mark Baldwin, in the words of Fernberger, "proposed the formation of a committee to consider the feasibility of cooperation among the psychological laboratories for the collection of mental and physical statistics" (43, p. 42). The committee that was appointed, chaired by Cattell, called itself "The Committee on Physical and Mental Tests," but the battery of tests they proposed for try-out to develop norms gained little acceptance so that after 1899 no further word was heard from this committee. Another committee for the purpose of establishing methods of testing was appointed in 1907 and continued until 1919. It made some progress, for example, sponsoring research on the Woodworth-Wells Association Tests, but it fell far short of the ostensible goal.

In 1915, on the motion of Guy M. Whipple, the Association went on record as "discouraging" the use of mental tests by unqualified individuals. In 1917 a committee to consider qualifications for psychological examiners was appointed, and two

years later one to consider certifying "consulting" psychologists. In 1919 the Section of Clinical Psychology within the American Psychological Association was formed (43). In large measure, it was a "special interest group" concerned with arranging programs at the annual meetings and the like. Its members were, however, drawn into the discussion, pro and con, of the merits of certification. After much maneuvering, favorable action on certification of clinical psychologists finally resulted, and the first certificates were granted after the 1921 meeting. However, only twenty-five psychologists applied, and the project was abandoned. The death blow was dealt by an APA policy committee which considered that certification was not practicable and, on vote of the APA membership in 1927, discontinued certification. In some measure at least, the decision was influenced by the realization that with certification went the problem of enforcement of the standards instituted, especially on psychological workers outside the membership. Thereafter, according to Fernberger (43), there was a period of some years without important action within the American Psychological Association on these problems.

Internship training, as distinguished from academic course work, is a manifestation of professional training. Morrow (78) indicates that Lightner Witmer was apparently the first to suggest practical work for the psychologist through training school and laboratory. However, the first actual internships were those offered by the Training School in Vineland, New Jersey, under the supervision of H. H. Goddard. This program began in 1908 and has continued down to the present time. In 1909 William Healy began accepting graduate students at the Juvenile Psychopathic Institute in Chicago, while the first internship in a psychiatric institution for adults was established in 1913 at the Boston Psychopathic Hospital under the direction of Robert M. Yerkes. Other earlier internships include those at Worcester State Hospital, McLean Hospital, the Western State Penitentiary in Pennsylvania, and the New York Institute for Child Guidance.

CLINICAL PSYCHOLOGY IN THE TWENTIES AND THIRTIES

In the twenties and thirties clinical psychology left the period of its lusty, disorganized infancy and entered its rather undernourished but rapid and stormy adolescence. As late as 1918 only 15 members or 4 per cent of the APA listed the field of clinical psychology as a research interest (*44*). This rose to 99 members or 19 per cent in 1937. In that year the newly instituted membership category of Associate showed 428 or 28 per cent interested in clinical psychology, the largest field of interest for this class of membership. In increasing numbers clinical psychologists were employed in hospitals, clinics, schools, penal institutions, social agencies, homes for the feebleminded, industrial plants, and the entire gamut of agencies concerned with human welfare. For example, Finch and Odoroff (*46*), in a survey concerning employment trends, indicate that of 1,267 members of the American Psychological Association in 1931, 286 or 26.9 per cent were not in teaching positions. In 1940 the number of nonteachers had swelled to 888 or 39.3 per cent of the membership. Clinical nonteachers increased from 95 to 272 during this ten-year period.

It was during this period that many psychologists did yeoman service for clinical psychology without being primarily identified with the field. Carl E. Seashore (*91*) may be used as an illustration. It has already been noted that he founded a psychological clinic at the University of Iowa about 1910. During the period now under consideration he was interested in the relationship between psychology and psychiatry and took the lead in organizing a national conference on this topic. He also aided in founding the Iowa Psychopathic Hospital and worked with Samuel Orton, Edward Lee Travis, and Wendell Johnson in speech pathology. Many other men such as Gardner Murphy, Goodwin Watson, Horace B. English, Albert T. Poffenberger, Kurt Lewin, Carney Landis, Robert M. Yerkes, Walter R. Miles, Gordon W. Allport, and Kurt Goldstein, although primarily associated with some other aspects of psychology, also performed services for the clinical field.

In spite of such developments as those just described, Loutitt (*70*) could indicate during the same period that "American Psychology, generally speaking, has not been greatly interested in practical problems of human behavior" (*70, p. 361*). This contention applied to clinical psychology with as much force as, or more than, it did to other applications of psychology. Most of the difficulties that clinical psychology went through during this period as it groped toward professional stature were internal to the field itself. Both rapid growth and some hostility from the dominant entrenched forces in psychology are imbedded in the history of the period and influence many of the specific developments now to be discussed.

THE PSYCHOMETRIC TRADITION

This period of the twenties was, in the words of Merrill, a "plateau . . . [following] the initial impetus given to testing when these first tools of the clinician were being subjected to evaluation, and the exaggerated expectations of over-enthusiastic users were being reduced in the crucibles of research" (*73, p. 283*). Studies of validity, investigations of the constancy of IQ, application of the tests to new populations, studies of individual differences, the nature-nurture controversy, racial differences, the development of group testing, achievement tests, interest measures, and personality testing of the questionnaire variety occupied this and the following decade and helped to consolidate the gains of the previous period. Theories of intelligence and factor analysis are also intimately related to this trend. It was a period, as the term plateau implies, of marked gain which prepared the way for the present period.

More and more objections began to be raised to the limitations entailed by this approach. The development of group tests during and after World War I placed a premium on easy reproduction, rigid standardization down to the slightest detail, and emphasis on the score obtained to the exclusion of all else. Measures of personality with these same characteristics were developed during the twenties and thirties. To some psychologists the results obtained were considered disappointing and sterile.

In 1927 F. L. Wells published *Mental Tests in Clinical Practice* (*108*), in which he stated vividly the major objection to a rigid psychometric approach:

An intelligent South Sea Islander, observing a psychometric examination, would be likely to regard it as a magic rite designed to propitiate friendly spirits in the patient's behalf. Should he observe a conscientious examiner in the apprentice stage, tightly clinging to forms prescribed, his idea would be confirmed, for none knows better than himself how slight a departure from the required formulae will not only destroy their beneficence but may well deliver the hapless sufferer into the hands of the malignant ghosts. Over against such esoteric views of psychometric methods is the customary and pragmatic one. The function of psychometrics is not the accomplishment of a ritual, but the understanding of the patient. The ceremony of mental tests is valuable so far as it serves to reach this end. When it fails, or stands in the way of doing this, proper technique demands that it be modified. Ability to do this intelligently is what distinguishes the psychologist, properly so called, from the "mental tester" (*108, p. 27*).

Further objections to exclusive reliance upon a psychometric approach arose from the emergence of projective techniques as an aspect of the dynamic tradition next to be considered.

THE DYNAMIC TRADITION

Many of the present developments in clinical psychology—the emphasis on understanding of personality functioning, the attempt to relate present behavior to experiences of which the patient is unaware, the evaluative use of incidental verbalizations and physical behavior of the patient, and the artistic element in psycho-diagnostic appraisal—stem in large measure from the dynamic tradition.

In terms of the sources of these influences, Sigmund Freud, of course, looms largest. He and his fellow analysts profoundly affected the thinking of many clinical psychologists, who were for the most part passive recipients of this influence. No longer did they share leadership with their medical colleagues as during the first twenty years of the century. The influence of psychoanalysis was felt directly on three of the specific manifestations of the dynamic tradition directly involving the psychologist—projective techniques, the Harvard Psychological Clinic, and the American Orthopsychiatric Association. The first, an approach to personality, the second, a clinic, and the third, a professional organization, share responsibility as the most important manifestations of the dynamic tradition in psychology of the day. Each will be considered in turn.

Hermann Rorschach, a Swiss psychiatrist, published with Oberholzer on the specific but intricate relationships which exist between his inkblot technique and psychoanalysis. The technique itself occupied much of his time between 1911 and his untimely death in 1922. In the United States pioneering work with the Rorschach was done by David M. Levy, a child psychiatrist, with whom Samuel J. Beck became associated beginning in 1927. In 1930 Beck presented the first Rorschach study in this country as his doctoral dissertation, and during the thirties the Rorschach technique came more and more into prominence in clinical circles. Along with Beck, pioneer American psychologists who made major contributions to Rorschach literature during this period, were Bruno Klopfer, Marguerite Hertz, and Zygmunt Piotrowski.

Two reasons are given by Beck (*18*) for the increasing preoccupation of psychologists with the Rorschach technique as compared to psychiatrists. There is, first, the division of labor with the

Rorschach as one of the diagnostic testing instruments and, second, the fact that its use spread outside the narrowly psychiatric area into the schools, work with delinquents, industry, and the like. Other projective techniques, notably the Thematic Apperception Test, also appeared during the thirties.

In the meantime the psychodynamic emphasis began to be a part of the intellectual armamentarium of the psychologist. The article by L. K. Frank, "Projective Methods for the Study of Personality" (*48*), published in 1939, offered a rationale for the projective approach and stimulated both research and theoretical efforts in the decades to follow. Merrill summarizes other reasons for the rapid spread of projective testing as having

> . . . had to do with significant changes that have been occurring in the clinician's self-concept and his changing perception of his role as his social responsibilities grow and expand. Projective tests have become important tools for the psychotherapists. These tests command the attention and respect of our colleagues in the medical fraternity, the psychiatrists. They constitute moreover, the basic technological structure upon which is being built a new systematic point of view, projective psychology with its own theory of personality. This new projective psychology has been aptly characterized as a psychology of protest. As both behaviorism and Gestalt psychology came about as protests against the established psychologies called structural, so this emerging projective psychology runs sharply counter to the traditions that have characterized individual psychology in America. Having something to push against, it can move (*73, p. 286*).

In 1927 the Harvard Psychological Clinic was founded by Morton Prince. Its express purpose was to bring together academic and clinical psychology. Henry A. Murray took over headship of the clinic early in the thirties and with a large group of collaborators, including Donald W. MacKinnon, Saul Rosenzweig, R. Nevitt Sanford, and Robert W. White, carried on a brilliant research project in personality functioning. This culminated in 1938 in the well-known *Explorations in Personality* (*81*).

The American Orthopsychiatric Association is an organization with ties to child guidance in particular and to the dynamic tradition in general. It was founded in 1924 with many of the leaders of the child guidance movement present (*71*). William Healy was elected president during this year and served through 1926. Later presidents included Karl Menninger, David Levy, and in 1931, the first psychologist to be president, Augusta F. Bronner. Other psychologist presidents were

Edgar A. Doll, Samuel Beck, and Morris Krugman. After thinking through the problem of membership, originally restricted to psychiatrists, the pattern emerged in 1926 of having as full members "psychiatrists, psychologists, and other professional persons whose work and interests lie in the study and treatment of conduct disorders" (*71, p. 199*). Both the letter and spirit of this method of organization for work interchange, support, and advance have continued to the present day. However, there has never been any question, as might have been foretold from the original organization, but that psychiatrists were dominant in it. For example, twenty-one of the first twenty-six presidents held the M.D. degree, only four being psychologists and only one a social worker. This organization continues to wield much influence both through its journal, *The American Journal of Orthopsychiatry*, and through its annual meetings which are characteristically attended by far more nonmembers than members.

PSYCHOLOGICAL CLINICS

This was a period during which psychological clinics reflected the plateau of the psychometric tradition. Some new clinics appeared; others closed their doors (*70*). In 1934 a survey report of a questionnaire of psychoeducational clinics by Witty and Theman (*115*) appeared. On the basis of their returns they estimated that there were about 50 such clinics. This figure may be contrasted with the approximately 20 found by Wallin in 1914 (*105*). In 1932 the median length of time the clinics had been in existence was four years. Located in colleges, universities, teachers colleges, and normal schools, their stated purposes involved (2) providing schools, social agencies, and individuals with diagnostic test services and remedial methods in order to bring about educational, vocational, and social adjustment; (b) training students in giving and interpreting tests; and (c) research with emphasis on the study of deviates, causes and treatment of learning difficulties, and work with remedial materials. It would appear that this survey epitomizes the work of psychological clinics of the day, featuring emphasis on testing and remedial education.

CHILD GUIDANCE

The period 1922–1927 was one in which the National Committee for Mental Hygiene on behalf of the Commonwealth Fund established demonstration clinics in a variety of cities and rural areas for the purpose of showing both their need and the work they could do (*99*). For the first time they were called "child guidance clinics." Eight clinics were permanently established directly as a result, and many others were at least partially stimulated by this effort. It was the announced intention from the very beginning that eventually expenses for their maintenance would be absorbed by the community in which they were located. Deliberate experimentation as to method of organization in relation to other agencies was carried out—some were attached to the courts, others to local charities, to university and to teaching hospitals. The child guidance clinic plan of organization called for the professional personnel to include at least a psychiatrist, a psychologist, and a social worker. These activities in their formative stages continued roughly over the decade 1920–1930. To be sure, their influence and organization continued thereafter, but this period marked the heyday of their unique contribution.

An important shift of focus of attention had been occurring during this period. No longer was the delinquent of primary interest. Nor was there much concern with mental defectives, epileptics, or neurological cases. Instead, emphasis was placed upon maladjustment in school and home, especially that centering around parent-child relationships.

The clinics began to concentrate upon problems of the individual who may be spoken of as falling within the normal range of intelligence, the roots of what may in some measure be traced to emotional difficulties.

THE PSYCHOLOGIST IN MENTAL HOSPITALS

In 1921 Wells left McLean Hospital for Boston Psychopathic Hospital where he served as head psychologist until 1938. This hospital also became a center of clinical activity and training. A pioneer in present-day clinical psychology, David Shakow, now of the Illinois Neuropsychiatric Institute, is still very active. For a period of nearly twenty years, Shakow served as director of psychological research at Worcester State Hospital. His activities, along with his research efforts, included direction of an internship training program. It apparently was the closest in spirit to the modern internship program, and his experience derived in this setting was of great value in formulating present-day practices concerning internship.

A gradual increase in the number of clinical psychologists in mental hospitals was taking place. However, the geographical isolation of most such hospital psychologists apparently accentuated an isolation on other grounds so that the effect of this aspect of the development of clinical psychology was not as important as it was to be in the decades to come. Nevertheless, some psychologists were beginning to suspect that their approach was unduly limited. As a result, there were serious attempts at broadening the scope of testing efforts, to escape the atomistic tradition by means of research and theorizing concerning the personality of their patients.

MENTAL DEFICIENCY

In 1919 Goddard was succeeded by Stanley D. Porteus as director of the Vineland Laboratory. Under both his direction and the subsequent direction from 1925 until 1949 of Edgar A. Doll the clinical problems of feeblemindedness received intensive and extensive study.

It was precisely in the field of intelligence testing that clinical psychology was most advanced during this period. Psychometric testing of suspected mental deficiency was widely accepted, and the psychologist was the authority in this field (28). Nevertheless, as Buck (28) indicates, appreciation of the complexity, rather than the simplicity, of the diagnosis of mental deficiency emerged during these two decades.

The fact that a person was doing some clinical psychological work with mental defectives unfortunately indicated almost nothing about the nature of the training and experience of the practitioner in question. In 1940 Hackbusch (56) reported an inquiry concerning psychological work in state and private institutions for the mentally defective. Of the approximately 100 institutions which replied apparently all were doing some form of psychological testing. However, less than half had a psychologist on their staff. The remainder had their testing done by outside sources, or by teachers, social workers, and physicians on their own staffs. It is also noteworthy that the "psychologists" apparently varied widely in the nature of their background. Some had less than a A.B. degree, while others had an A.B. or an M.A. in addition, but very few held the Ph.D. degree. Therefore, despite the acceptance of their work, the status of psychologists and psychological work in the twenties and thirties was somewhat confused.

PSYCHOLOGY AS A PROFESSION

The origins of professional activity, as has been indicated, were centered within the American Psychological Association. This period extended from 1895 to the mid-twenties. Founded to advance psychology as a *science*, the Association had not been singularly successful in reflecting the interests of its members either in applications of psychology or in their professional aspirations. The twenties and thirties were characterized by the advent of other organizations more directly concerned with professional problems.

In 1917 a group of psychologists interested in the advancement of the practice of psychology met in Pittsburgh, Pennsylvania. Leta S. Hollingworth took the initiative in bringing the group together, and prominent charter members included Bronner, Fernald, Healy, Kuhlmann, Pintner, Terman, Whipple, Wells, and Yerkes. To quote Symonds, "After a brief history of two years, during which a bitter struggle went on in the American Psychological Association over the question of authority for certification of psychologists for clinical work, the American Association of Clinical Psychologists became defunct through the adoption by the APA of a report recommending the establishment of the AACP as a Section of Clinical Psychology" (*100, p. 337*). According to the same writer, the next step was the slow development of various local groups concerned with applied and professional matters in several states.

In 1930 the Association of Consulting Psychologists was reorganized from a still earlier association founded in 1921 (*40, 52*). Gradually it extended its membership beyond New York and environs and became one of the more important elements later to merge into the American Association for Applied Psychology (AAAP). The organization meeting of this association took place in 1937. Many of the difficulties in organizing centered upon the standards for membership. Then, as now, there was the dilemma of maintaining standards and yet not setting them so high as to exclude the majority of those doing work in the applied fields. Eventually this was settled, and a national organization concerned with all aspects of the application of psychology came into being and became the dominant national professional organization. A divisional structure was followed with clinical, educational, industrial, and consulting sections.

The Journal of Consulting Psychology was at first a publication of the Association of Consulting Psychologists and then of the AAAP. Papers in clinical, educational, industrial, and consulting psychology appeared, but a considerable portion of space was devoted to organizational and professional matters (*100*).

Thus, there existed at the close of the thirties two major psychological societies—one dedicated to the advancement of psychology as a science and the other to its application. Generally speaking, members of the latter also had membership in the former but sincerely felt the essential nature of their applied organization. The Psychometric Society and the Society for the Psychological Study of Social Issues were also founded during this period. In part at least, these organizations arose because of their interests in the American Psychological Association. So the thirties closed with at least the possibility of dangerous rifts in the ranks of psychologists. However, as is well known, this danger passed in the forties with all of these organizations integrated into the reorganized American Psychological Association (*116*). In 1945 this reorganization went into effect. Both in spirit and in practice the American Psychological Association represents psychology as a science and as a profession.

THE PSYCHOLOGIST AND THERAPY

During the twenties and thirties there appeared to be a gradual increase in the number of clinical psychologists engaging in therapy. From the time of Sidis and Scott at the turn of the century some psychologists had been so employed. In many instances psychotherapeutic practice grew out of the psychologist's educational function. Considered as expert both in matters of learning as a subject of investigation and in education as a field of endeavor, the psychologist worked with patients, particularly children, with whom remedial education was necessary. A similar process took place to a lesser extent in psychiatric clinics. It was in the hospitals that this development lagged, partly because the sheer press of numbers of patients confined the psychologists to psychodiagnostic tasks and partly because psychotherapy, except at a few institutions, was not practiced at all.

There was relatively little difficulty in interprofessional relations with psychiatry during this period. In large measure this was because there were few psychologists practicing therapy, and these few were doing so under institutional auspices and exceptional circumstances. Then too, the psychiatrist himself was more isolated both from his medical colleagues and from the public than he is today. More concerned with the psychotic and the adult than with the neurotic and the child, his path did not as often cross that of the psychologist as it did in the forties and fifties.

No continuity in the development of psychotherapists among psychologists is discernible from generation to generation. Neither Sidis nor Scott stimulated psychologists to work with psychotherapeutic problems. In later years individual psychologists prominent in psychotherapy gained in stature, not unaided to be sure, but also not from combined efforts of any group or from the work of one senior individual. Phyllis Blanchard, for example, an acknowledged leading therapist, as attested to by her presence in leading symposia and by books on the topic, neither received her training in therapy from psychologists nor participated in the training of psychologists in therapy. Other therapist-psychologists, also, developed along individual lines. The work of Carl Rogers, although begun in the thirties, did not reach national prominence until the forties.

PSYCHOLOGISTS IN THE ARMED SERVICES AND THEIR EFFECT UPON PSYCHOLOGY IN THE POSTWAR PERIOD

About 1,500 psychologists served in the armed services during World War II. About one out of four psychologists thus was called upon to function in an applied field—that is, psychology applied to the very practical problem of war. Moreover, this group was predominantly young, averaging about 32 years of age (*24*), thus including many individuals just reaching professional maturity. It is not unduly optimistic to suppose that some of their experiences during these tours of duty carried over in attitude and practice to the postwar years.

To appreciate properly certain changes of attitude, it must be remembered that a considerable number of psychologists in uniform were products of an academic tradition whose isolationist tendencies in regard to professional application prior to the war they were quite willingly and even complacently furthering. In fact, Andrews and Dreese (*16*) found that almost 90 per cent of the psychologists in military service were in academic or governmental work prior to the war.

From the process of learning to apply their psychological training to the military situation, later consideration revealed at least two major trends that have had, and will continue to have, profound effect upon contemporary psychology. They discovered to their mild surprise, and to the considerable amazement of their colleagues from other disciplines, that their general training in psychological methods was capable of application to many problems which at first seemed utterly alien to the background. From aircraft instrument-panel design to selecting underwater demolition teams, psychologists found that they, in collaboration with specialists from other fields, had something valuable to contribute. Realization was forced upon them that an experimental background in psychology is capable of transfer to intelligent and capable handling of many sorts of problems.

Paradoxically, however, they gained added respect for the clinical approach. In this connection it must be realized that almost half of the psychologists used clinical and counseling procedures during some part of their period in uniform (24). Many psychologists, willy-nilly, were placed in a position where they functioned in selection and assignment, sat as members of discharge boards, worked as members of clinical teams, conducted therapeutic sessions, both group and individual, and in these and many other ways used diagnostic and treatment methods. Concrete expressions of this interest can be found in an article by Britt and Morgan (24) concerning the results obtained from a questionnaire mailed to every psychologist in uniform. They conclude that there was an overwhelming interest in having more practical postwar graduate training. Nearly 24 per cent of the suggestions for new courses for graduate study were clearly within the general clinical field. At least some of the armed services psychologists who had previously not been particularly receptive came to understand and appreciate the contributions, past and potential, of the clinical method. This impression is verified by the finding in a survey by Andrews and Dreese (16) that three times as many military psychologists engaged in clinical work after the war as had done so in the prewar period.

CLINICAL PSYCHOLOGY TODAY

With the coming of the forties and World War II, one leaves the realm of history and enters the present. It would be both hazardous and presumptuous to attempt to trace in detail the events from this time on. Nevertheless, certain factors in the foregoing account may be related to present trends. Clinical psychology as a method, as an attitude, and as a field of endeavor is reflected in its past.

It would appear that clinical psychology and academic psychology have influenced each other markedly, with a reciprocal, symbiotic relationship having been formed. Other disciplines, notably the medical and particularly the psychiatric and psychoanalytic, influenced and vitalized clinical psychology.

Through the thirties certain predominant aspects may be referred to as "child," "psychological," and "clinical" as contrasted with "adult," "psychiatric," and "institutional" functions. Distinctively psychological clinics and work with children are not only important because of their service and scientific value, but also for the community orientation that they manifest and the preventive emphasis that they maintain. And yet since the thirties the emphasis has shifted.

The "adult," "psychiatric," and "institutional" aspects of clinical psychology appear to be dominant today, but this is by no means an unmixed blessing. Many of the more vocal leaders of the field, including to some extent the official committees of the American Psychological Association, have fostered emphasis upon the former. The extremely valuable support rendered by the Veterans Administration to our training and practice has emphasized the current trend. Work with adults in a psychiatrically oriented institution is a specialty, albeit an important one, in the broader field.

With the forties also came the domination in the history of clinical psychology of one of the trends previously sketched. This was the emergence and implementation of a concept of a profession of psychology. One illustration will suffice. Until after World War II, there was relatively little demonstrable agreement about the training, nature, duties, or status of the clinical psychologist. To quote Eysenck, "A person who called himself a 'clinical psychologist' might be someone of great eminence, highly qualified academically and with 20 or 30 years of practical experience in the fields of diagnostic testing, research, and therapy, or he might be a student just graduated from the University, without any kind of relevant experience, capable only of grinding out Binet I.Q.'s without even an adequate understanding of their relevance to the clinical problem presented" (41, p. 711). The facet of the professionalization of a psychologist, although not completely defined today, has reached a degree of precise formulation undreamed of a few years ago.

Current issues and accomplishments, stabilizing trends, and unresolved problems may be related to the emergence of psychology as a profession. Factors making for the present stabilization include the agreement of the great majority of interested parties concerning diagnostic appraisal as a task of the clinical psychologist (7, 9, 12, 55, 94), the present organization and function of the American Psychological Association (4, 116), current efforts directed toward the training of clinical psychologists (9, 10, 12, 14), present activities looking toward codification of ethical problems (5, 6, 17, 21, 61), and the influence of such institutions as the American Board of Examiners in Professional Psychology (2, 3), state societies (11), the United States Public Health Service (42, 104), the Veterans Administration (1, 58, 103), and the armed services (102). On the other hand, currently unresolved issues face the profession today. The problems on which there are differences of opinion both in psychology and in other professions include psychotherapy as a task of the psychologist and the nature of the relation of psychology to psychiatry and medicine (7, 13, 54, 55, 72, 87, 94),

the nature of the relation of psychology to social work (33), the question of the advisability of certification and licensure (31, 47, 60, 109, 112, 117), the question of the desirability of private practice (38, 39), the position and function of non-Ph.D.'s in clinical psychology (15, 20, 35, 67, 69, 98), and the "imbalance" in psychology between scientific and professional demands (63, 87, 88, 89). Not only do these problems have roots in the past, but they are also an expression of the period of professionalization of large segments of psychology today.

World War II focused the needs and demonstrated what could be done in clinical psychology; the period after the war is still feeling the pressure of these social needs and is witnessing the reactions, adaptive and otherwise, of a beginning profession to these demands.

REFERENCES

1. ADLER, M. H., FUTTERMAN, S., & WEBB, R. Activities of the mental hygiene clinics of the Veterans Administration. *J. Clin. Psychopath.*, 1948, 9, 517–527.
2. AMERICAN BOARD OF EXAMINERS IN PROFESSIONAL PSYCHOLOGY, INC. *Official Bulletin.* 1948, No. 1.
3. AMERICAN BOARD OF EXAMINERS IN PROFESSIONAL PSYCHOLOGY. The work of the American Board of Examiners in Professional Psychology: annual report of the Board to the members of the APA. *Amer. Psychologist*, 1951, 6, 620–625.
4. AMERICAN PSYCHOLOGICAL ASSOCIATION. By-laws for the American Psychological Association (as amended through September, 1951). In *Directory, American Psychological Association.* Washington, D.C.: American Psychological Association, 1951.
5. AMERICAN PSYCHOLOGICAL ASSOCIATION. *Ethical standards for psychologists.* Vol. 1: *The code of ethics.* Washington, D.C.: American Psychological Association, 1952.
6. AMERICAN PSYCHOLOGICAL ASSOCIATION. *Ethical standards for psychologists.* Vol. 2: *Source book of ethical problems, incidents, and principles.* Washington, D.C.
7. AMERICAN PSYCHOLOGICAL ASSOCIATION, *Ad Hoc* Committee on Relations between Psychology and the Medical Profession. Psychology and its relationships with other professions. *Amer. Psychologist*, 1952, 7, 145–152.
8. AMERICAN PSYCHOLOGICAL ASSOCIATION, Committee of Clinical Section. I. The definition of clinical psychology and standards of training for clinical psychologists. II. Guide to psychological clinics in the United States. *Psychol. Clin.*, 1935, 23, 2–140.
9. AMERICAN PSYCHOLOGICAL ASSOCIATION, Committee on Training in Clinical Psychology. Recommended graduate training program in clinical psychology. *Amer. Psychologist*, 1947, 2, 539–558.
10. AMERICAN PSYCHOLOGICAL ASSOCIATION, Committee on Training in Clinical Psychology. Annual report of the Committee on Training in Clinical Psychology. *Amer. Psychologist*, 1951, 6, 612–617.

11. AMERICAN PSYCHOLOGICAL ASSOCIATION, Conference of State Psychological Associations. *CSPA Newsletter*, April 1952. (Mimeo.)
12. AMERICAN PSYCHOLOGICAL ASSOCIATION, Conference on Graduate Education in Clinical Psychology, Boulder, Colorado. *Training in clinical psychology.* New York: Prentice-Hall, 1950.
13. AMERICAN PSYCHOLOGICAL ASSOCIATION, Division of Clinical and Abnormal Psychology, Committee on Psychotherapy. Report. *Newsletter, Div. Clin. abnorm. Psychol.*, 1950, *4*, No. 2, Suppl. (Mimeo.)
14. AMERICAN PSYCHOLOGICAL ASSOCIATION, Education and Training Board. Doctoral training programs in clinical psychology. *Amer. Psychologist*, 1952, *7*, 158.
15. AMERICAN PSYCHOLOGICAL ASSOCIATION, Policy and Planning Board. Annual report: 1951. *Amer. Psychologist*, 1951, *6*, 531–540.
16. ANDREWS, T. G., & DREESE, M. Military utilization of psychologists during World War II. *Amer. Psychologist*, 1948, *3*, 533–538.
17. ANON. Discussion on ethics: a little recent history. *Amer. Psychologist*, 1952, *7*, 426–428.
18. BECK, S. J. Rorschach's test in this anniversary year. In L. G. Lowrey (Ed.), *Orthopsychiatry*, 1923–1948: *retrospect and prospect*. New York: American Orthopsychiatric Association, 1948. Pp. 422–455.
19. BEERS, C. W. *A mind that found itself.* New York: Longmans Green, 1908.
20. BLACK, J. D. A survey of employment in psychology and the place of personnel without the Ph.D. *Amer. Psychologist*, 1949, *4*, 38–42.
21. BOBBITT, J. M. Some arguments for a code of ethics. *Amer. Psychologist*, 1952, *7*, 428–429.
22. BORING, E. G. Edwin Garrigues Boring. In E. G. Boring, H. S. Langfeld, H. Werner, & R. M. Yerkes (Eds.), *A history of psychology in autobiography.* Vol. IV. Worcester: Clark University Press, 1952. Pp. 27–52.
23. BRILL, A. A. Introduction. In A. A. Brill (Ed.), *The basic writings of Sigmund Freud.* New York: Modern Library, 1938. Pp. 3–32.
24. BRITT, S. H., & MORGAN, JANE D. Military psychologists in World War II. *Amer. Psychologist*, 1946, *1*, 423–437.
25. BRONNER, AUGUSTA F., HEALY, W., LOWE, GLADYS M., & SHIMBERG, MYRA E. *A manual of individual mental tests and testing.* Boston: Little Brown, 1927.
26. BROTEMARKLE, R. A. (Ed.) *Clinical psychology: studies in honor of Lightner Witmer.* Philadelphia: Univer. of Pennsylvania Press, 1931.
27. BROTEMARKLE, R. A. Clinical psychology 1896–1946. *J. consult. Psychol.*, 1947, *11*, 1–4.
28. BUCK, J. N. The present and future status of the psychologist in the field of mental deficiency. *Amer. J. ment. Def.*, 1949–1950, *54*, 225–229.
29. CATTELL, J. M. Mental tests and measurements. *Mind*, 1890, *15*, 373–381.
30. CATTELL, J. M. Retrospect: psychology as a profession. *J. consult. Psychol.*, 1937, *1*, 1–3; 1946, *10*, 289–291.
31. COMBS, A. W. A report of the 1951 licensing effort in New York State. *Amer. Psychologist*, 1951, *6*, 541–548.
32. CORIAT, I. H. Some personal reminiscences of psychoanalysis in Boston: an autobiographical note. *Psychoanal. Rev.*, 1945, *32*, 1–8.
33. COWAN, E. A. Correspondence. *J. consult. Psychol.*, 1945, *9*, 64–65.
34. COWLES, E. Progress during the half century. *Amer. J. Insanity*, 1894, *51*, 10–22.
35. DARLEY, J. G., ELLIOTT, R. M., HATHAWAY, S. R. & PATERSON, D. Are psychologists without Ph.D. degrees to be barred from membership in the APA? *Amer. Psychologist*, 1948, *3*, 51–53.
36. DENNIS, W., & BORING, E. G. The founding of the APA. *Amer. Psychologist*, 1952, *7*, 95–96.

37. DOLL, E. A. (Ed.) *Twenty-five years: a memorial volume in commemoration of the 25th anniversary of the Vineland Laboratory, 1906–1931.* (Publ. Ser. 1932).

38. ELLIS, A. The psychologist in private practice and the good profession. *Amer. Psychologist*, 1952, *7*, 129–131.

39. ELLIS, A. (Chm.) Report of the Committee on Private Practice. *Newsletter, Div. clin. abnorm. Psychol.*, 1952, *5*, No. 4. (Mimeo.)

40. ENGLISH, H. B. Organization of the American Association of Applied Psychologists. *J. consult. Psychol.*, 1938, *2*, 7–16.

41. EYSENCK, H. J. Function and training of the clinical psychologist. *J. ment. Sci.*, 1950, *96*, 710–725.

42. FEDERAL SECURITY AGENCY. *National Mental Health Act. Five years of progress, 1946–1951.* Washington, D.C.: 1951. (Mimeo.)

43. FERNBERGER, S. W. The American Psychological Association: a historical summary, 1892–1930. *Psychol. Bull.*, 1932, *29*, 1–89.

44. FERNBERGER, S. W. The scientific interests and scientific publications of the members of the American Psychological Association. *Psychol. Bull.*, 1938, *35*, 261–281.

45. FERNBERGER, S. W. The American Psychological Association, 1892–1942. *Psychol. Rev.*, 1943, *50*, 33–60.

46. FINCH, F. H., & ODOROFF, M. E. Employment trends in applied psychology. *J. consult. Psychol.*, 1941, *5*, 275–278.

47. FOWERBAUGH, C. C. Legal status of psychologists in Ohio. *J. consult. Psychol.*, 1945, *9*, 196–200.

48. FRANK, L. K. Projective methods for the study of personality. *J. Psychol.*, 1939, *8*, 389–413.

49. FRANZ, S. I. The present status of psychology in medical education and practice. *J. Amer. med. Assn.*, 1912, *58*, 909–911.

50. FRANZ, S. I. Shepard Ivory Franz. In C. Murchison (Ed.), *A history of psychology in autobiography.* Vol. II. Worcester: Clark Univ. Press, 1932. Pp. 89–113.

51. FREUD, S. The origin and development of psychoanalysis. *Amer. J. Psychol.*, 1910, *21*, 181–218.

52. FRYER, D. (Chm.) The proposed American Association for Applied and Professional Psychologists. *J. consult. Psychol.*, 1937, *1*, 14–16.

53. GALTON, F. *Inquiries into human faculty and its development.* London: J. M. Dent, 1883.

54. GREGG, A. The profession of psychology as seen by a doctor of medicine. *Amer. Psychologist*, 1948, *9*, 397–401.

55. GROUP FOR THE ADVANCEMENT OF PSYCHIATRY, Committee on Clinical Psychology. The relation of clinical psychology to psychiatry. *Amer. J. Ortho-Psychiat.*, 1950, *22*, 346–354.

56. HACKBUSCH, FLORENTINE. Responsibility of the American Association on Mental Deficiency for developing uniform psychological practices in schools for mental defectives. *Amer. J. Ment. Def.*, 1940–41, *45*, 233–237.

57. HALL, G. S. Laboratory of the McLean Hospital. *Amer. J. Insanity*, 1894, *51*, 358–364.

58. HAWLEY, P. R. The importance of clinical psychology in a complete medical program. *J. consult. Psychol.*, 1946, *10*, 292–300.

59. HEALY, W., & BRONNER, AUGUSTA F. The child guidance clinic: birth and growth of an idea. In L. G. Lowrey (Ed.), *Orthopsychiatry, 1923–1948: retrospect and prospect.* New York: American Orthopsychiatric Association, 1948. Pp. 14–49.

60. HEISER, K. F. The need for legislation and the complexities of the problem. *Amer. Psychologist*, 1950, *5*, 104, 108.

61. HOBBS, N. The development of a code of ethical standards for psychology. *Amer. Psychologist*, 1948, *3*, 80–84.

62. Hoch, A. A review of psychological and physiological experiments done in connection with the study of mental diseases. *Psychol. Bull.*, 1904, *1*, 241–257.

63. Hunt, W. A. Clinical psychology—science or superstition. *Amer. Psychologist*, 1952, *6*, 683–688.

64. James, H. (Ed.) *The letters of William James.* Vol. II. Boston: Atlantic Monthly Press, 1920.

65. James, W. *The principles of psychology.* New York: Holt, 1890.

66. James, W. *The varieties of religious experience.* New York: Longmans Green, 1902.

67. Kelly, G. A. Single level versus legislation for different levels of psychology training and experience. *Amer. Psychologist*, 1950, *5*, 109, 111.

68. Kraepelin, E. *Lehrbuch der psychiatrie.* Leipzig: Verlag von Johann Ambrosius Barth, 1899.

69. Longstaff, H. P., Speer, G. S., McTeer, W., & Hartson, L. D. A survey of psychologists in four midwestern states. *Amer. Psychologists*, 1950, *5*, 422–423.

70. Louttit, C. M. The nature of clinical psychology. *Psychol. Bull.*, 1939, *36*, 361–389.

71. Lowrey, L. G. The birth of orthopsychiatry. In L. G. Lowrey (Ed.), *Orthopsychiatry, 1923–1948; retrospect and prospect.* New York: American Orthopsychiatric Association, 1948. Pp. 190–216.

72. Menninger, W. C. The relationship of clinical psychology and psychiatry. *Amer. Psychologist*, 1950, *5*, 3–15.

73. Merrill, Maude A. Oscillation and progress in clinical psychology. *J. consult. Psychol.*, 1951, *15*, 281–289.

74. Meyer, A. G. Stanley Hall, Ph.D., LL.D. *Amer. J. Psychiat.*, 1924–25, *81*, 151–153.

75. Meyer, A. August Hoch, M.D. *Arch. Neurol. Psychiat.*, 1919, *2*, 573–576.

76. Meyer, A. Organization of community facilities for prevention, care, and treatment of nervous and mental diseases. *Proc. First Inter. Cong. ment. Hyg.*, 1932, *1*, 237–257.

77. Morris, L. *William James: the message of a modern mind.* New York: Scribners, 1950.

78. Morrow, W. R. The development of psychological internship training. *J. consult. Psychol.*, 1946, *10*, 165–183.

79. Murchison, C. (Ed.) *The psychological register.* (2 vols.) Worcester: Clark Univer. Press, 1929, 1932.

80. Murphy, G. *Historical introduction to modern psychology.* (Rev. Ed.) New York: Harcourt Brace, 1949.

81. Murray, H. A., et al. *Explorations in personality: a clinical and experimental study of fifty men of college age.* New York: Oxford Univer. Press, 1938.

82. Norsworthy, Naomi. The psychology of mentally deficient children. *Arch. Psychol.*, N.Y., 1906, No. 1.

83. Peterson, J. *Early conceptions and tests of intelligence.* Yonkers, N.Y.: World Book Co., 1925.

84. Pintner, R. *Intelligence testing: methods and results.* (New Ed.) New York: Holt, 1931.

85. Pintner, R., & Paterson, D. G. *A scale of performance tests.* New York: Appleton-Century, 1917.

86. Roback, A. A. *History of American psychology.* New York: Library Publishers, 1952.

87. Rogers, C. R. Where are we going in clinical psychology? *J. consult. Psychol.*, 1951, *15*, 171–177.

88. Rosenzweig, S. Imbalance in clinical psychology. *Amer. Psychologist*, 1950, *5*, 678–680.

89. ROSENZWEIG, S. Balance in clinical psychology: a symposium in correspondence. *Amer. Psychologist*, 1951, *6*, 208–212.
90. SCOTT, W. D. An interpretation of the psycho-analytic method in psychotherapy with a report of a case so treated. *J. abnorm. Psychol.*, 1909, *3*, 371–377.
91. SEASHORE, C. E. *Pioneering in psychology*. Iowa City, Iowa: Univer. of Iowa Press, 1942.
92. SHAKOW, D. One hundred years of American psychiatry: a special review. *Psychol. Bull.*, 1945, *42*, 423–432.
93. SHAKOW, D. Clinical psychology: an evaluation. In L. G. Lowrey (Ed.), *Orthopsychiatry, 1923–1948: retrospect and prospect*. New York: American Orthopsychiatric Association, 1948. Pp. 231–247.
94. SHAKOW, D. Psychology and psychiatry: a dialogue. *Amer. J. Orthopsychiat.*, 1949, *19*, 191–208, 381–396.
95. SHARP, STELLA E. Individual psychology: a study in psychological method. *Amer. J. Psychol.*, 1899, *10*, 329–391.
96. SIDIS, B. Studies in psychopathology. *Boston med. & surg. J.*, 1907, *156*, 321–326, 357–361, 394–398, 432–434, 472–478.
97. SMITH, T. L. The development of psychological clinics in the United States. *Ped. Sem.*, 1914, *21*, 143–153.
98. SPEER, G. S. A survey of psychologists in Illinois. *Amer. Psychologist*, 1950, *5*, 424–426.
99. STEVENSON, G. S., & SMITH, G. *Child guidance clinics: a quarter century of development*. New York: Commonwealth Fund, 1934.
100. SYMONDS, J. P. Ten years of journalism in psychology, 1937–1946; first decade of the Journal of Consulting Psychology. *J. consult. Psychol.*, 1946, *10*, 335–374.
101. TERMAN, L. M. Trails to psychology. In C. Murchison (Ed.), *A history of psychology in autobiography*. Vol. II. Worcester: Clark Univ. Press, 1932. Pp. 297–332.
102. U.S. Dept. Army, Office of the Surgeon General. The U.S. Army's senior psychology student program. *Amer. Psychologist*, 1949, *4*, 424–425.
103. VETERANS ADMINISTRATION. Cooperative training program for clinical psychologists in association with part-time work in VA stations where neuropsychiatric cases are treated. *V.A. Tech. Bull.*, 1948, TB 10A–146.
104. VESTERMARK, S. D. Training and its support under the National Mental Health Act. *Amer. J. Psychiat.*, 1949, *106*, 416–419.
105. WALLIN, J. E. W. *The mental health of the school child*. New Haven: Yale Univ. Press, 1914.
106. WATSON, R. I. The professional status of the clinical psychologist. In R. I. Watson (Ed.), *Readings in the clinical method in psychology*. New York: Harper, 1949. Pp. 29–48.
107. WATSON, R. I. *The clinical method in psychology*. New York: Harper, 1951.
108. WELLS, F. L. *Mental tests in clinical practice*. Yonkers, N.Y.: World Book Co., 1927.
109. WENDT, R. G. Legislation for the general practice of psychology versus legislation for specialties within psychology. *Amer. Psychologist*, 1950, *5*, 107–108.
110. WHIPPLE, G. M. *Manual of physical and mental tests*. Baltimore: Warwick and York, 1910.
111. WHITEHORN, J. C. A century of psychiatric research in America. In J. K. Hall (Ed.), *One hundred years of American psychiatry*. New York: Columbia Univer. Press, 1944. Pp. 167–193.
112. WEINER, D. N. The Minnesota law to certify psychologists. *Amer. Psychologist*, 1951, *6*, 549–553.
113. WISSLER, C. The correlation of mental and physical tests. *Psychol. Monogr.*, 1901, *3*, No. 6 (Whole No. 16).

114. WITMER, L. Clinical psychology. *Psychol. Clin.*, 1907, *1*, 1–9.
115. WITTY, P. S., & THEMAN, VIOLA. The psycho-educational clinic. *J. appl. Psychol.*, 1934, *18*, 369–392.
116. WOLFLE, D. The reorganized American Psychological Association. *Amer. Psychologist*, 1946, *1*, 3–6.
117. WOLFLE, D. Legal control of psychological practice. *Amer. Psychologist*, 1950, *5*, 651–655.
118. WOODWORTH, R. S. *Personal Data Sheet.* Chicago: C. H. Stoelting, 1917.
119. WYATT, F. Clinical psychology and orthopsychiatry. In L. G. Lowrey (Ed.), *Orthopsychiatry, 1923–1948: restrospect and prospect.* New York: American Orthopsychiatric Association, 1948. Pp. 217–230.
120. YERKES, R. M.(Ed.). *Psychological examining in the United States Army.* (Memoirs of the National Academy of Sciences, Vol. 15.) Washington, D.C.: U.S. Govt. Printing Office, 1921.
121. YOUNG, K. The history of mental testing. *Ped. Sem.*, 1924, *31*, 1–48.

2. *A Historical and Theoretical Analysis of Some Broad Trends in Clinical Psychology*

JULIAN B. ROTTER

A QUARTER of a century has passed since the publication of C. M. Louttit's *Clinical Psychology* [79] in 1936. Louttit's book is considered by many to be one of the earliest major attempts to present a standard text of a broad field of psychological application which has been called "clinical psychology." Where previous articles and volumes had dealt specifically with mental tests, special disorders, abnormal psychology, etc., Louttit attempted to relate and describe systematically a field of application which had been formalized only a few years before, over some objections, in the organization of a clinical section of the American Psychological Association.

A comparison of Louttit's book with the treatises on clinical psychology published recently indicates that a tremendous change has taken place in the activities, interests, and ideas of the people who now consider themselves clinical psychologists. It is quite clear from a review of the intermediate years that the period of change is not over, but that clinical psychology is currently in an extremely active period of growth and change.

In order to determine the sources of these changes as well as their nature and interrelationship with other fields, an historical analysis seems most appropriate. A science of practice accumulates methods to meet contemporary challenges and sometimes maintains them long past their period of immediate usefulness. As a result, an examination of the theoretical, cultural, and socioeconomic influences on the behavior, ideas, and practices of clinical psychologists over the course of time appears to provide the best approach to understanding the present status and underlying bases of current clinical psychological study.

Reprinted from Sigmund Koch (Ed.), *Psychology, a Study of a Science*, Vol. 5 (New York: McGraw-Hill, 1963), pp. 780–830, by permission of the McGraw-Hill Book Company. Dr. Rotter is Professor of Psychology and Director of the Clinical Psychology Training Program, University of Connecticut.

To define or delimit clinical psychology on either logical or practical grounds is to attempt a task which would be likely to please very few, if any. A narrow logical definition would be rejected by many clinical psychologists. A broad but loose definition would overlap heavily with such fields as educational psychology, social psychology, counseling psychology, psychiatry, and industrial psychology. On the other hand, a definition of clinical psychology in terms of what it is that people who call themselves clinical psychologists actually do would probably overlap with all the fields of psychology—applied and theoretical. No attempt will be made, therefore, to provide a neat, logical definition of clinical psychology which adequately differentiates it from all other applied fields in psychology or other sciences.

Possibly the most general definition of what the clinical psychologist is concerned with can be broadly described as "the psychological adjustment of individuals." The interest in the individual's adjustment includes two general functions, the first of which could be called "assessment" or "description" and sometimes is referred to as "diagnosis," and the second is one of therapy or management.

The extensive changes in clinical psychological practice in the last twenty years have involved changes in methods. Perhaps more importantly, they have been changes in emphasis on the age and types of patients dealt with under these two general functions and in the relative importance attached to treatment as compared to diagnosis. A brief overview of these historical trends will help orient the reader to the sections that follow.

HISTORICAL TRENDS

During the 1930s and prior to World War II, the larger proportion of psychologists who identified themselves as clinical psychologists worked primarily with children's problems. They did so in settings such as university clinics, community clinics, traveling clinics operated by state departments of public welfare and sometimes by state departments of education, as well as in institutions for the feebleminded, clinics for the physically handicapped, speech pathology clinics, and institutions for the delinquent or predelinquent. Their major job was psychological testing with a great emphasis on intellectual ability and deficit. In many instances, rather thorough case studies were obtained, utilizing either their own or social workers' case materials in addition to tests. The information obtained was used to make recommendations—usually to teachers, parents, therapists involved in some special handicap training, referring physicians, and juvenile authorities. The university training of most of the clinicians tended to be limited to courses on group testing, the Stanford-Binet, abnormal psychology, and perhaps child psychology or child development. Most of the training in practical clinical skills was obtained as field experience on the job or, in some rare instances, as genuine internship [Shakow, 125].

Rarely did the clinical psychologist do extensive face-to-face therapy with children. In a few instances [Louttit, 80], such therapy was carried out in community clinics and was limited primarily to a rather eclectic approach to play therapy. Occasionally something approaching psychotherapy was carried out by clinical psychologists working with adolescent delinquents and persons having speech problems, particularly stutterers.

Work with adults was distinctly less common than work with children. Primarily, clinical psychologists working with adults had some institutional placement, usually a state psychiatric hospital in which their primary job was giving tests to aid the psychiatrist in making a diagnosis. Other positions were in prison systems where the psychologist combined the functions of classification and clinical assessment of inmates. Prison psychologists occasionally did individual or group psychotherapy. In the psychiatric hospital, individual or group psychotherapy tended to be rare; if present at all, it was only a minor aspect of the psychologist's job. Psychologists in institutional positions frequently found themselves involved in problems of selection of attendants, aides, or other personnel, with particular emphasis placed upon the personality adjustment or emotional stability of the applicants.

Toward the latter thirties, emphasis or personality testing, particularly with adults in mental hospitals, began to increase, but it was still heavily

outweighed by the emphasis on tests for ability and deficiency, tests purporting to determine the presence of deterioration, brain damage, or disabilities, and tests for special skills. Most books published in this period in the general area of clinical psychology were test manuals. Extensive reports of the diagnostic value of some tests of intellectual functioning appeared later. Psychologists rarely were involved in the publication of descriptions of methods of face-to-face treatment.

The advent of World War II, the war itself, and its aftermath—all of these produced important changes in the practices of clinical psychologists. One of the important early effects resulted from a large migration in the late thirties of both psychologists and psychiatrists, many of whom were escaping the totalitarian regimes. Several of this group had psychoanalytic interests and training (Freudian, Adlerian, Jungian). Although they did not initiate psychoanalytic thinking in this country, their activities and writings led to an increased interest in personality and personality development in general and psychoanalytic concepts in particular. Individual personality tests such as the Rorschach also were reintroduced to psychologists and psychiatrists in this period and some of the German and Austrian psychologists brought in a German characterological approach to personality. The general effect on the clinical psychologists and psychiatrists with whom they came in contact was to reduce the emphasis on intelligence, deficit or ability testing and to increase the emphasis on personality development, dynamics, and description.

The war itself led to an increased interest in clinical psychology and in the potential contribution of clinical psychologists to the treatment of mental patients. The large number of rejections in the draft for reasons of instability and intellectual deficiency created a national concern with the general problem of prevention and amelioration. After the war, this concern led to a greatly enlarged budget for the Institute of Public Health. Psychologists made a strong impression on people working in the mental health field because of their techniques, which could be used for selection, and because of their general knowledge of research methods. The U.S. Public Health Department, in making grants during the postwar period and advising the states on the use of these grants, placed great stress upon hiring clinical psychologists for both clinical and research purposes.

Within the Armed Forces, a large number of psychological breakdowns preceding or during combat found the medical services inadequately equipped to deal with the problem. Psychiatrists were few; consequently, both psychiatrists and clinical psychologists were trained in short courses to deal with the problem. Again the psychologist, with his selection techniques and his knowledge of research methods, created a strong impression on the people working in this field. Plans for an expanded program for the care and treatment of veterans included substantial sums for the training and hiring of clinical psychologists.

Support for training of clinical psychologists, both from the U.S. Public Health Service and from the Veterans Administration, went to universities which undertook an extensive program at the Ph.D. level for training clinical psychologists. Many of the students supported themselves—through the Veterans Administration —by working in Veterans Administration facilities which were scattered throughout the states. As their clinical material, these students had adults who had been psychologically incapacitated to some extent by their Army experience. Since the Veterans Administration training program was the largest program supporting the training of clinical psychologists, a major trend after the war was toward an interest in the personality problems of adults. The Veterans Administration was willing to hire the psychologists who finished in approved programs at salaries which generally exceeded those obtainable in schools, prisons, or community centers. Consequently, there was a marked increase in interest and training for working with adults who had personality breakdowns or problems in the postwar period.

During the war, the practical necessity of returning as many men as possible to combat led to a number of expedient attempts to do psychotherapy on patients. When clinical psychologists were available, they were frequently pressed into group psychotherapy [Bijou, 15] and, in some cases, individual therapy in the Army setting.

The work of Carl Rogers [108] during and immediately following the war in the field of psychotherapy—particularly his emphasis on publishing actual therapy protocols—created widespread interest. The somewhat sterile approach to diagnosis yielded—at least for many psychologists —to a strong desire to do therapy and to do something which could be immediately seen as helpful to the patient. This interest in adult psychotherapy, stimulated by new translations of European writings and by the presence of lay and medically trained analysts from the Continent, opened up the area of long-term face-to-face treatment of adults for clinical psychologists.

This was a province of practice which previously was almost the exclusive domain of a few psychoanalytically trained psychiatrists. That one had neither to be psychoanalyzed, nor psychoanalytically oriented, nor have an M.D. in order to do such treatment was readily accepted by clinical psychologists.

The U.S. Public Health Service supported a conference on the training of clinical psychologists at Boulder, Colorado, in 1949 [Raimy, 104]. This conference resulted in a number of general agreements, one of which was to try to make the Ph.D. a minimum requirement for an individual calling himself a clinical psychologist. Thus, the Ph.D. began to be required, either formally or informally, for clinical psychologists in universities and in all kinds of practical settings. Many of the universities lost interest in training clinical psychologists below the Ph.D. level. Due to the large number of openings available, it was natural that most clinical psychologists, with their greater investment in training, would enter the positions with the best economic future. Since these did not include community clinics, prison systems, school systems, clinics for the physically handicapped, etc., a general drift began toward work with adults and adult problems. More and more clinical psychologists accepted positions in the Veterans Administration, state hospitals, universities, university medical schools, private practice, and industrial consulting firms which emphasized the individual adjustment of executives.

In summary, then, since the early thirties, a general shift took place (1) away from a major emphasis on children's problems and handicaps to problems of adult adjustment, (2) away from a strong emphasis in intelligence testing, testing for psychological deficits and interference in intellectual functioning to an interest in testing for personality description and adjustment, and (3) away from an interest in diagnosis and description with an emphasis on the psychologist's function as a tester to an interest in psychotherapy and the actual management of cases.

Of course, each new emphasis in clinical interest resulted in a revised approach to older methods. For example, in the period between 1945 and 1950, literally scores of studies were done with intelligence tests such as the Wechsler-Bellevue Scale [Rabin and Guertin, 102], attempting to use these tests for purposes of diagnosis or personality assessment, thus indicating a markedly revised interest in intelligence testing.

In discussing the source and nature of the theory and research currently being applied by clinical psychologists, it is both logically and historically appropriate that we consider this theory under three large headings: (1) intelligence testing, (2) personality measurement and description, and (3) psychotherapy. Not only does this trichotomy provide some convenience in organizing this chapter, but the theory itself which is utilized in these three areas of application reflects differences which are understandable in light of social forces present at the different times at which they became the focus of interest for clinical psychologists.

An assessment of the major trends in clinical psychology both as to the techniques in use and the source of concepts employed by clinical psychologists in one brief chapter requires the neglect of many aspects of both practice and theory. Consequently, it is difficult to justify the selection of both the techniques and the ideas which will be surveyed and the selection of influences which have had a major effect on clinical psychological practices and theory. The following discussions deal with general trends, not including all important concerns of clinical psychologists; the more specific topics should be regarded as examples of these trends rather than descriptions of the most important developments in clinical psychology.

THE MEASUREMENT OF INTELLIGENCE

The earliest phase of the applied movement which now is known as clinical psychology was concerned primarily with the measurement of intelligence for purposes of studying individual adjustment. Although psychologists had earlier been concerned with the measurement of individual differences on a variety of mental, sensory, and motor tests, clinical psychology in this country is usually considered to have begun with Lightner Witmer's establishment, in 1896, of a clinic to deal with the adjustment problems of children. The major concern of this clinic and succeeding ones was handicapped children—the deaf, the blind, the mentally defective, and the physically handicapped. With the advent of intelligence testing, particularly the Binet-Simon method, the role of the psychologists in the clinic clearly became one of measurement of intellectual capacities and potentialities. The earliest employment of clinical psychologists was in university clinics, institutions for the feebleminded, child guidance clinics, and the like. Somewhat later, psychologists found jobs testing individual patients in mental hospitals.

Although clinical psychologists performed functions other than ability testing, mental testing dominated the majority of their practice and almost all of the books published in this area before 1930 were essentially manuals of tests such as those of Whipple in 1910 [151], Terman in 1916 [141], Pintner and Paterson in 1917 [99], Goodenough in 1926 [35], Wells in 1927 [150], and Bronner, Healy, Lowe, and Shimberg in 1927 [19]. In work with adult mental patients, some use was being made of inventories and the word-association method, but there was relatively little testing of personality characteristics for purposes of individual case study.

Although the prediction of individual "mental capacity" is still an important area of practice for the clinical psychologist, the purpose of giving tests has expended to a considerable extent during the last thirty years. The early theory of intelligence and mental abilities, however, has persisted to a large degree in current thinking, and the understanding of current conceptions requires some knowledge of the *theory* of the early mental testing movement.

There seems to be general agreement that the early work on the measurement of mental abilities stems from the German, Scottish, French, and English "faculty" psychologists. What the tests intended to measure were faculties of the mind, sometimes conceived in some over-all fashion as the intellectual faculties, including judgment, reasoning, memory, discrimination, etc., and sometimes conceived of as relatively specific characteristics. These were thought to be innate in character but affected by experience to some extent, particularly by central nervous system and sensory disorders. Strangely enough, Binet and Simon, although referring to intelligence as a "faculty," frequently made reference to the fact that they did not believe that this ability was entirely a matter of inheritance but that it also reflected training and opportunity. Peterson [96], in his early book on intelligence, referred somewhat skeptically to statements made by Binet regarding the intellectual gains of presumably feebleminded children being trained by Binet. However, Binet's feeling that this innate capacity was subject to training had little effect and essentially was neglected until later developments in American psychology.

Referring to intelligence as an innate faculty of the mind does not necessarily include the notion of a faculty as a kind of force impelling the individual to action, as some writers thought. Rather, we are using the term to describe a presumed inherent characteristic of the "mind," a built-in way of perceiving and reacting which defined not only what the individual would do, but also what he could not do on a genetic and neurological basis. This early conception contained the notion that there are other faculties such as emotions and will, and their relative strength in any given individual affected the intellectual faculties by domination and inhibition. For example, intellectual functioning was affected in mental disorders because of the domination of emotional faculties or deterioration of the will (motivation). In general, there was more reliance on the idea that the emotions, or lack or disintegration of the will interfered with the expression of the intellect and intellectual faculties and abilities that there was on the conception that the individual's life experience determined the kind and degree of development of a variety of skills.

In his early work, Binet needed to use some measure of serious retardation in intellectual functioning. He arbitrarily selected two mental age years as a criterion of such retardation [Stoddard, 137]. It was soon apparent that such a criterion would be differential at different age levels; to correct this, Stern [136] suggested dividing the mental age by the chronological age and so gave birth to the IQ. It is Stoddard's opinion, probably well founded, that Stern's "innocent contribution" has created much more difficulty in the area of mental testing than could have been foretold at the time of its inception.

A rather active controversy was carried out in the late twenties and early thirties regarding the nature of intelligence. Was it made up of specific abilities [Thurstone, 144; Thorndike, 143] or was it determined largely by a general factor [Spearman, 135]? This discussion, as far as clinical psychology is concerned, was relatively academic because general intelligence and the IQ were by this time "entitized" and reified to a considerable extent, and the conception of some general over-all faculty was implicitly accepted, as indicated by the actual practice of clinical and educational psychologists. Although it was believed that general intelligence was made up of different, highly correlated specific abilities, it was also widely believed that under normal conditions some general factor or trait adequately described the individual's potential to learn.

Once the IQ was reified, discussion did not center around whether or not this was a useful construct, but around what intelligence *really* was, and every psychologist had his own private meaning for the term. This situation led Johnson to write:

Thus, the word *intelligence* has been used—and is currently used—to refer to a bewildering variety of activities and assumed qualities. Discussion about intelligence, therefore, drips with controversy, invective, and obfuscation: animals have intelligence; animals cannot have intelligence; intelligence is hereditary; it is environmentally determined; the rate of mental growth is increased in an enriched environment, decreased in an impoverished one; it is not; intelligence is comprised of a general factor together with a number of specific factors; it consists of specific factors only; it is mainly a verbal affair; its verbal aspects are relatively unimportant, etc. [56, p. 115].

Not only was it thought that the IQ of an individual was a meaningful and useful construct, it was also accepted that—barring the advent of some kind of "physical" or "mental" pathology—the IQ should remain constant. Although such constancy was difficult to empirically demonstrate [Bayley, 11; Sontag, Baker, and Nelson, 134], the "ideal" instruments were constructed and refined in such a way as to not *test* this assumption but to *build* it into each scale. In this way, a test was considered to be better, more valid, and more acceptable if it could demonstrate such constancy over long periods of time. Tests were devised not so much to obtain an adequate sample of what the child could do or what he had learned, but presumably (although this now seems a little ridiculous) to measure his really true innate capacity and, if possible, to minimize the aspects of experience and training.

Of course, the next step in such reasoning was to assume that if the individual did not function as well in life situations—in school, on the job, etc.—as he should according to his innate ability, then he was a victim of some kind of mental or physical pathology. If it could be demonstrated or assumed that his functioning relative to others at one time was higher than it was currently, he was likewise the victim of pathology. The concept of intelligence being made up of specific abilities also has its place here, since it was conceivable that under different kinds of pathology, different kinds of specific abilities would be more affected than others. The pattern of different abilities (i.e., verbal versus performance, new memory versus old memory, concrete versus abstract, etc.) could be used not only to indicate the presence of pathology, but also to indicate the specific nature of the pathology so that particular diagnostic groups presumably would show a specific pattern of discrepancies.

It is on these two basic principles that much of the work of the clinical psychologist concerned with adjustment was based. Of course, there were applications in addition to those seeking to "diagnose" pathology or maladjustment. For example, tests were devised to measure presumed innate capacity for individuals with various language, physical, and sensory limitation in order to make predictions about educability.

The foregoing analysis is to some extent an oversimplification. The notion of specificity was more accepted by some, and many of the omnibus-type tests were analyzed for special abilities and tests were created to measure specific abilities, for example, sensori-motor functions, memory, judgment, verbal ability, etc. The profile of these various abilities was used for the purpose of indicating particular kinds of pathology, and also for the purpose of making predictions and suggestions about training, education, placement, and other forms of management of individuals.

Psychology, like the other social sciences, frequently reflects the social and political thought of the times. The concept of intelligence was no exception to this. The idea of innate unchanging characteristics (the constant IQ) was not consistent with the social and political thought of the thirties, and it was attacked by both sociologists and psychologists. Early studies on racial differences in intelligence yielded to studies on changes in intelligence as a function of education and other environmental changes. Particularly influential in changing attitudes were the studies on changes in the intelligence of Negroes moving from the South to the North [Klineberg, 65]. Within psychology this emphasis was crystallized into "the nature-nurture controversy" [Skeels, 131].

A group of investigators at the Iowa Child Welfare Station (B. Wellman, H. Skeels, M. Shodak, G. Stoddard, R. Updegraff, H. Williams, and others) completed a number of studies demonstrating an increase in IQ as a result of early stimulation by foster parents or preschool attendance. These studies made a considerable dent on belief in both the constancy of the IQ and the innate nature of intelligence.

Along with the studies of the Iowa group, a new look was taken at the previously convincing studies of the Jukes and the Kallikaks [Louttit, 79]. They were now regarded as very flimsy evidence for the inheritance of feeblemindedness. Later studies such as those of Schmidt [122] and Axline [8], although themselves heavily criticized, emphasized that many of the so-called "mentally deficient" were in reality "emotionally blocked." Controversies about the inheritance of feeblemindedness where there is no known organic pathology and the total influence of heredity in intelligence are still going on, but the earlier concepts of the innateness and constancy of the IQ have been severely shaken. In current clinical practice, there is a general acceptance of the idea that training and the environment have a large influence on development of the ability to score on intelligence tests. However, it is also generally believed that the influence of environment is maximum in the early years and minimum by the time adolescence appears.

In the forties, the sociologists and social psychologists continued to emphasize the importance of cultural influence on intelligence and attempted the development of "culture-free intelligence tests" [Eells, Davis, Havighurst, Herrick, and Tyler, 25]. Actually, these tests were apparently no more successful than others in providing materials which equalized or controlled previous experience. It is somewhat surprising that the emphasis on culture and training did not result in a discarding of the notion of over-all intelligence and the IQ in favor of a clear understanding of the value of varied tests in assessing what has been learned and what each test can predict. Rather, the early trend to entitize and reify the IQ continued. *That is, it is surprising that the pressure from sociology and from the social-political thought of the times was to break down the emphasis on the innateness of intelligence, but not to reject the concept of general intelligence itself or its constancy for the later years of development.*

A strong indication of dissatisfaction with this older conception of intelligence can be seen in a recent article by Liverant [77]. He summarizes his penetrating reexamination by concluding that the genetic model representing the antecedent conditions of intelligence is essentially untestable and not in accord with recent conceptual advances in both genetics and psychology. Liverant also states that the majority of the evidence indicates that the concept is not capable of subsuming the great variety of behaviors now assumed to be related to intelligence. He feels that the behavior realm typically ascribed to intelligence should be incorporated into a social learning theory with a focus of interest on the situational conditions which facilitate or hinder the acquisition of various problem-solving skills and the conditions which hinder or facilitate the performance of these skills.

INTELLIGENCE ESTIMATES
FROM PROJECTIVE TESTS

The advent of projective tests for the assessment of personality and for the purposes of diagnosis did result in some change or addition to the prevailing concepts of intelligence for many clinicians. However, these changes seemed to reintroduce more strongly the old faculty psychology. Although estimates were made from projective tests purporting to approximate the scores that might be obtained from tests such as the Stanford-Binet or Wechsler-Bellevue Intelligence Scale, it was generally assumed that such approximations were not substitutes for the formal tests already in widespread use. However, going back to the older faculty ideas, a reintroduction was made of the concepts of imagination, emotions, and will or drive as separate faculties. Presumably, some projective tests, particularly the Rorschach, are able to assess both present functioning and "true limits of capacity," with an emphasis on imaginative and integrative ability [Klopfer, Ainsworth, Klopfer, and Holt, 66, chap. 12]. These true limits may not be reached by the individual because of his lack of drive (will), lack of control of emotions, or lack of contact with reality. The typical intelligence test is seen by some clinicians as measuring efficiency rather than true capacity. The projective tests then were included in the testing battery of these psychologists not only for an assessment of personality deviations, but also for an assessment of intellectual dysfunction or loss as a result of some pathological condition and as a method of assessing "true intellectual capacity."

THE CURRENT SITUATION

Although the assessment of intelligence of individuals for the purpose of predicting their education or occupational achievement is still part of the function of the clinical psychologist, it no longer is his major interest. The latter emphases on dynamics, adjustment, and psychopathology has led to (1) the widespread use of intelligence tests as indicators of the extent or nature of the maladjustment or to explain the reason for some problems of adjustment, (2) the analysis of test profiles to relate specific disabilities to specific diagnoses, including whether or not low-level functioning is a true feeblemindedness or a functional limitation imposed because of an emotional disorder, and (3) the development of tests based on the work of neurologists and physiological psychologists and purporting to indicate damage to the brain.

The tests of brain damage are in part based on theories of brain functioning but, to a large extent, they have been accepted on rather shaky empirical grounds. These measures will be discussed briefly in the section on diagnosis. The many studies attempting to relate patterns of performance on point scales, such as the Wechsler-Bellevue, to diagnoses are almost purely empirical in nature and have usually failed to cross-validate on repeated tests with new populations.

One result of this interest in profiles or patterns for measuring pathology has been the greater reliance in clinical practice on point scales. Point scales such as the Wechsler Adult Intelligence Scale [148] and Wechsler Intelligence Scale for Children [147] are supplanting age scales such as the Stanford-Binet because of the greater conveniences in analyzing and comparing subtests.

The tendency in recent research is to avoid or neglect explicit theory in justifying the method of measurement of intellectual dysfunction psychologically or neurologically described. Empirical findings are reported but turn out to be nonsubstantial on repeated and careful objective testing. The methodologies of research are probably less at fault in this failure to cross-validate instruments than the concepts of pathology (i.e., treating brain damage as if it were some type of entity with similar characteristics, regardless of the individual or the locus, or the extent or nature of the brain pathology) and diagnosis (Kraepelinian), which are unreliable and do not actually abstract pathological behavior in a useful way for prediction.

In general, theorizing in the area of intellectual performance has remained relatively isolated and sluggish, and it seems that theories of intelligence have changed little in fifty years. Anastasi [6] has carefully argued that genetic determinants have at best only a distant relationship to complex intellectual behavior. However, we still seem primarily to measure faculties, innate in origin and general in nature, except that two additions to this theory have been accepted in the last thirty years. First, the specifics which make up the general characteristics of intellectual ability are differently affected in different kinds of psychopathology or psychophysiological pathology. Second, innate ability can be affected—sometimes considerably affected—by environment or culture, particularly in the early years.

Little use has been made of constructing tests specifically to measure variables of an intellectual nature which could be deductively arrived at from logical, systematic analyses of the theories of brain functioning or newer theories of psychological dysfunction. This is probably because logical and systematic theories in these areas are scarce.

As to the measurement of intellectual ability itself, surprisingly little use has been made of the tremendous body of knowledge accumulated by psychologists in the area of learning. Although the tests presumably measure the ability to learn, they almost always measure what *has been learned* rather than measuring or observing the individual in the process of learning. Only a few tests of "recent memory" and some problem-solving items that are really novel provide measures of the ability to learn some new material during the test itself. Tests for higher-level learning skills, such as those suggested by Harlow [41] and Schroder and Rotter [123] have not been made. Nor has there been attempt to break through the rigid categories of faculty psychology and devise constructs and tests which conceptualize the individual as solving problems in a variety of situations—without theoretical bias toward generality or innate limitations.

DIAGNOSIS

The clinical psychologist has met the problem of diagnosis with a set of personality variables and with an armamentarium of tests. Until recently, however, the tests he used were not clearly developed as operations for explicit theoretical variables. When they were so developed, they were often used for purposes different from those for which they were intended, accruing a variety of nonsystematically related concepts. Although it will result in some overlap, the following sections will discuss the source and nature of the concepts involved in personality tests separately from a discussion of the kinds of instruments in current practice. A final brief section will deal with concepts and tests utilized in the diagnosis of brain damage.

THE SOURCE OF CONCEPTS FOR PERSONALITY DIAGNOSIS

While the early work in intelligence testing was rooted in faculty psychology, the problem of diagnosis—even in its beginnings—appeared to draw on medicine or medical pathology for its orientation. The clinical psychologist was initially concerned with using his tests of intelligence and abilities, verbal and nonverbal, to discriminate the feebleminded (i.e., pathological individuals who could not be expected to benefit from normal educational or training procedures) and the more educable individuals (i.e., the blind or partially sighted, the deaf or partially deaf, the crippled, etc.) from those with less potential. Although the problems themselves were drawn from the medical approach to treating illness, the early work was oriented toward application in the field of education and training. Later on, when intelligence tests were beginning to be widely accepted, the clinical psychologist became involved in some problems of selection. With the growth of universal education and changing philosophies of education, his tests were also used to "diagnose" the superior child or the genius. The superior child was studied since he, too, required a special kind of handling or training in the school system.

With wider and wider acceptance of intelligence testing, clinical psychologists began to be hired in both institutions for the feebleminded and clinics and schools to make objective appraisals of abilities. Once hired, the clinical psychologist found himself being called on not merely to provide estimates of intelligence, but also to help make so-called "differential diagnoses." Was the limitation on ability permanent or temporary? Was the limitation on ability a result of a pathology or disease which was considered to be mental rather than physical, or "functionally psychotic" rather than "organic"?

In order to answer these questions, the clinical psychologist began to study the profile of responses to different kinds of test items, performance as compared to verbal, old memory to new learning, abstract to concrete, perception of form relationships compared to rate of manipulation. Tests were devised to sample the learning potential of individuals handicapped in hearing instructions, understanding English, seeing stimulus materials, manipulating form boards, etc. The standard intelligence tests gave way to a large variety of verbal and performance tests and the compilation of manuals for intelligence testing cited earlier.

As the clinical psychologist began the attempt to differentiate the source or kind of pathology from the patterning of intellectual tests, he also became involved in discovering limitations of performance resulting from functional conditions such as emotional inhibitions, psychoneurosis, and psychosis. It was a short step from here into positions in the mental hospitals to aid the psychiatrist in the diagnosis of patients.

Some psychologists worked in penal institutions, where they weeded out the individuals who belonged in either mental hospitals or institutions for the feebleminded and selected those most able to profit from education and training.

In this new diagnostic function, the clinical psychologist not only drew his problems from the fields of pathology and medicine, but made his application in the same field. For the most part, his function was to help the psychiatrist or another physician diagnose the patient's disease (sometimes this resulted in differential administrative management but rarely in differential face-to-face psychotherapy). In doing so, he took on the terminology and the concepts of psychiatry which had changed little since the middle of the nineteenth century and, in the opinion of some [Lewin, 75; Kantor, 59; Rotter, 115], he made a step in a direction which would limit his contributions for some time to come. That is, by accepting the disease-entity approach to behavior and tailoring his own tests and thinking to these concepts, the clinical psychologist may well have become involved in a relatively fruitless area of investigation and application.

The disease-entity approach to personality description is a true carryover of medical thinking into the psychological realm. Basically, the disease-entity approach in medicine deals with assumed specific diseases with regular symptom patterns caused by foreign organisms or resulting from specific structural defects. Applied to mental disorders or psychologically deviant behavior, it is assumed that a person so afflicted is a victim also of a disease in a literal sense. The disease might be inherited, based on a genetic weakness or some exogenous factor affecting the nervous system, or it might possibly be partially the result of early traumatic experience. It was made manifest by a constellation of symptoms which might be overlapping, as in the case of measles and scarlet fever, and making a differential diagnosis—particularly in an early stage of the disorder—was consequently a highly subjective "art."

The failure really to understand and develop methods of treating these "diseases" led to the substitute activity of classifying them for a long period of time. Here the psychologist could find a function. Was a disorder a true split from reality, genetically based and presumably of lifetime duration—or was it temporary and within the normal range, although extreme? Was it a side effect of structural attack on the nervous system, malingering, or what? Was the apparent depression, although cyclical, a true depression which reflected extreme personality deviation of lifelong duration—or was it merely the apathy of an individual whose interests in the outside world disintegrated as his disease advanced? Was the patient's refusal to communicate related to a deep depression, stuporous withdrawal, or major damage to the brain resulting in total aphasia?

The problem presented by the psychiatrist, in

which he asked the help of the psychologist, was to identify the true underlying disease. Since the textbook-defined cases were quite rare, the method was to describe the many symptoms and hopefully to arrive at a best guess of the "true diagnosis." In the late thirties and early forties, these were the major concepts with which the clinical psychologist worked. His traits were the symptoms of the various disorders of the psychiatric diagnostic schema. These included the nonpsychotic classifications of the hysterical, obsessive, neurasthenic, and psychasthenic neurosis, and various classifications of psychopathic deviate. The present method of classifying psychopathological behavior is considered to have originated with Kraepelin [68] in the late nineteenth century. Zilboorg and Henry [154] have shown that Kraepelin's diagnostic schema was a natural outgrowth of work in the preceding century. To the many classifications of mental disorder extent at the time and based largely on symptomatology, Kraepelin added the principle of classification by prognosis. Following Moebius [Rosanoff, 112], he stressed division of mental disorders into exogenous and endogenous categories and leaned heavily on the concept that mental abnormalities were disease entities. This latter concept had been a part of lay and learned thinking, at least since the time that mentally disturbed people were considered to be possessed by devils. Symptom, etiology, and prognosis were combined, not in any systematic way, but largely following the mode of the times. Kraepelin believed strongly that dementia praecox was an organic or endogenous disease and was incurable. Additions to and reinterpretations of the Kraepelinian system have been made from time to time, but the method of classification has changed little. The formulation of the nature of dementia praecox was changed considerably by Bleuler [Zilboorg and Henry, 154], and the "disease" was renamed "schizophrenia." Zilboorg and Henry in explaining the success of the Kraepelinian system state:

The Kraepelinian system was a true triumph of a settled question. Historically and psychologically the triumph was very great because it brought about, in textbooks at least, the fulfillment of the age-long ambition of bringing mental disease into medicine, carrying it through the front door, so to speak, bringing about a complete union of psychiatry and medicine.

It is easy to think in terms of categories and entities; now that the nosological approach to psychological abnormality has been incorporated into the textbooks of medicine, psychiatry, and abnormal and clinical psychology, getting rid of it is extremely difficult.

A second source of concepts came from the influence of psychoanalysis, which was becoming stronger in the thirties and became prominent after World War II. Of course, from a much earlier time, the concepts of Adler [1], particularly as applied in child guidance clinics, and the concepts of Freud, particularly applied to work with adults, were being utilized by psychologists operating in the field of adjustment and treatment. Some techniques for measuring the kinds of variables involved in the Adlerian and Freudian formulations had been developed [Symonds, 139]. The technique perhaps most frequently used and specifically developed to describe variables peculiarly psychoanalytic was the word-association technique. It was developed by Jung to discover the presence of specfic "complexes" postulated in the psychoanalytic conception of maladjustment. Interestingly enough, the same technique was more widely used [Kent and Rosanoff, 63] as a tool to aid in the diagnosis of schizophrenia.

The influx of psychoanalysts from Central Europe as a result of Nazi persecution had a profound effect on psychiatry and, through psychiatry, on clinical psychology. As a result of this influence, psychiatrists could be graded on a continuum from those who used purely the psychiatric diagnostic schema and its lists of symptoms as their conceptual tools to those who used purely a description of psychoanalytic dynamics for their description and understanding of mental abnormality. The presumed problems, as viewed from the psychoanalytic point of view, lay in the unconscious and were not readily amenable to interview techniques, questionnaires, etc. The psychologist had no way to get at these unconscious attitudes until the development of a new mode of testing—now known as projective tests—presented an opportunity which was enthusiastically accepted. The development of the projective technique did provide the psychologist with a set of tools to use for the description of personality from a psychoanalytic point of view, as well as new tools to deal with the older psychopathological concepts.

Two other general sources of concepts for the measurement of personality should be mentioned, although they have been less popular and less influential in general, except as they have been incorporated either into the psychoanalytic or psychiatric nosological approach. One of these may be called "trait theory" which, in its most limited aspect, involves typological conceptions.

The description of traits of character, which historically also has its roots in faculty psychology, has been of interest in the general field of personality theory for some time. However, clinical psychology, with its origin in medical and educational problems of pathology, had no ready utility for lists of traits, except as they related to various disease entities or reflected the internal dynamics of the psychoanalyst. Because of this, rather elaborate schemata such as those provided by Allport [5], Cattell [21], and the personalistic psychology of Stern [136] did not lead to the development of special diagnostic tools widely used by the clinical psychologist.

The early descriptions of mental diseases probably were partially influenced by some of the general typological thinking of the nineteenth century; in this sense, they are incorporated in the disease-entity approach.

Although typologies have flourished from the time of the early Greeks, present-day typological concepts in psychology are predominantly influenced by the French school, represented by the work of Rostan in 1828, and by the German school of Kretschmer [Sheldon, 128], whose typology followed closely that of Rostan. Rostan categorized into a digestive type, a muscular type, a respiratory type, and a cerebral type. These types correspond rather closely to Kretschmer's "pyknic," "athletic," "athletic-asthenic," and "asthenic types." Even when the typology has a more-or-less quality, so that a given person may be thought of as having a place on the continuum of a single trait or as having various degrees of characteristics of several types, one is still faced with a narrow, limited, and crude method of describing human behavior.

The present-day development of the Rostan and Kretschmer typology is best exhibited in the work of Sheldon [128, 129]. Although Sheldon has worked out one of the most elaborate typological systems and has fitted it out with the most objective referents for classification purposes, his typology remains subject to the usual criticisms.

Jung's [57] typology of extrovert and introvert is based primarily on psychological rather than constitutional determinants, in contrast to the typologies discussed above. It overlaps heavily, nevertheless, with the description of the psychological characteristics of the constitutional types.

Another classification schema has been developed based on the typing of individuals for their predominant sensory imagery. In modern times, this development traces back to the work of Galton [29], published in 1907. People who tended to image things predominantly in one sensory modality were classified into types such as: a visual imagery type, an auditory imagery type, a kinesthetic imagery type, etc. Rorschach [111], who was influenced both by the Jungian introvert-extrovert typology (which he called "introversive" and "extratensive") and by the imagery psychology popular in this time, combined the two and oriented his tests around the primary and basic characteristics of the *Erlebnistypus:* Testees on the Rorschach who tended to see things in movement (kinaesthesis) were considered to be introversive; those who tended to see percepts on the cards utilizing color were extratensive. The balance of these factors was the major descriptive variable of the test.

These general types found their way into abnormal psychology via Kraepelin [68] in 1913 and Kretschmer [70] in 1925. The asthenic or leptosomic body build was associated with the potential for dementia praecox, and pyknic body build was associated with the tendency toward manic-depressive psychosis. Body type itself became one of the characteristics of the "disease" and often helped establish a differential diagnosis in difficult cases. For the most part, typological thinking represents only a minor trend in present-day psychology. It still, however, has a basic influence in traditional abnormal psychology and in the area of psychiatric diagnosis.

Psychoanalysis has also developed its types (oral character, anal character, etc.), which are based on the individual's early experiences. For the most part, the typological thinking of importance to clinical psychologists has come from the disease-entity and psychoanalytic approaches to deviant behavior.

Mention should be made of the application of learning theory to problems of psychopathology or of the attempt to understand stable personality characteristics as a result of learning. The works of Mowrer [88] and Dollard and Miller [23] are perhaps best known in this connection. There have been many attempts to describe specific abnormal behaviors as a result of conditioning or association processes, but in general, these attempts provided no new concepts for describing personality. Rather they provided a description of the process involved in the development of the abnormal behavior as conceived in psychiatric terms, psychoanalytic terms, or both.

Of growing interest, but still considerably limited in actual clinical application, is a conception of personality in terms of needs or goal-directed responses [Murray, 91; Rotter, 115]. Although these theories undoubtedly originated in part in the psychoanalytic movement (including the Adlerian and Rankian conceptions), they have achieved a relative independence of specific analytic concepts and have developed some measures for their basic constructs. Partly as a result of the influence of Kantor [59], Lewin [75], Adler [2], and role-theory conceptions of sociology such as those of Thomas [142], the problem of pathology is not approached in terms of the diseases of the psychiatric diagnostic schema or the internal conflicts of analysis, but in terms of the interactions of the individual and his social field. The problem of maladjustment and adjustment does not involve merely a search for causes within the individual; there is a search for explanation in the individual's interaction with his particular social field or life space.

Other conceptions of personality are relatively recent—at least in their details of development. The Rankian movement, including Frederick Allen, Carl Rogers, and others, provides examples but such influence has been felt more in the development of therapeutic technique than in the development of diagnostic tools.

In general, the major influence on the concepts which the clinical psychologist used in differential diagnosis or in testing for descriptive purposes has come from the people who hired him to do the job, that is, from medically trained individuals with or without psychiatric training. These physicians were concerned for the most part with the classification or identification of the particular illness from which the patient was suffering. The psychoanalytically trained psychiatrist was interested in identifying the conflict, fixation, or instinctual anomaly from which the patient was suffering. Although the psychologist has added conceptual tools from other sources to some extent, these have not been the dominating ones in his repertoire. There are current signs, however, that the psychologist, by his own research tools and training in theoretical systematization, is beginning to bring to bear concepts of his own to deal with the problem of describing relatively stable behavioral characteristics of individuals. Examples of the building of test instruments around such concepts are the Level of Aspiration tests [Rotter, 114; Escalona, 26], originating in the work of Lewin, and the Edwards Personal Preference Schedule [24], originating in Murray's personality theory. A partial step in this direction is the attempt of some psychologists to statistically purify psychiatric concepts by factor analysis of clinical descriptions [Wittenborn, 152] and to develop tests such as the Minnesota Multiphasic

Personality Inventory (MMPI) [Hathaway, 44], which are ultimately aimed at substituting for subjective psychiatric diagnoses rather than merely predicting them.

In his earlier operations, the clinical psychologist's interest in personality was secondary to his work in assessment of ability. He paralleled the psychiatrist in the use of case history material and the interview as his source of information regarding the personality (the relatively stable characteristics other than intellectual) of his patients. Some techniques for evaluation of personality were developed quite early, but these were the tools of the psychologist concerned with research and selection (as in the case of the Woodworth-House questionnaire in World War I) more than they were tools for the clinical psychologist in his individual casework. Some questionnaires were, however, adapted for the clinic. A description of these tests is provided in Symonds [139]. One of these techniques, the Pressey X-O Test [101] was a forerunner of some of the later projective techniques.

As the clinical psychologist's interest began to turn toward differential diagnosis of functional disorders, new instruments were needed. One of the first widely used methods was the word-association technique. Symond's chapter on this test is still a standard reference. Naturally, the first attempts to widen the psychologist's diagnostic potential came from the reanalysis of techniques he used for intellectual assessment. The studies of Roe and Shakow [107] and Babcock [10] on analysis of the Stanford-Binet with pathological cases and of Jastak [52] and Bijou [14] on profile analysis of behavior problems are classical illustrations of this trend. Application of some of the work of physiologists and psychologists in the realm of emotions was tried out experimentally. These experimental procedures were not widely used as regular clinical techniques. The adjustment questionnaires obviously had their limitations. It was hardly worthwhile for the clinical psychologist to discover that the case already in the hospital or clinic was maladjusted, and he could make no particular use of the fact that the maladjustment score was 10 percentiles higher or lower than that of another patient. For feebleminded and psychotic patients, the questionnaire technique did not seem particularly applicable and so-called "psychopaths" could not be relied upon to tell the truth. As clinical psychologists became more and more

involved in the problems of diagnosis of psychiatric groups or in assessing the analytic dynamics of a patient, a vacuum developed in their repertoire of measurement techniques which was filled, in part, by the development and wider use of what has come to be called "projective tests."

Projective Techniques. The term "projective test" is loosely applied to a variety of test which are differentiated from other personality tests by all, some, or one of the following characteristics: (1) disguised purpose, (2) freedom of response, (3) global nature, usually encompassing a large number of specific variables, and (4) absence of detailed explicit norms and subjective scoring and interpretation.

The early forerunner of these tests was the previously cited word-association method. The Rorschach test, developed by a Swiss psychiatrist and introduced in this country through the writing of David Levy, Emil Oberholser, and Samuel Beck [Krugman, 71], was the instrument on which many of the more widely used current tests were modeled. Through courses by Samuel Beck and later Bruno Klopfer and Marguerite Hertz, clinical psychologists became acquainted with this instrument in the later thirties. During the war, it was taught to clinical psychologists in training in the Army and immediately following the war, it became a standard part of the clinical psychologist's techniques and training.

Work involving the use of inkblots to study personality antedates the development of the Rorschach test by many years. However, Rorschach was the first to develop an instrument specifically developed for clinical purposes. Rorschach was a psychiatrist who was interested in the problem of diagnosis of mental disease. He tried to construct an instrument that could be used to differentiate various kinds of mental disorders, ranging from organic brain disease to neurosis and including all of the so-called "functional psychoses," epilepsy, and feeblemindedness. Most of this work was done around 1916, and the theoretical concepts employed by Rorschach were the theoretical concepts current in Europe at that time. Although Rorschach makes some reference to psychoanalysis, he was predominatly influenced by the approach to mental disorder of Kraepelin, as somewhat revised by Bleuler. He conceived of the various mental disorders as disease entities, some functional and some organic in origin. The functional disorders were largely predetermined by constitution and inheritance, and each disease or disorder was so global in its nature that all of the affected person's activities were in part a reflection of its all-pervasiveness. Along with this adherence to disease-entity thinking was an implicit acceptance of faculty psychology current in his day and still relatively influential in present-day psychology. He speaks of the will, the emotions, the intellect, and the imagination as separate aspects or faculties of the organism that are sometimes struggling within the individual for dominance.

The dynamic aspect of Rorschach's theory is not the dynamics of the psychoanalyst or the dynamics of the field theorist, but the dynamics of the internal struggle among faculties and the attempt to describe behavior in terms of the relationships among faculties. A third source from which Rorschach drew his theories was that of the typologies referred to earlier. For the most part, however, Rorschach's "theory" (as it is sometimes referred to) is more a conglomerate than a systematic approach to personality. Certainly, it was less of a theory than that being developed by Freud or Adler around the same time.

In the late thirties, L. K. Frank [27] wrote an article on the new procedures, which he called "projective techniques." This label is now generally regarded as a misnomer. Along with the Rorschach test and some play techniques developing out of child therapy, he included some new tests developed by Henry A. Murray and his co-workers. Murray was developing a personality theory based on psychoanalysis but differing in its systematization. In 1935, Morgan and Murray [87] published a description of the Thematic Apperception Test; in 1937, Murray [90] described a variety of methods for the purpose of eliciting fantasies. Murray's goal was to obtain the same kind of material which appeared in dreams and presumably gave more ready access to unconscious ideation. One of these in particular, the Thematic Apperception Test, caught on and led to the development of a variety of other projective techniques which were mainly concerned with discovering the content of the subject's deeper or less obvious motivations.

Immediately following World War II, with the impetus of the Veterans Administration training program and its concern with serious problems of adjustment in adults, these methods achieved a high degree of popularity; the clinical psychologist could be as easily identified by his Rorschach or Thematic Apperception Test cards as he could by the Stanford-Binet or Wechsler-Bellevue Intelligence Scales. During this time, a large number of new projective tests were constructed and manuals written—usually following the two trends we have already outlined. They were either primarily concerned with obtaining information about unconscious motivation ("He has strong, passive, dependent needs," for example) or they were concerned with determining diagnoses, helping in the problem of making differential diagnoses, or describing the traits considered to be important for making psychiatric diagnoses. In a crude way, these two purposes have been systematized as dealing with the structure (diagnostic category) of personality or the content (psychoanalytic conflicts) of personality. The joint use of the Rorschach test to obtain structural information and the Thematic Apperception Test or a similar instrument to obtain content material was suggested by Harrison [42] and later by others.

For the most part, the universities rejected psychoanalysis and the projective techniques when they first made their appearance. This rejection in part accounts for the fact that the concepts and tools of the clinical psychologist came largely from psychiatry, medicine, and neurology, rather than from psychological theories of learning or perception. However, with the support for clinical psychology coming from the Veterans Administration and the U.S. Public Health Service, the large universities began to develop major training programs in clinical psychology. For the most part, earlier clinical psychologists did their research in traditional problems of psychology—then went out and practiced clinical psychology, which apparently bore little relationship to the research they had done at the university. The students in these new programs were able to do research with their own techniques and concepts. The projective tests were subjected to a great deal of testing at about the same time these methods were at the height of popularity. Most of the carefully done validation research resulted in relatively negative findings. However, with the typical cultural lag which takes place between research and application, it was still several years before a more skeptical and conservative attitude began to be taken toward the projective methods. As a result of the negative findings, clinical psychologists began to turn to other techniques. Particularly for research purposes they made increased use of techniques [Incomplete Sentences Blank of Rotter and Rafferty, 119]; Blum's Blacky Test, 16; Rosenzweig's Picture Frustration Test, 113] which were considered to have some of the advantages of projective instruments, but were capable of objective scoring.

The decline in the widespread enthusiasm for projective tests coincided with the increasing interest of clinical psychologists in psychotherapy. The over-all result has been not so much a rejection of projective tests and search for new methods as it has been a decline in the general concern and interest with diagnostic testing and a greater concern and interest with the problems of psychotherapy.

The effects of operationism in psychology and of the appearance of systematic behavior theories, such as those of Lewin and Hull, had their indirect effect on the clinician's attitude toward personality tests. This was more apparent for the more recently trained clinicians. Many of these clinical psychologists began to look for more explicit operational variables and theories with which to conceptualize their problem and to regard tests as operations for systematic variables. A general orientation toward regarding tests as referents or operations for theoretical constructs has been emphasized by Cronbach and Meehl [22] and Rotter [115, chap. 8].

Personality Questionnaires. Along with the development of projective tests, more refined and clinically oriented questionnaire methods were devised. An outstanding example of this is the MMPI [Hathaway, 44]. This method, borrowing again from the psychiatric diagnostic schema, set up nine empirically derived scales on the basis of psychiatric classification of patients at the University of Minnesota Hospital. Additional scales were set up to measure the consistency and honesty of the respondent. Although it was a somewhat lengthy test, it did have the advantage of dealing specifically with the categories or concepts in which the psychiatrist was interested. The difficulty with this and other similar scales lies in the unreliability of the criteria on which they were developed. Numerous studies demonstrating this limitation have been made [Rotter, 115, chap. 2] and cross validation of these scales on different populations usually resulted in inconsistent findings. Humm and Wadsworth [48] developed a similar scale for use in industrial selection, based on Rosanoff's psychiatric classification of types; the Guilford-Martin Test [38], based on a factor analysis and a trait approach, was also used in some clinics for high school children.

A more recent development in personality questionnaire tests is that of Gordon [36], Edwards [24], and Liverant [76], who tried to avoid the problem of a respondent giving the answer which they felt to be most socially acceptable by developing a forced-choice questionnaire in which the choices are presumably of equal social desirability. The Edwards scale attempted measurement of some of Murray's list of needs. Liverant measured some need constructs from social-learning theory,

and Gordon based his on a factor analysis of empirically derived items. In general, the evolution of forced-choice questionnaires in the personality realm is relatively new, but it appears to be a promising trend.

Another recent development is that of behavioral tests, for the most part instigated by the work of Lewin and his students. The best known of these is the level-of-aspiration technique, which is used to some extent in practical clinical situations. Behavioral tests are essentially work sample tests. They place the subject in a situation involving self-evaluation or frustration, and observations are made of his behavior in that situation rather than from his verbal statements about his feelings and attitudes or from his imaginative productions. The novelty of some of these instruments partly accounts for their lack of general popularity. However, their less general use in clinical practice also stems from the fact that they are relatively specific in nature and not simply relatable to the more generally used psychiatric and psychoanalytic concepts.

Structured versus Unstructured Tests. At the present time, some controversy continues between the advocates of projective tests and advocates of questionnaire methods. The controversy has two aspects, although they are often confused. One is the relative merit of subjective "clinical" versus actuarial or statistical [Meehl, 84] scoring and interpretation. The second is the relative merit of the structured direct test as compared to the indirect or unstructured test.

The categorization of structured and unstructured tests is somewhat confusing, and it would be better to substitute some other terms. The Stanford-Binet and the Rorschach can be regarded either as structured or unstructured, depending on how they are used. It appears that the difference lies in the degree of ambiguity of the instructions or the task presented to the subject and whether or not the method of scoring and interpretation is objective or subjective rather than the test materials.

For example, if one should ask a subject to count the Rorschach cards, one has an unambiguous test; if one should hand a subject the MMPI cards and ask him to put together the ones that he thinks should go together, one has an ambiguous test. Obviously, combinations of ambiguity and objectivity are possible—as are unambiguous and subjective interpretations.

The major differences between ambiguous and unambiguous tests can be regarded as twofold. The first of these is disguise of purpose. In some instances it is, of course, of value to hide the purpose of the test so that the subject cannot consciously or without awareness try to create some definite impression of himself. Numerous studies indicate that conscious control is a matter of degree, and subjects can change their responses in a specfic direction in both objective and projective kinds of tests.

Along with the possible gain from disguise of purpose is a loss which may well outweigh the gain. Some studies suggest very strongly that the subject does not take an ambiguous test passively. He attributes some purpose to the test, and the purpose he attributes to it may well hinge on odd bits of information, the setting of the test, differential emphasis on the words in the same instructions, and so forth. In fact, it is just because the subject is not sure of the purpose of the test that his own hypotheses hinge on minor clues, frequently ones of which the examiner is not aware. In short, as it strongly suggested by the study of Henry and Rotter [46], these tests may be much more susceptible to slight differences in the conditions of testing than structured tests, and their utility may be sharply curtailed if the individuals using them are not aware of this susceptibility.

This suggests that these tests are dangerous tools to use in selection and in research where they are presumed to be valid instruments measuring one or more personality variables. However, they may be ideally suited to research on the influence of the psychological situation on test responses and to some research relating various experimental conditions to perception.

The second characteristic of many of these tests is their omnibus quality. That is, instead of measuring a single or a few specific variables, these tests can produce responses which allow the subject to be placed in some rough high or low positions on a great many variables.

While it seems obvious that the ambiguous test cannot compete with carefully constructed unambiguous tests in measuring some clear and simple criterion for which the unambiguous test has been constructed, such a test can be of great value for the clinician, particularly one who is involved in some general assesment of the subject's personality. The clinician does not have available one test to measure the subject's hostility toward father, another for hostility toward mother, one for dependence on wife, another for anxiety over masculinity, etc. Even if he did have such tests available, he would never have the time to give them all. He relies instead on the hypothesis—which should be tested with each instrument—that what the subject *does* in a free-choice situation reveals the variables on which he is most different from others. However, since the responses of subjects can be so different and scored on so many different variables and since criteria for the things he is interested in are so difficult to obtain, validation of his judgments are hard to come by. Properly used, these instruments have value at the present time in providing the clinician with hypotheses—leads for further investigation. Such leads can be tracked down through additional testing, sometimes with more specific tests and with case history material. At least for some kinds of therapy, they may be invaluable to the psychotherapist in increasing the efficiency of his treatment.

In regard to actuarial versus clinical interpretation and scoring, both the evidence and logic argue for the fact that when one is predicting some specific, measurable criterion and has previous data on test responses and the criterion from a truly representative sample of a relatively homogeneous population, then a multiple correlation, regression equation, or other statistical device will predict the same criterion from another representative sample better than will subjective judgment—if the same conditions of testing hold.

In most practical testing situations, however, one rarely finds these conditions, namely, a specific, easily measured criterion, available or easily obtainable data and norms, a population on which norms have been obtained that is truly representative of the population they will be applied to, a relatively homogeneous population, and identical conditions of testing. Consequently, it is possible that there are practical testing situations in which the clinical or subjective method may be superior for certain purposes. Obviously, whether the clinical method is superior in any specific instance is at least partially dependent on the clinician.

What makes for a good clinician is not, however, a matter of general agreement or even of much discussion, although the study of Kelly and Fiske [61] made one empirical approach to the problem. It seems to this writer that, in theory, a "good" clinician has at least two frequently neglected advantages over the regression equation or multiple correlation. In practice, however, he is not very often specifically trained to make use of these advantages.

The first advantage is that he supplies informal or implicit norms from his experience that the objective scoring fails to supply. For example, let us take a personality questionnaire used to predict success at college. Where the test supplies different norms for men and women and possibly for age, he may consider differences in the meaning of a particular response for students from rural versus urban homes, for wealthy versus poor, for high school athletes versus nonathletes, for students of Italian versus Jewish extraction, for a single individual who went to the university school and probably had taken the same test before versus all the rest, etc. It can be argued, of course, that all these things can be done—by the accumulation of more norms or scores, feeding them into the multiple correlation, etc.—except that they are neither practical nor economical. In many instances, the number of cases in any group would be too small to develop meaningful statistical norms. However, the clinician can bring his experience to bear with variables that he has obtained from other groups and from his reading and general scientific knowledge.

The second major skill the clinician may add is the interpretation of the effects on response resulting from differences in testing conditions. A recent trend in validity testing indicates that a great variety of situational factors will significantly affect test responses [Lord, 78; Sarason, 121; Gibby, Miller, and Walker, 31; Mussen and Scodel, 92; Rotter, 116; Phares and Rotter, 97; Masling, 82]. These conditions include not only many characteristics of the examiner, the place, and the time of testing, etc., but the set, attitude, previous knowledge, etc., of the subject toward the test. For example, he can estimate for one subgroup or an individual the effect of an examiner who is likely to create hostility, the effect of time of administration (i.e., early Monday morning, just before lunch, late in the afternoon), or even the effects of recent changes in the draft law on the motivation of draftable college students. In general, such considerations give him information about the amount of effort and cooperation of the subject and, perhaps more important, the subject's purposes in taking the test. Again, many of these factors could be entered into an equation if enough data were gathered, but again, it would not be practical or economical in many cases. Quantification is always superior to no quantification if it is practical and economical, but the interpretation of or prediction from quantified scores and variables in many practical situations can be improved upon by a good clinician.

For both types of tests, a serious theoretical gap has been noted by several authors [Peak, 93; Butler, 20; Jessor and Hammond, 55] between the actual behavior of subjects taking tests and the inferences made from such behavior. Consider-

ing this problem in a recent analysis of the failure to predict goal-directed life behavior from personality tests, Rotter [118] has stressed the failure to apply our theories and knowledge about behavior in general to the test-taking behavior of subjects, as well as to the variables presumably being measured. The analysis emphasizes the failure to systematically differentiate expectancy for reinforcement from reinforcement, reward, or incentive value as *test constructs* and as influences on behavior in the testing situation. Current testing and prediction procedures also fail to recognize the major importance of the psychological situation both in analyzing the meaning or significance of test behavior and in determining what are the life situations to which prediction can be reasonably anticipated.

Summary of Personality Tests. Most of the tests mentioned in the foregoing sections have failed to establish themselves as having high utility or validity for practical prediction. This is partly the result of the fact that so many of them have been developed against the criteria of psychiatric diagnoses which themselves have poor reliability, and serious doubts have been raised about the value of these psychiatric concepts. Some have failed to demonstrate experimental validity because they have been developed in an attempt to discover unconscious motivations and "deeper" conflicts. For such instruments, the problems of finding adequate criteria are so great that they have rarely been surmounted. Some new trends have appeared in testing—tests are being developed for the measurement of less global or complex concepts than schizophrenia or anxiety, and there are promising studies in objective scoring of some projective tests, in the forced-choice personality questionnaire, and in behavioral testing. The projective tests should not be written off, however, as useless. Although they have limited value as instruments of known validity for research purposes, they can be extremely useful when the clinician regards his findings from these instruments as hypotheses for purposes of further exploration, rather than as independent and objective indications of generalized character traits residing within the individual.

Perhaps the greatest promise for the future of personality tests lies in the variety of criticisms on theoretical grounds of present procedures and the application of psychological principles of behavior to test construction. While new advances in statistics and test construction procedures can be of considerable value, they cannot supplant an adequate theory of complex social behavior applied to the test-taking behavior itself.

THE DIAGNOSIS OF BRAIN DAMAGE

In the realm of brain damage, the clinical psychologist's concepts also developed from a medical orientation. However, his concepts came from the neurologist rather than the psychiatrist. Hypotheses on the psychological effect of brain damage were formulated by such men as Jackson [51], Kleist [64], and Head [45], among the important early workers, and by Goldstein [32] and Weisenberg, together with the psychologist Katherine McBride [149] in the thirties. The concepts which these neurologists applied basically involved the same general faculty approach that was being applied in the area of intellectual abilities. Abstract reasoning, form perception, verbal ability, judgment, memory, etc., were the characteristics which would or would not be affected by particular kinds of damage to the brain. The early trend was toward strict localization, and the kind of intellectual dysfunction presumably revealed the localization of the damage. In addition to these concepts, the work of the gestalt psychologists introduced concepts such as disorders in figure-ground relationships, disintegration of gestalt images, distortions of figures, and abstract versus concrete reasonings.

Lashley's [72] doctrine of "equipotentiality" and Goldstein's [33] gestalt approach reduced some of the emphasis on strict localization of mental functions. Coupled with the additional influence of the psychiatric classificatory approach, this led to a generalizing of the nature of any damage to the brain. In consequence, brain damage is commonly regarded in practice as another kind of disease. This trend took place, although the work of Weisenberg and McBride [149] appears to have established the relevance of the distinction of dominant vs. nondominant hemisphere, as well as the relevance of broad concepts of localization, particularly whether or not the damage was anterior or posterior to the Rolandic fissure. As a result of this generalized view, numerous studies by psychologists have recently compared brain-damaged patients to patients with neurological disorders, making the assumption that brain damage, like schizophrenia, is an entity. The brain-damaged patients are expected to have some characteristic way of behaving, regardless of the nature, size, or location of the damage. The greater part of the evidence does not support this generalized view of the effect of malfunctioning of parts of the cerebral cortex.

Tests of Brain Damage. With the extreme difficulty of making neurological studies of the brain, the neurologist and psychiatrist turned to the psychologist for help, at least in the preliminary diagnosis of brain disorders. Since the intelligence testing movement had already developed some considerable diversification in terms of measuring specific abilities and disabilities, the items of standard intellectual tests were broken down into groupings so that memory functioning could be separated from new learning, language ability from performance, etc. Separate scales for memory function, such as the Wells Memory Scale [150] were developed and later revised by Wechsler [146]. Special tests developed by neurologists, particularly in the field of aphasia, were adapted by psychologists [Halstead, 39], and techniques like the Vigotsky Test [Hanfmann and Kasanin, 40] and the BRL Sorting Test [Bolles, Rosen, and Landis, 17] were in occasional use to study the possible loss of the higher processes of abstracting. More recently, specific tests were devised applying some of the work in experimental psychology [Hunt, 49] in the general field of perception and concept formation and many of them were largely influenced by gestalt psychology and the principle of isomorphism [Goldstein and Sheerer, 34]. Tests utilizing memory for designs seemed to be particularly useful, and the work of Bender [12] was extended in the development of a test instrument, the Bender-Gestalt. Graham and Kendall [37] have also devised such an instrument. Projective tests, such as the Rorschach, have been adopted to this diagnostic problem [Piotrowski, 100; Harrower-Erikson, 43], but these attempts have not stood up well on cross validation.

The validation of all these instruments for diagnosing brain damage has been badly handicapped by the difficulty of establishing criteria. The absence of a useful schema for delimiting different kinds of brain dysfunctioning and the difficulty of obtaining comparable control groups or accurate predamage data for patient groups are two of the major obstacles.

PSYCHOTHERAPY

EARLY TRENDS AND PSYCHOANALYTIC INFLUENCES

The earliest form of psychotherapy in which psychologists regularly were involved might best be called the "management of children." The early child guidance clinic was involved with problems of intellectual ability and concerned with advising parents and teachers and suggesting placements. The clinicians relied primarily on what might be called "common-sense principles." Gradually the ideas of Freud and Adler began to infiltrate into the guidance clinics. Particularly in the psychological clinics offering advice and recommendations, the ideas of Adler [1] seemed to hold more sway in dealing with children. By 1931, Woodworth could write:

> However true and adequate Adler's psychology may or may not be in the ultimate sense, it certainly embodies much proximate truth that is immediately applicable to life. One might say that his conceptions are easier than Freud's, easier to grasp and easier to apply. Especially in assisting children to master their problems, Adler's line of approach has proved its value, so that he has already won a position of influence in the educational field [153, p. 168].

However, in face-to-face treatment of children, Freudian-trained psychiatrists were beginning to adapt the techniques of Anna Freud and Melanie Klein, and play therapy with children was begun by psychologists working in child guidance clinics. The rather extreme approach involved in a more literal translation of psychoanalytic methods to children was not immediately popular, and play therapy with children varied considerably in the degree of conformity to the Freudian technique advocated by Melanie Klein and Anna Freud. Adler contributed concepts such as style of life, position in the family, sibling rivalry, inadequacy, inferiority, or insecurity feelings, displacement by other siblings, pampering, overprotection, co-operation, responsibility, and social interest. The Freudians contributed concepts such as catharsis, castration, transference, resolution of the Oedipus complex, and repressed hostility in dealing with children's problems.

Of particular importance was the notion of catharsis and repressed hostility. Many of the techniques relied heavily on expressive methods in which it was assumed that improvement would follow from the catharsis of repressed hostility [Levy, 74; Shaw, 126; Solomon, 133; Bender and Woltmann, 13]. Such catharsis was accomplished through finger painting, breaking balloons, playing in sand and mud, watching puppet shows, venting aggression against doll figures, etc.

For the most part, the treatment of children has not changed greatly in the last fifteen years, with the exception of the addition of new techniques which are derived from the Rankian group and which will be discussed below. Techniques vary from complete emphasis on treatment of parents with little face-to-face therapy with children, perhaps typified mostly by the Adlerian group, to extensive long-term child analyses with or without

extensive treatment of parents, typified by the more orthodox psychoanalytic school. In between these extremes are all varieties of treatment methods, many of them borrowing from psychoanalysis, with particular emphasis on catharsis. It is interesting that many of the neo-Freudians and Freud himself began to reject the importance of catharsis. Alexander and French [3] and Dollard and Miller [23] raised the question of whether expression of "repressed" feeling actually follows, rather than leads to improvement. These writers place greater emphasis on insight and attribute to catharsis only the role of leading to the potential for insight. In spite of the rejection of the importance of catharsis by some leaders of the analytic movement, much of the face-to-face therapy with children still relies heavily on catharsis itself as a major treatment concept.

Psychotherapeutic work with adults was more rarely attempted by clinical psychologists in the early development of this applied field. With few exceptions, psychotherapy with adults was practiced only by psychiatrists and a few lay analysts until the late thirties in this country.[2] Treatment by hypnosis, originating in work of the French school and via Freud's early work, was occasionally practiced by psychologists, but it never got a strong foothold. It is only rarely relied upon at the present time, although an upsurge of such treatment methods occurred during World War II, particularly in reference to the treatment of soldiers who experienced traumatic combat conditions [Brenman and Gill, 18]. In most cases, such hypnotic treatment was applied as a short method for speeding up the process of catharsis. In some cases, catharsis was the goal of the treatment itself, in others it was the first step leading to interpretation and attempts to accomplish insight.

The influx of both medically trained and lay analysts to this country in the thirties resulted in the treatment of didactic analyses of a number of psychologists, some of whom began to practice some form of analytic therapy. A multiplicity of schools of neo-Freudians developed. Ansbacher [7] has perhaps more aptly designated members as "neo-Adlerians." Horney [47], Fromm [28], Kardiner [60], and Sullivan [138] were included in these schools. For the most part, these writers broke off from traditional psychoanalysis by placing less emphasis on the importance of cleaning out the unconscious and by the rejection of the theory of instincts and by the rejection of a sexual basis for all motivation. They did rely on some version of Adler's concept of inferiority, usually in terms of security, and in some concept like Adler's "social interest," usually in terms of love for others. Clinical psychologists in contact with these various schools, either through their own analyses or professional association, developed all varieties and shades of psychoanalytic methods. The advent of World War II resulted in an increased interest in psychotherapy, and the writings of Carl Rogers were very influential in getting many psychologists involved in the actual practice of psychotherapy. Conceptually, Rogers seems to fit into a general movement stemming from Rank, which will be discussed below.

THE RANKIAN MOVEMENT

Like most of the others who broke away from Freudian psychoanalysis, Rank [105] objected to the primacy of sexual drive as a basic explanation of motivated behavior in humans. He also, like Adler, tended to reject importance of the unconscious as a storehouse of energy and the cleaning out of the unconscious as a first step in psychotherapy. For Adler, this meant more direct dealing with the patient at what the psychoanalyst would call the "ego level"; consequently, there was more direct interpretation and shorter psychotherapy. Rank carried these ideas even further.

From the point of view of the sociology of knowledge, it is interesting to note that when Rank came to this country he had considerable contact with schools of social work. Here his task was to advise on teaching social workers who were working with indigent families how to deal with the personal problems of their clients. Orthodox analysis was obviously highly inappropriate, and the major problem many of these patients faced could be conceptualized as one of dependency. The social workers themselves did not have the time for extensive training in psychodynamics, and any methods they employed would have to be suitable to the level of training and knowledge they had in this area. It is not surprising, therefore, that Rank's ideas began more and more to be directed toward a method which did not involve complex analysis of unconscious motivation and past experience.

Rank asserted that delving into the past served no useful purpose, but fixated the patient in the painful situations of the past, leaving him powerless to deal constructively with his current problems. He therefore rejected not only catharsis, but insight into the origin of current conflicts, feeling that they were neither necessary nor particularly useful in accomplishing change in the client. It was also clear to Rank that it would be hard to break off therapy with highly dependent individuals involved in the typical analytic "transference" and to get them to stand on their own feet. He felt that the relationship between the patient and the therapist from the very beginning should be one which stimulated the patient toward independence.

Rank's method of therapy, as it gradually evolved, placed great emphasis on a discussion of the relationship between the patient and the therapist with a partial rejection by the therapist of the patient's attempts to lean on him. Content centered around the analysis of current problems rather than analysis of the past. Without catharsis and insight, however, to explain why people should get better, Rank utilized the concept of will power, a prevalent concept in Europe at the time. His concept of will was conceived as another human faculty explaining man's efforts toward the obtaining of his goals. He felt that everyone had such a faculty and that if it were directed into constructive channels, it would allow him to make a better solution of his problems. He therefore considered the purpose of therapy to be awakening the patient's "constructive will" by the therapist's role as a "counter will." Rank's work was translated by Jessie Taft, a social worker who wrote *The Dynamics of Therapy* [140], in which she described Rank's ideas and applied them to social work. She introduced the term "relationship therapy" to describe this method.

Rank and Taft's work apparently had some influence on Carl Rogers and on Frederick Allen [4], a young psychiatrist who applied Rank's ideas to play therapy with children. The term "constructive will," however, was not an acceptable one in American psychology, and Allen essentially substituted a "creative acceptance" of oneself. Such acceptance was accomplished by freeing the individual of "anxiety" and "disorganized feelings" and through a generalization of the relationship achieved by the therapist in play therapy. Allen drew an analogy from the biology that the growth process is one of differentiation and integration and that before psychological growth could proceed, it was first necessary for the client to differentiate himself from others, particularly the adults controlling his environment.

Carl Rogers [108, 109], essentially in the Rankian tradition, accepted the general principle that therapy could proceed—without an analysis of the past—through the client's ability to solve his problems as he saw more deeply into them as a result of the therapist's reflection of his feelings. Inherently, Roger's conception still emphasized the dependent nature of the client and the importance of the client's differentiating himself from others. Like Rank and Allen, he explained the basis for change as the freeing of the patient's "growth potential." Later he dropped this term in favor of "self integration" to describe the internal process which accounts for the patient's getting better as a result of therapy. The notion of the self he uses can be related to Jung [58], Lecky [73] and Raimy [103]. Rogers carried the rejection of the importance of the past further than the relationship therapists did. He not only felt that the therapist need not explore the past for the patient's benefit, but that it served no useful purpose for the therapist. In fact, a diagnostic orientation on the part of the therapist would interfere with his intuitive understanding of the patient's feelings, which he should reflect back to the patient. It is apparent that such a view of therapy required an attitude and frame of mind or particular kind of personality on the part of the therapist more than some form of special training. Rogers's approach to therapy opened the way for people of many disciplines to engage in treatment without a long training program, personal analysis, or medical background. His early book *Counseling and Psychotherapy* [108], published a few years prior to the rapid growth of clinical psychology after World War II, was widely read. Rogers also brought the psychologists' interest in research and research orientation into the field of therapy, and his published use of recorded therapy interviews opened the door to psychologists to do research in this area.

One interesting side effect of the Rogerian movement was the denial of the necessity for diagnosis or even description of the individual's personal characteristics. The more a clinical psychologist accepted Rogers's orientation, the less he was concerned with or interested in diagnostic methods. In addition, the gradual disillusionment with the validity of techniques in common practice resulted in greater and greater interest in psychotherapeutic techniques, particularly in the settings where psychotherapy was possible.

Although Rogers's work led many psychologists to feel that psychotherapy was a legitimate field for them, they often differed strongly with Rogers's methods and the more complete phenomenological theoretical formulations [110] which he gradually evolved. As a result, other therapeutic approaches were also more widely explored. Frequently without the requirement of didactic and control analysis, many clinical psychologists began to

practice and teach some self-understood version of one of the psychoanalytic techniques. Sometimes these methods followed classical lines, sometimes a rather personal version of the methods of Freud, Adler, Horney, Sullivan, Jung, and others.

One rather different orientation is that of G. A. Kelly, who has some theoretical commonality with the Rankian school. Kelly [62] has lately published a personality theory which is based, like that of Rogers, on a phenomenological approach. Both Rogers and Kelly stress that the true concern of psychology is the internal perceptions of the subject, his internal frames of reference, or his subjective contructions of events, not prediction of behavior stemming from external stimuli. Where Rogers emphasizes feelings, Kelly is concerned with the subject's "personal constructs" or verbal and preverbal abstractions. He also has much in common with semanticists such as Korzybski [67]. Interestingly enough, Kelly's orientation to therapy involves the restructuring by the therapist of the patient's roles, following a study of the nature and content of the patient's personal constructs. The directiveness and methods of the therapist are quite different from those of Rogers, although both apparently start with much common theoretical ground.

The presumed difference between an S-R (objective- or stimulus-orientated psychology) and a phenomenological (experience- or subjective-orientated psychology) approach is being used increasingly as a basis for justifying different therapeutic techniques, although Jessor [53] has argued quite convincingly that the two theoretical approaches are much less different in operation than is usually believed.

Within the past few years, several American clinical psychologists have become interested in the variety of therapy methods, mostly originating on the Continent, which are loosely categorized as "existential analysis" [May, Angel, and Ellenberger, 83]. The general orientation has much in common with phenomenological approaches, although many variants deal with the unconscious life and use historical techniques. Such methods are based on the writings of continental philosophers such as Kierkegaard, Heidegger, and Nietzsche. It is difficult, however, to determine what many of these methods have in common— each borrows from different aspects of different writers—and most of the theoretical justification for the approach is obscure and laden with value terms. Perhaps the common ground for these approaches is the primary emphasis on the inner experiencing of the patient and a rejection of stereotyped approaches, "canned" interpretations, and psychiatric labels.

LEARNING THEORY APPROACHES

Particularly in the areas of diagnosis and psychotherapy, the conceptual thinking of the clinical psychologist has been borrowed, for the most part, from psychiatry and psychoanalysis. However, as psychologists became more involved in psychotherapy, the possibilities of more strictly psychological approaches began to appear since the process of psychotherapy itself can so readily be understood as a learning process. It is not surprising that the beginning writings in this area take psychoanalysis as a point of departure. Two major contributors of this kind were Mowrer [89] and Dollard and Miller [23].

Although Mowrer started with psychoanalysis, he rejected the notion that the problem in psychoneurosis was one of an overly strong superego leading to excessive repressions; rather, he felt that neurotics had "learned" social taboos but not assimilated them. The psychopath or criminal presumably has neither learned nor assimilated social taboos. Exactly what the distinction between learning and assimilation is or how it can be predicted it is not clear. Nevertheless, Mowrer's theorizing has brought him to the conclusion that that problem of psychotherapy was not one of weakening the superego but strengthening it; consequently, his method of therapy is more directive. It is, in many ways, closer to that of Adler, who felt that the patient had to give up his struggle for superiority in favor of interest in society.

Dollard and Miller have attempted to reinterpret much of psychoanalysis, using concepts derived primarily from Hull's learning theory. To do so, it was necessary to reject some of the notions of Freud, particularly the emphasis on instincts as differentiated from drives and, to some extent, the importance of catharsis. Primarily, their contribution was one of reinterpreting psychoanalysis in learning terms, but in discussing psychotherapy, they placed much more emphasis on its problem-solving character.

In a later development, Rotter [115] described a social-learning theory and its implications for psychotherapy, but formulated no extensive descriptions of specific psychotherapeutic techniques. This theory utilizes an expectancy and a reinforcement principle, but accepts an empirical law of effect rather than drive reduction. Behavior potential, expectancy, reinforcement value, and the psychological situation are the four basic descriptive variables.

From this point of view, the patient's maladjustment does not lie within him, but in his relationship to the social environment. Potentially, the problem can be approached both through changes in the patient's attitudes and behavior and through changes in the attitudes and behavior of the people around him. This emphasis leads to implications regarding the treatment of other individuals in the patient's environment, such as the teacher, parents, wives, husbands, etc. In individual face-to-face psychotherapy with adults, there is an increased emphasis on an understanding of the consequences of behavior, particularly so that delayed negative reinforcements or dissatisfaction and pain can be related to their logical source. There are also attempts to achieve insight into the origin of maladaptive behaviors. One implication of social-learning theory is that psychotherapy must include considerably more discussion of alternative methods of dealing with life's problems leading to the patient's trying out new behavioral solutions to his problems, including the development of "higher level" problem solving skills. Relatively less stress is placed on how the problems arose and the reduction of internal conflict through catharsis and insight. The latter is considered important only as the understanding of origins and motivations helps the particular patient achieve a position where he is more willing and ready to change his own behavior. If the patient can be helped to see and try out new solutions in his daily living, then he can determine for himself which changes will provide him with more satisfaction in the long run. Although this view of therapy has not been extensively tested, a number of laboratory studies [Rotter, 115, chaps. 5, 6] have dealt with principles which appear to be logically related to the therapeutic methods.

A recent book of Phillips [98] describes an approach to psychotherapy rejecting Freud's depth theory and drawing on "conflict theory." Phillips places great importance on the role of the therapist in helping the patient to structure the assumptions implicit in his behavior and to resolve his own conflict through the investigation of alternative methods of behaving. Although differing from social-learning theory on many points, Phillips, like Rotter, has attempted to build psychotherapeutic implications out of a human learning model rather than to reinterpret other methods by loosely translating them into learning terms. Shaffer [124], Shaw [126], and Shoben [130] have also urged the greater application of human learning principles to psychotherapy and H. B. Pepinsky and P. N. Pepinsky [95] have more extensively applied an anxiety-drive model to counseling.

One of the consequences of World War II was that clinical psychologists in military settings were asked, primarily because of lack of other personnel, to conduct group psychotherapy. Such groups were formed in prisons, convalescent centers, hospitals, and training centers. For the most part, these meetings were referred to as "gripe sessions"; more than anything else, it was assumed that if the patients could get rid of suppressed hostilities, express them, or talk them out, they would generally be less hostile to or more understanding of the authority demands of their situations. Although the success of these sessions has been questioned (some observers felt they did more to increase hostilities than to dissipate them), they served to introduce many clinical psychologists into the practice of group psychotherapy. Since World War II, they have continued to function rather broadly, working with both children and adults.

It is not possible to discuss here the great variety of techniques and concepts employed in group psychotherapy. In addition to the application of individual psychotherapy concepts such as Slavson's [132] application of psychoanalysis and Axline's [8] application of Rogers's methods to a group situation, concepts and techniques were borrowed from many sources. Moreno's [86] psychodrama technique and various derivatives of it are widely used, as well as principles of leadership and group interaction derived from sociology, social psychology, sociometry, and group dynamics.

Although the principles have not been clearly formulated, there has been an increasing trend to focus on group psychotherapy as a kind of therapy which provides special opportunities. The tendency is no longer to regard group therapy as a kind of mass situation with the same goals as individual psychotherapy. Rather it is regarded as a special situation where the patient has the opportunity to learn group norms, where he can be reinforced for social interest, and where he is able to learn about other's reactions to his own social behavior.

Although it is not customary, any general survey of psychotherapy should include reference to the values inherent in current practices. If the psychologist is to treat individuals, he must first decide what maladjustment and adjustment are. In other words, who should be treated, and what is the goal of treatment?

There is no logical or systematic way of determining the nature of maladjustment from theories of behavior. What behavior or which people we would call "maladjusted" or "adjusted" depends primarily upon value judgments (judgments of good and bad), at least at some level of theorizing. To state that something requires a value judgment is not to imply that it may be avoided. The clinical psychologist must make such a value judgment for himself. Do we consider as maladjusted the nonconformist who has few or no friends but writes excellent poetry, the man who is caught in the illegal act of putting a slug in the subway, the apparently self-accepting homosexual, or the patient in a mental hospital who, though confused from an outsider's point of view, seems to be happy and relaxed after years of hospitalization? Our answer will depend upon our basic value judgments on the nature of adjustment. Of course, there is an implication here that maladjustment represents more than a label. The judgment implies that someone should do something about it, that society or the clinical psychologist operating as an individual should make some attempt to change the person. Were we to assume that nobody should attempt to change someone else unless that person seeks the change, then we could get rid of the concept of maladjustment entirely and empty a large portion of our mental hospitals.

With some exceptions, psychologists (and certainly society in general) do believe that they have a responsibility to try to help people, or at least to help them discover that they would be better off with some changes. In addition to the people who seek psychological help, there are many others who would benefit from it, for example, the mother who is overprotecting her child; the person who is a danger to himself or to others; the only child, happy as the center of attention of indulgent parents and grandparents, who is heading for difficulties later in life; and the expressly miserable adult who is apparently convinced that his difficulties are physical and seeks no help of a psychological nature. If we equate maladjustment or the concept of maladjustment with the concept of those who need to be treated, helped, or changed, we must determine the kinds of behavior or people we would include in this category.

With the exception of Rogers and some of the followers of Adler, most clinical psychologists have avoided the problem of defining their own values. Instead, they rely on the concept of disease borrowed from medicine. By some ultimate criterion not made explicit, specific behaviors or constellations of behaviors are indications of disease, and anyone having a specific disease needs treatment. Therefore, we have the illness of the psychopath, immature personality, nervous disposition, psychotic, compulsive neurotic, and the rest. Diseases themselves are identified by authorities and may be found described in certain textbooks.

The importance of psychologists becoming more explicit about their values has been recently discussed by Jessor [54]. The three value concepts broadly conceived which appear to be *implicit* in the practice of psychotherapy might be called the "conformity approach," the "self-centered approach" and the "social-centered approach."

The conformity criteria for adjustment implies that a man should accept the values of his culture and that he is maladjusted when he fails to accept the mores, the goals, and the beliefs of his society. Although few clinical psychologists would admit to such a belief themselves, like others in our society,[3] they may frequently rely on conformity as the criterion of adjustment in the absence of other explicit value concepts.

The self-centered approach holds that the internal feelings of happiness, well-being, harmony, and freedom from pain and internal conflict are the criteria for adjustment. The person who feels more unhappy is more maladjusted, the behavior that results in the feeling of unhappiness or lack of well-being is the maladjusted behavior. The psychoanalytic and client-centered approaches to psychotherapy have emphasized these criteria by implication if not by overt statement.

The social-centered point of view stresses the social contribution of the person and his behavior. Does the person contribute to the welfare of others, to society as a whole? Does he fulfill some useful function in society? The same criterion can be applied to some specific behavior. Is it, in a broad sense, contributive to the society the person lives in? This was the emphasis of Alfred Adler and his concept of social interest. Adler [2] felt that the problem of treatment or psychotherapy was one of building social interest in the patient, and Sullivan [138] and Mowrer [89] have also by implication accepted the same value conception. Sullivan did this by relating adjustment to the ability to love others; Mowrer did so by relating adjustment to the acceptance of social responsibility.

Although these value concepts are more frequently complementary than incompatible, as good social scientists clinical psychologists still need to explore more thoroughly both their own value systems and the implications of these value systems for the practice of psychotherapy.

RESEARCH IN PSYCHOTHERAPY

Although many of the concepts and methods of clinical psychology have been borrowed from other disciplines, clinical psychologists have contributed the major effort and methodology to research on the effectiveness of psychotherapy and the nature of the process. The problems and limitations of this research have been described in the *Annual Review of Psychology* for 1960 [117] and in previous issues and in a recent symposium of the conference on psychotherapy published by the American Psychological Association [Rubenstein and Parloff, 120].

Such research on therapist variables, patient variables, process variables, treatment outcomes, and criteria for improvement is proceeding vigorously, and many dissertations which would have been concerned with projective tests in an earlier period now deal with some aspect of psychotherapy. Particularly favored are studies varying therapist characteristics and laboratory analogs to psychotherapy, since these areas of investigation are more amenable to inexpensive short-term research. In the latter category are studies of verbal conditioning, an application of Skinner's work on instrumental conditioning, recently reviewed by Krasner [69]. These investigators have been particularly effective in demonstrating possible subtle effects of therapist behavior.

PSYCHOTHERAPY—SUMMARY

Although most of the specific techniques used in psychotherapy stem from Freud, the general trend is toward the development of less time-consuming and presumably more efficient techniques and methods than classical psychoanalysis. The general over-all trend is toward less emphasis on investigation of the past and interpretation of symbolic manifestations of the unconscious and more emphasis on dealing with the present, using the patient's relationship to the therapist in therapy as a source of learning. More recently, there has been increased interest in conceiving of the patient's difficulties in terms of inadequate solution of problems. Sullivan and Rotter place particular emphasis—possibly derived originally from Adler, Lewin, and Kantor—on viewing the patient's difficulty in terms of his relationships with others and seeing maladjustment as lying not necessarily so much inside the patient as in his relationship with others.

At any rate, it is clear that clinical psychologists are beginning to feel some security in this general area and to contribute ideas that are more strictly psychological in nature. They seem ready to tamper with some of the highly valued taboos that derive from Freudian psychoanalysis.

One of the striking aspects of most of the psychotherapeutic techniques in common usage is their relatively loose relationship to theory. Although two or more psychoanalytically oriented therapists can argue from the same theory, they can emerge with considerably different techniques. The situation is similar for the more nonanalytic approaches, as illustrated by the considerably different emphasis in treatment of Kelly and Rogers, both of whom start their theorizing from a somewhat extreme phenomenological point of view. Although learning theory and perception theory are likewise beginning to lead to formulations of new or revised techniques of psychotherapy, it is probably safe to say that none of the theories of the nature of personality and its development are at this time so carefully structured and systematized that their implications for psychotherapy may be regarded as purely logical deductions from the theory.

Many of the recent attempts to reconceptualize the variables of therapy appear to have little as a goal other than the justification of previously learned techniques by using more widely accepted psychological concepts. However, they are also beginning to lead to new methods. The reconceptualization itself in many cases has the salutary effect of suggesting methodology for the validation of the principles of psychotherapy, either directly with patients as subjects or through laboratory experiments which provide "near analogies" to the psychotherapeutic situation.

AN OVERVIEW

The field of clinical psychology has changed considerably in its short history, and it appears that the change itself has been rapidly accelerated since World War II. Changes reflect the effects of such broad cultural conditions as wars at home and abroad, economic conditions, the broad trends of professionalization in psychology as a whole, the degree of interest of the university in training for a relatively new profession, and the kind of support government is giving the university. The issue of whether or not clinical psychologists are primarily practitioners or scholars and researchers is still an open one. The development of the profession also reflects the changing culture concepts regarding education, psychological disorders, and treatment.

It appears to this writer that psychiatry and psychoanalysis and its schools have played a much heavier role than traditional psychology in providing the practicing clinical psychologist with his conceptual tools. It should be remembered, however, that the university has been interested in training clinical psychologists only for a very short period of time. Prior to World War II, except for work in intelligence testing, the university provided the clinical psychologist with very little training for the practical jobs he was to do. Since he obtained his training in the clinical setting, he assimilated also the concepts of the people who had been working in that setting for a longer period of time.

The contributions of experimental and theoretical psychology, however, have not been negligible. The work in psychophysics has contributed heavily to the development of testing procedures and methods of measurement—for the more standardized tests in particular. The gestalt work in perception was a major source of theory and research in the development of tests for brain damage and also exerted a strong influence in the development of some of the projective techniques. More recently psychologists have been going both to learning theory and to perception theory to find a logical or sounder theoretical basis for their personality theories and psychotherapeutic techniques. Particularly promising is the fact that they are beginning not merely to look for justification for techniques and theories which have been previously accepted on an authoritative and subjective basis but also to derive new methods of treatment and new concepts from preexisting theory and research.

We have not discussed in any detail the actual established validity of the clinical psychologist's practices in the field of intelligence testing, diagnosis, and psychotherapy. In the latter two fields, it is hard to establish what this may be, but attempts to validate instruments in common use, for the most part, have been only slightly successful. Experimentally established validities—when they occur—are generally at such a low level as to hardly warrant their use in individual predictions. As for the field of psychotherapy, research itself has been so difficult that there are available neither sufficient data as to its effectiveness, nor established principles which have been tested independently in the laboratory and which can be logically and confidently applied to the complex psychotherapeutic situation.

The over-all picture, however, is not necessarily discouraging. To some extent, progress has been limited by the inadequacy of the constructs or conceptual tools with which the clinical psychologist has been working in the past and only recently has begun to challenge. New conceptual tools may bring new methods, and both may bring higher validities and greater utility. In any case, the more thorough training now required of clinical psychologists and some of the recent attempts to carry basic theory and research into the area of application under complex conditions may hold considerable promise for the future.

NOTES

1. I am greatly indebted to Dr. June E. Chance and Dr. Richard Jessor for their many helpful suggestions following their critical reading of this manuscript.

2. It is significant that in the two-volume handbook *Personality and the Behavior Disorders*, edited by Hunt [50], which was the standard source book in the training of clinical psychologists immediately after the war, only 1 chapter out of 35 was concerned with psychotherapy. This chapter was entitled "Psychiatric Treatment" and it was written by a psychiatrist. Recent texts in clinical psychology by psychologists such as Pennington and Berg [94], Wallen [145], and Garfield [30] devote about one-quarter of the text, on the average, to psychotherapy.

3. Mills [85] and Reisman [106] have described such conformity trends among American social scientists.

REFERENCES

1. ADLER, A. *Guiding the child on the principles of individual psychology.* New York: Greenberg, 1930.

2. ADLER, A. *Social interest: a challenge to mankind.* New York: Putnam, 1939.

3. ALEXANDER, F., & FRENCH, T. M. *Psychoanalytic therapy.* New York: Ronald, 1946.

4. ALLEN, F. *Psychotherapy with children.* New York: Norton, 1942.

5. ALLPORT, G. W. *Personality: a psychological interpretation.* New York: Holt, Rinehart, & Winston, 1937.

6. ANASTASI, ANNE. Heredity, environment and the question "how?" *Psychol. Rev.*, 1958, *65*, 197–208.

7. ANSBACHER, H. L. "Neo Freudian" or "Neo Adlerian"? Report on a survey conducted among members of the American Psychoanalytic Association. *Amer. Psychologist*, 1953, *8*, 165–166.

8. AXLINE, V. *Play therapy.* Boston: Houghton Mifflin, 1947.

9. AXLINE, V. Mental deficiency—symptom or disease? *J. consult. Psychol.*, 1949, *13*, 313–327.

10. BABCOCK, H. *Time and the mind.* Cambridge, Mass.: Sci-Art, 1941.

11. BAYLEY, NANCY. On the growth of intelligence. *Amer. Psychologist*, 1955, *10*, 805–818.

12. BENDER, L. A visual motor gestalt test and its clinical use. *Res. Monogr. Amer. Orthopsychiat. Assn.*, 1938, No. 3.

13. BENDER, L., & WOLTMANN, A. Use of puppet shows as a therapeutic method. *Amer. J. Orthopsychiat.*, 1936, *6*, 341–354.

14. BIJOU, S. W. Behavior efficiency as a determining factor in the social adjustment of mentally retarded young men. *J. genet. Psychol.*, 1944, *65*, 133–145.

15. BIJOU, S. W. *The psychological program in AAF convalescent hospitals.* U.S. Army Air Force Aviation Psychology Program Research Reports, 1947, No. 15.

16. BLUM, G. S. A study of the psychoanalytic theory of psychosexual development. *Genet. Psychol. Monogr.*, 1949, *39*, 3–99.

17. BOLLES, M. M., ROSEN, G. P., & LANDIS, C. Psychological performance tests as prognostic agents for the efficacy of insulin therapy in schizophrenia. *Psychiat. quart.*, 1938, *12*, 733–737.

18. BRENMAN, M., & GILL, M. M. *Hypnotherapy*. New York: Josiah Macy, Jr. Foundation, 1944.

19. BRONNER, A. F., HEALY, W., LOWE, G. C., & SHIMBERG, M. E. *A manual of individual mental tests and testing*. Boston: Little, Brown, 1927.

20. BUTLER, J. M. The use of a psychological model in personality testing. *Educ. psychol. Measmt.*, 1954, *14*, 77–89.

21. CATTELL, R. B. *Personality: a systematic theoretical and factual study*. New York: McGraw-Hill, 1950.

22. CRONBACH, L. J., & MEEHL, P. E. Construct validity in psychological tests. *Psychol. Bull.*, 1955, *52*, 281–302.

23. DOLLARD, J., & MILLER, N. E. *Personality and psychotherapy: an analysis in terms of learning, thinking, and culture*. New York: McGraw-Hill, 1950.

24. EDWARDS, A. *Personal preference schedule*. New York: Psychological Corp., 1954.

25. EELLS, K., DAVIS, A., HAVIGHURST, R. J., HERRICK, E., & TYLER, R. *Intelligence and cultural differences*. Chicago: Univer. Chicago Press, 1951.

26. ESCALONA, S. K. *An application of the level of aspiration experiment to the study of personality*. New York: Teachers Coll., Columbia Univer., Bureau of Publications, 1948.

27. FRANK, L. K. Projective methods for the study of personality. *J. Psychol.*, 1939, *8*, 389–413.

28. FROMM, E. *Man for himself*. New York: Holt, Rinehart, & Winston, 1947.

29. GALTON, F. *Inquiries into human faculty and its development*. New York: Dutton, 1907.

30. GARFIELD, S. L. *Introductory clinical psychology*. New York: Macmillan, 1957.

31. GIBBY, R. G., MILLER, D. R., & WALKER, E. L. The examiner's influence on the Rorschach protocol. *J. consult. Psychol.*, 1953, *17*, 425–428.

32. GOLDSTEIN, K. The significance of the frontal lobe for mental performance. *J. neurol. Psychopath.*, 1936, *17*, 27–40.

33. GOLDSTEIN, K. *The organism*. New York: American Book, 1939.

34. GOLDSTEIN, K., & SHEERER, M. Abstract and concrete behavior: an experimental study with special tests. *Psychol. Monogr.*, 1941, *33*, No. 239.

35. GOODENOUGH, F. *Measurement of intelligence by drawing*. Yonkers, N.Y.: World, 1926.

36. GORDON, L. V. *Gordon personal profile*. Yonkers, N.Y.: World, 1951.

37. GRAHAM, F. K., & KENDALL, B. S. Performance of brain damaged cases on a memory-for-designs tests. *J. abnorm. soc. Psychol.*, 1946, *41*, 303–314.

38. GUILFORD, J. P., & MARTIN, H. G. *The Guilford-Martin Personnel Inventory*. Beverly Hills, Calif.: Sheridan Supply Co., 1943.

39. HALSTEAD, W. C. Preliminary analysis of grouping behavior in patients with cerebral injury. *Amer. J. Psychiat.*, 1940, *96*, 1263–1294.

40. HANFMANN, E., & KASANIN, J. Conceptual thinking in schizophrenia. *Nerv. Ment. Dis. Monogr.*, 1942, No. 67.

41. HARLOW, H. F. The formation of learning sets. *Psychol. Rev.*, 1949, *56*, 51–65.

42. HARRISON, R. The thematic apperception and Rorschach methods of personality investigation in clinical practice. *J. Psychol.*, 1943, *15*, 49–74.

43. HARROWER-ERIKSON, M. R. Personality changes accompanying cerebral lesions. I. Rorschach studies of patients with cerebral tumors. *Arch. Neurol. Psychiat.*, 1940, *43*, 859–890.

44. HATHAWAY, S. R. *The Minnesota Multiphasic Personality Inventory*. Minneapolis, Minn.: Univer. Minn. Press, 1943.

45. HEAD, H. *Aphasia and kindred speech disorders*. Vols. I & II. New York: Macmillan, 1926.

46. HENRY, E. M., & ROTTER, J. B. Situational influences on Rorschach responses. *J. consult. Psychol.*, 1956, *20*, 457–462.

47. HORNEY, K. *New ways in psychoanalysis.* New York: Norton, 1939.

48. HUMM, D. G., & WADSWORTH, G. W. The Humm-Wadsworth temperament scale. *Personnel J.*, 1934, *12*, 314–323.

49. HUNT, H. F. *The Hunt-Minnesota Test for Organic Brain Damage.* Minneapolis, Minn.: Univer. Minn. Press, 1943.

50. HUNT, J. McV. *Personality and the behavior disorders.* Vols. I & II. New York: Ronald, 1944.

51. JACKSON, J. H. *Selected writing of Hughlings Jackson.* James Taylor (Ed.). London: Hodder, 1932.

52. JASTAK, J. School test patterns of clinic children. *Del. State med. J.*, 1939, *11*, 114–119.

53. JESSOR, R. Phenomenological personality theories and the data language of psychology. *Psychol. Rev.*, 1956, *63*, 173–180.

54. JESSOR, R. Social values and psychotherapy. *J. consult. Psychol.*, 1956, *20*, 264–266.

55. JESSOR, R., & HAMMOND, K. R. Construct validity and the Taylor Anxiety Scale. *Psychol. Bull.*, 1957, *54*, 161–170.

56. JOHNSON, W. *People in quandaries.* New York: Harper, 1946.

57. JUNG, C. G. *Psychological types.* New York: Harcourt, Brace, 1923.

58. JUNG, C. G. *Modern man in search of a soul.* New York: Harcourt, Brace, 1933.

59. KANTOR, J. R. *Principles of psychology.* Vols. I & II. New York: Knopf, 1924.

60. KARDINER, A. *The psychological frontiers of society.* New York: Columbia Univer. Press, 1945.

61. KELLY, E. L., & FISKE, D. W. *The prediction of performance in clinical psychology.* Ann Arbor, Mich.: Univer. Mich. Press, 1951.

62. KELLY, G. A. *The psychology of personal constructs.* Vols. I & II. New York: Norton, 1955.

63. KENT, G. H., & ROSANOFF, A. J. A study of association in insanity. *Amer. J. Insanity*, 1910, *67*, 37–126.

64. KLEIST, K. Gehirnpathologische und lokalisatorische Ergebnisse uber Horstrorungen. Gerquschtaubheiten und Anusion. *Mach. f. Psychiat. u. Neuro.*, 1928, *68*, 853–860.

65. KLINEBERG, O. Cultural factors in intelligence test performance. *J. Negro Educ.*, 1934, *3*, 478–483.

66. KLOPFER, B., AINSWORTH, M. D., KLOPFER, W. G., & HOLT, R. R. *Developments in the Rorschach Technique.* Yonkers, N.Y.: World, 1954.

67. KORZYBSKI, A. *Science and sanity.* (2nd ed.) New York: International Non-Aristotelian Library, 1941.

68. KRAEPELIN, E. *Lectures on clinical psychiatry.* London: Baillière, 1913.

69. KRASNER, L. Studies of the conditioning of verbal behavior. *Psychol. Bull.*, 1958, *55*, 148–170.

70. KRETSCHMER, E. *Physique and character.* London: Routledge, 1925.

71. KRUGMAN, M. Out of the inkwell: the Rorschach method. *Charact. & Pers.*, 1940, *9*, 91–110.

72. LASHLEY, K. S. *Brain mechanisms and intelligence: a quantitative study of injuries to the brain.* Chicago: Univer. Chicago Press, 1929.

73. LECKY, P. *Self-consistency; a theory of personality.* New York: Island Press Co-operative, Inc., 1945.

74. LEVY, D. Trends in therapy—release therapy. *Amer. J. Orthopsychiat.*, 1939, *9*, 713–736.

75. LEWIN, K. *A dynamic theory of personality.* New York: McGraw-Hill, 1935.

76. LIVERANT, S. The use of Rotter's social learning theory in the development of a personality inventory. *Psychol. Monogr.*, 1958, *72* (Whole No. 445).

77. LIVERANT, S. Intelligence: a concept in need of re-examination. *J. consult. Psychol.*, 1960, *24*, 101–110.

78. LORD, E. E. Experimentally induced variations in Rorschach performance. *Psychol. Monogr.*, 1950, *64*, No. 10.

79. LOUTTIT, C. M. *Clinical psychology.* New York: Harper, 1936.

80. LOUTTIT, C. M. The nature of clinical psychology. *Psychol. Bull.*, 1939, *36*, 361–389.

81. LOUTTIT, C. M. *Clinical psychology of exceptional children.* New York: Harper, 1957.

82. MASLING, J. The influence of situational and interpersonal variables in projective testing. *Psychol. Bull.*, 1960, *57*, 65–85.

83. MAY, R., ANGEL, E., & ELLENBERGER, H. F. (Eds.). *Existence.* New York: Basic Books, 1958.

84. MEEHL, P. E. *Clinical vs. statistical prediction.* Minneapolis, Minn.: Univer. Minn. Press, 1954.

85. MILLS, C. W. *White collar: the American middle class.* New York: Oxford, 1951.

86. MORENO, J. L. Psychodrama and psychopathology of interpersonal relations. *Psychodrama Monogr.*, 1945, No. 16.

87. MORGAN, D., & MURRAY, H. A. A method for investigating phantasies: the Thematic Apperception Test. *Arch. Neurol. Psychiat.*, 1935, *34*, 289–306.

88. MOWRER, O. H. *Learning theory and personality dynamics.* New York: Ronald, 1950.

89. MOWRER, O. H. (Ed.). *Psychotherapy: theory and research.* New York: McGraw-Hill, 1953.

90. MURRAY, H. A. Techniques for a systematic investigation of fantasy. *J. Psychol.*, 1937, *3*, 115–145.

91. MURRAY, H. A. Toward a theory of interaction. In T. Parsons & E. A. Shils (Eds.), *Toward a general theory of action.* Cambridge, Mass.: Harvard Univer. Press, 1952.

92. MUSSEN, P. H., & SCODEL, A. The effects of sexual stimulation under varying conditions on TAT sexual responsiveness. *J. consult. Psychol.*, 1955, *19*, 90.

93. PEAK, HELEN. Problems of objective observation. In L. Festinger & D. Katz (Eds.), *Research methods in the behavioral sciences.* New York: Dryden, 1953.

94. PENNINGTON, L. A., & BERG, I. A. (Eds.). *An introduction to clinical psychology.* (2nd ed.) New York: Ronald, 1954.

95. PEPINSKY, H. B., & PEPINSKY, P. N. *Counseling theory and practice.* New York: Ronald, 1954.

96. PETERSON, J. *Early conceptions and tests of intelligence.* Yonkers, N.Y.: World, 1925.

97. PHARES, E. J., & ROTTER, J. B. An effect of the situation on psychological testing. *J. consult. Psychol.*, 1956, *20*, 291–293.

98. PHILLIPS, E. L. *Psychotherapy: a modern theory and practice.* Englewood Cliffs, N.J.: Prentice-Hall, 1956.

99. PINTNER, R., & PATERSON, D. *A scale of performance tests.* New York: Appleton-Century-Crofts, 1917.

100. PIOTROWSKI, Z. A. The Rorschach ink-blot method in organic disturbances of the central nervous system. *J. nerv. ment. Dis.*, 1937, *86*, 525–537.

101. PRESSEY, S. L. A group scale for investigating the emotions. *J. abnorm. soc. Psychol.*, 1921, *16*, 55–64.

102. RABIN, A. I., & GUERTIN, W. H. Research with the Wechsler-Bellevue test, 1945–1950. *Psychol. Bull.*, 1951, *48*, 211–248.

103. RAIMY, V. C. Self reference in counseling interviews. *J. consult. Psychol.*, 1948, *12*, 153–163.

104. RAIMY, V. C. (Ed.) *Training in clinical psychology.* Englewood Cliffs, N.J.: Prentice-Hall, 1950.

105. RANK, O. *Will therapy.* New York: Knopf, 1936.

106. REISMAN, D. *Individualism reconsidered.* Glencoe, Ill.: Free Press, 1954.
107. ROE, A., & SHAKOW, D. Intelligence in mental disorder. *Ann. N.Y. Acad. Sci.*, 1942, *12*, 361–390.
108. ROGERS, C. R. *Counseling and psychotherapy.* Boston: Houghton Mifflin, 1951.
109. ROGERS, C. R. *Client-centered therapy, its current practice, implications, and theory.* Boston: Houghton Mifflin, 1951.
110. ROGERS, C. R. A process conception of psychotherapy. *Amer. Psychologist*, 1958, *13*, 142–149.
111. RORSCHACH, H. *Psychodiagnostics.* W. Morganthaler (Ed.). New York: Grune & Stratton, 1942.
112. ROSANOFF, A. J. *Manual of psychiatry and mental hygiene.* (7th ed.) New York: Wiley, 1938.
113. ROSENZWEIG, S. The picture association and its application in a study of reaction to frustration. *J. Pers.*, 1945, *14*, 3–23.
114. ROTTER, J. B. Level of aspiration as a method of studying personality. II. Development and evaluation of a controlled method. *J. exp. Psychol.*, 1942, *31*, 410–422.
115. ROTTER, J. B. *Social learning and clinical psychology.* Englewood Cliffs, N.J.: Prentice-Hall, 1954.
116. ROTTER, J. B. The role of the psychological situation in determining the direction of human behavior. In M. R. Jones (Ed.), *Nebraska symposium on motivation.* Lincoln, Neb.: Univer. Neb. Press, 1955.
117. ROTTER, J. B. Psychotherapy. In P. R. Farnsworth & Q. McNemar (Eds.), *Ann. Rev. Psychol.*, *11*, Palo Alto, Calif.: Annual Review Inc., 1960, 381–414.
118. ROTTER, J. B. Some implications of a social learning theory for the prediction of goal directed behavior from testing procedures. *Psychol. Rev.*, 1960, *67*, 301–316.
119. ROTTER, J. B., & RAFFERTY, J. E. *Manual for the Rotter Incomplete Sentences Blank, college form.* New York: Psychological Corp., 1950.
120. RUBENSTEIN, E. A., & PARLOFF, M. B. (Eds.). *Research in psychotherapy.* Washington, D.C.: American Psychological Association, 1959.
121. SARASON, S. The test situation and the problem of prediction. *J. clin. Psychol.*, 1950, *6*, 387–392.
122. SCHMIDT, B. G. Changes in personal, social and intellectual behavior of children originally classified as feebleminded. *Psychol. Monogr.*, 1946, *60*, No. 5.
123. SCHRODER, H. M., & ROTTER, J. B. Rigidity as learned behavior. *J. exp. Psychol.*, 1952, *44*, 141–150.
124. SHAFFER, L. F. The problem of psychotherapy. *Amer. Psychologist*, 1947, *2*, 459–467.
125. SHAKOW, D. An internship year for psychologists (with special reference to psychiatric hospitals). *J. consult. Psychol.*, 1938, 2, 73–76.
126. SHAW, F. J. Some postulates concerning psychotherapy. *J. consult. Psychol.*, 1948, *12*, 426–431.
127. SHAW, R. F. *Finger painting.* Boston: Little, Brown, 1934.
128. SHELDON, W. H. *The varieties of human physique: an introduction to constitutional psychology.* New York: Harper, 1940.
129. SHELDON, W. H. *The varieties of temperament: a psychology of constitutional differences.* New York: Harper, 1942.
130. SHOBEN, E. J. Some observations on psychotherapy and the learning process. In O. H. Mowrer (Ed.), *Psychotherapy: theory and research.* New York: Ronald, 1953.
131. SKEELS, H. M. Some Iowa studies of the mental growth of children in relation to differentials of the environment: a summary. *The thirty-ninth yearbook of the National Society for the Study of Education. Intelligence: its nature and nurture.* Bloomington, Ill.: Public School, 1940.

132. SLAVSON, S. R. *An introduction to group therapy.* New York: Commonwealth Fund, 1943.

133. SOLOMON, J. C. Active play therapy. *Amer. J. Orthopsychiat.*, 1938, *8*, 479–498.

134. SONTAG, L. W., BAKER, C. T., & NELSON, VIRGINIA L. Mental growth and personality development: a longitudinal study. *Monogr. Soc. Res. Child Develpm.*, 1958, *23*, No. 68.

135. SPEARMAN, C. *The abilities of man.* New York: Macmillan, 1927.

136. STERN, W. *General psychology from the personalistic point of view.* New York: Macmillan, 1938.

137. STODDARD, G. D. *The meaning of intelligence.* New York: Macmillan, 1943.

138. SULLIVAN, H. S. *The interpersonal theory of psychiatry.* New York: Norton, 1953.

139. SYMONDS, P. M. *Diagnosing personality and conduct.* New York: Appleton-Century-Crofts, 1931.

140. TAFT, J. *The dynamics of therapy.* New York: Macmillan, 1933.

141. TERMAN, L. M. *The measurement of intelligence.* Boston: Houghton Mifflin, 1916.

142. THOMAS, W. I. *Social behavior and personality.* E. H. Volkert (Ed.). New York: Social Science Research Council, 1951.

143. THORNDIKE, E. L., et al. *The measurement of intelligence.* New York: Teachers Coll., Columbia Univer., Bureau of Publications, 1927.

144. THURSTONE, L. L. *The nature of intelligence.* New York: Harcourt, Brace, 1926.

145. WALLEN, R. W. *Clinical psychology.* New York: McGraw-Hill, 1956.

146. WECHSLER, D. *The Wechsler Memory Scale.* New York: Psychological Corp., 1945.

147. WECHSLER, D. *Wechsler Intelligence Scale for Children.* New York: Psychological Corp., 1949.

148. WECHSLER, D. *Manual for the Wechsler Adult Intelligence Scale.* New York: Psychological Corp., 1955.

149. WEISENBERG, T., & McBRIDE, K. E. *Aphasia.* New York: Commonwealth Fund, 1935.

150. WELLS, F. L. *Mental tests in clinical practice.* Yonkers, N.Y.: World, 1927.

151. WHIPPLE, G. M. *Manual of mental and physical tests.* Baltimore, Md.: Warwick and York, 1910.

152. WITTENBORN, J. R. Symptom patterns in a group of mental hospital patients. *J. consult. Psychol.*, 1951, *15*, 290–302.

153. WOODWORTH, R. J. *Contemporary schools of psychology.* New York: Ronald, 1931.

154. ZILBOORG, G., & HENRY, G. W. *A history of medical psychology.* New York: Norton, 1941.

3. *Recommended Graduate Training Program in Clinical Psychology*

COMMITTEE ON TRAINING IN CLINICAL
PSYCHOLOGY, AMERICAN PSYCHOLOGICAL
ASSOCIATION

AT the meeting of the Board of Directors of the American Psychological Association in Ann Arbor, March 28–30, 1947, the President was authorized to appoint a special Committee on Training in Clinical Psychology to perform the following tasks:

a. Formulate a recommended program for training in clinical psychology.

b. Formulate standards for institutions giving training in clinical psychology, including both universities and internship and other practicum facilities.

c. Study and visit institutions giving instruction in clinical psychology, and make a detailed report on each institution.

d. Maintain liaison with other bodies concerned with these problems, including the committees of the American Orthopsychiatric Association, the National Committee for Mental Hygiene, and others.

The undersigned persons constitute the Committee as finally appointed. The Committee, because of the relatively short period that it has had to work, has limited itself in this report to presenting a recommended program of training in clinical psychology.

The work of our Committee insofar as it relates to a training program grows naturally out of the activities of several previous committees and groups. The historical aspects of the development

Report submitted to the American Psychological Association, Detroit, September 9–13, 1947. Reprinted from *American Psychologist*, 1947, *2*, 539–558, by permission of the American Psychological Association and David Shakow, committee chairman. Dr. Shakow is Chief, Laboratory of Psychology, National Institute of Mental Health, Bethesda, Maryland. Committee members were Ernest R. Hilgard, E. Lowell Kelly, Bertha Luckey, R. Nevitt Sanford, and Laurance F. Shaffer.

of clinical psychological training has been thoroughly covered by Morrow (9). Of particular relevance are the 1943 "Proposed Program of Professional Training in Clinical Psychology" of the Committee on Training in Clinical (Applied) Psychology (1) and the 1945 Sub-committee Report on "Graduate Internship Training in Psychology" (4). A recent issue of the Menninger Bulletin (July 1947) describing "The Menninger Foundation School of Clinical Psychology" and the July 1946 "Internship and Externship Programs" issue of the *Journal of Consulting Psychology* are also of considerable importance in this context. The report of the Committee on Graduate and Professional Training (10), although more directly related to future activities of our Committee, in some respects also bears on the present report.

The program here presented is especially timely because of the existing ferment in the field of psychology, particularly in the area of clinical psychology. The Harvard University Commission's report (6) suggests some of the possibilities which lie ahead of psychology in the near and distant future. With respect to clinical psychology, one sees on the one hand the breathless preoccupation with actual training which has resulted largely from the Veterans Administration and United States Public Health Service programs, and on the other hand the deep concern with the goals and trends of this training both within the Psychological Association and on the part of organizations interested in the fields with which clinical psychology is associated. The Josiah Macy Jr. Foundation has held the first of a series of Conferences on Clinical Psychology (8); the American Psychiatric Association and the Group for the Advancement of Psychiatry have Committees on Clinical Psychology and the American Orthopsychiatric Association and the National Committee for Mental

Hygiene are engaged in activities which in one respect or another involve the evaluation of the functions of clinical psychologists. It is, therefore, especially desirable that the Association set forth its own official policy in this important matter of training and that it play the major role in determining the content and goals of such a program.

We are cognizant of the great difficulties which the shift from an academic to a professional program involves in a university setting. We recognize that this change must take much effort and time and that even were it possible to set up a fairly fixed schedule of training, such a step would at present be both premature and ill-advised because of the great need for experimentation in ways of implementing a sound program. We are therefore emphasizing the goals and principles of what we consider a desirable program rather than attempting to lay out a detailed blueprint. We have decided to limit our present consideration of training to a program at the four-year doctoral level because of our firm conviction that professionally qualified persons cannot be given adequate background training in less time. This is in line with a decision independently arrived at by the Policy and Planning Board (2) that further training of clinical psychologists at the MA level be discontinued. It should be emphasized however, that this decision does not preclude the training of persons to apply psychological principles in specialized areas such as remedial teaching, vocational and educational counseling, educational testing, etc. However, such persons are in our opinion not clinical psychologists and the present report is not concerned with their training. We have further decided not to let our program be determined in any way by present practices in training which arise from special situations such as those created by the financial arrangements of the Veterans Administration. We have, rather, tried to present what we consider ideally desirable in the present state of our knowledge, and we have left to the university the practical working out of the program according to local conditions.

PRE-PROFESSIONAL REQUIREMENTS

In that wise volume, "Medical Education," (5, p. 176), Abraham Flexner says ". . . . the medical school cannot expect to produce fully trained doctors; it can at most hope to equip students with a limited amount of knowledge, to train them in the method and spirit of scientific medicine and

to launch them with a momentum that will make them active learners—observers, readers, thinkers, and experimenters—for years to come. . . . The general arrangement of the curriculum, if sound, can make this task a bit easier, or if unsound, a bit harder; but in general much more—very much more—depends on teacher and student than on curricular mechanics or teaching devices."

If we substitute clinical psychology for medicine, this statement expresses the essential point which we wish to make in this report. Our task is to find good teachers to give good students good training that will start them off in the first stages of their careers as clinical psychologists. This report will be concerned in some detail with ways of meeting the problems that arise in attempting to achieve this task.

What specific goals do we have in mind in the preparation of the clinical psychologist? Clinical psychology seeks to acquire systematic knowledge of human personality and to develop principles and methods by which it may use this knowledge to increase the mental well-being of the individual. If we recognize that clinical psychology is both a science and an art calling for scientific rigor tempered by personal and social sensitivity, we can specify these goals fairly clearly. The more carefully the present scene is examined and the more thoughtfully the future is viewed, the more convinced are we of the need for preparing the clinical psychologist with a combination of applied and theoretical knowledge in three major area: *diagnosis, therapy* and *research.* The purpose is not to develop persons with encyclopedic proficiencies nor is it directed at disproving the contention of some that the scientific and therapeutic attitudes mix poorly in the same person (a view which we are unwilling to accept until definite proof is forthcoming). Rather is it our purpose to see that the necessary broad training is provided that will make later specialization on a sound foundation possible. It becomes increasingly clear that persons having a specialized background in only part of one of these fields, for instance, Rorschach testing, or counseling, or electroencephalographic research, cannot function adequately. We go even beyond this and say that broad training, if it is in only one of the three major areas, is quite inadequate for ordinary clinical psychological work, to say nothing of teaching and preventative endeavors, two major fields of activity which require special attention.

The ability to carry out effectively the combination of functions called for depends upon the clinical psychologist's being the right kind of person, a person who has a relevant informal experience background into which has been integrated the proper formal education, both undergraduate and graduate.

What characteristics does the "right kind" of person possess? As yet, we do not know definitely, for research on this important problem has only begun. It is generally agreed, however, that especially important are the personality qualifications represented by a reasonably well-adjusted and attractive personality. Until dependable research data are available, the following list, which includes the kind of specific qualities experienced observers believe clinical work calls for, may be useful:

1. Superior intellectual ability and judgment.
2. Originality, resourcefulness, and versatility.
3. "Fresh and insatiable" curiosity; "self-learner."
4. Interest in persons as individuals rather than as material for manipulation—a regard for the integrity of other persons.
5. Insight into own personality characteristics; sense of humor.
6. Sensitivity to the complexities of motivation.
7. Tolerance; "unarrogance."
8. Ability to adopt a "therapeutic" attitude; ability to establish warm and effective relationships with others.
9. Industry; methodical work habits; ability to tolerate pressure.
10. Acceptance of responsibility.
11. Tact and cooperativeness.
12. Integrity, self-control, and stability.
13. Discriminating sense of ethical values.
14. Breadth of cultural background—"educated man."
15. Deep interest in psychology, especially in its clinical aspects.

The list is formidable but in the present state of our knowledge, represents the kind of selection goals towards which we must work. Characteristics of this type seem a necessary foundation for work in a field which requires so much in the way of maturity, sensitivity, and knowledge.

How are we to obtain such persons for training? Problems of both recruitment and selection are involved. The problems of recruitment are more difficult than they are in such major professional fields as medicine and law, since the latter are well-established and known to youngsters from quite early years. For the present, the major effort in recruiting will have to be made at the college level through teachers of psychology and vocational advisors who are on the lookout for promising

candidates. In coming years, growing general acquaintance with the field and the multiplication of earlier courses in psychology at the secondary level are likely to lead the student to think of clinical psychology as a lifework. The first rough selection could then come in the secondary schools.

Beyond the problem of recruiting a sufficiently large number of persons to maintain the necessary supply of clinical psychologists lies the major task of proper selection at the point of entrance into graduate work. Here, besides the ordinary selective devices such as are provided by the credentials of the candidate, the Graduate Record Examination and the devices which are being developed in the "Research Project on the Selection of Clinical Psychologists under contract with the Veterans Administration" under the auspices of the University of Michigan (7) should be of help in selecting the best candidates. It is not necessary to elaborate on the obvious point that besides rigorous selection at the point of entrance into graduate work a process of selection must go on throughout the program.

Given the proper kind of person, what may we expect of him in the way of informal background experience which may be considered relevant? For the present we shall devote our attention to the nonacademic experiential background of the person. Since it seems reasonable to expect the clinical psychologist to be interested in people and have a broad base of human contacts, he should have had experiences, particularly in his college years (summer holidays and other spare time), involving close relations with both ordinary and unusual persons in field, factory, institution, or laboratory. In addition to direct contact with people of various kinds he should have had the indirect acquaintance with people that comes from immersion in great literature, because of the emphasis which such portrayals place on the molar aspects of behavior and the insights into human nature that they give. Anything that reading may accomplish to broaden his acquaintance with the wide range of psychological expression, whether in relation to individuals or cultures, is so much relevant background for him.

What can we say about the formal educational background which we may expect from the candidate who is entering the graduate program? Two distinct points of view are generally expressed. On the one hand, there is some demand that students come with a common, fairly defined background, especially in psychology, in order to make graduate instruction easier. On the other hand, some hold that, for the broad development of the field, to cast all the participants in the same mold would be undesirable. Medicine, the proponents of this view indicate, has experimented with a rather rigid prerequisite program but is raising more and more question about its desirability. The solution probably lies somewhere between the two points of view. It seems to us that certain general requirements for the undergraduate program which the student could ordinarily be expected to meet can be laid down. In exceptional cases, provision to waive these should, of course, be made.

The undergraduate program must be recognized as at most *pre*-professional. The professional and the more advanced courses in psychology should in general not be open to the undergraduate. The undergraduate program should be directed at providing a broad cultural and scientific base for specialized graduate study. The courses should help the student to attain a first insight into the structure and dynamics of human behavior, an understanding of the biological and social development of the individual, and a preliminary acquaintance with the principles and methods of collecting and evaluating data.

More specifically, as an example of what a basic undergraduate program might include, the following is presented:

1. *Psychology*. An approximate optimum of twenty semester hours, to consist essentially of courses for undergraduates. The student must be permitted to take a sufficient number of psychology courses to enable him to acquire a fair acquaintance with the content of the field of psychology, both in its general and in its laboratory aspects, but he should not be permitted to concentrate heavily in it. The main emphasis should be on courses in dynamic psychology[1] which consider crucial human problems at a fairly rigorous scientific level. Mass "titillating" courses directed at the general student body are definitely not what we have in mind here.

2. *Biological and physical sciences*. Approximately twenty semester hours of which the major part should preferably be in biology including genetics, and the balance in physics and chemistry. Satisfactory secondary school preparation in the latter two would reduce the amount required at the college level.

3. *Mathematics and statistics*. Approximately nine semester hours in mathematics and statistics, with special emphasis on their logical principles.

4. *Education*. Approximately six semester hours in the fundamentals of educational philosophy, and experimental didactics in the form of practice teaching, if this can be arranged.

5. *Social sciences*. Approximately twelve semester hours in sociology, anthropology, and economics. (Political science or history might be substituted for the last.)

6. *History of culture*. Approximately nine semester hours in history of civilization, comparative literature, comparative religion, philosophy, etc.

7. *Psychology as revealed in literature*. Approximately six semester hours in "literary psychology" if this can be arranged.

8. *Languages*. Reading knowledge of French and German. (Some consideration should, however, be given to the desirability of substituting other languages, for example, Spanish and Russian.)

We wish to emphasize that the undergraduate program cannot be appraised according to credit hours or in relation to specific courses. Each candidate's record must be examined on its merits to see how far it meets the spirit of the background requirements of breadth, good introductory acquaintance with psychology, and fair acquaintance with the biological and social sciences. If a choice is to be made between the latter two groups, there seems some reason for postponing further study of the social sciences to the graduate period. The student, being more mature at this time, is better able to grapple with its relatively greater uncertainties.

GRADUATE PROFESSIONAL PROGRAM

GENERAL PRINCIPLES

The general principles which underlie the graduate program appear to us of primary importance—in fact much more important than the details of the program. If clarity in the formulation of goals exists, there should be relatively little difficulty about agreeing on the means for implementing them. As has already been indicated, it is the opinion of the Committee that the setting up of a detailed program is undesirable. Such a step, if accepted generally, would go far in settling clinical psychology at a time when it should have great lability. Considerable experimentation with respect to the personality and background of students as well as the content and methods of courses will for a long time be essential if we are to develop the most adequate program. Our aims are rather to achieve general agreement on the goals of training and encourage experimentation on methods of achieving these goals and to suggest ways of establishing high standards in a setting of flexibility and reasonable freedom. We also hold that the goals should not be determined by special situations and special demands, but should be oriented toward the question of what is the best training for the clinical psychologist.

Against this general background the principles which we consider important are the following:

1. A clinical psychologist must first and foremost be a *psychologist* (2) in the sense that he can be expected to have a point of view and a core of knowledge and training which is common to all psychologists. This would involve an acquaintance with the primary body of psychological theory, research, and methods on which further training and interdisciplinary relationships can be built.

2. The program of education for the doctorate in clinical psychology should be as rigorous and extensive as that for the traditional doctorate. In general this would represent at least a four-year program which combines academic and clinical training throughout but which includes intensive clinical experience in the form of an internship.

3. Preparation should be broad; it should be directed to research and professional goals, not to technical goals. Participants should receive training in three functions: diagnosis, research and therapy, with the special contributions of the psychologist as a research worker emphasized throughout. Although many will probably tend to specialize in one or another of these areas after obtaining the degree, the Committee feels strongly that there should be training in each of these areas during the graduate period. We are particularly concerned that training shall be of such a quality as to eliminate the possibility that a technician, whether in the sense of a directive or nondirective counselor, a Multiphasic specialist, a Binet tester, a Rorschach specialist, or a remedial instructor, will be turned out as a clinical psychologist, and so depended upon for a range of work he will be unable to do.

4. In order to meet the above requirements the program calls for study in six major areas: a. General psychology; b. Psychodynamics of behavior; c. Diagnostic methods; d. Research methods; e. Related disciplines; f. Therapy. Such a program should go far towards reducing the dangers inherent in placing powerful instruments in the hands of persons who are essentially technicians, persons who from the standpoint of the academic group have no real foundation in a discipline, and who from the standpoint of the clinical group have no well-rounded appreciation of the setting in which they function.

5. The program should concern itself mainly with basic courses and principles rather than multiply courses in technique. It is simple to organize a program that includes innumerable courses of the latter type and come out in the end with a poorly trained person. The stress should be laid on fewer, well-integrated courses which subtly but inevitably leave the student with a sound background, on which he can build knowledge of techniques as he needs them. The courses should be so arranged that more advanced courses really call for knowledge acquired in preceding courses and are built on these. This has too infrequently been true in psychology graduate programs with the result that students have not had the clear notion of progress towards a goal that law students and medical students have. The relationship of the course material to personality theory should be constantly emphasized and unless the whole program is oriented in this direction we doubt its final effectiveness for achieving the stated goals.

6. Courses should be scrutinized for their content, rather than judged by their titles. Equally important is the way the content is handled, that is, the quality of the teaching. Other factors to be evaluated are the internal integration of the course and its integration with other courses, both academic and field. Departments of psychology have perhaps been too much concerned with providing their instructors with freedom to organize their courses as they saw fit under an assigned title. This has frequently resulted in considerable duplication in courses and in the omission of important areas. In either case the student suffered. Without in any way infringing on the instructor's fundamental freedom, it would seem possible, through department and individual conferences, for instructors to lay out courses which are complementary and supplementary to the others given, rather than overlapping because they are ignorant of the general content of colleagues' courses. Courses should as much as possible involve active student participation in preference to merely requiring listening or even watching demonstrations. Individualization of instruction, detailed personal supervision, and the encouragement of initiative and self-reliance must be recognized as important aspects of the teaching. The student should come in contact with a number of instructors representing a variety of points of view and types of experience.

7. The specific program of instruction should be organized around a careful integration of theory and practice, of academic and field work, by persons representing both aspects. Just as there is great danger, in the natural revolt against "acade-

mic" dominance, of ending up with a "practical" program, so is there danger in the continued dominance of the academy. It is important to break down the barriers between the two types of approach and through their smooth integration impress the student with the fact that he is taking *one* course of training provided by *one* faculty.

8. Through all four years of graduate work the student should have contact, both direct and indirect, with clinical material. This can be accomplished in the theoretical courses through the constant use of illustrative case material with which the instructor has had personal contact. The student should from the first year be provided with opportunities for actual contact with human material in naturalistic, test, and experimental situations in the setting of practicum, clerkship, and internship. Throughout, the effort should be made to maintain and to build upon that most valuable quality, the naive enthusiastic interest in human beings, with which the student first comes into the training program.

9. We have just made the point that the student should have contact with clinical material throughout the four years of training. Equally important is the need for contact with normal material. Opportunities should be provided to enable the student to become acquainted with the range of normal and borderline persons who never establish clinical contacts. Such training is essential in order to keep the student balanced in his interpretation and understanding of the abnormal.

10. The general atmosphere of the course of training should be such as to encourage the increase of maturity, the continued growth of the desirable personality characteristics earlier considered. The environment should be "exciting" to the degree that the assumed "insatiable" interest in psychological problems is kept alive, the cooperative attitude strengthened, and the passivity usually associated with so much of traditional teaching kept at a minimum. The faculty must recognize its obligation to implant in students the attitude that graduate work is only the beginning of professional education.

11. A distinct weakness in the training of psychologists, when compared with that of physicians and social workers, is the lack of sufficient feeling of responsibility for patients and clients.[2] The program should do everything possible to bring out the responsibilities associated with the activities of the psychologist. There should be persistent effort to have the student appreciate that his findings make a real difference to a particular person and to that person's immediate group.

12. A systematic plan should be laid to use representatives of related disciplines for teaching the trainee in clinical psychology, and opportunities for joint study with students in these disciplines should be provided. Through these approaches the student learns to work closely and in cooperative fashion with those whose methods may be different but whose goals are quite similar. In these settings he learns to acquire modesty about his own contribution, and to value the "team" approach to the problems of both a service and research nature that he meets, problems which, because of their difficulty and complexity, require a concentrated group attack. In the service aspect he must learn that the team approach calls for the coordinated thinking of various specialists on the problems of a particular patient and that participation in such group activity involves not only immediate, but continuing, responsibility for the client, whether direct or delegated, on the part of all of the members of the team.

13. Throughout the course of training there should be an emphasis on the research implications of the phenomena with which he is faced, so much so that the student is finally left with the set constantly to ask "how" and "why" and "what is the evidence" about the problems with which he is faced. There is probably no more important single task placed on the teaching staff than this direction towards research.

14. In addition to the research implications of the data he should become sensitive to their social implications; he must acquire the ability to see beyond the responsibilities he owes to the individual patient to those which he owes to society. Medicine has developed a code which is admirable so far as concerns responsibility to the individual patient, but has paid relatively less attention to the other type of responsibility. It is our hope that psychologists will gradually acquire more of the medical attitude towards individual patients but develop a high degree of social responsibility as well.

PROGRAM OF GRADUATE TRAINING

As has already been indicated, the program of graduate training falls naturally into six major instructional areas: general psychology, dynamics of human behavior, related disciplines, diagnostic methods, therapy, and research methods. For purposes of exposition of the general plan it seems best to consider the program according to these categories rather than by school year. Under each heading will be discussed the progressively advancing courses falling roughly into the particular category. The classification is, of course, arbitrary and there is a considerable amount of overlapping in both the theoretical and practical aspects. The description of an experiment in perception, for instance, can be significant not only because it points up fundamental perceptual theory, but it can also do the same for psychodynamic theory, research methodology, and physiological relations and—it is not inconceivable—the therapy.

Although it is not our intention to encourage filling up the student's time with courses to so great an extent as is the present practice, for instance, in the medical program, it is still our belief that graduate students in this program can carry heavier schedules than are ordinarily called for by graduate schools. The students must be given time to read and think but we believe these goals need not be sacrificed—in fact they might even be strengthened—if the program were thought of as requiring more semester hours of teaching contact through the year in order to get in *necessary* course work.

A. *General psychology.* In view of the fundamental tenet accepted by the Committee, namely, that clinical psychologists are primarily psychologists, it is clear that due attention must be paid to preparation in the general aspects of psychology. It is our hope, however, that in the presentation of the general courses now under consideration instructors will keep in mind the need for including material related to personality theory and that they will consider the implications of the phenomena they are discussing in the context of total behavior. It is our hope, too, that the trend of the past towards emphasizing the segmental aspects exclusively will be considerably reduced. The courses[3] in this category which should generally be included are:

1. General, physiological, and comparative psychology.
2. History of psychology and contemporary schools of thought.
3. Developmental psychology — Fundamental theories of genetic development: child, adolescent and adult; individual differences.
4. Social psychology.

B. *Psychodynamics of behavior.* If we are to develop the kind of clinical psychologist this program aims for, considerably more emphasis than in the past will have to be placed on permeating the program with theory of personality and psychodynamics. There is no other aspect of the program that is more important and that has so many ramifications. If a dynamic orientation is what we are after, then there can be no half-measures. To accomplish such a purpose it is necessary that as many of the instructors as possible be well acquainted with psychodynamic theory and that they present their material in the light of such theory both in the classroom and in the field. The suggested courses in this area are:

1. Dynamic psychology—Fundamental theories of personality and motivation of normal and abnormal behavior.
2. Experimental dynamic psychology—Conferences and laboratory work. Starting with a selected group of classical experiments in general psychology that bring out fundamental experimental principles, the course might go on to the consideration of the theory and design of clinical research and experiments on personality characteristics and dynamics. It should also involve the critical analysis of published studies and the application of experimental techniques to actual problems in the clinical field. Some university might perhaps be interested in the experiment of conducting this course concurrently with the previous course—conceivably even as a single unit.
3. Psychopathology — The consideration of symptoms and sympton complexes in various mental disorders with emphasis on nosology to some extent but more particularly on the mechanisms and dynamics behind symptoms. The course should be organized largely around actual case presentations.

C. *Diagnostic methods.* Diagnostic study has taken on an increasingly important role in the functioning of the clinical psychologist. This statement may seem somewhat anomalous considering the fact that for a long time "testing" was widely considered the only function of the clinical psychologist. The difference lies in the fact that whereas the functions of the clinical psychologist have been broadened considerably there has been an equal broadening of the concept of what testing involves and a great expansion of the variety of procedures available to him. Besides standard tests there are work samples, psychodrama, real life segments, and situational tests among the methods now at his command. At one time diagnosis implied merely a type of "pigeon-holing." At present this represents only a minor aspect of what is called for. Now diagnosis concerns itself with the origin, nature, and especially the dynamics of the conditions under investigation, and with suggesting hypotheses as to outcome under varying forms of disposition. Its important contribution to personality research, to psychiatric diagnosis, and to therapy are being recognized increasingly. The need for detailed and intensive training in this area is obvious. How shall this training be carried out?

There is a certain logical order in the steps of training which seem to us to be essentially these: Principles and theory, demonstrations, preliminary laboratory experience (in the sense of practice by students on each other and on any other available subjects), practicums in the form of clerkships (organized short periods of part-time training at established field centers) and internships (organized, full-time, extended periods of training at established field centers).

The devices with which the student should become acquainted and in which he should attain proficiency are many and of varying degrees of difficulty. Increasing experience with students in this field convinces us, however, that before actually beginning to work on diagnostic devices the student should have a preliminary and fairly extensive period of training devoted to naturalistic observation and description, procedures on which these devices are fundamentally based. Because so much of clinical psychology (and psychiatry) depends on the description of the complexities of behavior, we would recommend that a considerable portion of the time to be set aside for diagnostic devices in the first year be spent rather in training students in careful observation and report. For this purpose one-way screens, paired observers, and recording devices of both sound and visual types, should be used in settings where individuals and groups are under observation in free and controlled situations. Constant checking of observer's reports against each other, against supervisor's observations, and against the mechanical devices should be standard practice. It is important that a healthy respect for careful observation and report be developed in students who are going to work in a field where a good share of the time the major instrument, in both respects, is the observer himself. With regard to reporting, both in this connection and in connection with diagnostic study, strictness and insistence on high standards of succinctness and accurate terminology are essential. A further argument for early training in observation is suggested by a reading of Flexner (5, p. 253), who, quoting Wenkebach's statement, "Das Wissen verdrängt das Sehen," points out the dangers which come from the early acquisition of technical terms and how frequently such knowledge serves as a barrier to accurate observation of the conditions with which the student is concerned.

Concurrent with the observational field work of the first year might come a broad survey course in clinical psychology whose purpose it would be to provide the student with a perspective of the whole field of clinical psychology. This would include a consideration of the varieties of duties and responsibilities which may be involved in different settings in relation to clients, other professions, and the public. Such a course might be followed by instruction in the technique of taking histories and interviewing, at least in part given under the guidance of experienced social workers and psychiatrists. The preparation of an autobiography during this period is also to be recommended.

After this preliminary background, which has emphasized molar techniques and has provided acquaintance with some clinical material, there follows naturally a systematic course in the theory and practice of diagnostics. Such a course should begin with a consideration of the theory and philosophy of diagnostics; it should provide an understanding of the place of diagnostic procedures in systematic psychology, its relationship to other forms of directed acquisition of knowledge such as naturalistic observation and experiment, its history in detail, and its strengths and weaknesses as a scientific method and as an applied technique. A presentation of the theory and practice of test construction might follow.

The student should then acquire an extensive, if superficial, acquaintance with the wide variety of test and other diagnostic devices: sensory and motor; intelligence: verbal and performance, individual and group; educational and vocational guidance; personality: objective, projective, and situational; and some general notions about their applicability, roughly in the stated order. He should, of course, have a more intensive acquaintance with the selected devices generally used in clinical settings. Whereas he may acquire knowledge of the former from general test survey courses, his knowledge of the latter should be acquired from specialized courses devoted to these techniques. In this connection, the faculty must resist pressure from the students who will put up considerable clamor to be permitted to do projective testing (just as some press for therapy) before they have the necessary relevant clinical and theoretical background for the proper use of these complex techniques. Knowledge about tests should not be derived from didactic teaching alone nor from occasional practice on fellow-students tacked on to the course. Practicums and clerkships, as has repeatedly been emphasized, must be recognized as essential and integral parts of the university training, and periods of practice with subjects in clinical settings must be provided. The general emphasis during the university period should, however, not be on too intensive practice in any one device nor with any one type of subject; rather, it should be directed toward getting across to the student the "feel" of contact with a variety of types of patients as well as the "feel" of a variety of types of test procedures. With this in mind the university should have available many neighboring clinical centers for clerkships, such as schools, child guidance units, schools for the feebleminded, psychopathic and other psychiatric hospitals, mental hygiene clinics, general medical and surgical hospitals, educational and sensory-motor disability clinics, prisons, industrial units and vocational guidance centers. Each student should rotate among at least four of these.

During the internship or externship it is inevitable, and in fact desirable, that a certain amount of the activity of the previous years is duplicated. The student should at the time he commences the internship have, besides a general background in basic general and dynamic psychology, a broad acquaintance with test techniques and an elementary appreciation of their application. He has now come to a setting whose major contribution is to throw him into direct, constant, and intensive contact with human material—a setting in which he can apply both his theoretical knowledge and his beginning skills.

In this environment, where the emphasis is on the individual patient, rather than the problem or the technique, there are certain goals related to test procedures which one expects the student will reach. It is expected that besides acquiring skill, through repeated practice, in the administration and understanding of a wide variety of tests, he will learn when tests are called for and when they are not, what tests and combinations of tests are required in specific problems, and that he will learn their weaknesses as well as their strengths. Besides acquiring a sensitivity to the diagnostic and prognostic aspects of his test findings one hopes that he will become sensitive to their therapeutic implications as well. In fact, there should be an effort to develop in him a "therapeutic attitude" towards his diagnostic work; an attitude that involves learning to avoid probing and carrying out misplaced therapy; an attitude that involves leaving the patient the better rather than the worse for the experience—this without violating the controls or the spirit of good diagnostic procedure. It is expected that he will acquire some sense of balance between the extremes of rigorous pedantic exactness and sloppy guessing, that he will recognize that different problems lend themselves to differing degree of control, and that there

are times and stages of development when a rough negative correlation appears to obtain between psychological meaningfulness and degree of control. It is to be hoped that he will learn that what is important, while working always for reasonably greater control in the clinical setting, is to be honest about the degree of control obtained at the particular time, to admit that one is ignorant or merely hypothesizing when such is the case. His supervisors should strive to have him attain enough security about presenting tentative conclusions so that he does not escape into meaningless profundities or into exactness about the insignificant when he is overcome by the complexities and the difficulties of the significant.

These courses are suggested for the diagnostic series:

1. Observational techniques and reporting.
2. Survey of clinical psychology.
3. Methods of case study, case analysis and interviewing.
4. Theory and practice of psychological diagnostics:
   a. Theory of testing and test construction
   b. Verbal "intelligence" tests
   c. Non-verbal ability tests
   d. Tests of sensory and perceptual function
   e. Tests of motor function and motor skill
   f. Educational achievement tests
   g. Vocational tests
   h. Clinical tests of psychological deficit, aphasia, conceptualization, etc.
   i. Projective and other personality procedures
   j. Clinical analysis and integration of diagnostic devices.

D. *Therapy.* It is our thesis that no clinical psychologist can be considered adequately trained unless he has had sound training in psychotherapy.[4] The social need for the increase of available therapists is great. Clinical psychologists are being called upon to help meet this need, as well as the greater research need, and we anticipate that many will devote a part of their time to some form of psychotherapy. Our strong conviction about the need for therapeutic experience grows out of the recognition that therapeutic contact with patients provides an experience which cannot be duplicated by any other type of relationship for the intensity and the detail with which it reveals motivational complexities. A person who is called upon to do diagnostic or general research work in the field of clinical psychology is seriously handicapped without such a background; a person who is called upon to do research in therapy (a field to which psychologists of the future must, for various reasons, devote themselves prominently) cannot work at all without such a background.

Many important problems of an interdisciplinary, social, and legal nature are raised by such a program, questions which are not pertinent to the discussion here. There is no reason, however, why these cannot be taken care of eventually by the various Committees and Conferences concerned with the problem. We feel that members of other groups, such as psychiatrists, psychoanalysts, and social workers, who have been concerned predominantly with problems of therapy should be called upon, to as great an extent as possible, to take an important role in the teaching of the clinical psychologist. A by-product of this association could not help but be a reduction of some of the difficulties raised by the mentioned problems.

Because of the greater complexity and inexactness of the therapeutic process it would seem reasonable that study in this area begin not before the second year. The work might be introduced by lecture and discussion courses on theory and methods, follows by practicums on simpler therapeutic techniques and on problems such as those which are involved in remedial work and guidance. Therapeutic activity of a more advanced (though still simple) kind should perhaps be left for the internship and fourth years of the program. During the internship, the student should be in an institution where detailed and close supervision is available. In the fourth year he has gained sufficiently in background, maturity, and appreciation of his responsibilities to the client, and to his own and other professions. Really advanced training in therapy is, with few exceptions, a problem of the post-doctoral period which requires considerable thought devoted to it.

The courses which should be included are:

1. Therapeutic theory and methods—Lectures and discussion. Introductory course in therapy and counseling; methods and techniques; evaluation of results. There should be considerable emphasis on different points of view in therapy and on common factors in the various forms of therapy.

2. Remedial aspects of special disabilities—Lectures and systematic supervised practice.

3. Techniques of guidance and counseling—Lectures and systematic practice under supervision in individual personality guidance and counseling of minor problems.

4. Personality therapy—Detailed consideration of case material in seminars; carefully supervised practice.

5. Techniques of group therapy—Lectures, systematic participation, and supervised practice.

E. *Research methods.* Because of the academic background of psychology, a natural development has been that of all the disciplines in the mental hygiene field it is psychology which has been most concerned with research. It is important that this interest in research on the part of psychology continue, for as one surveys the scene the likelihood that the major burden of research will fall on the psychologist becomes clearer. If he permits himself to be drawn off into private therapeutic practice as has the psychiatrist, or into institutional therapeutic work as has the social worker, the outlook for research is dim in a field where the need is enormous. As has already been indicated, if a social need for therapy exists, then the need for research is even greater. The fact that there is not equal pressure for the latter is mainly due to the excusable but still short-sighted outlook of the public. The universities, with their more far-sighted orientation, have a serious responsibility to develop research interests and abilities in the clinical psychologists they train. The interest should be in research on the laws of human behavior primarily and on technical devices and therapy secondarily. Throughout the course of training, research attitudes and problems should permeate all aspects of the program, in the diagnostic courses and in therapy, as well as in the courses in general psychology and psychodynamics. The emphasis on personality theory, already mentioned, is closely related and should serve as further support to this point of view. Only from a concentrated attempt to build up such an attitude can we expect to draw from our training programs a substantial number of psychologists who will be interested in devoting themselves primarily to research, and a further number who will devote at least part of their time to such activity.

The courses in this area should include:

1. Experimental psychology—Conference and laboratory course of a basic kind in experimental techniques, devoted mainly to the consideration of the more meaningful problems in general psychology, e.g., learning, reaction mechanisms, work activity, etc. Consideration should be given to variability of response—to the significance of the extremes of the distribution as well as to the modal and typical response—and to the clinical implications of these general problems.

2. Advanced statistics and quantitative methods in psychology and psychopathology.

3. Research in dynamic psychology—Conference and laboratory course which considers the

theory and design of experiments in personality characteristics and dynamics; application of experimental and other research methods to the problems in the clinical field.

4. Dissertation—Preliminary work on the dissertation including the setting of the problem, preparatory reading, and the outlining of the project in detail during the second year. Actual experimental work on the dissertation carried out during the third (internship) year under joint supervision of university and field center. Final work on the dissertation during the fourth year.

F. *Related disciplines.* Because of the problems with which he is constantly faced there is no psychologist who needs a broader background than the clinical psychologist. He works in a setting with medical specialists of many kinds: psychiatrists, physiologists, neurologists, to mention the most prominent, and with representatives of other disciplines such as social workers and educators with all of whom he has the closest contacts. On the one hand, his work may have specific physiological implications, on the other, broad educational and social aspects. He cannot be narrow; he must be able to meet his colleagues on common ground and at the same time see what the remoter implications of his findings are. That an adequate training program could be organized which does not include in it some of the background which such an assignment calls for is inconceivable. It has already been suggested that some of this background should have been acquired during the undergraduate period. But the greater part must necessarily come during the graduate period. Here, too, representatives from other disciplines should be used as much as possible in the training; in fact, it cannot be carried out without them.

The program should include:

1. Physiological sciences—Lectures and demonstrations. Selected aspects of physiology and anatomy: especially neurophysiology, neuroanatomy, autonomic nervous system, endocrinology, etc.

2. Introduction to clinical medicine—Lectures. Introductory course in clinical medicine to acquaint the psychologist with the major characteristics of the clinical pictures of various diseases and with technical medical procedures which he will hear about in the settings where he works. Special attention should be given to those diseases which today are usually referred to as psychosomatic.

3. Social organization and social pathology—Lectures and field visits. A course to acquaint the psychologist with social structure; the pathological

aspects of this structure as seen in crime, poverty, etc., and the agencies set up to take care of these. The major part of this course could most effectively be given by psychiatrically oriented social workers rather than sociologists.

4. Influence of culture on personality—Lectures on cultural anthropology's contribution to the understanding of personality.

We might summarize what has been presented in the preceding section, which covered the content of the program according to areas, by a brief statement of the content according to year levels.

The primary purpose of the first year of study is to lay the systematic foundation of knowledge of psychology, to achieve some degree of acquaintance with the physiological and other sciences needed for professional clinical work, and to train the student in good observational technique.

The program of the second year of graduate work is directed mainly at providing the student with the necessary background in the experimental, diagnostic, and therapeutic approaches to the problems of clinical psychology. Although a certain amount of teaching may still be carried on in the form of lectures, the major emphasis is on direct contact with patients, clients, or other subjects, either in the diagnostic or in the experimental setting. Practicum courses and clerkships in different clinical settings are essential element of this year's program.

The third year consists of an internship whose content is discussed in fuller detail in a later section. The Committee believes that the third year spent in an internship and the fourth in a final year at the university is the most desirable arrangement, although other patterns should be experimented with. The advantages of this proposal are many: (1) The student is enabled to complete the analytic and final work on his dissertation at the university. (2) It permits the final integration of the experiences acquired during the internship with the more theoretical principles emphasized by the university, and emphasizes the unity of the course of training. Otherwise the internship may be considered as a mere appendage. (3) The return of graduate students with internship background to the university should have some influence in integrating the kind of training provided by the university and the internship center. It might also serve as a reciprocating educational influence upon the nonclinical university group, both students and instructors. (4) The student is placed geographically close to the agency which already has an established placement service and is therefore in a better position to aid him in the consideration of employment opportunities.

The program of the fourth year should be
relatively elastic and could include most of the
following:

1. Final work on dissertation.
2. Cross-discipline seminars (attended by representatives of psychology, anthropology, sociology,
social work, psychiatry, etc.) that devote themselves to the discussion of psychology's relation to
the other sciences concerned with the adjustment
problems of the individual and the group. The
purpose of these seminars should be to integrate
the major principles of previous study and to point
out the broader implications of the course of
instruction for the personal and social scenes.
3. Seminar on professional problems—standards, ethics, etc.
4. Additional courses in psychology as needed
to round out the individual student's program.
5. Additional courses in related fields as needed
to round out the individual student's program.
6. Advanced therapeutic work, if indicated.
7. A program of self-evaluation, if indicated.
(See later discussion of the problem of personal
analysis.)

SPECIAL PROBLEMS

Since certain aspects of the program raise special
questions they are considered in this section. The
first of these is the internship.

INTERNSHIP

What are the aims of a psychological internship?[5] Underlying all of its aims is the principle
now recognized for the whole clinical psychology
program, but particularly true for the internship,
namely, that the knowledge essential to the practice
of clinical psychology cannot be obtained solely
from books, lectures, or any other devices which
merely provide information about people or about
ways of studying them. Rather, extensive and
intensive experience *with* people is held to be
essential if the student is to acquire a proper
perspective and the ability to apply effectively the
scientific facts and techniques which he has acquired
in the academic setting. It should be pointed out
that the internship is not a "repair shop" in which
the failures of the academic center are taken care
of. The university must adequately carry out its
function of providing the necessary training in tool
subjects so that the student may take the fullest
advantage of what the internship is set up primarily
to provide, namely, material on which to use these

tools. Before he can become either a competent
practitioner or investigator, the student must become sensitive to the many relevant aspects of the
real person under actual study and learn to view
him as an individual. In this process, he also learns
to view himself as an essential instrument in the
study of other persons. Because of the recognition
of these needs, clinical clerkships and internships,
the only devices that can accomplish these goals
adequately, have been made integral parts of the
program.

The major contribution of the internship is the
provision of extended practical experience of gradually increasing complexity under close and competent supervision. The building up of an apper-
ceptive mass of experience which gives concrete
meaning to general principles can be attained only
by volume and variety of contact with actual clinical
problems in association with other disciplines. The
program should provide the student with a broad
base for later specialization by throwing him into
full-time contact with human clinical material,
contact of a much more intensive kind than he can
possibly achieve during the clinical clerkships of the
second year. This aspect of the instruction gains
its value from being organized around the case
material to be found in the institution, that is, the
person rather than the condition is made the center
of interest. Not only is the person seen in cross-
section but it is possible to follow him longitu-
dinally, either as the psychological processes
develop and unfold, or as they may have been
previously conditioned.

The content of the internship program comprises
two major categories of activity: that involving
contact with the patients or clients and that involving the acquisition of experience in the administrative sphere.

Contact with clients is of two types: *direct*—the
acquisition of information from the patient by the
investigator himself; *indirect*—the acquisition of
information from and about the patient through
other investigators and sources.

In direct contact with clients the main avenues
of approach are those concerned with diagnosis
and those concerned with disposition. Each of these
requires separate consideration.

A most important aspect of the education of the
intern is the further instruction he receives in the
use of *diagnostic procedures*, the procedures directed
at acquiring knowledge about the origin and nature
of the patient's condition. Under this heading are
included a great variety of techniques of different
levels of objectivity and degrees of complexity
among which history-taking, interviewing, clinical

psychometrics and analytic and projective techniques are of particular importance.

An equally important aspect of his direct contact with clients is that involving *disposition:* what is to be done about the presented problem on the basis of the findings obtained through the use of the various diagnostic procedures. The worker himself may be directly concerned with disposition or he may serve in the role of consultant. In the former, the direct execution of the implications of the diagnosis may be at a technical aid level, at a therapeutic aid level, or at a quite advanced professional thereapeutic level. In the latter instance, when the intern acts as a consultant, the recommendations which frequently are part of a much broader set of recommendations deriving from studies made by several disciplines, are carried out by another person. In such a case the intern should have the opportunity to find out how effective are the actions taken with respect to the recommendations he has made, that is, he should at least be able to follow the case through written or oral reports. One of the advantages of the full-time internship is that the student is in a position to follow personally the evaluation and disposition made of the patient whom he has studied. A major disadvantage of part-time appointments is the likelihood of lapses in this follow-up process— the experience in too large a part consists of a succession of unclosed gestalten.

The direct contact with subjects just discussed lends itself to two different types of approach, each with a different end in view. The first is the *service* approach, that is, the study of the patient with the aim of solving his particular problem without regard for the general implications involved. Most of the work which is done by the intern is at this level. The second is the *research* approach, that is, the study of the patient not only for himself but for the general implications which his particular problem presents to psychology and psychopathology. This may be based either on a very thorough study of the client as an individual case or as a unit in a series of cases. Research experience, as has been indicated, is an essential part of the background of the clinical psychologist and a considerable part of the intern's time—perhaps up to one-third— should be devoted to the study of a problem on which he can accumulate a body of data during the course of the year's internship. This material, as suggested earlier, may very well be used for a dissertation. One of the most valuable contributions of the internship is the repeated opportunity which it affords for intensive team work, for intimate association with members of related disciplines on specific cases and problems. Such practical opportunities for coordinated activity and thinking are indispensable for proper training.

In addition to these direct contacts with clients a considerable part of the instruction which the student receives involves only *indirect* contact with them, that is, is about patients with whom he himself has had no direct association. This includes experience of three kinds: (1) individual—about a particular subject; (2) general—about classes of subjects; and (3) technical—about methods used with such subjects.

Indirect contacts with *individual* patients may arise either within the setting of the institution's psychology department or outside the department. In the former are included conferences and department staff meetings which consider the diagnostic or therapeutic aspects of cases carried by other members of the department. In this type of relationship with clients the extra-departmental contributions are usually the more extensive. A major contribution to the student's education is the knowledge which he acquires from regular attendance at the institution staff meetings which consider patients for initial orientation, for diagnosis, for disposition, or for special pedagogic purposes. At these, the student has the opportunity to become acquainted with the contribution made towards the understanding of a case by other disciplines, such as psychiatry, social work, pediatrics, education, occupational therapy, or nursing, and the manner in which the various contributions integrate with the psychological findings.

Contact of the *general* kind, that is, about general problems and classes of subjects, is obtained by the intern both in and out of the institutional psychology department through lectures, courses, and seminars in one or more fields, such as psychiatry, psychosomatics, neurophysiology, experimental psychopathology, and re-education and rehabilitation, and in the approaches to the problems of clinical psychology from the standpoints of particular disciplines, namely, social work, neurology, psychiatry, internal medicine, pediatrics, education, pastoral work. The student thus continues his "academic" education in the setting of concrete material and personal day-by-day meaningful illustration. This education has the further advantage of being carried on without the interruptions which shifts back and forth in geographical setting entail. During the internship year opportunity is afforded for extensive seminar study of advanced techniques in therapy, and advanced work in diagnosis with such devices as the Rorschach and the Thematic Apperception Test, techniques about which only the first essentials are actually learned in the first courses which are taken at the university.

Another aspect of this indirect contact with patients is the instruction which may be provided in sessions which consider new *technical* procedures. Here, too, the emphasis should be on the exemplification of the techniques by case material from the clinical setting.

An important point which administrators of internship centers must keep in mind is the necessity for constantly providing experience with normal material. The institutional personnel, by serving as subjects in psychological experiments and tests, frequently offers a rich source in this respect.

There is one other type of experience which is of some importance. We refer to the *administrative* aspects of department activity, including the mechanics of relationships with colleagues, superiors, members of other disciplines, and the institutional administration. At the start of the course of internship the supervision should be close and the supervisor should assure himself of the ability of the student to handle even the simplest problems or procedures. As the student shows increasing competence, the supervision should be proportionately reduced and greater responsibility placed on the students to supervise each other with only a final check by the supervisor. The latter should, however, always be available for consultation. The importance of competent supervision cannot be overemphasized and any institution which accepts the responsibility of providing an internship program must recognize this as one of its important tasks. In the intra-departmental sphere each intern should carry some of the responsibility for departmental functions. This may be in the nature of assisting in the supervision of other interns (rotated regularly among the group), the teaching of students who are serving clinical clerkships, and the care of departmental records of patients.

A fundamental purpose which must lie behind the process of instruction of the intern is the gradual development in him, through judicious supervision, of a sense of a responsibility and self-reliance in handling clinical problems. The program as a whole should be organized to provide the student with increasing responsibilities commensurate with his growth in the ability to accept these. Such a task requires constant knowledge by the supervisor of the state of the student's progress through active contact; absentee, routinized, or overloaded supervision cannot achieve this goal. The optimum number of students that a supervisor can handle depends on the nature of his other

responsibilities; in general, five is about right. As soon as possible, the student should become a productive staff member, one who contributes practically to the service activities of the department. Even if his contribution is limited, as it necessarily is at first, the psychological effect on the student in giving him a sense of responsibility and a feeling of usefulness is great. Such contributions also make the administrators of internship centers more receptive to the establishment and maintenance of internship opportunities.

Another important aspect of the problem of the mechanics of instruction is the way in which the internship is organized. A full consideration of the various types (concurrent as opposed to block or consecutive, straight as opposed to rotating) leaves the Committee with the judgment that the block system, in which a full year is devoted solely to the work at the institution, especially that involving residence there, is to be preferred. As suggested earlier other forms should, however, be experimented with. For the present, too, it seems preferable to concentrate on the straight internship, if for no other reason than because of the much greater simplicity of its organizational aspects as compared with the rotating type. (In the latter the problem is complicated because the student has to move at intervals from institution to institution.) In the medical field rotation has in many instances been found to result in a "smattering of knowledge." This, as well as many other important aspects of the problem, is discussed in some detail in the Subcommittee Report (4), and should be referred to.

What kind of institution is to be preferred for the internship—child or adult, state or private, mental disease or mental deficiency, out-patient or in-patient? Careful consideration of the problem impresses the Committee that it is not the type of institution which should be the major determining factor but rather the nature of the particular institution. "Good" institutions, that is, those providing opportunities for diagnosis, research, and therapy with a reasonably varied population under adequate supervision, of any type are better than poor institutions of what might be considered a favored type.

These general goals can of course most easily be achieved in large training centers where various disciplines are represented. Too much training in psychology has gone on in starved environments and a change in this respect is long overdue. A major characteristic of the "rich" environment is that concurrent training is provided in a variety of related disciplines, such as psychiatry, social work, nursing and occupational therapy, as well as in psychology. For the latter, it is most important that at least the first two be represented. Such a setting provides the possibility for students of several disciplines to work jointly, under supervision, on common cases. Some of the most profitable learning about the case itself, about the relative and complementary contributions of the different disciplines, and about ways of working together effectively for the benefit of the client comes from these contacts. Besides the appreciation of the complexity and many-sidedness of the problem which comes from the different philosophies and points of view which are ordinarily represented, there is considerable learning by example from the other disciplines. Instances of this are the appreciation of rigorous experimentation that is derived from the physiologist and biochemist, the appreciation of the importance of meaningfulness as represented in the systematic viewpoint of the psychoanalyst towards molar data, and the sensitivity to the practical social implications of the problem that comes from the social worker.

OPTIONAL COURSES

Although the four-year program should have a common core for all those training in clinical psychology, and should in general be similar for all students in the program at a particular university, it is important that a certain degree of option for special courses be permitted. This can ordinarily be worked out most satisfactorily in the fourth year, but should be possible at other points in the program. One may expect that the concept of what constitutes desirable clinical training programs will change with the years and it is best to permit students, through elective courses, to do a certain amount of experimenting with their programs as one aspect of this search for the most satisfactory program.

DISSERTATION

Because of our interest in developing a research-oriented professional person it is quite important to retain the feature of the dissertation as part of the requirements for the doctorate. However, universities will have to rethink the whole question of the nature of the dissertation and its proper function, especially as it relates to the present type of program. With respect to its place in the proposed program, advantage should be taken of the opportunity provided by the internship to carry out a research project in the field of major interest to the student, both because of this interest and because it is important for him to obtain research experience in the clinical field. The student can learn as much about the nature and rigors of methodology and make an equally significant contribution to knowledge in working on some problem in personality or in psychopathology as he can in the more conventional fields. Although a dissertation on some aspect of personality which is based on normal subjects in the university laboratory should of course be acceptable, the Committee feels that preference should be given to projects involving clinical material since the student must receive as much training as possible in research with such material. The present program is so organized that research on clinical material could probably be carried out most economically in time if the internship period were utilized for this purpose. In the ordinary course of events, the student would, during his second year, do whatever preliminary work was necessary on his dissertation: he would select the problem with the aid of the faculty and the supervisor at the prospective internship center, and draw up a project outline. If preliminary experimentation is necessary it might be possible to carry this out at the university or at one of the clerkship centers. During the internship year, the student would collect the data for the dissertation. Supervision of his project should continue a joint responsibility of the university and the field training center. When the student returns to the university for his fourth year of work, he would be in a position to do the final analytic work and writing.

It is our hope that as a result of the more extensive and careful selective devices which this program is advocating, the dissertation will become much less of a major hurdle than it has heretofore been. As in professional schools, the student should by the end of the second year be so certain of having been carefully screened and of having met the requirements as to capacity and achievement, that, given conscientious attention to the balance of his program, there should be little doubt about his completing the course. The development of such an atmosphere would do a great deal to reduce the anxiety with which the latter part of the PhD program is so heavily laden, an anxiety which is largely created by the multiple and generally illogical uncertainties connected with the dissertation. If such an atmosphere can be developed the productivity of students during this period would certainly become greater.

INTEGRATION OF ACADEMIC
AND FIELD PROGRAM

After what has already been said in different sections of this report it is unnecessary to discuss further the importance of integrating the two parts of the program. The techniques of implementation, however, require additional consideration. The problem of integration arises with respect to three aspects: (1) content, (2) supervision, and (3) accrediting and certification.

For the program to be most effective the content provided by the two teaching centers must be well integrated. In this respect, faculty members have in the past been quite lax. They have left too much to the student the task of correlating and integrating the material in the variety of courses which he has taken at the university. The integration of university and field center activities has been neglected even more. If training is to be optimally effective, strenuous effort will have to be directed at correcting the situation. In order to achieve such integration the whole group must become essentially *one* faculty. Arrangements for reciprocal visits and conferences between the staffs should be made to discuss such problems as the points of view to be emphasized, the techniques of teaching, and the avoidance of overlap. It is most important for the instructors at each place to know the general content of the teaching at the other. Such mutual acquaintance would go far towards making easier for the student the transition to the internship center and back to the university.

In the matter of supervision an integrated program must also be achieved. The supervisor at the internship center must obviously be held responsible for the major part of the student's activity. If the candidate is to use his available research time at the institution for work on his dissertation, a very close relationship between supervisors and agreement as to the division of supervisory responsibilities must be achieved by the two groups. The appointment by the university of several of its instructors, on a rotating basis, to act as field supervisors should be considered. It would be their responsibility to hold scheduled conferences with the interns in order to maintain contact with them and help supervise their dissertations.

All of the aspects requiring integration point to the obvious need for a combined responsibility in setting and maintaining standards. Such unification can only be achieved by accepting the internship center as an institution of comparable status with the university and in some respects an integral part of it. This can be achieved by interchange of personnel, joint conferences, and by interchange of student visits. There is no better way of achieving integration than through an interchange of staffs. The teaching staff of the university should be encouraged to spend summers or other periods at the institution on guest appointments. The staff of the institution should be given temporary full-time or permanent part-time appointments at the university on a regular faculty or lectureship basis. The latter arrangement is generally quite practicable and does not become too involved in the problems of university administration.

SELF EVALUATION

As psychologists become more involved in the clinical field, they become increasingly impressed with the importance of the observer as instrument. An important aspect of this problem, one which arises particularly in dealing with motivational questions, is the degree to which one's own biases, affects, and problems, frequently only different from the patient's in intensity, color the material provided by the patient. It has become obvious to those working in the clinical field that some kind of control of this source of error is necessary. Psychiatrists and social workers, from their more extended experience with this type of material, have long accepted the principle of the need for intensive self-evaluation as a prerequisite for their work, especially their therapeutic work.

Psychologists, in our opinion, must come around to the acceptance of some kind of intensive self-evaluation as an essential part of the training of the clinical psychologist. We are not prepared to recommend any special form of such procedure, although some of us believe that whenever possible this should take the form of psychoanalysis because of its relative completeness. Others of us believe that shorter methods of self-evaluation, because they may be less time-consuming and less indoctrinating, are preferable. Whatever the form, training should include detailed self-examination under the competent guidance of persons relatively free from dogma who have an interest in psychological theory as well as in therapy.

Psychologists can adopt from social work practice a procedure that has been found effective in achieving at least partial self-knowledge. We refer to their use of detailed case supervision of students. As a result of almost daily contacts with the student on his own cases a relationship is established between the sensitive supervisor and student which may indirectly have therapeutic benefits. Such a setting makes it possible for the student to examine critically his own behavior and interpretations as they grow out of his handling of case material and provides an opportunity for considerable personal growth. The profit from these personal contacts is increased when backed up by classroom discussion of cases on a less personal motivational basis.

Administrators of training programs should make an effort to promote such supervisory practices and canvass the possibilities for the more intensive type of self-evaluative experience in their own regions. Students, during the last part of their doctoral training, or immediately after this training, should be encouraged to undertake such a program.

PROFESSIONAL RESPONSIBILITIES

No group can become a profession overnight, a fact which clinical psychology is in the process of discovering. What really counts in the making of a profession—professional ideals and practices— cannot (un)fortunately be taught in courses. Proper technical training, professional certification and state certification, of course, play important roles. More important, however, are identification with a group having high ideals, and constant association in the actual work situation with persons having professional goals. It is in the work relationship that the student can learn to think of himself as a professional person. It is here that the student can gain an appreciation of how people meet such problems as maladjustment, illness, and handicaps and in this context gain a feeling of responsibility about his work because he understands that his findings really make a difference in what happens to a particular individual and his family. It is here that he learns to carry, in addition to this responsibility for the individual, the broader social one which transcends the need of the individual patient. It is in this setting, too, that another important aspect of professional training, his relationship with other professions, is constantly brought to his attention. He learns the techniques and importance of the group attack on problems: how best to work with other professional groups for the benefit of the individual client and the frequent necessity for identifying himself with a group even broader than his own professional group, namely, the "team."

If the student, after having achieved strong identification with psychology, learns to divest himself of this identification in order to become part of larger wholes for the benefit of a patient or a group, then he may be said to have achieved true professional growth. It is in this setting that ethical problems constantly arise and that the greatest learning in dealing with them naturally occurs. When this opportunity for "field" learning has been afforded, then "talk" learning becomes profitable. Seminars on professional and ethical professional problems have a contribution to make and should generally be made available during the fourth year. In these courses the ethical problems that arise from relationships with clients, and those that arise from relationships with other psychologists and with other professions and the public should be considered, especially as they develop from concrete situations.

STUDENT RELATIONSHIPS

We have stressed, in one context or another, the importance of the development of a sense of responsibility. Such a sense comes only in proportion to the opportunities for practice afforded a person. Besides those we have already discussed, another area where students may exercise responsibility is in helping to shape the program in which they are enrolled. Such thinking about professional problems, whether group or individual, should be encouraged, as should the organization of colloquia which the students themselves administer. The opportunity to express themselves freely on policy will insure reduction in the dissatisfactions and irritations which naturally arise in any program.

Another aspect of this problem has to do with the individual problems of the students—whether personal, or connected with the program. Provision should be made for adequate conferences on such problems when they arise. In fact, each student should have an active advisor whose responsibility it would be to keep track of the student's progress and who would be readily available to consider his individual problems.

EVALUATION OF ACCOMPLISHMENT

A problem which necessarily follows the organization of a program such as the one outlined is that of accrediting and certification, that is, the official recognition of the adequacy of those who take part in it—the student, the university, the field center.

For the student, at the various levels of individual advancement, some appropriate symbols of achievement seem necessary. The following are suggested:

1. Doctoral degree following the four-year course of professional preparation. Although there

are some professional groups, notably the legal, which practice on the basis of a bachelor's degree, there are various considerations which make it doubtful if anything less than a doctoral degree would be satisfactory for the practice of clinical psychology.

2. Membership in the special division of the professional association of the group, the American Psychological Association's Division of Clinical and Abnormal Psychology. The first grade of active membership, Associateship, as recommended by the Policy and Planning Board (2), would come for participants in this program, with the attainment of the doctorate; the second, Fellowship, with an additional five years of acceptable experience—essentially at the level of diplomate as discussed later.

3. After a year's post-doctoral experience would come state certification as recommended in the Policy and Planning Board Report (2). Closely linked with the problem of study beyond the doctoral degree is that resulting from the establishment of the American Board of Examiners in Professional Psychology (3). This Board has as its function the certification of candidates who after five years of actual experience, three years of which have been spent in recognized training centers, have passed examinations in stated aspects of the field of clinical psychology. (The nature of this advanced residency type of training requires special consideration and is not directly pertinent to the present problem. We hope to consider the matter in a later report.) Diplomas of the Board would serve as evidence of competence in the specialty of clinical psychology. Such a program emphasizes the important point that the attainment of the doctoral degree is only a step in the process of professional education, an education which continues through to specialist rating and beyond; in fact, throughout professional life.

Training universities and field centers as well as students must be evaluated. The universities should be evaluated according to their ability to meet the requirements set forth by this program. (Our Committee has been charged with such an evaluation and hopes to be able to commence this task shortly.) Not only the formal meeting of standards with respect to the courses given but the actual quality of the courses, as it relates both to content and instruction, should be carefully scrutinized.

The field centers should be given the same careful scrutiny as the schools. Standards as to content, quality, and amount of supervision, facilities (personnel, clinical, library, teaching), and

living arrangements, should all be carefully set up and used in the evaluation. Since it is likely that the degree of expansion of clinical psychological training will depend to a great extent upon the number of really adequate internship centers which are available, considerable effort should be directed by universities to encouraging their development.

RECOMMENDATIONS

The Committee on Training in Clinical Psychology believes that the program outlined in the present report, if effectively carried out, should provide the basic background for clinical psychologists who will undertake both teaching and practice functions in the diagnostic, therapeutic, and research aspects of the field. This program, it believes, should also prepare persons who can eventually contribute to its preventive aspects, a goal towards which more and more of our future efforts must be directed.

The Committee on Training in Clinical Psychology therefore recommends to the Council of Representatives:

1. That the present report be endorsed.

2. That the program here outlined be presented to the universities offering doctoral training in clinical psychology as a recommended program.

3. That the report be recommended for publication in The American Psychologist.

NOTES

* The Committee wishes to acknowledge with gratitude the aid received from the following persons who read preliminary drafts of the report: Mrs. Ethel L. Ginsburg, Mrs. Elizabeth H. Ross, Drs. Alan Gregg, Robert R. Holt, James G. Miller, and David Rapaport.

1. We shall have occasion to refer repeatedly to "dynamic psychology," a term which has to some extent taken on the "blessedness" of James's old lady's "Mesopotamia." Because of this, the term is not in good repute with some persons. However, we find no term so satisfactory for describing what we have in mind—the "how" and "why" of human behavior as opposed to the static, structural "what." Without getting involved in what would in the present context be merely irrelevant semantics, the definition given in Warren: "A systematic interpretation of mental phenomena, regarded as a succession of causes and effects with emphasis upon internal drives and motives," or the definition provided by one of us: "Fundamental theories of motivation, conflict, and resolution of conflict, applied to an understanding of normal and abnormal behavior" essentially describes what we refer to as "dynamic psychology."

2. The words "patient" and "client," although not quite satisfactory terms for the person with whom the psychologist established "interpersonal relationships," are used throughout this report, either together or singly, but always interchangeably. Because of the variety of situations in which the clinical psychologist is called upon to work—medical and non-medical, normal and abnormal—neither term accurately designates all the persons with whom he deals. The old psychological term "subject" is sufficiently broad, but unsatisfactory because of its implications of exaggerated dominance and direction; the other old term "observer" is even more unsatisfactory because of the implication of emotional distance and marked non-dependence which it carries. For the present, to avoid awkwardness in expression, we must be satisfied with "patient" or "client," with the understanding that either term carries the broader meaning here indicated.

3. At this point and elsewhere when specific courses are considered we have deliberately refrained from indicating the semester hours to be devoted to them. We conceive of some of these as being three-hour courses and others as much as 12-hour courses. The decision as to their length had best be left to the individual university.

4. Psychotherapy is a process involving interpersonal relationships between a therapist and one or more patients or clients by which the former employs psychological methods based on systematic knowledge of the human personality in attempting to improve the mental health of the latter.

5. The term internship (residence appointment) is used in this report interchangeably with externship (non-residence appointment).

REFERENCES

1. AMERICAN ASSOCIATION FOR APPLIED PSYCHOLOGY. Committee on Training in Clinical (Applied) Psychology. (B. V. Moore, Chairman.) Proposed program of professional training in clinical psychology. *J. consult. Psychol.*, 1943, 7, 23–26.

2. AMERICAN PSYCHOLOGICAL ASSOCIATION. Annual Report of the Policy and Planning Board: 1947. *Amer. Psychologist*, 1947, 2, 191–198.

3. AMERICAN PSYCHOLOGICAL ASSOCIATION: Committee on the American Board of Examiners in Professional Psychology: Report. *Amer. Psychologist*, 1946, 1, 510–517.

4. AMERICAN PSYCHOLOGICAL ASSOCIATION AND AMERICAN ASSOCIATION FOR APPLIED PSYCHOLOGY COMMITTEE ON GRADUATE AND PROFESSIONAL TRAINING: Subcommittee report on graduate internship training in psychology. (D. Shakow, Chairman.) *J. consult. Psychol.*, 1945, 9, 243–266.

5. FLEXNER, A. *Medical education.* New York: Macmillan, 1925. Pp. ix + 334.

6. GREGG, A. (Chairman). The place of psychology in an ideal university. The report of the University Commission to advise on the future of psychology at Harvard. Cambridge: Harvard University Press, 1947. Pp. 42.

7. KELLY, E. L. Research on the selection of clinical psychologists. *J. clin. Psychol.*, 1947, 3, 39–42.

8. KUBIE, L. S. (Chairman). Training in clinical psychology. Transactions of the First Conference, March 27–28, 1947, New York, N.Y. New York: Josiah Macy, Jr. Foundation, 1947. Pp. 88.

9. MORROW, W. R. The development of psychological internship training. *J. consult. Psychol.*, 1946, 10, 165–183.

10. SEARS, R. R. Clinical training facilities: 1947. A report from the Committee on Graduate and Professional Training. *Amer. Psychologist*, 1947, 2, 199–205.

II
TRAINING AND
BACKGROUND

The hallmark of an established profession is standardization of the training of its members. A profession cannot expect acceptance from the community until it provides reasonable assurance that every individual who has the moral (and preferably the legal) right to identify himself with that profession has undergone a prescribed, minimum program of education and training.

Prior to World War II, the training of psychologists, clinical or otherwise, had been heterogeneous. The postwar demand for the clinical psychologist's skills sharply increased pressure on the profession to standardize training. Since its initial effort in this direction in 1947 (e.g., the Shakow Committee report in Part I), clinical psychology has continued to be highly concerned with the training of its members. Lloyd and Newbrough summarize the several national conferences that directly reflect this concern. Pumroy and Alexander and Basowitz review contemporary views on training, and other articles in this part discuss certain specialized kinds of training.

The goals of clinical training have continued to develop and mature in the two decades since the Shakow Committee report. The current, consensual view—the training of a "scientist-professional"—is detailed by Hoch, Ross, and Winder.

Until very recently, psychologists have not questioned the assignment to the medical setting of the internship or other practicum aspects of clinical training. The final paper of this part suggests a drastic revamping of this position. While Albee's statement probably would not be endorsed at this time by a consensus of clinical psychologists, it may well designate the path that training in clinical psychology will follow at some time in the future.

4. Current Characteristics of the Education of Clinical Psychologists

DONALD K. PUMROY

THIS report is based upon two different papers. The first paper was entitled "Current Characteristics of Practicum Instruction in Clinical Psychology" and was presented in a symposium chaired by Thomas M. Magoon at the APA Convention of 1960. Magoon was the chairman of a committee to study the practicum training in clinical, counseling, industrial, and school psychology program for Division 2; the author was responsible for the section of clinical psychology. The second part of this report is concerned with the results of a questionnaire which was sent to the departments of psychology that had been approved by the Education and Training Board of APA. This questionnaire primarily focused on the courses offered in clinical psychology but also contained some other questions relating to the department's current position which our committee judged to be important for clinical psychology. This second part was prepared for the Corresponding Committee of Fifty by a committee composed of: Stuart E. Golann, University of Maryland; Robert J. Murney, Medical Center for Federal Prisoners, Springfield, Mo.; Albert W. Silver, Eastern Michigan University; and the author who served as chairman. This second part was presented at the Corresponding Committee of Fifty meeting at the APA Convention, Philadelphia, 1963.

PART I: CURRENT CHARACTERISTICS OF PRACTICUM INSTRUCTION IN CLINICAL PSYCHOLOGY

The same questionnaire was used to obtain information about practicum instruction in the four specialties of clinical, counseling, industrial, and school psychology. Only the clinical psycho-

logy information will be covered in the following order: (1) numerical findings for each graduate year; (2) observations of the author about responses to the write-in questions; (3) comparisons between schools approved by the APA for clinical training and those not approved.

The questionnaire was mailed to the academic departments listed in the December 1958 issue of the *American Psychologist* as giving a Ph.D. in clinical psychology. There were 69 schools listed which were sent the questionnaire. Returns were obtained from 61 (88%).

RESULTS AND DISCUSSION

In response to the first question about whether or not students typically get practicum experience, 96 percent of the schools answered "yes." Of these, it was required for all but two. It is important to note that the practicum experience here includes internship. The median number of credits that a student would have accumulated by the completion of the Ph.D. was $7\frac{1}{2}$; the median clock hours in practicum was 2250. Most schools (85%) used both university and non-university agencies for their practicum instruction.

During the first year of graduate school about half the students began practicum work. Thus, to the question about whether or not a typical student took practicum in his first year, 48 percent of the schools said "yes" and 52 percent said "no." The students who took practicum spent a median of 5 hours per week with it. While there was a great deal of variation in what the student did during the beginning of practicum work, it frequently started with the following: orientation to the functions of the agency, observation of the staff at work, attendance at staff and case conferences, and some testing if the student had the necessary

Reprinted from *Training in Clinical Psychology: The Matter from Several Perspectives* (Washington, D.C.: American Psychological Association, 1964), 48–69, by permission of the American Psychological Association and the author. Dr. Pumroy is Associate Professor, Psychology Department, University of Maryland.

training. The supervision most employed was sitting-in while the student performed practicum activities (65%) and the use of a one-way screen to observe (68%). The tape recorder was used rather less (22%). This is understandable since the supervisors were most concerned here with the techniques of test administration; thus, actual observation of the student was important. The median supervisory time given each student per week was 1¾ hours. About one-half of the departments requiring practicum during this first year examined the student at the end of the practicum and for most of the departments (87%) grades were given. Again it should be noted that the subject material was largely testing and the examination was usually on this material. Only a few schools (13%) used any sort of a pre-post testing to evaluate student improvement.

In the second year, practicum instruction was much more frequent (86%). The median hours per week spent by the students was 10, with a range of 3½ to 30. The type of supervision for this period tended to change more toward tape recording (64%), but one-way vision screen was still used frequently (66%) as well as sitting-in with the student. Conferences with the student in which he presented his testing or therapy case were also frequently mentioned. The median supervision time per week was three hours. The practicum experience seemed to be of two kinds: one was the orientation and testing for the students who began their practicum in the second years; the other category was made up of individuals who were in their second year of practicum training. This latter group became involved in therapy, both group and individual, as well as continuing with their testing work. Also, the latter group was more likely to be obtaining their experience somewhere other than an academic setting. This was reflected in the fact that 30 percent of the schools gave exams while 64 percent of them did not. Even so, grades were given in 73 percent of the schools and not given in 25 percent; the grades were frequently given on the basis of some evaluation or rating given by the practicum supervisor.

The third graduate year contained a mixture of types of practicum, but the students typically took practicum in 85 percent of the schools. The median time per week was 21 hours. During this period the student in the diagnostic testing work was beginning to be viewed as a junior staff member, particularly with the administration of the tests. More emphasis was placed on therapy. This is reflected in the type of typical supervision; the tape recorder was used most (74%), the one-way vision screen next (55%), and sitting-in (29%). Conferences between the student and supervisor to discuss a case were also mentioned by 45 percent of the respondents. The median hours the student experienced supervision was 3½. The students were rarely given exams at the end of practicum; only 7 percent of the schools said "yes," while 91 percent said "no." Even though exams were not given, many of the schools did give grades (55%).

While with some schools the fourth year is the internship year, with other schools the third year is used. In the latter case, the student can return to the academic department and be in a position to work closely with his advisor.

When the fourth year was the internship, 65 percent of the schools said their typical student took practicum during this year while 28 percent said "no." The median time per week for practicum work was 24½ hours. Supervision during this fourth year was mostly done with the tape recorder (73%); next was the one-way screen (52%), and sitting-in with the student (30%). The median supervisory time per week was four hours. Relatively few schools gave exams at the end of this period; only 5 percent did so, but grades were given for practicum work in 43 percent of the schools.

Only 18 percent of the schools reported that their typical student took any practicum work beyond the fourth year. The median time the student spent on practicum at this level was 16. The median supervisory time per week was three hours. The reduction in supervision time is also evident in the way supervision was conducted; mostly done by tape recorder (67%) with some one-way screen observation (42%). Exams were given in only 18 percent of the schools, but grades were given in 36 percent of them. During these later years the student was more on his own, functioning as a junior staff person. A few schools mentioned that the training in the later stages focused on the psychologist's role in the consultation function.

The above discussion describes the typical situation with regard to the provision of practicum training. It seemed worthwhile to include some of the problems expressed by the individuals responsible for practicum training. They are as follows:

1. Many supervisors mentioned that adequate supervision required a tremendous amount of time. This was particularly mentioned with reference to listening to tape recordings of the student's psychotherapy. They were concerned that the heavy burden on the instructor was not adequately reflected in his course load. One of the respondents summed it up succinctly as: "staff needs sleep and finds little time for it."

2. Another problem mentioned by several is the difficulty encountered when a student is sent to an agency for his internship. At times the student gets so engrossed in the service aspects of the agency that he neglects to do his thesis; particularly if the agency is some distance from the school. One of the respondents described this as a "flight into clinical service."

3. The problem of individuals who do well in their academic work but are poor in their clinical work, and vice versa, was reported. This is sometimes handled by discouraging the bright student from continuing in clinical work.

4. Problems with scheduling were mentioned by several departments. The difficulty was that service agencies' business hours and the university class schedule were often in conflict. This was particularly true when the agency was some distance away and wanted the student to work a block of time. For example, if the university scheduled a class for Monday, Wednesday, and Friday, the student could only work Tuesday and Thursday (not a block of time). In some cases the distance traveled worked a hardship on the students.

An attempt was made to see whether there was a difference in practicum instruction between the schools with APA approval and those without APA approval. It would seem that the effects of such factors as the committee review, the discussions of their own programs and comparisons with other programs, and the desire to meet the standards for approval would lead the approved department to structure its programs in a way different from those not yet approved. To determine this, the questionnaires were divided into Approved (75%), and Non-approved (25%). Contrary to what was expected, there was relatively little difference between the two groups. One difference, although slight, seemed to be that the students from the Approved schools spent more time in practicum instruction than did the students from the Non-approved schools. Another difference was that the Approved departments had more agency facilities available to them to use than did the Non-approved departments.

SUMMARY

I have pointed up that (1) practicum instruction in clinical appears to be taught in a similar manner in the different graduate schools in the U.S.; (2) there are problems in teaching practicum that differ from the problems encountered in other courses; and (3) there does not seem to be much difference in practicum instruction within schools that are APA approved and those that are not.

PART II: THE CURRENT PICTURE OF CLINICAL TRAINING IN APA-APPROVED SCHOOLS

In our field, which is apparently in a continuous state of change, it seemed to the committee that the determination of the current situation in clinical psychology was a large and difficult undertaking. A manifestation of the change was the very existence of the Corresponding Committee of Fifty itself. One apparent reason for its establishment was an appreciation for some dissatisfaction among the younger clinical psychologists. Perhaps this dissatisfaction has been reflected in other ways: Some of these ways would seem to be the recent trend for psychologists in private practice to join Division 13 (Division of Consulting Psychology), the interest and joining of psychologists in PIAP (Psychologists Interested in the Advancement of Psychotherapy), and the increased activities in local clinical groups in the large metropolitan areas. A concomitant, yet different, aspect of clinical psychology that has received attention has been the discussion of a special clinical psychology degree different from the Ph.D. degree.

All of these factors seem to indicate that many changes regarding clinical psychology are at least being considered and it seemed worthwhile to attempt to ascertain some picture of how clinical psychologists were currently being trained. To this end, we decided to seek this information from the place that clinical psychologists are being trained, the psychology departments. As the attitudes and values of the departments frequently are reflected in their curricula, it was decided to collect this information as well.

METHOD

The schools selected were those listed as offering clinical programs that were approved by the American Psychological Association's Education and Training Board. A questionnaire, sent to each of these schools, was designed to collect information about the current curricula for clinical training. The questionnaire was reviewed by members of the committee and by several of our colleagues for breadth and clarity. The questionnaire was made as objective as possible so that it would be less of a burden to the respondent. Questions were included on new areas or problems such as the pre-doctorate degree and on the type of employment the new clinical Ph.D. typically took as his first job.

The questionnaire was mailed, in early 1963, to 59 schools that were listed in the December 1962,

American Psychologist as offering doctoral programs approved in clinical psychology by the
Education and Training Board. There was one
follow-up; on the basis of this, 55 questionnaires
were completed and returned (a 93% return).

RESULTS

One area of focus was the clinical courses taught.
(The respondents were instructed that "student" as
used in the questionnaire was to be interpreted to
mean the "typical Ph.D. student in Clinical Psychology"). Our questions and the percent answering
them "yes" or "no" were:

1. Does your student take a course in the area of
   personality theory?
   Yes, 100%; No, 0%.
   This course was required in 85 percent of the
   schools reporting. The number of credits given
   for the course was somewhat difficult to report
   since the schools were on semester, trimester,
   and quarter plans. In the quarter and semester
   system the mode was three credits.

2. Does your student take a course in individual
   intelligence testing?
   Yes, 91%; No, 9%.
   Individual intelligence testing was required by
   87 percent of the schools. It is interesting to
   note that it would be possible for a student to
   receive a Ph.D. in clinical psychology without
   having taken a course in individual intelligence
   testing. The number of credits given for this
   course vary widely; the mode was three credits

TABLE 1. NUMBER OF SCHOOLS REQUIRING A
STUDENT TO ADMINISTER A CERTAIN NUMBER
OF TESTS

Number of Tests Required	WAIS	WISC	Stanford-Binet	Total
30–35	1	1	1	3
20–29	1	2	6	9
11–19	7	3	4	14
10	13	11	9	33
9	1	1	1	3
8	3	0	0	3
7	2	1	2	5
6	6	4	4	14
5	10	14	12	36
0–4	2	6	5	13
Not listed	9	12	11	32
Total	55	55	55	165

for the quarter and semester systems. Table 1
shows the number of tests that a student was
required to administer.

3. Does your student take a course that covers
   objective personality testing?
   Yes, 76%; No, 24%.
   Objective personality testing is required in 55
   percent of the schools, and not required in
   27 percent. The remainder of the schools (18%)
   did not reply. Several alternative explanations
   are possible here. Perhaps it is taught at the
   undergraduate level. Or it may be assumed
   that the student learns this in a practicum
   situation. Three credits was the mode for this
   course under both the quarter and semester
   systems.

4. Does your student take a course that covers
   projecting testing?
   Yes, 98%; No, 2%.
   Projective testing was required by 91 percent of
   the schools. Under the quarter system the
   modal number of credits was 6. Under the
   semester system there was a wide range of
   credits; the distribution was almost bimodal
   with peaks at 3 and 6 credits. It seemed that
   many of the schools on the semester system
   offered two courses on projective tests, one
   each semester.

5. Does your student take a course in psychotherapy?
   Yes, 98%; No. 0%; No Answer, 2%.
   A course in psychotherapy was required in 85
   percent of the schools; it was not required in
   13 percent. The respondents were asked whether
   this course was more didactic or technique
   oriented. Fifty-seven percent of the schools
   replied didactic, 13 percent said technique, and
   14 percent said both. On the quarter system,
   the modal number of credits was 3 and 4.
   With the semester system schools, there was,
   again, a bimodal distribution with peaks at 3
   and 6. Most schools had the course listed for
   3 credits; the next most frequent situation was
   a year course, 3 credits each semester.

6. Does your student take a practicum course
   that is given on campus?
   Yes, 85%; No, 15%.
   A practicum course was required in 76 percent
   of the schools, and not required in 13 percent.
   Twelve percent did not answer this item. With
   both the quarter and semester systems the

student typically took this course for an academic year (3 quarters or 2 semesters). The number of credits given varies widely; here the quarter system distribution was bimodal with peaks at 9 and 18 credits. In the semester system the mode was 6 credits with a great deal of variation. The respondents were asked whether this practicum included experience in test administration and interpretation; 85 percent replied "yes," 4 percent said "no." Eleven percent did not answer. They were also asked whether the practicum provided experience in therapy; 84 percent said "yes," 7 percent said "no," 9 percent did not respond. Since there has been an increased interest in child clinical work, the departments were asked whether the practicum included work with children (below 12 years). Seventy-eight percent said "yes," 9 percent said "no," 13 percent did not respond.

7. Does your student take a practicum course off campus?
   Yes, 69%; No, 27%; No Answer, 4% (2 schools).
   The respondents were equally divided on whether academic credit was given; 40 percent said "yes," 40 percent said "no." The question was intended to cover any applied experience outside of an academic setting. It should have covered internships. The question apparently was not clear since some of the respondents answered as though it included an internship, while others did not. This yielded a range of hours spent in this activity from 4 hours to 5,000 hours. The responses to the question whether this practicum experience involved test administration and interpretation were 67 percent "yes," 15 percent "no," and 18 percent "no response." This practicum experience involved therapy in 62 percent of the cases, did not in 11 percent, and 27 percent did not respond. They were also asked whether this practicum included work with children; 38 percent said "yes," 31 percent said "no," and 31 percent did not reply.

In the past the pattern was that the student first received his academic training and then his practical training (i.e., internship). It would now seem that the situation has been changing. This was probably reflected in the confusion about answering the question on practicum outside of school. Three terms are used to cover practical applied training; they are

"practicum," "clerkship," and "internship." Some schools appear to use "practicum" to cover all applied training. Others use "practicum" for practical courses taught by the faculty of the school. "Clerkship" is used if the student is in the first two years and spends most of his time observing or helping with data. "Internship" usually means that the student is spending full time in a clinical setting and is working as a junior staff person. The distinction between practicum and internship was much clearer when the student did not receive any applied training until he went on his internship.

Lately there has been a tendency to merge academic and applied work earlier in the students' graduate work. This usually has meant an increase in applied training and a decrease in academic work as the student progresses through graduate school. In order to get some indication of this on the questionnaire, the respondents were asked which procedure was followed by their typical clinical student. The question was presented as follows:

8. There appear to be several different ways in which the academic and practicum work are integrated in the student's training. These seem to be the ways that are most common:

A. The situation where the student completes his academic work and then goes on an internship and then returns to the campus for his dissertation.

B. The situation where the student completes three years of academic work and then goes on an internship and works on his dissertation while away from campus.

C. The situation where the practicum work and academic work are merged together starting the first or second years and the student tends to take less academic work and more practicum work as he advances toward his degree.

D. The situation where the internship is post-doctoral.

E. No internship.

F. No fixed pattern, much variation.

G. Other (please indicate).

The respondents were asked to check which of these procedures were most like the one followed by their students. The responses are presented in Table 2.

TABLE 2. Responses To the Question on Integration of Academic and Practicum Training

	A	B	C	D	E	F	G
Alone	8	2	23	0	0	4	5
In combination	9	9	8	1	0	2	3

Alone indicates the number of schools which stated that their typical student followed one of the procedures listed. As some of the schools checked two or more, *In combination* indicates the number of schools selecting that procedure in combination with others. Thus it appears that the merging of academic and applied training was the most typical.

An attempt was made to assess the departments' position on clinical training versus research training for their clinical student by the next question.

9. Some departments feel that the clinical psychologist should be primarily a research psychologist while other departments have emphasized the clinical aspect of the training. Would you please check the statement that represents your department's point of view on this issue?
   A. Our students are trained with an equal amount of emphasis on research and clinical activities.
   B. Our students are primarily trained for research work.
   C. Our students are primarily trained for clinical work.
   D. Our students are primarily trained for research work but they are qualified upon graduation to do clinical work.
   This question represents an attempt to assess the position of the department on the matter of clinical versus research training for their clinical students. The responses to this question are presented in Table 3.

TABLE 3. Responses To Item on Clinical versus Research Training

	A	B	C	D	Total
No. of schools	34	0	1	17	52

Three schools replied that did not check one of the above. One school checked A and D, another checked B and D, and the third checked the reverse of D. An equal emphasis on research and clinical training was the most typical

response, with 62 percent of the schools checking this category. Thirty-one percent said their students were primarily trained for research but were qualified to do clinical work.

10. In the last few years there has been some talk about establishing a subdoctoral technician degree for psychologists. We are concerned with your department's position on this.
    A. We have taken no action on this issue.
    B. We have a committee appointed to study this.
    C. We are studying the issue.
    D. Other (please indicate).
    The responses to this question are presented in Table 4.

TABLE 4. Responses To Item on Subdoctoral Training

	A	B	C	D	Total
No. of schools	24	3	10	13	50
Percent of schools	44	5	18	24	91

Four schools responded with combinations, one with C and D, two with A and D, and one with B and C. The "other" responses were quite varied. Nine of the departments were opposed and four of them were not interested in establishing such a program at their school. Two said that they were planning to establish a clinical doctoral degree.

11. About what percent of all of your students are in the clinical program?
    A. (0–20) 2%   D. (61–80) 13%
    B. (21–40) 18%   E. (81–100) 3%
    C. (41–60) 64%
    Half of the graduate students appear to be in clinical programs.

12. About what percent of your recent clinical Ph.D. students (since 1955) have taken a first post-degree position involving professional duties?
    A. (0–20) 7%   D. (61–80) 25%
    B. (21–40) 18%   E. (81–100) 12%
    C. (41–60) 38%

13. About what percent of your recent clinical Ph.D. students (since 1955) have taken a first post-degree position involving primarily teaching or research duties?
    A. (0–20) 13%   D. (61–80) 9%
    B. (21–40) 38%   E. (81–100) 2%
    C. (41–60) 38%

While more of the students take their first job in applied areas, the difference between them and the number of students taking a position in teaching and research is not marked.

DISCUSSION

What then are some conclusions that can be drawn from the data obtained from these two studies? It is difficult, of course, to generalize from such relatively simple data to the complex and intertwined problems of clinical training. I will attempt to present my conclusions in the light of earlier work done on clinical training. Certainly the three outstanding discussions of clinical training have been the *Training in Clinical Psychology* (Raimy, 1950) commonly called the Boulder Conference; *Psychology and Mental Health* (Strother, 1956), the Stanford Conference; and *Graduate Education in Psychology* (Roe, 1959) usually referred to as the Miami Conference.

When the current study is compared with the earlier reports there seems to have been little change in clinical training between the Boulder Conference and the present. There was considerable congruence between the course work recommended at the Boulder Conference and what was reported in our survey. (One methodological reason for congruence may have been the structure of the questionnaire. This was mentioned by one of the respondents.) It would seem that there is less emphasis on testing than has been the case in the past. Although practicum training was emphasized as important at both the Boulder Conference and Miami Beach Conference, it would seem that the schools have not viewed it as such. This was inferred from the fact that instructors responsible for practicum are usually of junior rank; as they acquire more rank, they tend to become more involved in other activities. Consistent with this observation is the view that less course credit is given to an instructor in practicum than an instructor in an academic course.

The difficulty of training for research versus training for clinical service is a persistent problem. The responses to this question indicated equal positions for research and service. This is similar to the view expressed at the Boulder and Miami Beach Conferences. At Boulder, the doing of research was emphasized, while at the Miami Beach Conference, the point of view appeared that the graduates should have a research orientation with less emphasis on the actual "doing." The

problem will probably continue to be with us for some time since approximately half of the graduate students in those schools with APA approved programs are in the clinical program and the majority of the new Ph.D.'s in clinical go into a service position.

One of the most popular solutions to the problem has been the interest in establishing a new degree (e.g., Doctor of Psychology) or a sub-doctoral degree to designate those individuals primarily involved in service activities. The Ph.D. degree then would be retained as designating the individual who is primarily engaged in research activities. Two schools mentioned that they were planning to establish a clinical doctorate program in the near future. The subdoctoral training has been discussed for some time. The Boulder Conference mentioned the definite need for people with training less than a doctorate degree. On the other hand, they stated that by filling positions with partially trained persons, it would de difficult to up-grade professional standards.

As was mentioned earlier, the questionnaire elicited little in the way of new or unique ideas about the training of clinical psychologists. Perhaps there is more change than has been reflected in the answers to the questionnaire. Perhaps the Education and Training Board, even though they appear to have encouraged innovation, have, by the very nature of their existence, caused departments to conform to a model. One innovation was mentioned, however, although not in any detail. This is what has been labeled "mental health." This would seem to include an orientation to the community and training in consultation. This particular avenue of development would seem consistent with the changing views of mental illness, the area of major activity for clinical psychologists.

SUMMARY

This paper was concerned with the current curricula for training clinical psychologists. The report was based on information collected in two different surveys of graduate schools giving a doctoral degree in clinical psychology. The first survey was concerned with practicum training and the second was primarily concerned with courses taken by graduate students in clinical programs. The results of these surveys were presented and some conclusions were drawn from the findings.

REFERENCES

RAIMY, V. C. (Ed.). *Training in clinical psychology.* New York: Prentice-Hall, 1950. (Conference on Graduate Education in Clinical Psychology held at Boulder, Colorado, August, 1949.)

ROE, ANNE, GUSTAD, J. W., MOORE, B. V., ROSS, S., and SKODAK, MARIE. (Eds.). *Graduate education in psychology.* Washington, D.C.: American Psychological Association, 1959. (Miami Beach Conference.)

STROTHER, C. R. *Psychology and mental health.* Washington, D.C.: American Psychological Association, 1956. (Stanford Conference.)

5. *Current Clinical Training Practices: An Overview*

IRVING E. ALEXANDER AND HAROLD BASOWITZ

To have been totally concerned with support of graduate education in psychology, and especially with clinical psychology, for a combined total of 9 years covering the period 1958–1964 has been a multifaceted experience for the authors. During this time we have had occasion to examine hundreds of documents describing training programs and we have enjoyed the privilege of visiting, between us, virtually every institution in this country which purports to train clinical psychologists. Countless hours have been spent in discussion with people in the field, with each other, and with former colleagues about the problems of our emerging field. We have been alternately encouraged and discouraged about future prospects, although usually not in phase with each other. From it all there remains a hard core of information and a residue of impressions from which we shall try to distill a meaningful communication. Our task, as we see it, is to illuminate current university training practices as they relate to the problems that face us today.

The broad outlines of future clinical psychology programs were sketched in 1947 in the ground-breaking report of the American Psychological Association committee chaired by David Shakow and augmented in greater detail by the Boulder Conference Report of 1950. The history of the next decade is one of university departments adopting the curricular recommendations combined in these reports in order to live up to the objectives of training the scientist-practitioner. By 1958 it seemed apparent from the summary of the Miami Conference that despite the expressed need for more

Reprinted from *Professional Preparation of Clinical Psychologists*, E. L. Hoch, A. O. Ross, and C. L. Winder (Eds.), (Washington, D.C.: Americal Psychological Association, 1965), 15–20, by permission of the American Psychological Association and the authors. Dr. Alexander is Professor and Chairman, Department of Psychology, and Director of Clinical Training, Duke University. He was formerly Training Specialist in Psychology, National Institute of Mental Health. Dr. Basowitz is Professor of Psychology, New York University, and also was formerly Training Specialist in Psychology, National Institute of Mental Health.

flexibility in programing, the basic curricular lines were set. In accord with the dictum that all students should be "psychologists first" before specializing, clinical students were initially prepared through a series of course experiences in the more traditional area of general psychology and in experimental design and data analysis. This had already become the prevailing model for the first year of graduate training, modified in some institutions by a traditional course or sequence in intelligence testing. It may be noted that the objectives of this first year of study frequently became distorted. Instead of retaining the aim of basic preparation for any kind of specialization, they rapidly assumed in many institutions the properties of a *rite de passage*. The first-year program became the proving ground to determine whether the student had enough seriousness of purpose and enough intellectual scope to convince even the most hard-headed of our colleagues that despite his "poor" choice of a specialty area, the student would have the possibility of being a creditable member of the profession.

More recently, the first-year pattern seems to be changing. Fewer core courses are required; more choice is permitted; and the core course requirements tend now to be distributed over a two-year time span. Relevant specialty material, usually psychological assessment or personality theory, is now introduced at the beginning of graduate training. The remnants of the old first-year ordeal tend to be perpetuated in newly emerging clinical programs where literal adherence to the recommendations contained in prestigeful public documents is accepted as the most direct route to public approval, namely accreditation. It is also found in those institutions where selection is still a major problem and where it is used as an effective screening device.

The increased flexibility in first-year course programing has come about as a result of pressure from both students and faculty. Students reported morale problems when their participation in work related to their central interest was delayed for a year. Clinical faculties were frustrated in their desire to facilitate early relevant research participation in the clinical fledgling who was overloaded with core courses. The dissertation experience was frequently the only research exposure a student had in his graduate career. All too often doctoral research was done in fields outside of the student's major area of interest with the sole purpose of completing a degree requirement. The unusually high ratios of clinical students to clinical staff necessitated the search for dissertation advisors from other areas. In most departments clinical students constituted at least half of the student population while clinical staff rarely exceeded four or five full-time members. Unusually heavy administrative and clinical supervisory burdens, in addition to full-time teaching duties, tended to cut down the research productivity of the clinical staff members, adding still further difficulties in exploring meaningful research problems with their students. In recent years steps have been taken to remedy this situation. Faculty-student ratios have been reduced, to some extent as a function of pressure from the Education and Training Board to maintain accreditation, and research participation has been demanded in the first year of study or certainly no later than the second. Most institutions now require at least one bit of evidence of research competence before the dissertation is undertaken, either in a research apprenticeship model or in the formality of a master's thesis or its equivalent. While this change in curriculum may have a salutary effect on future research production, it has not been without its effects on clinical staff selection which, as we shall later have occasion to point out, has influenced in turn the more clinical content in graduate training programs.

A second noticeable change in clinical curriculum planning has taken place with regard to the emphasis placed on the teaching of diagnostic skills. From a multiplicity of testing courses designed to produce competence in the use of particular tests (Rorschach, TAT, Wechsler, Binet, MMPI, etc.), the trend has turned toward compression. The modal clinical program now includes a two- or three-semester sequence in "Assessment" in which students are "introduced" to a wide variety of techniques and their use with different populations with the hope that competence will be gained through individual supervision in the practicum and internship experiences. The reasons for this change are multiple and can only be touched upon here. It is attributable partly to the disillusioning results of empirical tests of the power of clinical instruments as reflected in the "clinical versus statistical" prediction controversy of the late fifties. Another contributing factor is found in the changing status of the diagnostic role in clinical facilities as opportunities for research, psychotherapy, and administration have become available to clinical psychologists. A third element is the increasing emphasis on the psychologist's role as a psychotherapist. In this role, following the model of two influential schools, psychoanalysis and client-centered therapy, the importance of psychodiagnostic information to the therapeutic process is minimized. Also to be considered is the unwillingness of senior clinical staff members in graduate departments to spend their teaching time in technique courses. The usual practice is to relegate this task to the new clinical staff member who typically has limited clinical experience in the use of these techniques.

The change in emphasis on testing courses should not, however, be construed entirely in a negative light. It becomes increasingly apparent that the clinical psychologist of the present day is no longer being trained to work primarily in a medical setting where, at least at one time, the diagnostic function was of paramount importance. Present opportunities for employment in schools, industry, community settings, and private practice as researcher, administrator, consultant, and psychotherapist have forced additions to already crowded curricula which make it almost impossible and perhaps unnecessary to provide the slow, methodical grounding in testing techniques exemplified by the full semester course in Binet testing so prevalent 10 or 15 years ago.

The consequences of this change have been interesting to observe. It has tended to push off the major responsibilities for diagnostic skills training to the practicum and internship agencies. This is especially true for those departments where clinical facilities are not under their own control. In such instances the diagnostic role is further undermined since the clinical identification models within university departments are rarely involved in this activity. What is most unfortunate, however, is that when the student does get to the practicum agency he frequently finds that here, too, the diagnostic function is not highly valued. Without question, the clinical student of today is less concerned than the student of 10 years ago with the problems of diagnosis, less skilled in the use of fantasy material for personality assessment, but more conversant with objective, machine-scored measures used for these purposes.

A third major modification in predoctoral clinical programs is to be found in internship training patterns. While formerly the full-year block internship in a single clinical facility was the prevailing standard, we now find a variety of practices in use. Some institutions, cognizant of the need for continuity in research activity, prefer to encourage their students to complete internship requirements through a two-year, half-time arrangement in a single nearby facility. Others will plan shorter but more varied experiences in a number of clinical settings. The old practice of continuing a student through the Veterans Administration training program throughout his graduate years is less frequently found today. Full-year internships in distant training centers still tend to be the mode in remote university settings where local facilities are not in abundance. In metropolitan centers or in large university complexes, students are likely to stay close to home for internship experience.

Perhaps the most striking modifications in curriculum over the past 10 years are reflected in the increased numbers of opportunities available for psychotherapy training, for divergent practicum experiences, and for research participation through apprenticeship. Whereas in former days individual therapy was the predominant model we now have, as a result of the impact of the mental health movement, a wide variety of therapies being taught in graduate programs. Courses or practica devoted to group, individual, family, and community techniques are now more widely available. While it is true that exposure to many approaches has become the fashion, we are still faced with the continuing problem of the intensity or depth of the experiences provided. Time, facilities, personnel, as well as program intent are frequently given as the reasons why a graduate student finishing a degree in clinical psychology is not adequately prepared to assume the therapist's role. Most clinical faculties are ill suited to undertake this heavy burden which requires intensive individual supervision and accessible clinical populations, while most predoctoral practicum and internship staffs have too little time with the students to do this job adequately. Thus the clinical student frequently comes away from his graduate days with a whetted appetite, a limited exposure to various therapeutic techniques, and a lack of competency feelings about his ability to perform as a therapist. In our attempts to prepare a "generalist" we have consistently discouraged those students with committed interest in psychotherapy from preparing themselves thoroughly while in predoctoral status. Whether this need necessarily be the case is a matter that should be carefully evaluated.

Certainly it should be pointed out that people currently in training have for the most part richer practicum resources than ever before. The mushrooming of clinical facilities all over the country has enlarged the practicum and internship pattern formerly limited largely to Veterans Administration and mental hospital settings. Students are now being sent wherever competent role models are functioning. These include community clinics, child guidance centers, schools, general hospitals, disability centers, prisons, homes for juvenile delinquents, and facilities for the mentally retarded. The standard fare of the departmental clinic or the local Veterans Administration installation is being supplemented by these new possibilities. As a result of this trend toward broader practicum training it seems fair to say that the clinical student of today is probably less attuned to the problems of severe psychopathology than were his predecessors, but more aware of other potential arenas of psychological application.

Despite the changes in content and structure outlined above, we would say that the scientist-practitioner objective continues to be the stated one for the vast majority of clinical training programs. Some few will boldly emphasize the scientific aspect, with little or no regard for building the skills of the practitioner. Still fewer will frankly announce their interest in training clinical service people. In actual fact, even these apparently divergent views are not clearly reflected in curricular differences. In basic outline, at least on paper, all clinical programs tend to be more alike than they are different.

Earlier in this presentation we alluded to the effect that clinical staff selection has had on the evolution of graduate training programs. It is no secret that in screening new candidates for staff positions departments are concerned mainly with their research promise and all too little with their clinical acumen or interest. It is also well known that new clinical faculty, under the stress of course preparation and research productivity from which the academic rewards are obtained, rarely have the opportunity to enhance their clinical experience by active participation in clinical work. These conditions have important ramifications. Our students are probably being better prepared in clinically relevant research than ever before, in personality, if not psychopathology, but the role model for the effective scientist-practitioner is fast disappearing. Within a short period of time young faculty clinicians identify themselves as personality researchers and tend to depreciate the clinical role largely through their lack of clinical sophistication.

Since they are responsible for a fair share of the training in most programs, it becomes apparent why so many clinical students suffer an identity crisis sometime during their training. These particular circumstances relating to the loss of adequate role models may have more to do with the present dissatisfaction with the scientist-practitioner goal of clinical training than has been recognized heretofore.

If one asks where one finds excitement in present day clinical programs, the answer is not likely to come in terms of curricular description, but rather in terms of people and attitudes. As we have pointed out previously, there is almost a monotony involved in reading clinical curricular outlines. All require some proficiency in general psychology, research design, and data analysis. All attend in some fashion to personality assessment, psychotherapy, and clinical research. All involve practicum experience and an internship. The critical questions revolve around who are the people offering the work in the specialty area; what is their level of competence; and what are their attitudes toward their subject matter? Over and above these aspects, what is the prevailing climate of opinion in the department toward clinical psychology and the student's prospective role in this field? Those programs in which excitement is generated usually have staff members who are working creatively in their special areas of interest, whether this work results in empirical research, theoretical speculation, or in practical use. Successful programs tend to be those in which clinical psychologists do not have to justify their existence in terms of a strict scientism where methodology is the be-all and end-all of the approach to significant human problems. Desirable clinical programs are more likely to exist in departments where clinical psychology is seen as still another acceptable special area of inquiry in a total field that ranges from biological to social and from mathematical to humanistic approaches to man.

We cannot leave the subject of current clinical training practices without observing that the perspective of history inevitably is sobering in its effect. Even for a field with so brief a life as modern clinical psychology, it provides a constant reminder that ultimate truths and final solutions to vexing questions are the exception rather than the rule—if they ever occur at all. Although there is much one can comment upon in this connection, limitations in space permit us to draw attention to but a few issues whose implications, in our view, require the most serious consideration both conceptually and from a pragmatic standpoint.

A fundamental problem destined to be with us for a long time relates to the balance between generalization and specialization in education and training. The problem is a recurrent one inherent in the nature of any changing field, with its expansion of knowledge, discovery of new areas of investigation, and opportunities and demands for application. As such, it is hardly peculiar to psychology but a matter of major preoccupation in all scientific disciplines. In response to this press, there has been in recent years a noticeable trend toward the decentralization of graduate training in psychology as fields have become more specialized. In some institutions "area" committees are set up to work out basic requirements for students in their own specialties, and programs are becoming more tailored to fit the individual student, his prior preparation, his capacity, and his rate of progress. Experimental psychologists are being led much more to study mathematics, physics, and physiology as part of their graduate programs. Students in physiological psychology are spending more time in the basic medical sciences at the expense of breadth in developmental, personality, or social psychology. The reduction in core courses and the modifications in clinical curricula mentioned earlier appear to reflect the same movement. Perhaps this in the long run will tend to have positive effects upon clinical training practices. When one is no longer concerned that the student have a smattering of knowledge in all things psychological, it may be possible to prepare him intensely in his own area of interest. Yet the reconciliation of such a development with a healthy reluctance to foster an undue narrowing or fragmentation of the entire discipline poses a dilemma from which there is no easy escape.

In similar vein, the scientist-practitioner model, although never intended to be rigidly binding, has lately evidenced remarkable elasticity in its implementation. The actual practices of certain institutions, as distinguished from their avowed purposes, seem to suggest training paradigms for either scientists or practitioners, rather than a felicitous blending of the two. If so, then it may at the very least be clarifying to inquire whether different models in training programs—for scientists, for practitioners, and for scientist-practitioners—could exist in different university departments and each be deemed as perfectly acceptable within the general rubric of clinical psychology. Further, what differences in training are to be expected should such alternate models be pursued? And what problems exist in accommodating these prospects with current American Psychological Association accreditation procedures and with existing state licensure and certification of psychologists?

Finally, no matter what models are contemplated, it is clear that the question of university training facilities, the auspices under which they operate, and the primary functions they are designed to serve, warrant careful reexamination. This question is compelling whether the facilities are viewed as laboratories for research in human problems or as miniature clinical units where the craft is to be learned—if such a distinction is to be made. Regardless of whether one subscribes to Albee's recent proposal (see position paper by Albee) in this respect, namely, the creation of psychological centers, at least his paper presents the issue sharply. It hardly seems necessary to point out that adequate faculty models, as well as relevant student training activities, are critically dependent upon appropriate facilities.

In our view there has been a fair amount of progress in clinical training over the years and this progress has reflected, albeit slowly, the changing nature of the field. We have now the solid beginnings of training in the child-clinical specialty in several institutions. Others have begun to prepare people for a career in community mental health work. It is clear in both cases, but especially in the latter, that in order to develop expertise it may be more important to lead students into allied areas of study at the expense of broader psychological knowledge. If we seek a unified solution involving a set curriculum to solve the multiplicity of problems we face, we are destined for unhappiness and failure. The scientist-practitioner model becomes the focus of the issue only if we demand that it remain as the only model and that it be adequate to produce any kind of professional person demanded in the present market. Multiple models are possible and should be encouraged in different institutions and even within single large institutions. Perhaps we should strive more to do what we can do well rather than dissipating our energies by attempting in our training programs to prepare our students, although admittedly unsuccessfully, to be all things to all men.

6. Previous Conferences on Graduate Education in Psychology: A Summary and Review

DEE NORMAN LLOYD AND J. R. NEWBROUGH

THIS paper was prepared to provide an overview of the issues and recommendations of previous national conferences on graduate education that have relevance to clinical psychology and to the Conference on the Professional Preparation of Clinical Psychologists (Chicago). In addition to the conferences bearing directly on clinical psychology (Boulder, Palo Alto, Miami Beach), we have included brief discussions on two conferences on training in counseling (Northwestern and Greyston) and one on training in school psychology (Thayer) to provide information of comparative value. The information contained in the summaries of these conferences was taken from the original conference reports (Raimy, 1950; Strother, 1956; Roe et al., 1959; APA, 1952; Thompson and Super, 1964; Cutts, 1955). Because of the extent to which these reports are condensed, this review should serve only as an introduction to the conferences; the reader interested in more detailed information should consult the appropriate report.[1]

Information about the participants at the conferences are portrayed in Tables 1 and 2. In Table 1, the number of persons attending each conference are categorized by their major professional affiliation. (This refers to their job site and not to the board or agency that they represented at the conference.) Table 2 groups the participants by their area of professional training.[2] In Table 3, which follows the summaries of the conferences, we have indicated the major issues and topics discussed at each conference, including those proposed for the Chicago conference (Subcommittee on Issues, 1965).

TABLE 2. PROFESSIONAL AREA MEMBERSHIP OF CONFERENCE PARTICIPANTS

Professional Area

Conference	Psychology				Gen. Med.	Psych-iatry	Soc. Wrk.	Nurs.	Educ.	Total
	Clin.	Couns.	School	Other[1]						
Boulder	49	2	2	16		1	1	1		72
Northwestern	5	36		1						42
Thayer	11	3	11	6	1	1	1		15	49
Stanford	53	8		3		4				66
Miami Beach	53	10		56					3	122
Greyston	7	49		3					1	60

1. Includes APA Central Office representatives.

Reprinted from *Professional Preparation of Clinical Psychologists*, E. L. Hoch, A. O. Ross, and C. L. Winder (Eds.), (Washington, D.C.: American Psychological Association, 1965), 122–139, by permission of the American Psychological Association and the authors. Dr. Lloyd is Project Director and Dr. Newbrough was Chief, both of the Community Projects Section, Mental Health Study Center, National Institute of Mental Health, Adelphi, Maryland. Dr. Newbrough now is Associate Professor of Psychology, George Peabody College for Teachers.

TABLE 1. MAJOR ORGANIZATIONAL AFFILIATION OF CONFERENCE PARTICIPANTS

Organizational Affiliation

Conference	College & University					Federal			State Agency[3]	Serv. Agency[4]	School Systems[5]	Organiz. Outside U.S.[6]	Total[7]
	Dept. Head	*Dept. Staff*	*Couns. Center*	*Med. School*	*Other[1]*	*NIMH*	*VA*	*Other[2]*					
Boulder (1949)	12	38			3	3	3	2	1	4	2	1	72
Northwestern (1951)	2	17	9		6	1	1			4	2		42
Thayer (1954)	6	10			6	3			3	2	15	2	49
Stanford (1955)	5	26	7	6	1	6	10		4	2			68
Miami Beach (1958)	36	40	5	6	4	7	5	5	8	5	3	1	122
Greyston (1964)	1	22	20		2	2	2	6	1	2	1		60

1. Deans, administration, and other departments, student personnel, etc.
2. Department of Defense, Office of Education.
3. State hospitals, health departments, and city health services.
4. Private clinics, foundations, and industry.
5. Public and private school systems.
6. United nations and Canadian universities.
7. Includes representatives of APA Central Office.

MAJOR CONFERENCE SUMMARIES

THE BOULDER CONFERENCE: GRADUATE EDU-
CATION IN CLINICAL PSYCHOLOGY

The Boulder Conference, held in August 1949, was the first of the national conferences on training in psychology and was concerned specifically with clinical. Following World War II, training institutions were attempting to meet an unprecedented demand for persons professionally trained in the mental health fields. Since clinical psychology training was highly variable at that time, there was an acute need for determination of policies and for planning of programs. The specific impetus for this conference was the request of the VA and the PHS for APA to furnish the names of universities with satisfactory training programs and to produce a recommended program of training and a procedure of accreditation. There were 72 participants representing, primarily, the approved training programs. Organizational affiliations of the participants are found in Tables 1 and 2. The two-week conference consisted of general sessions held twice daily, followed by small group meetings. Participants were randomly assigned to groups for each of the smaller meetings: The conference discussed and attempted to arrive at positions on the following 15 issues: (1) social needs and clinical psychology, (2) professional training in light of a changing science and society, (3) kinds and level of training, (4) professional ethics and problems of training, (5) background preparation for clinical psychology, (6) the core curriculum in clinical psychology, (7) training for research, (8) training for psychotherapy, (9) field training, (10) selection and evaluation of students, (11) staff training, (12) relations with other professions, (13) relations with governmental agencies, (14) accreditation of training universities, and (15) licensing and certification.

Discussion and Conclusions. In defining clinical psychologists, the conference took a very operational point of view. The title should be used only by persons with a doctoral degree based upon graduate education in psychology received from a recognized university. The conference agreed that there were three social needs to be served by trained clinical psychologists: (1) immediate help for persons in need of assistance, (2) prevention of conditions requiring treatment, and (3) contributions to the development of positive mental health. As well as providing professional services to meet these ends, the clinical psychologist would make research contributions to them. The conference made the important decision that research

should be given a place of equal and coordinate importance with practice because first, the primary functions of some clinical psychologists will be the execution and direction of research, and second, the clinical psychologist who is primarily engaged in service activities must be able to evaluate the development and assessment of new clinical techniques, primarily because these tools were at a very primitive stage of development. This position led to considerable discussion, questioning, and expression of divergent opinions. At the end of the conference, however, there seemed to be a recognition and acceptance of the importance of research training in the preparation of all clinical psychologists.

In evaluating professional training, the conference tried to produce a recommendation to include both uniformity and diversity. Uniformity was desired to give a particular meaning to "clinical psychology." Diversity was seen as necessary because of the process of rapid development and change occurring in society and psychology that would make crystallization of clinical functions premature. It was felt that uniformity would be achieved by setting minimal standards for training. This would allow diversity to be attained by the ways in which training departments would go beyond the minimal standards to develop their particular approaches to the professional field. To protect diversity, the conference adopted a resolution urging that APA create a committee to review the educational philosophy in graduate education of all specialties in psychology and to have the power to review accreditation policies and practices.

The conference recognized the need for and gave serious consideration to the functions of people trained at a sub-doctoral level. It suggested that sub-doctoral training programs should (1) have specific curricula to avoid diverting failures from the doctoral program to it, (2) be carried out within university departments, not professional schools, (3) be of 2-year duration, and (4) yield a certificate which specifies level of accomplishment and areas of competence. Recommendation was made to APA to carry out a study of the proper functions and titles of such persons and the extent of the relative and absolute needs for both trained psychologists and such assistants.

Professional ethics was given prominence in discussion since psychology was rapidly admitting large numbers of newly trained members who were facing constantly increasing public responsibilities. Attention was directed toward the university's responsibilities in selecting students of good character, in training them to be ethical and in weeding out unethical students. The ethics involved in professional practice where problems of working with and studying people are many and subtle were considered in some detail. Cooperation with members of allied professions was considered to be an ethical necessity based on three points: (1) the extreme complexity and variety of mental health problems, (2) the equally wide variety of skills and techniques required to effectively serve the individual, (3) the fact that the current training of any one profession cannot possibly insure mastery of all these techniques.

Discussions revealed increasing dissatisfaction with "one best way" of arranging curricula; it was questioned whether the goal of the entire training program (to produce a broadly educated and scientifically oriented professional person) could be met with this approach. The conference wished, therefore, to emphasize the need for experimentation in structuring curricula. For undergraduate training, the conference preferred to de-emphasize specialization courses and technical courses such as testing. Undergraduate students, however, should receive a sound grounding in basic psychology courses. There was agreement on the need for a common core of knowledge and skill in basic psychology in the graduate program. In discussing the structure of the core curriculum, the conference relied heavily on the proposals in the 1947 Shakow Committee Report (APA, 1947). The goal of the core curriculum should be to educate students to deal with psychological problems in a scientific manner, and should be centered around the areas of theory construction, conceptual tools, and scientific methodology. Twelve areas were listed, with the major emphasis being given to the integration of theory and field experience. Theory was highlighted many times in the discussion as the means to provide the student with the adequate conceptual tools to organize his work and to evaluate his techniques. There was discussion about the monitoring of courses in order to see that they covered certain areas. Considerable concern developed about this as an interference with academic freedom.

Training for research was described as, perhaps, the most challenging part of a curriculum. Discussion of this topic quickly became polarized between research and service. Five points were identified as basic to this conflict: (1) Students should, it was thought, receive training in both areas so that they could work in both or either. (2) The general lack of dependable knowledge about personality demands further research. (3) It is very difficult to obtain interest and competence in both areas, but careful selection of high-quality students may possibly achieve this. (4) Effectively performed service brings psychologists into intimate contact with significant research problems. (5) Effective service functions will probably provide the means for clinical research in psychology and psychiatry. It was recognized that teaching research to clinical students presents special problems, and it was suggested that departments should deal with these problems specifically in order to capitalize on the student's motivation. The master's degree was discussed because some universities were no longer awarding it. It was seen as the first important step in learning how to do research. Group research was discussed as an alternative method for training students to tackle complex problems. When engaging in this, however, the student must demonstrate his independent proficiency. Research skills believed to be necessary in clinical psychology included: (1) relevant analyses of clinical phenomena in order to develop fruitful concepts and hypotheses, (2) careful definitions of concepts as a check on intuitive judgments, (3) explicit formulation of research problems and design of appropriate investigations in the field of personality and clinical problems, (4) competence in statistical analyses of data, and (5) the ability to communicate research findings effectively in writing. The doctoral dissertation was discussed as one of the major, yet perhaps one of the weakest, points in clinical training. Often the student comes to the dissertation really unprepared to cope with it. He should have had previous research experience and should define and begin to work on an area for the dissertation at least by his third year. There was an acknowledged need to improve the quality of doctoral research.

It was generally agreed that all students in doctoral programs should have training in the theory and practice of psychotherapy. It was seen to be the university's responsibility to introduce the student to carefully supervised experiences, but it was recognized that technical skills must be received in supervised post-doctoral training. The conference strongly emphasized the need for a carefully planned and organized program of training in therapy to follow from a series of supervised experiences which had been integrated with academic preparation. Emphasis was given to the need to have qualified supervisors, beneficial aspects of a self-analysis, and careful training in the ethics of psychotherapy. The conference also strongly recommended that psychologists genuinely collaborate with physicians.

Field training was discussed as an integral part of the training received at the university. It should be a set of experiences closely related to the classroom and a part of a continuum of developing responsibility and skill. The first experience should be a laboratory, next a clerkship, and then an internship. There should also be training experience with as many patient groups and institutional situations as possible. Clerkship and internship, it was thought, ought to be described as "practicum experience" with an accompanying de-emphasis of the word "internship." It was seen to be the university's responsibility to have the student prepared to use clinical skills when he arrived at the practicum agency and to see that the student was properly placed. Internship was viewed as best coming before the dissertation, unless it were on a part-time basis as with the VA, so that the student could return to the university to complete his dissertation. The conference discussed the structure and organization of field work placements and standards for field work training, and it recommended that APA take over accreditation of field training facilities.

Selection and evaluation of students was a focus of consideration because of existing difficulties in both areas. The ratio of applicants to openings was about 10 to 1, so it became necessary and desirable to select the best students. From the Kelly study of VA trainees, undergraduate marks seemed to be one of the best predictors (Kelly, 1947; Kelly and Fiske, 1951). Participants also stated a preference for students showing strong theoretical and social motivation, rather than those with economic or status motives. There was an apparent problem with multiple applications to various universities. It was thought that a central clearinghouse for applicants or at least a common date for announcing acceptances would be ways of coping with the problem. The point was referred to the APA with the request to work out a standard date for announcements. Competence of the teachers of clinical psychology was recognized as a problem since many of the specific skills are not stimulated or well-used in the academic environment. There was emphasis upon the staff relating to the practicum agencies, becoming involved in short-term institutes, and when possible, taking leave to work in the clinical field. There was also need for experience and training in the arts of teaching; an experience which should begin while a graduate student.

Relations with other professions were stressed as a paramount concern. The conference dealt with five major professions: (1) psychiatry and other medical groups, (2) social work, (3) counseling and guidance, (4) school psychology, and (5) industrial psychology. Representatives from all of these, save industrial psychology, were in attendance. The conference noted that psychology and psychiatry had advanced to the point where representatives could meet and talk on a realistic basis. It was felt that the two professions must work as collaborators, not with one subservient to the other. Social work was described as having an entirely service-oriented tradition with quite different values from those of psychology. In considering counseling, considerable overlap between the two fields was noted. The core seemed common, but the differences centered around counselors dealing with more limited objectives of educational and vocational adjustment, having somewhat less training typically, and having little or no experience with the psychiatrically ill. The relationship of clinical to school psychology was noted as a complex one, often differing only in job title and setting. The major differences, however, may be in the knowledge about and experience with educational principles and practices. An extensive report on psychiatric nursing was presented to the conference. It served to introduce the profession to psychologists and to increase the awareness of the need for closer collaboration. The matter was referred to APA to establish proper liaison.

Relations with the Federal Government were noted to be of considerable importance. The government was seen to have large influence, but little demonstrated coercion. The VA had the largest impact with 700 students in 41 universities and 130 consultants from university departments. The PHS was providing stipends at the pre-doctoral level. The Army and PHS had limited programs for training and use of clinical psychologists. Generally, the effect of governmental support has been to expand the training program within the university department. This led to concern about possible disastrous effects should federal support be removed. The principle of forward financing was seen to be desirable, but it was realized that this was contingent upon congressional approval.

Accreditation of training universities was viewed as a somewhat mixed blessing. It had been established because of the needs of the VA and the PHS to know about suitable training programs. But the lack of APA approval in clinical often did not reflect well upon departments which provided good training in other areas. There was concern about the power of the approval arm of APA, and a recommendation was sent to APA that the two functions, setting standards and accrediting, be separated into two committees. It was also suggested that APA publish again the description of the areas of interest of each graduate department of psychology.

The conference participants were generally agreed that licensing or certification would be an inevitable development in clinical and perhaps in other applied areas of psychology. It was recognized, however, that it was in all cases a state issue. The conference recommended that APA increase its efforts through advisory services and financial support to state associations in the furtherance of legislation of psychologists.

Specialization was recognized as developing within clinical psychology. Child clinical was identified as a most important area. Private practice was a minor but developing aspect of clinical psychology; an aspect, however, that the conference did not particularly favor. The medical orientation was seen to be an extensive one in clinical psychology; there was strong belief, however, that clinical psychology was broader than medical psychology.

STANFORD CONFERENCE:
PSYCHOLOGY AND MENTAL HEALTH

In August 1955, the Institute on Education and Training for Psychological Contributions to Mental Health was held at Stanford University. The three factors which led to this conference were: (1) the trend toward specialization manifested in the Boulder, Northwestern, and Thayer conferences and its implication for graduate training, (2) the recommendation of the Boulder Conference to review the policies and procedures which it developed, and (3) the rapid growth of the mental hygiene movement.

Six major issues were discussed at the conference: (1) training needs of psychologists in community mental health programs, (2) specialization in training, (3) practicum training, (4) training for therapy, (5) training for research in the mental health field, and (6) problems of departmental organization.

This was not a formal conference, and the intent was not to reach decisions or to formulate policies. Rather, it was to reflect the opinions, views, and suggestions present within the profession and to provide the opportunity for representatives of universities and of federal agencies to examine some of the implications of the mental health movement for psychology.

Discussion and Conclusion. Participants unanimously agreed that the mental health movement would have even more far-reaching effects on psychology than did the post-war demand for clinical psychologists and that public concern over mental health would make greatly increased demands on the behavioral sciences and on the mental health professions.

Although there will be an increasing demand for a larger number of practitioners, the conference opinion was that research on the nature and treatment of mental illness and the development of preventive programs were of primary importance and should receive higher priority. This conclusion stemmed from the recognition that knowledge of the factors involved in mental illness is inadequate and that the demand for practitioners even with improved therapeutic techniques would continue to surpass the supply.

Emphasis on mental health research and on the preparation of personnel for these programs was seen to require changes both in the scientific and in the professional training of psychologists. Both on the undergraduate and on the graduate levels, more emphasis will need to be placed on familiarity with concepts and methodologies from all the social sciences. Such a background will be equally necessary for research psychologists and for the mental health practitioners.

Psychology curricula should include more emphasis on social factors in behavior, exploratory research, development of new tools and methods for the mental health field, work in the clinic and community as well as in the laboratory, and interdisciplinary research. In order to provide broader research training, content of undergraduate and graduate courses in experimental psychology should place more emphasis on problems and methods in the areas of personality, social psychology, and psychopathology. Active research programs in clinics and other field facilities should be encouraged, and opportunities provided for students to become involved in research in these settings.

The Boulder Conference decision to attempt to integrate professional with scientific training was reviewed. The participants were in almost unanimous agreement that this had proved to be a wise decision. "No support was apparent for proposals to separate professional from scientific training."

On the issue of specialization, the conference strongly favored efforts to define a common core of professional training that would provide basic preparation for various professional fields. This "basic professional core program" would not preclude special training in the area of the student's major interest during doctoral training; full competence in any specialty, however, would undoubtedly require some post-doctoral training.

In view of the present and projected expansion

of mental health programs, the conference felt that some form of sub-doctoral training in psychology would be unavoidable. Although this need for and the potential contributions of individuals with sub-doctoral training was recognized, no enthusiasm was expressed by participants for the development of such programs. Efforts in this direction were felt to have the disadvantage of weakening the present doctoral programs.

Concerning improvement of practicum training and training in psychotherapy, the conference considered the following: (1) closer coordination between universities and practicum agencies, (2) improvement of practicum training facilities, and (3) the breadth of training required. It was felt that the solution to difficulties in coordinating programs between universities and practicum agencies could be found in improved communication and increased interaction. Criteria of good training, accreditation of internship agencies, and extensity vs. intensity in internship training were discussed. Majority opinion favored a diversity of experience, both in terms of functions performed and types of patients seen. Six months at not less than 20 hours a week was considered a minimum time to spend in any one agency when the intern was rotated among agencies to diversify his experience. It was felt, however, that diversity could be achieved in a single agency if clientele and functions were sufficiently varied.

Differences of opinion among participants on the issues concerning training in psychotherapy were by no means reconciled at the conference. Substantial agreement was found on the following propositions: (1) training in psychotherapy is essential for psychologists working in the mental health field, (2) it is the responsibility of the university to provide initial training in psychotherapy, (3) training must be experimental and should begin fairly early in the graduate program, and (4) post-doctoral training will be required for the development of professional competence in therapy. It was also felt that students should have some appreciation of the importance and role of various other approaches to modification of behavior that are related to psychotherapy—mental health education, preventive intervention to counteract environmental influences, personal counseling, group therapy, and utilization of a therapeutic environment.

MIAMI BEACH CONFERENCE: GRADUATE
EDUCATION IN PSYCHOLOGY

The Miami Beach Conference, held in December 1958, attempted to define, evaluate, and propose solutions to the major issues in graduate education in psychology as perceived at that time. Events of the prior decade with increasingly new roles for psychologists, licensing laws and certification, growth in the number of psychologists and pressing manpower demands were seen as the factors giving rise to the need for this conference. The conference did not focus on training in any single specialty but on the entire field of graduate education. Participants were chosen from a wide variety of working situations and academic settings in order to provide a major interplay of diversified points of view. Each department with a doctoral program, individuals outside of the university, and each state association were invited to nominate participants. Every effort was made to obtain a balance in areas of emphasis and geographical location. The conference lasted 8 days, during which discussions of issues were conducted both in small groups and by the conference as a whole.

The issues were organized into five major topics: (1) roles of psychologists, including evaluation of roles currently being trained for, the extent to which training should be adjusted to the needs of society, training for new roles, and the relationships to other professions; (2) the common core of training, including evaluation of how much should be common for all students and for all departments, the proportion of time and phasing of the core, the role of the master's degree in the doctoral program, and aspects of the dissertation and internship applicable to all specialities; (3) training for specialization, including evaluation of the differentiating and common aspects of the specialties, a professional core, coursework outside of psychology, field work experiences, alternative degrees in place of the Ph.D., and standards for internships and post-doctoral programs; (4) sub-doctoral training programs, including evaluation of the psychological service needs of society, level of training they require, functions for which technicians should be trained, and standards for training and supervision; (5) standards, accreditation, and control, including evaluation of current accreditation procedures, extent and desirability of controls by APA, state legislation, ABEPP, federal agencies, and other professions, and special controls for certain specialties.

Discussion and Conclusions. The rapidly growing and presumably continuing discrepancy between demands for psychologists and the number presently or potentially available produced a realization of the need for reappraisal of the appropriate roles for psychologists. The conference defined the problem as how best to deploy limited forces in the interest of both psychology and society. Because of the rapidity with which changes occur in what psychologists do, the conference concluded that it was impossible to anticipate future directions that may come about. There was agreement, however, that the roles of psychologists should not derive solely from society's demands for services, but that psychologists must decide what roles to emphasize, to change, or to abandon.

There was strong consensus that doctoral education in psychology "should continue to educate psychologists as broadly as possible, limited only by the major aspects of the type of position to which the student is initially oriented." In order to obtain maximum return from psychologists and prepare students for the development of new roles, the conference agreed that psychology departments should continue to stress research training, and should devote attention to preparing students for a variety of ways in which they might participate in the broad dissemination of psychology. Mainly from the manpower restrictions that were foreseen, the conference emphasized the need to foster innovation in devising ways which are more efficient than person-to-person relationships for meeting mental health needs. "A whole variety of approaches such as therapeutic modification of social environment, group psychotherapy, and various attempts at primary prevention of mental disorder must be explored and evaluated." The need for innovation in service roles implies the strong desirability of a well-grounded research orientation among psychologists performing service functions.

The conference felt that a need exists for sub-doctoral personnel who can perform specific psychological functions and that serious attention should be given to preparing personnel to perform these functions. Master's programs should be evaluated for possible expansion or change for the training in a variety of psychological, technical specialties. Psychologists in all specialties should examine their functions and identify those skills and techniques which can be learned adequately and applied effectively without the broad background and research training which the conference unequivocally supported for doctoral level training. The conference encouraged innovations in further developing existing technical specialty programs. There was agreement that sub-doctoral training should be provided only in those specialty areas in which doctorally trained personnel are available to supervise and direct training. The conference did not identify skills nor offer curricula for sub-doctoral training; it did recommend, how-

ever, that the Education and Training Board of APA begin working on these problems. It was recognized that many difficulties could arise from the implementation of sub-doctoral programs involving such matters as titles, status, supervisory control and legal control, but it was recommended that at least a start should be made in coping with these.

The conference agreed that there is a common basic subject matter of psychology and that this core is important to any program of training. It is through the core that students can see themselves and be seen by others as members of a culturally identifiable sub-group. Additions to and deletions from the core represent the process by which psychology is defined and re-defined. Specialization, outside of the core, determines in what directions psychology will be applied. Because of psychology's ties to many fields of knowledge—biology, medicine, education, etc.—it is difficult to specify what is the unique core of psychology. Lists of content areas were prepared by sub-groups, but the conference as a whole would not specify the core in terms of course content. There was general agreement that in the best interest of promoting innovation and development in training, each department should be free to select from the totality of psychological knowledge which sampling best fits the needs of its program and students and the capacities of its faculty.

There was strong acceptance that the defining characteristic of the Ph.D. psychologist was his research training. In view of this position that research is not a specialty but an element common to the training of psychologists, the conference concluded: (1) that research should be broadly defined to be a continuum of methodologies, including not only rigorous hypothesis testing, but also clinical and naturalistic devices for the formulations of communicable and testable generalizations; (2) that early experience with research is desirable regardless of later specialization; and (3) that some relaxation of traditional specifications for the doctoral dissertation might be desirable, such as accepting research which yields negative findings, is primarily exploratory in nature, is the product of teams, or is not an empirical study. There was majority acceptance that the doctoral dissertation should be directed only by staff having considerable experience in the particular area of research. Although only a bare majority favored the suggestion that departments should consider a reduction in their formal course requirements to provide students with research experience in a variety of settings, it was agreed that some means should be found to increase research experience prior to the dissertation. There was considerable agreement that modifications to the research requirements should be sought for those in primarily applied areas so that the experience would be more instructive and rewarding. The apprenticeship for research training described in the Estes Park Report met with general approval (Taylor, Hunt, and Garner, 1959). It was also thought that universities could make more use of practitioners as official faculty members to insure their participation in the educational process and to make possible more effective apprentice relations in professional training.

It was agreed that the structure of specialty training for the Ph.D. should be congruent with the goal of developing well-rounded psychologists. Specialization should not interfere with students' understanding of basic psychological principles; rather, it should be carried out in such a way as to illustrate and clarify the application of psychological principles. How well this goal can be achieved should determine how early in the doctoral program specialization training should occur. It was felt that specialization is a threat to the development of psychology as a unified discipline only when it takes the form of training to perform service functions without regard for the goals of scientific inquiry. Specialty training was seen as promoting the development of psychology by bringing new topics and data from real life situations. It was also noted that clinical and counseling students may have the most broadly based experience because they have experimental training as well as specific field experience.

The conference agreed that psychologists engaged in the professional specialties have a common core not specifically shared by other specialties, a core which is transmitted to students primarily by means of experience in practicum or internship. The conference noted the types of internships presently in use, but took no stand on the proper timing of the internship for those specialties which require one. Experimentation and innovation were approved, and it was felt that accrediting agencies should not restrict this. It was agreed that in specialties with internships, a carefully planned clerkship at the university should precede internship training. It was also agreed that the university department was primarily responsible for selection of internship agencies and the coordination of work in the internship facility with that at the university. Several dissatisfactions were expressed about internship training. The inadequacy of Ph.D. training as sole preparation for a career in psycho-

therapy was especially stressed; it was generally assumed that post-doctoral training for this function was essential. The conference was not willing, however, to go on record as recommending an additional year of supervised internship. The feeling was that both the new Ph.D. and his employer should be aware of his limitations and continuing need for supervision. The major discussion on pre- vs. post-doctoral training centered around a proposal to introduce a two-year internship following the Ph.D., after which an individual would be designated a clinical psychologist. The residency program proposal was accepted as a worthwhile suggestion for exploration and trial. The development of training centers at this level, however, should be very gradual. There was disapproval of any moves to formalize post-doctoral training as a requirement. Improvement and increase of facilities for post-doctoral education in all specialties was favored, and the conference affirmed the principle that the professional development of any psychologist involves continued learning throughout his career.

The issue of granting a professional degree in psychology was raised at the conference. There was full agreement that the Ph.D. is a research degree and should be retained as such. The proposal that a non-research degree is needed largely met with indifference, and the conference as a whole did not feel it to be a crucial issue.

Concerning controls, the conference agreed that some form of accreditation was necessary, that APA was the most appropriate agency to accredit, that extension of accreditation to post-doctoral centers should be made, and that accreditation of sub-doctoral programs should be inaugurated as these develop. The general feeling was that present accreditation policy should not be inflexible, but extensions beyond it should be made with great circumspection.

RELATED CONFERENCES

NORTHWESTERN CONFERENCE: STANDARDS FOR TRAINING COUNSELING PSYCHOLOGISTS

The Northwestern Conference was held August 1952, to review the functions of counseling psychologists as they relate to society and to clarify training standards for this specialty at the doctorate level. The goal of counseling psychology is to foster the psychological development of the individual, including work with people on the continuum from those who function at tolerable levels of adequacy to those suffering from more severe psychological disturbances. Emphasis is on the positive, the preventive, maximizing of personal and social effectiveness and forestalling psychologically crippling disabilities. Educational facilities were seen as the most important setting for counseling psychologists. Other settings include industry, hospitals, community agencies, vocational guidance centers, and rehabilitation clinics. The conference felt that training programs should qualify a Ph.D. counseling psychologist to work effectively in such varied areas. In addition to service functions, the roles of consulting to other professional workers, formal teaching, training, and collaboration with people in many professional settings were emphasized. The conference felt it to be imperative that psychological counseling remain firmly within the basic psychological science. Research must, therefore, continue to be a basic job of the counseling psychologist and a basic element in his training. Concerning graduate curriculum, the conference was in favor of a core of basic concepts, tools, and the techniques common to all psychologists. In addition, specific subject areas representing a counseling specialty core were outlined for doctoral programs: (1) personality organization, (2) knowledge of social environment, (3) individual appraisal, (4) counseling and psychotherapy, (5) professional orientation, (6) practicum, and (7) research. To develop and improve standards and experiences in training, the conference encouraged training institutions to experiment with their programs. Further study of post-doctoral training and relationships to other specialties was also recommended.

GREYSTON CONFERENCE: PROFESSIONAL
PREPARATION OF COUNSELING PSYCHOLOGISTS

In January 1964, the Division of Counseling Psychology convened another conference to examine the issues in the work and training of counseling psychologists and to make recommendations for their improvement. The conference consisted of a four-day workshop wherein independent committees were assigned responsibility for recommendations concerning large segments of the areas under discussion. The discussions and conclusions were grouped under the topics of (1) roles of counseling psychologists, (2) content of professional preparation, (3) organizational aspects, and (4) unity and diversity.

From an analysis of the developments in counseling over the past decade, it was felt that although changes in the roles of counseling psychologists have occurred, "the basic objectives of counseling psychology as enumerated in the Northwestern Conference and subsequent statements of Division 17 were still valid." In comparison with the early 50's, counseling in 1964 was viewed as similar in scope, but changing in emphasis in response to increasing social demand for a wider variety of counseling services. In the future, more involvement can be anticipated with crucial domestic and international social issues such as unemployment, training underdeveloped and underprivileged populations, and delinquency. With these increasing demands there will be the need for new role models. It was also felt that more service will have to be indirect rather than direct.

Many of the conclusions concerning graduate curriculum were a reaffirmation or expansion of those of the Northwestern Conference. The conference re-affirmed the recommendation for training in the foundations of psychology as a behavioral science. Because of the specialized interest of counseling psychology, however, greater emphasis should be placed on (1) developmental psychology, (2) individual differences, (3) personality theory, and (4) learning theory. Because of counseling's concern with everyday problems, more than usual study should be included in the areas of (1) sociology, (2) the world of work, and (3) education. Training of counseling psychologists should include early and continuous experiences in a variety of meaningful research projects and a familiarity with research design and statistics. The conference agreed that counseling psychology should embrace far more than traditional functions of individual appraisal and individual interviews. Although competence in these basic functions is needed, other ways of facilitating personal and social development are also important.

Guides for practicum training were described in terms of three levels: (1) pre-practicum laboratory experiences, (2) field work, and (3) internship in an agency. Practicum training should develop competence in the sequence of roles leading to progressively increasing responsibility in counseling functions. Practicum experience should be obtained in a wide variety of settings with diverse clients having varied problems and needs. Although there was a majority agreement that variety was desirable, there was not agreement on the amount of variety when applied to the preparation of an individual trainee. The extremes of highly concentrated experience with a limited number of functions or a superficial exposure to a wide variety of settings are both undesirable. Supervision of practicum programs, effective liaison between universities and practicum agencies, and the integration of didactic and practical training were also discussed. The conference stressed the need for close integration of coursework, skill training, and professional experience. Practicum experience should be scheduled early and should be continuous with the rest of graduate training. This model was presented as an alternative to the traditional model in which the first graduate year is spent entirely in the basic science, the second mostly on laboratory practice, and the third and fourth in intensive internship experience. Several programs were identified as already successfully experimenting with this pattern of simultaneous training.

The conference recommended that training institutions seriously consider initiating and developing two-year professional training programs leading to a Master of Science in counseling, a Master of Psychology degree, or some other certification of competence. These programs should emphasize a professional service orientation, development of counseling skills, and training in relevant content areas such as adjustment factors and personality functioning. Need was also expressed for more formally organized post-doctoral training and in-service professional development programs, including both full- or part-time internships and short-term institutes for maintaining professional skills. Conflicts between goals and demands of psychology as a science and as a profession were discussed. In counseling, training is already developing under two auspices, graduate departments of psychology and schools or departments of education. The conference did not make strong recommendation concerning future direction of training in counseling with respect to degree labels and locations. From the scope and variety of training experiences and settings considered desirable, however, it was inferred that there would be no fundamental objection to a professional degree granted by a professional school, so long as "sound training in the science as well as the profession were provided and competence in research as well as the service aspects of counseling were assured." Selection and recruitment, identity of counseling as a specialty, unity and diversity within counseling and the problems involving support from official and university sources were also discussed at the conference.

THAYER CONFERENCE: FUNCTIONS,
QUALIFICATIONS, AND TRAINING OF
SCHOOL PSYCHOLOGISTS

The Thayer Conference was held over a 10-day period in West Point, New York, in August 1954.

There were 48 participants, and the format was closely patterned after the Boulder Conference. Five issues were identified for discussion: (1) definition of functions, (2) specification of competencies, (3) selection, training, and experience, (4) administrative and professional relationships, and (5) professional development, recognition, and accreditation.

A school psychologist was defined as "a psychologist with training and experience in education. He uses his specialized knowledge of assessment, learning, and interpersonal relationships to assist school personnel to enrich the experience and growth of all children, and to recognize and deal with exceptional children." His function is to promote sound mental health, to provide counsel on curriculum and school programs and to work primarily with the staff, rather than the children. Research was described as a "moral obligation" of the school psychologist, but the conference accepted the fact that it is not always possible for him to carry it out.

Qualifications were stated in the general terms of high intelligence, emotional stability and sound training. The need for sub-doctorally trained personnel was recognized, but there was interest in limiting the title "School Psychologist" to the doctorally trained. Professional training was specified for the graduate level; it should include work with an experienced school psychologist and include practicum. Training should be broad in cultural, psychological, and educational matters. Although few universities had formal doctoral programs, this was thought to be desirable. The model was that of clinical training, being at least four years in length, including an internship and yielding a major research contribution. Two-year training programs to produce specifically trained technicians were discussed. Universities were cautioned to provide an adequate program and not to undertake it lightly. In-service training was regarded as important, especially for those with sub-doctoral training.

Some concern was expressed that safeguards for the practice of school psychology were not generally existent. Less than half the states had certification for school psychologists. The conference emphasized teaching of ethics to students and establishing accreditation procedures for training programs.

The future was discussed in terms of upgrading school psychology. Emphasis was placed on the quality and training of individuals entering the field. It was hoped that the conference would serve to raise standards and institute ways to maintain them.

DISCUSSION

In Table 3, we have summarized the major issues and topics in training across conferences. Analysis of the recommendations, positions, and conclusions of the various conferences with respect to these issues reveals only minor differences from conference to conference. The differences seem to be found in the kind of discussion about the issues and the relative importance of the issues of a particular conference.

SOCIAL NEED

All conferences have expressed concern about changes in society which result in increased service demands on psychologists: At Boulder, the increase in clinical activities following World War II; at Stanford, the increasing specialization reflected in the Northwestern and Thayer conferences and the growth of the mental health movement; at Miami Beach, the further increases in manpower demands, the expanding services of psychologists and the accompanying legal involvements of certification and licensing. At each conference, it was felt that the increasing service needs could not be met with presently or foreseeably available manpower. From this recognition of the inability to, and perhaps the

inadvisability of, fulfilling service needs there has been increased discussion devoted to *research training*, *sub-doctoral training*, and *curriculum*.

RESEARCH TRAINING

At Boulder, research was given an equal position with service training for clinical psychologists. The reason given for this was the need of practitioners to be able to evaluate methods and to develop new techniques for treatment. At Stanford, these reasons were reiterated, and the additional recommendation made that research training within clinical psychology should be emphasized more than training for service since techniques and methods still did not seem to be effective. At Miami Beach, the need for innovation and development of treatment methods was again emphasized, the importance of the research function reasserted, and the recommendation made to broaden the definition of what is acceptable or valuable research in graduate training. Reading between the lines, it can be seen that over the years since Boulder, there has been a continuing discrepancy between what has been reaffirmed at the conferences and what occurs in actual training practice. The discussion of this issue at all the conferences has centered on the problems of integrating service and research

TABLE 3. Major Issues in Training Treated at Conferences

Issues

Conference	Social Needs[1]	Research	Psychotherapy	Professional vs. Scientific	Professional School	Professional Degree	Practicum[2]	Practicum Agencies	Sub-doctoral[3]	Post-doctoral[4]	Graduate Curriculum[5]	Selection[6]	Staff Training	Relations with Other Professions	Relations with Gov. Agencies	Controls[7]
Boulder	X	X	X	X			X	X	X	X	X	X	X	X	X	X
Northwestern	X	X	X	X			X	X			X	X		X		X
Thayer		X		X			X		X		X	X	X	X		X
Stanford	X	X	X	X			X	X	X	X	X			X		
Miami Beach	X	X		X	X	X	X	X	X	X	X	X			X	X
Greyston	X	X		X	X	X	X	X	X	X	X	X	X		X	X
Present Conference	X	X	X	X	X	X	X	X	X	X	X		X			

1. Training to meet manpower demands, professional roles, etc.
2. Breadth vs. intensity, timing, specialty, etc. in both internship and clerkship.
3. Psychological technician, expansion of mental health program.
4. Requirements, specialties.
5. Breadth vs. intensity, sequence and integration, core, etc.
6. Undergraduate preparation, selection, and recruitment.
7. Accreditation, licensing, certification, and ethics.

functions in training. It is difficult to determine whether this debate has increased over the years for it was an active one in 1949. The final positions, however, have been the same—an emphasis on the importance of research.

SUB-DOCTORAL TRAINING

There appears to be a clear relationship between the expansion of service functions, the social demands upon psychology and discussions relating to the training of master's level, psychological technicians. Discussions on this topic have been characterized by both growing concern and reluctance to recommend anything specific. At Boulder, recommendation was made to APA to study the possibility of such programs. At Stanford, it was felt that increasing service demands would make some form of sub-doctoral training unavoidable; participants were reluctant, however, to support development of such programs. At Miami Beach, the subject was fully discussed and recommendations again made to APA. There was also, as at Stanford, much concern about the implications of such programs for the profession and for doctoral programs.

CURRICULUM

The graduate curriculum to date has been patterned after that suggested by the Shakow Committee (APA, 1947) and recommended at Boulder. The common core concept has not been seriously questioned, and a curriculum specific to professional specialties has been recognized. Further recommendations for training have been concerned with broadening the experience within the social sciences and innovating new techniques and methods for meeting mental health needs.

PRACTICUM TRAINING AND PRACTICUM AGENCIES

Although discussed at each conference, the formulations on practicum training have changed little since Boulder. The ways in which the practicum relates to the entire curriculum structure, the adequacy of the agencies providing the experience, and the lack of closeness between the classroom and field experiences have always been discussed and probably always will be so long as the field training is administratively separated from the department. With increased emphasis on diversity of experience and community service, the practicum possibilities have broadened. This

has intensified the problem of assessing their quality and of monitoring the programs provided for the students.

PSYCHOTHERAPY

Discussions of psychotherapy have been minor variations on the same theme. Psychotherapy has been accepted as part of graduate training, with post-doctoral training seen as the requisite way to become competent in this area. Conferences since Boulder have increasingly stressed the need for training in a broader concept of psychotherapy than the traditional dyadic relationship.

POST-DOCTORAL TRAINING

Post-doctoral training has received consideration at the conferences mainly in connection with gaining necessary skills and competence in specialty areas, particularly psychotherapy. Each conference, however, has been unwilling to extend the training process by formally proposing that post-doctoral experience be part of everyone's training.

STAFF TRAINING

Between Boulder and the Chicago Conference, there has been no major concern with competence of the training staff. In 1949, there were few properly trained clinicians in universities to staff the training programs. Now that clinical practice has become so diverse, training departments again appear to be in a position of not having properly trained staff.

PROFESSIONAL VS. SCIENTIFIC TRAINING

This issue is central because it is concerned with a model of training which has effects on all the previous topics discussed. The Shakow Report and Boulder Conference established the model which integrates the two concepts. Although the merits and disadvantages of this model have been vigorously debated at all conferences, each time the majority has reaffirmed the established model. The primary reason has always been the needs for research, mentioned above. At the Boulder Conference, the proponents in favor of stronger professional training were largely service-oriented men from publicly structured and supported agencies. Now, over a decade later, the number of community-oriented practitioners has greatly increased and has been joined by a new group of proponents, the private practitioners. Evidence for the growing concern with this issue is found in the recent appearance at conferences of discussion about professional schools and professional degrees. The recent Clark Committee Report (APA, 1965) and the statement of issues for the Chicago Conference are directed at a serious deliberation of these growing issues.

CONCLUDING COMMENTS

What do conferences accomplish? Historically, they do not seem to have been held solely for the formulation of actions to be carried out. Only the initial conferences, Boulder and Northwestern, have clearly accomplished this. If subsequent conferences were to be judged by this criterion only, they would appear ineffective. Initial conferences, however, organized procedures from a state of nascence and formalized a system. In effect, this meant that later conferences had to start any discussion from within a frame of reference and had to assess or monitor an ongoing process. So, the purposes for each conference and the criteria on which its effectiveness should be judged may differ. This, then, leads to a different perspective for the functions of conferences.

Generally stated, a conference may be viewed as a response to forces at work both within and without the profession. It serves the function of mediating agent for these forces; its effect results from the interaction of these forces in the conference process. A response to forces internal to the profession is the need to survey the current climate of opinion within psychology. This seems to be present at all conferences and in part represents a monitoring function. It may also reflect a need for the reaffirmation of the identity or unity of psychology, which finds its specialties becoming increasingly diverse. In this way a conference can be a device for accommodation which provides a means for disparate elements to come together, have a shared experience in the professional ferment, and go away with strengthened ties to the profession. This may include concerns to change emphasis in the existing system and to pull diverging elements back.

The other set of forces at a conference are those from outside the profession. If one takes major governmental actions prior to past conferences as indices of social change (e.g., establishment of the NIMH and VA clinical training before Boulder, the VA counseling program before Northwestern, and the mental retardation, community mental health, and poverty program prior to the Chicago Conference), then it can be hypothesized that conferences are stimulated by and are a response to changes in society.

An example of the interplay of external and internal forces may be seen in the issue of sub-doctoral training. This involves both social need and demand and psychology's concern with the protection of its public image. Psychology has generally been committed to upgrading itself with continuing emphasis on doctoral training. Individuals with lower levels of training represent a threat to this process since the public may not be able to distinguish them from the doctorally trained. All conferences have recognized the objective merit of sub-doctoral programs, but movement in the direction of actually instituting them has been very slow. This may be due both to the fact that psychology has not devised satisfactory ways of protecting its image and to the fact that social events have not provided for such a significant change in the profession.

It is interesting to consider how the issues and forces are focused for the profession to deal with them. This may be done, not in the conference itself, but by the intense work of a small committee which presents a public report to the profession just prior to the conference. The Shakow Committee Report (APA, 1947) seemed to serve this purpose for Boulder. Because of the model established at Boulder, any committee report prior to a subsequent conference, in order to be effective for change, would necessarily have to provide a focus which differs from the values of the existent structure. The Chicago Conference is the only national conference since Boulder which has been preceded by such a report, the Clark Committee Report (APA, 1965). Since this report seems directed at change, the proposed model is divergent from currently held values, and one would predict that it will be received differently from the way Boulder dealt with the Shakow Report. In this context, the effect and influence of the Clark Committee Report on the Chicago Conference is open for speculation.

We have tried to illustrate the point that a conference should be seen as a mediating instrument in the process of a profession's development. It gathers its identity from the forces, internal and external, that it mediates. Its effect on the profession is dependent upon the interplay of these forces. Considering the present complex of inter-acting forces in the profession and society, what will the Chicago Conference serve to mediate?

NOTES

1. For a comparison and contrast of issues across conferences, see Blank, 1964.

2. The information for both tables was taken from the list of participants in each conference report or from the major affiliation listed in the APA Directory for the year of the conference. Although this categorization is crude and admits inaccuracies because of the overlap that exists in both training and affiliation, we thought that it would add to the reader's understanding of the recommendations and conclusions reached at each conference.

REFERENCES

AMERICAN PSYCHOLOGICAL ASSOCIATION, Committee on Training in Clinical Psychology. Recommended graduate training program in clinical psychology. *Amer. Psychologist*, 1947, *2*, 539–558 (David Shakow, Chairman).

AMERICAN PSYCHOLOGICAL ASSOCIATION, Division of Counseling and Guidance, Committee on Counselor Training. Recommended standards for training counseling psychologists at the doctorate level. The practicum training of counseling psychologists. *Amer. Psychologist*, 1952, *7*, 175–188 (Northwestern Conference).

AMERICAN PSYCHOLOGICAL ASSOCIATION, Committee on the Scientific and Professional Aims of Psychology. Preliminary Report. *Amer. Psychologist*, 1965, *20*, 95–100 (Kenneth E. Clark, Chairman).

BLANK, L. Clinical psychology training, 1954–1962: Conferences and Issues. In L. Blank, and H. P. David (Eds.), *Sourcebook for training in clinical psychology*. New York: Springer, 1964. Pp. 1–42.

CUTTS, N. E. *School psychologists at mid-century*. Washington, D.C.: American Psychological Association, 1955 (Thayer Conference).

KELLY, E. L. Research on the selection of clinical psychologists. *J. clin. Psychol.*, 1947, *3*, 39–42.

KELLY, E. L., and FISKE, D. W. *The prediction of performance in clinical psychology*. Ann Arbor: University of Michigan Press, 1951.

RAIMY, V. C. (Ed.). *Training in clinical psychology*. New York: Prentice-Hall, 1950 (Boulder Conference).

ROE, ANNE, GUSTAD, J. W., MOORE, B. V., ROSS, S., and SKODAK, MARIE (Eds.). *Graduate education in psychology*. Washington, D.C.: American Psychological Association, 1959 (Miami Beach Conference).

STROTHER, C. R. *Psychology and mental health*. Washington, D.C.: American Psychological Association, 1956 (Stanford Conference).

SUB-COMMITTEE ON ISSUES, Conference on the Professional Preparation of Clinical Psychologists. Issues in the professional training of clinical psychologists. 1965 (Mimeo. draft).

TAYLOR, D. W., HUNT, H. F., and GARNER, W. R. Education for research in psychology. Report of a seminar sponsored by the Education and Training Board. *Amer. Psychologist*, 1959, *14*, 167–179.

THOMPSON, A. S., and SUPER, D. E. (Eds.). *The professional preparation of counseling psychologists—Report of the 1964 Greyston Conference*. New York: Teachers College, Columbia University, 1964.

7. Conference on the Professional Preparation of Clinical Psychologists: A Summary

ERASMUS L. HOCH, ALAN O. ROSS AND C. L. WINDER

THE Conference on the Professional Preparation of Clinical Psychologists was convened at this time as a result of a combination of factors, among them the following.

1. Psychologists in general, and psychologists in the applied areas in particular, seem increasingly to be feeling a sense of social commitment. While this feeling may always have existed, it has recently undergone a renaissance, is being more clearly articulated, and presumably will serve as a major motivating force in mapping psychology's future roles and functions.

2. Clinical psychology, despite its long history within psychology, has come into prominence mainly within the past 2 decades. It presses vigorously not only for greater recognition but for more room in the house of psychology as well.

3. In the face of their rapid growth as a profession and the demands made on them by society, clinical psychologists feel the urgency and immediacy of more and better genuine training, in clinical practice as well as in scientific aspects.

4. The universities, for their part, are similarly concerned. As a result they are either reassessing the present training programs or are actually planning variations, some of which seem like radical departures.

5. Compounding all of the foregoing is the general manpower problem which the Joint Commission on Mental Illness and Health has taken pains to point up and of which the Conference has been acutely aware.

Without countenancing the lowering of standards as such, the conferees have sought for a responsible position in the face of the dilemma presented by the foregoing combination of circumstances. Brought together for the purpose were not only clinical psychologists and their colleagues in applied areas, but experimental and social psychologists as well, together with representatives of such other disciplines as psychiatry and social work, a group including both suppliers of clinical psychologists and consumers.

NATURE OF THE PROBLEM

The overall problem with which the Conference struggled was a double-edged one.

1. On the one hand, clinical psychology is still busily putting its own house in order. There is the painful and urgent problem of identity. There is widespread concern that ours be a fully independent profession. There is need to produce enough PhDs to meet the social need which even now outstrips the numbers being trained.

2. Quite apart from internal pressures, developments in the community are already creating newer, bigger problems to be confronted. (a) A live concern with mental health keeps demands for psychological services mounting. (b) An even newer concern— the prevention of psychological disorders—has added further problems and opportunities. (c) Now it turns out that the newest concern of all—that of "community psychology," the more effective utilization of human potential—calls for clinical psychologists to fill still newer and more unaccustomed roles while not yet having resolved some of the present dilemmas.

A responsible profession does not allow itself to be shaped solely, or even mainly, by social forces.

Reprinted from *American Psychologist*, 1966, *21*, 42–51, by permission of the American Psychological Association and the authors. Dr. Hoch is Professor of Psychology and Administrative Officer of the Department of Psychology at the University of Michigan; Dr. Ross is Chief Psychologist at the Pittsburgh Child Guidance Center and Adjunct Professor of Psychology at the University of Pittsburgh; and Dr. Winder is Professor of Psychology at Michigan State University.

Rather, it makes thoughtful decisions of its own, taking account of social forces and self-knowledge. In other words, the mature profession recognizes an obligation to be responsive to the needs of the community which houses it, seeking at the same time to keep such responsiveness appropriately controlled and carefully planned.

Confronted with a mass of contemporary social developments, each of which has psychological implications, the problem of the profession lies in "picking up the right options," as Nicholas Hobbs put it in his opening address to the Conference. Opportunities for psychology are everywhere; what is not so clear is whether and how to rise to this one or that. The poverty program represents not so much a plan of financial assistance as an educational campaign with tremendous psychological implications. The civil rights movement involves not simply a guarantee of constitutional privileges but an invitation to meaningful psychological research in human interaction and a good opportunity for both students and professionals to develop important functions. Population control goes beyond contraceptives practices to problems of attitudes and motivation. A growing awareness of the rights of children represents not only a discharge of responsibilities but a new philosophy of mental health—one in which emphasis is less on cure, more on prevention, less on pathology, more on the maximization of potential.

Our responsibilities are not discharged by rising enthusiastically to every social challenge, well intentioned but ill prepared. The problem, as the Conference saw it, was to decide which challenges to accept and, more importantly, how psychologists are to be prepared to react responsibly, effectively, and flexibly to human needs in our rapidly changing society.

CHARACTER OF THE SOLUTION

In the course of their deliberations, the conferees attempted to sketch a prospectus for producing a corps of well-trained, rigorous, professionally skillful, science-valuing clinical psychologists whose responsiveness to social needs would rest on careful, systematic observations of meaningful, often complicated, problems.

Thus oriented, the conferees adopted a formal resolution stressing that practice should be based to the greatest extent possible on science and reaffirming the abiding interest of the Conference in the scientific and the professional components of graduate education.

In such a spirit the Conference undertook its discussion of the character of education and training in clinical psychology, not only at the doctoral level but at postdoctoral, subdoctoral, and even undergraduate levels as well.

PROFESSIONAL PREPARATION OF CLINICAL PSYCHOLOGISTS

UNDERGRADUATE EDUCATION

Previous conferences have sometimes been criticized for neglecting to come to grips with the problem of nondoctoral education. The present Conference, therefore, made it a special point to deal with subdoctoral education and, indeed, conferees attempted to give attention to the undergraduate level as well. Unfortunately, Conference time constraints and the scope of the problem did not permit the extensive consideration that undergraduate education warrants. One work group undertook to prepare a statement, which it proposed for endorsement.

The tenor of the statement, which, it should be stressed, was not acted upon by the Conference in view of limitations of time, can be gleaned from a representative paragraph:

Within the framework of a liberal arts major in psychology, we recommend that the curriculum be expanded to include training in the competent utilization of some of the basic skills of psychology, such as psychological assessment, group leadership, field work, and interviewing as well as experimentation and statistical analysis. It is expected that the acquisition of these skills would not only enrich the education of the student in the best sense of a liberal arts degree but also permit the graduate of such a program to be prepared for either a temporary termination of his formal education (with the competence to earn a living using these skills in appropriate settings under professional direction and supervision) or to be well prepared for more advanced work in the field of psychology. In no way, however, is it implied that a holder of only a baccalaureate degree is prepared to engage in the professional activities which require much more extensive preparation and training.

Clearly, some unknown but significant proportion of Conference participants believed that improved and more comprehensive undergraduate preparation deserves to be considered both in its own right, as part of the solution to problems of better graduate education, and as part of the overall strategy of dealing with the manpower problem.

In making proposals pertaining to undergraduate education, the conferees were well aware of possible obstacles to their implementation. University departments have their respective ideas about the advisability of extending down to the undergraduate level acquaintance with such functions as administration of individual intelligence tests and learning of such skills as interviewing. Nonetheless, at the same time, the conferees reminded themselves of the success that Harvard and Brandeis have had with such projects as the use of undergraduate students as volunteer therapeutic aides in mental hospitals. Many conferees hoped universities would experiment open-mindedly with enlarged opportunities for undergraduate psychology majors to learn enough to earn a living by using their skills in appropriate settings.

In any case, the Conference agreed that graduate education should take cognizance of undergraduate preparation, granting advanced standing where warranted. Particularly to be avoided is the repetition of courses and instructional material at both educational levels.

Recognizing that various proposals (including specific curricular suggestions) merited more extensive discussion than could be carried out in the time available, the Conference recommended instead that the American Psychological Association, presumably through its Education and Training Board, be enjoined to study the general problem of undergraduate education in psychology carefully, exploring in detail such suggestions as noted above. It was hoped that, in conjunction with such a study, it might be possible to convene an early conference of those who are concerned with undergraduate education, a conference which would include competent representation of other disciplines and of liberal arts administration.

SUBDOCTORAL GRADUATE EDUCATION

In the case of subdoctoral graduate education, the Conference dealt with the issues in some detail, adopting a statement which not only spells out practices to be avoided but suggests some positive steps as well, though here, too, time did not allow coming to grips with all of the underlying issues and problems. The statement that follows, then, implies acceptance of responsibility to explore alternatives for psychological contributions to training at other than the doctoral level. It should be interpreted not as an expedient for simply producing more manpower as such but rather as a strategy for meeting manpower needs while maintaining "quality control."

The Conference is opposed to master's level training of clinical psychologists [though not opposed to a master's degree in psychology which may include elective courses from the clinical field]. The Conference

further condemns the practice of giving a consolation master's degree to students who are dropped from doctoral programs in clinical psychology. If such students are judged suitable for master's level training, they should complete the requirements of the specialty program awarding the degree.

There is a growing number of nonprofessional and subdoctoral specialty areas having functions that are in part psychological. Other disciplines have established such programs (e.g., in guidance counseling and in rehabilitation). Clinical psychologists are encouraged to seek opportunities to participate in such training as consultants, teachers, and field instructors.

It is the feeling of the Conference that large university departments should consider the development of programs to train such nonprofessional and subdoctoral workers, though it is recognized that they may not easily be able to develop them because of other pressures and demands.

In general, the preference is to designate individuals completing such programs by occupational titles which do not use the term "psychology" and which designate fairly specifically the work done (personnel specialist, counselor aide, statistical technician, mental health worker, interview coder).

In so recommending, the Conference intended legitimization of attention to subdoctoral and subprofessional education, encouraging university departments to explore some alternatives. The understanding, however, was that (a) people trained at such levels would perform clinical services not autonomously but under appropriate supervision and (b) they would be labeled in such a way as not to be misidentifiable as "clinical psychologists."

The Conference by no means wished to suggest that university departments remove safeguards to which they had grown accustomed simply in order to produce more pairs of hands. At the same time, however, it did not seem out of order to suggest that departments might (a) look anew at some of their previous assumptions and (b) consider experimentation with new modes of training. Implicit in the suggestions was the notion that, despite their trepidations, university departments and the profession at large might now consider loosening some of the usual constraints sufficiently to gather empirical evidence as a basis for judging the feasibility and advisability of moving in some of the suggested directions. For here, after all, might lie some major opportunities for psychology to expand training in a socially significant way.

POSTDOCTORAL EDUCATION

Unlike the case of subdoctoral education, there was no debating the advisability of postdoctoral education. Indeed, the latter was in effect regarded as an ethical responsibility for those who aspire to the status of "expert" in selected areas of professional function.

In view of the fact that an increasing number of psychologists with nonclinical PhDs have requested training to prepare them to become clinical psychologists, it is necessary to distinguish such *postgraduate* education from the *postdoctoral* training taken by the clinician to extend existing skills. With respect to postgraduate education, the Conference made the following recommendations, among others.

1. Postgraduate training should definitely be offered by university psychology departments.

2. Internships or experiences in field stations should not be accepted, in and of themselves, as adequate preparation.

3. With respect to subject matter and professional skills, the postgraduate psychologists must meet all of the requirements of PhD training in clinical psychology, but recognition should be given to previous preparation which forms the central core of all doctoral training in psychology. Such preparation includes course work in languages, research, thesis, and the rest.

4. The university department assumes the responsibility of evaluating the student's previous preparation when he enters a course of clinical training, and of fashioning individualized courses of training designed to update his knowledge and skills.

5. Stipends for postgraduate students should be made available to enable nonclinical PhD psychologists to return to school without undue financial burden.

6. At the end of training, when all requirements have been satisfactorily met, the university should mark the achievement by awarding a document which indicates successful completion of such a course of study.

It should be noted especially that the foregoing recommendations for specialized postgraduate training in clinical psychology might offer a model broadly applicable for any doctoral level psychologist who wishes to expand his area of competence by pursuing specialty training in any other area of psychology.

Having clarified the distinction between postgraduate programs and postdoctoral education, the Conference took specific positions regarding the need for postdoctoral training.

The Conference supports the need for postdoctoral training for a specialty area or for advanced training beyond the journeyman level attained on receipt of the PhD degree. The content of such programs should be much more advanced and specialized than is the usual curriculum of a graduate program. The programs should achieve a standard of excellence that is of highest quality. It is the responsibility of psychology to develop appropriate mechanisms to maintain these standards.

Specialty training in such broad areas as psychotherapy, child clinical psychology, special clinical problems, research, and community mental health practice is already offered in varying degrees, particularly at institutions somewhat separate from university programs. This type of training continues to need support. It is recommended that universities develop such programs. The concept of the psychological service centre [to be discussed in detail in a later section] should be supported as one way of providing such specialized postdoctoral training.

The Conference emphasized that postdoctoral programs are needed to supplement predoctoral training. Use of postdoctoral training resources to provide what is essentially predoctoral training was noted and discouraged.

The Conference resolves that postdoctoral programs should not be required to make up for deficiencies in training on the doctoral level. Doctoral programs should prepare a clinical psychologist fully for journeyman entry into the field so that postdoctoral specialty programs can concentrate on the appropriate goals of enhancing, reinforcing, and expanding a core of existing skill.

In defining the obligation for postdoctoral training, the Conference felt it appropriate to add the following.

Although postdoctoral training is desirable for all clinical specialists, it is deemed essential for those anticipating independent professional practice and also for those who are to teach and supervise in specialty clinical courses.

DOCTORAL TRAINING

While the primary focus of the Conference was on doctoral training, the matter was approached in ways which differed significantly from the efforts of earlier conferences. Specifically, four alternative models for doctoral training in clinical psychology were presented in the *Preconference Materials* (Cook, Bibace, Garfield, Kelly, & Wexler, 1965), as described in a later section.

Again, the rubrics under which discussion was to take place were of different character from those of previous conferences. The "core curriculum" was no longer the coin of the realm it had been earlier; the present conferees chose to speak of chunks of knowledge and areas of subject matter rather than of courses per se. Nor was the practicum, as such, discussed in detail; instead, concern was more with the general setting in which psychological experience was to be gained, and in particular, with the psychological service center as the setting of choice, supplemented by appropriate experience elsewhere (as discussed below).

With such a set, the Conference did not proceed to list the "characteristics of a good doctoral training program"; it elected instead to consider first the "conditions important to the implementation of good doctoral training." As will be seen from what follows, the difference is not just in the choice of words but rather in the general orientation.

CONDITIONS IMPORTANT TO THE IMPLEMENTATION OF GOOD CLINICAL TRAINING

FACULTY

Here the sense of the meeting was summarized by the conferees as follows.

To implement doctoral training in clinical psychology satisfactorily, it is necessary to present the student with adequate role models distributed over all of the scientist-professional continuum. This implies and requires inclusion on the faculty of skilled, mature, and dedicated practitioners who have an investment in the professional as well as the scientific phases of clinical psychology.

Universities should attract and retain appropriate faculty through the use of measures such as:

1. According the professional activities of clinical practice the same recognition and rewards as are now extended to other aspects of academic endeavor
2. Recognizing the complexity and far-reaching effects of clinical teaching and supervision and their demanding, time-consuming character
3. Acknowledging the scholarly aspects of the application of psychological knowledge and methods in the area of practice
4. Rewarding excellence in clinical practice

There were two further considerations, as the conferees saw them.

Training in clinical psychology requires faculty members who are skilled in clinical practice and who maintain their skills by continuous involvement in clinical activity. Such attributes should be given serious consideration in appointments and recommendations for advancement of clinical faculty members.

Whenever possible, university faculty should not only serve as consultants to field stations but should also render some actual service in these stations. Conversely, field-station psychologists should be utilized as clinical teachers in the university settings.

SETTING

Extensive concern with details of the practicum was perhaps less apparent than might otherwise have been the case as a result of the full endorsement given by the Conference to the establishment of the psychological service center as an ideal setting for training. The resolution follows.

To improve the effectiveness of clinical psychological training, we recommend the establishment of psychological service centers, serving a broad range of populations with a variety of psychological problems, administered by psychologists, and having a close association with a university or universities. While designed primarily to meet the training needs of graduate students, the center should serve significant social needs, at the same time providing an appropriate setting for research.

The center should provide the experiential underpinning for a broad segment of the clinical curriculum and should engage students at various levels of training. It would provide encouragement and opportunity for faculty to continue to develop clinical knowledge and skill, while serving as a forum for clinical ideas and an appropriate setting for clinical inquiry and experimentation with new procedures. The services provided by the center should be in the best tradition of clinical practice. To do otherwise would be to present to students inadequate role models of professional work.

To achieve such ends, the best talent should be utilized—from within the psychology department and elsewhere in the university, from practicing psychologists in the community, and from appropriate members of related professions. The variety of psychologically supervised experiences in the center should complement but not supplant experience in off-campus settings which may be required for adequate breadth and depth of training.

In line with the above, a highly desired outcome of the development of such centers, involved as they would be with a range of psychological problems, would be the accelerated interaction of psychologists representing various domains of application. Industrial, counseling, clinical, school and educational, social, and experimental psychologists, to cite only some, need to have better opportunities to work shoulder-to-shoulder on common problems.

In addition to whatever else it represents, the above constitutes an endorsement of psychology as an independent, fully responsible profession.

At its final plenary session, the Conference considered also broadening the concept of such centers to include those under nonprofit auspices in the community. The centers might serve as multiple-function agencies in which many specialty fields of psychology are represented. In addition to services carried out within the center, programs could be extended into the community and its institutions. Thus, services and action programs for schools, members of labor unions, the disadvantaged, the disabled (including the mentally disabled), among others, could be developed by a psychological service center whose staff consisted of clinical, school, industrial, social, and other types of psychologists.

Research—particularly evaluation of programs, with feedback of results to make for a self-correcting system—would be initiated and encouraged within these centers. If such centers were developed, close affiliative ties with one or perhaps several university psychology departments would be highly desirable. As such, the center could provide practicum and research training experience for both graduate and postdoctoral students in a number of specialty areas or fields of psychology.

EXPERIENCE

With near unanimity the Conference reaffirmed the principle that in order to qualify as acceptable, a clinical psychology training program must include a predoctoral clinical internship of at least 1 year, which is coordinated and integrated with the rest of the graduate student's training.

Discussion of the nature of clinical experience led to a series of fairly specific propositions, some of which follow.

1. Practicum training should begin as soon as possible, so that most of the academic work of clinical students can be related directly to the experiences, needs, and questions arising from such training.

2. Attention should be given to developing explicit measures of clinical competence, so the student may learn to improve his performance on the criterion measures.

3. Early evaluation of the student's progress in all aspects of his program is encouraged to facilitate the most productive relationship between student and faculty.

4. Basic to effectiveness and efficiency is the development of ways of continuously integrating and interrelating clinical training with relevant research training throughout the entire program. Ideally, both aspects should be included in courses, seminars, laboratory practicum, and research experiences.

5. Substantial instruction and training in didactic and practicum laboratory settings should be devoted to theory, techniques, and research in psychological analysis of individuals, groups (including the family), and discrete social systems. Such training should include observation (including participant observation), the interview, psychological assessment, experimental analysis, sociocultural analysis and synthesis, and communication.

6. There should also be comparable instruction and training with appropriate clinical problems in the therapy and behavior modification area, including dyadic interaction, group approaches, alteration of the environment, and behavior control methods.

The Conference further reaffirmed the value of internship placements in off-campus facilities, provided the student's university department takes the responsibility for careful placement so as to meet his individual training needs, and provided further that the off-campus experience is closely coordinated with the on-campus work through genuine collaboration between training supervisors and faculty members.

It was urged that when on-campus psychological clinics are used for internship placements, the same standards of accreditation now applied to independent training centers be used in their evaluation. In order to qualify as acceptable, an internship setting should be one which is staffed by highly experienced clinical psychologists who have professional autonomy.

While supporting the responsible development of emerging subspecialties in the mental health field, the Conference favored the exposure of all students in clinical psychology to both normal and psychologically disturbed individuals, to varieties of psychopathology, to a wide range of age groups in both sexes, and to individuals from various ethnic and social backgrounds.

The conferees recognized the increasing emphasis on clinical work with children and the importance of such work from the point of view of developing, enhancing, and maintaining human effectiveness. In view of the rapidly increasing need for clinical psychologists competent to work with children, the Conference urged that greater emphasis be placed on the important subspecialty of clinical child psychology.

The conferees further noted a developing need for specialized training in dealing with problems of community mental health and of community psychology. Inasmuch as few training centers currently train clinical psychologists for such special functions as consultation, planned change, facilitation, mental health education, community organization, crisis intervention, and epidemiological research, the Conference urged that the profession take cognizance of the deficiency.

The desired end product of all of this?

The PhD training program must prepare a clinical psychologist whose style of practice is ethical and whose psychological activities involve a constant drawing on theory, a conscientious attention to definable procedures, the evaluation of his clinical work via acceptable scientific procedures, and a felt responsibility for reporting his results to his colleagues. In addition to his evaluation of clinical processes, the scientist-professional would be encouraged to make creative theoretical contributions.

NATURE OF GOOD TRAINING

Though it did not spell out a list of courses, the Conference left no doubt as to its intentions. Two themes, for example, recurred a number of times.

1. A "core" of courses need not specifically be enumerated, provided the essential areas of know-

ledge they represent are underscored; translation of such areas into course terms may then be left to university departments themselves.

2. There is strong reaffirmation of the position that clinical psychology must have its base in general psychology. Clinical skills, important as they are, must never be taught in isolation from their scientific base.

Against the background of such general points of view, the Conference could then be more explicit about the nature of academic preparation. Some of its observations follow.

PROFESSIONAL PREPARATION

Curriculum.

The notion of a core curriculum is no longer viable, but clinical training must include knowledge of many important concepts from other areas of psychology, such as learning, developmental, and social psychology. Clinical training cannot be carried out in isolation from general psychological knowledge.

During the first graduate year, clinical students must have substantial training in basic substantive areas of psychology in both its biological and social aspects, even though clinical training must also begin in the first year.

For clinical students, the content of traditional courses should be made as relevant as possible to the understanding of human behavior.

In order that they may develop in relationship to social needs, programs will usually need to incorporate increased emphases on developmental processes, group processes, social structures and cultural systems, and methods for producing individual change through changing social systems.

The Conference approved the following statement as reflecting the consensus of the participants:

With general advances in the state of our knowledge gained from infrahuman and human studies, there is an increased recognition within the field of psychology that an appreciation of and intimate acquaintance with developmental psychology is of vital importance for the proper training of the psychologist, regardless of his field of specialization. Important as such knowledge is for all psychologists, it is considered crucial for the clinical psychologist, and absolutely basic for the clinical child psychologist.

Sequence.

Clinical components of training, research training, and general psychological training should be arranged to occur continuously from the beginning of graduate study, with maximum attention to integration, drawing of relationships, and mutual relevance. In other words, from the outset of graduate study, training should include continuous integration of clinical practice, theory, and research.

Selection.

Recognizing the primacy of the human interaction over the clinical interaction and the fact that humanitarian concern and sensitivity cannot readily be taught, the conferees favor the selection of qualified students who have sought out a significant social experience such as living with or serving members of disturbed or disadvantaged groups.

Self-awareness.

There is need for encouraging and assisting each student to develop awareness of his own personality and behavior, his effects upon others, ability to suspend judgment, tolerance for error (by self and others), and similar characteristics. Psychotherapy, sensitivity training, clinical supervision, and role playing are among the means to these ends.

RESEARCH TRAINING

Fully committed to the thesis that good clinical training must rest on an appreciation of the scientific base of psychology, the Conference gave careful attention to the character of training in research. The general tenor of the discussion is reflected in the following.

The primary purpose of research training is to teach the individual to contribute to knowledge. Research training should serve also as a method of helping clinical psychologists formulate problems and issues as well as get and use feedback on the results of their own work. The canons of science and scholarship rather than any specific methodological paradigm should be the determining factor in research training and in evaluation of the merits of research.

While it is recognized that research in the clinical area is difficult to mount and conduct, it is our concern, in the interests of good training in clinical psychology, that students be encouraged, and given the opportunity, to address the significant problems of their field with full knowledge of the present state of its sophistication or complexity.

1. We recommend, therefore, that university faculties of psychology be encouraged to study their practices in the teaching of research and in the choice of thesis and dissertation topics and methods. We urge that, if such practices prove to be antithetical to the students' involvement with problems of major concern to them, the range of problems and/or methods be broadened and other appropriate solutions to these problems be devised.

Among the methods we suggest for consideration are: (a) the techniques and methods of inquiry available to the clinician and, in a sense, peculiar to him; (b) the natural setting as well as the laboratory, so as to enhance the significance of findings as they affect the human condition; (c) action research; (d) significant evaluation and follow-up studies of demonstration projects.

2. It is also recommended that research training be so embedded in the program that research orientation becomes an integral part of the clinical psychologist's

mode of professional behavior. Such may best be accomplished when (a) the clinical faculty is itself engaged in research activities which articulate with their clinical activities, (b) courses on statistics and research design encompass a wide range of clinical problems and methods, and (c) research training includes an emphasis on important problems that arise in professional practice.

The conferees labored under few illusions regarding the implementation of such worthy measures. In part, the suggestions, innocent though they might seem, represented major new emphases in academic circles. With near unanimity the conferees voted to reaffirm the classical definition of a dissertation as (a) an original contribution to knowledge which (b) demonstrates the competence of the contributor. At the same time, the conferees pointed out that the present assumption that "original contribution" necessarily implies the collection of empirical data is only one possible interpretation of the definition; other interpretations, which may be equally consonant with clinical involvement and scientific advancement, warrant consideration. Examples are to be found in original contributions which are theoretical, historical, evaluative, or scholarly in other ways. It should be noted that the Conference participants included graduate deans, who were of the opinion that such recommendations, though no small concessions to ask, could be implemented at many universities.

In no way was any of the foregoing to be construed as a lessening of emphasis on science in graduate education. The Conference specifically reaffirmed the position that clinical psychology must have a broad scientific base. Within such a context it was hoped that dissertation possibilities might be broadened, nonempirical contributions to knowledge accepted, exploratory, hypothesis-forming as well as hypothesis-testing designs recognized, and similar liberalized attitudes brought about. The conferees were particularly concerned, however, that if such changes could be wrought, they not be interpreted as decreasing emphasis on research competence under the scientist-professional model of clinical training.

TRAINING IN PSYCHOTHERAPY

In the context of the present Conference, it seemed difficult, if not impossible, to discuss training in psychotherapy without, at the same time, considering "related approaches to the modification of behavior." The latter were intended neither to replace nor to derogate what at earlier conferences had been a rather heavy emphasis on training in psychotherapy per se. Indeed, by way of reaffirming the essential role which training in psychotherapy plays in the preparation of the clinical psychologist, the conferees voted that the development of competence in dyadic psychotherapy should continue as a major goal of training, while students should be exposed also to other techniques of behavior modification, such as selective reinforcement of behavior, community and environmental techniques, and the like.

Taking the broader view then, the Conference stated its overall position as follows.

1. Major goals of training in psychotherapy and related approaches to the modification of behavior should be to: (a) develop therapeutic competence in students; (b) help the student develop greater ability to enter a meaningful relationship with others; (c) increase self-awareness, sensitivity, and understanding of themselves and others; (d) develop the ability to recognize and conceptualize human problems.

2. Training in clinical psychology should prepare students not only to deal with problems in the area of psychopathology but also to assist in maximizing human potential and in devising techniques of prevention of human problems insofar as possible.

3. In each clinical training program there should be training in one-to-one psychotherapy and in one or more of a variety of other approaches to effecting change in persons, such as group psychotherapy, community psychology approaches, the alteration of environment, and the selective reinforcement of behavior.

4. While clinical psychology students should have experience in one-to-one relationships, they should also be exposed to relationships which result in indirect influence on individuals, groups, or institutions through the mediation of people whom they affect and who in turn affect many other people. Small and large social groups also offer possibilities for innovation in behavior modification.

5. It is considered essential that each clinical program should include, among the regular faculty, some supervising clinical psychologists who are actively engaged in the practice of psychotherapy and related approaches to the modification of behavior.

Having thus established for itself the nature of good doctoral training and the conditions important to its implementation, the Conference was in better position to assess "models" of doctoral programs being proposed for its consideration. In so doing, the conferees were particularly concerned that, with the emergence of new approaches to the training of clinical psychologists, the content, rationale, and aim of each program be clearly articulated and made public. Such information should be made readily available to potential students, undergraduate advisors, and accrediting agencies, with the latter viewing a factual, up-to-date program description as a requirement for accreditation.

ALTERNATIVE MODELS OF DOCTORAL TRAINING

Having reaffirmed its emphasis on a broad scientific base for clinical psychology and the continuing importance of research competence under the scientist-professional model, the conferees nonetheless faced up to the question of going beyond the single image of the clinical psychologist to a consideration of further models, namely, those of the professional psychologist, the psychologist-psychotherapist, and the research-clinician. Two historical facts hung over the discussion.

On the one hand, it was noted, the scientist-professional model has, contrary to the original hope, all too often failed to result in the integration of the research attitude in all that the clinical psychologist does. Instead, there seems to have developed a situation in which many psychologists remind themselves periodically that they must take "time out to do research." The notion of stopping whatever one is doing at intervals in order to honor a commitment to research implies an artificial conception of what had been intended as a very real and thoroughgoing involvement. No such Jekyll-Hyde split had been envisioned. What *had* been intended, conferees kept pointing out, was that whatever the scientist-professional did would be research oriented, that is, characterized by a certain style of problem solving, an orderly process of inquiry.

On the other hand, the Conference noted, even where clinical psychologists had been duly trained under the scientist-professional model, their actual professional roles all too often found them behaving more in the character of the professional-psychologist or even psychologist-psychotherapist models, both of which seemed to net greater reward, or at least to meet expectancies, in the settings in which they worked. According to many "working clinicians," their training had failed to prepare them adequately even for the latter roles.

The conferees examined all three of the alternative models in the process. Of two, they made relatively short shrift. The psychologist-psychotherapist impressed few, if any, as an adequate model for clinical psychology. In its very narrow conception of the psychologist's role, it seemed to do justice neither to the doctorally trained psychologist nor to the setting in which he would contribute. The conference did take a positive stand regarding the possible development of a new doctoral level profession of psychotherapy, however.

The Conference took the position that competence in any single professional function, whether psychotherapy, research, or psychodiagnosis, does not constitute clinical psychology. Accordingly, training programs preparing students for only one such function should not be identified as programs in clinical psychology. In the view of the conferees, clinical psychology includes the following broad functions: psychological analysis and assessment for decision-making purposes; psychotherapy and other forms of behavior modification; psychological investigation (research and evaluation); training and education; consultation; administration. It was understood that any individual clinical psychologist need not be equally competent in all of these functions, but that a comprehensive training program should introduce him to each of them and prepare him well for several of them.

The research-clinician model was rejected for different reasons. If it meant what it said, then it seemed just another term for the scientist-professional (with emphasis here perhaps on *scientist*-professional rather than scientist-*professional*). If, instead, it was meant to characterize a nonclinical psychologist making a research contribution in a clinical setting, then such a person might be described more directly as what he was, for example, "experimental psychologist working in a clinical setting."

The professional-psychologist model, however, provoked long, hard discussion. So that its conception may be clear, it is redescribed here, as it appears in the *Preconference Materials* (Cook *et al.*, 1965).

The distinctive feature of this pattern of doctoral training would be the effort to prepare a broadly trained psychological clinician prepared to intervene in a wide variety of settings for the purpose of fostering change and forestalling psychological problems. His training would include psychological science but would stress those areas in which clinical methods find their support. It would also include relevant material from related disciplines, such as medicine and sociology. He would be introduced to a variety of diagnostic, remedial, and preventive procedures. His training would include analysis of the manner in which clinical methods are developed with the intent to make him a sophisticated evaluator of new methods developed in the future. Because he would not carry out a doctoral dissertation or learn foreign languages, he would have more time available for professional training and experience. Should he wish to develop the competence of a specialist in specified diagnostic, remedial, or preventive procedures, he will need additional training—either on the job or in formal postdoctoral training programs.

We would expect a clinical psychologist trained in this manner to devote full time to professional practice oriented toward treatment, prevention, or both. He would use diagnostic instruments, carry out psychotherapy, engage in milieu therapy, use behavior therapy, consult in community mental health projects, work with groups, organizations, and communities—as the occasion demanded. He would, as far as his limited scientific training would permit, keep abreast of new methods as they developed and critically appraise them prior to adoption. He would contribute to the development of methods of practice by sharing his professional experience with that of his colleagues [pp. 21–22].

Although it considered the above as a possible additional model under which clinical psychologists might be trained, the Conference actually underscored its continuing endorsement of the scientist-professional pattern under which the student is trained in a PhD program as both a professional psychologist and a research scientist. Within the scientist-professional pattern, the conferees felt, the time has come to broaden and elaborate training and to diversify training opportunities, so as to make it possible for different students to build on their different interests in their professional preparation.

Discussion was extensive, however, on the issue of whether such efforts should proceed to the point of offering a professional degree (not the PhD) in a program oriented primarily toward service rather than toward research. The conferees were obviously troubled by the question. Some favored experimentation with such programs; others opposed such moves. Accordingly, in an effort to scale the attitudes, it was found that they ranged from endorsement or encouragement of such experimentation, through tolerant acquiescence to the idea, to (in some cases) opposition to it. After prolonged open discussion and a determined effort to arrive at a representative Conference position, the following statement was adopted.

This conference recognizes the development in recent years of new methods in clinical psychology. Among these we note behavior therapy, milieu therapy, community psychology, group therapy, and new approaches to individual therapy.

We recognize, also, the ever-widening opportunities for clinical psychologists to render professional services. New opportunities are continually developing in hospitals, clinics, private practice, community mental health programs, schools, work settings, the various components of the poverty program, and in many other areas of life. It is clear that, in addition to added skill in the established techniques of assessment and therapy in dyadic relationships, clinical psychologists need new knowledge and skills to meet the ever-changing challenge presented by these service opportunities.

For this reason, we strongly recommend diversification of training opportunities in doctoral programs in clinical psychology. The objective of such diversification would be to provide the opportunity for different students to stress different knowledge and methods in their professional preparation.

We believe that training in clinical psychology should integrate professional and scientific education leading to a PhD degree. Within the context of this doctoral level training, innovation and diversification are encouraged in order to produce proficiency in professional and scientific skills meaningful to the field of clinical psychology.

It is recognized that other pilot or experimental programs in university psychology departments may be attempted.

The experiences with and the results of such programs will provide the only bases on which their effectiveness in producing clinical psychologists should be evaluated.

In effect, the conferees were taking account of the possibility that training departments might experiment with programs of the above sort and, in fact, possibly explore doctoral programs of still other types. If seemed, therefore, that evaluation of such experimentation should properly be based on the success which such programs might achieve.

What the Conference was saying, in short, was that (a) the scientist-professional model represents the endorsed form of training in clinical psychology, but (b) if university departments wish to engage in exploration, that is their prerogative, and (c) psychology ought to keep an open mind, letting the results speak for themselves.

Whether all of the foregoing would prepare the clinical psychologist to "pick up the right options," the Conference could not be certain. That it had attempted to discuss the problems responsibly, however, it was sure.

NOTES

1. Editors' note: This advance summary of the deliberations of the Chicago Conference of August 27–September 1, 1965, is presented in response to the intense and widespread interest in an early report of Conference outcomes. The reader should bear in mind that the present account, a preliminary one, which must of necessity compress a great deal of discussion, is to be followed by separate publication of detailed Conference Proceedings. The latter will attempt to provide the perspective from which the conferees viewed the issues in the course of their deliberations.

REFERENCE

COOK, S., BIBACE, R., GARFIELD, S., KELLY, G., & WEXLER, M. Issues in the professional training of clinical psychologists. In C. N. Zimet & Frances M. Throne(Eds.), *Preconference materials: Conference on the Professional Preparation of Clinical Psychologists*. Washington, D.C.: American Psychological Association, 1965. Pp. 17–30.

8. Integrating Scientific and Professional Training at the Graduate Level

FORREST B. TYLER

SINCE World War II considerable thought and attention has been given to graduate training in psychology, with special emphasis on training in applied areas such as clinical. A major concern has been meeting both scientific and professional training goals which have been outlined and discussed at the Boulder Conference (9), the Stanford Conference (13), and the Miami Beach Conference (10).

In spite of these conference ruminations, the devising of training programs to meet both scientific and professional training goals with some degree of adequacy and within a reasonable time period has proven difficult. These implementation difficulties seem to have stemmed in part from the fact that the academic-scientific aspects of training and the applied-professional aspects of training have seldom been integrated. That is, it has been assumed in setting up training programs that a student cannot be trained scientifically and professionally at the same time. The contrary assumption that it is possible to train simultaneously for both scientific and professional objectives has been used as the basis for developing one aspect of a graduate training program which is to be reported here.

Although the general nature of goals for applied psychology training has been discussed in the conference reports noted, few specific programs have been described in professional journals. Dawson (2) described a practicum training program at a state mental hospital, and Luchins has written extensively (6, 7) about a "functional approach" to clinical psychology training. Luchins (7) argues for a rather extended training period in which the student's training is centered around "the structure and activities of a clinical installation," and involves studying the institution and thereby contributing to

its service goals. By conceptualizing the psychologist's role as one of "student of behavior and of social processes, rather than as technician or diagnostician" he has to some extent broadened the goals of practicum-type training. At the same time he has emphasized the importance of the student's contributing to the service goals of the institution on an ongoing basis. In this latter regard his approach seems characteristic of professional training in most universities and service agencies in its focus on the actual performance of psychological services. Further, the emphasis seems to be on the performance of the service *per se* as important, rather than on the performance of the service as of value in developing a skilled professional practitioner. One somewhat contrasting view has been presented by Holzberg (4) in his discussion of research training during the clinical psychology internship. He emphasized the importance of providing equal status and belongingness *in its own right* to research in relation to more traditional professional activities such as diagnosis.

The present effort to train for both scientific and professional goals in one context involved an intensive summer program organized around an advanced graduate course in abnormal psychology.[1] Although clinical psychology has grown in status, its Siamese twin of earlier days, i.e., abnormal psychology, has been looked on with less favor. It is still retained as an undergraduate and graduate course and still required for admission to a number of graduate schools (11), yet it has almost disappeared as a professional entity. There is agreement that all clinical psychologists must have familiarity with this area of knowledge; however, relatively little attention was given to it at the Boulder or San Francisco conferences. At universities the "abnormal" course has characteristically been taught in the academic setting and supplemented with more-or-less systematic trips to a nearby mental hospital. These trips—and the course—have ordinarily been sandwiched into an already busy schedule and been

Reprinted from *Journal of Clinical Psychology*, 1963, *19*, 116–120. Dr. Tyler is a Training Specialist with the Behavioral Sciences Training Branch of the National Institute of Mental Health and was formerly Director of the Clinical Training Program at Southern Illinois University.

of necessity somewhat disjointed and "unreal."

Until recently the present writer shared this general disinterest in abnormal psychology. This perspective came to be re-examined only under the pressure of supervising this summer training program designed for pre-intern clinical students who had a minimum of one academic year of graduate training. An important rationale underlying this program has been that by increasing the interest of students in hospital work, the psychological services programs in Illinois state mental hospitals will be benefited in the future. Consequently, no immediate service return to the hospital has been necessary to justify the program. Consistent with this orientation, the training grant obtained to support the program included funds for hiring a supervisor for the trainees. Thus the service functions of the hospital staff were not materially interfered with by the necessity of supervising practicum students, but neither were they substantially augmented by the presence of the students.[2]

The resulting position of having a group of students in the midst of a hospital setting for two months with unlimited opportunities to observe, explore, ask questions, and otherwise learn at leisure, seemed to offer unlimited possibilities. Since there was ample time available, it was felt that a fairly ambitious goal could be set for the program. That goal was the systematic exploration of both scientific and professional perspectives about a representative group of descriptive, explanatory, and management problems in the field of psychopathology. As noted, traditional abnormal psychology courses are academically oriented. Clinical practica, on the other hand, are often dominated by the pressure to "be clinical" and suppress scientifically learned cautions about the adequacy of measuring instruments, validity indices, etc., in order to make decisions about the cases being seen. Here the purpose was to help the students develop a perspective which included an awareness of the reality of human pathology and existing methods of treatment, plus an awareness of scientific methods and the limits of scientific knowledge about all behavior, including that which we call pathological. In other words, it was hoped to aid the student to work out some basis for incorporating both scientific and professional perspectives without compartmentalizing them and becoming a "professional clinician" on one day and a "scientist" on the next (5). Once this goal was formulated it then became evident that the program could be of value to general psychology students, whose interests were limited to theory and research, as well as to clinical students, whose interests included profes-

sional service as well as scientific psychology. Presumably, a broad perspective on psychology as a base for further learning should be as valuable to the general psychologist as to the clinical psychologist. Consequently, the program was opened to general psychology students, too.

As to the practicum functions of the program, all student case workups and diagnostic tests were filed as part of the hospital records and could be referred to for professional purposes if desired, yet the students had no active responsibility for making decisions about patients. Information obtained by students was treated professionally, as it would have been had it been gathered by any hospital staff member, but the students were not required to solve actual case "problems". Such an arrangement retained the reality of professional responsibility for competent assessment and reporting, but relieved the student of the pressure of professional responsibility for decisions about the care and treatment of the patient. Further, since no service demands had to be met, there was freedom to modify the nature and amount of any such professional work consistent with the needs and desires of the student. General psychology students (required to have only a minimal knowledge of the Wechsler scale and of report writing) could do a limited amount of clinical-type practicum activities with the more modest goal of familiarizing themselves with such an approach to data gathering. Thus they would have a better understanding of the nature of clinical assessment and would also acquire skills useful to them in interacting with patient (or other) research subjects. In addition, the general psychology student was guided in working out a research practicum, which included the exploring of possible research problems as well as research techniques for studying theoretical (or other) problems in the understanding of pathological and normal behavior. Clinical students could do more clinical case studies, and more extensive diagnostic studies, and could give more thought to understanding the nature of professional clinical work. However, they too were encouraged to think about research and explore research possibilities.

Although the summer program could have been organized around other didactic courses, none seemed quite as appropriate as an advanced course in abnormal psychology, particularly since the stimulation of the hospital environment seemed most likely to lead to questions about that area. Consequently, the course focused on the immediate setting, which a course in personality or advanced clinical would not have done, yet it was not as narrow nor as specialized as a diagnostic testing or therapy course would have been. In attempting to attain a broad perspective on the field of psychology via the medium of abnormal psychology, all aspects of the course were considered. Beginning with selection of textbooks, it was felt that books should be used which represented the traditional clinical service, or procedural evidence, or orientation to pathology. In addition, the orientation stemming from an adherence to traditional experimental criteria—what Rychlak (12) calls *validating evidence* —should also be represented. A choice of procedural evidence based texts was readily made since the diagnostic procedures of the hospital itself are based on the *Diagnostic and Statistical Manual for Mental Disorders* of the American Psychiatric Association (1) and since each professional hospital staff member is provided with a copy of *Modern Clinical Psychiatry* by Arthur P. Noyes and Lawrence C. Kolb (8). These texts seemed adequately to represent the procedural evidence perspective on abnormal psychology and at the same time to provide the same framework for the student as for the hospital staff member.

The provision of a text or texts to provide a more validating evidence based perspective on abnormal psychology was less easy. Eysenck's (3) *Handbook of Abnormal Psychology* seemed most clearly to meet that criterion, although there may well be many psychologists who doubt that "all roads lead to support" for Eysenck. The book provides students with a better acquaintance with English research than they would otherwise get, although this acquaintance is provided at times at the expense of equally relevant American research. In spite of these limitations, the book provides a very valuable collection of research studies on important descriptive, differential, and explanatory problems in the area of pathology. It also provides useful critiques of these studies from the perspective of generally rigorous validating evidence standards. Finally, it contributes greatly to defining the status of knowledge and research in the areas covered, and points clearly to important unanswered questions (from the validating-evidence perspective) about the nature and nurture of human pathology.

Formal class sessions took the form of presentations (by the supervisor, his assistant, or one of the students), plus discussions and questioning. Since the program was not defined in terms of the usual classroom time segments, meetings and discussions could continue at length as enthusiasm and interest warranted. It was also possible to break up into smaller units as different foci of concern developed. A topic could be explored further through observation or interaction with patients, or through reading. It could also be terminated briefly, without guilt or concern, as boredom and disinterest or active opposition to continuing became evident.

Topics included classification of disorders, various therapies (i.e., shock therapy, drug therapy, psychotherapy, etc.), cognitive disorders, the psychoneuroses, schizophrenia, the affective disorders, motivational and "ego-function" abnormalities, etc. An attempt was made to cover representative topics and to bring to bear as many different points-of-view as possible on each topic. For example, consideration of the topic of the classification of mental disorders began with direct contact with patients themselves, at first on the hospital grounds in informal conversation. An early and natural outgrowth of such interactions was a concern with why these persons were hospitalized and why "labelled" as they were. Throughout the summer the students (and supervisors) attended regularly the four-times-a-week intake diagnostic staff meetings which served to diagnose tentatively and to provide recommendations for disposition of all incoming patients. These meetings provided an impetus to study and to understand the rationale for diagnosis, the nature of the generally accepted diagnostic schemata used, the nature of the personality and of the particular pathological problems of each patient, and the critical determinants in making different diagnoses. Inevitably, questions arose about the current medical disease conceptions of pathological processes and the utility of the attendant classification system. Eysenck's (3) chapter on classification, and the alternatives to present day systems that he has advocated, provided a markedly different reference point from which to view the problems of diagnosis. Since even Eysenck's factor-analyzed scheme is based primarily on symptomatic material, the question of the adequacy of symptoms as a base for classification was raised. The alternative perspective of traditional psychology in studying human behavior was presented. Specifically, the notion of S-O-R (stimulus-organism-response) models was considered, as was the tendency of psychologists to incorporate stimulus data and organism data (inferred from a knowledge of the organism's history of environmental conditioning) into their thinking about the determinants of any responses. The contrast between this approach and that of relying on response data or symptoms in classifying pathology was then noted and discussion directed toward possible systematic incorporation of more data, especially stimulus data and conditioning data, as a basis for more effective classification of pathological disorders. Thus it was possible through focus on a specific problem in pathology to bring together apparently unrelated conceptions (e.g., traditional S-O-R conceptions and diagnostic classification systems for hospital patients) and thereby to increase understanding of both the conceptual systems discussed and the problem itself.

A wide range of topics was covered, but always from the focus of abnormal psychology. Each topic was analyzed in such a way as to provide for a broad perspective on various aspects of pathological behavior, and to provide for a wide range of information—both theoretical and research—on that topic. It was hoped thereby to enable the student to assimilate information from both validating-evidence perspectives and from procedural-evidence perspectives without the device of compartmentalization and "changing hats" back and forth from professional to scientific. This goal was accomplished in part by beginning with the assumption that professional and scientific goals can be achieved together. Neither the practicing professional nor the researching scientist has all

the answers about psychopathology, and neither is out of contact with reality. Both are competent and have something to offer; both are human and have limitations. Their competencies and limitations can best be identified if they are neither revered nor rejected, but if the knowledge they offer is brought to bear in a straightforward way on problems of concern—in this instance those of abnormal psychology.

NOTES

1. This program is conducted at Anna State Hospital, Anna, Illinois, and is jointly sponsored by that hospital and Southern Illinois University. It is financed primarily by Illinois Mental Health Fund grant 2911 to the hospital with some support from University funds.
2. In spite of the fact that this program was "in principle" self-contained, it should be evident to any reader that the inquisitive graduate students and one all-too-human supervisor could acquire real nuisance value when dropped suddenly into the midst of ongoing hospital routines. A great deal of credit for success of this program belongs to Dr. R. C. Steck, Superintendent of the Anna State Hospital, and to his professional staff for their cooperation and support.

REFERENCES

1. AMERICAN PSYCHIATRIC ASSOCIATION. Committee on Nomenclature and Statistics of the American Psychiatric Association. *Diagnostic and statistical manual for mental disorders.* Washington, D.C.: American Psychiatric Association, 1952.
2. DAWSON, J. G. A practicum training program. *Amer. Psychologist,* 1957, *12,* 532–535.
3. EYSENCK, H. J. (Ed.). *Handbook of Abnormal Psychology.* New York: Basic Books, Inc., 1961.
4. HOLZBERG, J. D. The role of the internship in the research training of the clinical psychologist. *J. consult. Psychol.,* 1961, *25,* 185–191.
5. KELLY, G. I itch too. *Amer. Psychologist,* 1955, *10,* 172–173.
6. LUCHINS, A. S. A functional approach to clinical psychology. *J. genet. Psychol.,* 1956, *89,* 153–163.
7. LUCHINS, A. S. *A Functional Approach to Training in Clinical Psychology.* Springfield, Ill.: Charles C. Thomas, 1959.
8. NOYES, A. P. and KOLB, L. C. *Modern clinical psychiatry.* Philadelphia: W. B. Saunders Company, 1958.
9. RAIMY, V. C. (Ed.). *Training in clinical psychology.* New York: Prentice-Hall, 1950.
10. ROE, ANNE, GUSTAD, J. W., MOORE, B. V., ROSS, S., and SKODAK, MARIE (Eds.). *Graduate Education in Psychology.* Washington, D.C.: American Psychological Association, Inc., 1959.
11. ROSS, S. Educational facilities and financial assistance for graduate students in psychology: 1961–62. *Amer. Psychologist,* 1960, *15,* 800–823.
12. RYCHLAK, J. F. Clinical psychology and the nature of evidence. *Amer. Psychologist,* 1959, *14,* 642–648.
13. STROTHER, C. R. (Ed.). *Psychology and Mental Health.* Washington, D.C.: American Psychological Association, 1956.

9. *Training Psychologists for the Therapeutic Community*

SHERMAN E. NELSON

THE therapeutic community or therapeutic milieu movement has had a profound and extensive effect on mental illness and its treatment in recent years. Some institutions frankly designate themselves as therapeutic communities. Many other hospitals have therapeutic community wards or sections, and it is hard to find a progressive mental hospital today which does not subscribe to some therapeutic community concepts.

Elements which all therapeutic community endeavors have in common are "open doors," the deliberate attempt to make all aspects of the patient's day as therapeutic as possible, emphasis on the patient's strengths and independence rather than his weaknesses and dependence, and maximum use of the patient's potential for being therapeutic to his fellow patients through the use of formal and informal group techniques.

FUNCTIONS OF THE PSYCHOLOGIST IN THE THERAPEUTIC COMMUNITY

THE MAXIMUM USE OF GROUPS RATHER THAN INDIVIDUAL PSYCHOTHERAPY

The term "group psychotherapy," as used in the therapeutic community, includes not only small groups of patients meeting with one or two therapists, but groups of all sizes and compositions with a wide variety of purposes. In addition to more traditional group psychotherapy, there are activity, government, living unit management, and informal groups as well. Individual psychotherapy may be practiced, but its duration is usually brief, and its

Reprinted from *Preconference Materials Prepared for the Conference on the Professional Preparation of Clinical Psychologists* (Washington, D.C.: American Psychological Association, 1965), 54–56, by permission of the American Psychological Association and the author. Dr. Nelson is Director of Psychological Services, Fort Logan Mental Health Center, Denver, Colorado.

purpose is often to aid and support the patient in gaining the maximum benefit from the many group opportunities available.

THE USE OF ONESELF IN AS THERAPEUTIC A WAY AS POSSIBLE IN A WIDE AND VARIED NUMBER OF SITUATIONS

In the therapeutic community setting, interactions with patients occur throughout the day in all activities. Psychotherapy does not begin and end in the psychologist's office or in a small group room. In the course of a typical day the psychologist may participate in occupational, recreational, and work therapies, as well as in many informal contacts with patients on the living unit. He is constantly examining and trying to perfect his treatment skills in every contact he has with patients.

ASSESSMENT OF THE PATIENT'S PROBLEMS BY USING INFORMATION FROM A VARIETY OF SOURCES

Psychological tests may be used in the therapeutic community, but in general on a far more limited basis than in more traditional facilities. Continuous and close participation and involvement with patients provide many vivid opportunities for a direct observation of their problems as they are acted out in the living situation. The psychologist also draws on the observations of other staff and patients, on family members, and on community informants for his evaluation. Inferences from test stimuli are often unnecessary.

ACTIVE INVOLVEMENT OF RELATIVES IN THE PATIENT'S TREATMENT

Relatives participate in treatment as much as possible, and individual contacts with relatives, patient and spouse groups, and total family programs are stressed. Work with relatives may be carried on to provide better support for the patient through greater tolerance and understanding of his difficulties, or in a number of cases may actually be direct treatment of a disturbed marriage or family situation of which the patient is only a part.

THE USE OF COMMUNITY RESOURCES

The psychologist is often expected to know, to work with, and to influence professionals and agencies outside of the institution throughout the course of the patient's treatment.

TEACHING THERAPEUTIC COMMUNITY SKILLS TO OTHER PERSONNEL

The psychologist is one of the most highly educated professionals in the therapeutic community. He is called on constantly to teach other staff members, either in class, informally, or by example.

RESEARCH AND PROGRAM EVALUATION

Although its forerunners can be found far back in the history of the treatment of mental illness, the therapeutic community is regarded as a new concept and modality. The high motivation of its adherents has accounted for great progress in a rather short time. However, as with all approaches to the complex problem of mental illness and its treatment, constant and extensive research is needed to evaluate its success, identify elements which are effective or ineffective, and point the way to changes and modifications. Of all the professionals involved in the approach, the psychologist is best equipped by training to carry on direct research and to consult on research by colleagues in other disciplines.

CHANGES NEEDED IN THE PREPARATION OF PSYCHOLOGISTS FOR THE THERAPEUTIC COMMUNITY

The author feels that a solid grounding in general psychology prior to clinical specialization can only enhance the eventual effectiveness of the psychologist who is headed for therapeutic community work. However, he has some major objections to the model which presently characterizes so much of clinical training. There are two major points of view on clinical preparation for therapeutic community work. One is that present programs, with their emphasis on intensive study of the individual case, tests, individual psychotherapy, and "intrapsychic" research are not only adequate, but also provide the eventual therapeutic community psychologist with the only basic preparation he needs. His motivation and his adaptability will presumably enable him to pick up the additional skills required in the job situation. The other point of view, which the author favors, is that present clinical training programs should be drastically modified to better prepare the psychologist for therapeutic milieu work.

Not all of the intrapsychic or one-to-one elements in theoretical, assessment, or psychotherapy training should be abandoned. However, the therapeutic community approach, while it will undoubtedly undergo many changes, is here to stay and is growing rapidly in influence and utilization. An increasing number of psychologists will be needed to meet the challenges in these areas. If the present predominant clinical training model remains unchanged, psychologists preparing for therapeutic community work may be handicapped not only by training which has stopped short of their future job demands, but which has also prepared them for clinical work of a nature better suited to the private consulting room.

The author strongly recommends that those responsible for clinical training programs recognize the growing importance and tremendous future potential of the therapeutic community approach for psychologists and institute the following changes:

1. A greater emphasis on evaluating and treating the individual as part of a psycho-social field. Intrapsychic dynamics should not be abandoned, but training should give greater stress to family, social, and cultural factors. The ideal therapeutic community psychologist of the future may be as much a social as a clinical psychologist. All of mental illness is not encompassed in a test battery or in cloistered office interviews.

2. Greater stress on group dynamics and group psychotherapy theory and technique in formal course and practicum work. Exclusive emphasis on formal one-to-one psychotherapy does not prepare the trainee for a rapidly increasing trend toward group treatment.

3. Recognizing that psychotherapy does not reside solely in structured office or small group contacts and encouraging and helping the student to develop his treatment skills in a wide variety of situations and settings.

4. The development of knowledge and skill in the use of community resources.

5. The development of skill in communicating with and teaching less highly educated mental health personnel and lay people. Some psychologists have demonstrated this ability, but they did not acquire it in graduate school.

6. Encouraging and promoting action and program evaluation research by the student, rather than laboratory and basic research alone.

10. Graduate Training in Community Mental Health

JAMES G. KELLY

COMMUNITY mental health as a scientific and professional field is primarily concerned with preventing negative adaptations to stress and promoting positive adaptations to stress. These aims are based on the premise that mental health services should be allocated in accordance with knowledge of the social organization of communities and the social structure of population groups. The present position paper is also based upon the following assumptions which are considered essential to psychologists' work in this field: (a) Basic research on the relationship between sociocultural variables and personality functioning will create valid knowledge about the positive mastery of stress. (b) The ability to effectively analyze and reduce negative adaptations to stress requires—in addition to psychotherapies—the creation of innovative services for those specific population segments which evidence maladaptation. (c) Strengthening such local institutions as schools and churches, so that they can develop effective social organizations which will reduce negative adaptations to stress in local communities.

PRINCIPLES FOR GRADUATE TRAINING

Postdoctoral training is highly recommended for the psychologist seeking a career in community mental health. Graduate preparation should provide training in both research and practice sufficient to enable him to pursue his future career in work with either a research or practice orientation. Certain principles must be followed in such a training program if it is to achieve the highest scientific-professional standards. Here are six basic tenets:

Reprinted from *Preconference Materials Prepared for the Conference on the Professional Preparation of Clinical Psychologists* (Washington, D.C.: American Psychological Association, 1965), 59–61, by permission of the American Psychological Association and the author. Dr. Kelly is Associate Professor of Psychology, University of Michigan.

1. Community mental health training requires intensive, rigorous preparation in such areas of psychology as perception, cognition, learning, child development, social psychology and quantitative methods. Only by achieving basic competence in these areas can the psychologist understand the range of human behavior that can be expressed in different settings.

2. Training in community mental health emphasizes competence in dealing with the concepts of human ecology and epidemiologic methods. The psychologist's understanding of this subject prepares him to generate research or innovative services which are meaningfully related to changing expressions of individual behavior in different settings.

3. Training in research and practice is based upon the tutorial method in addition to successful performance in a sequence of core courses. The present position paper stresses the importance of a colleague relationship between faculty and student as a means of encouraging critical thinking on the part of both students and faculty and strengthening the student's commitment to professional goals and values.

4. Training for both research and practice requires exposure to new types of laboratory experiences. These can utilize such research sites as action research projects, or such practicum settings as settlement houses or city planning councils. Many of these settings are currently often not considered when students are placed in laboratory situations. Exposure to these settings would give the student firsthand knowledge of additional resources he can use to understand and produce change in individuals.

5. Training encourages psychology students to participate in laboratory work and seminars with students from other university departments. While the form of the training activities varies, all students must become familiar with substantive interests and professional points of view that contribute to the field of community mental health but which

originate outside psychology. University departments likely to share such an interest are sociology, anthropology, education, economics, preventive medicine, public health, social work, and psychiatry.

6. All training in psychology encourages the student to expose himself to divergent viewpoints. Community mental health work in particular requires the utmost awareness of alternative professional and personal points of view. The graduate student who has an opportunity critically to evaluate controversial or deviant community interests or atypical proposals for research or practice will be able better to analyze the demands for social change as well as the resistances to it. The community mental health training program can help achieve this aim by encouraging the availability of lecturers and the introduction of ideas which propose analyses or solutions to social problems that seem to conflict with present positions and practice.

PRIORITIES FOR GRADUATE TRAINING

The quality of a training program rests more heavily upon the talents, convictions and tolerances of its faculty than upon its course catalogue. Instead of proposing a specific curriculum, which can easily become outdated, I will therefore suggest priorities for a training program. These are designed to create new knowledge and to prepare psychologists to deal with rapid changes in their profession —and among their clients. I believe that the purpose of a 4-year doctoral program is to (a) develop competence in the primary content areas of psychology; (b) develop skills for integrating knowledge gained from research and practice; (c) produce research knowledge on the relationship between individual behavior and the social environment.

Specific priorities for a community mental health program are as follows:

Clinical methods courses are primarily concerned with (a) methods for assessing social settings; (b) analysis of adaptations to stressful events; and (c) analysis of behavior change. These courses should begin during the first year of graduate work. Emphasis in all three is upon looking at settings, events and behavior change as problems of human ecology. Then on the basis of ecological concepts and methods, the student will be able to begin to formulate hypotheses about the range and uniqueness of the behavior that is displayed from one setting to another. This initial preparation can help students begin to plan

research or to develop alternative therapeutic services for a variety of individuals and social settings.

An expanded range of placements is advocated for the predoctoral internship year. Examples are: community mental health centers here and abroad, action research projects and selected research laboratories which are intensively studying problems of human ecology. The community mental health centers which are currently emerging in this country can provide the student with an opportunity to participate in comprehensive mental health programs. These provide different services to specific segments of the population; or they are oriented to particular community problems. Participation in action research can expose students to nontraditional modes of community analyses and social intervention. Research laboratories can provide them with an extended period during which they can become involved with research other than that being done at the university.

During the fourth year, while the student is completing the doctoral dissertation, he can also benefit from two other types of experience. One is to help supervise the practicum training for first-year graduate students. The second is to attend interdepartmental research seminars as a faculty participant. Community mental health work is likely to place heavy demands upon the new PhD for teaching and interprofessional collaboration. By including a place for such activities in his graduate career, he can anticipate those functions which will be expected of him when he begins professional work.

SUMMARY

This position paper emphasizes scientific and research training for psychologists in community mental health. As a focus for explaining and predicting behavior the paper stresses the importance of ecological studies, including an account of relevant social settings. Important elements of such training are: (a) diverse practicum and internship settings; and (b) opportunities for interprofessional work. The primary goal for graduate training is to prepare psychologists for scholarly careers in research and practice. Psychology's unique contribution to community mental health is its traditional emphasis on scholarship and critical analysis and its commitment to research work. Community mental health's contribution to psychology is to extend the scope of clinical methods.

The further rationale for the described training is that continuous and simultaneous training in research and practice assists the integration of scientific concepts. From this will emerge a more creative researcher or a more innovative practitioner. Psychologists in community mental health work are expected to work in diverse settings, to assume leadership in the creation of knowledge and to adapt professional skills to changing roles imposed by themselves as well as by society.

11. A Postdoctoral Residency Program in Clinical Psychology

JOSEPH D. MATARAZZO

THE purpose of the present paper is to provide a description of one training center's approach to postdoctoral training for the professional aspects of clinical psychology, as seen through the eyes of one of the faculty members in this training program. The reader interested in the general topic of postdoctoral training of clinical psychologists in the United States should consult the preliminary but informative reviews of this newly developing area by Santostefano (1960), Basowitz and Speisman (1964), Blank and David (1964), Mayman (1964), and Alexander (1965). The paper by Alexander offers a thumbnail description of 20 institutions which currently offer continuing 1- or 2-year National Institute of Mental Health—supported postdoctoral training programs to graduates of departments with American Psychological Association—approved programs in clinical psychology who have had a full year of internship. The program to be described below is one of these 20 postdoctoral programs. As yet, none of the 20 postdoctoral programs has been accredited by any outside agency, although, like our own program, many of them are offered in agencies with concurrent predoctoral internship programs which have been accredited by the Education and Training Board of APA.

While there appears, since the Boulder Conference, to be some basic core similarity among the goals and actual training programs which exist for predoctoral internships in clinical psychology, such a common core appears not yet to have emerged for these 20 postdoctoral training programs. At this early stage in the development of professional clinical psychology, the diversity of approach to specialized postdoctoral training appears healthy; for the number and kinds of institutions and independent settings in which psychologists carry professional responsibility and the range and varieties of responsibilities they are undertaking are changing and growing at a rapid pace. Some of the postdoctoral training programs appear designed to train clinical psychologists who can assume greater responsibilities in traditional psychiatric settings; others in community mental health programs; still others in child guidance settings; while others appear to be training psychologists for independent practice responsibilities in the areas of psychological assessment, consultation, or psychotherapy.

In many of these postdoctoral settings, training programs for research clinical psychologists also are offered. In our own department, concurrent with the postdoctoral residency program to be described below, we offer a 4-year program leading to a PhD degree[1] in general-experimental psychology, a 1-year predoctoral internship program in clinical psychology, and a 1- or 2-year training program devoted exclusively to research in clinical psychology or physiological psychology. Thus, our postdoctoral residency training program in clinical psychology, while devoted almost exclusively to professional training, is offered in a setting which also strongly stresses training in the science-related aspects of psychology.

Neither the writer nor any of his colleagues hold up this postdoctoral residency program, and underlying philosophy, as a model for all clinical psychology and for all training centers. There are many other models for such training in other settings. The program to be described below is the unique outgrowth of, on the one hand, the philosophies of particular psychologists with personal commitments, and some healthy areas of disagreement, to a specialized type of training for a limited number of psychology students and, on the other hand, a combination of local conditions (an unusually favorable environment for the full and effective

Reprinted from *American Psychologist*, 1965, *20*, 432–439, by permission of the American Psychological Association and the author. Dr. Matarazzo is Professor and Chairman, Department of Medical Psychology, University of Oregon Medical School.

growth of psychology in a medical school) which may or may not exist in other settings.

TWOFOLD TRAINING MODEL

In our medical school setting we offer 1 or 2 years of postdoctoral residency training to prepare the young clinical psychologist to engage in professional practice in two areas:

1. As a *psychodiagnostician-clinician-consultant* to others, e.g., on referral from other psychologists, physicians in private practice and hospital practice, the schools, governmental agencies, attorneys, judges, family members or friends of former patients and clients, or those from the latter groups and others who consult him directly, etc.

2. As a *psychotherapist* helping his patients and clients, through a process of further social learning or unlearning, to achieve greater effectiveness in interpersonal relations, planning life goals, etc.

PSYCHODIAGNOSTICIAN ROLE MODEL:
PSYCHOLOGIST AS CLINICIAN-CONSULTANT

Over the years, the training model of the clinical psychologist as diagnostician which has evolved for me is one which differs from the traditional post-Boulder-Conference one. In my training function I assume that our postdoctoral resident has had, in a predoctoral internship, good training in the use of such psychological assessment techniques as the interview, objective and projective measures of intelligence, personality, interest, and related dimensions. Therefore the emphasis in my training of the psychodiagnostician postdoctoral resident is in helping him assess the patient's (or client's) strengths and weaknesses *within the context in which he lives or is operating.* In order for him to adequately assess the major elements of the patient's life context, the clinical psychology resident typically must establish contact and work collaboratively with other professional and nonprofessional persons, including family, social agencies, ministers, physicians, etc., and then, himself, begin to make professional decisions and take responsibility for these decisions.

THE QUESTION OF A PSYCHODIAGNOSTICIAN
ROLE MODEL

The answer to the question of which role model a psychology resident learning assessment and consultation skills in this setting is to emulate, while carrying out clinical responsibilities in such

hospital services as pediatrics, surgery, psychiatry, obstetrics-gynecology, medicine, etc., has been slow to emerge for me, and is still emerging. Following World War II the assessment faculty psychologist in medical centers was in large part a psychodiagnostician offering a type of laboratory consultation service (Matarazzo & Daniel, 1957, p. 98). Patients were referred to him much as they were to the clinical pathology laboratory or to the radiology department, often, in fact, for a "routine" examination.

However, the writer and his clinical psychologist colleagues at our Medical School, very likely in common with psychologists in similar hospital settings, have developed for themselves, over the past 7 years, a new model for psychologists as consultants. In contrast to industrial-clinical, and university-clinical training settings, in a medical center such as ours this model quite appropriately has some features in common with that of the medical clinician-teacher, or clinician-consultant to a medical, surgical, psychiatric, pediatric, or other service. Thus, for example, a senior neurologist in a medical center or general hospital is rarely referred a patient "for a neurological examination." Rather, in common with colleagues from other departments, he is "called in consultation" as part of the further understanding of a patient on whom much other information already has been collected. While the neurologist undoubtedly will carry out a neurological examination (one, incidentally, geared specifically to the needs of this patient as will be determined from a careful reading of what other colleagues have already written into the patient's hospital chart about his medical-social characteristics), he is called in consultation both as a neurologist-clinician (adding his skills to the solution of a clinical problem) and as a teacher (helping other senior consultants and their residents in training to learn more about his specialty). Since our clinical psychology faculty members also have *formal* appointments as attending staff to our several medical school teaching hospitals, and thus are called in consultation to see patients in the same way as are their medical colleagues, it is possible for us to train, by example, our psychology resident in similar consultation skills. Thus, the generic term "clinician-teacher" is used to describe this professional role model for the training of the psychology resident.

The process of assimilation of this new clinician-teacher, professional-service role has not been completed; it is still only 7 years old and we expect to continue to develop and modify it to better fit the needs and responsibilities of professional psychology. Yet, one important by-product of this new model merits mention: Whereas in many parts of the country (traditional) psychodiagnosis is disparaged (this is especially true among predoctoral students and new PhDs), the writer (in common with his students) finds considerable satisfaction in this type of work as an assessment clinician-consultant-teacher.

The actual mechanics of the training program in consultation skills could be described at this point. Yet to do so would be to present merely a list and description of many of the standard elements of most training programs in clinical psychology. For example, teaching skills: (*a*) for establishing rapport with, and presenting a professional model in relation to nurses, physicians, other colleagues, and, of course, the patient; (*b*) for establishing privacy and confidentiality; (*c*) for the most effective utilization of interviewing skills, tests, and other assessment techniques; (*d*) for writing brief summaries of one's findings and opinions directly into the hospital chart, following those contributed by the last consultant or colleague who saw the patient, and in a nonspecialized language which is meaningful to nurses, medical colleagues, and attorneys and judges in instances involving medical-legal, or psychological-legal participation, etc.; (*e*) for also communicating such findings quickly and effectively in more informal ways as, for example, by telephone, in corridor conversations, and in the lunchroom, as well as providing appropriate analysis and discussion of such findings in daily or weekly conferences, etc.

The above elements are to be found in many training programs. The somewhat unique feature of the training program here being described is the acceptance of the psychology resident in these activities by his colleagues in this hospital setting, beginning with the hospital administrators and sifting down imperceptibly through chiefs of services, attending staff, nurses, residents, interns, and other professionals with whom he comes into daily contact. The same acceptance holds true for the psychotherapist model described below. In the writer's opinion it is this *atmosphere for training* which is one of the most important features of every training program. In my opinion the positive nature of this atmosphere constitutes the greatest asset of our training program.

It is probably clear that many predoctoral interns, in view of their age and level of professional development, cannot make optimal use of this advanced type of tutorial training. It is for this reason that we introduced, initially in very embryonic form, a postdoctoral fellowship training

program. We have trained nine postdoctoral fellows to date and currently have two others in training. Only in 1964, after almost 7 years of experience and experimentation with the program, did we feel we could call it a residency. When we finally felt we were ready and proposed the change of name to the hospital administration, we won immediate agreement that our program was comparable to other hospital programs and should be included among the hospital's residency offerings. For those readers who object to the term "resident" for the psychology fellows being trained in our medical school setting, I can only say that to call them by any other name in this setting would be unduly partisan and probably serve no purpose. However, as will be discussed below, while we call him a resident in clinical psychology, our program stresses training in the *generic* aspects of applied psychology and, thus, hopefully prepares him for professional work in a variety of the nonmedical settings in which he may be working as a psychologist years later.

PSYCHOTHERAPIST ROLE MODEL

Although in describing our program for the training of the resident for this role we use the traditional term "psychotherapist," the training in this skill in our setting is in many ways nontraditional. Saslow and Matarazzo (1962) described the treatment philosophy which underlies the training for psychotherapy of psychiatrists and psychologists, as well as other professionals, on an open psychiatric ward in our general (teaching) hospital. The psychotherapist model for which we train is somewhat different from the classical two-person, patient-psychotherapist approach, with its emphasis upon uncovering and the working through of intrapsychic conflicts (i.e., the model of the psychoanalyst in practice). The approach to personality and behavioral change to which we introduce our psychotherapy postdoctoral resident is a social-learning one: i.e., the model of the psychologist or psychiatrist, or other mental health consultant, who attempts to facilitate personality and behavioral change through explicit recognition of the often *low generalizability* of new psychotherapeutic insights and behaviors outside of the two-person psychotherapy office. The approach to therapy stresses, as its main ingredient, the deliberate use of a patient's human milieu (be it on the ward, at home, or at work) in his psychotherapy. It uses, as adjuncts to individual psychotherapy, social influences such as family, employers, friends, other hospital patients, staff, teachers, and others in the rehabilitation of persons who are receiving treatment on this open psychiatric ward.

In our setting we also give our psychology resident, in common with his psychiatric counterpart, concurrent supervised psychotherapeutic experience in our adult and family outpatient clinics, where this same focus on the social context as an adjunct to psychotherapeutic rehabilitation is maintained. In addition, as part of his training, the psychology resident is allowed to observe, either by sitting in the same room or through a one-way window, the psychotherapy conducted by a senior faculty member.

It is our hope that he will learn from the mixture of these varied experiences that some patients require long-term psychotherapeutic help—in isolated cases including transfer to a staff member or another resident at the end of the resident's 1- or 2-year period of training—while the majority of patients require, or seek, his therapeutic effort over a much briefer period of time. He hopefully also will be in a better position to differentiate these two types of patient needs than he was before his residency. He also learns that, unlike the post-Boulder-Conference model of, for example, the Veterans Administration hospital psychologist conducting psychotherapy with patients in an institutional setting, the professional psychologist-psychotherapist of today must take responsibility, himself, for most of his own professional decisions involving his patients and clients.

Thus, for both the psychodiagnostician-consultant and psychotherapist role models, our training program pays considerable attention to the fact that the practice of general clinical psychology—be it as a consultant in a general hospital, or a psychiatric hospital, or a community mental health center, or a public school, or in one's own office—requires that the psychologist assume responsibility for his patients and clients, and his own professional actions and decisions involving them, at a level comparable to that assumed by such other "older" professionals as physicians and attorneys. Our profession has changed markedly in the past 5 years and has begun to show that it finally is acquiring its own individuality, formal professional structure, and security. In a very real sense we believe our training program thus mirrors a segment of the zeitgeist in clinical psychology in America today.

One of the major features of this zeitgeist deserves further discussion: namely, the fact that possibly without our being fully aware of it, one of the significant differences between the clinical psychologist of 20 years ago and today is that the latter is a much more independent professional than was the former. However, independence demands responsibility and this, in turn, demands that those of us who teach young professional clinical psychologists pay particular attention to the ways in which we can train for such responsibility.

TRAINING FOR FULL PROFESSIONAL RESPONSIBILITY

After a dozen years of watching psychologists, including myself, slowly gain the professional security, acceptance, and confidence required in order to take full professional responsibility for patients and clients, I have concluded that one of the most critical deficits in my own training and, for that matter, in most of our present training programs, was and is the failure to emphasize explicitly this need to train young psychologists for such responsibility. The reasons for this are clear. Training for such responsibility can be provided typically only after a profession has developed to a point where its older representatives are themselves functioning in such a manner. Many indices suggest to me that the latter has happened to clinical psychology in the 2 decades since the Boulder Conference. One index of the maturing of professional psychology, but by no means the most important index, is the fact that, as of 1964, 25 of the 50 states of the US certify or license psychologists by statute. In addition, the psychologists in another 17 states have voluntary certification of their members for professional practice. Four Canadian provinces also certify psychologists by statute. The accelerating number of states and provinces establishing such laws in the past 5 years indicate that very soon most, if not all, states and provinces will license or certify the professional psychologist.

How does a new profession train its younger members to assume responsibility for the welfare, and sometimes the lives, of their fellow men? The answers to this question obviously are complex, and involve important issues currently being raised, discussed, and analyzed by students of the sociology of professions. Yet one point is clear: A professional is trained in a setting of some type.

Two decades ago Shakow and associates (APA, 1947), recognizing the infancy of professional clinical psychology, had this to say about the features of the practicum setting in which young clinical psychologists might best be trained:

No group can become a profession overnight, a fact which psychology is in the process of discovering. What really counts in the making of a profession—professional ideals and practices—cannot (un)fortunately be taught in courses. Proper technical training, professional certification and state certification, of course, play important roles. More important, however, are identification with a group having high ideals, and constant association in the actual work situation with persons having professional goals. It is in the work relationship that the student can learn to think of himself as a professional person. It is here that the student can gain an appreciation of how people meet such problems as maladjustment, illness, and handicaps and in this context gain a feeling of responsibility about his work because he understands that his findings really make a difference in what happens to a particular individual and his family. It is here that he learns to carry, in addition to this responsibility for the individual, the broader social one which transcends the need of the individual patient. It is in this setting, too, that another important aspect of professional training, his relationship with other professions, is constantly brought to his attention [p. 556].

Shortly after the publication of the statement of these general requirements for an adequate practicum training setting for clinical psychologists, Kubie (1948) added that the best settings then existing for such training were those provided by our sister profession of medicine. He wrote:

There is only one place where this atmosphere and feeling of therapeutic responsibility, this dedication to healing, has been cultivated, namely in medical schools and hospitals, where everyone functions as part of a complicated therapeutic team. This atmosphere is so important in training for therapy of any kind, that without it all intellectual and technical equipment is of little value [p. 49].

Therefore training for medical psychology and especially its clinical diagnostic and therapeutic phases, should be given in medical schools and teaching hospitals [p. 49].

As a matter of fact, with the exception of the Counseling Center of the University of Chicago, and possibly one or two other similar centers, during the 20 years since Boulder there have been few well-established practicum settings for the training of clinical psychologists which have not been predominantly medical centers. However, as another index of the growing maturity of professional clinical psychology, there are indications today that psychologists may soon be training many of their students in predominantly psychological centers. Examples of these are the professional postdoctoral training programs recently instituted by psychologists at New York University and at Adelphi University, as well as by the Los Angeles Society of Clinical Psychologists.

As Albee (1964) aptly has pointed out, most of today's well-established professions (e.g., medicine, law, dentistry, social work) provide their *own* facilities for training the younger members of their professions. Albee strongly urges the establishment of psychological centers for the training of applied psychologists. While I agree with Albee's aim, it is well for us to remember that a truly effective professional culture or atmosphere in the training settings of these other professions, in the sense described by Shakow and Kubie, was not achieved overnight or lightly by these "older" professions. Until psychological centers have achieved their own experience, history, and other cultural supports for training the young clinical psychologist for professional responsibility, it is apparent that some training programs in medical settings, such as our own, will continue to be required for such training.

The writer hopes that it is clear to the reader that the postdoctoral training in clinical psychology which we offer our psychology resident in this medical setting does not, ipso facto, mean that the young psychologist is being trained in a medical model. With the at first necessary and important help of the professor of psychiatry and the dean of our medical school, as well as our other colleagues, psychology became an autonomous and independent department of the Medical School in 1961. Developments such as this one in our own Medical School were predicted by participants at the Miami Conference on Graduate Education in Psychology (Roe, Gustad, Moore, Ross, & Skodak, 1959, p. 64). Following this development at our Medical School it became possible for psychology, in its clinical activities, to explore on a small scale in this setting its potential new roles and usefulness to society. As others have pointed out in the past, only when an individual, a group, or a profession has achieved the opportunity to explore its potential independently will these same individuals also have the opportunity to discover newer and more unique ways to make effective contributions. Also in the process new knowledge often is gained. In our own setting, as one by-product of this new independence, and in addition to their work as attending psychologists on the wards and in the clinics, our clinical psychology faculty members are developing what appear to me to be highly individualistic professional activities. One faculty clinical psychologist is applying operant-conditioning techniques as important adjuncts to psychotherapy. Another is developing new approaches to the education of youngsters in an experimental school for retarded children. Still another is beginning to develop new approaches to family diagnosis and therapy. Two of these three faculty members, in conjunction with a senior psychiatrist colleague, are exploring a highly promising method of teaching psychotherapeutic skills to residents in psychiatry and psychology by the use of a miniature radio transmitter and receiver (the latter worn near the ear of the resident). Other clinical faculty psychologists, including the writer, are practicing and studying their own brands of clinical psychology. The training that the psychology resident receives from *each* of these clinical psychologists is instrumental: i.e., it serves the purpose of exposing him to a broad range of clinical experiences. It is not expected that he will become a professional exactly like any of his clinical teachers.

Thus, neither the medical school setting itself nor the interests of the individual faculty psychologists lend themselves to training the psychology resident in a particular model, let alone a medical model. Since the human problems to which we expose our psychology resident, and for which problems we train him to assume responsibility, are generic, our resident receives training which is general and, hopefully, one which he later can apply in a myriad of professional settings. No one can predict what new roles and new responsibilities the clinical psychologist trained today will be carrying out in the future. There are many indications that he most probably will not be a person spending most of his professional time in a one-to-one assessment or psychotherapeutic relation. For that reason it seems to me that residency training programs must train him generically for a broad range of future possible professional responsibilities.

I have been asked how the above training program differs from the program for training psychiatric residents who someday will also serve as diagnostician-consultants and psychotherapists in a variety of new roles which society asks of them. It is my observation that in my own actual everyday professional work in these two roles I reflect more my own training background in the science and profession of clinical psychology than I do the training background in the science and profession of medicine of most psychiatrists. Yet I, like most readers, can identify some psychiatrists of my own acquaintance whose day-by-day professional practices (and teaching and research) cannot easily be differentiated from mine or those of some clinical psychologists of *similar* postdoctoral training and experience. Likewise, the same is true of some practicing clinical psychologists for whom psychiatrist counterparts can be found, often in the same or a nearby office (e.g., the psychologist who practices psychoanalytic psychotherapy exclusively). Except for the drugs and electroshock therapy used by the generalist psychiatrist in therapy, and a whole range of assessment techniques used by the generalist psychologist in psychodiagnosis, there is little which today differentiates the practices of many representatives (practitioners) of the two professions. Nevertheless, I believe this may become increasingly less so after the establishment of the psychological centers mentioned above. This belief is based on the assumption that many new postdoctoral training programs for psychologists will emphasize consultation roles to meet a variety of community needs, whereas the training programs for many psychiatric residents will continue to emphasize the two-person, doctor-patient consultative role so traditional in medicine.

One final point perhaps should be mentioned in order to clarify my use of the terms "residency" and "patient" and, thus, the apparent emphasis on a medical context in this paper. I have previously indicated that I did not wish to suggest the adoption of a medical model for the postdoctoral training of all clinical psychologists, especially not those clinical psychologists who eventually will work in industry, the schools, mental health centers, marital counseling centers, and other settings. Nevertheless, I do wish to acknowledge that for that small, or large, segment of today's pool of young clinical psychologists who wish to work with *patients*, the adoption of some features of a medical model is today still clearly necessary. One cannot effectively work with the wide range of patients today being referred to clinical psychologists, including those with clear medical conditions in and out of general hospital settings (e.g., serious depression, process schizophrenia, essential hypertension, and other psychosomatic conditions), without acknowledging these medical realities.[2]

The latter point is intimately related to the question of "patient" versus "client" which seems to be, from the many journal references to it, a perennial problem for clinical psychology. Yet in actual professional practice it rarely has seemed a problem to me and, I suspect, to other professional psychologists. If I see an individual in a hospital, I call him what he, himself, and everyone else calls him: namely, a patient. If instead I see him in my office (after referral by an attorney, industrial firm, high school principal, a judge, or by self-referral) I refer to him as a client. If he is referred to my office by a physician who is continuing to see him medically, and my role is that of a collaborating consultant, I call him a patient. Thus, the *context* of the individual referral determines patient versus client status—not partisan professional considerations. In like manner, when I am called in consultation to see a person in jail and awaiting trial I refer to him as "prisoner" or by his given name, and not patient or client. A school child seen in school is referred to as "the student," and an executive in industry as, for example, "the Vice President for Marketing." This *same* executive, when sent to me by his physician for a serious depression, with its multitude of medical signs and symptoms, is a patient. If he consults me for a nonmedically related marital difficulty, he is a client. I believe that practising clinical psychologists have less trouble with these distinctions than do those psychologists who are not engaged in active professional pursuits. For the latter, whether a person seen by a psychologist is a patient or a client appears to be a matter for endless debate. As mentioned earlier, similar comments can be made to those readers who object to the term "resident" to describe our psychologist trainee. To call him by any other name in our setting would be inappropriate. He has, in some ways, as much in common with the medical resident as do, for example, the residents in surgery, psychiatry, pathology, or radiology. He also is as uniquely different from them as each is from the other. It is probably fair to say that some of the so-called medical specialties are sufficiently different today, one from the other, as almost to constitute separate professions. There already are indications that in the future the same may be true in psychology. For example, how much do present professional clinical psychologists in clinics, industry, and the schools have in common? I see the purpose of our residency training program to prepare the young clinical psychologist to be able to assume a responsible role in any of these, and other, settings.

The reader may ask why I have not spelled out more of the details of how one actually trains a young psychologist resident to accept and discharge responsibility at a level comparable to that taught to students in other professions. The reason can be stated as clearly as hopefully it was in the earlier section which dealt with the mechanics of teaching consultation skills. I have not described it because it is a very complex process. It is a skill still taught best by *example*. How it is done can be demonstrated in a number of ways during any given day or week, but the process is very difficult to articulate. It has been my impression that the legal and medical professions also teach their students more by example than prescription the complex aggregate of personal-social philosophy, skills, and attitudes which make up responsible action. Mature professional decisions and actions reached with and executed after an appropriate balance among the needs of the patient, society, other colleagues, and social institutions can be guided, but, in my opinion, cannot as yet be taught by well-developed formal methods.

One of the inevitable challenges faced by every professional person is that of dealing effectively with real-life problems, no two of which ever are alike, and for which ready-made solutions rarely exist. Consequently, one of the important skills his teachers must help the psychology resident to learn is how to *live with uncertainty*; how to initiate a problem-solving approach in every instance in which he must make professional decisions even though the amount of helpful information available to him is minimal. In addition, we must teach him that to *deliberately* postpone action when one has no basis upon which to take responsible action is itself a responsible professional action. To wait until one has collected more clues, even when the pressures on him to do something *now* are great, is a difficult action, but one which in some instances is the action of choice. Clearly, like more experienced professionals, residents will differ among themselves in both their tolerance for ambiguity and in their ability successfully to discriminate procrastination from responsible action. Close preceptorship training, coupled with gradually increasing levels of responsibility across a sufficiently diversified range of human problems, hopefully, will help him learn the skills necessary to deal with and, inevitably, to live with uncertainty and ambiguity—one of the hallmarks of a professional.

Thus, because the resident is older than the typical predoctoral intern, and because our particular setting provides him with the daily opportunities to exercise his professional judgments, albeit with decreasing levels of guidance, by the end of his training period he hopefully will be making most, if not all, professional decisions without help from his clinical teachers. To go beyond this general description of how to train for responsibility would be as difficult for me at this time as, for example, it would be for a more senior corporation attorney to describe how a new law school graduate joining his firm learns to take responsibility for his own actions, or how a surgeon teaches a new surgical resident to become a surgeon. We all know that the setting for such training is a variable of major importance, and that on-the-spot guidance, when the rarely-to-happen-in-the-same-way-twice event occurs, is a crucial element for teaching the attitudes and skills which, through day-after-day reinforcement, result in a new set of values appropriate to responsible professional actions.

Thus, while the postdoctoral training program in clinical psychology described here takes place in a department of psychology of a medical school, it nevertheless is the writer's belief that the training given—most of it by preceptorship on the wards, in the clinics, in the library, and in the corridors and conference rooms, as well as in the offices of our faculty—offers an adequate beginning to the hopefully lifelong and never-ending training for the professional practice of general clinical psychology. Over the years the writer expects the graduates of this program to be practicing their profession in a variety of community settings: those calling for clinical, consultation, research, and administrative skills. It is also his belief that from the outset the graduates of this program will find it easier, less threatening, and professionally more rewarding to assume professional responsibility for their patients and clients than did his own generation of immediately post-Boulder-Conference clinical psychologists. For us, similar training was obtained primarily during a predoctoral internship, and at a time when the profession of psychology was just beginning to try to chart its identity. Whatever skills we later developed for responsible professional action, we acquired primarily through on-the-job experience and informal association with colleagues. Hopefully, for those who go through it, our residency training program will lessen the time required for acquiring such skills.

In closing, I wish to reiterate a point made earlier: While I believe our residency training program provides generic training in clinical psychological skills, those which can be used in a variety of new settings, I do not hold up this program as a model for a large segment of tomorrow's clinical psychologists. Our profession clearly is still in a state of rapid change. The program here described is but one of the experiments in training called for at Boulder, Miami, Stanford, Princeton, and in numerous meetings of the Education and Training Board of the APA. Training programs in other models, many of them also generic, currently are available or being developed. I see this heterogeneity in training models, in contrast to the homogeneity of the past 2 decades, as one of clinical psychology's greatest current assets.

NOTES

1. These PhD degrees, along with those in anatomy, biochemistry, physiology, and several other basic sciencies, are awarded by the University even though our Medical School has faculty and budgetary autonomy.

2. The arguments extant as to whether neurotic or psychotic conditions are behavioral or medical are, in my opinion, partisan debates which sometimes submerge the sufferer's interest to those of the professionals involved. No clinical psychologist who wishes to deal professionally with neurotic or psychotic conditions can be impervious to the physiologic, biochemical, or medical concomitants of these conditions (i.e., the fact that behavior can have multiple determinants), even though he acknowledges that he is not professionally qualified to deal with them. Many scientists, including Bush (1962) in the following passage, have presented convincing evidence that biochemical dysfunctions often mimic purely behavioral ones: "The increases in concentrations of cortisol in plasma and in the excretion rate of metabolites of cortisol that are seen during such relatively common and mild periods of anxiety as being given an oral examination or interview for a senior position are such as are seen otherwise only in patients with severe Cushing's syndrome. Much further work is needed to elucidate the question of what part this phenomenon might play in psychosomatic disease [p. 322]." Thus, if psychological centers someday replace today's medical centers for training those clinical psychologists who wish to take professional responsibility for *patients*, these psychological centers will need, as is the case today, to continue to provide consultative teaching to their students from representatives of medical and medically allied professions. This will not, of course, be necessary for those clinical psychologists being trained to work with clients in the schools, industry, counseling centers, and similar settings.

REFERENCES

ALBEE, G. President's message: A declaration of independence for psychology. *Ohio Psychologist*, 1964, *10*, No. 4.

ALEXANDER, I. E. Postdoctoral training in clinical psychology. In B. B. Wolman (Ed.), *Handbook of clinical psychology*. New York: McGraw-Hill, 1965, in press.

AMERICAN PSYCHOLOGICAL ASSOCIATION, Committee on Training in Clinical Psychology. Recommended graduate training program in clinical psychology. *American Psychologist*, 1947, *2*, 539–558.

BASOWITZ, H., & SPEISMAN, J. C. Program support for training by the National Institute of Mental Health: 1947–1963. In L. Blank & H. P. David (Eds.), *Sourcebook for training in clinical psychology*. New York: Springer, 1964. Pp. 43–60.

BLANK, L., & DAVID, H. P. (Eds.). *Sourcebook for training in clinical psychology*. New York: Springer, 1964.

BUSH, I. E. Chemical and biologic factors in the activity of adrenocortical steroids. *Pharmacological Reviews*, 1962, *14*, 317–445.

KUBIE, L. S. Elements in the medical curriculum which are essential in the training for psychotherapy. *Journal of Clinical Psychology*, 1948, *4*(Monogr. Suppl. No. 3), 46–51.

MATARAZZO, J. D., & DANIEL, R. S. Psychologists in medical schools: Personal, professional, academic and scientific characteristics. *Journal of Neuropsychiatry*, 1957, *4*, 93–107.

MAYMAN, M. Postdoctoral professional training: How and why? In L. Blank & H. P. David (Eds.), *Sourcebook for training in clinical psychology*. New York: Springer, 1964. Pp. 140–151.

ROE, ANNE, GUSTAD, J. W., MOORE, B. V., ROSS, S., & SKODAK, MARIE (Eds.). *Graduate education in psychology*. Washington, D.C.: American Psychological Association, 1959.

SANTOSTEFANO, S. Postdoctoral training in clinical psychology: A preliminary report by an interest group. *American Psychologist*, 1960, *15*, 213–215.

SASLOW, G., & MATARAZZO, J. D. A psychiatric service in a general hospital: A setting for social learning. *International Journal of Social Psychiatry*, 1962, *8*, 5–18.

12. *Survey of Psychotherapy Training and Activities of Psychologists*

BERNARD LUBIN

PROBLEM

THE evolving role of the clinical psychologist in the United States has come to include the practice of psychotherapy. This has come about partly in response to the great need for mental health personnel (1) and partly through the conviction of psychologists that psychotherapy, concerned as it is with the study and modification of behavior, also is within the sphere of their interest and competence. (4) Although the amount of psychotherapy done by psychologists has increased within the past 25 years, no data are available to indicate the amount and the nature of the training of psychologists in psychotherapy.

The development of adequate training programs for clinical psychologists by the universities and by the practicum agencies was greatly facilitated by the creation of the Evaluation and Training Board (ETB) of the American Psychological Association. In order to prevent premature standardization of training policies and procedures, the ETB purposely has avoided the promulgation of specific requirements and recommendations in the area of training for psychotherapy to the universities and practicum agencies. (3).

In 1956, the APA Division 12 Committee on Psychotherapy surveyed the universities which had approved graduate programs in clinical psychology with the purpose of assessing the nature and extent of the training in psychotherapy which they offered to psychologists. The Committee's report (2) reflects differences among the universities in matters of general philosophy and procedures.

Another factor which has worked toward increasing the diversity in psychotherapy training of clinical psychologists is the trend toward the development of specialty training programs at the postdoctoral level (7). A considerable number of psychologists have taken additional training in psychotherapy by means of these postdoctoral programs or through private arrangements for supervision in psychotherapy. The present investigation was initiated to collect current information about the psychotherapy training and activities of psychologists.

METHOD

In the spring of 1960, a one-third random sample of the 1959 APA Directory listing of the membership of the Division of Clinical Psychology was surveyed by mail questionnaire. A cover letter, a four page questionnaire, and a stamped return envelope were sent to the sample (N = 776). The questionnaires were to be completed anonymously and returned within one month. Of the 776 questionnaires mailed, 32 were returned because the individual was deceased or because no current address was available. One month later, a follow-up letter was sent to the entire sample requesting completion of the questionnaire if this had not as yet been done. Eight percent of the respondents returned their questionnaires after the follow-up letter was sent. A total of 546 completed questionnaires were returned. Ten of these marked "retired" were discarded since the information would not represent the training, practice, or opinions of working psychologists. Considering the effective sample to be 744, the remaining 536 questionnaires represent a 72 percent return.

Reprinted from *Journal of Clinical Psychology*, 1962, *18*, 252–256, by permission of the *Journal of Clinical Psychology* and the author. Dr. Lubin is Director of the Division of Research and Training, Indiana Department of Mental Health, and Associate Professor, Indiana University School of Medicine.

RESULTS AND DISCUSSION

CHARACTERISTICS AND REPRESENTATIVENESS OF THE RESPONDENTS

Seventy-five percent of the respondents were male, 86 percent possess the Doctorate (Ph.D. or D.Ed.), 37 percent have Diplomate status, and 30 percent are Fellows of Division 12. They range from 26 to 70 years of age, median 41 years. Fifty-six percent received their highest degree since 1949.

The twenty universities at which the highest degrees were obtained and which comprise 71 percent of the sample are, listed in descending order of frequency: Columbia University Teachers College, New York University, University of Chicago, University of Minnesota, State University of Iowa, University of California (L.A.), University of California (Berkeley), Harvard University, Ohio State University, Purdue University, University of Michigan, Western Reserve University, Northwestern University, University of Pennsylvania, Stanford University, University of Pittsburgh, University of Texas, Yale University, University of Kansas and Boston University. Seventy-eight percent of the respondents were residing in the following 13 states which are listed in descending order of frequency: New York, California, Pennsylvania, Ohio, Illinois, Massachusetts, Maryland, Texas, Florida, Michigan, New Jersey, Kansas and Connecticut.

Forty-one percent indicate that at least half of their work schedule consists of psychotherapy. Seventeen percent are in full-time private practice and 12 percent have part-time private practices.

When asked to characterize their therapeutic orientation, the results were: eclectic (19%), neo-analytic (27%), classical psychoanalytic (12%), Rogerian (5%), learning theory (5%), and no response (2%). Fifty-seven percent have had personal psychotherapy with 46 percent having had one year or more. Those who have had personal

psychotherapy describe the orientation of their therapists as: neo-analytic (40%), classical psychoanalytic (39%), eclectic (14%), Rogerian (6%), and learning theory (1%). Comparison of some of the major characteristics of the respondents (sex, age, residence, percentages of Ph.D's, Diplomates, and Fellows of Division 12) with other data (5,6) reveals no serious bias in the present group.

TRAINING IN PSYCHOTHERAPY

Overall, the sample has had significantly more supervised experience in psychotherapy with adult patients in individual psychotherapy than with children in individual psychotherapy, with adults in group therapy, or with children in group therapy (Table 1). The order is as indicated. McNemar tests for the significance of the difference between correlated proportions were well below the .001 level in each analysis.

Table 2 shows the percentages of the sample having varying amounts of supervised training in each of the areas. In the case of individual therapy with adults and children, 80 to 60 percent of the sample respectively have had supervised training, but only 43 percent have had supervised training in group therapy with adults, and 91 percent have had no supervised training in group therapy with children. Group methods of treatment clearly lag behind individual methods as an area of practicum training for psychologists.

Table 2 presents data as to the number of cases in each of these areas on which supervision was received. As expected (Tables 1 and 2), individual therapy, both adult and children, have the highest medians. The upper ends of the ranges, 200 cases in individual therapy with adults and children and 50 groups in group therapy with adults and children, suggest that these respondents might have interpreted the term supervision in a different and less demanding manner. However, these extreme

TABLE 1. YEARS OF SUPERVISED PSYCHOTHERAPY EXPERIENCE (N = 536 AND DF = 1 FOR ALL ANALYSES)

Comparison	χ^2	p*	Higher Frequency
Individual Therapy with Adults vs. Group Therapy with Adults	233.00	< .001	Individual Therapy with Adults
Individual Therapy with Adults vs. Individual Therapy with Children	94.94	< .001	Individual Therapy with Adults
Individual Therapy with Adults vs. Group Therapy with Children	355.13	< .001	Individual Therapy with Adults

*p .001 = 10.83

TABLE 2. SUPERVISED PSYCHOTHERAPY EXPERIENCE PERCENTAGES REPORTING IN YEARS
AND CASES (N = 536)

Area	Years				Cases	
	None	1	1 to 2	< 2	Median*	Range
Individual Therapy: Adults	20	07	22	51	10	1–200
Individual Therapy: Children	38	15	25	22	7	1–200
Group Therapy: Adults	57	17	16	10	2	1–50
Group Therapy: Children	91	04	04	01	3	1–50

* Based on those reporting supervised experience.

cases did not seem to effect the medians materially.

Where was most of the supervised training received? Table 3 reveals that more than half of those respondents who have had supervised psychotherapy experience with adults in individual therapy received most of their training at the postdoctoral level, either in their work setting, by private arrangements, or through postdoctoral programs for training in psychotherapy. The major sources of training in group therapy with adults are the internship and postdoctoral programs. By contrast, the major sources of training in psychotherapy with children are at the predoctoral level, at the university or during the internship.

Table 3 indicates that supervision was provided more frequently by psychologists in the areas of group therapy with adults and individual therapy with children. Psychiatrists were more frequently the supervisors of individual therapy with adults. Three of the small number of respondents who claim supervised training in group therapy with children wrote in that most of their supervision was done by social workers.

Since about half of the respondents indicated that they received supervision from psychologists, it would be important to know something about the distribution of supervisory experience among psychologists. Table 4 reveals that slightly less than half of the sample have supervised students in individual therapy with adults, one quarter have supervised students in individual therapy with children or in group therapy with adults, and only three percent claim to have supervised students in group therapy with children.

Unfortunately, data on the psychotherapy training of the other mental health professions are not available for comparison. It would be of interest, for example, to know if the larger amount of training in individual psychotherapy with adults is true of other professions as well.

It should be noted that "supervision," a key term in this investigation, has not been defined. Cursory observation indicates that supervisory activity varies a great deal from situation to situation. For the purpose of this investigation, it was felt that a restrictive definition of supervision would be premature.

Since it has been estimated that a considerable number of psychologists engaged in clinical activities are not affiliated with Division 12, information about these non-affiliates is necessary before the findings of this investigation can be generalized with confidence beyond the present population.

TABLE 3. MAJOR SOURCE OF TRAINING (PERCENTAGES)

Area	University	Internship	Postdoctoral	Psychologist	Psychiatrist
Individual Therapy: Adults	16	31	53	41	59
Individual Therapy: Children	33	44	23	53	47
Group Therapy: Adults	09	42	49	60	40
Group Therapy: Children	25	49	26	50	50

TABLE 4. NUMBER OF YEARS IN WHICH RESPONDENTS SUPERVISED THE PSYCHOTHERAPY OF OTHERS (PERCENTAGES)

		Years	
Area	*None*	*1-3*	*3>*
Individual Therapy with Adults	55	17	28
Individual Therapy with Children	76	13	11
Group Therapy with Adults	75	16	09
Group Therapy with Children	97	02	01

SUMMARY AND CONCLUSION

A one-third random sample of the 1959 membership of Division 12 of APA was surveyed by mail questionnaire concerning their psychotherapy training and activities. Characteristics of the 72 percent of the sample that responded are described. Among the more salient findings were that the respondents have had significantly more supervised experience in individual methods of treatment and with adult patients.

NOTES

* This investigation was supported by a grant from the Association for the Advancement of Mental Health Research and Education, Inc. Appreciation is expressed to James Norton, Harry Brittain, Eugene E. Levitt, Gordon A. Barrows, William U. Snyder, and Frederick C. Thorne for assistance and suggestions.

REFERENCES

1. ALBEE, G. W. *Mental health manpower trends*. Report of The Joint Commission on Mental Health. New York: Basic Books, 1959.
2. AMERICAN PSYCHOLOGICAL ASSOCIATION, Division of Clinical Psychology. Report of the Committee on Psychotherapy (Dittoed), July 17, 1956.
3. AMERICAN PSYCHOLOGICAL ASSOCIATION, Education and Training Board. Criteria for evaluating training programs in clinical or in counseling psychology. *Amer. Psychologist*, 1958, *13*, 59-60.
4. ELLIS, A., NUDES, J. and RIESS, B. F. Qualifications of the clinical psychologist for the practice of psychotherapy. *J. clin. Psychol.*, 1955, *11*, 33-37.
5. KELLY, E. L. Clinical psychology—1960: report of survey findings. *Newsltr* (Division of Clinical Psychology of APA), 1961, *14*, 1-11.
6. MENSH, I. M. Clinical psychology in transition. *Newsltr* (Division of Clinical Psychology of APA), 1960, *13*, 9-10.
7. SANTOSTEFANO, S. Postdoctoral training in clinical psychology: a preliminary report by an interest group. *Amer. Psychologist*, 1960, *15*, 213-215.

13. *A Declaration of Independence for Psychology*

GEORGE ALBEE

PSYCHOLOGY has reached a crucial choice point in its development. We are pressing the limits of growth imposed by our present structure. Indeed, developmental distortions have been occurring for a long time. Like the ancient Chinese habit of binding women's feet, the distortion of our field, particularly of clinical psychology, has come to be regarded by many as beautiful and proper.

We see attempts to perpetuate and institutionalize the distortions by splitting off a separate profession of applied clinical psychology from its home in a discipline rooted in scientific and philosophic origins.

In my recent OPA presidential address I examined some of the cultural forces which affect the appropriateness and timeliness of our psychotherapeutic approaches and suggested that while a concern with psychotherapy is of great significance to the development of psychological theory it should not become the blind alley into which our training efforts are diverted.

I would like to advance the hypothesis that most of our present problems are derived from one clear-cut error which we made nearly twenty years ago when we decided to train clinical psychologists in medical settings. Let me elaborate this argument and urge a solution. The next decade is the crucial one for us. If we permit clinical psychology to be split off, or if we drive it off, the power and strength of our science-profession will be dissipated. If on the other hand we find a way to increase the centripetal force there are practically no limits to our horizons.

Most of the strong established professions control their own field work resources. Every medical school has a controlling interest in a complex of first-class University Hospitals where students of medicine receive excellent practicum training. As a general rule professors of medicine

and professors of surgery at the medical school head these departments in the affiliated hospitals. Sometimes medical schools work out agreements with other community hospitals where they place students and invariably the school arranges appointments in such a way as to have a tremendous influence on the hospital.

Other professions have long ago discovered the importance of controlling their own practicum facilities. Schools of Dentistry operate dental clinics as part of their ongoing training resources.

The profession of social work sends its students outside the university for their field work experience and while this represents a different pattern from the training of professional physicians and dentists in captive clinics and hospitals, a great many social work students are trained in agencies where the director is a social worker and the power structure is controlled by social workers.

It is when we come to the so called "ancillary" professions—nursing, occupational therapy, rehabilitation therapy, recreational therapy, etc.—that we find students being trained in agencies completely dominated and controlled by some profession other than their own.

Whether we like it or not clinical psychologists' training is much closer to the pattern of the "ancillary" professions than it is to the powerful independent professions. Clinical psychology students are guests in other peoples' agencies and hospitals.

In many places the patterns and grooves are so well worn as to be perfectly comfortable and natural-seeming. For years trainees in many clinical settings have been "completely accepted" and allowed to perform all of the tasks and techniques which psychology has insisted should form a part of their training. Other places, not so smoothly honed, are always struggling to achieve Freedom Now for psychologists. We all know these places where the official policy is that psychology students may engage only in diagnostic testing, but where the departments from which the students are sent

Reprinted from *The Ohio Psychologist*, June, 1964, by permission of *The Ohio Psychologist* and the author. Dr. Albee is Professor and Chairman, Department of Psychology, Western Reserve University.

understand that this official policy can usually be "handled" on a personal basis by the captive psychologist-supervisor who personally vouches for the acceptability of the given student and gets exceptions to policy made by the powers that be.

The pattern of training that was set by the Veterans Administration Clinical Psychology Program in 1945 has nurtured and strengthened psychology more than anything else. It may seem odd and belated to begin asking questions about whether we would do it over again if we could choose.

A large generation of clinical psychologists has been trained as guests in houses not our own. Psychology in the VA is strong and viable and it continues to be a major source of support for our graduate students in clinical psychology.

But it, like most field work agencies, is a setting under the total and sometimes incompatible control of medicine. Living in such settings psychologists have become nimble as pickpockets, adaptable as rats, and quick-witted as con-men, but they have not developed a separate professional image for themselves.

In many ways, too, clinical psychologists, like well-treated slaves in other empires, have unconsciously adopted the values, the language, and the manners of their owners and masters. A few of us have been arguing for years that disturbed people are not *sick*, that they should not be regarded as *patients* to be *treated* etc., etc. Only recently have I realized that only as we escape from the bondage imposed by our training requirements will we be able to stop speaking the language of our Egyptian masters!

The depth of the brain-washing to which the present generation of clinical psychologists has been exposed is evidenced by the degree to which our thinking accepts without resistance the medical model and the primacy of medicine's responsibility for the field of mental disorder.

The plain fact is that nearly all of the people seen in psychologists' offices or on the wards of "mental hospitals" are *not* sick. While the concept of mental illness had a sort of temporary usefulness in counteracting the older explanations of sinfulness and taint it is now a millstone around our neck.

I am leading up to the proposition that psychology, to free itself of the devastating handicap of training clinical psychology students on other peoples' territory must soon find a way of establishing its own captive practicum training center. The captive center must be big, expensive, and must include *all areas of psychology*, not just applied,

within its walls. It will not fit into an attic or into a basement, nor even into some of the new steel and glass buildings which now house psychology departments on our campuses. It must be a Psychological Center, perhaps semi-autonomous but with university faculty members occupying important positions within the Center and with private practitioners in the community coming in to donate teaching services in exchange for the relief and stimulation such activity will offer from the lonely life of the psychotherapist or the solitary life of the industrial psychologist surrounded by businessmen.

The Psychological Center will have many obvious advantages. It will be administered and controlled by psychologists and its program can be organized in such a way as to provide excellent and varied training to our students.

The Center will solve several of the most persistent and damaging characteristics of clinical training available up to the present. One has been the lack of opportunity for graduate students in clinical psychology to obtain ongoing research experience during most of their graduate program. Whatever ways this problem has been hidden it is certainly true that in most graduate psychology programs ample opportunities for on-the-job or in-the-lab research training have been available in experimental, physiological, industrial, and even social psychology, but the student in clinical psychology has been placed in settings where the choice of clients, and their handling, was organized not at all for his training but for other purposes. I know of very few university settings where clinical psychology students could participate in significant research with disturbed children or adults as an across the board and regular part of their training. This situation is reflected in Kelly's discovery that most practicing clinical psychologists (members of Division 12) were not doing any research. Other psychologists do research because they were reinforced for doing so as students. Most clinical psychology students are barred from doing significant research because guests can't help themselves. Those that survive and finally manage to do a dissertation to get their degree have found research something less than rewarding.

A Psychological Center must offer a variety of services. There will be a wing occupied by the industrial consultants, a floor occupied by social psychologists, and separate sections for engineering psychology.

The experimental people doing research on grants will occupy the whole of higher floors where animal odors will blow away. And the clinical people will offer a variety of services for children including diagnostic testing, play therapy, and parental counseling. Referral service for pediatricians and other professionals in the community, will be available. It will offer adult counseling (I hope we can get rid of the term psychotherapy but I am not optimistic) in some quantity.

A whole new psychological vocabulary will come into its own. The people coming to the Psychological Center for service will not be called patients, because it will be *Our* center and not *Theirs*. The air will be fresh and free. In the cafeteria psychologists will talk with psychologists, and we will all return to the practice of educating each other by talking with each other.

Parapsychological personnel will have to be employed, of course! They will be treated with acceptance, dignity, and respect, though it will be made clear that decisions affecting the policies of the Center will be dictated primarily by considerations which affect the adequacy of training of the students in psychology. Other professions will be allowed to engage in counseling provided they have the genuine collaboration of a qualified psychologist.

Another part of the Psychological Center will be an experimental school. Components may include nursery schools for normal children and for special groups of children such as the academically talented, emotionally disturbed, and mentally retarded. An ungraded first three years should also be included. It is time for psychology to return to its rightful place in symbiotic relationship to education.

Among the benefits to be derived from the availability of a Psychological Center affiliated with graduate psychology programs is the expansion of professional training made possible. Despite attempts at increasing the output of trained psychologist over the past 15 years our output is still far below society's demand for trained psychologists.

So much of the support of our present training programs comes from federal training and research money that there is the danger that some future economy-minded Congress could destroy the whole training edifice in one economy action. By diversifying the sources of support, by drawing on client fees, children's tuition, endowment, and other local sources of support, in addition to federal grants, the opportunity for expansion would be paralleled by the strength that diversification of funding provides.

One of the most persistent demands from clinical psychologists is for post-doctoral training.

The practicing clinician, whether he works in an agency or in his own private office, feels a strong need to keep up with developments in the field and to sharpen and refine his techniques and knowledge. This is especially interesting when viewed against the difficulty that medicine has had in trying to get physicians interested in keeping up with the proliferation of knowledge in medicine.

Psychologists are exceedingly demanding in their search for continued training and education.

The availability of a Psychological Center would go a long way toward handling the need for post-doctoral training.

Zoltan Gross is quoted in the *PPP Newsletter* (February, 1964) as saying that psychology must develop a professional school inside the university. He recognizes clearly what Flexner pointed out 50 years ago—that any group which aspires to be a separate profession must have a theory, and also neophytes carefully selected, thoroughly rooted in the academic setting. No profession can survive unless its roots are in the academic community.

One of the problems that besets psychology is the fact that it has grown up in the context of the Graduate School where it is one department among many.

This sibship status has had the effect of limiting the size of our graduate programs. Even though we have grown faster than any other academic discipline there are limits to our growth imposed by the understandable reluctance of other departments long established in the academic tradition to see our new field outdistance the rest. All sorts of subtle controls are imposed on psychology whether it be resistance to the expansion of its faculty, opposition to a separate building, or simply the problems of communicating with deans who frequently are naive about the subject matter and growth trends of psychology.

Not being a separate school most departments are forbidden to conduct fund-raising drives. Although departments of psychology now are at least as large in terms of budgets, number of students, number of degrees, or whatever criterion we accept as a measure of size, as many of the separate professional schools, they cannot raise their own capital endowment funds for their own purposes. This may be one of the ultimately convicing arguments for a separate professional school because of the need to finance the Psychological Center.

I want to make it clear that I am not proposing that Psychological Centers be exclusively part of University departments. There is no question that psychology is going to offer more service to the public rather than less as we discover new methods and techniques and as the public comes to view psychology as a source of help.

The pattern of private practice involving an individual practitioner in a private office seeing an endless stream of middle-aged neurotics for psychotherapy need not be the institutional structure under which psychological services are made available to the public. I would like to urge private practitioners to examine the feasibility of constructing a Psychological Center of the sort I am proposing where diversified services could be offered and where all of the advantages of a heterogeneous co-operative program would be available. It is my conviction that psychologists are sufficiently intelligent to be able to devise patterns which retain most of the advantages of individual practice while at the same time taking advantage of the strength to be found in centralized intake, shared case work services, ease of referral, public visibility, and such public service programs as emergency intake, suicide prevention, centralized accounting and business operation, etc.

Perhaps at first the Psychological Center would claim only the part-time co-operation of individual practitioners in clinical and industrial psychology. I am confident that before long it could absorb practically all of the time of any number of psychologists.

What I am suggesting is that just as a university center would provide the setting for training students it also may provide a model of excellence for other private centers to emulate.

I am sure that I do not have to spend more time itemizing the advantages of central psychological operations. In the clinical field let us take the example of a central record room. One of the problems in evaluating the effectiveness of psychotherapy, or of evaluating most forms of clinical procedure has been the unavailability of comparable records. By drawing on the enormous reservoir of knowledge in psychology it would be easy to set up routine procedures for the recording of detailed information on clients—on their performance on tests, their family history, educational background, etc.

I believe that one of the most compelling reasons for the sort of Center that I am proposing is that it will bring clinical psychological training back into psychology and well re-establish the valid principle that the essential functions of the clinical psychologist are diagnosis, therapy and research.

III
ROLES AND
FUNCTIONS

The traditional major functions of the practicing clinical psychologist have been diagnosis (primarily by means of formal test devices), psychotherapy, and research. These are presented respectively by Klopfer, Sundberg, Ayllon, and Schofield. Ayllon's paper was selected because it describes a form of therapy usually termed *behavior modification*, which has been developed largely by psychologists. The survey by Schofield is now fifteen years old. A more current account of the research interests of clinical psychologists is, unfortunately, not available. It is possible that these interests have changed since 1952. Schofield's survey serves, nevertheless, to give some idea of the traditional scope of clinical psychology's research endeavors.

In recent years, the functioning of the clinical psychologist has been extended in response to demand. Some of these newer functions, like administration and consultation, are noted by Mill and in the report of the American Psychological Association Ad Hoc Planning Group.

Clinical psychologists are found today in an ever increasing number of settings. Many of these—the university clinic, state hospital, the correctional institution, the school, industry, government, and private practice—are discussed in various papers in this part. There are both constant and idiosyncratic elements of functioning of the psychologist in these diverse environments. The reader should bear in mind that the roles presented by no means exhaust the burgeoning variety of settings in which the clinical psychologist is currently employed.

14. *Mental Health and the American Psychological Association*

AD HOC PLANNING GROUP ON THE ROLE
OF THE APA IN MENTAL HEALTH PROGRAMS
AND RESEARCH

THE mission of the Ad Hoc Planning Group on the Role of the APA in Mental Health Programs and Research was to aid the Board of Directors in its task of formulating policies. As the history of the Ad Hoc Planning Group during the past two years shows all too clearly, its work has been full of difficulties and frustrations. Many of the group's problems and resistances have been due to the complexity of the field of mental health itself and to the shortcomings of its label. "Mental health" means many things; communication and thinking are impeded when different persons, or the same persons at different times, apply different meanings to the term.

With awareness of the complexities of its task, the Ad Hoc Planning Group has had to consider: (*a*) what mental health is, (*b*) what roles psychologists can play in mental health, (*c*) what the APA as an organization might do about mental health, and (*d*) what the functions are of a committee on mental health within the APA.

WHAT IS MENTAL HEALTH?

While all thoughtful psychologists agree that many of the meanings implied by the words "mental health" are of great importance, few of them like the term. Many feel that both of the words have obsolete—even obnoxiously obsolete—connotations. "Mental" implies that the field has to do with a separate part or property of a human being, his "mind." Without espousing a radical

Reprinted from *American Psychologist*, 1959, *14*, 820–825, by permission of the American Psychological Association. Harold M. Hildreth was Chairman of the Planning Group, which included Jerry W. Carter, Jr., Andie L. Knutson, Fillmore H. Sanford, Laurance F. Shaffer, M. Brewster Smith, and Albert S. Thompson.

behaviorism, psychologists generally agree that the hypothesis of a "mind" apart from a "body" does not represent the best conceptual structure of our science. "Health," too, is a dubious word that inevitably evokes an image of its opposite, "illness." These are medical terms; and, even apart from any jurisdictional factionalism, most psychologists doubt that all of the attributes of human interpersonal living which run from effective satisfaction to fruitless distress are appropriately categorized on a continuum from "well" to "sick." Many psychologists wish that better terms could be devised and win acceptance.

But we are probably stuck with "mental health" and "mental illness," and they are perhaps no worse historical accidents than, say, "psychophysics." Having given vent to our repugnance, we may abandon quotation marks and settle down to the task of understanding what these strange words signify in our culture's language.

HISTORICAL DEVELOPMENT

A salient consideration is that mental health and its predecessor mental hygiene are terms with changing meanings. They do not have the same meaning today as they did a generation ago, and their significance is still in the process of evolution. In succession, the words have meant the humane care of psychotic patients; the treatment, cure, and rehabilitation of all mental patients; and the prevention of mental illness of any degree. The most recent meanings have included the establishment of conditions conducive to effective and satisfying individual lives and the improvement of society so as to facilitate widespread satisfaction and effectiveness. The significance of the term mental health has grown by accretion. As new meanings have been added, the old ones have not been relinquished.

Mental health, then, means not one thing but many things, and it is probably futile to argue that one meaning is better or higher than another. Instead, psychology and other professions must attend to the wide range of issues that the term implies.

Serving the Mentally Ill. A continuing mental health activity is, and will be for unpredictable years to come, the identification, treatment, and rehabilitation of a distressed segment of the population labeled (unsatisfactorily) as mentally ill. The concept of treatment has expanded in recent years to include children and adults in the community who may benefit from professional help, as well as patients in hospitals and clinics. In spite of the recent emphases on the newer meanings of mental health, remedial efforts with identified deviates consume more professional services, including those of psychologists, than the other aspects combined.

Preventing Mental Illness. The prevention of overt illness is a goal of all hygienic enterprises, as exemplified in some of the greatest triumphs of medicine: the control of smallpox, of yellow fever, and more recently of poliomyelitis. The not inconsiderable efforts now devoted to preventive mental health—through consultation and education with families, schools, and communities—are, frankly, characterized by untested methods and unknown results. At their best, they are based on laudable zeal and on a conviction that it is better to apply our present meager knowledge than to do nothing. Although there are many doctrinaire theories about prevention, scientists generally recognize that it represents a virgin area for research.

Aiding Personal Growth. Psychologists—and many psychiatrists, sociologists, educators, and others as well—are not satisfied with the negative aim of minimizing mental illness. They feel that a more positive objective is needed, of aiding the development of persons who are creative, free, happy, foresightful, and socially responsible. No one can deny the merit of such aims for the fulfillment of individual aspirations. These aims are not the exclusive property of the mental health professions but are shared with philosophy, religion, education, and the social sciences. Except for a general conviction that interpersonal learning processes are involved, however, no one really knows how to achieve the objectives.

Improving Social Conditions. The most recently recognized task of mental health is to bring about individual well-being by modifying communities and larger units of society. This worthwhile aspiration recognizes that the possibility of contributing to the self-realization of a person is limited if his culture is a destructive one. Here, as in the preceding aim, hopes have run ahead of soundly established knowledge. Of course, there are enough obvious social evils to correct so that action does not have to wait indefinitely.

Mental health, logically, is an aspect of public health, although it has been publicized without evident relationship to the general public health movement. One feature that commends the amalgamation of mental health with public health is the social orientation of the latter field. Public health places emphasis on prevention and on the changes in public attitudes that are required before preventive measures will be accepted and thereby made effective. The earlier and perhaps narrower aims of mental health in treating or even in preventing psychoneuroses and psychoses tend to imply work with single individuals. The newer concepts of personal development and social evolution are more harmonious with the methods used by general public health for education and community action.

PSYCHOLOGISTS IN MENTAL HEALTH

Mental health is not simple, and neither are the roles that psychologists play in it. Within each of the four types of mental health activity that have been named, psychologists may perform several functions. They may be researchers, practitioners, educators, persuaders, organizers, or administrators. Just as no single discipline or profession encompasses the mental health problem, no one specialty in psychology has a monopoly on relevance to it. Furthermore, psychologists may serve the aims of mental health, in any of their roles and specialties, in a number of settings such as hospitals, government agencies, universities, schools, and communities.

In the view of the Ad Hoc Planning Group, therefore, psychologists can make their greatest contribution to mental health in the long run simply by *being* psychologists, by pursuing the many curiosities, engaging in the many activities, sustaining the lively concerns with people and their behavior that have become characteristic of psychology as science and profession. So long as the effectiveness of existing ameliorative approaches remains substantially unproved, the scientific attitude of skepticism and experimentation will be an important ingredient of the psychologist's contribution. Psychologists will do well to maintain the identity of psychology as a science and profession, and their own identity as non-hyphenated psychologists.

At the same time, there are obviously special directions of activity and interest that bear more directly on mental health problems. The various roles of service and practice with individual clients have in recent years proved attractive to many. The present need is for psychologists to interest themselves in roles through which they have a more widely ramifying impact on people. Psychologists can use their background and skills to great advantage as identifiers and crystalizers of community problems. For those who will use their imagination along these lines and anticipate, as well, the problems emerging, there is a virtually limitless field of psychological contribution. To be effective, however, they will need to become students of community organization as well as of individual propensities and behavior.

This view of the prospects suggests that psychologists will not need to fight aggressively to win recognition for their potential contribution to society's mental health problem. The better mousetrap, when psychologists have one, quickly produces the well-worn path. As individuals as well as in their national and state organizations, psychologists may increasingly find it necessary to set priorities, to choose carefully among the competing demands that are likely to be made on them.

RESEARCH

The description of mental health activities reveals the many gaps in our knowledge. We are not totally ignorant, of course. Some considerable knowledge exists in the areas of the identification, treatment, and rehabilitation of frankly disordered persons. Psychological research has made substantial contributions to the solution of these problems. We have some useful foundations from general and social psychology than can contribute to the newer mental health objectives by providing understandings of motivation, learning, and the assessment and modification of attitudes in normal as well as in disordered persons. But our present knowledge is far from adequate. Inventive as well as evaluative research is critically needed.

Among the professional persons concerned with mental health, psychologists are, by tradition and training, better equipped than most to design and carry out research studies. Although other professions also contribute to research, psychology's most distinctive contribution which least overlaps that of others lies in the task of investigation.

The need for research and psychology's distinctive capacity for it lead to the conclusion that the major role of psychologists in mental health should be in the designing and carrying out of research studies. Research is of many kinds, and basic studies not originally conceived in relation to mental health will continue to make indispensable contributions. Research on normal psychological development has particularly direct relevance. More explicitly applied research does not, however, develop without a real awareness of the problems to be attacked. For this reason, if for no other, psychologists must become involved directly in community enterprises. Since the community is a natural laboratory for the study of man in his relations to other men, closer involvement of psychologists in the community should advance theoretical understanding as well as applied research in the areas of mental health.

SERVICE

Large numbers of psychologists are already involved in providing mental health services. A view of the future seems to suggest, however, that the individual approach now common—the therapist and one client at a time—will never meet the needs of mental health fully. New graduates in psychology who are entering community services need to be convinced in attitudes and trained in skills that will permit a more efficient use of time. Lacking research, the exact course of more efficient practice is not clear. Perhaps it will be in the work of a highly trained person with groups of persons; or indirectly by training and supervising less expensively educated and more available workers; or by serving with and through community leaders such as teachers, clergymen, and the like.

COMMUNICATION

Psychologists are, in the main, very good communicators with one another. No cognate field has more journals or better attended professional meetings. But communication among various specialties within psychology needs further improvement. Psychologists concerned with mental health need to communicate their problems more effectively to those engaged in some areas of basic research and, in turn, need fuller acquaintance with relevant research opportunities and findings. Planned steps toward joint meetings and shared publications are clearly desirable.

Psychologists do not seem to have any special aptitude for communication with other disciplines, except in local face-to-face contacts. (Indeed, does any profession?) If the sharing of psychiatric, sociological, and other viewpoints with that of psychology is conducive to accomplishment in mental health, improvements in communication are needed.

Communication with the public is a third area within which psychologists may serve mental health. They may well assume increasing responsibility for speaking to local groups and participating in community enterprises.

THE APA AND MENTAL HEALTH

"The objects of the American Psychological Association shall be to advance psychology as a science, as a profession, and as a means of promoting human welfare." If mental health as broadly conceived is a major enterprise in promoting human welfare, then Article I of its By-Laws surely indicates that the APA has a concern for mental health. What specific activities in mental health should engage the attention of the APA, which does not as an organization conduct research or provide services to the public? Several may be suggested.

FACILITATION OF RESEARCH

Since research is probably the psychologist's most distinctive contribution to mental health, the APA's major function may well be the facilitation of research. Several specific activities fall in this category. Support for mental health research comes mainly from federal legislation and to a lesser extent from state appropriations. Contacts with government agencies responsible for research and with the Congress as by giving testimony at hearings are worthy of the most intensive and well planned efforts. Assistance may be given to state psychological associations for performing similar functions. Representations to foundations and other fund granting agencies and the circulation of information concerning sources of support may also be worthwhile activities.

It has sometimes been said in recent years that as much money for the support of research is available as psychologists can use constructively. Such a situation may exist with respect to the small grants typically given to individuals for the pursuit of limited projects. But some kinds of research most needed in the field of mental health must be on a large scale and extended over long periods of time. Examples are longitudinal studies from birth to adulthood to observe influences affecting mental health, and well controlled and well measured projects on a substantial scale to determine the effects on various indices of mental health of planned innovations in education and other community services. Such enterprises, if skillfully designed, might throw light on some issues that small studies will never solve. They would require financial support of a magnitude not now conceived.

EDUCATION FOR RESEARCH AND SERVICE

Since World War II, the APA has had much influence on graduate education in psychology through conferences and through a series of committees, now represented by the Education and Training Board. Without setting undesirably inflexible requirements, much could be done to influence the training of psychologists for research and service in mental health. It is inappropriate for this Ad Hoc Planning Group to spell out the details. Special meetings such as those recently held at Estes Park and Miami Beach, symposia at conventions, communications from the E&TB to universities, and other means can nudge the course of training for clinical and counseling psychologists, and perhaps for social psychologists and those in other relevant areas, toward a greater awareness of community mental health problems and their potentialities for research.

As in the case of facilitation of research, the APA can play a role in encouraging fuller financial provision for education toward research and service careers in mental health. Particularly desirable—and costly—is further long term support to promising individuals to launch them, post-doctorally, on research careers.

FACILITATION OF COMMUNICATION

Another contribution to mental health that might be made by the APA is the facilitation of communication through publications, symposia, and interdivisional and interdisciplinary meetings. The APA as a whole makes such resources available now. What is needed is their more intensively directed use for the specific goals of mental health. The function of communication might become a major concern of an APA committee on mental health.

RELATIONS TO OTHER ORGANIZATIONS

The relations of the APA to other national and international organizations that deal with mental health offer difficult problems. A few such organizations properly evoke mixed attitudes. Some of their activities have been highly constructive, as in increasing the public's awareness of mental health problems and in increasing the acceptability of mental health services. Other features are regarded less favorably by psychologists: the raising of substantial sums by national fund raising drives little or none of which is spent on research, their apparent pre-emption of mental health for psychiatry, and their concern for status.

The APA should surely maintain relations with the National Association for Mental Health and the World Federation for Mental Health. It seems important, however, to base the relationship on a substantive recognition of what psychology can offer to mental health, mainly in research although also in services. A contest for status or a "demanding of the rights" of psychologists, on the other hand, will predictably lead to hostility and continued distance. It does not seem overoptimistic to believe that psychology will win recognition more quickly by a display of its functional contributions than by self-seeking diplomacy.

The American Public Health Association seems to offer an immediately congenial relationship, because of its research orientation and its already interdisciplinary character. The relationship should be cultivated in a sincere effort to contribute to mental health, and not as a weapon in a contest for status.

THE STATUS OF PSYCHOLOGISTS

It is proper for the APA to be involved in the welfare and status of all psychologists as well as in the advancement of all psychology. A wise policy, however, would separate the concern for the status of psychologists who are engaged in mental health activities from the concern for making contributions to mental health. This consideration suggests that a committee that deals with mental health cannot also be charged with problems of status.

AN APA COMMITTEE ON MENTAL HEALTH

Exhortations that "the APA" do something are empty unless the doer is specified. As a corporate association, the APA does nothing; its deeds are performed by living persons: its officers, directors, representatives, Central Office staff, editors, boards, committees, and members. Who, then, should do something about mental health? The Ad Hoc Planning Group, at the request of the Board of Directors, makes these recommendations.

COMMITTEE ON MENTAL HEALTH RESEARCH AND PROGRAMS

It is recommended that the Board of Professional Affairs consider renaming the existing APA committee as the Committee on Mental Health Research and Programs, to give emphasis to the view that research is psychology's greatest potential contribution to mental health. The major objectives of the committee might well lie in the area of communication. As examples of its functions, but not in limitation of them, the committee might evoke the preparation of a series of articles summarizing research on various aspects of mental health, both to make the positive results more available to users and to display gaps which would stimulate new studies. It might encourage symposia, addresses, and reports not only on research but also on mental health needs and programs.

A major task might be the cultivation of interprofessional relationships. To this end, the APA's representatives to any interprofessional bodies dealing with mental health might well be members of the committee. Representation on other bodies might lead to a desirable exception to the customary APA practice of systematic rotation of committee membership. If a representative to another organization has achieved a position of responsibility in it, his continuance on the committee is in the interests of the APA.

The Committee on Mental Health Research and Programs could be charged to think and make recommendations about any matters relevant to its mission. Inventive contributions arise from a feeling of freedom to explore afield. Some functions of the APA in mental health, however, are best assigned to other bodies. Mental health is a large problem, and many branches of the APA need to become involved in it.

OTHER APA FUNCTIONS

The function of the facilitation of financial support for research and education in mental health will probably be exercised most effectively by staff members of the Central Office, under the guidance of the Executive Secretary and the Board of Directors. Only a continuing staff located in Washington will have sufficient acquaintance with conditions and persons.

The Education and Training Board needs to become involved with the improvement of training for research and service in constructive mental health. The Ad Hoc Planning Group sees no need for a new curriculum for a "mental health psychologist" and, indeed, sees danger in fractionation. But existing programs in clinical, counseling, and social psychology and perhaps in some other areas may need stimulation to prepare students for more effective research and participation in preventive and constructive mental health enterprises. One useful and inexpensive step would be the collection and circulation of accounts of the features of existing training programs which seem to contribute to education for roles in the promotion of positive mental health.

The status of psychologists and the setting of appropriate standards of training by civil service and other large employers remains an important function of the Board of Professional Affairs. It should not be confused with the contributions of psychology to mental health.

All committees and divisions of the APA should be made more aware of mental health in its newer and broader meanings. They may then see it not as a minor "clinical" specialty but as a human enterprise that merits the best contributions of psychologists generally.

15. *Toward an Understanding of Clinical Psychology*

CYRIL R. MILL

PSYCHOLOGISTS are understandably concerned that their professional discipline be understood and accepted by others. Recent studies show that the psychologist is still regarded by many persons in the medical profession as a "mental tester" (1). It is true that one of the chief contributions which can be made by a clinical psychologist (and there are five or six other sub-specialties in the field such as industrial psychology, experimental psychology, social psychology, educational psychology, and military psychology) is the skill and special techniques which he can bring to the problem of diagnosis of emotional maladjustments and learning problems. But this should not lead to the neglect of several other areas in which some psychologists can provide distinct service, such as consultation, training, research, administration, and individual and group psychotherapy. These and other services, in addition to the diagnostic function, are being provided in the clinics and hospitals of the Department of Mental Hygiene and Hospitals by persons trained in the field of psychology.

A few illustrations might show some of the varied activities in which psychologists in this Department are presently engaged.

CONSULTATION

Community groups and social agencies have called upon psychologists for consultation regarding problems of juvenile delinquency, to assist with the formation of a local Family Service Society, and for other problems related to mental health. Schools use psychological consultation for case conferences, workshops for parents on child development, and for the recommendations they can give in the operation of special classes, sheltered workshops, and facilities for cerebral palsied children.

Physicians interested in research have used psychological consultation to sharpen their hypotheses and plan their experimental design. Psychologists are coming to be seen as a source of information and consultation by an increasing number of civic groups, and are serving on boards of many social agencies.

TRAINING AND EDUCATION

Many psychologists enjoy teaching and affiliate themselves with universities or extension programs wherever possible. Training others to a better understanding of emotional maladjustments and what to do about them is a part of many psychologists' daily job. They may be called upon to speak to a one-shot affair, as at a P.T.A. meeting, in a workshop lasting eight to ten hours spaced out over several weeks, or in a more traditional course covering a semester. Many types of students are receiving this training, including psychiatric aides, policemen, housewives, nurses, medical students, teachers, and lawyers and ministers. Several psychologists in Virginia are now trained to use some of the newer instructional methods of group dynamics which have proven to be more effective than the traditional lecture method.

RESEARCH

The current survey of research in mental health in the South which is being conducted by the Southern Regional Education Board has pointed up the strong role of psychologists in research. Out of a total response to the survey of 576 individuals in the southern states, 325 held the Ph.D. degree, as compared to 128 who held the M.D. Most of these Ph.D's are psychologists, although not all are clinical psychologists. In Virginia the last few years have seen an increase in research activity both in the number of projects completed and the total number of psychologists engaged in research.

Reprinted from *Virginia Medical Monthly*, 1959, *86*, 708–710, by permission of the *Virginia Medical Monthly* and the author. Dr. Mill is Program Director for Consultation, National Training Laboratories.

Projects are presently underway on several psychological tests of intelligence and personality, on factors related to reading problems and underachievement, and on the effects of various drugs on perception, cognition, and intellectual functioning.

ADMINISTRATION

No one, these days, comes into the professional fields of mental health with specific training in administration. Yet everyone is aware of the desirability of good administrative practices for organizing an efficient and happy unit. Very often physicians are burdened with administrative duties for which they are not prepared or which they do not enjoy. In some clinics either the psychologist or the psychiatric social worker is delegated many administrative duties to everyone's satisfaction. In hospitals the psychologists are also found serving on committees and taking some of the administrative burden which does not entail the making of medical decisions. More of this could be done, and medical administrators could well consider ways and means of utilizing the administrative potential that exists among their psychological staffs.

INDIVIDUAL AND GROUP PSYCHOTHERAPY

In some of Virginia's hospitals more patient-hours of psychotherapy are provided by psychologists than by the medically trained staff. Group psychotherapy is being offered to patients just before discharge, and to the aged with gratifying results. Group and individual psychotherapy with children in hospitals as well as play therapy is largely the result of interest of psychologists in this field.

In some of the mental health clinics, all members of the team engage in psychotherapy, with group psychotherapy making this service available to greater numbers of people.

DIAGNOSIS

The role of the psychologist in diagnosis should not be omitted in this discussion. The unique contribution made by the psychologist to an understanding of a case is through his use of tests. Usually, in clinical procedure, different facets of the patient's problems of adjustment are contributed by each member of the team. Different diagnostic recommendations occasionally are offered by each team member but this is a reflection on no one, arising as it does from the fact that varying aspects are focused upon through the social history, through the psychiatric interview or neurological examination, and the psychological examination. The discussion of these differences provides for stimulating staff meetings and a clear understanding of the case dynamics. The final diagnostic labelling is a psychiatric responsibility.

The practice of referring all cases for a psychological examination is disappearing. Such a "shotgun" means of referral is wasteful of valuable time, and as referring sources gain an understanding of the kinds of questions best answered by making a psychological referral, wiser referrals result.

Harlow and Salzman (2) suggest that a request for a psychological evaluation of personality functioning would be appropriate under the following circumstances:

1. For evaluating possible underlying pathology, e.g., the suspicion of what appears to be neurotic symptomatology masking a schizophrenic process.
2. For evaluating the relative strength of different pathological trends in a patient, e.g., whether a depression observed clinically is primary or incidental to other pathology also present clinically.
3. For obtaining information about a patient which may be unobtainable through interview, e.g., the "hyper-repressive" patient.
4. For investigating the etiology of a symptom, e.g., the meaning of a conversion reaction.
5. For evaluating the advisability of initiating, continuing, or terminating hospitalization, e.g., when there is a question concerning the possibility of further decompensation.
6. For planning a psychotherapeutic approach, e.g., for deciding between supportive or interpretive therapy, e.g., by alerting the therapist to the forms of resistance and defense likely to be employed.
7. For an evaluation of change as a result of the therapeutic process.

Appraisal of intellectual functioning is appropriate:

1. For making a differential diagnosis, e.g., for legally declaring a patient a mental defective.
2. For making a disposition of a case, e.g., whether a patient has the intellectual capacity to utilize certain types of psychotherapy.
3. For evaluating the relationship between a patient's current functioning to his potential abilities, e.g., when a person failing in school is felt to have the capacity to perform more adequately.
4. When there is a question of disturbed thought processes, e.g., when schizophrenia is suspected.
5. For evaluating impairment of, or deterioration in, ability to perform cognitive functions, e.g., when organic involvement is suspected.

It is probable that within the next ten years the American Psychological Association will set the Ph.D. degree as the minimum essential for psychology as a profession. In clinical psychology, the Ph.D. means at least three years of graduate study, plus a one-year internship, plus research training in the preparation of a doctoral dissertation. In the near future, the Commonwealth of Virginia must review its standards for the employment of psychologists and adjust the pay scale to a level appropriate for psychologists who are fully trained.

Each year sees more effort by psychologists to improve the quality and quantity of their services.

The first step toward this end in any local situation is to establish satisfactory role-relationships based upon understanding of the other fellow and his job. This seems elementary, but a recent study revealed that in some hospitals in Virginia physicians new to the psychiatric setting did not know the difference between a psychologist and a social worker! As working relationships develop over a period of time, and each member learns more about how to ask the right question of the other, medical and psychiatric personnel find that they are deriving greater and more valuable services from their psychological colleagues.

REFERENCES

1. ZANDER, ALVIN, COHEN, ARTHUR R., and STOTTLAND, EZRA. "Role Relations in the Mental Health Professions." Ann Arbor: U. of Mich. 1957.
2. HARLOW, ROBERT G., and SALZMAN, LEONARD F. "Toward the Effective Use of The Psychological Consultation." *Am. J. Psychiat.*, 115, 3, Sept., 1958.

16. The Role of Diagnostic Evaluation in Clinical Psychology

WALTER G. KLOPFER

It has become fashionable during recent years among some clinical psychologists to derogate the diagnostic evaluation as a professional activity. The purpose of the present article is to examine the various reasons given for this lowering of diagnostic evaluation on the hierarchy of professional activities and to see whether they will bear close scrutiny. Thus, cited below are the six major arguments given on behalf of the pessimistic position, each argument being followed by a critical evaluation.

1. "Diagnostic testing is a relatively simple activity which requires less skill and training than other responsibilities of the clinical psychologist, such as psychotherapy and research."

Recent reviews by Masling (1959) and Guertin et al. (1962), have demonstrated that psychological tests are not the simple laboratory procedures they are sometimes assumed to be. Not only are projective instruments subject to transient and situational influence, but even such seemingly objective instruments as intelligence tests can be manipulated while remaining within the standard administrative regulations. In order to interpret psychological tests properly it is necessary not only to have a great deal of clinical skill and experience, but also to be keenly aware of the limitation of predictive efficiency imposed upon the clinician by the normative data upon which predictive hypotheses are based, the level of awareness being tapped, the previous experience of the patient in taking tests, his current motivation and set, and of course, the biases, predispositions, and interprofessional relationships of the clinical psychologist doing the test interpreting. Viewed in this light the process becomes considerably more complex. It is the firm

conviction of this author that nowhere does the clinical psychologist utilize more of his resources than in the area of diagnostic evaluation. Psychotherapy, for all its complex theoretical bases, is still practiced mainly as an art at the functional level. Research can be ingenious and creative, but is often carried out at the hack level. However, to do an effective job of diagnostic evaluating requires the use of all the clinical psychologist's scientific and clinical training, plus the best intuition he is capable of bringing forth.

2. "Diagnostic evaluation, although of value, is not as worthy of taking up the psychologist's time as other activities of greater direct service to society, such as psychotherapy."

Of course there are many different ways of doing psychotherapy. The client-centered therapist has maintained stoutly that having available facts about the patient, whether these be anamnestic data or psychological test data, is of little value since the therapist does not plan the treatment but merely provides an atmosphere within which the patient can mature and grow on his own. It is outside of the scope of this paper to examine this particular assumption in detail, except to point out that only some patients can progress under these circumstances, and that it may be important to determine in advance which patients may or may not benefit from such a procedure. In order to answer this question, a diagnostic evaluation is a prime requisite.

Another method of psychotherapy, the orthodox psychoanalytic one, operates mainly at the intrapersonal or intra-psychic level. Thus the patient is in effect asked to shake hands with his own unconscious and to gain conscious control over his various motives so that he may not be overwhelmed in the future and his ego weakened by stresses from within. This seems to necessitate at least some diagnostic evaluation, even though this evaluation can be limited to intrapersonal types of evaluations such as are carried on by means of projective techniques.

Reprinted from *Journal of Projective Techniques and Personality Assessment*, 1962, 26, 295–298, by permission of the *Journal of Projective Techniques and Personality Assessment* and the author. Dr. Klopfer is Professor of Psychology, Portland State College, Portland, Oregon.

The third and more currently common approach to psychotherapy embraces a realistic evaluation on the part of the therapist of the entire phenomonological world of the patient. This includes his inner stresses, his adaptation to reality, his characteristic interpersonal methods, and the social acceptability of his behavior. A typical psychotherapist today feels that he is a responsible liason agent between interpersonal reality and the patient, and tries to be flexible in the stance he takes, so that the patient may learn the maximum amount from his association with the therapist. The therapist having the latter goal is likely to want a great deal of diagnostic information about his patient as soon as possible. This will include not only information about the patient's unconscious, but also the more conscious information about his self-concept, his characteristic attitude towards other people, the ego strength he is able to bring to bear in various situations, his social stereotypes, etc. Thus, the therapist would seemingly benefit from the entire array of psychological information which could be obtained from a comprehensive battery of psychological tests.

Further, it seems an unwarranted assumption that diagnostic evaluation is of value only in connection with psychotherapy planning. Certainly many times important administrative decisions can be aided by the presence of such data, clinical diagnoses with many behavioral implications can be made more accurately, and research can be carried on which will enable psychologists to show more understanding and utilize their time more productively as a result. There seems to be no necessary inconsistency between spending time in diagnostic evaluation or in research since, as was once pointed out to me by one colleague, "I am amassing research data every time I sit down to evaluate a patient."

3. "Diagnostic evaluation is so time consuming and lengthy and clumsy that it engages the psychologist far beyond the point of diminishing returns."

There is some justification in this criticism if one takes as a framework the typical activity of the psychologist of 15 years ago in carrying on diagnostic evaluation. I am sure that many readers will recall the time when it was not unusual to spend days, if not weeks, on administering, scoring and interpreting a group of projective tests and trying to gain every little nuance of "psychodynamic significance." However, this is not current psychological practice. In an effort to meet the needs of a situation as described above, the typical kind of evaluation carried on today relies in large part upon self-administered instruments such as the MMPI, the Sentence Completion Test, various adjective check lists, self-administering TAT's, and other such instruments. Typically, some of this information will be scored, tabulated and graphed by clerks and the time of the clinical psychologist is restricted to administering tests like the Rorschach, Bender and WAIS, and interpreting these together with others as a whole battery. In reading answers to questions on the ABEPP examination, the present author has discovered that the practice described above is quite typical of ABEPP candidates. They seem to feel that it gives them maximum information, and is still parsimonious as to time. This is in line with the current practice of emphasizing multi-level assessment of the individual, including evaluation of his public image, his conscious self-concept, and his underlying motivational system. Sticking strictly to projective or to intellectual instruments without integrating these with anamnestic data, interview data and the results of objective instruments of appraisal would seem to be frivolous in terms of the time consumed, and less accurate and important in terms of the information desired.

4. "There is little point in engaging in diagnostic evaluation because of the unknown and questionable validity of the various instruments involved."

This argument, of course, can always be brought to the fore, and contains some justice. Some clinical psychologists engaged in diagnostic evaluation tend to over-evaluate the accuracy of their instruments, and to give a false impression of finality to the recipients of their reports. However, it is possible to hierarchically arrange the tests and the interpretations from the tests in terms of the degree of evidence available for validity. Certainly one can make predictions with greater accuracy from the MMPI than from the DAP. At least the probability of the truth of the prediction can be specified in quantitative terms. Further, in comparing our science with other sciences that deal with probabilities, we need feel no shame regarding the status of diagnostic evaluation methods. For example, the medical science of obstetrics is not only unsuccessfully attempting to explain spontaneous abortions in many instances, but is still trying to get a rationale for the usual nine-month gestation period. Certainly, social sciences such as anthropology and sociology are often forced to fly by the seat of their pants to at least as great an extent as our science of clinical prediction. Further, the critics of diagnostic evaluation on the lack of validity basis often are enthusiastic psychotherapists. To claim that there is more evidence for the efficacy of psychotherapy than for the predictive accuracy of psychological tests is to be blind indeed.

5. "Diagnostic evaluation has no demonstrated value in helping to make administrative decisions, and is consequently a waste of time."

This criticism hurts because it is so often justified! All too often the clinical psychologist in submitting the report of his findings talks within a self-contained frame of reference of his own, and completely fails to be responsive to the needs of the referrer for specific recommendations. When the question involves hospitalization or outpatient treatment, promotion or non-promotion, execution or non-execution of a criminal, and other similarly significant decisions, it is of very little value to have the psychological report refer to the patient's latent homosexuality, masturbatory anxiety, confusion in sexual role, difficulty in interpersonal relationships, and other similar "psychodynamic" stereotypes that are so dear to the heart of many clinical diagnosticians.

However, it is the belief of the present writer, as documented in his recent book (Klopfer, 1960), that clinical psychologists can do better than this and can respond directly to the referral problems in a clear concise way. Thus, the present writer would agree that this criticism is justified, but not that it is insurmountable.

6. "Psychological reports are of no value since they are totally incomprehensible to anyone other than a psychologist."

This criticism is the unkindest cut of all, but unfortunately is justified all too often. Many of the recipients of our information find themselves alienated by the esoteric jargon and the flights of fancy so dear to the heart of clinical psychologists. They somehow sense that this is an exercise in mental masturbation rather than an attempt to communicate significant information that will have practical value. Whether our incomprehensibility is due to lack of real understanding of the concepts involved or whether it constitutes an attempt to maintain psychological distance between us and our referrers is difficult to say. At any rate, as long as such incomprehensibility continues to be manifest, it will serve as a barrier to the full acceptance and utilization of diagnostic evaluation by clinical psychologists.

CONCLUSIONS

Human behavior continues to be as complex as ever. There is no particular evidence of the increased sophistication of clinical psychologists in finding short-cuts to the alleviation of human suffering which will obviate the necessity of thorough idiographic evaluation. This article has expressed some doubts as to the wisdom and justification of by-passing diagnostic evaluation in clinical practice. Certainly the use of psychological tests continues to be an essential element in psychological research. A trend has been noted which consists of the greater integration of objective and real-life methods of diagnostic evaluation with those that are more projective and indirect. This trend leads to greater parsimony in the use of the psychologists' time and more detailed information available to the referrer, leading to better decisions and less waste of human resources. Finally, the present author has stated his position that the clinical psychologist uses his resources both as a scientist and as a clinician to the greatest extent in his function as a diagnostician. There is no aspect of the job of clinical psychologist which is more complex, more difficult, and more challenging.

REFERENCES

GUERTIN, WITT, et al. Research with the Wechsler Intelligence Scale for Adults, 1955–60. *Psych. Bull.*, 1962, *59*, 1–27.

KLOPFER, W. G. *The psychological report: Use and communication of psychological findings.* New York, Grune & Stratton, 1960.

MASLING, J. The influence of situational and interpersonal variables in projective testing. *Psych. Bull.*, 1960, *57*, 65–85.

17. The Practice of Psychological Testing in Clinical Services in the United States[1]

NORMAN D. SUNDBERG

WHICH tests are most used in clinical work these days? How do practices compare with earlier times? In what ways do clinical services differ? These questions come to mind in considering the practice of testing in hospitals and clinics in the United States. If one is to evaluate clinical practice, one must know what is going on. Yet the literature is very scanty. The most recent survey of clinical testing practices was done by Louttit and Browne (1947). Their 1946 study was based on returns from 43 institutions which were mainly college clinics. They also refer to a survey done in 1935. A few studies report on tests in special settings: Darley and Marquis (1946) surveyed practices in veterans guidance centers shortly after World War II; Swenson and Lindgren (1952) reported on the use of psychological tests in industry. Other than the studies reported by Louttit and Browne, there has been no general survey of clinical testing for at least 25 years.

PROCEDURES AND SAMPLE

The survey form consisted of a questionnaire about the agency and its testing practices and a check list for reporting the usage of specific tests. The check list included the most used tests from the Louttit and Browne study, tests with a high number of publications (Buros, 1953), and spaces for adding other tests. For each test, the respondent made a rating on the frequency of usage like that used in the Louttit and Browne study: 0 (never used), 1 (used occasionally), 2 (used frequently), or 3 (used with the majority of cases). The first survey request and one follow-up were conducted in the spring of 1959. Of the total of

304 agencies and hospitals, usable responses were obtained from 185 or 61%.

The intent of the sampling procedures was to obtain a broad selection of clinical agencies and hospitals from all over the United States. To this end, five different kinds of clinical services were selected from four different sources of information (American Board of Professional Standards in Vocational Counseling, 1958; American Psychological Association, 1959; Moore, 1958; National Association for Mental Health, 1955). Each state was sampled and additional random selections were made for every multiple of eight agencies listed. The respondents totaled 10% of all the agencies and institutions listed in the directories, and the original sample was 16% of the total. The numbers in the final sample on which this analysis is based were as follows: 27 Veterans Administration stations (all hospitals except for 3 clinics), 66 hospitals and institutions (including 39 state mental hospitals and 13 institutions for mental defectives), 53 outpatient clinics (37 of which were primarily child clinics), 23 counseling centers (of which one-third were affiliated with universities and most of the rest were community counseling agencies sponsored by organizations), and 16 university training clinics. In the total sample there was almost an exact balance between outpatient and inpatient services, and between adults and children (including adolescents) seen for testing.

FINDINGS AND COMMENTS

As might be expected from such a heterogeneous sample, testing practices differed greatly. The number of tests used by any single agency varied from 5 to 82 different tests. The median number of different kinds of tests was 26. The total number of tests administered in a year ranged from 18 in one small outpatient clinic to 14,230 in a large

Reprinted from *American Psychologist*, 1961, *16*, 79–83, by permission of the American Psychological Association and the author. Dr. Sundberg is Professor of Psychology and Associate Dean of the Graduate School, University of Oregon, Eugene.

TABLE 1. TESTS USED BY TEN PERCENT OR MORE OF THE TOTAL SAMPLE ($N = 185$)

Name of Test	Usage Rating Totals[a]			Total Mentions	Weighted Score	TM Rank	WS Rank
	1	2	3				
Rorschach	24	36	110	170	426	1	1
Draw-A-Person (Machover)	37	46	77	160	360	2.5	2
Thematic Apperception Test	50	63	47	160	317	2.5	4
Visual Motor Gestalt Test (Bender)	33	58	67	158	350	4	3
Stanford-Binet	69	46	31	146	254	5	6
WAIS	33	46	53	132	284	6	5
MMPI	55	42	26	123	217	7.5	8
Wechsler-Bellevue	64	30	29	123	211	7.5	9
Draw-A-Man (Goodenough)	67	29	23	119	194	9	10
WISC	33	34	47	114	242	10	7
Kuder Preference Record	66	26	16	108	166	11	12
House-Tree-Person	60	23	21	104	169	12	11
Goldstein-Scheerer Tests of Abstract & Concrete Thinking	74	18	1	93	113	13	16
Sentence Completion Tests (of all kinds)	(44)	(26)	(21)	(91)	(159)	(13–14)	(12–13)
Vineland Social Maturity Scale	42	32	8	82	130	14	13
Otis Self-Administering	52	21	7	80	115	15	14.5
Gray Oral Reading	61	14	3	78	98	16	18
Vocational Interest Blank for Men (Strong)	42	23	9	74	115	17	14.5
Porteus Maze Test	63	6	3	72	84	18	22
Rosenzweig Picture Frustration Study	60	10		70	80	19	25
Arthur Point Scale of Performance Test	62	5		67	72	20.5	28
Kohs Blocks	49	16	2	67	87	20.5	20.5
Kent Series of Emergency Scales	52	9	4	65	82	22.5	24
Make-A-Picture Story	52	13		65	78	22.5	26
Minnesota Clerical	44	15	3	62	83	24	23
Minnesota Paper Form Board	39	18	4	61	87	25.5	20.5
Sentence Completion (unnamed)	31	16	14	61	105	25.5	17
Kent-Rosanoff Word Association	52	8		60	68	27.5	29
Test of Mechanical Comprehension (Bennett)	34	24	2	60	88	27.5	19
Vocational Interest Blank for Women (Strong)	40	11	5	56	77	29	27
Gesell Developmental Schedule	42	9		51	60	30	31.5
Concept Formation (Hanfmann Kasanin)	42	3		45	48	31	40

Name of Test	Usage Rating Totals[a]			Total Mentions	Weighted Score	TM Rank	WS Rank
	1	2	3				
Ishihara Color Blindness	42	2		44	46	32.5	42
Purdue Pegboard	36	6		44	54	32.5	34
Differential Aptitude Test (Bennett)	28	13	2	43	60	34.5	31.5
Hunt-Minnesota Test for Organic Brain Damage	42	1	2	43	44	34.5	44
Stanford Achievement	30	10	2	42	56	36	33
Shipley Institute of Living Scale	26	10	5	41	61	37	30
Meier-Seashore Art Judgment	39	1		40	41	39	45
Minnesota Rate of Manipulation	34	5	1	40	47	39	41
Szondi Test	30	7	3	40	53	39	35.5
Study of Values (Allport-Vernon-Lindzey)	28	7	3	38	51	41	38
Minnesota Spatial Relations Test	29	5	2	36	45	42.5	43
Mooney Problem Check List	24	9	3	36	51	42.5	38
Primary Mental Abilities (Thurstone)	31	4		35	39	44	46.5
Childrens Apperception Test	16	16	1	33	51	45	38
Personality Inventory (Bernreuter)	27	1	2	30	35	46	52.5
Blacky	22	6	1	29	37	47.5	50
Pseudo-Isochromatic Plates for Color Perception	27		2	29	33	47.5	55
Adjustment Inventory (Bell)	23	1	4	28	37	50	50
Cattell Infant Scale	22	5	1	28	35	50	52.5
Wide Range Achievement	12	7	9	28	53	50	35.5
Healy Picture Completion, II	23	4		27	31	53	56.5
Leiter International Performance	18	7	2	27	38	53	48
Wechsler Memory Scale	17	10		27	37	53	50
California Test of Personality	20	4	1	25	31	55	56.5
General Aptitude Test Battery	19	4	1	24	30	56.5	58
MacQuarrie Test for Mechanical Ability	21	3		24	27	56.5	59
Babcock Test of Mental Deterioration	20	2		22	24	58.5	61
Symond's Picture Story Test	12	8	2	22	34	58.5	54
Monroe Diagnostic Reading	21			21	21	61	62
Rotter Sentence Completion	8	8	5	21	39	61	46.5
SRA Mechanical Aptitudes	16	5		21	26	61	60

[a] Usage Ratings: 1. Occasionally; 2. Frequently; 3. With Majority of Cases.

TABLE 2. SUMMARY OF THE TWENTY MOST USED PSYCHOLOGICAL TESTS IN EACH OF THREE DECADES
$N(1935) = 49$; $N(1946) = 43$; $N(1959) = 185$

Name of Test	Total Mentions			Total Mention Order			Weighted Scores		Weighted Score Order	
	1959	1946	1935	1959	1946	1935	1959	1946	1959	1946
Arthur Performance	67	29	26	20.5	15.5	3	72	58	28	7.5
Bell Adjustment Inventory	28	26	11	50	18.5	19.5	37	42	50	19.5
Bernreuter Personality Inventory	30	25	11	46	20	19.5	35	41	52.5	21
Binet-Simon	—	—	17	—	—	12	—	—	—	3
Draw-A-Man (Goodenough)	119	36	—	9	3.5	—	194	74	10	3
Draw-A-Person (Machover)	160	—	—	2.5	—	—	360	—	2	—
Gesell Developmental	51	24	20	30	22	8.5	60	45	31.5	17
Goldstein-Scheerer	93	4	—	13	97.5	—	113	4	16	100
Gray Oral Reading	78	32	7	16	8	34.5	98	63	18	6
Healy Picture Completion, I	—	19	17	—	35	12	—	28	—	38.5
Healy Picture Completion, II	27	30	24	53	12	4	31	44	56.5	18
Herring-Binet	—	7	16	—	77.5	14	—	7	—	90
House-Tree-Person	104	—	—	12	—	—	169	—	11	—
Ishihara Color Blindness	44	30	—	32.5	12	—	46	42	42	19.5
Kent EGY	65	30	—	22.5	12	—	82	50	24	12.5
Kent-Rosanoff Free Association	60	27	6	27.5	17	43	68	36	29	28
Kohs Blocks	67	26	6	20.5	18.5	43	87	47	20.5	15
Kuder Preference Record	108	23	—	11	25	—	166	46	12	16
Kuhlmann-Anderson	1	15	20	—	47.5	8.5	1	25	—	40.5
Kuhlmann-Binet Revision	18	11	19	—	61	10	26	14	—	65.5
Merrill Palmer	123	22	22	7.5	28.5	6	217	40	8	22
MMPI	—	29	—	—	15.5	—	—	50	—	12.5
Otis Intelligence	80	21	12	15	31.5	17.5	115	38	14.5	23.5
Otis Self-Administering	—	33	12	—	7	17.5	—	55	—	10
Pintner-Patterson Performance	72	12	22	18	54	6	84	20	22	53
Porteus Mazes	170	30	27	1	12	2	424	48	1	14
Rorschach	70	34	—	19	5.5	—	80	68	25	4
Rosenzweig Picture Frustration Study	42	—	—	36	—	—	56	—	33	—
Stanford Achievement	146	34	22	5	5.5	6	254	58	6	7.5
Stanford-Binet	—	43	49	—	1	1	—	112	—	1.1
Stenquist Mechanical Aptitude	74	13	17	17	50	12	115	21	14.5	48.5
Strong VIB (Men)	160	31	7	2.5	9	34.5	317	57	4	9
TAT	—	36	—	—	3.5	—	—	64	—	5
Terman Group	—	11	15	—	61	15	—	13	—	68.5
Thurstone Personality	—	10	14	—	66	16	—	11	—	74
Vineland Social Maturity	82	30	—	14	12	—	130	54	13	11
Visual Motor Gestalt (Bender)	158	12	—	4	54	—	350	15	3	60.5
WAIS	132	—	—	6	—	—	284	—	5	—
Wechsler-Bellevue	123	41	—	7.5	2	—	211	103	9	2
WISC	114	—	—	10	—	—	242	—	7	—

TABLE 3. TESTING PRACTICES OF DIFFERENT PSYCHOLOGICAL SERVICES, 1959

Name of Test	UAC % [a]	UAC FUI Rank [b]	CC %	CC FUI Rank	OPC %	OPC FUI Rank	H & I %	H & I FUI Rank	VA %	VA FUI Rank	Total %	Total FUI Rank
Rorschach	69	1	57	10	100	1	100	1	100	1	92	1
Draw-A-Person (Machover)	75	3	57	13.5	94	2	91	3	93	5	86	2
TAT (Murray)	69	2	61	12	100	3	83	7	100	6	86	4
Visual Motor Gestalt Test (Bender)	56	9	43	15	94	4	97	2	93	27.5	85	3
Stanford-Binet	56	6.5	70	13.5	87	6	91	6	56	3	79	7
WAIS	50	4	65	7.5	58	9	80	4	93	2	71	5
MMPI	75	12.5	74	10	43	11	73	11	85	4	66	8
Wechsler-Bellevue	56	11	83	7.5	51	13	71	8	78	8	66	9
Draw-A-Man (Goodenough)	56	9	48	16.5	66	7	80	9	41	22	64	10
WISC	50	5	48	16.5	72	5	85	5	4	27.5	62	6
Kuder Preference Record	69	9	87	1	40	22	52	17.5	82	7	58	12
House-Tree-Person	44	16.5	22	19	60	8	64	10	67	12	56	11
Goldstein-Scheerer Test of Abstract & Concrete Thinking	50	16.5	22	21.5	38	22	55	15	89	14.5	50	23.5
Sentence Completion Tests (Combined)	(38)	14	(17)		(43)		(50)		(93)		(49)	13
Vineland Social Maturity Scale	31	24	39	18	70	10	39	12	19	27.5	44	16
Otis Self-Administering	38	24	83	3	26	29.5	35	20.5	67	9	43	23.5
Gray Oral Reading	38	12.5	35	21.5	60	12	33	22.5	37	27.5	42	15
Vocational Interest Blank for Men (Strong)	56	29	78	2	21	22	26	27.5	70	11	40	34.5
Porteus Maze Test	38	20	13	28	38	22	47	17.5	44	17	39	38
Rosenzweig Picture Frustration Study	50	29	17	28	40	17.5	33	27.5	56	19.5	38	51
Arthur Point Scale of Performance Test	38	29	26	28	45	29.5	45	20.5	4	27.5	36	23.5
Kohs Blocks	44	24	13	21.5	30	15.5	44	16	44	17	36	27.5
Kent Series of Emergency Scales	6	24	26	21.5	21	29.5	53	14	44	22	35	27.5
Make-A-Picture Story	44	24	9	28	34	15.5	41	19	41	22	35	32
Minnesota Clerical	25	20	87	10	13	26	15	25	78	17	34	20.5
Minnesota Paper Form Board	25	16.5	91	4.5	8	26	20	29.5	70	14.5	33	18
Sentence Completion	31	6.5	17	28	19	14	42	13	52	10	33	14
Kent-Rosanoff Word Association	31	29	17	28	23	22	39	22.5	48	19.5	33	44
Test of Mechanical Comprehension (Bennett)	19	20	87	4.5	6	26	20	29.5	78	12	32	17
Vocational Interest Blank for Women (Strong)	50	16.5	74	6	23	19	21	31	19	27.5	30	20.5
Gesell Developmental Schedule	19	24	22	24	40	17.5	32	25	4	27.5	28	41
Concept Formation (Hanfmann-Kasanin)	31	29	4	28	9	29.5	27	25	59	27.5	24	56.5

Ns: Veterans Adm. Stations 27
Hospitals and Institutions 66
Outpatient Clinics 53
Counseling Centers 23
University Affiliated Clinics 16
185

[a] % = Percent mentioning using the test (Total Mentions divided by *N*).
[b] FUI Rank = Rank on Frequent Usage Index (Weighted Score minus Total Mentions).

counseling center. The median number was 868 test administrations per year. The average number of persons tested annually varied from 153 for outpatient clinics to 578 for counseling centers. Table 1 presents the 62 tests used by 10% or more of the respondents. The Total Mentions column refers to the number of agencies mentioning the given test, and the Weighted Score column is the total of the ratings multiplied by the frequency with which agencies checked these ratings. The rank-difference correlation between the two is high (.96 for the 62 tests). Among the leading 10 tests there are 4 projective techniques and 5 intelligence tests. The other test is the MMPI. The Rorschach outstrips its competitors very clearly both on number of places using the test and on amount of usage. A number of interesting tests which are rather new do not appear on Table 1 but were mentioned among the 375 different tests listed by the total group.

Table 2 presents data on the 20 most used psychological tests in each of three decades. The data from 1935 and 1946 were taken from the Louttit and Browne report (1947). Among the 40 tests listed there were 13 tests that have appeared on all of the test lists in the three decades. Of these the leader in all-time use in the clinic has been the Stanford-Binet. The Goodenough Draw-A-Man Test also has enjoyed a high position. The instability of testing preferences is indicating by the turnover rate in the top 20 tests. Between 1935 and 1946 there was a turnover of 60%. Between 1946 and 1959 there was a turnover of 38%. Between 1935 and 1959 there was a turnover of 76%. This figure means that among the tests which undoubtedly account for the majority of clinical test administrations in the United States, three-fourths of the tests have changed in 25 years. There are, however, some differences in samples which would be likely to affect the results. The earlier ones were smaller and at least the 1946 sample had relatively few psychiatric hospitals. The present sample is much more representative of clinical services of all kinds.

It is interesting to see the shift in kinds of tests used in the three decades as revealed by the complete lists. Intelligence tests dropped from 55% of the totals listed for 1935 by Louttit and Browne to 24% of the tests in use in 1959. The other striking change has been in the number of projective techniques starting with almost none in 1935 and rising to 23% of the total in 1959. Other percentages have remained almost constant. There has been a general increase in adult testing as compared with tests for children and a slight decrease in performance testing.

Table 3 shows the testing practices of the different psychological services with the 31 leading tests. The percentage of the given psychological agencies which are using the test is given, and also the rank on the Frequent Usage Index (FUI), which is an attempt to provide a more pure measure of usage by eliminating the distorting effect of the checking of tests which were rarely used. FUI uses only the ratings for frequent usage and usage with a majority of cases. The differences among the agencies on some tests are quite distinct. For instance, notice the counseling center column as compared with the outpatient clinics and hospitals and institutions columns in the usage of the Rorschach and the Kuder. Table 4 presents the intercorrelations on the FUI ranks among the different kinds of psychological services. The figures which stand out most prominently are the correlations between counseling centers and the two predominantly psychiatric organizations. This table gives support for a real difference between

TABLE 4. INTERCORRELATIONS AMONG DIFFERENT KINDS OF PSYCHOLOGICAL SERVICES ON FREQUENT USAGE OF TESTS

	VA	H & I	OPC	CC
H & I	.46			
OPC	.30	.78		
CC	.51	.04	.08	
UAC	.47	.68	.74	.50

Note.—The 31 most frequently used tests and their FUI Ranks were used for these rank-difference correlation figures.

counseling psychology and psychiatry-affiliated clinical psychology. The vocational and educational problems facing counseling psychologists require different kinds of tests. VA services and university training clinics occupy intermediate positions.

DISCUSSION

Psychological testing is a large activity in the United States. It is interesting to see what this sample implies if the numbers are extrapolated on the assumption of a 10% sampling of clinical services in the country. The picture would be as follows: nearly 7,000 clinical and counseling psychologists are seeing 1,300,000 people every year for all kinds of psychological service; of these, psychological tests are administered to 700,000 persons. Even this large number is only a fraction of the total figure on psychological testing if one would bring in industrial, military, educational, and private clinical work.

Such a survey as this raises many questions. Why are some tests widely used and others ignored? Levy and Orr (1959) have shown that institutional affiliation affects the kind of research psychologists do with tests. The social psychology of test usage would be equally interesting to explore. What is the relation between test usage and number of publications? The most widely used test, the Rorschach, also has the largest number of publications (Buros, 1959). Its rate has remained at almost three publications in English per week for a decade (Sundberg, 1954). For the tests listed in Table 1, the rank-difference correlation between FUI and Publication Rate for the last 7 years as taken from Buros (1959), was .46. This matter assumes greater importance since number of pub-

lications probably reflects highly of the amount of research. Some tests are much published and others are underpublished. In the latter category is the Draw-A-Person Test which is much used but has very few publications and little research; there is much criticism of the test (Swenson, 1957) which needs answering (Arbit, Lakin, & Mathis, 1959). Another question is the implication of these findings for training. Certainly popularity does not mean validity. This survey does not mean that these tests should be used. It does say which tests are the leading ones, and it seems that students should be familiar enough with them to read the literature critically and evaluate the clinical testing practices that they are bound to meet.

NOTES

1. This study was partially supported by Public Health Service Grant M-2825(A).

REFERENCES

AMERICAN BOARD OF PROFESSIONAL STANDARDS IN VOCATIONAL COUNSELING, INC. *Directory of vocational counseling services, 1959–60.* Washington, D.C.: APGA, 1958.

AMERICAN PSYCHOLOGICAL ASSOCIATION, INC. *1959 Directory.* Washington, D.C.: APA, 1959.

ARBIT, J., LAKIN, M., & MATHIS, A. G. Clinical psychologists' diagnostic utilization of human figure drawings. *J. clin. Psychol.*, 1959, *15*, 325–327.

BUROS, O. K. (Ed.) *The fourth mental measurements yearbook.* Highland Park, N.J.: Gryphon, 1953.

BUROS, O. K. (Ed.) *The fifth mental measurements yearbook.* Highland Park, N.J.: Gryphon, 1959.

DARLEY, J. G., & MARQUIS, D. G. Veterans' guidance centers: A survey of their problems and activities. *J. clin. Psychol.*, 1946, *2*, 109–116.

LEVY, L. H., & ORR, T. R. The social psychology of Rorschach validity research. *J. abnorm. soc. Psychol.*, 1959, *58*, 79–83.

LOUTTIT, C. M., & BROWNE, C. G. Psychometric instruments in psychological clinics. *J. consult. Psychol.*, 1947, *11*, 49–54.

MOORE, B. V. Educational facilities and financial assistance for graduate students in psychology, 1959–60. *Amer. Psychologist*, 1958, *13*, 741–760.

NATIONAL ASSOCIATION FOR MENTAL HEALTH, INC. *1954–55 Directory of outpatient psychiatric clinics and other mental health resources in the United States and territories.* New York: NAMH, 1955.

SUNDBERG, N. D. A note concerning the history of testing. *Amer. Psychologist*, 1954, *9*, 150–151.

SWENSON, C. H., JR. Empirical evaluations of human figure drawings. *Psychol. Bull.*, 1957, *54*, 431–466.

SWENSON, W. M., & LINDGREN, E. The use of psychological tests in industry. *Personnel Psychol.*, 1952, *5*, 19–23.

18. Intensive Treatment of Psychotic Behaviour by Stimulus Satiation and Food Reinforcement

T. AYLLON

UNTIL recently, the effective control of behaviour was limited to the animal laboratory. The extension of this control to human behaviour was made when Lindsley successfully adapted the methodology of operant conditioning to the study of psychotic behaviour (Lindsley, 1956). Following Lindsley's point of departure other investigators have shown that, in its essentials, the behaviour of mental defective individuals (Orlando and Bijou, 1960), stutterers (Flanagan, Goldiamond and Azrin, 1958), mental patients (Hutchinson and Azrin, 1961), autistic (Ferster and DeMyer, 1961), and normal children (Bijou, 1961; Azrin and Lindsley, 1956) is subject to the same controls.

Despite the obvious implications of this research for applied settings there has been a conspicuous lag between the research findings and their application. The greatest limitation to the direct application of laboratory principles has been the absence of control over the subjects' environment. Recently, however, a series of applications in a regulated psychiatric setting has clearly demonstrated the possibilities of behavioural modification (Ayllon and Michael, 1959; Ayllon and Haughton, 1962). Some of the behaviour studied has included repetitive and highly stereotyped responses such as complaining, pacing, refusal to eat, hoarding and many others.

What follows is a demonstration of behaviour techniques for the intensive individual treatment of psychotic behaviour. Specific pathological behaviour patterns of a single patient were treated by manipulating the patient's environment.

THE EXPERIMENTAL WARD AND CONTROL OVER THE REINFORCEMENT

This investigation was conducted in a mental hospital ward, the characteristics of which have been described elsewhere (Ayllon and Haughton,

1962). Briefly, this was a female ward to which only authorized personnel were allowed access. The ward staff was made up of psychiatric nurses and untrained aides who carried out the environmental manipulations under the direction of the experimenter. Using a time-sample technique, patients were observed daily every 30 minutes from 7:00 A.M. to 11:00 P.M.

The dining room was the only place where food was available and entrance to the dining room could be regulated. Water was freely available at a drinking fountain on the ward. None of the patients had ground passes or jobs outside the ward.

SUBJECT

The patient was a 47-year-old female patient diagnosed as a chronic schizophrenic. The patient had been hospitalized for 9 years. Upon studying the patient's behaviour on the ward, it became apparent that the nursing staff [2] spent considerable time caring for her. In particular, there were three aspects of her behaviour which seemed to defy solution. The first was stealing food. The second was the hoarding of the ward's towels in her room. The third undesirable aspect of her behaviour consisted in her wearing excessive clothing, e.g., a half-dozen dresses, several pairs of stockings, sweaters, and so on.

In order to modify the patient's behaviour systematically, each of these three types of behaviour (stealing food, hoarding, and excessive dressing) was treated separately.

EXPERIMENT I: CONTROL OF STEALING FOOD BY FOOD WITHDRAWAL

The patient had weighed over 250 pounds for many years. She ate the usual tray of food served to all patients, but, in addition, she stole food from the food counter and from other patients. Because

Reprinted from *Behaviour Research and Therapy*, 1963, *1*, 53–61, by permission of *Behaviour Research and Therapy* and the author. Dr. Ayllon is Director of

Clinical Research, Behavior Research Laboratory, Anna State Hospital, Anna, Illinois.

the medical staff regarded her excessive weight as detrimental to her health, a special diet had been prescribed for her. However, the patient refused to diet and continued stealing food. In an effort to discourage the patient from stealing, the ward nurses had spent considerable time trying to persuade her to stop stealing food. As a last resort, the nurses would force her to return the stolen food.

To determine the extent of food stealing, nurses were instructed to record all behaviour associated with eating in the dining room. This record, taken for nearly a month, showed that the patient stole food during two thirds of all meals.

PROCEDURE

The traditional methods previously used to stop the patient from stealing food were discontinued. No longer were persuasion, coaxing, or coercion used.

The patient was assigned to a table in the dining room, and no other patients were allowed to sit with her. Nurses removed the patient from the dining room when she approached a table other than her own, or when she picked up unauthorized food from the dining room counter. In effect, this procedure resulted in the patient missing a meal whenever she attempted to steal food.

RESULTS

Figure 1 shows that when withdrawal of positive reinforcement (i.e. meal) was made dependent upon the patient's 'stealing', this response was elimin-

ated in two weeks. Because the patient no longer stole food, she ate only the diet prescribed for her. The effective control of the stealing response is also indicated by the gradual reduction in the patient's body weight. At no time during the patient's 9 years of hospitalization had she weighed less than 230 pounds. Figure 2 shows that at the conclusion of this treatment her weight stabilized at 180 pounds or 17 per cent loss from her original weight. At this time, the patient's physical condition was regarded as excellent.

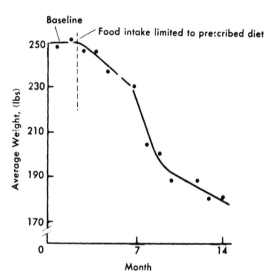

FIG. 2. The effective control of food stealing results in a notable reduction in body weight. As the patient's food intake is limited to the prescribed diet her weight decreases gradually.

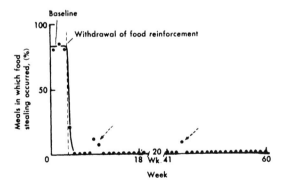

FIG. 1. A response, food stealing, is eliminated when it results in the withdrawal of food reinforcement. The dotted arrows indicate the rare occasions when food stealing occurred. For purposes of presentation a segment comprising 20 weeks during which no stealing occurred is not included.

DISCUSSION

A principle used in the laboratory shows that the strength of a response may be weakened by the removal of positive reinforcement following the response (Ferster, 1958). In this case, the response was food-stealing and the reinforcer was access to meals. When the patient stole food she was removed from the dining room and missed her meal.

After one year of this treatment, two occasions of food stealing occurred. The first occasion, occurring after one year of not stealing food, took the nurses by surprise and, therefore the patient 'got away' with it. The second occasion occurred shortly thereafter. This time, however, the controlling consequences were in force. The patient missed that meal and did not steal again to the conclusion of this investigation.

Because the patient was not informed or warned of the consequences that followed stealing, the nurses regarded the procedure as unlikely to have much effect on the patient's behaviour. The implicit belief that verbal instructions are indispensable for learning is part of present day psychiatric lore. In keeping with this notion, prior to this behaviour treatment, the nurses had tried to persuade the patient to co-operate in dieting. Because there were strong medical reasons for her losing weight, the patient's refusal to follow a prescribed diet was regarded as further evidence of her mental illness.

EXPERIMENT II: CONTROL OF ONE FORM OF HOARDING BEHAVIOUR THROUGH STIMULUS SATIATION

During the 9 years of hospitalization, the patient collected large numbers of towels and stored them in her room. Although many efforts had been made to discourage hoarding, this behaviour continued unaltered. The only recourse for the nursing staff was to take away the patient's towels about twice a week.

To determine the degree of hoarding behaviour, the towels in her room were counted three times a week, when the patient was not in her room. This count showed that the number of towels kept in her room ranged from 19 to 29 despite the fact that during this time the nurses continued recovering their towel supply from the patient's room.

PROCEDURE

The routine removal of the towels from the patient's room was discontinued. Instead, a programme of stimulus satiation was carried out by the nurses. Intermittently, throughout the day, the nurses took a towel to the patient when she was in her room and simply handed it to her without any comment. The first week she was given an average of 7 towels daily, and by the third week this number was increased to 60.

RESULTS

The technique of satiation eliminated the towel hoarding. Figure 3 shows the mean number of towels per count found in the patient's room. When the number of towels kept in her room reached the 625 mark, she started taking a few of them out. Thereafter, no more towels were given to her. During the next 12 months the mean number of towels found in her room was 1.5 per week.

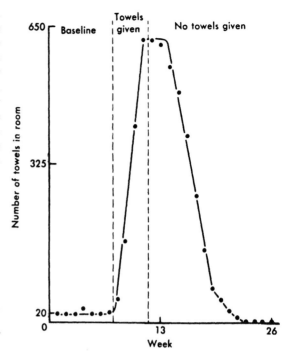

FIG. 3. A response, towel hoarding, is eliminated when the patient is given towels in excess. When the number of towels reaches 625 the patient starts to discard them. She continues to do so until the number found in her room averages 1.5 compared to the previous 20 towels per week.

DISCUSSION

The procedure used to reduce the amount of towel hoarding bears resemblance to satiation of a reinforcer. A reinforcer loses its effect when an excessive amount of that reinforcer is made available. Accordingly, the response maintained by that reinforcer is weakened. In this application, the towels constituted the reinforcing stimuli. When the number of towels in her room reached 625, continuing to give her towels seemed to make their collection aversive. The patient then proceeded to rid herself of the towels until she had virtually none.

During the first few weeks of satiation, the patient was observed patting her cheeks with a few towels, apparently enjoying them. Later, the patient was observed spending much of her time folding and stacking the approximately 600 towels in her room. A variety of remarks were made by the patient regarding receipt of towels. All verbal statements made by the patient were recorded by the nurse. The following represent typical remarks made during this experiment. First week: As the nurse entered the patient's room carrying a towel, the patient would smile and say, "Oh, you found it for me, thank you". Second week: When the number of towels given to patient increased rapidly, she told the nurses, "Don't give me no more towels. I've got enough". Third week: "Take them towels away. . . . I can't sit here all night and fold towels". Fourth and fifth weeks: "Get these dirty towels out of here". Sixth week: After she had started taking the towels out of her room, she remarked to the nurse, "I can't drag any more of these towels, I just can't do it".

The quality of these remarks suggests that the initial effect of giving towels to the patient was reinforcing. However as the towels increased they ceased to be reinforcing, and presumably became aversive.

The ward nurses, who had undergone a three year training in psychiatric nursing, found it difficult to reconcile the procedure in this experiment with their psychiatric orientation. Most nurses subscribed to the popular psychiatric view which regards hoarding behaviour as a reflection of a deep 'need' for love and security. Presumably, no 'real' behavioural change was possible without meeting the patient's 'needs' first. Even after the patient discontinued hoarding towels in her room, some nurses predicted that the change would not last and that worse behaviour would replace it. Using a time-sampling technique the patient was under continuous observation for over a year after the termination of the satiation programme. Not once during this period did the patient return to hoarding towels. Furthermore, no other behaviour problem replaced hoarding.

EXPERIMENT III: CONTROL OF AN ADDITIONAL FORM OF HOARDING THROUGH FOOD REINFORCEMENT

Shortly after the patient had been admitted to the hospital she wore an excessive amount of clothing which included several sweaters, shawls, dresses, undergarments and stockings. The clothing also included sheets and towels wrapped around her body, and a turban-like head-dress made up of several towels. In addition, the patient carried two to three cups on one hand while holding a bundle of miscellaneous clothing, and a large purse on the other.

To determine the amount of clothing worn by the patient, she was weighed before each meal over a period of two weeks. By subtracting her actual body weight from that recorded when she

was dressed, the weight of her clothing was obtained.

PROCEDURE

The response required for reinforcement was stepping on a scale and meeting a pre-determined weight. The requirement for reinforcement consisted of meeting a single weight (i.e. her body weight plus a specified number of pounds of clothing). Initially she was given an allowance of 23 pounds over her current body weight. This allowance represented a 2 pound reduction from her usual clothing weight. When the patient exceeded the weight requirement, the nurse stated in a matter-of-fact manner, "Sorry, you weigh too much, you'll have to weigh less". Failure to meet the required weight resulted in the patient missing the meal at which she was being weighed. Sometimes, in an effort to meet the requirement, the patient discarded more clothing than she was required. When this occurred the requirement was adjusted at the next weighing-time to correspond to the limit set by the patient on the preceding occasion.

RESULTS

When food reinforcement is made dependent upon the removal of superfluous clothing the response increases in frequency. Figure 4 shows that the patient gradually shed her clothing to

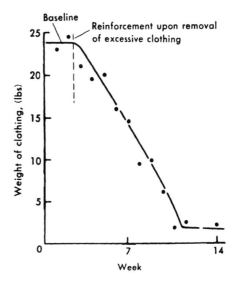

Fig. 4. A response, excessive dressing, is eliminated when food reinforcement is made dependent upon removal of superfluous clothing. Once the weight of the clothing worn by the patient drops to 3 pounds it remains stable.

meet the more demanding weight requirement until she dressed normally. At the conclusion of this experiment her clothes weighed 3 pounds compared to the 25 pounds she wore before this treatment.

Some verbal shaping was done in order to encourage the patient to leave the cups and bundles she carried with her. Nurses stopped her at the dining room and said, "Sorry, no things are allowed in the dining room". No mention of clothing or specific items was made to avoid focusing undue attention upon them. Within a week, the patient typically stepped on the scale without her bundle and assorted objects. When her weight was over the limit, the patient was informed that she weighed "too much". She then proceeded to take off a few clothes, stepped on the scale again, and upon meeting the weight requirement, gained access to the dining room.

DISCUSSION

According to the principle of reinforcement a class of responses is strengthened when it is followed by reinforcement. A reinforcer is such when it results in a response increase. In this application the removal of excessive clothing constituted the response and the reinforcer was food (i.e. access to meals). When the patient met the weight requirement she was reinforced by being given access to meals.

At the start of this experiment, the patient missed a few meals because she failed to meet the weight requirement, but soon thereafter she gradually discarded her superfluous clothing. First, she left behind odd items she had carried in her arms, such as bundles, cups and handbags. Next she took off the elaborate headgear and assorted "capes" or shawls she had worn over her shoulders. Although she had worn 18 pairs of stockings at one time, she eventually shed these also.

During the initial part of this experiment, the patient showed some emotional behaviour, e.g., crying, shouting and throwing chairs around. Because nurses were instructed to "ignore" this emotional behaviour, the patient obtained no sympathy or attention from them. The witholding of social reinforcement for emotional behaviour quickly led to its elimination.

At the conclusion of this behaviour treatment, the patient typically stepped on the scale wearing a dress, undergarments, a pair of stockings and a pair of light shoes. One of the behavioural changes concomitant with the current environmental manipulation was that as the patient began dressing

normally she started to participate in small social events in the hospital. This was particularly new to the patient as she had previously remained seclusive spending most of the time in her room.

About this time the patient's parents came to visit her and insisted on taking her home for a visit. This was the first time during the patient's 9 years of hospitalization that her parents had asked to take her out. They remarked that previously they had not been interested in taking her out because the patient's excessive dressing in addition to her weight made her look like a "circus freak".

CONCLUSIONS

The research presented here was conducted under nearly ideal conditions. The variables manipulated (i.e. towels and food) were under full experimental control. Using a time-sample technique the patient was observed daily every 30 minutes from 7:00 A.M. to 11:00 P.M. Nurses and aides carried out these observations which were later analysed in terms of gross behaviour categories. These observations were in force for over a year during which time these three experiments were conducted. The results of these observations indicate that none of the three pathological behaviour patterns (i.e. food stealing, hoarding and excessive dressing) exhibited by the patient were replaced by any undesirable behaviour.

The patient displayed some emotional behaviour in each experiment, but each time it subsided when social reinforcement (i.e. attention) was not forthcoming. The patient did not become violent or seclusive as a consequence of these experiments. Instead, she became socially more accessible to patients and staff. She did not achieve a great deal of social success but she did begin to participate actively in social functions.

A frequent problem encountered in mental hospitals is overeating. In general this problem is solved by prescribing a reduction diet. Many patients, however, refuse to take a reduction diet and continue overeating. When confronted with this behaviour, psychiatric workers generally resort to two types of explanations.

One explanation of overeating points out that only with the active and sincere co-operation of the patient can weight reduction be accomplished. When the patient refuses to co-operate he is regarded as showing more signs of mental illness and all hopes of eliminating overeating come to an end.

Another type of explanation holds that over-eating is not the behaviour to be concerned with. Instead, attention is focused on the psychological 'needs' of the patient. These 'needs' are said to be the cause of the observable behaviour, overeating. Therefore the emphasis is on the removal of the cause and not on the symptom or behaviour itself. Whatever theoretical merit these explanations may have, it is unfortunate that they fail to suggest practical ways of treating the behaviour itself. As a consequence, the patient continues to overeat often to the detriment of his health.

The current psychiatric emphasis on the resolution of the mental conflict that is presumably at the basis of the symptoms is perhaps misplaced. What seems to have been forgotten is that behaviour problems such as those reported here prevent the patient from being considered for discharge not only by the hospital personnel but also by the patient's relatives. Indeed, as far as the patient's relatives are concerned, the index of improvement or deterioration is the readily observable behaviour and not a detailed account of the mechanics of the mental apparatus.

Many individuals are admitted to mental hospitals because of one or more specific behaviour difficulties and not always because of a generalized 'mental' disturbance. For example, an individual may go into a mental hospital because he has refused to eat for several days, or because he talks to himself incessantly. If the goal of therapy were behavioural rehabilitation, these problems would be treated and normal eating and normal talking reinstated. However, the current emphasis in psychotherapy is on 'mental-conflict resolution' and little or no attention is given to dealing directly with the behavioural problems which prevent the patient from returning to the community.

NOTES

1. This report is based, in part, on a two-year research project (1959–1961), conducted by the author at the Saskatchewan Hospital, Weyburn, Saskatchewan, Canada, and supported by a grant from the Commonwealth Fund. Grateful acknowledgment is due to H. Osmond and I. Clancey of the Saskatchewan Hospital. The author also thanks E. Haughton who assisted in the conduct of this investigation, and N. Azrin and W. Holtz for their critical reading of the manuscript.

2. As used in this paper, 'nurse' is a generic term including all those who actually work on the ward (attendants, aides, psychiatric and registered nurses).

REFERENCES

AYLLON, T. and MICHAEL, J. (1959). The psychiatric nurse as a behavioural engineer. *J. exp. anal. Behav., 2,* 323–334.

AYLLON, T. and HAUGHTON, E. (1962). Control of the behaviour of schizophrenic patients by food. *J. exp. anal. Behav., 5,* 343–352.

AZRIN, N. and LINDSLEY, O. (1956). The reinforcement of cooperation between children. *J. abnorm. (soc.) Psychol., 52,* 100–102.

BIJOU, S. (1961). Discrimination performance as a baseline for individual analysis of young children. *Child Develpm. 32,* 163–160.

FERSTER, C. B. (1958). Control of behaviour in chimpanzees and pigeons by time out from positive reinforcement. *Psychol. Monogr., 72,* 1–38.

FERSTER, C. and DeMYER, M. (1961). The development of performances in autistic children in an automatically controlled environment. *J. chron. Dis., 13,* 312–345.

FLANAGAN, B., GOLDIAMOND, I. and AZRIN, N. (1958). Operant stuttering: The control of stuttering behaviour through response-contingent consequences. *J. exp. anal. Behav., 56,* 49–56.

HUTCHINSON, R. R. and AZRIN, N. H. (1961). Conditioning of mental hospital patients to fixed-ratio schedules of reinforcement. *J. exp. anal. Behav., 4,* 87–95.

LINDSLEY, O. R. (1956). Operant conditioning methods applied to research in chronic schizophrenia. *Psychiat. Res. Rep., 5,* 118–139.

ORLANDO, R. and BIJOU, S. (1960). Single and multiple schedules of reinforcement in developmentally retarded children. *J. exp. anal. Behav., 3,* 339–348.

19. Research in Clinical Psychology

WILLIAM SCHOFIELD

THIS is the fourth annual review of research in clinical psychology published in six psychological journals (48, 49, 50). As in previous reviews the journals covered are: *Journal of Clinical Psychology, Journal of Consulting Psychology, Journal of Abnormal and Social Psychology, Journal of Applied Psychology, Journal of General Psychology,* and *Journal of Psychology.* Again, an attempt was made to apply a stable definition of research; papers were included in the survey if they constituted "systematic investigation of a specifically described group of subjects and the derivation of normative or comparative data from psychometrics, case histories, or therapeutic interviews; or analysis of administration, scoring, and interpretation of a given instrument" (47).

The distribution of the 181 studies found in the six journals of 1952 is reported in Table 1 according to the major research areas represented. Comparable data for 1951 are also presented in this table. The increase in the total number of studies over 1951 is in part a reflection of the thirteen papers carried in the Morton Prince Memorial Supplement to the *Journal of Abnormal and Social Psychology.* The rank order correlation between the first nineteen categories of Table 1 with respect to frequency of studies for 1951 and 1952 is +.838. As compared with values of *rho* = +.681 for 1949–50 and rho = +.543 for the 1950–51 ranks, the higher correlation between the ranks of the various research areas for the last two years suggests a stability, possibly temporary, in the major patterns of clinical research.

For the fourth consecutive year, validity studies of projective techniques lead the list. The average per cent of all studies falling in this category for the four years, 1949–1952 inclusive, is 19.2%. The frequency of studies in this area has been remark-

ably constant, with approximately one-fifth of all the studies tabulated each year being concerned with validity of various projective devices.

Eleven of the 34 studies in category 1, or approximately one-third, are concerned with the Rorschach. This is less than the usual frequency of Rorschach validity researches which in the previous three years have accounted for a half of the studies in this category (cf. Table 2 of the 1951 review (50)). Notable among the papers in this category are those by Thiesen, Allen *et al.*, and Matarazzo *et al.* The study by Thiesen (55) involved application of a simple pattern analysis to twenty of the more objectively scored Rorschach variables in an attempt to elicit configurations which would distinguish between a group of 60 adult schizophrenics and 157 gainfully employed adults. Numerical values of each Rorschach variable were reduced to three categories of magnitude by use of sigma distances to set defining limits. An inspectional technique was applied to the discovery of recurring combinations and triads of categories which appeared discriminating. Five patterns were selected which met the specification of at least 10 per cent frequency in the patient group with less than 2 per cent frequency in the normals, and a significance level of .01 for the normal-patient difference. Only 3.2 per cent of the controls showed one or more of the five distinguishing patterns as contrasted with 48.4 per cent of the patients. This study is one of the earliest applications of objective, quantified pattern analysis to the Rorschach and should prove somewhat chastening to those who have decried any effort at statistical validation of projectives on the grounds that such an approach does violence to the configurational, wholistic quality of an instrument such as the Rorschach.

The paper by Allen *et al.* (1) is another study of the influence of color in the Rorschach, this one concerned with the effect of presence or absence of color on the consistency of responses from test to retest. An achromatic series was prepared by the Swiss publisher of the standard Rorschach, using

Reprinted from "Research in Clinical Psychology: 1952," *Journal of Clinical Psychology*, 1953, *9*, 313–320, by permission of the *Journal of Clinical Psychology* and the author. Dr. Schofield is Professor, Departments of Psychiatry and Psychology, University of Minnesota.

TABLE 1. Distribution of 181 Research Studies Reported in Six Selected Journals in 1952, by Areas of Research Represented, with Comparative Data for 1951

Area	No. of Studies	% of Total	% of 1951 Total	Rank 1951
1. Validity (projective techniques)	34	18.8	21.0	1
2. Normative study (personality)	30	16.6	12.6	2
3. Validity (structured personality tests)	20	11.0	7.7	3.5
4. Normative study (intelligence)	18	9.9	7.7	3.5
5. Normative (projective techniques)	13	7.2	2.8	11.5
6. Objective evaluation of therapy	12	6.6	4.9	7.5
7. Normative (structured personality tests)	9	5.0	7.0	5.5
8. Intertest relationships	8	4.4	7.0	5.5
9. Validity of psychiatric diagnosis	7	3.9	2.8	11.5
10. Validity (prognostic indicators)	6	3.3	4.9	7.5
11. New test (projective)	3	1.7	2.1	13.3
12. Abbreviated intelligence tests	3	1.7	1.4	15.5
13. Detection of malingering	3	1.7	—	17.5
14. Validity, W-B diagnostic patterns	2	1.1	4.2	9.5
15. Test standardization	2	1.1	4.2	9.5
16. New tests (intelligence)	2	1.1	2.1	13.3
17. Differential diagnosis of feebleminded	1	.5	2.1	13.3
18. Validity of W-B Deterioration Index	1	.5	—	17.5
19. Analysis of recorded interviews	0	0.0	1.4	15.5
20. Miscellaneous	7	3.9	4.1	20.0
	181	100.0	100.0	

the same presses and plates and same black ink as used in printing the standard cards. Subjects were 25 university students who were tested and re-tested with the standard and achromatic series, in AB-BA order, over a six week interval. No reliable differences were found between the consistencies of responses to either the colored or non-colored cards in either the standard or experimental, achromatic series. The consistency of test-retest responses ranged from 27 per cent to 35 per cent which agrees well with the data reported by Mons (35).

The study of Matarazzo *et al.* (31) is of particular interest because it constitutes an effort at experimental validation of the perceptual significance as well as personality correlates of the major Rorschach scoring categories. Subjects were both normal controls and psychiatric patients who were rated for anxiety-proneness by a psychiatrist, similarly rated on the basis of their Rorschach protocols, and subsequently submitted to inter-mittent photic stimulation with white light at frequencies ranging from 2 to 30 flashes per second. Record was made of the subjective experiences reported by the subjects at each frequency of photic stimulation. These included seeing color, movement, and patterns. These subjective experiences were scored for each subject in terms of Hertz's system, without knowledge of the subject's Rorschach protocol. The controls showed significant relationships between their Rorschach and "photic" responses involving color and movement. These relationships are reported as "disturbed" in the patients and anxiety-prone normals. The flicker variables per se did not distinguish the normals from the anxiety patients. The implications of this type of research for validity of Rorschach variables and for personality theory based on perceptual types are considerable, and it is to be hoped that this work will be extended.

The TAT and Szondi are represented in category 1 by seven papers each. Garfield *et al.* (20) report an investigation of the influence of two methods of administration and of the sex of subject and examiner on TAT protocols. Administration of the 20 cards in a single session or in two sessions separated by a two-day interval was found not to affect the protocols significantly. Neither sex of examiner, sex of subject, nor the interaction of these two significantly affected the records obtained with the twelve cards used with both sexes; significant sex differences in level and mood of stories were found for the eight cards which are used differentially with the two sexes.

Using the standard set of TAT cards and modified sets in which the central character of the picture was altered so as to appear obese or crippled, Weisskopf and Dunlevy (58) tested the hypothesis that bodily similarity between story teller and central pictorial figure would increase the amount of projection. Their subjects were college students who were obese, crippled, or of normal height and weight and without physical defect. While obese central figures elicited less projection than either normal or crippled figures, the hypothesis of enhanced projection with bodily similarity between subject and pictorial figure was not supported.

Webster (56) reports an interesting application of Rao's multiple discriminant technique to TAT variables, demonstrating the possibility of losing discrimination when there is failure to control or randomize personality variables other than the independent variable under study. Using questionnaire data for separation of subjects into four groups on the basis of submissiveness and security variables, Webster was able to show the differential discrimining power of various TAT variables applied to the homogeneous sub-classes.

Of the seven Szondi studies included in category 1, four are concerned with validation of basic assumptions involved in the scoring system, vector interpretation, etc. (2, 14, 16, 41). The remaining three are studies of its diagnostic utility when applied to epileptics, homosexuals, and neurotics (13, 24, 36). In all seven studies the authors interpret their findings to indicate lack of validity of the Szondi!

The remaining studies of category 1 include two on the H-T-P test, two papers on figure drawing, one each on the Rosenzweig P-F, Bender-Gestalt, and a sentence completion technique, and a report on a large-scale, door-to-door validation of an instrument based on the Rosenzweig P-F study. The latter paper by Sanford and Rosenstock (46) deserves attention because it reports the application of the large-scale sampling techniques of opinion polling to the standardization and validation of a projective device designed to elicit attitudes of political import. Many of the instruments of clinical psychology, in particular those concerned with personality assessment, would benefit greatly from the development of norms from this kind of controlled sampling.

The thirty papers included in category 2 of the table (Normative studies of personality) cover a considerable range of topics. Six of the papers might be generally classified as concerned with psychosomatic disorders. These include case studies or psychometric analyses of peptic ulcer (26, 30), anorexia nervosa (39), dermatosis (37), and dysmenorrhea (27). The paper by Palmer et al. (39) provides a summary of the previous literature on anorexia nervosa and gives a detailed presentation of the case histories and psychometrics for five patients. The patients were remarkably homogeneous with respect to age, nature of onset, previous medical history, and certain aspects of family structure and personal history. In view of this extensive homogeneity, the lack of any clear uniformity in the Rorschach psychograms warrants analysis. The authors are sensitive to the implications of this finding for test validity and briefly rationalize it by suggesting the Rorschach protocol is better considered a measure of thought processes rather than a clue to content of emotional conflicts.

Two of the studies in category 2 are concerned with personality investigations of prison inmates. The study by Fry (19) involved administration of the MMPI, Rosenzweig P-F Study, and the TAT to large samples of college students and adult prisoners of both sexes and the elicitation of reliable response differences for sex, racial, and civil status groups on all three instruments. Driscoll (15) used the MMPI and a special "Prison Projective Test" in a study of prison inmates; of interest is the finding of reliably *lower* scores on the D, Mf, and Pa scales of the MMPI for inmates rated as having poor adjustment as compared with a "good adjustment" group.

The hypothesis of "perceptual defense" as a phenomenon in schizophrenia is tested by two very different researches included in category 2. Sanders and Pacht (45) utilized non-language perceptual stimuli in the form of squares in five colors and five sizes, exposed at two distances, with comparison required against a standard series of black squares. Their subjects were V. A. psychotics and neurotics and university undergraduates. Analysis of variance applied to color, size, sequence, and normality, and interactions of these variables, demonstrated a different size constancy index for each of the groups and led to the suggestion that "with increasing personality disturbance there is increasing perceptual defensiveness in terms of overcompensation." McGinnies and Adornetto (32) report a study of male schizophrenics and employed firemen, in which they utilized lists of neutral and taboo words and tachistoscopic exposure to test for "defensiveness." The patients gave higher recognition thresholds than the normals for both neutral and taboo words. The controls gave higher thresholds for the taboo words than for the neutral words. An interesting analysis was made of the frequency and type of pre-recognition hypotheses generated by the two groups of subjects. The general support of the perceptual defense hypothesis rendered by these two methodologically disparate studies should stimulate further research in this area of psychopathology.

A study by O'Connor (38) merits attention because of the imaginative test battery used to predict stability and anxiety-aggressiveness in high-grade defectives. The battery included the Progressive Matrices Test, the U. S. E. S. tests of hand and finger dexterity, Heath's Rail-Walking test, Fessard's Hand Dynamometer test of Persistence, Eysenck's Leg Test of Persistence, the Eysenck-Furneaux adaptation of Hull's test of postural suggestibility, and a Track Tracer Test. An intercorrelation matrix of these tests was factor analyzed to determine which contributed most heavily to variance in the two criteria. The most useful tests in predicting stability were the sway test, the rail-walking test, and the dynamometer persistence test. Variance in the two-point rating of anxiety-aggressiveness was chiefly related to the Progressive Matrices and the Rail-Walking preformances.

Included in category 2 is a paper by Speroff and Kerr (53) on the application of sociometric techniques to determine the relationship between "interpersonal desirability values" of steel mill workers and their accident records. Subjects were members of nine 4-to-6 men teams on the finishing end of a hot strip mill. Two major subgroups were represented: a group of negroes and a group of Spanish-speaking manual workers. Each subject was asked to name, within his racial group, the man he would most like to work with and the one he would least like to work with. From these nominations a desirability value was computed for each worker. These values were found to correlate − .54 with the number of accidents on the workers' records, those least frequently selected as desirable having the greater number of accidents. The authors add to the effectiveness of their study by avoiding the common pitfall of casual interpretation of their coefficient and by proposing three hypotheses which might account for the relationship they demonstrated.

It may be noted from Table 1 that category 3 (Validity of structured personality tests) represents a slight increase in rank over that held by comparable studies in the 1951 survey. Last year's review commented on the marked increase in the number of studies in this area over the number published in the two previous years, and the suggestion was made that accumulating research findings from sophisticated analyses were encouraging renewed attention to the possibilities in the much maligned questionnaire approach (50). The 20 studies in category 3, nearly double the number for last year, would seem to support this view.

Of the 20 papers included in category 3, fourteen, or 70 per cent, involve the MMPI, modifications of

the MMPI, or scales developed from the MMPI item pool. Of particular interest among these papers are those by Buechley and Ball, Clark, Freeman and Mason, Geist, Seeman, Sullivan and Welsh, and Welsh. Buechley and Ball (7) report on the development of a new validity check for the group form of the MMPI. This is a test-retest (Tr) scale based on the sixteen items which are exactly repeated in the booklet form. The Tr scale correlates only + .63 with the F scale and is reported by the authors to distinguish "subjects whose high F scores resulted from random responses from those whose responses may be validly and consistently bizarre." Clark (9) reports on the MMPI profiles of three groups of Army general prisoners. While all three samples were considerably alike in their general MMPI profiles, certain scales yielded reliable mean differences among the "emotional instability," "anti-social personality," and "no NP disorder" groups. Freeman and Mason (18) report a cross-validity study of Clark's (8) recidivism key on a sample of prisoners at Washington State penitentiary. The scale failed to discriminate between recidivists and first offenders, and Freeman and Clark were unsuccessful in using their criterion groups and later samples to develop a new recidivism scale.

The paper by Geist (21) reports application of the inverted factor technique to determine the relationship between scores on the Bernreuter, Bell, Guilford-Martin, MMPI, and psychiatric diagnosis. Composite profiles of negatively and positively loaded cases on the four factors extracted by centroid method from the inverted matrix of Pearsonian coefficients were compared with MMPI profiles extracted from the literature, with good agreement resulting. It is unfortunate that such a complex analysis was carried through on a very small sample of patients, viz. 25. Seeman's (51) study is an experimental demonstration of the validity of the notion that structured personality inventory items can partake of the quality of subtlety which is popularly considered to be an exclusive property of projective devices.

Sullivan and Welsh (54) develop a relatively simple and promising technique for configural analysis of MMPI profiles which represents a midpoint between the configural item scoring possibilities suggested by Meehl (33) and the configural analysis represented by experienced clinical interpretation. By use of their technique, which involves rank comparisons of the coded scales of individual profiles, Sullivan and Welsh were able to discover signs (e.g., Hs > D; Hs > Sc; D > Hy) which reliably discriminated ulcer patients from a control group

The technique would seem to have particular promise for special problems of clinical differentiation or for the analysis of personality tendencies associated with particular medical phenomena such as hypertension. Welsh's (59) paper reports two indices based on simple arithmetic manipulations of scores on the clinical MMPI scales. The Anxiety Index (AI) seems to be reliably associated with clinical appraisals of anxiety, and the Internalization Ratio (IR) as a reflection of amount of "somatization" of conflict appears highly related to response to therapy.

Included in category 3 are papers by Brodman et al. (5, 6) on the utility of the Cornell Medical Index-Health Questionnaire for detecting psychiatric factors in general hospital patients; and a paper by Gleser and Ulett (23) on the Saslow Screening Test for anxiety proneness, an instrument of construction and content somewhat comparable to the Cornell but with more circumscribed purpose. It is of considerable interest that the authors of the latter paper report the Saslow test to be a good measure of anxiety-proneness as rated by psychologists and psychiatrists but not highly related to an over-all evaluation of maladjustment. This finding encourages awareness that capacity for anxiety is not equivalent in any linear sense with actual operation of anxiety as a source of maladjustment. This awareness seems frequently lacking in experiments designed to extend knowledge of psychopathology. Roberts (42) reports an experimental validation of the Index of Adjustment and Values designed by Bills, Vance, and McLean (3). By use of a voice key and chronoscope to measure reaction times to trait words previously indicated by the subjects as fitting their self-concepts and "Ideal selves," data were obtained suggesting that discrepancy between self-concepts and concepts of the ideal self is a good index of emotionality. Another intriguing paper in category 3 is a study by Lee (29) which explores the possibility of using scores on the Bennett Test of Mechanical Comprehension as a subtle measure of masculinity-femininity. Scores on the Bennett were found to correlate +.57 with scores on the Terman-Miles M-F Test.

Category 4 of Table 1 (Normative studies of intelligence) includes three factorial studies of the Wechsler-Bellevue and a report of centile norms for a large sample of university students. Cohen (10) reports centroid factorizations of W-B subtest correlation matrices for samples of neurotic, schizophrenic, and brain damaged patients respectively. Age range was 20 to 40. Three identical factors (verbal, non-verbal, and distractibility) were found

to account for the subtest relationships in all three groups. A general factor of present intellectual functioning was found to be present in all groups but to vary in its relationships with the common factors in the different patient samples. In a separate paper, Cohen (11) analyzes the rationale of the W-B subtests in terms of his factorial findings and concludes that Wechsler (57) and Rapaport (40) "imply a specificity of measurement for each of the subtests which is untenable in the light of the appreciably high order of subtest intercorrelation." A distinct contrast to Cohen's data is reflected in the factorial study of Birren (4) who applied centroid analysis to the W-B subtest intercorrelations obtained with a sample of men and women in the age range 60 to 74. Four factors were obtained and were identified as verbal comprehension, closure, rote memory, and induction. Except for the first of these factors, there appears to be little overlap with Cohen's factors. The finding of more rather than fewer common factors in an elderly "normal" as compared with a younger pathologic sample raises a question as to whether there is increasing heterogeneity in patterns of intellectual function with advancing age. The subjective aspects of factorization should not be overlooked in attempting to account for apparently divergent findings in studies of this type (12). Birren attempted an alignment of W-B factors with those of Thurstone and concluded that the W-B is of limited use for studies of age changes in intellect because it does not tap all of the "known" primary mental abilities.

Merrill and Heathers (34) report centile score equivalents for W-B IQ's obtained on 257 veteran and 193 non-veteran students at the University of Washington Counseling Center. The median W-B IQ for these students was 122. Centiles are also reported for raw scores on the 1949 ACE for entering freshmen. Gellerman (22) reports marked discrepancies between the scores yielded by Forms I and II of the Arthur Performance Scale when used with mental defectives; because of excessive difficulty or unreliability of Form II subtests, Gellerman suggests the Form I M.A. to be a more valid measure of mental level. Kent (28) presents valuable normative data for the Lincoln Hollow Square Test and a Color Cube test administered to 629 public school children in the 7–11 year age range.

The 102 studies included in the first four categories of Table 1 account for more than half (56.3%) of the total number of clinical research studies carried in the six journals in the past year. Space does not permit comment on all of the remaining categories. Note should be made of the continuing low rank for frequency in the last two years of studies concerned with use of the W-B for differential psychiatric diagnosis (category 14) and with the validity of the W-B Deterioration Index (category 18). Since these researches were tied for fifth place in the 1950 rankings, their more recent rankings possibly reflect growing recognition of the generally negative findings which have resulted. Also notable is the return to a high rank for frequency of normative studies of projective techniques (category 5). Of the thirteen studies in this category, seven are concerned with the Rorschach. Of these, the papers by Roe (43) on group Rorschach data for university faculties in the biological, physical, and social sciences, and by Hales (25) on a standard scoring, profile patterning and coding system appear to be of major import to clinical workers and researchers. Also included in category 5 is a paper by Rosenzweig and Rosenzweig (44)

reporting normative data on the P-F study for 152 problem children. Graphic reporting of the major score distributions by two year age intervals leads to several tentative conclusions concerning the developmental pattern for socialization.

In view of the great need for knowledge of a factual nature in the field of psychotherapy, it is encouraging to find that the frequency of research reports concerned with objective evaluation of the effects of psychotheraphy remains high (category 6). Eysenck's (17) recent provocative summary should prove challenging rather than discouraging to clinicians and should operate to enhance collaborative investigation by psychologists and psychiatrists who need to *demonstrate the evidence* which underlies their subjective convictions that psychotherapy is a socially useful function in which to be engaged.

REFERENCES

1. ALLEN, R. M., MANNE, S. H., and STIFF, MARGARET. The influence of color on the consistency of responses in the Rorschach test. *J. clin. Psychol.*, 1952, *8*, 97–98.
2. BARRACLOUGH, PATRICIA, COLE, D., and REEB, MILDRED. The influence of test instructions on Szondi results. *J. clin. Psychol.*, 1952, *8*, 165–167.
3. BILLS, R. E., VANCE, E. L., and McLEAN, O. S. An index of adjustment and values. *J. consult. Psychol.*, 1951, *15*, 257–261.
4. BIRREN, J. E. A factorial analysis of the Wechsler-Bellevue Scale given to an elderly population. *J. consult. Psychol.*, 1952, *16*, 399–405.
5. BRODMAN, K., ERDMANN, A. J., LORGE, I., GERSHENSON, C. P., and WOLFF, H. G. The Cornell Medical Index-Health Questionnaire. III. The evaluation of emotional disturbances. *J. clin. Psychol.*, 1952, *8*, 119–124.
6. BRODMAN, K., ERDMAN, A. J., LORGE, I., GERSHENSON, C. P., and WOLFF, H. G. The Cornell Medical Index-Health Questionnaire. IV. The recognition of emotional disturbances in a general hospital. *J. clin. Psychol.*, 1952, *8*, 289–292.
7. BUECHLEY, R. and BALL, H. A new test of "validity" for the group MMPI. *J. consult. Psychol.*, 1952, *16*, 299–301.
8. CLARK, J. H. Application of the MMPI in differentiating AWOL recidivists from non-recidivists. *J. Psychol.*, 1948, *26*, 229–234.
9. CLARK, J. H. The relationship between MMPI scores and psychiatric classification of army general prisoners. *J. clin. Psychol.*, 1952, *8*, 86–89.
10. COHEN, J. Factors underlying Wechsler-Bellevue performance of three neuropsychiatric groups. *J. abn. soc. Psychol.*, 1952, *47*, 359–365.
11. COHEN, J. A factor-analytically based rationale for the Wechsler-Bellevue. *J. consult. Psychol.*, 1952, *16*, 272–277.
12. CURETON, E. E. The principal compulsions of factor-analysts. *Harvard educ. Rev.*, Vol. 9, No. 3, 1939.
13. DAVID, H. P. and RABINOWITZ, W. Szondi patterns in epileptic and homosexual males. *J. consult. Psychol.*, 1952, *16*, 247–250.
14. DAVIS, N. ELAINE and RAIMY, V. C. Stimulus functions of the Szondi cards. *J. clin. Psychol.*, 1952, *8*, 155–160.
15. DRISCOLL, P. J. Factors related to the institutional adjustment of prison inmates. *J. abn. soc. Psychol.*, 1952, *47*, 593–596.

16. DUDEK, F. J. and PATTERSON, H. O. Relationships among the Szondi test items. *J. consult. Psychol.*, 1952, *16*, 389–394.

17. EYSENCK, H. J. The effects of psychotherapy: An evaluation. *J. consult. Psychol.*, 1952, *16*, 319–324.

18. FREEMAN, R. A. and MASON, H. M. Construction of a key to determine recidivists from non-recidivists using the MMPI. *J. clin. Psychol.*, 1952, *8*, 207–208.

19. FRY, F. D. A normative study of the reactions manifested by college students and by state prison inmates in response to the Minnesota Multiphasic Personality Inventory, the Rosenzweig Picture-Frustration Study, and the Thematic Apperception Test. *J. Psychol.*, 1952, *34*, 27–30.

20. GARFIELD, S. L., BLEK, L., and MELKER, F. The influence of method of administration and sex differences on selected aspects of TAT stories. *J. consult. Psychol.*, 1952, *16*, 140–144.

21. GEIST, H. A comparison of personality test scores and medical psychiatric diagnosis by the inverted factor technique. *J. clin. Psychol.*, 1952, *8*, 184–188.

22. GELLERMANN, S. W. Forms I and II of the Arthur Performance Scales with mental defectives. *J. consult. Psychol.*, 1952, *16*, 127–131.

23. GLESER, GOLDINE and ULETT, G. The Saslow Screening Test as a measure of anxiety-proneness. *J. clin. Psychol.*, 1952, *8*, 279–293.

24. GOLDMAN, G. D. The validation of the paroxysmal vector of the Szondi test. *J. abn. soc. Psychol.*, 1952, *47*, 475–477.

25. HALES, W. N. Profile patterning and coding of the Rorschach test: Preliminary report of research methods and materials. *J. consult. Psychol.*, 1952, *16*, 37–42.

26. HECHT, I. The difference in goal striving behavior between peptic ulcer and ulcerative colitis patients as evaluated by psychological techniques. *J. clin. Psychol.*, 1952, *8*, 262–265.

27. HERZBERG, F. I. A study of the psychological factors in primary dysmenorrhea. *J. clin. Psychol.*, 1952, *8*, 174–178.

28. KENT, GRACE H. Performance tests as clinical instruments for children. *J. Psychol.*, 1952, *33*, 3–26.

29. LEE, MARILYN C. Relationship of masculinity-femininity to tests of mechanical and clerical abilities. *J. appl. Psychol.*, 1952, *36*, 377–380.

30. MARQUIS, DOROTHY P., SINNETT, R., and WINTER, W. D. A psychological study of peptic ulcer patients. *J. clin. Psychol.*, 1952, *8*, 266–272.

31. MATARAZZO, RUTH, WATSON, R. I., and ULETT, G. A. Relationship of Rorschach scoring categories to modes of perception induced by intermittent photic stimulation—A methodological study of perception. *J. clin. Psychol.*, 1952, *8*, 368–374.

32. McGINNIES, E. and ADORNETTO, J. Perceptual defense in normal and in schizophrenic observers. *J. abn. soc. Psychol.*, 1952, *47*, 833–837.

33. MEEHL, P. E. Configural scoring. *J. consult. Psychol.*, 1950, *14*, 165–171.

34. MERRILL, R. M. and HEATHERS, LOUISE B. Centile scores for the Wechsler-Bellevue Intelligence Scale on a university counseling center group. *J. consult. Psychol.*, 1952, *16*, 406–409.

35. MONS, W. *Principles and Practice of the Rorschach Personality Test*. J. B. Lippincott, 1948.

36. MUSSEN, P. and KRAUSS, SHIRLEY R. An investigation of the diagnostic validity of Szondi Test. *J. abn. soc. Psychol.*, 1952, *47*, 399–405.

37. NARCISO, J. C. Some psychological aspects of dermatosis. *J. consult. Psychol.*, 1952, *16*, 199–201.

38. O'CONNOR, N. The prediction of psychological stability and anxiety-aggressiveness from a battery of tests administered to a group of high grade male mental defectives. *J. gen. Psychol.*, 1952, *46*, 3–17.

39. PALMER, J. O., MENSH, I. N., and MATARAZZO, J. D. Anorexia nervosa: Case history and psychological examination data with implications for test validity. *J. clin. Psychol.*, 1952, *8*, 168–173.

40. RAPAPORT, D. *Diagnostic Psychological Testing.* Vol. 1. Yearbook Publishers, Inc., 1945.

41. RICHARDSON, HELEN M. The discriminability of the "drive factors" represented in the Szondi pictures. *J. clin. Psychol.*, 1952, *8*, 384–390.

42. ROBERTS, G. E. A study of the validity of the Index of Adjustment and Values. *J. consult. Psychol.*, 1952, *16*, 302–304.

43. ROE, ANNE. Group Rorschachs of university faculties. *J. consult. Psychol.*, 1952, *16*, 18–22.

44. ROSENZWEIG, S. and ROSENZWEIG, LOUISE. Aggression in problem children and normals as evaluated by the Rosenzweig P-F study. *J. abn. soc. Psychol.*, 1952, *47*, 683–687.

45. SANDERS, R. and PACHT, A. R. Perceptual size constancy of known clinical groups. *J. consult. Psychol.*, 1952, *16*, 440–444.

46. SANFORD, F. H. and ROSENSTOCK, I. M. Projective techniques on the doorstep. *J. abn. soc. Psychol.*, 1952, *47*, 3–16.

47. SCHOFIELD, W. Research trends in clinical psychology. *J. clin. Psychol.*, 1950, *6*, 148–152.

48. SCHOFIELD, W. Research in clinical psychology: 1949. *J. clin. Psychol.*, 1950, *6*, 234–237.

49. SCHOFIELD, W. Research in clinical psychology: 1950. *J. clin. Psychol.*, 1951, *7*, 215–221.

50. SCHOFIELD, W. Research in clinical psychology: 1951. *J. clin. Psychol.*, 1952, *8*, 255–261.

51. SEEMAN, W. "Subtlety" in structured personality tests. *J. consult. Psychol.*, 1952, *16*, 278–283.

52. SHATIN, L. Psychoneurosis and psychosomatic reactions: A Rorschach contrast. *J. consult. Psychol.*, 1952, *16*, 220–223.

53. SPEROFF, B. and KERR, W. Steel mill "hot strip" accidents and interpersonal desirability values. *J. clin. Psychol.*, 1952, *8*, 89–91.

54. SULLIVAN, P. L. and WELSH, G. S. A technique for objective configural analysis of MMPI profiles. *J. consult. Psychol.*, 1952, *16*, 383–388.

55. THIESEN, J. W. A pattern analysis of structural characteristics of the Rorschach Test in schizophrenia. *J. consult. Psychol.*, 1952, *16*, 365–370.

56. WEBSTER, H. Rao's multiple discriminant technique applied to three TAT variables. *J. abn. soc. Psychol.*, 1952, *47*, 641–648.

57. WECHSLER, D. *The Measurement of Adult Intelligence.* Williams and Wilkins Co., 3rd edition, 1944.

58. WEISSKOPF, EDITH A. and DUNLEVY, G. P. Bodily similarity between subject and central figure in the TAT as an influence on projection. *J. abn. soc. Psychol.*, 1952, *47*, 441–445.

59. WELSH, G. S. An anxiety index and an internalization ratio for the MMPI. *J. consult. Psychol.*, 1952, *16*, 65–72.

20. Psychologists in Medical Education: 1964

NATHANIEL N. WAGNER AND KAREN L. STEGEMAN

A STRONG, unverified impression has existed among psychologists in medical education that their number has increased substantially since Matarazzo and Daniel's (1957) survey of January 1955. They found 346 psychologists in the 78 medical schools in the United States. The present report is the first part of a larger survey of psychologists in medical education.

On November 1, 1963, a letter was sent to one or more key individuals in the 87 medical schools in the United States requesting a list of all psychologists employed at that school. Following the earlier survey, the letter defined psychologists as those holding actual *staff* positions. Interns and practicum students were not to be included, but "graduate students and other psychologists who are part of your permanent staff, e.g., a person who has been working for his degree but who holds a research position for two years" were included.

By March 4, 1964, lists of psychologists had been received from 84 of the 87 medical schools in the United States. After telephone conversations with representatives of the 3 schools who had not replied to the November 1 letter or the two subsequent

Reprinted from *American Psychologist*, 1964, *19*, 689, by permission of the American Psychological Association and Dr. Wagner. Dr. Wagner is Chief Psychologist and Associate Professor, University of Washington Medical School. Miss Stegeman was Research Assistant, Department of Psychiatry, University of Washington Medical School, at the time this article was written.

follow-up letters, a complete list was obtained.

Table 1 lists the present number of psychologists in each medical school and the comparable 1955 figures. The total now is 993, an increase of 187% over the 1955 total of 346. Eighty-six of the 87 approved medical schools employ psychologists in varying numbers ranging from 1 to 51. (The lone school with no psychologists is a 2-year institution, i.e., all students complete their medical training by transfer to a 4-year school.) The mean and median numbers of psychologists per medical school now are 11 and 9. In 1955 the range was 1 to 17 psychologists in 68 of the 78 medical schools which employed psychologists. The mean and median were both 4.

During this same 9-year period, two other factors related to the growth of psychologists in medical education need to be considered. The number of medical schools has increased by 11%, from 78 to 87. Second, APA membership has increased by 65%, from 13,475 on January 1, 1955, to 22,174 on January 1, 1964. It is clear that the impression of substantial increase in the numbers of psychologists in medical education is verified, even when these other factors are considered.

An extensive questionnaire has been sent to the 993 psychologists named in the preminary survey. Analysis of these data should indicate areas, within medical education, of greatest expansion, i.e., research, teaching, service, and possibly clarify some of the factors responsible for this striking increase.

REFERENCES

MATARAZZO, J. D., & DANIEL, R. S. Conference on psychology in medical education survey psychologists in medical schools: Personal, professional, academic, and scientific characteristics. *Neuropsychiatry*, 1957, *4*, 93–107.

TABLE 1. PRELIMINARY SURVEYS

School	Matarazzo and Daniel 1955 Number	Wagner and Stegeman 1964 Number	School	Matarazzo and Daniel 1955 Number	Wagner and Stegeman 1964 Number
1. Medical College of Alabama	0	4	48. Columbia University	2	19
2. University of Arkansas	1	6	49. Cornell University	5	9
3. California College of Medicine[a]	—	1	50. Albert Einstein College of Medicine of Yeshiva University[a]	—	42
4. University of California, Los Angeles	9	51	51. New York Medical College	6	19
5. University of California, San Francisco Medical Center	12	29	52. New York University	10	8
6. Loma Linda University	4	4	53. University of Rochester	7	11
7. University of Southern California	1	1	54. State University of New York (Downstate Medical Center), Brooklyn	11	19
8. Stanford University	3	7			
9. University of Colorado	10	20	55. State University of New York (Upstate Medical Center), Syracuse	3	11
10. Yale University	8	14			
11. George Washington University	3	2	56. Bowman Gray School of Medicine of Wake Forest College	4	5
12. Georgetown University	5	2			
13. Howard University	3	12	57. Duke University	4	19
14. University of Florida[a]	—	25	58. University of North Carolina	4	22
15. University of Miami	3	3	59. University of North Dakota	0	0
16. Emory University	0	4	60. University of Cincinnati	4	19
17. Medical College of Georgia	3	5	61. Ohio State University	2	9
18. Chicago Medical School[a]	—	7	62. Western Reserve University	4	11
19. University of Chicago	4	13	63. University of Oklahoma	1	22
20. University of Illinois	6	16	64. University of Oregon	1	15
21. Northwestern University	15	14	65. Hahnemann Medical College	1	2
22. Stritch School of Medicine of Loyola University	0	2	66. Jefferson Medical College of Philadelphia	2	10
23. Indiana University	9	25	67. University of Pennsylvania	3	13
24. State University of Iowa	9	11	68. University of Pittsburgh	15	18
25. University of Kansas	5	12	69. Temple University	5	15
26. University of Kentucky[a]	—	7	70. Woman's Medical College of Pennsylvania	1	2
27. University of Louisville	7	10			
28. Louisiana State University	1	5	71. Medical College of South Carolina	0	3
29. Tulane University	6	7	72. State University of South Dakota	0	1
30. Johns Hopkins University	6	31	73. Meharry Medical College[a]	—	4
31. University of Maryland	4	12	74. University of Tennessee	3	7
32. Boston University	5	14	75. Vanderbilt University	3	5
33. Harvard University	8	47	76. Baylor University	2	15
34. Tufts University	1	10	77. University of Texas		
35. University of Michigan	7	38	Galveston	11	9
36. Wayne State University	2	11	Houston	3	
37. University of Minnesota	17	25	78. University of Texas Dallas	3	7
38. University of Mississippi	0	6	79. University of Utah	7	6
39. University of Missouri	0	5	80. University of Vermont	0	1
40. Saint Louis University	2	3	81. University of Virginia	1	5
41. Washington University, St. Louis	10	22	82. Medical College of Virginia	3	10
42. Creighton University	1	5	83. University of Washington	6	19
43. University of Nebraska	8	9	84. West Virginia University[a]	—	1
44. Darmouth Medical School	0	4	85. Marquette University[a]	—	2
45. Seton Hall College of Medicine and Dentistry[a]	—	2	86. University of Wisconsin	5	5
			87. University of Puerto Rico[a]	—	2
46. Albany Medical College of Union University	4	3			
47. State University of New York at Buffalo	4	5	Total	346	993

[a] Not part of the 1955 survey.

21. The Role of Psychologists in University Counseling and Psychotherapy

EMORY L. COWEN

THIS study reports a fact finding survey concerning the activities and functions of psychologists in facilities for personal counseling and psychotherapy for undergraduates within university mental health programs. It is clearly recognized, in practice and theory, that university mental health problems are not the exclusive province of any single discipline. Psychiatrists, for example have long been concerned with such problems. Farnsworth (1) presents an historical overview of this interest, as well as a detailed consideration of the potential role of psychiatry in a university mental health program. Data indicating the extent to which psychiatrists and other mental health specialists have actually participated in the health programs of 1157 American colleges are also available (3). Recognizing beforehand the breadth of contributions from other disciplines, the aim of the present investigation is to determine more precisely the role of psychologists in this area.

METHOD

Our basic data derive from a questionnaire distributed to the Director of Clinical Training at each of the 52 colleges and universities listed in the June 1958 *American Psychologist* as having an APA approved Ph.D. training program in clinical psychology.

The questionnaire covered a variety of areas including: structure of the various service facilities, nature and size of staff, number of people seen, types of referrals, and participation of graduate student trainees. In order to maximize the likelihood of a good return, the questionnaire was kept brief and part responses were encouraged even if all items could not be answered. Thirty seven responses were received within one month, at which time a follow-up was distributed to the remaining 15 schools. Within three weeks completed questionnaires were received from 13 additional schools for a total of 50 responses from the original group of 52. Some respondents, as anticipated, did not answer one or more questions; accordingly, the number of responses varies from item to item. Where answers seemed unclear or implausible, individual follow-up letters were sent to the respondent for clarification.

RESULTS

All 50 schools answered affirmatively to the question "Do you provide counseling or psychotherapy[2] for undergraduates[3] with personal, social and emotional problems?" This offers an encouraging confirmation of the anticipation that mental health functions would increasingly become a responsibility of the university (1, 2).

TYPES OF FACILITIES

All 50 respondents indicated which of four categories best described the services referred to in the preceding response. The four "approximate paradigms" utilized were as follows:

1. *Psychological.* Characteristically within a psychology department, administered and staffed by psychologists, with minimal psychiatric participation, *i.e.*, there may be a psychiatrist on call, or one who attends staff and/or case conferences, but such a person is not involved in actual work with students (N = 18).

2. *Psychiatric.* Typically within a medical setting, with the bulk of the student contact work being done by psychiatrists. Although there may be one or more psychologists on the staff, the latter do not appear to have a major role in the counseling and therapeutic aspects of the program (N = 5).

Reprinted from *Journal of Clinical Psychology*, 1960, *16*, 66–70, by permission of the *Journal of Clinical Psychology* and the author. Dr. Cowen is Professor of Psychology and Director of Clinical Training, University of Rochester, Rochester, New York.

3. *Separate.* Refers to those schools which maintain independent facilities of the psychological and psychiatric variety as described above, each of which is actively involved in undergraduate counseling and therapy (N = 22).

4. *Integrated.* Those facilities which include both psychologists and psychiatrists on their functional staff, which are housed in a single setting, and in which members of each discipline are actively involved in a major portion of the treatment program. The administrative directorship of the integrated clinic may be either psychological or psychiatric in nature (N = 5).[4]

The ratio of one type of facility to another would doubtless vary as a function of the sample of schools tapped. Quite probably the relatively high percent of "psychological" facilities reflects the fact that the responding institutions house highly developed graduate training facilities in clinical psychology. "Separate" psychological and psychiatric facilities, however, are modal. This may be attributable in part to the relatively large undergraduate enrollments characterizing our sample, or because facilities in a given school may evolve relatively independently within disciplines, without co-ordinated overall planning.

Several questions were asked about the nature and use of psychiatric consultation. These refer to the 18 psychological facilities and to the 22 essentially psychological organizations in schools with separate facilities; they are not relevant to the psychiatric or integrated facilities. Thirty-seven of these 40 schools answered the items; of these 28 had psychiatric consultation and nine did not. Schools with psychiatric consultation described the nature of such consultation as ranging from token participation to active participation in a variety of non-contact functions. At ten schools the psychiatric consultant took part regularly in case conference or staff meetings. Seven stated that the major role served was that of being available for consultation on difficult or complex matters. Another ten schools reported that the psychiatric consultant was available on a "call", "stand-by" or "emergency" basis. Some of these indicated quite frankly that there was little or no actual contact with the consultant, and that the relationship existed more in principle than in fact. Three schools indicated that psychiatric consultants were used primarily for trainee supervision, and other single schools stated reasons such as "training", "instructional", and "screening".

Considerable ingenuity has gone into the development of titles for these university service facilities. Fourteen different titles were given by the 42 respondents who identified their organiza-

tions by name, and it is only by assuming a license in grouping that consistencies emerge. Clearly the most popular title is Psychological Clinic (N = 15). By using either the word University or Student before, and Bureau or Service after the word Counseling (as the fixed middle term) we may account for another 12 schools. Seven more organizations go under the title Counseling (and Testing) Center, while an additional four are called Psychological Service Centers (or Bureaus). The remaining facilities have non-duplicated titles.

FACILITIES FOR WHOM AND ON WHAT BASIS

All respondents indicated that facilities in counseling and psychotherapy were available for undergraduates; all but one provide comparable services for graduate students. Twenty-one of the centers also offer therapeutic services for community adults while 15 provide such facilities for children; the latter two, however, are likely to be on a fee basis. Thirty-four of the 48 respondents provide therapeutic help for undergraduates without charge, four do so on a fee basis, while the remaining 12 indicate that services may be either on a fee or non-fee basis depending on their nature and extent. All 46 of the responding institutions offer individual psychotherapy; 18 also provide group therapy.

Thirty-five of the schools estimated the approximate percents of students coming from various referring sources. Using each school as a unit without weighting for overall size of operation, it is clear that self referrals constitute the single preponderant source (54%). Referrals from administration, including deans' offices, dormitory advisors, and student service facilities account for an additional 21%. Faculty referrals total to about 12%, these splitting fairly evenly between psychology and other university faculty. Approximately 10% of the referrals came from medical sources, while the remaining 3% came from the advisor system used in some schools.

STAFF

Determination of the amount of staff time devoted to counseling and psychotherapy with students poses a complex challenge. For one thing, staff time is not always neatly divisible into the categories student *vs.* non student, making it quite difficult to determine precisely what percent of total staff activity is directed to student problems. Moreover staff time in a counseling service may combine service and training functions. Too, many staff people who are full time at an institution, devote only a portion, sometimes variable, of their time to such activities.

Estimates were gathered separately for post-doctoral, sub-doctoral (non-graduate student), and graduate student time. The data based on the 44 schools providing answers to these items are summarized in Table 1. For reasons cited above, the

TABLE 1. STAFF HOURS IN UNDERGRADUATE COUNSELING AND PSYCHOTHERAPY WORK PER WEEK

	Post Doctoral	Sub Doctoral	Grad Student	Total
Mean	103	35	85	223
Median	70	15	50	135
Range	0–520	0–160	0–600	16–800

mean figures doubtless overestimate the actual amount of time spent in student contact work. Nevertheless a sizable number of psychologist man-hours are currently devoted to student mental health matters at the universities sampled. As one studies staff "profiles" from the responding institutions it becomes clear that the individual patterns are virtually legion. At some schools at least 90% of the total staff man-hours is contributed by graduate student trainees, while at others we find 100% post Ph.D. staff. Other patterns are observed in which, for example, the brunt of service is provided by sub-doctoral non-graduate student personnel.

An item was included to determine what percents of undergraduate counselees are seen by psychology staff, graduate students and other personnel. Once again the percent estimates provided by the 35 responding institutions were averaged as units without weighting for size of operation. On this basis we find 49% are seen by psychology staff, 45% by graduate students and 6% by other personnel, usually medical. These overall figures do not however capture the variation among schools; for some, 100% of the under-graduate therapy is done by staff while for others it is all done by graduate students. Moreover the data are overweighted by exclusively psychological facilities, or by the psychological facility in a university which is also known to have separate psychiatric facilities. Doubtless they would change drastically with inclusion of comparable information from the many student health psychiatric facilities actively in operation.

EXTENT OF SERVICES

A series of questions attracting anywhere from 33–38 respondents explored the extent of therapeutic services offered by the universities. This is likely to be influenced both by the size of the school and the amount of support for mental health activities provided by the institution. The universities range in size of undergraduate enrollment from approximately 725 to 26,000 with a median around 8,500. The number of students seen for personal counseling and therapy per year ranges from 15 to 750 with a median around 125. The average number of interviews per student seen is nearly 11; however the median figure, six, is a more accurate reflection of central tendency in this instance. The range for mean number of interviews runs from about 2.5 to 95 sessions; a rough mode for range of sessions would be from one to about 40 or 50 sessions.

PRACTICUM FOR STUDENTS

Forty-two of 46 respondents indicated that practicum courses in counseling and psychotherapy were required in their clinical Ph.D. program. A series of more specific questions about these practica followed, each attracting 40 respondents. Evaluation of the latter data are complicated. Practicum courses may include both diagnostic and therapeutic activities; often it is difficult to determine how much of each. Some schools are individualized in their approach to the problem of required practicum courses, and students with differing backgrounds and experience have different practicum requirements. Too, there are more mundane problems such as trying to convert semesters and quarters into common credit units for comparative purposes. These considerations necessitated some dependency upon the "educated guess" or the "mental coin flip" in trying to make finer discriminations. Within this framework of limitations the picture that emerges is summarized in Table 2. A very prevalent pattern is for schools to require two semesters of therapy practicum totalling to six hours of graduate credit. One

TABLE 2. SEMESTERS, CREDIT HOURS, AND SIZE OF REQUIRED THERAPY PRACTICA

	Semesters	Credit Hours	No. Students
Mean	2.7	6.5	8.9
Median	2	6	7
Range	1–6	0–18	1–25

heartening aspect of these data is the rather small size of the typical therapy practicum group, with the consequent implication of relatively close supervision. In 30 instances therapy practicum supervision is provided exclusively by psychologists, in one case by psychiatrists only, and in the remaining nine by both groups.

Thirty-three respondents were able to estimate the percent of undergraduates seen by graduate students in their therapy practicum courses. In twelve schools no undergraduates whatsoever are seen by graduate students through such courses, and in another nine institutions the figure is less than 25%. However there are 10 schools in which 75% or more of the people seen therapeutically by graduate students in their practica are undergraduates; in most of these instances the actual percent figure is close to 90. Thus for 31 of the 33 schools either the particular practicum is virtually exclusively devoted to work with undergraduates, or else its constituents are likely to have only infrequent opportunities to work with undergraduates.

OVERVIEW AND SUMMARY

A striking and encouraging finding of the present survey is that all 50 responding universities housing APA approved Ph.D. training programs in clinical psychology provide counseling and psychotherapy service for undergraduates with personal, social, and emotional problems. This datum implies a recognition of the intimate relation between the emotional well-being of the student and his ability to profit maximally from his educational experience. We may hope that parallel progress will soon be identifiable in the area of preventive work, as part of a more comprehensive program of mental health within the university.

Our survey suggests that psychologists (doctoral and sub-doctoral) as well as graduate student trainees are exercising an active role in therapy in student mental health programs. Our ability to plan more adequate programs will be enhanced by the accretion of comparable information from other mental health related disciplines.

There are many different patterns of student health programs at the various universities. Part of this is attributable to vicissitudes of size, geography and tradition. It is doubtful that there can be any single "best" pattern of therapeutic facilities which overrides these factors. Nonetheless, one wonders about the relative infrequency of the so-called "integrated" structure. It is not clear from the present survey to what extent "separate" (psychological and psychiatric) facilities are non-overlapping in function. In principle, at least for the relatively smaller universities, the integrated type of facility may be a parsimonious one which could potentially reduce administrative waste resulting from overlap of function, as well as facilitate referrals for potential counselees themselves and for referring personnel.

In the main, psychotherapeutic services provided for undergraduates by psychologists are on a short-range basis, and are without charge. At some institutions graduate trainees are actively involved in therapeutic work with undergraduates, while at other schools such work is done virtually exclusively by staff members. Inherent in each of these facts are issues warranting more careful consideration. Illustratively, to what extent should universities consider the desirability of longer term treatment facilities? What is the potential role of fee and/or insurance programs, with respect to the extension of therapeutic service to a larger proportion of students who might be expected to profit from such help?

By and large the present data appear to reflect an active and growing role for psychology in university mental health work. Doubtless, the potential for expansion of activities in this field is considerable.

NOTES

1. Grateful appreciation is expressed to Drs. John Flavell, S. D. S. Spragg and Melvin Zax, each of whom read an earlier draft of the manuscript and commented constructively thereupon.

2. No attempt was made to differentiate between counseling and psychotherapy, since the terms have a considerable amount of interchangeability in current usage. We did however specifically orient this question, and the entire questionnaire in fact, to personal-social-emotional problems so that our interests could be more clearly delineated for the respondents.

3. One APA approved Ph.D. training institution in clinical psychology has no undergraduates at all. For this and subsequent data summaries, its graduate students are treated as if they were undergraduates.

4. Since the respondents had only the category titles and not their full descriptions, the final classifications made by the author differed in several instances from those made by the respondent. Illustratively, the category "integrated" was checked by a few schools simply on the basis of their having a psychiatric consultant. Such a classification was changed to psychological, when it was clear that the consultant was not actually involved in student contact work.

REFERENCES

1. FARNSWORTH, D. L. *Mental health in college and university.* Cambridge, Mass.: Harvard Univ. Press, 1957.
2. GILBERT, W. M. The clinical psychologist in a student counseling bureau. In *Survey of clinical practice in psychology.* New York: International Univ. Press, 1954.
3. MOORE, N. S. and SUMMERSKILL, J. *Health services in American universities.* Ithaca, N.Y.: Cornell Univ. Press, 1954.

22. The Hospital Psychologist—
Present Problems and Future Solutions

THE scarcity of well-trained psychiatrists, psychologists, and social workers in our mental institutions has reached staggering proportions. In part, this shortage is due to the reluctance of many professionals to work in mental hospitals; they have multiple, well-founded reasons for employing their talents elsewhere. This paper will focus on the special problems encountered by clinical psychologists in mental hospitals; although, some of its conclusions may have relevance to other professions as well. The author presents this analysis with the hope that it might inspire corrective measures to overcome some of the major reservations that many psychologists have about functioning in a mental hospital.

There are several commonly mentioned sources of job dissatisfaction, such as relatively low salaries imposed by the hospital's limited budget and the frustrating amount of institutional red tape. But this discussion will be restricted to a consideration of the professional aspects of the clinical psychologist's work.

The typical graduate from a sound doctoral program in clinical psychology seeks in his job an opportunity to develop his scientific understanding of the behavior of living organisms. He will be attracted to and remain with the kind of mental hospital that permits him to exercise his skills and pursue his interests in a personally and socially rewarding manner.

One of the psychologist's major clinical skills is that which enables him to formulate a dynamically oriented evaluation of a disturbed individual's personality. In doing so, he relies heavily on his understanding of psychopathology; his ability to evaluate and integrate relevant research data; and

Reprinted from *Mental Hospitals*, 1961, 313–320, by permission of *Mental Hospitals* and the author. Dr. Tolor is Director of the Research Institute and Associate Professor, Fairfield University, Fairfield, Connecticut.

his competency to use psychodiagnostic techniques, such as special tests and interview methods. Potentially, this function is one of the most rewarding, interesting, and genuinely significant to the psychologist; unfortunately, when practiced in a mental hospital setting, it also can be the source of a great deal of dissatisfaction.

Many times the hospital psychologist is inundated by a large volume of referrals for evaluation. Too often, referrals are prompted by nothing more than a desire to fulfill certain technical requirements or a supervisor's wishes, without much appreciation on the part of the referring source of the amount of time and energy required to prepare a single thorough evaluation. Moreover, the failure of the referring source to understand what can and what cannot be accomplished by psychological evaluations sometimes leads him to present problems that defy solution.

FRUSTRATION AND ISOLATION

The psychologist may respond with frustration to the discrepancy existing between what reasonably may be expected of him and the need of the referring physician. He also may respond to unreasonable expectations by making unwarranted or sweeping conclusions as a defense against appearing to be ignorant or inadequate in the eyes of professional colleagues.

Another difficulty arises when psychologists sometimes fail to derive an experience of closure in work with hospital patients and may even begin to perceive themselves as interlopers in the patient-physician relationship. This self-perception results when hospitals exclude psychologists from intake conferences and fail to provide them with constant feedback information concerning the patient's course, both during hospitalization and after discharge, as well as significant developments in psychotherapy. Under these conditions it is small wonder that patients' names and faces can become meaningless to the psychologist and that he eventually may visualize patients more as psychograms than as real persons.

In some hospitals, the psychologist may feel that his evaluations and suggestions are given little weight in psychiatric staff decisions and, therefore, represent virtually useless intellectual exercises. When the psychologists' reports are used primarily to confirm psychiatric impressions which will prevail irrespective of deviant psychological findings, the pressure on the psychologist to arrive at an agreement with the psychiatric findings and to disregard psychological test data becomes an important factor in dissatisfaction. Moreover, the work then becomes routine, tedious, and objectionable to the more talented psychologists.

In the role of psychotherapist, the psychologist's primary dissatisfaction with mental hospital work springs from the lack of coordination between the various professions, especially between the therapist and the medical administrator. Too frequently the phrase "team approach" has a hollow ring in the mental hospital and becomes a travesty on the philosophy of a well-coordinated approach. The large number of patients who receive some type of drug treatment in conjunction with psychotherapy underscores the importance of integrating psychotherapeutic interventions with ongoing somatic treatments. The absence of such unified planning often produces deleterious effects which may discourage the psychotherapist who is working toward specific goals with his patient. Similarly destructive consequences may result when, without prior consultation with the therapist, the staff reassigns a patient from one type of ward to another or from one activity program to another.

The need to understand all of the possible effects of administrative decisions concerning the patient makes it vital to keep lines of communication open among the staff. When the therapist and the administrator do not enjoy a constant exchange of viewpoints, they are bound to suffer a variety of misconceptions about each other's intentions.

A special situation occurs when a psychologist functioning as a group therapist is deprived of a voice in making administrative decisions. As we all know, during group-therapy sessions, psychotic patients devote considerable time to discussing administrative policies, such as those relating to open or closed wards, the menu, and ground privileges. Admittedly, the therapist should avoid being sucked into the pros and cons of such issues as far as possible. However, if he is unable to participate in discussions with a flexible administrative staff, his position with the patients is seriously undermined, and his own morale is lowered.

NEGLECTED RESEARCH TALENTS

Research is one of the psychologist's areas of special training and competence; therefore, it should be a particularly attractive activity to him and yield much in the way of job satisfaction. But, the less-than-enthusiastic attitude of many hospital psychologists is reflected in the relatively meager and unimportant clinical research being carried out in their field. This, too, can be traced back to institutions that have failed to provide full support and cooperation to those who are most interested and talented in performing research.

Too many mental hospitals still assign primary importance to the so-called "service functions," even though they could benefit from gaining reputations as research centers and from the general enlightenment that accompanies scientific investigation. Thus the time allotted to research—even when the administration considers it to be a legitimate part of the psychologist's duties—is often so limited that only very superficial, non-complex, and unrelated problems may be tackled.

The hospital psychologist's excessive emphasis on test-oriented research is caused partially by the inaccessibility of clinical data in some hospitals and the disinterest of other professional personnel who may be too caught up in their own pressing needs to provide services. Test-oriented research probably adds little to the resolution of basic mental health problems. The elucidation and refinement of psychologists' diagnostic instruments represent goals far short of their hopes, but even these limited goals are often denied the clinician who is deprived of the staff cooperation necessary for an adequate study.

Other special problems are engendered by the relatively low professional status enjoyed by state, federal, or private-hospital clinical psychologists as compared to that of private practitioners or university clinical psychologists. The private-practice clinician enjoys a high degree of independence in his work and often achieves a much greater monetary reward than does the hospital psychologist. The psychologist in a university is spared many of the interprofessional rivalries existing in hospital settings; in most instances, he also is provided with unusual opportunities for further professional growth and intellectual stimulation which the hospital may not offer.

Some of this status differential can be reduced

by hospitals providing an ample supply of outside consultants and permitting psychologists to participate in the training of other professionals. Clinical psychologists should participate to the fullest extent in the training of psychiatric residents if an adequate foundation for understanding the clinical psychologist's functioning is to be insured. Sometimes residents resist such exposure since their expectations and the psychologists' self-perceptions seem to differ greatly.

THE IDEAL SITUATION

What kind of mental hospital, then, represents a desirable place of employment to a psychologist?

First, this model hospital promotes close integration of the clinical psychologist's activities with those of other professionals. In psychodiagnosis, it provides a team approach in fact rather than in theory by promoting the exchange and proper use of information. From the very start it welcomes the psychologist as an integral part of the evaluating team and its staff consults with him when important decisions are made.

In the ideal mental hospital, the psychologist maintains contact with the patient during the course of hospitalization and automatically receives any available follow-up information. Referrals for testing are well conceived, with due appreciation given to the strengths and weaknesses of psychological assessment techniques. Most important, the psychologist's findings are given equal consideration when a treatment program suited to the patient's needs is being formulated.

This model mental hospital, by closely co-ordinating administrative and therapeutic procedures, also encourages the psychologist to assume greater responsibility in the treatment program. (An example of this is the recent policy prevailing at many VA hospitals which permits psychologists to assume some of the administrative and psychotherapeutic responsibilities for patients on the wards.) Somatic treatments are well integrated with psychotherapy. Communication between the various disciplines flows freely and frequently.

The more attractive hospital encourages research by providing ample time, facilities, and professional support. Clinical material is readily available. The staff is acutely aware of the need for cooperation. The administrator considers coordination of the service staff and the research staff to be vital, especially in research where patients' somatic treatments or social contacts represent variables that must be controlled carefully.

The desirable mental hospital attempts to attract personnel by making the work situation a continuous learning process. It permits competent personnel to function as teachers or consultants. It encourages a constant infusion of ideas from the outside to prevent inbreeding and stagnation of thinking among staff members. It helps clinical psychologists to institute teaching programs which permit them to make important professional contributions and enhances their professional status.

The clinical psychologist in such a hospital might function in an advisory capacity to the administration concerning such matters as the selection of personnel and the morale of hospital employees. He also might assist in establishing closer liaison between the community and the hospital, thereby working toward improvement of public relations.

Two recent developments in mental hospital patient-care may have further profound influences on the clinical psychologist's future activities. First, the higher discharge rate and the more rapid turn-over of hospitalized patients suggests that the harried psychiatrist and psychologist will have progressively less time to spend with any one patient. Consequently, the psychologist should be encouraged to supply intensive training to attendants and nurses who have the most frequent daily contact with patients and, therefore, wield the most influence for better or worse. The psychologist should be urged to adjust his assessment techniques to make them more consistent with the patient's expected stay in the hospital or likely exposure to psychotherapeutic interventions; this would eliminate superfluous testing and provide a better opportunity for a thorough evaluation when indicated.

The second current trend of major significance to psychologists is that of locating new, smaller mental hospitals within the community rather than in isolated rural areas. The implication of this change for hospital psychologists is that they may consult with the patient and his family in the patient's home before hospitalization and prior to or after discharge. Such home visits would permit psychologists to make unique contributions which would extend beyond those made by social workers. Moreover, this approach would open unlimited new vistas for research.

The possibility exists of liberating numbers of well-trained, preventively minded psychologists from the confines of the hospital office and pitting them more directly against the problems of mental illness. Within this possibility lies the mental hospital's brightest hope for attracting and retaining the clinical psychologist of the future.

23. *The Psychologist's Function on a State Level*

ARTHUR J. BINDMAN, NORMAN A. NEIBERG,

RAYMOND R. GILBERT, AND DAVID W. HAUGHEY

VASTLY increased demands for varied rehabilitative services, coupled with shortages of professional personnel, are impelling mental health and correctional program administrators to re-evaluate the traditional functions of their professional staffs. As a result, during the last 15 years, clinical psychologists have steadily assumed larger and more complex responsibilities.

Who is a clinical psychologist, and what services can he render?[1] Today, the term "clinical psychologist" is usually applied only to those who have obtained a Ph.D. in psychology and are scientist-practitioners in the clinical aspects of human behavior. A clinical psychologist, to obtain his Ph.D., must complete at least four years of graduate study and practical field training in one of 56 training programs approved by the American Psychological Association. During his graduate training, he is given progressively more experience and responsibility which equips him to offer services beyond that of a mere "mental tester." In addition, he can achieve Diplomate status from the American Board of Examiners in Professional Psychology after completion of his Ph.D., five years of acceptable experience, and written and oral examinations.

This report will discuss six major areas of a clinical psychologist's role in Massachusetts as he collaborates with the other "helping professions": diagnosis, psychotherapy, research, education and training, consultation, and administration.

DIAGNOSIS

Clinical psychologists have made a major contribution to the diagnostic evaluation of patients. Through testing, they contribute importantly and uniquely to differential diagnosis, personality assessment, and the evaluation of thinking disorders in brain-damaged individuals. Although these services are usually performed at the intake phase, psychologists also help to assess continued-treatment techniques.

In most correctional institutions, the psychologist usually is the only person on the classification board who is trained to make systematic observations of the inmates' emotional problems and controls and provide useful information about their potentials for rehabilitation. By means of special tests he helps hospital patients or prison inmates to plan for educational or occupational activities after discharge.

EXAMPLES

A seven-year-old boy exhibited marked hyperactive, destructive behavior and posed a problem of differential diagnosis. Although the boy's case history was ambiguous in regard to physical or functional problems, the psychologist found test patterns suggestive of organic brain damage. Subsequent EEG studies confirmed these findings.

A patient was admitted to a hospital and diagnosed as schizophrenic. His schizophrenic episodes had been relatively acute, but because he very quickly regressed to infantile behavior, psychotherapy for him was questionable. Projective tests determined the degree of regression and revealed many personality strengths. These strengths indicated a favorable prognosis if the patient were to receive immediate psychotherapy which would continue over a long period of time. On the other hand, projective tests suggested that a similar patient was less treatable because his basic personality was much more infantile.

A sex offender was admitted to a correctional institution, and, after diagnostic testing, was placed in both group and individual psychotherapy. Tests were

Reprinted from *Mental Hospitals*, 1961, *12*, 6–9, by permission of *Mental Hospitals* and the authors. Dr. Bindman is Director of Psychological Services, Massachusetts Department of Mental Health; Dr. Neiberg is Director of Psychological Research, Division of Legal Medicine, Massachusetts Department of Mental Health; Dr. Gilbert is Professor of Psychology, State College at Boston; and Dr. Haughey is Associate Professor of Psychology, State College at Boston.

repeated several times throughout the treatment regimen and provided the best objective measure of personality change.

PSYCHOTHERAPY

Psychologists are trained and experienced in both group and individual psychotherapy, and receive psychiatric supervision during their professional training. In community mental health centers for children, they conduct play and activity group therapy and discussion groups for both parents and children. In hospitals or correctional institutions, they provide rapid, emergency psychotherapeutic techniques. In state schools, they give group counseling and educational therapy to patients and assist in vocational planning. While therapy and counseling are important during continued treatment, they are often equally valuable during aftercare, particularly if, in each period, they are performed by the same psychologist.

In a correctional institution, the psychologist may be the only person who is trained in psychotherapy. He conducts both individual and group therapy for inmates who need such assistance to adjust to the institution and, after release, to the community.

EXAMPLES

A probation officer referred an eight-year-old adopted boy to a community mental health center because the boy repeatedly set fires. A psychologist initiated contact with the boy through diagnostic testing and gave him weekly play therapy for two years. By learning to express his basic problem of self-identity and to accept his adoption, the boy improved markedly and his fire-setting ceased.

A young adult was admitted to a mental hospital during an acute schizophrenic episode. He seemed to adjust well to the hospital and was placed in intake group psychotherapy, led by a psychologist. He also received individual psychotherapy from a psychiatrist. In the group, the patient was able to revaluate some of his problems and to compare them with those of other patients. He recovered rapidly and returned to the community within two months. As an outpatient, he continued to visit the hospital for a year for group psychotherapy, and was then discharged.

A 20-year-old inmate in a correctional institution was placed in permanent segregation because of repeated assaultive behavior toward correctional officers and other inmates. A psychologist administered psychotherapy and continued it after the inmate was released from segregation. Although the inmate's basic problems have not been altered, he is making his first successful institutional adjustment in five years and is utilizing other treatment and training programs with an eye to his future release from the institution.

RESEARCH

Psychologists are trained as behavioral scientists and are experienced in research strategy, design, and methodology. Psychological research, based on significant and answerable questions, provides important information concerning the effectiveness of programs or treatment techniques, flaws in the social climate of a ward or prison which may impede rehabilitation, and the best methods for teaching defective children. A competent research staff obtains special grants from government and other agencies. These grants assist in attracting top-level personnel to institutions.

EXAMPLES

A mental health center became interested in the epidemiology of local juvenile delinquency. A staff psychologist initiated a project to obtain data about sources and distributions of delinquents in an urban population, and to develop a method of classifying the delinquents. This information provided a basis for developing and deploying services to meet the area's needs.

A psychologist in the Division of Legal Medicine faced the problem of improving a poor classification scheme and weak diagnostic categories for a wide variety of patients. He developed techniques which enabled agency personnel to better understand the kinds of patients with whom they dealt. He outlined schedules to assess and more precisely diagnose these patients, to provide better means of program evaluation, and to facilitate realistic program planning for the future.

The psychologist in a state hospital gathered information about the hospital's patient-population by means of objective observations. This information became the basis for developing specific hypotheses which could be evaluated by psychological tests and other methods. Results assisted the hospital to better understand the type of patient-population with which it was dealing and to provide more suitable treatment techniques.

TRAINING AND EDUCATION

With regard to hospital inservice training, psychologists provide courses, group discussions, lectures, and special programs for nurses, psychiatrists, social workers, and lay personnel. Psychologists play key roles in community mental health education programs; they plan, organize, and conduct programs to explain mental health principles, human development, and the nature of mental disorders. In correctional institutions, psychologists develop mental health training programs for correctional officers and educational groups for inmates.

Psychologists also help to train graduate students and new psychologists by supervising diagnostic testing, psychotherapy, consultation, and research. Such training programs, developed in close liaison with accredited universities, often channel new personnel into the state's mental health and correctional programs.

Officials of a mental health association asked the staff of a community mental health center to co-ordinate educational programs with the association's membership drive. The center's psychologist directed a program of movies and guest speakers on the theme of "normal child development." As a result, discussion groups were started with parents, bringing about better communication between the mental health center and the community.

The psychologist at a state hospital developed an intern program for graduate psychology students at a local university. From this program he obtained extra psychological services and potential staff members for the hospital, and was able to initiate important research projects. He in turn has been stimulated by his participation in the training program and by teaching at the university.

A psychologist in the Division of Mental Hygiene, who had public health training, developed an inservice training program to orient new professional personnel to public health aspects of community mental health.

A teacher was going to exclude a seven-year-old boy from the first grade because she was unable to control his aggressive behavior. She requested consultative help from the local mental health center. The psychologist consultant recognized the teacher's personal over-involvement in the problem and helped her to see the child's behavior as an understandable reaction to deprivation and rejection at home. No longer threatened and upset, the teacher was able to use her habitual skill in handling problem children, and helped the boy to settle down and do better in school.

A hospital superintendent was faced with the problem of developing a high-level training hospital. Because his psychology department was weak, he asked a psychologist consultant from a central department to discuss various methods of enhancing his program. During meetings over a period of five months, the consultant helped the superintendent to develop a better staff through more extensive inservice training and closer liaison with training universities. This in turn produced a more stimulating and challenging program for the entire hospital.

A new superintendent of a correctional institution wanted to improve the morale of staff and inmates by developing a counseling program. A psychologist consultant from the Division of Legal Medicine met with the superintendent to evaluate the institution's counseling needs and decide how to put necessary services into action. The consultant helped the superintendent to develop a personnel-training program, an alcoholism clinic, and individual and group therapy programs, utilizing mental health workers from both the institution and the Division.

CONSULTATION

Psychologists have demonstrated their skills in practicing the specialized techniques of mental health consultation. In community mental health centers, they develop contacts with professional agencies that care for large groups of children and give crisis consultation on children's specific adjustment problems. As an outgrowth of their consultant roles, psychologists also act as case-finding agents. In this way, without themselves getting involved in long-term treatment and case follow-up, they help other professional workers to use their own skills more effectively.

In the hospital, psychologists provide specialized consultation and technical assistance to various types of personnel. They assist the administrator of a hospital or correctional institution to improve programming. In many agencies, psychologists function as consultants to other professional workers in areas such as diagnosis, research, psychotherapy, and administration.

ADMINISTRATION

The role of psychologists in administration is a new and expanding one. Their theoretical knowledge, research training, and experience qualify them to organize and administer programs of clinical, consultative, and educative services. They also provide specific services to administrators, such as personnel evaluation and screening, and program analysis.

In the Division of Mental Hygiene, psychologists are administrators of some community mental health centers, maintaining liaison with community leaders and other agencies concerned with mental health. In hospitals, psychologists serve as administrative officers of wards or larger sub-sections, taking responsibility for the daily routine management of patient-activities and care. Psychologists are administrators of outpatient services or follow-up services of hospitals and state schools. Their administrative duties include the direction of psychology departments where they recruit personnel and take charge of program planning and training programs. They also coordinate particular aspects of their departmental programs with other segments of the total hospital program.

A psychologist directs a state-wide, multi-discipline program of nursery centers for mentally retarded children. Others assist in developing similar broad programs in the Division of Legal Medicine.

Psychologists in the correctional field function as deputy commissioners, administering a department-wide personnel and inservice training program or a classification and treatment program. They serve as institution superintendents, associate wardens or directors of treatment, and as administrators of specific clinical facilities.

EXAMPLES

A psychologist was named executive director of a community mental health center in the Division of Mental Hygiene. He assumed responsibility for the center's finances and its professional staff functions and standards; liaison with the local mental health association, mental health board, and care-taking agencies; and development of a total community mental health program. During a two-year period, the psychologist's position became well defined and highly accepted in the community, facilitating even closer relationships between the community and the mental health center. The center also became a training agency for a large university training program.

A psychologist in a large state hospital developed a major training and research program in collaboration with a local university's psychology training program. Through his administrative skill, he was able to develop pre-doctoral and post-doctoral training programs and a number of research programs which were subsidized by federal funds. These provided much-needed services for the hospital and guaranteed a pool of prospective employees. The psychologist also served as administrative assistant to the hospital's superintendent, taking charge of specific aspects of program development.

A clinical psychologist in the Department of Mental Health, functioning in relation to correctional problems, was promoted to a top administrative position in the Department of Correction where he could apply his skills in enhancing and developing the total treatment and classification program. Another psychologist is administrator of all personnel and training programs in the Department of Correction.

NOTES

1. For purposes of this paper the term "clinical psychologist" and "psychologist" will be used interchangeably. The authors realize the increasingly important roles that other psychologists—social, experimental, and counseling—are playing in the mental health and correctional fields, but will limit their statements primarily to clinical psychologists.

24. Psychologists' Concept of Their Role in Institutions Housing the "Criminally Insane"

LYMAN M. RIEGEL AND RAYMOND A. SPERN

IN the past decade there has been a marked growth in the number of psychologists and psychological services rendered in agencies for the treatment of the "criminally insane," paralleling the growth of the profession of psychology as a whole (Rogers, 1956, 1957; United States Department of Health, Education, and Welfare, 1954). However, this increase in personnel has not been accompanied by improved communication of specialized techniques and knowledge, although a start has been made in a closely related field (Corsini, 1956; Corsini & Miller, 1954; Sell, undated). The present study was undertaken to partially remedy this situation by publishing a list of those institutions or units of institutions which house the "criminally insane" and by surveying the psychologists' concept of their role in such agencies, including especial emphasis on psychotherapeutic functions.

A letter was sent to the Director of Mental Health in every state,[2] requesting a list of institutions or units of institutions in their states which house persons legally defined as "criminally insane," that is, those persons who have been adjudged not guilty of the commission of a crime by reason of insanity. It was known that the laws pertaining to the care of the "criminally insane" varied widely (Weihofen, 1954), and it was hypothesized that treatment facilities differed accordingly.

Upon receipt of this information, a questionnaire was mailed to the superintendents of 56 such institutions in 48 states[2] with the request that they pass it on to the psychologist most intimately acquainted with the division for the "criminally insane."[3] In the event there was no psychologist associated with this division, the department heads

Reprinted from *American Psychologist*, 1960, *15*, 160–163, by permission of the American Psychological Association and the authors. Mr. Riegel is Director of Inservice Training, State Hospital No. 1, Fulton, Missouri. Mr. Spern is Research Associate, Human Resources Research Office, Fort Benning, Georgia.

were requested to indicate the fact. After a follow-up of nonrespondents, the final return comprised 89 per cent of the 56 institutions.[4] Since seven of the replies indicated that no psychologists were closely connected with this service, the results reported are for the remaining 43 agencies.

In addition to asking for the number of patients, full-time and part-time psychologists and their academic degrees, psychiatrically trained physicians, and board certified psychiatrists, the questionnaire contained five questions (four multiple-choice) directly pertaining to psychologic functions. These were:

1. Rough percentage of your staff's time given over to clinical evaluation, research, therapy, consulting with other staff members, teaching and training, and other

2. How satisfied in your psychology staff regarding your administration's recognition, respect, and utilization of your professional skills? (very satisfied, satisfied, dissatisfied, very dissatisfied)

3. Does the administration of your institution encourage or favor the use of psychotherapy and/or counseling done by psychologists? (strongly approve, approve, disapprove, strongly disapprove)

4. Are the opinions of the psychology staff taken into consideration in plans concerning the treatment or discharge of patients? (always, usually, occasionally, rarely, never)

5. Protection of the public should be the *primary* consideration that determines the staff's decision as to the discharge of patients committed as "not guilty by reason of insanity." Your opinion: (agree, disagree). Administration's viewpoint: (agree, disagree).

RESULTS

The Directors of Mental Health (and the various psychologists) were very cooperative in forwarding information on the "criminally insane" in their respective states. A few made it clear that they were responsible for the mental health program and either had no official connection or little contact with the hospitals. Others apparently had well coordinated programs.

At this point, it might be well to stress the great differences which prevail between institutions of this type. New York, for example, has two state hospitals for the "criminal insane," both under the supervision of the Department of Correction. Dannemora serves male convicts declared mentally ill while serving a sentence for a felony. Matteawan houses the "criminally insane," plus mentally ill male nonfelons, mentally ill female prisoners, and various patients from state hospitals.

The Men's Reformatory in Iowa, under the Board of Control, houses the "criminally insane" in addition to a number of mentally ill persons who must remain there until they are adjudged competent to stand trial for legal offenses. In those other states which keep some "criminally insane" in prisons, the motive appears to be security; the state hospital may retain technical custody. In many states, mentally ill prisoners can be transferred to mental hospitals for treatment; the time spent there may or may not count toward their sentence.

Table 1 summarizes the data on the number of patients, psychologists, and medical psychiatric personnel. In addition, it presents the ratio of patients per psychologist and per medical psychiatric staff member. The range in number of patients and ratio to staff varies widely from one institution to another: 14 institutions have 300 or more patients with only Lima, Ionia, Farview, and Matteawan State Hospitals housing over 1,000 patients; 41 per cent of the psychologists are full-time, while 56 per cent of the units have only part-time psychologists.

Table 2 depicts the percentage of total time devoted by psychologists to their various duties. It is immediately apparent that the major activity is psychodiagnosis and secondarily that of psychotherapy, although 21 per cent of the institutions reported no psychotherapy or counseling.

TABLE 1. NUMBER OF PATIENTS, PSYCHOLOGISTS, AND PHYSICIANS; AND RATIO OF PATIENTS TO PSYCHOLOGIC AND MEDICAL STAFF

Item	Number of Respondents	Range	Mean	Median
Number of patients	39	5–2,000	318	150
Number of psychologists	27[a]	0–3	1.3	1
Number of physicians	27[a]	0–13	2.6	2
Patients per psychologist	27[a]	5–2,000	307	276
Patients per physician	27[a]	5–782	155	138

[a] Mean number of patients 396; median 276

TABLE 2. STAFF DUTIES OF PSYCHOLOGISTS IN PERCENTAGES

(33 Respondents)

Activity	Range	Mean	Median
Evaluation	1–97	49	50
Therapy and/or counseling	0–40	17	20
Consulting	0–25	9	10
Teaching	0–20	5	5
Research	0–20	5	3
Other	0–30	3	0

Table 3 indicates that medical administrations have strongly favorable attitudes toward psychologists performing psychotherapy and that as a whole psychologists working with the "criminally insane" are fairly well satisfied in their relations with their administration. The apparent discrepancy between the attitudes of the administration toward psychologists doing psychotherapy and the percentage of time actually spent in this activity may be due to the disproportionate amount of time

TABLE 3. RELATIONSHIP BETWEEN MEDICAL ADMINISTRATION AND PSYCHOLOGY

(39 Respondents)

Question	Response category			
Administration's attitude toward psychotherapy by psychologists	Strongly	Approve	Disapprove	Strongly disapprove
Percent agreement	36	61	3	0
Consideration of psychologists' opinion in planning[a]	Always	Usually	Occasionally	Rarely
Percent agreement	23	56	18	3
Satisfaction with administrations' utilization of skills	Very	Satisfied	Dissatisfied	Very dissatisfied
Percent agreement	36	49	15	0

[a] A "Never" category was not used by respondents.

devoted to the routine but very important job of psychological evaluation.

The administrations' view on the subject of the protection of the public in relation to the discharge of patients (as perceived by the respondents) and that of the psychologists do not closely coincide. Psychologists apparently tend to judge each case more upon its individual merits than do the administrators. Of the psychologists, 53 per cent agreed that the protection of the public was the primary consideration in discharging patients, while they felt that 71 per cent of the hospital heads agreed with this philosophy.

In attempting to determine what factors entered into the attitude of administrations toward psychotherapy conducted by psychologists, comparisons were made between those institutions reporting an attitude of "strong approval" as contrasted to those which only "approved." No significant difference was found in the percentage of time spent in psychotherapy. No significant relationship between the degree of administrative approval of psychotherapy and the educational level of the psychology personnel (master's versus doctoral level) was apparent. There was no systematic relationship between the degree of approval and the absolute number of medical personnel in the institutions; however, there was a more favorable attitude in those institutions having a smaller ratio of patients and physicians. No relationship appeared between the geographic location of hospitals (north vs. south, east vs. west) and the degree of approval of psychotherapy done by psychologists.

DISCUSSION

The initial assumption that treatment facilities for the "criminally insane" varied widely was borne out by the study. It is evident that there are a few large institutions and many smaller units. Other data reveal that: 3 western states have no provisions for treatment of the "criminally insane," 3 states have separate hospitals for the Negro insane, 3 states use prison wards, and at least 11 states house the "criminally insane" in their regular hospital population. Only California specifically listed special facilities for women, although it is assumed that all states segregate on the basis of sex within hospital units of this type.

The percentage of time spent by individual psychologists in their various activities differs considerably from institution to institution. It is of interest that the median time spent in these activities corresponds closely with the allocation of psycho-

logical staff time in state institutions for the mentally retarded (Berger & Waters, 1956). The lack of time spent in research perhaps reflects the strong emphasis placed upon service functions, such as psychodiagnosis, rather than a disinterest in this vital area. A considerable part of the psychologists possess the PhD degree. However, it could be argued with solid support from the facts that even research trained clinicians value "helping others" above their research role. It is an interesting commentary that, while clinicians in training are taught that their "unique contribution" is research, in reality most of them seem primarily motivated to "help people." There are few productive clinicians researchwise (Clark, 1957).

Although the competence of psychologists in psychotherapy is widely accepted, the investigators endeavored to find out what attitudes prevailed in institutions for the "criminally insane." The fact that institutions reporting differences in the degree of approval tend, nevertheless, to report similar percentages of time spent doing psychotherapy could reflect a lack of discrimination between the rating categories of "strongly approve" versus mere "approve." The difference in the ratio of psychiatric personnel to patients in institutions "strongly favorable" as contrasted to those that only "approve" suggests there may be a real distinction, however. The administrations of those institutions in which there is a more favorable ratio of physicians to patients may have a more "enlightened" attitude regarding psychotherapy in general and the role of their psychological personnel in particular, although service demands for psychological evaluation remain high and therefore limit the time that can be spent in psychotherapy.

No meaningful relationship was established between the psychologists' degree of satisfaction with the administrations' utilization of their professional skills and with the extent to which their opinions were taken into consideration. In fact, the one psychologist who replied that his opinion was rarely considered indicated that he was very satisfied! The overall degree of reported job satisfaction is surprisingly high since in the maximum security treatment situation the conflicts between therapeutic and custodial philosophies are maximized.

It should be kept in mind that, as a matter of courtesy and convenience, the questionnaires were sent through the superintendents of the various hospitals. Methodologically, a distorted picture could be obtained if replies went back through official channels. The authors feel that this did not occur except in one case, and even then the psychologist wrote in "at the moment" after "satisfied." Typically, a returned questionnaire would be accompanied by a page or more of additional information, qualifications, comments, and criticism. It was later impossible to write to the homes of the reporting psychologists since provision had been made for anonymity.

More than anything, these findings might indicate that, just as institutions vary in size and scope of treatment, so do the satisfactions and tribulations of working in institutions for the "criminally insane" vary from psychologist to psychologist. That is, there may be selective factors which attract some clinicians to this type setting. If state institution psychologists acquire lower status through association with their patients, one would expect their status needs to be highly frustrated in units for the so-called "criminally insane," since it is difficult to imagine any other group which the public holds in more opprobrium. On the other hand, a psychologist may gain some notoriety and be viewed as one who can "handle himself" with such reputedly dangerous individuals.

Jacobson, Rettig, and Pasamanick (1959) suggested that state institution psychologists may be oriented toward public service. To a clinician, work with the "criminally insane" may be a challenge, an opportunity for service to a long neglected group, and an ideal chance to conduct research with a "captive" population. Depending upon the extent to which intellectual stimulation and professional freedom are lacking in the maximum security setting, clinicians may tend to move elsewhere. Further research might be conducted on the sociological structure of such units and on the comparative length of stay of psychological personnel.

NOTES

1. This study was completed in partial fulfillment of the requirements for a course in Professional Problems under the supervision of Robert S. Daniel, Chairman of the Department of Psychology at the University oe Missouri; it was approved and underwritten by thf Research Committee of State Hospital No. 1, Fulton, Missouri, where the authors were employed in the Psychology Department. The authors also wish to thank C. Scott Moss, Chief Psychologist at State Hospital No. 1, and others for their constructive suggestions.

2. Alaska and Hawaii were not states at the time of the study.

3. The authors wish to thank Donald L. Leslie, Chief Psychologist, Lima State Hospital, Lima, Ohio, for supplying a partial listing of hospitals and hospital units for the "criminally insane."

4. A list of hospitals and hospital units for the "criminally insane" has been deposited with the American Documentation Institute. Order Document No. 6150 from ADI Auxiliary Publication Project, Photoduplication Service, Library of Congress, Washington, D.C. 20025, remitting in advance $1.25 for microfilm or $1.25 for photocopies. Make checks payable to: Chief, Photoduplication Service, Library of Congress.

REFERENCES

BERGER, A., & WATERS, T. J. The psychologist's concept of his function in institutions for the mentally retarded. *Amer. J. ment. Defic.*, 1956, 60, 823–826.

CLARK, K. E. *America's psychologists.* Washington, D.C.: APA, 1957.

CORSINI, R. J. Clinical psychology in correctional institutions. In D. Brower & L. E. Abt (Eds.), *Progress in clinical psychology.* Vol. II. New York: Grune & Stratton, 1956. Pp. 260–265.

CORSINI, R. J., & MILLER, G. A. Psychology in prisons, 1952. *Amer. Psychologist*, 1954, 9, 184–185.

JACOBSON, F. N., RETTIG, S., & PASAMANICK, B. Status, job satisfaction, and factors of job satisfaction of state institution and clinic psychologists. *Amer. Psychologist*, 1959, 14, 144–150.

ROGERS, L. S. Psychologists in public service and the public. *Amer. Psychologist*, 1956, 11, 307–313.

ROGERS, L. S. Psychologists in public service and how they grew. *Amer. Psychologist*, 1957, 12, 232–233.

SELL, D. E. (Ed.) *Manual of applied correctional psychology.* Columbus: Dept. Mental Hygiene and Correction, State of Ohio, undated.

UNITED STATES DEPARTMENT OF HEALTH, EDUCATION, AND WELFARE, Public Health Service, National Institute of Mental Health. *Patients in mental institutions 1950 and 1951.* Washington, D.C.: United States Government Printing Office, 1954.

WEIHOFEN, H. *Mental disorder as a criminal defense.* Buffalo: Dennis, 1954.

25. The Expanding Role of Psychologists in Juvenile Corrections

DON G. LEDERMAN

THE field of juvenile corrections is seeking more and more well-trained psychologists who are needed to function in a variety of roles.

Some installations have a psychology department which provides a ratio of one psychologist per 50 children. The institutions themselves have become open, homelike settings structured on the basis of small cottage units. Many of them utilize emotionally healthy married couples as cottage parents. The atmosphere is a non-punitive one of warmth and acceptance, designed to break into the repetitive cycle of rejection-hostility and to promote a feeling within the child that he is a respected member of society rather than a convict. Active treatment programs, based on etiological factors and unconscious motivation in addition to behavior, are in the ascendance. To this end, greater efforts are being put forth in the diagnostic area; labeling a child and assigning him to a program is no longer considered sufficient classification. More and more, the institution is becoming professionalized and treatment oriented. Some even have progressed to the point where they are successfully defying the strong tide of traditionalism which dictates the absolute separation of treatment and custody. That is, the happy incorporation of the custodial aspects of the program (cottage or home life department) within the clinical services department is being tried with much success. The individual cottage units are each supervised by a professionally trained person who assumes a position of leadership in the team approach to rehabilitation. Finally, even administrative personnel, including the superintendent, are now professionally trained.

In this new institution the functions of the psychologist are: [diagnostics, consultation and training, administrative consultation, therapy, research, committee assignments, community contacts, and administration.]

DIAGNOSTICS

As part of the routine intake process, and on special referral, the psychologist is responsible for thorough psycho-diagnostic evaluations. He is given sufficient time to administer individual projective techniques, to conduct depth interviews, and to interpret and integrate this material into a comprehensive word-picture of the child. He tries to answer, in everyday language, three major questions: "What, if anything, is wrong with the child? How did he get that way? What can we do about it while he is here?" Based on his understanding of the subject's conflicts, needs, and motivations, as well as the etiology of his problems, the psychologist makes detailed recommendations to the child's therapist or counselor, his cottage parents, his teachers, and his recreational supervisors. The recommendations provide guidelines for these staff members in their individual and cooperative efforts to interact most therapeutically with the child. In addition to the wide circulation of the report and its direct use by other staff, it also functions as an important resource available to the psychologist in his role of consultant and teacher.

CONSULTATION AND TRAINING

Since the new philosophy holds that all staff is involved in the treatment process, the psychologist is kept quite busy consulting with and training both professional and non-professional personnel. The results and implications of psychological examinations are sometimes orally presented and interpreted to social workers, cottage parents, and other interested parties. The social worker-counselor

Adapted from Donald G. Lederman, "The Expanding Role of Psychologists in Juvenile Corrections," *Correctional Psychologist*, 1965, *1*, 5–7, by permission of *Correctional Psychologist* and the author. Dr. Lederman is Clinical Psychology Consultant, Office for Children and Youth, Pennsylvania Department of Public Welfare.

often requests consultation with the psychologist regarding an immediate problem with a child, as well as on-going consultation and guidance of their therapeutic efforts, both individual and group. Frequently, the psychologist will advise teachers and cottage parents regarding their relationship with a particular child or their handling of a group.

In addition to providing guidelines for immediate treatment goals or problems, these consultative efforts unquestionably also incorporate elements of an informal training device. For example, if a suggestion made by a psychologist to a cottage parent bears fruit, then the content of the suggestion at least, and, hopefully, the clinical insight behind it, are likely to become part of the cottage parent's permanent skills. Staff or team meetings, organized to discuss a particular child, and chaired by the psychologist, very often have as their chief value the opportunity they afford to expose lay staff to clinical concepts. Finally, the psychologist assumes more formal teaching responsibilities in the form of lectures and discussions during professional seminars and in-service training programs.

ADMINISTRATIVE CONSULTATION

The psychologist is often a member of the superintendent's advisory board. It is this board which formulates the top-level administrative policies and treatment philosophy of the institution. His counsel is sought also on a more formal basis by the superintendent and the heads of other departments. This level of consultation affords the psychologist the very rewarding experience of being involved as a prime mover in the progress of the total institution toward a treatment milieu. Further, the administration often asks the psychology department to take an active part in personnel selection.

THERAPY

The institutional psychologist cannot hope to do therapy with his share of the total population, even when this is only 50 clients. The resistance on the part of these stoical young people to traditional therapeutic approaches is legend. The new philosophy holds that the entire institutional staff should be part of the treatment cadre and all-too-often most of the non-professionals are inadequately trained in this role. Thus, the psychologist may most economically and valuably use his time and skill by letting one-to-one therapy take a back seat to working with the child's other "therapists" (in the form of consultation and training). By communi-

cating a child's problems and needs to other staff members, and then directing their endeavors, the psychologist is able to spread himself much thinner, and the impact of his special knowledge and skills is felt by more children than would be possible through office-type therapy.

The psychologist, however, is never in danger of losing his skill as a psychotherapist for lack of practice. There are more than ample numbers of children among this very diversified clientele who fit the classical "intelligent neurotic" mold, or who do not respond to the treatment "milieu." The most interesting (the sickest) children are referred for both group and individual therapy. Enough are referred, in fact, to allow the psychologist to select among them for clients he believes would be most responsive. Nevertheless, the writer does not believe that there is any danger of the therapist role crowding out the consultant role. The difficulty and frustrations inherent in "reaching" this type of client rather quickly persuade the psychologist that he would be better off devoting more time to environmental manipulation and staff guidance as his preferred mode of operation. Even if the therapist is lucky enough to "reach" the client, he often discovers that his efforts are continually nullified by the experiences the child has outside the therapy office (in his cottage or classroom). To protect the fruits of his own labors, therefore, the psychologist is again pushed toward a greater emphasis on consultation and training.

RESEARCH

In the progressive institutions, the psychologist is encouraged to conduct both immediately practical and basic research. In addition to being allowed to indulge his own interests in this area, he quickly realizes that in an institutional setting, it is the psychologist who is the recognized expert in matters pertaining to research. Administrators, psychiatrists, and social workers all seem to be aware of their educational shortcomings in this regard and come to him for help with theory, test construction, research design, and statistics. Thus, psychologists are finding that research provides another important outlet for their consultative role.

COMMITTEE ASSIGNMENTS

The psychologist is asked to serve on or chair all types of institutional committees. These would include classification, diagnostic, discipline, transfer, recreation, etc. Here again, perhaps the most important value of psychological participation in these functions lies in the opportunity it affords to promulgate clinical insights and approaches among the committees' non-professional members. The skillful psychologist may even be able to help transform a discipline committee into an instrument for treatment.

COMMUNITY CONTACTS

If such activity is desired, the psychologist will find ample opportunity to address community and service organizations regarding delinquency (its causes, prevention, and treatment) and the training school program. In so doing, he becomes an integral part of the important public relations efforts of the institution. He also is making a valuable contribution to the rehabilitation process itself, since community response to the parolee is of prime importance in solidifying institutional gains and preventing recidivism. And, as we all know, parole and other community services are the weakest links in the rehabilitation chain.

ADMINISTRATION

Since the purpose of this paper is to discuss the role of a psychologist employed as such, administrative opportunities will be mentioned only briefly. For those interested, top-level correctional positions are beginning to open for those in the psychological profession. They take the form of Intake Director, Clinical or Treatment Director, Program Director, Assistant Superintendent, Superintendent, and director of a statewide psychology program for a multi-institutional system. This type of position provides the psychologist with a very broad base for disseminating and implementing his philosophy of treatment.

In general, the entire field of juvenile corrections has so recently opened for the psychologist, and progress is so rapid, that the beginning professional is in the enviable position of being able to create his own job description. That is, he is usually allowed to emphasize those aspects of the expanding role discussed above that are most interesting and rewarding to him.

26. *Clinical Child Psychology in the Schools*[1]

HERSHEL BERKOWITZ

WHILE the educational psychologist has been the psychologist most typically involved in the schools, clinicians have evinced an increasing interest in the area of education (Sarason, Davidson, & Blatt, 1962) and have contributed to a significant extent to the recent role changes and developments in the schools. It may in fact be argued that certain aspects of clinical training enable the child clinician to make a unique and helpful contribution to the schools. I would like to pursue this argument further at a later point.

First, however, I would like to emphasize that the clinician's attraction to and involvement with the schools are not without ambivalence. Complaints about teachers' lack of understanding and rigidity are quite frequent. Reports on such programs of consultation in the schools as those of Losen (1964) and Newman (1965) often sound more like projects for the infiltration of enemy territory than descriptions of attempts to cooperate with, and lend advice to, fellow professionals.

On the other hand, while educators have become increasingly open in asking for advice and assistance in dealing with children manifesting emotional disturbances or difficulties in learning, they too have not been unambivalent in their reactions toward clinicians. Diagnostic services have been widely accepted, but when clinicians have attempted to formulate courses of action in the schools on the basis of their evaluations, a divergence of educational reaction has occurred (Leaverton, 1965). Anecdotes range from those instances in which clinicians have been regarded as helpful persons in the enterprise of dealing with and helping difficult children within the classroom to instances in which educators have indicated that the most helpful service which some clinicians could render would be the removal of their patients and themselves from the school system.

Now, there is no question but what some children are so disruptive to normal school procedures that a great deal of anger and resentment is generated toward the clinician who suggests that they be dealt with in the classroom situation. This may be the case even when keeping the child in the class is, objectively, the most feasible available alternative. Under such circumstances resentment and resistance directed toward the clinician is readily understood as a displacement of the frustration and anger which the difficult child has aroused. Often the problem is complicated when a dearth of facilities prevents the removal from the classroom of children that are better treated in special educational settings. In such cases the clinician may be resented because he is the interpreter of a frustrating and disappointing reality circumstance. Nor is there any question but that many educators—teachers, principals, and administrators alike—are threatened by psychologists and find it difficult to work with them. There is a fear that collaboration with psychology may subvert the educational system from its primary goal of education. Psychologists are often regarded as persons who condone the inappropriate and inadequate in behavior. Educators maintaining such a point of view fear and resent the psychologist as a person who might encourage teachers to accept their charges' failures to achieve, instead of seeking ways to remedy the situation (Bower, 1946). A further source of educational resentment of psychologists is a tendency for psychologists to be regarded as mindreaders, persons who constantly scrutinize and criticize the behavior of those around them. As a result of this attitude many educators feel exposed, vulnerable, and threatened by the psychologist and hence are unable to freely discuss classroom problems or cases with him.

It seems clear that much of the friction between educators and their erstwhile psychological collaborators is due to situational limitations and to the educator's lack of familiarity and understanding of the role and manner of the functioning of the

Reprinted from *Psychology in the Schools*, 1966, *3*, 223–228, by permission of *Psychology in the Schools* and the author. Dr. Berkowitz is Instructor in Clinical Psychology, University of Colorado Medical Center.

psychologist. One might thus conclude that improved facilities and better education of the educators might be all that is necessary to render the psycho-educational collaboration a fruitful one.

I do not believe this to be the case. The difficulties are not as one-sided as the preceding discussion might suggest. Many clinicians seem to find it extremely difficult to communicate in a meaningful and helpful manner with educators (Bower, 1964), even about children who are not severely disturbed or who need not be exceedingly difficult to deal with in the classroom. Such difficulty in communication seems to occur, in my own experience, even when educators are not particularly threatened or unsympathetic to the clinician's contribution. Why is this so?

Bower (1964) suggests that the source of some of these difficulties might lie in the basically different approaches which educators and clinicians maintain in the course of their duties. Bower maintains that the educator's stance is task oriented, emphasizing cognitions and discipline above affects and affective expression. The clinician, on the other hand, is more concerned with affective expression and tends to place a generally higher priority upon feelings. Bower believes that this relative difference in emphasis may lead to difficulty when the psychologist is called upon to render assistance in matters pertaining to the classroom. I believe that Bower's interpretation of the basic difference between the educational and clinical position is essentially to the point, at least at present. This need not necessarily continue to be the case however. The recent increase in emphasis upon ego-functions in psychoanalytic theory has resulted in an increased emphasis upon the cognitive and structural aspects of functioning in clinical psychology. Such a shift in emphasis may well serve to lessen the distance between the positions of clinicians and educators and to increase the ease of communication between the two professions.[2] On the other hand, educators are becoming increasingly concerned with the need for more emphasis upon the individual child in teacher training. It is in this area that the clinician brings to the classroom an emphasis and skill which the educator lacks. Here also, however, a second problem arises, for the clinician's concern with the functioning of the individual is most often coupled with a total lack of appreciation for the pressures and demands of the classroom situation in which educators must work.

The typical public school teacher is faced with the task of imparting intellectual contents and skills to a relatively large group of children. The clinician more often than not is concerned with the

difficulties of learning or adjustment of one individual child. In a series of informal discussions with teachers in the University of Colorado Medical Center's Day Care unit, and with principals and administrators in the Denver public schools, the most frequent complaints expressed about clinicians concerned their failure to appreciate that the tasks and methods of the classroom were, of necessity, different from those of the clinic playroom. While appreciation was expressed for the value of clinical tools and insights, it was emphasized that their fruits were often rendered useless because of a failure to give consideration to the situation in which they might be implemented. To quote one administrator, "clinicians bring an important emphasis on the individual to the classroom; but a psychologist with a true appreciation of classroom problems is much more valuable than a more highly trained clinician without such an appreciation."[3]

In my observations both at the Day Care Center and the Children's Clinic of the University of Colorado Medical Center, it appeared that all too often clinicians of all disciplines tended to think first of the emotional needs of their patients and only secondarily, and in passing, of the situation in which the teacher was called upon to deal with them. All too often therapists assumed that what was good procedure in the playroom was ipso facto good procedure in the class. Perhaps the most blatant example of the consequences of this assumption is that of the clinician who, when told by a public school teacher of his patient's tendency to have tantrums in the classroom, suggested "when he's like that when I see him, I take him out for a walk around the block or an ice cream cone— couldn't you try that?" He was quite serious in making this suggestion to a teacher responsible for a class of over twenty children. He was also a relatively sensitive and adequate clinician, however, he erred in generalizing too directly from his experience in the playroom to the school situation. The playroom does not typify all of life; while the skills and outlook of psychotherapy and diagnosis are invaluable for the understanding of disturbed behavior, the techniques of psychotherapy, individual or group, are not necessarily those which are best suited for dealing with that behavior in the classroom.

Admittedly, the foregoing example was of a gross lack of appreciation for the nature of the classroom situation. Such extreme misunderstanding hopefully is rare. As educators are all too willing to testify, however, more subtle and yet still quite disruptive failures on the part of clinicians to appreciate the demands and pressures of the classroom abound. All too often clinicians ask that teachers meet patients' needs by behaving in ways which, if carried out, would lead to the grossest neglect of their duties to the other children in the classroom. Teachers are asked to function as substitute parents, as ancillary therapists, to understand and condone behaviors which are extremely disruptive and annoying, and to devote unrealistically large amounts of time in efforts to meet needs for attention and control.

This is not to say that emphasis upon individuality and the needs of the individual is necessarily impossible or even bad in the classroom. Quite the contrary. The point is that while the clinician is apt at recognizing the individual's needs, he must, if he is to be of help to the educator, also become cognizant of the demands of the classroom and must develop an appreciation for the sort of techniques appropriate to meeting the needs of the individual child within that situation. I am reminded of an extremely skillful teacher who succeeded admirably in dealing with a child who was incessant in his disruptive demands for attention. The teacher dealt with and solved this problem by simply patting the child on the head every now and then as he walked around the classroom in the normal course of his duties. The child's need for recognition was met and yet the teacher was quite free to meet the needs of the other twenty-some-odd children in the class.

What does all of this mean for training in child clinical psychology? I do not intend a criticism of basic modal training in the area; rather I would argue that as an additional part of such training the child clinician needs to learn more about the problems and demands of the school situation. In the course of this training the contemporary child clinician has hopefully been exposed to a solid grounding in psychological and developmental theory and to an emphasis upon the value of dispassionate inquiry and an attitude of critical scrutiny. As a result of intensive training in psychodiagnosis and psychotherapy, he has developed a greater sensitivity to that which is uniquely individual in the expression of cognitions, affects, and motivations. Hopefully, these different experiences and aspects of training blend so that the mature and well trained child clinician is endowed with an openness and sensitivity towards behavior and an interest in understanding it thoroughly and at many levels of inquiry. This endowment should enable the child clinician to make a valuable contribution to the schools if it were only combined with an appreciation for the nature and demands of the school situation.

Such a combination of the clinical training and familiarity with the school situation would enable the child clinical psychologist to assist educators in a number of areas which require a sensitive understanding of inter- and intra-personal processes. He would be able to render valuable assistance in the early diagnosis of many learning, cognitive, and emotional disturbances. He would be able to offer valuable suggestions for remedying such disturbances in their early stages, perhaps within the school situation itself. In the role of consultant he would be ideally suited to assist educators in understanding, explaining, and coping with the often puzzling and frustrating behavior of some of their charges. In all of these endeavors the use of classroom observation as a diagnostic technique would greatly assist the clinician in his attempt to translate diagnostic impressions into concrete advice about techniques for dealing with and assisting children in the classroom. The ability to render such advice is essential for the clinician who would work in the schools. It is a skill, however, which can only be acquired as a result of a thorough familiarization with the school situation.

Such familiarization could probably be best brought about if the clinician in training were afforded the opportunity to spend some time in observing actual classes of children in a context where he could engage in relatively free communication with teaching personnel. He could thus become acquainted, in a meaningful manner, with the goals of the educational process and the techniques best suited to furthering those goals. If the teachers involved were skillful and if disturbed children were an important element in the classroom being observed, the clinician's understanding of the nature of the techniques suitable for dealing with such children within the school situation would be greatly furthered. I believe that psycho-educational facilities, where disturbed children are dealt with from a task-centered orientation, would provide an ideal range of experience in this regard, although ideally the opportunity to observe classrooms of both normal and disturbed children should be afforded the clinician in training. Even more useful would be the opportunity to participate to some extent in the teaching process within such classrooms. I believe that in addition to preparing the child psychologist for working with the educator, such a training experience would provide an invaluable context for the integration of academically acquired knowledge about normal development with concepts of pathology and deviency.

Up to now I have mainly addressed myself to issues pertinent to the performance of diagnostic and consultative services in the schools. At this point I would like to illustrate the impact of experience within a psycho-educational setting upon one's functioning as a clinician with an example taken from my own experience in doing psychotherapy within such a setting. Wanda is a seven-year-old girl with some brain damage and history of parental neglect. She was referred to the Day Center by her public school, largely because of her regressive and angry behavior. While she appeared more depressed than angry upon admission to the Day Care program, she was quite regressive in her behavior, eating with her hands, engaging in much sexual provocation of other children and assuming an air of infantile dependency and stupidity. From the beginning of treatment the issue of regression was a focal point in the discourse between Wanda's teachers and myself. I saw my task as that of fostering regression and affective expression and was not at all concerned with Wanda's behavior outside of the playroom. I was a therapist! The teachers saw their task as one of socialization and education; they were disturbed by Wanda's regressive behavior. Midway through the first school semester a staff meeting was held wherein all personnel were encouraged to join in a campaign to socialize Wanda. I joined in this campaign, reversing my earlier position and making the playroom an extention of the class. Wanda began to show signs of interest in a more mature stance in life but her depression and passively expressed anger with adults began to interfere with her functioning in class. At this point I decided to reestablish the playroom as a place for affective expression and regression. My attitude was quite different from that at the beginning of treatment, however. I sensed that Wanda needed to engage in regressive activities, but also realized that she needed to work out some integration between her feelings and desires on the one hand and the reality demands of the classroom on the other. Far from separating treatment and education I began to regard them as complimentary aspects of the same process. I maintained an active interest in Wanda's class behavior and strongly encouraged her teachers to demand appropriate behavior from her. Through classroom observations I began to obtain a clearer picture of Wanda's response to reality demands and a more precise notion of the issues with which she was dealing. In the playroom I was able to assist her in dealing with those issues by encouraging regression and

helping her to work through her feelings, desires and frustrations within the context of a less task-oriented and demanding interpersonal situation. I was also able to help her teachers develop a plan for meeting her educational needs. Wanda is now becoming more appropriate and direct in her feelings and is beginning to seek gratification in a more age-appropriate manner. I do not believe that this progress would have been attained as quickly without the close collaboration which developed between the teachers and myself. In addition, this experience has assisted me in developing a broader outlook on psychotherapy and, I believe, a more useful notion of the nature and possible benefits of psycho-educational collaboration.

I have, in the course of this paper addressed myself chiefly to issues which might seem pertinent only to the child clinical psychologist interested in work in psycho-educational facilities or in the role of diagnostician-consultant to the schools. I do not believe that this is the case. The preponderance of children seen in individual psychotherapy in clinics and private practice are enrolled in the schools where they spend approximately one-third of their waking time. The importance of environmental influences in childhood disorders has long been acknowledged by most child clinicians. Few such clinicians would deny the importance of working with the parents of their charges in order to bring about a favorable home milieu. It would seem that close contact with the schools would enable the clinician to exert a favorable influence on still another important aspect of the child's life. Familiarity with the school situation should greatly enhance the value of such contact. Pertinent counseling and advice on the part of the therapist should help to avert further educational trauma, make the school experience more helpful to the child, stimulate an interest in mastery of the environment, and in some cases, greatly accelerate the process of treatment itself. Familiarity with the demands and pressures of the classroom should enable the clinician to engage in helpful consultation; school conferences could be useful and constructive instead of the frustrating, disappointing, and even hostile events they so often are at present. All too often child clinicians have criticized educators for their lack of understanding and tolerance. If we are to help them become more understanding, must we not first increase our own appreciation for the tasks and problems which confront them?

NOTES

1. This paper was presented in a symposium sponsored by the Corresponding Committee of Fifty on "The Diversity and Future of Child Clinical Psychology," American Psychological Association, Chicago, September, 1965.

2. Article in preparation by M. Rudnick: "Two disciplines in search of a language."

3. Dr. Franklin C. Vaughn, Director of Psychological and Social Services in the Denver, Colorado, public schools. Personal communication.

REFERENCES

BOWER, E. M. Psychology in the schools: conceptions, processes and territories. *Psychology in the Schools*, 1964, *1*, 3–12.

LEAVERTON, L. Can the home school provide adequate help for the emotionally disturbed child? *Psychology in the Schools*, 1965, *2*, 269–274.

LOSEN, S. The school psychologist—psychotherapist or consultant? *Psychology in the Schools*, 1964, *1*, 13–17.

NEWMAN, S. A demonstration project in school consultation: a preventative approach. *Psychology in the Schools*, 1965, *2*, 70–76.

SARASON, S. B., DAVIDSON, K., & BLATT, B. *The preparation of teachers.* New York: Wiley, 1962.

27. Psychological Consultation with Executives: A Clinical Approach

EDWARD M. GLASER

TRADITIONALLY, the attention of psychologists in industry was focused mainly on the study of job evaluation and criteria of performance; personnel selection and placement; employee training; monotony, fatigue, accident, and safety problems; and market research and advertising. Applied psychology in industry also has undertaken investigation of the relationships between people's interests, attitudes, and attributes and their behavior in certain situations or their performance of certain tasks. In most cases these studies have been concerned with classes of people—such as given populations of workers, trainees, consumers, etc.—not with individuals as such.

During World War II, some clinically oriented industrial psychologists shifted their attention to developmental counseling with key management personnel. The rationale for this development was the inference from empirical observation, which since that time has been supported by some experimental evidence (1), that many of the problems in connection with the human and with the long-run operational performance of an organization stem from the attitudes and actions of the managers. Since psychological services need to be performed within limits of time and expense, it appeared that effort invested first at this level might have greater effect on the overall functioning of the entire organization than a similar initial investment at lower echelons. With understanding and support at the top, subsequent application of psychological principles to other company problems—such as personnel selection, supervisory training, performance analysis, interaction skills, communications adequacy, and decision making—might take better root.

In some cases the shift in emphasis from personnel management problems to counseling with top executives came as much from the changing attitudes of managers who were evolving a professional concept of their jobs as from the observations by psychologists studying the determinants of organizational performance. A number of men in top positions seemed to be saying: "In addition to our wanting professional help in selecting and coaching others, we recognize some psychological limitations and developmental needs of our own; we want to deepen our insights into self and the reactions of others; we want to improve our own leadership ability and thereby enhance our managerial effectiveness."

CASE REPORTS

The purpose of this paper is to describe psychology in action at the executive level, pointing up some of the unique problems and opportunities. Rather than attempt an abstract description, it might be more informative to illustrate by case material how one group of clinically oriented psychological consultants functions with its clients. (The cases below were taken from the files of Edward Glaser & Associates, with substitution of fictitious names.)

CASE 1: JUPITER MANUFACTURING COMPANY

The President, Roscoe Miller, then 36 years old, was referred by the president of another client company. Miller's interest in talking with a psychological consultant at the time stemmed from a decision he had made that Jupiter needed a new director of manufacturing who would have potential for becoming Executive Vice-President. Miller's vague notion of what the consultants did led him to believe that they might help him recruit and select such a man.

Reprinted from *American Psychologist*, 1958, *13*, 486–489, by permission of the American Psychological Association and the author. Dr. Glaser is Managing Associate, Edward Glaser & Associates, Los Angeles, California.

Rather than accept the assignment at face value, the consultant asked Miller to tell him about his organization. The consultant was interested in noting the things the President chose as important in describing his company: which areas he stressed —product, sales, research, individual personnel, group integration; what his own hopes, concerns, and frustrations were; what he perceived his major present and future problems to be; whom he tended to blame or praise for failures and successes.

As the discussion progressed, Miller began to see his problem of executive procurement in a different perspective. He came to recognize that he had been focusing on only two parts of a complex situation: the requirements of the job and the qualifications of the man to be hired. Now it became clear to him that another important factor was the nature of the environment in which the new executive would function. If the consultant was to be in a position to do his best professional work in connection with executive assessment, he needed first to learn a good deal about the environmental soil in which that executive would be expected to perform. He needed to learn about the attitudes, values, and behavior patterns of the President (since the new man also would report to the President) and the five department heads already reporting to him. Miller saw the logic of this and invited a psychological assessment or description of himself so that the consultant could get to know him at a level of some depth and comprehensiveness. The President then wanted to tell his department heads to go through the same procedure.

At this point the psychologist proceeded to explore with Miller his leadership behavior. Miller began to gain some insights into himself and new perceptions of the possible impact of his behavior on others: for example, of the probable reaction of the department heads to his advising them without prior discussion that they ought to be assessed psychologically—a completely new idea to them.

Miller then talked over with the psychologist appropriate ways of offering consultation to his key executives on a voluntary basis. This culminated in a meeting at which the Jupiter top management group had an opportunity, before making any commitment, to discuss fully and openly with two psychologists from the consulting firm whatever questions they felt relevant. They were thus enabled to arrive at a better understanding of the consultants' role and methodology in working with organizations.

Later, among themselves, the management group decided they wanted psychological consultation. They also spelled out what they wanted from the service: personal assessments and developmental counseling to assist them toward better understanding of themselves and others; new ideas about how to function with less continuous tension in the fast pace of their rapidly growing company; conference leadership for a searching examination of the suitability of the organization structure in relation to its objectives and to the personalities of of its key people; training in how to attract and select superior people; counsel on how to maintain an environmental climate that would encourage continued *esprit de corps*, high productivity, and creativity as the company continued to expand.

Thus the consultants started to work with Jupiter at the point of the President's readiness, but quickly helped him add new perspective to his initial ideas. In addition to personal counseling, the President and his other executives now use the psychologists as a sounding board on a wide variety of problems including those mentioned in the preceding paragraph. The executive committee has invited one of the psychologists to sit in as a process observer and contributor-of-another-viewpoint at their weekly meetings. Consultation also has been rendered on special psychological problems which have arisen from time to time at lower echelons.

In the course of close contact with key personnel, the psychologists learned much about the interpersonal relations among the executives. Along with many healthy and positive forces, certain tensions, frustrations, anxieties, and distorted perceptions were disturbing some individuals and draining off a portion of their constructive energies. Counseling has been addressed to a reduction of these problems.

Both the client and the consultant have been aware of and concerned with the desirability and extreme difficulty of specifying meaningful dimensions of change in the organization and of finding ways of testing their possible causal relationship with the psychological consulting program. To date, workable and scientifically acceptable measurement procedures have not been evolved.

As an expedient for appraising progress, periodic collaborative assessments by the executive group and the psychologists have been made of the effectiveness of work to date. There has been general agreement as to the existence of the following phenomena and as to the attribution of some causal connection between them and the consulting program:

1. The management group has gained in effectiveness through improved mutual understanding, interpersonal relations, and communication among themselves and with the rest of the organization.

2. Most of the executives counseled have come to give increased attention to re-examining, defining, and appraising progress toward personal and organizational goals.

3. There has been a marked increase in freedom to give and accept constructive criticism, to initiate and face change with less anxiety.

4. As these company characteristics and their assumed consequences became known in the business community, Jupiter's recruiting problems in a tight labor market were much simplified.

CASE 2: RABER COMPANY

The next case describes intensive work undertaken with a single department within a company. The Sales Division Manager had asked the psychologist to evaluate the Training Director to find out if the latter was well qualified for the job. Instead of immediately accepting this assignment, the psychologist explored with the Division Manager his reasons for being uncertain about his subordinate's qualifications. This led to a discussion of the Manager's general dissatisfaction with the selection and training of salesmen. Upon the psychologist's suggestion, it was agreed that it might be of more value to focus on the general problem of the department's seemingly poor performance rather than merely to evaluate the Training Director. The consultant therefore was made available to the Salesman Selection and Training Department to help develop a program designed to reduce personnel turnover and raise sales productivity.

Subsequent interviews with the Training Director revealed that he felt most of the high turnover and low productivity of the salesmen were attributable to the field training and supervision they received after they left the home office training school. At this point, with the prior approval of the Training Director, the consultant recommended to the Sales Division Manager and the Executive Vice-President a plan incorporating the following procedures:

1. Obtain active participation of all departments concerned with recruiting, selecting, training, compensating, or supervising salesmen.

2. Involve people at all levels within each of these departments; meet with these people in groups so constituted that no person would be in the same group as his immediate superior.

3. Conduct these group meetings as "brainstorming" sessions to get ideas for lowering turnover and increasing productivity. The group agreed to abide by a rule for these meetings prohibiting any criticism of persons or any immediate evaluation of ideas in order to permit maximum flow of thinking.

4. Collect, classify, and tally ideas.

Five meetings were held, involving 40 people who produced 151 ideas. After the ideas were classified, the consultant recommended that the decisions on evaluating and implementing ideas with merit be assigned to a special task committee consisting of appointed representatives from every level.

As an immediate result of the project, radical changes were made in almost every phase of the sales program, i.e., recruitment, selection, home office and field training, compensation rates, forms and procedures, sales techniques, and methods of supervision. Other positive effects were: increased sales, a significant reduction in time required for salesmen to get into production, more effective communication among the different levels of the sales organization and especially between home office and field. Finally, many people reported that they felt much more motivated as a result of seeing so many needed changes put into effect.

PSYCHOLOGICAL DESCRIPTIONS

Since the philosophy and professional practice governing the utilization of psychological descriptions varies considerably, it might be of interest to describe the procedure used by this particular consulting group and, with some variation, by their professional affiliates.

Psychological descriptions may be done for at least three somewhat different purposes: (a) as a means of assisting individuals better to understand themselves and their development needs, (b) as an applicant selection tool, (c) as a manpower inventory tool, thereby contributing to more effective utilization and coaching of personnel as well as to internal selection for promotion or transfer.

Psychological descriptions usually require several hours and include an intensive interview covering work, education, general developmental history, current interests, future aspirations, and perceptions of other persons. Also included are some psychological tests. The report written from these data contains the psychologist's clinical description of the person, but does not contain the confidential data on which the professional opinions were based.

The psychologist initiating work with a new client makes it clear that the assessment situation is confidential. That is, although he may agree to furnish and orally interpret to top management a copy of each written report, this is done only after the report has been shown to and discussed with the individual and his consent obtained to discuss it with his superiors. Sometimes when an assessment program is set up, it is agreed that the written report will be shown only to the employee himself. This post-assessment feedback is held with all employees and with applicants who are hired, for the worth of the psychological description is perceived to lie primarily in its potential for contributing to the subject's self-understanding and, where desired, for initiating a developmental counseling relationship with the consultant.

The general orientation herein described is that in every situation involving the assessment of an employee, as distinguished from an outside-the-company applicant, the psychologist's professional loyalty is to the individual as well as to the company. There need be no conflict between these two loyalties if the consulting relationship is structured from the beginning on this basis. The company will be benefited as a psychological consultation contributes significantly to increased effectiveness of key personnel.

There is no feedback normally to an applicant who is not hired, although he may see the psychologist on his own if he so desires.

SOME SPECIAL PROFESSIONAL CONSIDERATIONS

One way to point up some of the special problems of the clinical psychologist in industry is by contrast with the situation of clinical psychologists in private practice.

1. The clients of the industrial consultant are principally organizations and their key personnel, while the clients of the private practice clinician generally are individuals. These individuals come requesting personal assistance and guidance in their adjustive efforts, whereas the initial help sought by the industrial client often is in "fixing up," selecting, motivating, or educating others. Somebody at or near the top of the client organiza-

tion wanted help of some kind or the consultant wouldn't be there, but not all the persons involved necessarily did. Is the psychologist in danger sometime of invading privacy when he sees people who did not first ask to see him—particularly if he communicates to their superiors about them, however constructively? The ethically concerned industrial consultant realizes there usually are overt or covert pressures on people from top management to consult with him despite efforts to structure this on a voluntary basis. He tries to minimize these pressures.

2. The private practice clinician generally is presented with behavior problems or anxieties of sufficient concern to have led the individual to seek professional help. The industrial clinician frequently has to define the problems. That is, as he becomes acquainted with an organization, he responds not only to the client's felt needs, but also frequently invites attention to areas where the application of psychological principles might be of real value. The job, the challenge, and the reward of the industrial clinician may be seen as helping effective people become more effective, particularly in their work roles.

3. The private practice clinician generally sees a person in isolation from that person's ordinary environments, whereas the industrial clinician counsels with an individual in the context of his work-life in an organization milieu and often is working simultaneously with some of the individual's superiors, coordinates, and subordinates. Thus the industrial clinician must be concerned with the dynamics of both individual personalities and the work groups of which they are a part, as well as with the formal organizational structure.

4. The very fact that to be maximally effective the industrial clinician must work closely with top management may give rise to another problem which needs to be recognized: a perception in which the consultant appears to some members of the organization as a sort of unofficial "super-management" because he has influence with the top executives. Even though the consultant has no decision making authority in any client organization, he may indeed have influence on some decisions involving people and, to that extent, power. How this influence or power is used can be the difference between a consultant "playing God," serving needs of his own, or properly taking the role of an applied behavioral scientist and psychological counselor.

These and many other problems which the clinician in industry faces must ultimately be viewed in terms of the practitioner's personal and professional integrity. Any failure to maintain ethical professional conduct with a client is bound to reduce the psychologist's effectiveness, aside from the damage that may be done to the reputation and the public image of psychology. By continued alertness to special problems arising from the psychological consultant's relationships with his clients, many of these pitfalls can be avoided.

The psychological consultant to management is in a position to share with the managers and supervisors of men in our society what psychologists tentatively know about promoting healthy human development and constructive interpersonal relations. In working with the normal problems of industrial managers, psychologists have a remarkable opportunity to learn more and to invest their efforts where the impact and consequences can be relatively far reaching.

REFERENCE

   1. LIKERT, R. Developing patterns of management: II. *General Management Series* (Amer. Management Assoc.), 1956, No. 182.

28. The Role of the Psychologist in Comprehensive Community Mental Health Centers: The National Institute of Mental Health View

STANLEY F. YOLLES

I AM very pleased to have the opportunity to join this Conference of State Chief Psychologists and Psychologists of the United States Public Health Service. Meetings such as this between state professionals and those in the Federal establishment typify our close alliance on behalf of public health, and I speak as a colleague devoted to a cause we share in common.

In your strategic posts as administrators and leaders of your profession throughout the states, you have been in key positions to affect the role of the psychologists in that most significant pursuit of interest to us all—the strengthening of the mental health of our society.

Today, the swift movement of events in both the fields of mental health and of social action presents all mental health professionals with fresh opportunity and equally fresh challenge. Just a few weeks ago President Johnson signed into law new mental health legislation which brings even closer to realization the community mental health services we have tried for many years to make available to all our citizens.

Under this new amendment to the Community Mental Health Centers Act of 1963, Federal aid will help pay the cost of staff as the centers get underway. This support, coupled with the Federal assistance for construction, means that the mental health professions can and must devise within the community mental health center model ways for the most effective practice of their respective disciplines.

It was the Roman General Fabius who said of his famous adversary, Hannibal, "You know, Hannibal, how to gain a victory, but not how to use

it." If the mental health of this nation has gained a victory in the current move toward community care and prevention of the mental illnesses, we are now called upon to use the skills and knowledge of all the mental health professions for the benefit of the people themselves who are in need.

At the outset, I should like to clarify the position of the National Institute of Mental Health on the role of the psychologist in the community mental health center. I do not intend to suggest, as the assigned title infers, a special "National Institute of Mental Health View." Indeed, NIMH superimposes no special view concerning the work of the mental health professions in the network of community mental health services to be established across the land. Rather, the role of each profession is being established in and by each profession itself, as witness this and many other conferences which are being held among leaders of training, and leaders of public health practice.

Each profession must undergo its own self-review, its own innovations in preparation and training, it own explorations as to how it can best serve as a member of the community mental health team.

In its effort to insure the effectiveness of the nationwide program, NIMH has and does lend its support to these endeavors. In psychiatry, the Institute is supporting various types of pilot training programs in community and social psychiatry. In psychology, the Institute is supporting various programs in community mental health training. In social work, training is being extended to expose students to elemental problems in mental health. In nursing, several pilot projects in community mental health nursing are being conducted under the auspices of universities or colleges.

In addition, as you all know, the Institute has supported many of the major conferences on training in the four mental health disciplines. In

Reprinted from *American Psychologist*, 1966, *21*, 37–41, by permission of the American Psychological Association and the author. Dr. Yolles is Director of the National Institute of Mental Health, Bethesda, Maryland.

psychology, this includes a number of major conferences beginning with the Boulder meeting in 1948 and continuing on to the Conference on the Professional Preparation of Clinical Psychologists which just ended here in Chicago. These conferences have, of necessity, paid major attention to the changing direction and needs in professional training and in professional services.

It is through such conferences, and other processes of self-examination and self-improvement, that guidelines to manpower utilization are developed—as well, of course, as from down-to-earth experience and demonstrations and studies of what works best.

The shortages of personnel in mental health, as well as in welfare and health services in general, have long since made evident the need for innovations in the roles of professional and nonprofessional manpower.

The Report of the Joint Commission of Mental Illness and Health (1961) reflected an awareness of this trend. Its statement on the use of mental health personnel may serve as a useful preamble for our discussion this morning. It is, in part, as follows:

psychiatry and the allied mental health professions should adopt and practice a broad, liberal philosophy of what constitutes and who can do treatment within the framework of their hospitals, clinics, or other professional service agencies [p. 248].

The Commission outlined the fundamental ABCs of the clinical functions of our respective callings. They are:

A. That certain kinds of medical, psychiatric, and neurological examinations and treatments must be carried out by or under the immediate direction of psychiatrists, neurologists, or other physicians specially trained for these procedures.

B. That psychoanalysis and allied forms of deeply searching and probing "depth psychotherapy" must be practiced only by those with special training, experience, and competence in handling these techniques without harm to the patient—namely, by physicians trained in psychoanalysis or intensive psychotherapy, plus those psychologists or other professional persons who lack a medical education but have an aptitude for, training in, and demonstrable competence in such techniques of psychotherapy.

C. That nonmedical mental health workers with aptitude, sound training, practical experience, and demonstrable competence should be permitted to do general, short-term psychotherapy—namely, treating persons by objective, permissive, nondirective techniques of listening to their troubles and helping them resolve these troubles in an individually insightful and socially useful way [p. 249].

"The *principle* that must guide us in questions of authority, professional prerogatives, and qualifications involved in treatment of the mentally ill," the Commission held, "is one of individual competence . . . [p. 248].

"The matter of competence applies equally to the psychiatrist, the psychologist . . . the social worker and occupational therapist . . . the nurse . . . and the ward attendant . . . [p. 248]" the Commission concluded.

Since mental and emotional problems vary so widely as to kind and degree, the Commission's view of individual competence as a guideline for appropriate types of treatment has been widely accepted by the mental health disciplines.

I am most aware that my audience here this morning is a highly sophisticated one in the employment and practice of psychology in public health. I shall, therefore, attempt to place my remarks within the framework of the role of the psychologist in the community mental health center.

To this end, we may clarify first just what a community mental health center program is, what it is intended to do, and what further potential it may have, if any, as it matures beyond the starting point.

I will begin with the statement that the community mental health center program is an entirely new approach to the care, treatment, and prevention of the mental illnesses. I say this knowing full well that there is a body of psychological opinion that the centers approach, is not revolutionary enough. The program is an integrated network of treatment services based in the community, where people live and work, where they can get proper care when they become ill, where they can be maintained, and where they can be helped to lead productive lives.

That is the treatment aspect of the center—giving to the mentally ill alternatives to lengthy hospitalization, alternatives to no care at all. With the use of psychoactive drugs, with the use of short-term intensive treatment in the psychiatric wards of general hospitals, with the opportunity to serve patients as the course and degree of their illness or difficulty requires—we hope at last to be able to put to use more broadly whatever skills and knowledge we now possess.

We know, for example, various psychiatric tenets which we have not been able to employ widely enough. Among them, we know that illness detected and treated early is more reversible than illness long ingrown. We know, too, that the often slow process of rehabilitation is a crucial factor in healing, and may need special attention, such as home nursing visits, or a special setting, such as the halfway house.

The treatment of illness, however, is but one phase of the mission of the community mental health center. It is also conceived as an instrument for the *prevention* of mental illness and the promotion of the community's mental health.

The center program is in fact not simply a medical step into the community—although that in itself would be new enough—it is a starting point for new departures in looking at problems of mental health.

An outstanding result of multidisciplinary mental health research has been our present knowledge concerning environment as a factor in producing illness or health. The behavioral and social sciences, as well as psychiatric research, have all pointed to factors of environment which help shape the individual's ability to withstand stress. Thus, the environment of the individual has become our laboratory. In psychiatry, we have been studying the immediate environment of the family, both as to the role of the family in the illness of one of its members, and in normal growth and development. In psychology, too, the family structure is under close study, as well as the wider environment of the community in which people learn and grow. A major contribution of psychology has been the theory of social competence—in what ways can we intervene to help people become competent within their society to withstand its stress and to realize their fullest potential?

An essential element of the community mental health centers program, therefore, is the provision of preventive services. In addition to the four treatment services—inpatient and outpatient care, partial hospital and emergency care—a vital preventive service is a requirement for Federal aid. That service is consultation to community agencies and professionals, and educational programs for the community at large.

Obviously this network of services is not entirely comprehensive. Full comprehensive services also include diagnostic and rehabilitative services, precare and aftercare, training, research and evaluation—categories in which psychologists as well as other behavioural sciences can make a major contribution.

The centers program is a workable and flexible nucleus. It is a core around which other important services may be offered as the centers become part of community life. We believe that the program as it now stands—and as it may be expanded—embodies both treatment and prevention of illness, and it can become an effective instrument for the promotion of mental health.

It is quite true that varying views have arisen

within some segments of the mental health professions concerning which of the comprehensive services should be considered most essential. In a long-neglected field of endeavor—the supply of services and the use of knowledge on behalf of community mental health—it is, perhaps, understandable to desire full comprehensive services all at once.

In some professional quarters, very healthy discussions have been taking place as to just how a pioneering program should look, where it should go, what it should accomplish. I say this is healthy because above all, the program is designed for maximum flexibility, to suit the community and the population it is to serve.

On one hand we have heard, from those who are oriented to the state mental hospital system, that the center program cannot work, that it is too "far out," too great a departure from the system of care as it is organized today.

On the other hand, we have heard from other serious practitioners of mental health—at times from the psychologist—that the center model is too medical, that it is not "far out" enough, that it is too restricted to the treatment of disease, that it cannot work as a positive agent for community mental health.

Personally, I am inclined to feel that a community mental health system that is subject to constructive questioning and exploration from both the treatment and the preventive points of view must be fairly rounded system that has a strong potential for both. While the program is not referred to as a "center" because it fulfills both functions, it appears, after all, that it may be a "center," too, in terms of its potential for serving both as a medical model and as a model in which the psychologist can practice his preventive as well as clinical skills.

A major point, therefore, that I should like to make about the role of the psychologist in the community mental health center is that the program need not limit, but in fact, can stimulate the creative practice of psychology as a tool for the prevention of mental illness and the promotion of mental health.

The clinical psychologist will, of course, participate in the treatment or therapy aspects of the program, as the ABCs of the Joint Commission make clear. But beyond that, he or his coprofessionals can contribute uniquely to the success of the overall program in whatever community it has been designed to serve. He can work in liaison with and in consultation with community agencies and with the new social action programs which have a direct bearing on people's lives. He can work with his colleagues in industry, in the schools, in employment centers. He can become one of the center's connecting links with the community, trained as he is in the preventive view of the competence of individuals as they go about their daily life.

While we in psychiatry will be trained to treat the mentally ill as part of the mental health team, the psychologist will seek to make of the centers program a true community agent of illness prevention and promotion of health. It is he who is the bridge between the medical and the behavioral and social sciences. It is he who has been trained to ask: What are the community social problems and the solutions? What are the problems of living and how does the individual deal with them? It is the psychologist who is trained not only to be a participant in the treatment process, but to be, to use a term that is becoming popular, a "conceptualizer," as well. To the psychologist, the mental health of the community is in the school room, in the juvenile court, in the home, and on street corners, as well. It is he, then, who will hold a key role in making of the community mental health center something more than a headquarters, however unique, for treating mental illness.

Leaders in the training of psychologists have already begun to develop and to explore curricula and programs out of which the community-oriented psychologist may emerge. For example, the clinical psychologist may, like the psychiatrist, need to add to his clinical training a social consciousness, an awareness of the workings of community structures, a willingness to apply his skills outside of the one-to-one individual treatment setting. In many instances, he may need to cross the many varieties of specialties within his profession to acquire the variety of skills needed to be most effective in community mental health work.

In exploratory conferences on training psychologists in community mental health—such as the one held recently in Boston—the psychologist is being discussed as the "creative generalist" of the community mental health center, and as such, some aspects of social psychology, behavioral psychology, and other specialties may become part of the community psychologist's skills.

The second point about the psychologist in the community mental health center is that he will function—as will each mental health discipline—as part of a mental health team. This may require that each profession modify and broaden its perspective. After all, a real team does not work together with separate points of view. In the new training programs, each of the professions—psychiatry, psychology, nursing, and social work—is examining its

training process, exploring its possibilities as effective helping agents in a community program setting, as part of the center's mental health team. We can and will arrive at a fruitful synthesis of all mental health professions in the community care system, and the psychologist is a major member of the team.

Finally, I should like to clarify the question of leadership of the community mental health centers program. Professional prerogatives are, we realize, no less dear to the heart of the psychiatrist and the psychologist than to other professions which invest years in highly specialized training. The question of leadership, however, is not predicated simply upon prerogatives. Even more, it has been of keen interest to the professions because of the prevailing belief that the discipline of the program head will determine what direction the program will take.

Whether justified or not—and that is another question—the fact is that the subject of leadership has appeared again and again in professional councils as a rather indestructible query which does not seem to yield easily to simple and direct response.

The simple and direct response is, of course, that leadership is based upon individual competence, and not upon membership in a particular discipline.

In the Federal regulations for construction aid to community mental health centers, for example, it is provided that a qualified *psychiatrist* will be responsible for the *clinical* program, with the medical responsibility for every patient vested in a physician. Nowhere in the regulations is it suggested that administrative leadership be limited to psychiatrists.

Furthermore, the new legislation similarly places no restriction on the leadership of the center program. Indeed, the Senate report on hearings for the staffing aid includes a very clear statement as to this point.[2]

"There is no intent in any way in this bill to discriminate against any mental health professional group from carrying out its full potential within the realm of its recognized competence," Senator Lister Hill reported from the Committee on Labor and Public Welfare in June.

"Even further," the report states, "it is hoped that new and innovative tasks and roles will evolve from the broadly based concept of the community mental health services. Specifically, overall leadership of a community mental health center program may be carried out by any one of the major mental health professions [p. 4]."

For its open view as to leadership, the new legislation was commented upon by Arthur Brayfield (1965), Executive Officer of the American Psychological Association. In the course of the hearings, he said, "we are pleased to see that this amendment places no restriction as to the administration of these centers, and it is not assumed that an MD must be placed in charge [p. 429]."

This open view illustrates an essential quality of the centers program: that is, flexibility. It is a flexible system not only as to program and leadership, but as to its entire staffing structure. The technical and professional personnel will, of course, represent the traditional mental health disciplines. But new departures within the disciplines and in the use of auxiliary personnel—such as volunteers and indigenous workers—will contribute to the success of our new community approach. The open view, then, is more than nonrestrictive; it is a positive recognition of developments in all the mental health professions that are sharpening their skills needed in community mental health work.

The new departures and the creative approaches of which I speak are already past the planning stage. They are at work in pioneering programs in various parts of the country. In Minnesota, for example, new community mental health centers will operate under program directors who are psychologists, with psychiatrists as heads of their clinical services.

Another state providing leadership positions for psychologists is Kansas.

At the South Shore Mental Health Center in Massachusetts, Leonard Hassol, a psychologist, actively working with a group of psychologists, has developed a program which is receiving wide attention from those interested in the needs of the profession to "tool up" for community mental health. The program has evolved out of a philosophy of planned social change in which community mental health plays an integral role.

The South Shore program includes mental health consultation in schools, and with police and court authorities. It includes aftercare services through a halfway house, an evening clinic, nursing service, social and recreational programs, drug and supportive therapy. It offers therapeutic tutoring for disturbed youngsters, and emergency services for children whose parents become hospitalized. It participates in the domestic peace corps, in Operation Headstart, in a well-baby clinic, in an anti-poverty program, and in the teaching of behavioral science in elementary schools.

The significant point is that the potential of a mental health program in its relationship to the community is bounded only by the skill, the competence, and the imagination of its director and its staff.

As I have suggested earlier, the mandate to the mental health professions has been made clear. Financial support for the centers can and will be worked out through Federal sources, through mental health and social and welfare programs, through local and state tax revenues, and through private funds. Finances are a problem, but not an insoluble one. An adequate supply of professional help can be forthcoming, too, through Federal support of mental health training and in-service training as well. Staffing may be a problem, but not an insoluble one.

I believe that the success of the new community mental health centers program will rest ultimately not on any one of these factors, but upon the skill and the competence and the creativity of each mental health profession as it takes its place in service to the community's mental health. From a public health viewpoint, of course, that service is to attack illness by devising means to help prevent it. In this, the psychologist as well as all health professions find their highest role.

NOTES

1. Prepared for Conference of State Chief Psychologists and Psychologists in United States Public Health Service, Chicago, September 2, 1965.

2. Hill, *Mental Retardation Facilities and Community Mental Health Centers Construction Act Amendments of 1965*, S. Rep. No. 366, 89th Congress, 1st Session (1965).

REFERENCES

BRAYFIELD, A. H. Community mental health centers "staffing" legislation. *American Psychologist*, 1965, *20*, 429–430.

JOINT COMMISSION ON MENTAL ILLNESS AND HEALTH. *Action for mental health.* New York: Basic Books, 1961.

A. INTRODUCTION

In his "1984" (12) Orwell describes an authoritarian society with dogmas which everyone is forced to believe in and live by. These are (*a*) war is peace; (*b*) freedom is slavery; (*c*) ignorance is strength. He also describes methods used to make sure that these dogmas are believed by all. The methods described are sure fire ways of making up history rather than describing it and they include three steps: (*a*) the past is erased; (*b*) the erasure is forgotten; (*c*) the lie becomes truth.

To some extent a reading of present day psychological literature all too often gives one the impression that psychology as a profession started just a few years ago by the people in practice today, as if it had no ancestry or no past, or else had come through the processes suggested by Orwell and had successfully erased all of the past. By so doing the danger is that we forget that our present needs can be better understood in the light of the knowledge of the past—what took place there and how we got this way. Growing up does mean selective outgrowing, but it does not mean throwing everything overboard that is marked historical or past. Growing up means interdependence with emerging realities and continuity as well as change for confronting present realities.

B. NEED FOR PERSPECTIVE

Our professional need in the sense of coping with the present reminds me of a story of a girl who considered herself smart, talking to a girl whom she considered to be very dumb. The dumb one seemed not to grasp readily the self-appointed sophisticated girl's talk about the facts of life. The bright one, fed up with the seeming inability of the dumb one to grasp what she said, came out with: "What's the use of talking to you You don't even know who made you!" The response of the so-called dummy was, "Do you mean originally or recently?"

"History," as Muller (11) likes to tell us, "has no meaning, in the sense of a clear pattern or determined plot; but it is not simply meaningless or pointless. It has no certain meaning because man is free to give it various possible meanings." Without getting lost in history it might be well for us to start with a historical look at how we started and how we carried on in a manner that led up to the present. De-emphasized in our presentation will be recent material readily available. Included will be material wittingly or unwittingly omitted in "America's Psychologists" (3) and supplementary material concerning private practice.

C. IN THE BEGINNING THERE WAS CATTELL

Of the greats in psychology, Cattell was the first to show interest in the development of an applied psychology. In 1929, as president of the Ninth International Congress of Psychology, Cattell looked over the field and announced that: "A history of psychology in America in the last fifty years would be as short as a book on snakes in Ireland since the time of St. Patrick. In so far as psychologists are concerned, America was then like Heaven, for there was not a damned soul there" (1, p. 441).

From the very beginning Cattell was interested in turning psychology into a profession as well as a science. In his later years, particularly, he took every opportunity to help it move that way. Some illustrative statements, selected in the form of key sentences, include the following:

It seems to me certain that experimental psychology has wide-reaching practical applications, not only in education, but also in medicine, in the fine arts, in political economy and, indeed, in the whole conduct of life (1, p. 482).

Reprinted from *Journal of Psychology*, 1958, *45*, 93–108, by permission of the *Journal of Psychology* and the author. Dr. Meltzer is Professor of Psychology, Washington University, and a consulting psychologist.

Psychology may supply economic values equal to those of the physical and biological sciences, human values of even greater significance (1, p. 484).

What we need is a science that will coördinate all efforts to control conduct with the effects of all changes in the environment. This is the primary business of psychology; it requires the coöperation of all the sciences and of all the professions (1, p. 489).

For the present the psychological expert should doubtless be a member of one of the recognized professions who has the natural endowments, special training, and definite knowledge of the conditions that will make his advice and assistance of value. But in the end there will be not only a science but also a profession of psychology (1, p. 207).

In the twenties a number of developments took place which moved the field in the direction of increasing professional emphasis. Cattell himself helped found and develop the Psychological Corporation in 1921. This organization, particularly in the administration of Dr. Paul Achilles, stimulated an interest in the application of psychology. In the early twenties newly organized child guidance clinics in selected cities in the United States, sponsored by the National Committee of Mental Hygiene and supported by the Commonwealth Fund[2] introduced the use of a team of professionals composed of psychiatrists, psychologists, and psychiatric social workers. This opened up a field where clinical psychologists could get experience in and also develop interests in clinical applications. The consequences of World War I helped yield an increased interest in professional application in industry as well as educational institutions. These and related developments moved in the direction of a good many people in the American Psychological Association of that day not being satisfied with the attention given the applied field by the parent body and moving in the direction of organizing the American Association for Applied Psychology.

D. MATURING WITH THE *AAAP*

The organization of the *AAAP* represented a new landmark for the field of applied psychology.[3] The purposes of the *AAAP* and its immediate predecessors are described in a report published in the first issue of the *Journal of Consulting Psychology* (6). The then existing national and regional associations of applied psychology, the Association of Consulting Psychologists and the Clinical Section of the Psychological Association amalgamated their interests in the new national society.

The lead article in the first issue of the *Journal of Consulting Psychology* was by Cattell, the title:

"Retrospect: Psychology as a Profession" (2). The follow-up article was fittingly enough by Cattell's successor at Columbia University, Dr. R. S. Woodworth, under the title of "The Future of Clinical Psychology" (22). In this article Professor Woodworth questioned the title of clinical psychology because it suggested bedside and argued that people coming to psychologists are neither bedridden, nor sick in the usual sense. His opinion at that time was that "consulting psychology" might be a better title, though not perfect. "Personal service psychology" had more appeal to him even though he could see flaws in this too. His impression at that time was that "the profession of personal service psychology is going to be a large, highly varied but unified profession. It will be large enough and unified enough and well enough equipped with knowledge and technique to stand on its own feet and to cooperate on terms of mutual respect with other professional groups which also engage in personal service." In this article, too, Woodworth warned about the vacuum being filled by an inrush of half-trained and semi-scientific practitioners unless the leaders in the profession are successful in their efforts to maintain and raise standards. "A legal right charlatans have in most states still," said he, and they still have. His hope was ". . . as the profession grows in competence and in numbers its influence and authority will increase." In a sense this can be said to be a more tangible addition to Cattell's more vague hope for psychology as a profession.

In a 1940 issue of the *Journal of Consulting Psychology*, Donald G. Paterson (13) already assumed that applied psychology had come of age. He divided the historical account of the growth of applied psychology into three periods: "The first period covers the prenatal stirrings of an embryonic science, extending from the last two decades of the nineteenth century until America's entrance into the World War" (p. 1). He adds:

It is our contention that the birth-labor of applied psychology began in April, 1917, and was completed on the day of the Armistice in 1918. The period of infancy, childhood, and adolescence occurred during the "golden twenties" and the "depressed thirties." We would insist that applied psychology has reached its majority on scheduled time and is now twenty-one years of age whether we calculate our dates from April 6, 1917, until the completion of organization of the American Association for Applied Psychology in September, 1938, or from November 11, 1918, until November 25, 1939.

In this article about applied psychology coming of age, Paterson actually listed what he considered outstanding names in the various applied fields at the time as well as listing historical characters such as William James, G. Stanley Hall, Munsterberg, Seashore, Cattell, Scott, and Thorndike. In child psychology he mentioned 11 names; in industrial and employment psychology, 18 names; in clinical psychology, 30 names; in highway safety and traffic control, three names; and in advertising, seven names. The *AAAP* is no more and now we have many divisions in the American Psychological Association with professional interests.

E. BACK TO THE *APA*

In the postwar period the *APA* was recognized as a kind of federation of 18 divisions and, with this reorganization, the *AAP* was swallowed up. The momentum for interest in professional psychology not only remained, however, but continued at an increased tempo. In the recently published *APA* sponsored study of *America's Psychologists* (3) data is presented which clearly indicates: "Persons whose interests resemble those of the founders of the *APA* (Developmental, Experimental and Physiological, General, Personality, Quantitative, and Social) are now outnumbered two-to-one by persons whose interests are in more recently developed applications of psychology (Clinical, Counseling, Educational, School, Human Engineering, Industrial, and Personnel)" (pp. 18–19). There is also data indicating "Almost three times as many of today's *APA* members identify with clinical psychology as with experimental psychology; contrasted to the early days of the *APA*, this is a startling shift, with many effects on the nature of the field and of the *APA*" (pp. 17–18). A picture of the rapidly growing profession is described; yet the role of the *AAAP* in influencing growth towards a professional direction is not only not considered, but it is not even mentioned.

The Policy and Planning Board of the *APA* recommended professions for national certification of members engaged primarily in the practice of psychology as distinguished from teaching and research in 1945. In 1947 the American Board of Examiners in Professional Psychology was incorporated. The Board was authorized to award diplomas to advanced students in three areas: clinical psychology, counseling psychology, and industrial psychology. In 1952 the Council of Representatives of the *APA* adopted "Ethical Standards of Psychologists" (4). The standards and incidents behind it are available from the American Psychological Association. The long form was published in 1953, and a shorter summary (5) was published some time later. The Association also is public relations conscious and has published a public information guide. Yet, in spite of this manifested interest in professional practice and public relations, on many campuses in the United States many graduate students still get the feeling that their professors, and even their departments, not only do not favor, but make active moves to restrict their interest in courses which may be helpful in practice or expressed early interest in practice. On the other hand some of the professors complain that too many of the graduate students too often want to jump the gun before they are ready for getting into practice. An interest in professional practice definitely implies having a set of ethical standards for any organization which has some concern for its welfare and healthy growth, but from the point of view of prospectives it might be interesting to ask how did those few psychologists who practiced years ago get along without the privileges and published codes that are available to new comers? What were used as guideposts and what kind of orientation served the purpose of an ethical code?

F. GUIDEPOSTS FOR PRIVATE PRACTICE IN 1935

If the foregoing remarks represent a fast touch and run review of psychology as a profession, particularly as seen by the leaders in its various stages of growth, it might be well now to take a look at private practice as such. The most tangible way of doing this is to take an actual person in practice, who is knowable, at the earliest possible time. In 1934 the writer moved into private practice after six years of public practice in a psychiatric child guidance set-up. Not unlike Cattell's description of psychology before 1880 as not having a damned soul there, in full time practice I was aware of the existence of only one man in the field, Dr. David Mitchell, a student of Dr. Witmer's, practicing in New York. I moved into private practice at the suggestion of a number of doctors, particularly pediatricians, who had used the public resources and felt a need for a private source of referral.

After one year of practice, at the suggestion of Dr. Achilles from the Psychological Corporation, I wrote a brief article on psychology in private practice, which may have some historical meaning for persons interested in moving into the field. The article included a consideration of community and personal needs for psychological services, illustrations of referrals and their sources, and a set of 11 guideposts or guiding principles for the practice of psychology. Of this article only the description of the situation as perceived in 1935 and the 11 self imposed guides for the practice are given. Omitted are the brief case study materials and descriptions and the listing of the sources of referrals. This appeared in 1935 and read as follows (9):

The Psychologist in Private Practice (9)

A large measure of insecurity characterizes almost every human relationship today. Frustrations, anxieties, and uncertainties are widespread. Numerous are the individuals who are confronted with crucial problems. An intelligent and sane solution of many of these calls for a knowledge of the dynamics of human nature. Large is the need for well trained individuals who can help people help themselves. The psychologist with a background of clinical experience and a first hand knowledge of factors in community organization which can be used in helping people who have difficulties in dealing with themselves and other human beings is in a strategic position to render useful services.

A psychologist thus equipped can be of service to doctors who are aware of their own limitations in training as well as time and see the need for psychological as well as medical aid for many of their patients. He can be of help to mothers who are in need of and are aware of the need for expert help in dealing with some behavior problems of their children. He can be of aid to social agencies directed by individuals who realize the need for supplementing their work with psychological services. Some of the other sources he can coöperate with are school teachers who see in children more than subject matter experts in the making; ministers who appreciate the possibilities of using expert service in helping some of the members of their congregations who come to them for help in their very personal problems; and business organizations directed by individuals who appreciate the significance of the human factor in industry and business.

In his work with practical problems it is well for the psychologist to be fully aware of the limitations as well as the possibilities of his methods for measuring and investigating problems of behavior and personality. And in the light of that awareness it is advisable for him to set up coöperative relationships with individuals and agencies which are relevant for a particular task. Because many psychologists in their training have learned much about the abilities of men and the changing of human nature through habit training, they at times tend to neglect other ways for studying and changing behavior. The psychologist in practice, therefore, should be doubly careful to consider the physical development of an individual in evaluating his personality organization and to consider situational factors in planning a program for changing it.

In this brief article it will be impossible to discuss adequately what the writer considers an intelligent plan of action for the psychologist in private practice. As a substitute, an attempt will be made in the following paragraphs to illustrate some of these considerations through fragments from case studies and comments about sources referred, methods used and coöperative

relationships instigated or responded to, and in the light of experiences of this nature to list a set of suggestions for practice. [Illustrative case studies omitted.]

In the light of experiences with cases of the foregoing nature the writer suggests the advisability of psychologists in practice keeping in mind that:

1. His interest is in the total personality of the individual client.

2. His level of interest is a working selection from the humanistic interest of the parent in his child and the objective interest of the laboratory psychologist in his research.

3. Characteristically causation is multiple not single; hence the need for a many sided study.

4. A many sided approach does not mean dealing with intangibles. Emotional and personality factors as well as physical and social factors are susceptible to critical evaluation if not reliable measurement.

5. The usefulness of tests is in the insights they yield about the personality under investigation.

6. A sense of relevance is often more important than a ritualistic "comprehensive" approach in testing or social history taking.

7. Integrated work often implies the need for coöperation with medical and other experts. That is, integration often means teamwork, not muddling through all aspects.

8. The facts of learning as discussed in educational psychology texts can be applied in practice. In many problems they do not suffice.

9. Of equal importance for the psychologist in practice are the facts of social learning as well as the mechanisms of mental adjustments called dynamisms by Dr. Healy.

10. Individual integrity is always related to, and at times dependent on, family integrity as well as neighborhood organization.

11. The need for the psychologist to grow with his client and permit the client to outgrow his need for the psychologist.

G. PSYCHOLOGICAL PRACTICE

One question asked by people who are interested in moving into private practice or in improving private practice is what kind of work is one confronted with? Some of the questions asked overlap with those asked by Vernon (20). What should the fees be? What kind of people come? Who refers them? How long does the usual treatment last? There is an interest in questions of this kind as manifested by the large attendance at *APA* meetings concerning private practice. There are, however, some facts available in published form which are not well enough known.

In 1945 Lee Steiner wrote a little book based on her own exploratory researching about where people take their mental troubles (14). She concerned herself mostly with relatively uninformed people. In getting this information she played the role of a patient, sponsor, or correspondent. By playing these roles she was able to get first hand

TABLE 1. Differences in Referrals in Psychiatric and Psychological Practice

	Psychiatrist		Psychologist	
Time consuming work	6 to 9 intensive cases		3 industrial organizations	
New patients	96		120	
Single occasions	71		14 (11.7%)	
Follow-up	Remainder 2 to 5 visits before disposition		55 (45.8%)	
Referral sources	Colleagues mostly		Clients	32%
	Social agencies	5	Former clients	28%
	Veterans' service	2	Agency-educational or social	16%
	Old patients	11	Self	9%
	Lawyers	4	Directory	8%
			Doctors	7%

experience with the array of "talent" in the psychological "underworld." With literary license she reports that "everyone and anyone came." She reports:

For the most part, they were young people who were loaded down with ambitions they could not fulfill, unmarried people in their thirties or forties who were having disturbing love affairs, or those who were disturbed because they had no love affairs, mentally retarded individuals who could not make the grade either socially or vocationally, and people who had troubles with in-laws or relatives. Some drug addicts, shop-lifters, and students on the verge of suicide also came. Most of them were shopping around and had already visited one of the several "psychologists" listed in the telephone directory. Mail-order business she also received. These people need direction and guidance in the selection of more legitimate as well as adequate help that is furnished by "agencies" and persons described by Steiner. In this task psychiatrists and psychologists through participation in community mental hygiene activities are in a position to help (10, p. 614).

To explore the problem of where relatively more informed people take their problems—people who can afford to pay, the kind of problems they come with, and who refers them—the writer made a study and reported his findings in an article included in Fryer and Henry's *Handbook of Applied Psychology* (10). In this study comparisons are made over the same one-year period between the psychological practice in St. Louis and the psycho-analytic practice reported by Dr. Ginsburg in New York (8). There are distinct differences. It might be of some value to report the information concerning differences in referrals in the two settings (Table 1).

A study of the problems and the sources of the referral of individuals who came to a psychiatrist and those who came to a psychologist shows distinct differences. Whereas the majority of the cases reported by the psychiatrist were either psychotic or psycho-

neurotic, more than 90 per cent of all the individuals who came to a psychologist in private practice were more often relatively normal people in relatively normal situations. Much more often were the individuals who came to a psychologist's office involved with other people, who also could be reeducated (10, p. 618).

H. PRESENT ISSUES AND VALUES

Even this brief description of experiences suggests differences in time and the range of possible attitudes and values on the part of psychologists in clinical practice and in industrial work as compared with most psychologists on the campus. In the *Dialogues of Whitehead* (21) there is a poem credited to Lady Margaret Hall which has some relevance here:

> If all good people were clever
> And those that are clever were good,
> This world would be nicer than ever
> We dreamed that it possibly could.
>
> But it seems as though seldom if ever
> Do the two hit it off as they should,
> The good are so harsh to the clever,
> The clever so rude to the good.

If all psychologists were equally clever, and equally clever for all purposes, as well as equally good in the ethical sense, perhaps this session would be completely unnecessary. But there are distinctive and marked differences even among psychologists in almost every respect. Psychologists are not equally good, not equally bright. They differ in shrewdness, in statistical sense, in knowledge. They differ in clinical insights. They differ in the sense of attitudes and values in political, economic, and philosophical considerations.

Some of the issues worth considering are the following:

1. *Privileges vs. Responsibilities.* National certification of experienced professionals is now provided for by way of the *ABEP* in three areas of specialization. An increasing number of states also have provisions for state certification. By these and related provisions, psychologists are given privileges which they previously did not have. The question has been justifiably asked whether the privileges being handed out are sufficiently related to acceptance of professional responsibility by the people who are receiving them. To what extent are the privileges, as now given, robbing, particularly less experienced and less trained people of a challenge to growth and maturity and acceptance of responsibility? Maternal over-protectiveness is not the best way of developing courage and integrity in children; giving relatively untrained young psychologists in practice guaranteed privileges is a form of over-protection unless they have had the kind of experience as well as training which makes them accept the challenge of self responsibility.

2. *Codes vs. Motives.* Realizing the need for ethical standards, the *APA* has in published form prescribed standards for use. Many contributions suggesting codes were made while the topic of ethical standards was kept alive. Of the many which have come to the attention of the writer, the most arbitrary and rigid one is the one suggested by Sutich (16). He offered a series of codes or a list of duties to be fulfilled prior to the establishment of the relationship with the client. Illustrative duties from his list include:

a. It is the duty of the psychologist to make a clear explanation of the nature of the democratic consulting relationship to the client before its establishment.

b. It is the duty of the psychologist to obtain explicit or implied approval or acceptance of the democratic consulting relationship, after he has described it to the client, and prior to its establishment.

c. It is the duty of the psychologist to inform the client, prior to the establishment of the relationship, that he cannot guarantee either complete or partial psychological readjustment or reorientation or any other result through cooperative analysis.

A rapid reading of such duties will make anyone who is at all realistic and understanding ask such questions as: What is the motivation for such lists? What purpose are they supposed to serve? Are they supposed to protect the client from receiving unprofessional services or being taken advantage of in any one way? Or are they more motivated by a feeling of need for untrained psychologists to protect themselves from getting in trouble with clients? In an actual clinical work situation, for example, if a potential suicide comes in should he, following the suggested code, be advised that the first need is for establishing a democratic consulting relationship before any work is attempted? Or should he be listened to and be given the feeling of desire to understand as well as the beginnings of understanding so he encourages himself to want the help he came to get or, at times, was sent to get? Or if a very depressed person comes in and expresses persistent worries that keep him feeling low, should he too be advised that the duty of a psychologist is to inform him prior to the establishment of a relationship that he cannot guarantee either complete or psychological adjustment cooperative results through analysis? Or should he be treated as a person who is in need of help, who came for help, and who is desirous of help and who begins to get a feeling of being understood from being listened to as the beginnings of a therapeutic process? Is a set of rituals in the form of a list of duties intended to safeguard the professional or proposed to really help the client?

3. *Fees for profit vs. fees for professionally acceptable service.* A number of cases have been reported which suggest that persons who pay profit more from therapy than those who don't. By paying they have something at stake, a motive for getting well because they want to get their money's worth. In the contemporary American scene psychologists, as well as psychiatrists, disregard the majority of the population's needs when they charge the highest possible prices. By so doing they cater to the rich, who can afford to pay these prices and who can also afford to prolong therapy and thus make it possible for the practitioner to get more than his share of money for work done. How about the middle classes who can't afford to pay these high prices? Most of these people who have a pride in wanting to pay but can't afford to pay the high prices also have too much pride to want to take services from social agencies without cost. The majority of people, therefore, are thus robbed of services they need because lack of funds prevents them from getting it the way they would like, by paying, or they are possessed by pride which keeps them from wanting to go to social agencies. The question is, of course, if professional services are supposed to satisfy community needs, should there not be provisions made for the middle classes as far as fees are concerned as well as for the rich and poor?

4. *Time arrangement for client vs. convenience of psychologist.* In the arrangement of time the usual practice is for mental hygiene specialists who

charge fees to have hours between nine and five. These are the exact hours when the working man cannot come in. Only people who are their own bosses or those who can arrange their own time, or people who are rich enough or have help enough can readily make time at the hours usually available. For people who are not in that fortunate position it would be easier for them not to have to excuse themselves before a boss or lose a day's pay if they could go after working hours. This usually means evening hours. Evening hours are sometimes available in outpatient clinic services, but rarely, if ever, in private practice. Again, community responsibility on the part of a professional would imply being available at hours possible for the client and not at hours that may be convenient for the psychologist in practice, regardless of how inconvenient and impossible they may be for the client.

5. *Overdependence vs. healthy attachment.* Listening to some relatively untrained inexperienced professional psychologists one would get the impression that they have some form of magic in their personalities with which they mesmerize their clients on the first visit. It is a fact that many clients get an overattachment for the psychologist on the first visit which may lead them to look for dependence to him as a source in which they have confidence. This is not a healthy road for maturing a client when the relationship built up is used too consistently. Unnecessary prolongation of treatment then results. Dynamics directed towards the fullest and healthiest style of self management for the client can be used to the advantage of the client's outgrowing the need for a psychologist at the earliest possible time without a loss of integrity or confidence. How to build a relationship with a client that moves in the direction of outgrowing the need of the psychologist and learning the ability to depend on himself with confidence is an important phase of therapeutic direction. The important thing, too, of course, is to make sure that the person who is being educated to mature and grow to manage himself does so with a full enough understanding to have a survival value without professional help. To brag about a dependent personality not being able to get along without the psychologist he has been going to for a long time is nothing that represents a practice that an honest profession would approve.

6. *Diversity vs. uniformity in training.* In the Boulder Conference of 1949 on graduate education in clinical psychology, the discussion of diversity versus uniformity led to the conclusion that training programs for clinical psychologists must reflect the changing needs of society, as well as the theoretical and technical changes taking place within the profession of psychology and its related fields. It was agreed "... in view of the wide gaps in our present knowledge, the validation of our working assumptions is a task of the utmost importance. In addition to research carried out by individuals, group or cooperative research would help in arriving more quickly at answers to pressing problems of human welfare. In order to keep the profession sensitive to changes in society and in psychology, diversified university training programs should be encouraged although a basic core of general and clinical psychology will be necessary to provide a certain amount of uniform background" (17, p. 33). There is nothing in the foregoing statement that can be criticized except that it is rather vague and intangible. More specific questions should be: What kind of work will the person in private practice be confronted with? What kind of training, therefore, should he have so that he can feel well equipped to do the work he will be called on to do? Practice in clinical psychology has improved substantially in the last few years, but very little, if any of it, is slanted in the direction of preparation for private practice. One thing seems clear, whatever need there is for reevaluation should include also the addition of a more specific kind of training that gives the graduate student an opportunity to learn what he will be called upon to do in settings resembling those that he will work in. Veterans Administration practice and hospital training are very relevant but they are not enough because a client coming to a *VA* or a hospital definitely does not come with the same attitude or the same purposes as do the people who come to the offices in private practice. In private practice there is the need for life going on at home and work while going for help, which calls for special considerations. The problem of interdependence with other professions in private practice also has its own unique characteristics. Practicing in an office associated with a group of doctors is different from practicing in one's own office and, again, may call for some differentiations in preparation which are typically not provided for in universities as they exist. An appraisal of resources would make it possible to develop such facilities which, at the present time, are neglected.

7. *Internship vs. work experience.* There are some psychologists who are consistent in arguing against the use of internships, particularly in industry, Uhrbrock (19) has consistently opposed internships. Work experience in an honest-to-God industrial setting, however, can be made available

for use in the training program. Whether this be called an internship or not, is not important. What is important is that one who works in industry obtains experience in the kind of settings in which he may more likely work, dealing with the kind of problems he will be confronted with when he is on his own. Potential resources of this nature can be made available if effectively explored.[4]

In the Boulder Conference, clinical psychology is described as being more client oriented than is industrial. In their wisdom the members of the Conference say: "As a consequence the clinical psychologist who works in the industrial field is frequently subjected to conflicts between his feelings of responsibility to the individual employee and his loyalty to the organization employing him. These conflicts are no different from those felt by any clinical psychologist who has some administrative responsibility or who works in a somewhat restrictive framework, but they are apt to be intensified in the industrial situation" (17, p. 156). What the members of the Conference fail to realize is that what they are really saying is that in our present graduate course set-up, no provisions are made for psychologists getting enough of a background in economics, labor problems, and industrial organization as deemed necessary by business groups as well as by psychologists. Given that kind of an enriched perspective, a person with clinical experience as well as with enough knowledge of industrial organization will have some problems that are distinctly different but also manageable. What conflicts of loyalties he develops will more often than not be of his own making because of a lack of perception of the nature of the people he deals with for the problems he is seeking to solve.

8. *Self-sufficiency vs. interdependence in practice.* In private practice there are some people who think that they have to have a set-up where they can serve and satisfy all psychological service needs. Generally speaking, that is neither the possible, nor the desirable thing to do. People who survive in private practice and grow, typically have more interdependent relationships with doctors, with educational agencies, with social agencies, and other human institutions interested in human welfare. This implies not only professional relations for public relations purposes, but also in an admittance that every human being has limitations. A sense of limitation will make it more readily possible for a psychologist to be most helpful to his client by referring him to sources that specialize in certain kinds of helping needs more than he can render himself. A psychologist is in a position differentially to select or supplement with persons or facilities equipped to deal with their specialty rather than be a one and only source of support in a pseudo self-sufficient manner.

9. *Understanding and management vs. diagnosis and treatment.* A study of the kind of problems which confront a psychologist in practice suggests that there is altogether too much emphasis on ritualistic diagnosis and treatment and that the concepts themselves, although useful in medical practice, are sometimes a handicap rather than a help as an intellectual reference point for dealing with human problems as they appear in the psychological services. Much more to the point and more honest would be to think in terms of understanding and management instead of diagnosis and treatment. The style of understanding usually predetermines the likely style of management. This is so in breadth as well as depth of understanding. A person who, for example, conceives of mental disease as being brought about by being possessed by the devil has relatively few types of courses of action open to him as far as management is concerned. His treatment is limited to ways of getting rid of devils, ranging all the way from near murder to prayer. Similarly, if a person has a wider perspective in the light of which he studies and interprets human problems, his understanding will be fuller and his management, therefore, more realistic and adequate. The concept of understanding and management is not only an advantage in actual private practice, but is also a conceptual framework that readily enough can be carried into other situations such as industry.

In the present day we have to consider the human being in all of his human surroundings, his economic realities, his political realities, his social realities, as well as his family realities. Approaching this problem in terms of the fullest possible understanding for the most effective possible management is the only road that makes for the kind of understanding which makes further understanding more possible both to the professional and to his client. For so doing a historical perspective is an important ingredient.

NOTES

1. In the main based on materials prepared for participation in the 1957 APA Symposium, "The Place of Private Practice in Professional Psychology," sponsored by Divisions 12, 13, and 17.

2. See Stevenson (15) for a description of the growth of the child guidance movement.

3. For a survey of professional psychology up to 1950, see (7), and the early issues of the *Journal of Consulting Psychology*, particularly the statement made by the editor in (18).

4. On a small scale resources of this nature are now available for graduate students at Washington University by arrangement with the Human Relations Research Foundation.

REFERENCES

1. CATTELL, J. McK. Man of Science. Vol. II, Addresses and Formal Papers. Lancaster, Pa.: Science Press, 1947.

2. ———. Retrospect: Psychology as a profession. *J. Consult. Psychol.*, 1937, *1*, 1–3.

3. CLARK, K. E. America's Psychologists: A Survey of a Growing Profession. Washington: American Psychological Association, 1957.

4. COUNCIL OF REPRESENTATIVES OF THE *APA*. Ethical Standards of Psychologists. Washington: American Psychological Association, 1953.

5. ———. Ethical Standards of Psychologists: A Summary of Ethical Principles. Washington: American Psychological Association, 1953.

6. FRYER, D. H. The proposed American Association for applied and professional psychologists. *J. Consult. Psychol.*, 1937, *1*, 14–16.

7. FRYER, D. H., & HENRY, E. R. Handbook of Applied Psychology. (2 vols.) New York: Rinehart, 1950.

8. GINSBURG, S. W. Some notes on the private practice of psychiatry. *Bull. Menninger Clin.*, 1946, *6*, 188–196.

9. MELTZER, H. The psychologist in private practice. *Psychol. Exch.*, 1935, *3*, 182–185.

10. ———. Psychiatrists and psychologists in private practice. In *Handbook of Applied Psychology* (Vol. II) Fryer, D. H., & Henry, E. R. (*Eds.*). New York: Rinehart, 1950.

11. MULLER, H. J. The Uses of the Past. New York: Oxford Univ. Press, 1952.

12. ORWELL, G. 1984. New York: Harcourt Brace, 1949.

13. PATERSON, D. G. Applied psychology comes of age. *J. Consult. Psychol.*, 1940, *3*, 1–10.

14. STEINER, L. R. Where Do People Take Their Troubles? Boston: Houghton-Mifflin, 1945.

15. STEVENSON, G. S., & SMITH, G. Child Guidance Clinics: A Quarter Century of Development. New York: Commonwealth Fund, 1934.

16. SUTICH, A. Toward a professional code for psychological consultants. *J. Abn. & Soc. Psychol.*, 1944, *39*, 329–350.

17. STAFF OF THE CONFERENCE ON GRADUATE EDUCATION IN CLINICAL PSYCHOLOGY. (Raimy, V. G., *Ed.*). Training in Clinical Psychology. New York: Prentice-Hall, 1950.

18. SYMONDS, J. P. Toward unity. *J. Consult. Psychol.*, 1937, *1*, 23–24.

19. UHRBROCK, R. S. Internships vs. field training for industrial psychologists. *Amer. Psychol.*, 1955, *10*, 535–538.

20. VERNON, W. H. D. Some professional problems of the consulting psychologist. *J. Consult. Psychol.*, 1946, *10*, 136–142.

21. WHITEHEAD, A. N. Dialogues of Alfred North Whitehead. (Lucien Price, *Ed.*). Boston: Little-Brown, 1954.

22. WOODWORTH, R. S. The future of clinical psychology. *J. Consult. Psychol.*, 1937, *1*, 4–5.

30. The Psychologist as a Mental Health Consultant[1]

ARTHUR J. BINDMAN

THE psychologist as a mental health consultant is a relatively new role requiring a breadth of knowledge and experience culled from a number of fields and applied in a wide variety of areas. In the remarks which follow, the historical background of mental health consultation, as a specific technique, will be sketched and differentiated from other types of consultation. Its application by psychologists and the unique aspects of psychological training which enhance or detract from this method will be described. Suggestions for future developments in mental health consultation will also be made.

Consultation is not a new word in our vocabulary, although it has received little attention from psychological theory or research. Secondly, the types of consultation which can be provided have frequently become confused, not only in the minds of those receiving consultation, but also among the various practitioners. If we think of our usual model of consultation, it is one of a professional asking another professional to see the former's client in order to make an appraisal and suggestions for problem resolution. The consultant may be called in because he is a specialist and can provide some specific knowledge or act in a technical assistant capacity. In the medical model, he may even follow through and provide a specific procedure.

Another type of consultation which is frequently noted in social agencies is the use made of one professional discipline, e.g., psychiatrists, who consult on cases or other problems, but who do not supervise these cases. Gilbert (1960) (8) has made this point quite clearly when she notes that a consultant in this latter role cannot become involved in the supervisory process if he is to remain a "pure"

consultant, i.e., having no decision making power or administrative role.

A third type of consultant is the individual who works in a particular agency in an administrative position who provides consultation to line personnel, but who also may have administrative responsibilities for these same personnel. This type of consultant is frequently seen in public health agencies, departments of education, and in industrial settings where they are known as intramural consultants, in contrast to the extramural consultants who come "from the outside." The intramural consultant usually cannot divorce his supervisory and inspection roles from his consultation role, and in a sense he is, therefore, not a "pure" consultant.

A fourth example of consultation which gives more breadth to our discussion is the type of consultant who becomes involved in a counseling relationship with the consultee, whom he views as the client. I would submit that this example, frequently seen where psychologists have transferred their clinical and counseling skills to the industrial setting, would not fall into the generic category of what is called consultation, although it may be so labeled by some practitioners.

How does mental health consultation relate to the general area of consultation? Mental health consultation is a type of consultation aimed at the reduction of mental health problems by involving the participation of the professional caretakers who deal with these problems in their own professional roles. The mental health consultant deals particularly with problems that induce "crises,"as well as providing assistance in early case-finding and special types of program consultation [Simmons (15)]. This is termed mental health case consultation which stresses work with a consultee around the problems of clients. Simmons points out that the consultant "is not viewed as a therapist or the giver of prescriptive advice. Instead, the consultant seeks to assist a co-professional deal

Reprinted from *Journal of Psychiatric Nursing*, 1964, *2*, 367–380, by permission of the *Journal of Psychiatric Nursing* and the author. Dr. Bindman is Director of Psychological Services, Massachusetts Department of Mental Health.

more effectively with that segment of the population which he serves by helping the consultee solve those problems in his work which have mental health implications." The mental health consultant can also provide technical assistance regarding mental health problems, so that consultees can become more skillful and gain knowledge in dealing with problems which concern them [Bindman (2)].

The technique of mental health consultation takes its base from writings by members of the Wellesley Human Relations Service, such as Klein (9, 10, 11), Lindemann (12), and more recently Simmons (15). Vaughan (18) and Bindman (1, 2, 3) of the Massachusetts Department of Mental Health, where mental health consultation is part of the department's community mental health program, have written about particular applications of this method of mental health practice. Caplan (4, 5, 6, 7) of the Harvard School of Public Health has provided the best theoretical model as gleaned from his research and from in-service seminars he has conducted over a period of years with the Massachusetts Department of Mental Health. It may be of interest that the techniques of mental health consultation have received ever-widening attention and are being offered in the curriculum of the Postgraduate Center for Psychotherapy (13), as well as being the subject of a conference sponsored by NIMH (16). Mental health consultation has only recently received more attention from psychologists, as far as the technical literature is concerned, and training in the techniques of mental health consultation for psychologists have only been noted in recent years.

What is unique about mental health consultation? How does it differ from other interpersonal techniques? How well trained is the psychologist in applying these techniques, and what further training does he need? Perhaps a definition will help in focusing upon the process. It has been defined as "an interaction process or interpersonal relationship that takes place between two professional workers, the consultant and the consultee, in which one worker, the consultant, attempts to assist the other worker, the consultee, to solve a mental health problem of a client or clients, *within the framework of the consultee's usual professional functioning*. The process of consultation depends upon the communication of knowledge, skills, and attitudes through this relationship, and therefore is dependent upon the degree of emotional and intellectual involvement of the two workers. A secondary goal of this process is one of education so that the consultee can learn to handle similar cases in the future in a more effective fashion and

thus enhance his professional skills" [Bindman (1, 2)].

It will be noted that stress has been placed on the words, "within the framework of the consultee's usual professional functioning." This implies that the consultant does not try to make a psychotherapist out of the consultee when the latter is confronted with a mental health problem. In fact, stress is placed upon the improvement of the consultee's use of his own professional skills in reducing mental health difficulties or in enhancing mental health in his client(s).

The definition of mental health consultation suggests that there is a relationship to education, psychotherapy, supervision and administration in this process. It is really none of these methods, although techniques may have been borrowed from each.

The following are some distinctive differences.

EDUCATION AND MENTAL HEALTH CONSULTATION

Education generally emphasizes a long-term systematic approach; the curriculum is usually planned; the problem area is usually well-defined and delimited and the teacher may "feed" information to the student. In mental health consultation, there is no highly structured, pre-planned approach. The consultant uses whatever opportunities he can to form a relationship with the consultee and to focus upon the problem. The meetings are usually few in number, and thus difficulties may result in delimiting the problem too quickly in terms of an expected outcome. Finally, the consultant may advise, but he usually does so in a non-directive fashion and in no case does he implement a plan for problem solution himself. Caplan (7) suggests that consultation does come close to the methods of a problem centered seminar, individual tutorial or individual and group supervision.

SUPERVISION AND MENTAL HEALTH CONSULTATION

There is an essential and basic difference between consultation and supervision. The supervisor must be responsible for the work of the supervised individual, but the consultant is not directly responsible. The supervisor directs the work of the supervisee and even assists him in a direct fashion, while the mental health consultant is problem-focused and is not expected to follow through to see if his suggestions are being used. This is a major difference; i.e., the supervisor must deal directly with the professional role of the person being supervised, while the consultant should remain focused on the problem if he is to maintain his role. As Rhodes (14) points out in writing about the process of consultation in general: Consultation . . . "does not explore or attempt to interact with other roles of the consultee. Whenever it does venture into other life roles of the consultee, it is no longer consultation." Perhaps a minor distinction between supervision and consultation is the frequency with which the consultant is from another professional discipline than the consultee. In mental health consultation he is usually from one of the so-called mental health professions and the consultee is not. In supervision, particularly in case work and nursing, the supervisor will be from the same profession. Finally, the consultee usually initiates mental health consultation, while in supervision the supervisory relationship is initiated "from above."

PSYCHOTHERAPY AND MENTAL HEALTH CONSULTATION

There are a number of differences between these two interpersonal methods. Psychotherapy is generally long term; it is concerned with a range of intrapsychic problems in a patient or client; it weakens or changes defenses; there may be interpretation and other psychological means of handling resistances. In mental health consultation, the time span is short and the consultant attempts to handle a specific problem of a client and then withdraws. Defenses are not weakened in the consultee, but rather they are bolstered and supported. The consultant rarely interprets and if he does it may be about the client's problems and not the consultee's.

Psychotherapy of the consultee should be avoided. The consultant may be aware of the consultee's personal difficulties, but he constantly focuses upon the problem, the client, or other aspects of the work situation and not upon the intrapsychic conflicts of the consultee. "If the consultant allows himself to get involved in the consultee's intrapsychic problems, he is falling into the trap which has been set for him; namely, that the consultee was not fully certain that he is to play the role of a patient, but now he has proved that he is to do so" [Bindman (1)]. Rhodes (14) also notes that there has been much confusion between these two methods. In fact, he remarks that consultants have been met with anger and rejection on the part of consultees when they have applied

their therapeutic skills to the consultee's intrapsychic processes instead of being aware of the consultee's need to focus upon the problem situation or client.

On the other hand, one cannot deny that in mental health case consultation there is the need to develop a close relationship with the consultee, just as in other interpersonal modes, although the consultant must do this as quickly and efficiently as possible and without the depth noted in intensive psychotherapy. Secondly, corrective emotonal experiences take place in both mental health case consultation and in psychotherapy, but once again in a much less intensive fashion in the former.

ADMINISTRATION AND MENTAL HEALTH CONSULTATION

In administrative practice, the administrator assumes responsibility for taking specific action, making decisions, promulgating policy, and in general taking leadership. Administration implies that a subordinate will follow directions of the administrator. Mental health consultation is best carried out when the consultant can clearly communicate to the consultee that there is a "take it or leave it" characteristic to their relationship with each having the right to withdraw. The consultant does not make decisions, assume responsibility for follow-up of results, or take a leadership role. Towle (17) indicates that in a true consultation relationship the person seeking advice is a free agent and he alone holds the responsibility for using the advice. The distinction between administration and consultation may become particularly nebulous in program consultation where there may be problems related to administration. The consultant should be wary lest he become the administrator instead of merely assisting in administrative planning. Of course, when the consultant is hired on an intramural basis this "pure" role of consultant may become impossible to maintain, especially when he acts in a line function and carries certain administrative responsibilities in his role. It would appear from our present knowledge that mental health consultation is best carried on in as "pure" a form as possible with the consultant on an extramural staff level.

TECHNIQUES OF MENTAL HEALTH CONSULTATION

One cannot discuss techniques of mental health consultation without relying heavily on the theoretical writings of Caplan (4, 5, 6, 7). He divides mental health case consultation into four major categories: case insight, action-help, consultee crisis, and social system consultation.

In case insight consultation, the consultee lacks understanding regarding a client's problems. The consultant attempts to increase the consultee's knowledge regarding the psychological functioning of the client, but in keeping with the consultee's professional background. One technique that is used is to jointly observe a client, and then discuss their perceptions. The hoped for result is that the consultee will then enhance the environment in such a way that it has a positive effect upon the client's behavior pattern. One example might be that of a teacher who does not understand why a child behaves aggressively on the playground in relation to younger children. She is helped by the consultant in her understanding of the child's sibling rivalry problems. The result is that she gives special attention to the child and helps him compensate for his feelings of rejection. Another example is that of a manager in industry who cannot understand why a particular subordinate is easily flustered and on the verge of tears at times. The mental health consultant might help the manager gain further understanding into the subordinate's feelings of low self-esteem and also provide suggestions which could help the employer become more effective.

In action-help consultation, the consultee lacks the skill or facilities in his work setting to deal with special mental health problems of a client. For example, he may not know what resource he can use in the community when a particular problem occurs. The mental health consultant collaborates with the consultee and assists him in working out a plan for the client. Nondirective techniques are used at first, but at a later stage the consultant may give more direct information in order to broaden the consultee's knowledge in assisting clients. In the long run, the consultee should become more effective in case finding and in the utilization of community resources in meeting the needs of his clients. One example is that of a school principal who is assisted by the mental health consultant in understanding a serious mental health problem of a child and how she can help the family to bring the child to a community health center. Another example in an industrial setting is that of a mental health consultant who helps a supervisor sharpen his skills in assessing problems of depression in older workers, and tells him how he can make inplant referrals for assistance or use outside facilities for referrals in some instances.

In consultee crisis consultation, a disturbed or disturbing situation in a client may trigger off a crisis in a consultee. Frequently, the client's behavior is the type which will cause similar problems which have been controlled to suddenly reemerge. The consultee may distort and stereotype his relationship with the client, the result being reduction in the consultee's effective functioning. The consultant uses two major techniques in working with the consultee. The first is "segmental tension reduction" (Caplan, 1959) (7) in which the consultant fosters discussion of the client's problems, which by implication are concerned with the consultee's problems. There is no explicit discussion of the consultee's feelings, but rather this implied method reduces the consultee's tension which in turn affects the client due to the close relationship between them. An example of this method might be the discussion of a child's mother by a teacher and mental health consultant, which in turn is meaningful for the teacher's own feelings in relation to the child.

The second method in crisis reduction is "dissipation of the stereotype" [Caplan (5, 6, 7)]. This consists of the consultant discussing with the consultee about the client's behavior in an attempt to encourage a more realistic appraisal and reduce stereotype. The aim is to have the consultee see the human aspects of the client as a person in need and not as a "monster" of some sort so that the crisis will be reduced. An example might be a hospital superintendent who stereotypes an aide as "shiftless and sloppy." The mental health consultant may use discussion and/or joint observation to help the superintendent see that this aide does not necessarily fit the pattern to which he has been relegated.

In social system consultation, one must consider whether crises or needs for action-help may have been engendered by difficulties in the social system of the consultee, such as communication problems, a vague or poor authority system, role conflicts, and disturbing personality problems. Usually, these problems have had a long history, but sudden changes in the equilibrium of the social system may require consultation. The consultant may use a case consultation approach, in which he is working indirectly, or he may work directly and provide administrative consultation in which organizational practices, personnel problems, and other management problems which may relate to the solving of a client's mental health problems will be discussed. An example of this approach would be mental health consultation with a superintendent of schools concerning the personnel practices in his school system which have resulted in an incompetent individual obtaining an important supervisory position which in turn is upsetting a very competent principal.

TRAINING IN MENTAL HEALTH CONSULTATION

Although mental health consultation is not exclusively a psychologist's function, it would appear that psychological training, particularly in clinical and counseling psychology coupled with supervised experience, is a strong base for this work. A background in casework or psychotherapy would be essential in order that the practitioner be experienced with human dynamics and be sensitive to unconscious processes and interpersonal elements in a relationship. However, stress should be placed upon training and experience with so-called normal behavior and its vagaries rather than merely pathological functioning.

In an earlier paper, it was suggested that the psychologist should have the following [Bindman (2)]:

1. Thorough knowledge and experience in personality functioning and psychodynamics.
2. Thorough knowledge and experience in psychotherapy, both individual and group, and sufficient supervision in these methods so that he understands himself and is able to control his relationships with others.
3. Thorough knowledge and experience in diagnostic appraisal and especially through the use of secondary cues and behavioral features.
4. Some training and experience in various aspects of educational methods, both in a didactic sense and in the use of other educational and promotional methods.
5. Some knowledge of social psychology and especially of social structures, communities, social groups institutional structures, and community organization.

A clinical psychologist with experience in a community mental health setting may frequently have much of the above, but in some areas the health educator, sociologist, social worker, or social psychologist will be more adequate. In addition, as the psychologist mental health consultant becomes more involved in administrative or social

system consultation, he sould be further trained in administrative principles, organization of community resources, industrial management, and mental health promotion techniques. In closing, let me add that there are still very few places where a psychologist can go to gain the necessary basic training and experience in mental health consultation, let alone advanced course work in this area.

A NOTE FOR THE FUTURE

The part that psychologists, as well as others working in the mental health field and functioning in a consultant capacity, are playing and will continue to play in developing, understanding, and evaluating mental health consultation would appear to be increasing. With the continuing demand for mental health services and the rapid burgeoning of community mental health programs, there is an ever increasing need for techniques which will possibly prevent problems in the mental health sphere, and to do this in a relatively quick and effective fashion. Mental health consultation may not be the complete panacea, but it does hold promise for positive change and deserves the interest of the professional psychologist. Although one should not make a prediction without sufficient data or at least a high degree of confidence in the data at hand, nevertheless the trend appears to be one of increased use of consultants in general and mental health consultants in particular. Once again, psychologists are faced with a dilemma—how can they best train themselves for the application of these techniques, if there is this increased demand for services? Perhaps more post-graduate training centers (13) are the solution in combination with on-going service programs. It is a difficult problem, and one which is barely being faced now. One wonders if this training opportunity will be grasped by psychology in the near future, or will it, like other chances, perish due to lack of interest.

NOTES

1. Presented at American Psychological Association Convention, New York, 1961.

REFERENCES

1. BINDMAN, A. J. Mental Health Consultation: Theory and Practice. *J. Consult. Psychol.*, 23, 473–482, 1959.
2. ———. Training in Mental Health Consultation. Paper read at the American Psychological Association Convention, Cincinnati, 1959.

3. BINDMAN, A. J., and KLEBANOFF, L. B. Administrative Problems in Establishing a Community Mental Health Program. *Amer. J. Orthopsychiat.*, *30*, 696–711, 1960.

4. CAPLAN, G. The Role of the Social Worker in Preventive Psychiatry. *Med. Soc. Wk.*, *4*, 144–159, 1955.

5. ———. Mental Health Consultation in Schools. In *Elements of a Community Mental Health Program*. Milbank Memorial Fund, N.Y., pp. 77–85, 1956.

6. ———. *Mental Health Aspects of Social Work in Public Health*. U.S. Children's Bureau, Washington, D.C., 1956.

7. ———. *Concepts of Mental Health and Consultation*. U.S. Children's Bureau, Washington, D.C., 1959.

8. GILBERT, RUTH. Functions of the Consultant. *Teach. Coll. Rec.*, *61*, 177–187, 1960.

9. KLEIN, D. C. Training the Psychologist in a Community Mental Health Center. Paper read at the American Psychological Association Convention, Chicago, 1956.

10. ———. Consultation in the Framework of Preventive Psychiatry. Paper read at the American Orthopsychiatric Association Annual Meeting, San Francisco, 1959.

11. ———. The Prevention of Mental Illness. *Ment. Hyg.*, *45*, 101–109, 1961.

12. LINDEMANN, E. The Wellesley Project for the Study of Certain Problems in Community Mental Health. In *Interrelations Between the Social Environment and Psychiatric Disorders*. Milbank Memorial Fund, N.Y., 1953.

13. *Postgraduate Center for Psychotherapy*. N.Y. Postgraduate Center for Psychotherapy, *Bulletin of Information*, 1960.

14. RHODES, W. C. Training in Community Mental Health Consultation. Paper read at the American Psychological Association Convention, Chicago, 1960.

15. SIMMONS, A. J. Consultation Through a Community Mental Health Agency. Paper read at the American Psychological Association Convention, Chicago, 1960.

16. *The Psychologist and Consultation*. Report of the Consultation Subcommittee of the Conference of Chief Psychologists in State Mental Health Programs. NIMH, Bethesda, 1959.

17. TOWLE, CHARLOTTE. The Consultation Process. Unpublished mimeographed manuscript. University of Chicago, 1950.

18. VAUGHAN, W. T. Mental Health for School Children. *Children*, *2*, 203–207, 1955.

31. *The Psychologist as a Ward Administrator: Current Status*

HORACE STEWART AND HENRY HARSCH

PROBLEM

The precise role of the clinical psychologist has never been rigidly defined and perhaps for a good reason. Brannon and Waites (1) have described a role for the clinical psychologist as a ward administrator. This role allowed for a fuller use of the psychologist's skills delegating him primary responsibility for special ward programs and authority to sign "Doctors Orders" for non medical matters, i.e., passes, ground privileges, access to funds, psychological treatment programs, and manipulation of ward environment. Webb and Hiram (6) found that using a psychologist as a ward administrator led to less morbidity, more ground privileges, more time on leave of absence, and more time out of the hospital for the patients. Ishijama, Denny, Prada, and Vespe (3) reported that patients in a mental hospital expected psychologists to engage in more therapeutic activities and be more active in dispositional decisions, while the other staff members expected an emphasis on psycho-diagnostic testing and a de-emphasis on treatment activities. The gain in status to ward administrator engendered staff hostility. Cowen and Schwartz (2) outline the precise role the psychologist played in administering a convalescent cottage which housed chronic patients. These studies indicate the expansion of the role authority and duties of the psychologist working in a clinical setting. The present survey is an attempt to ascertain the extent of duties now performed by the clinical psychologist as a ward administrator.

METHOD

This report is based upon a mail survey of institutions, state hospitals, and Veterans Administration hospitals where clinical psychologists were employed. The 1963 Directory of the American Psychological Association contained 186 such institutions. A questionnaire was sent to the chief psychologist of each of these institutions. One hundred and fifty-seven (84%) of the questionnaires were promptly returned.

The general instructions for the questionnaire included the following:

There appears to be an increase in the number of clinical psychologists who are becoming ward administrators. Ward administration is defined as having direct control over the patient's welfare in terms of psychological treatment, routine policy formulation, control over ward environment, discharge planning, transfer and placement of patients, and in general, being recognized as a major influence in the patient's care. This questionnaire is an attempt to ascertain the amount of ward administration being done at this time.

RESULTS

The first four questions of the questionnaire were directed toward the number of psychologists on the staff, the population of the hospital, the number of physicians and board psychiatrists on the staff of the various institutions. These four questions revealed that the state hospitals have fewer doctoral level staff, larger patient population, less staff physicians, and less board psychiatrists than are found in Veterans Administration hospitals. This finding is not striking but should be kept in mind in terms of progress in ward administration. Progress has been much the same in both the better and more poorly staffed institutions.

Question five, "*How many of your psychologists actively administer wards in your hospitals?*" No psychologist was administering wards in 119 (77%) of the responding institutions. Psychologists were presently administering wards in 35 (23%) hospitals. The number of psychologists so employed

Reprinted from *Journal of Clinical Psychology*, 1966, *22*, 108–111, by permission of the *Journal of Clinical Psychology* and Dr. Stewart. Dr. Stewart is Assistant Professor of Psychology, Augusta College, Augusta, Georgia. Dr. Harsch is in private practice in Atlanta, Georgia.

were 49 in state institutions and 44 in Veterans Administration hospitals. Although one state hospital reported 12 psychologists so employed, the median was two psychologists per institution in the role of ward administrator.

Question six, "*Do you feel ward administration is a desirable role for psychologists?*" Ward administration was opposed by 44 (29%) of the respondants, 67 (44%) approved with definite reservations and 5 (3%) had no opinion. Many of the chief psychologists who had reservations expressed the opinion that they did not want to see their staff become encumbered with administrative details, but would have them free to use their authority to utilize their knowledge of human behavior to the benefit of the patients.

Question seven, "*How many years has ward administration been a part of your hospital program?*" Ward administration had been instituted for a mean of 5.02 years in 40 institutions which had such a program although it may have been discontinued. There was a range from one to ten-plus years with a median of five years. Ward administration had been part of the program for more than six years in 15 institutions. Ward administration has been practiced, on the average, longer in the V. A. institutions.

Question eight, "*How do the psychologists on your staff feel about ward administration?*" This question was addressed to those psychologists who were actually engaged in ward administration. A positive response was given by 17 (42%) of the respondants, while 23 (58%) had mixed feelings or reservations about the role. There is much feeling about not being a "junior psychiatrist", but having a clear-cut status reflecting the training and competence of the clinical psychologist.

Question nine, "*Does the medical staff oppose the psychologist as a ward administrator?*" Definite opposition from the medical staff was expressed in only two (5%) of the replies, most of the medical staff opposed in two (5%), some medical opposition was elicited from 18 (45%) and no medical opposition to the psychologist as a ward administrator was given by 18 (45%). A common reply to this question was that, at first, there was much medical opposition to the psychologist as a ward administrator. However, in a short period of time most of the medical staff changed its opinion and approved of the psychologist in this role. The strongest opposition comes from the medical staff in the state hospitals. Other disciplines were not reported as engaging in ward administration to any appreciable extent, i.e., social service, nursing or attendant personnel.

Question ten was a rating scale for determining the extent and type of duties performed by psychologists in administering wards. Table 1 presents this tabulation. A ward administration program had been initiated by 40 (25%) of the respondants. This program had been discontinued in five institutions. The patterns for state hospitals *vs.* V.A. hospitals were not remarkably different. All of the 28 duties were reported as having been performed somewhere at some time.

Question eleven, "*Have there been, or do you anticipate, any legal problems on ward administration?*" There was no anticipation of legal problems in 95% of the respondants because of their ward administration activities. There was some apprehension as to the fact that psychologists do not enjoy legal protection for activities that may encroach upon medical practice. However, where the psychologist was doing a good job he felt that he would not be subject to legal difficulty.

Question twelve dealt with the psychology interns and their opportunity to learn ward administration. All but three of the institutions that reported ward administration had a psychology internship program. However, over one-half (58%) of these institutions were not giving any training in ward administration to their psychology interns. Therefore, specific training for ward administration must be sought out by those who feel it to be a valuable aspect of training.

DISCUSSION

It is difficult to ascertain the specific amount of authority the psychologist possesses due to the intricacies of the delegation of authority in medical settings. However, it becomes apparent that the psychologist is assuming a more important position in the treatment team. The delegation of authority to a particular psychologist is often the result of a good working relationship and demonstrated ability on the part of the individual psychologist to his medical colleagues. One psychologist reported that he was an acting superintendent of the state hospital in Larned, Kansas, for approximately six months (5). Although he represents an extreme example, this points out that the clinical psychologist can play an extremely important and powerful role even in the institutions that have been traditionally a strong-hold of the physician.

A crucial point of validity concerning the present study resolves itself into the actual authority that the clinical psychologist enjoys as a ward administrator. Because of a difference between an individ-

TABLE 1. Frequency and Extent of Duties Performed by Psychologists as Ward Administrators
(N = never, MA = with medical advice, S = seldom, O = often, A = always)

Duty	N	MA	S	O	A
1. Grant permission for telephone calls	2	3	5	13	17
2. Refer patients to occupational therapy	2	6	3	14	15
3. Refer patients to music therapy	4	5	1	12	14
4. Refer patients to vocational rehabilitation	2	5	3	12	18
5. Give permission for dances and movies	6	2	3	13	16
6. Give permission for walkouts	3	3	2	14	14
7. Authority to transfer patients	9	11	2	4	12
8. Write mental examinations which physicians have traditionally done	20	2	4	6	8
9. Write initial admission notes on patients	16	2	1	10	10
10. Write therapy and progress notes	0	0	0	13	27
11. Conduct ward staff conferences in regard to patient's treatment and ward problems	0	0	6	15	19
12. Give verbal orders to nurse or attendant	3	0	4	16	17
13. Write orders on doctor's order sheet	17	2	5	3	13
14. Perceived by relatives as patient's doctor	1	0	8	20	10
15. Authority to grant town visits	3	6	3	12	15
16. Authority to grant trial visits	7	14	0	9	8
17. Authority for furloughing patients	7	15	0	9	9
18. Sign the discharge or furlough papers	29	1	0	2	6
19. Recommend changes in E. C. T. or drug therapy which may interfere with psychotherapy	3	5	5	18	8
20. Psychologist's authority is equal to the physician's authority on the ward	7	1	7	15	8
21. Psychologist's authority greater than physician's on ward	19	2	5	11	1
22. Authority to transfer out unsuitable attendants	20	5	8	4	2
23. Are there professional staff conferences in regard to inter-professional problems	7	1	14	12	4
24. Do psychologists feel free to initiate new methods or techniques that may be therapeutic (patient government, ward projects)	1	1	1	20	17
25. Do the psychologist ward administrators also be psychotherapy with any of the patients on their ward	3	0	5	20	11
26. Does the psychologist select patients for psychotherapy	1	0	0	18	21
27. Do nurses resent a psychologist as an administrator	14	1	20	4	1
28. Do attendants resent a psychologist as an administrator	14	1	23	1	0

ual's perceived authority and his actual authority, it is difficult to ascertain the real position. The ultimate responsibility for patient care, in a state hospital, is often in the hands of the governor of the state. This authority is in turn delegated to a hospital superintendent who is traditionally a physician. The physician in turn, in some cases, is apparently able to delegate further authority to psychologists. Just how clearly this is delegated even to other staff physicians is seldom clearly defined. Kissinger (4) clearly makes the point that the delegation of authority even among the physicians is often confused and subject to unpredicted change, often disrupting working relationships. The psychologist as a member of a para-medical discipline often suffers from even minor fluctuations in the administrative organization.

The role of ward administrator is not extremely popular to the clinical psychologist, as over half of the psychologists so employed have definite reservations. The psychologist desires the authority of the position without engaging in the administrative duties *per se*. Recognition of competence is seen in the role, a recognition which would enable him to put into practice his knowledge of the scientific principles of behavior.

SUMMARY

The duties and attitudes of clinical psychologists acting as ward administrators were sampled in a mail survey. Ward administration was currently practiced in 23% of the institutions polled. It was practiced equally in both state and V. A. hospitals. This role was a controversial one with over one-half of the psychologists so employed being ambivalent about it. The psychologist is seen as attempting to find a place on the treatment team more compatible with his training.

REFERENCES

1. BRANNON, E. P. and WAITES, A. J. The role of the clinical psychologist in ward administration. *Amer. J. Psychiat.*, 1955, *112*, 497–501.
2. COWEN, JOSEPH and SCHWARTZ, LLOYD. An experiment in the utilization of a clinical psychologist as a ward administrator in a state psychiatric hospital. *Psychiat. Quart.*, 1960, *34*, 472–479.
3. ISHIJAMA, TOARU, DENNY, JAMES M., PRADA, RAYMOND and VESPE, RAYMOND. The role of the psychologist on mental hospital wards as defined by the expectant others. *J. clin. Psychol.*, 1962, *18*, 3–10.
4. KISSINGER, R. D. The un-therapeutic community: A team approach that failed. Paper read at Eastern Psychological Association, 1963.
5. PRATT, STEVE. Personal communication, 1964.
6. WEBB, WARREN W. and HIRAM, L. G. The utilization of the psychologist in ward administration. *J. clin. Psychol.*, 1957, *13*, 301–302.

32. *Psychologists and Government Programs*

EUGENE T. GENDLIN, HERMAN DIESENHAUS,

MARK OBERLANDER, AND LEONARD

PEARSON

THIS paper reports the results of a survey[1] of all APA members, concerning their possible interest in working in one of seven functions of psychologists in government and community programs. 2,649 respondents indicated interest in one or more of the functions, their preferred geographic location, and salary range. No specific blank of respondents' names was provided. By adding their names (and frequently other information), 1,717 respondents turned the survey into a request to be informed of this kind of job opening. Thus, roughly 10 per cent of APA members are actively interested in hearing about such positions. The findings also show that the seven categories do differentiate different sorts of interest. This field of psychology in community and government programs has not, as yet, any definitions of psychologists' job functions. Thus the survey was an attempt to test an original tentative set of such categories.

THE PROBLEM

Psychologists are being sought for a great variety of functions in government. The "New Society" and the new community approach to social problems involve many programs on federal, state, and local levels. Many such programs are already in operation and many more are now being planned. These developments are creating social change of New Deal proportions. Their impact on the roles and contributions of psychologists is only just beginning to be felt.

Reprinted by permission of the authors. Dr. Gendlin is Visiting Associate Professor, Departments of Psychology and Philosophy, University of Chicago; Dr. Diesenhaus is Medical Research Associate, Research Program in Child Development, Illinois Institute for Juvenile Research; Mr. Oberlander is Research Assistant, Department of Psychology, University of Chicago; and Dr. Pearson is Associate Professor of Psychology, Western Reserve University.

Most of these programs are looking for a psychologist. Some of the positions are high-level policy positions. So often, the ideal person to head up this or that would seem to be a psychologist. Other positions are team-contributing. A psychologist is needed as one specialist among others. For what function is he needed? He himself will have to define it. He is usually wanted precisely to keep the program effective and sensitive in those respects to which a psychologist would be sensitive. Other positions involve planning, training, and consulting.

Just what sort of psychologist is wanted? Child, clinical, experimental, assessment, personality, biological, etc.? The answer is any, all, or none of these. What is being looked for is a certain sort of person. Any of these old psychological slots will do. None of them express what is wanted. As long as the individual is a psychologist, what then counts is his motivation, interest, ability, and willingness to feel his way with a new program under new circumstances.

Psychologists cannot help being vitally interested in these developments. Not only the field but the nature of our society will be strongly affected. We want these developments to include what a psychologist would be sensitive to, and that is just what the various programs also seek! But it has been difficult to connect these programs with those among the more than 19,000 APA member psychologists who might be interested. No effective channel exists.

This problem is not a matter of job seeking. Most of the psychologists who would be interested probably have a perfectly satisfactory position. They might have this position only out of interest, challenge, and long-standing concern for socially significant problems. How many psychologists are so describable and who are they? How might we connect them to the programs and agencies who are searching for them?

The usual definitions and areas of specialization in psychology do not fit the present problem. There is a major conceptual problem involved, mirrored by how employment listings now divide psychology. Either populations are divided (child, personality, social, rehabilitation, aging) or the divisions follow differences in method (experimental, clinical).

But, the problems of working more effectively with all these different populations involves problems of institutionalization, isolation from the community, community attitudes, and so on, i.e., roughly *the same* community approaches are always involved. No wonder the programs are quite often not looking for this or that specialist.

The new community approaches of these programs find that all groups in the community must be worked with simultaneously, and that research—where possible—is as important as practice. Who would be more likely to come up with a pertinent research program, the experimental or the clinical psychologist? Who can say? It depends on the man. Shall our community health program be headed by a child specialist or a specialist on aging? It doesn't matter; it depends on the man.

Only a few years ago, psychologists (for example, those who worked in hospitals) were (and still are) frequently saying: "It's no use; you'd have to change the whole system if you really wanted to help even just this one patient effectively." By "changing the whole system" we meant both the hospital structure and the attitudes and programs in the community. We really meant the equivalent of "impossible." But today exactly that sort of change in basic structure is the national trend.

As psychotherapists, many of us have long been dissatisfied with our inability to do much for the poor, the lower-class individual, for the aged, the delinquent, the alcoholic, the drug addict, the epileptic, the retarded, the disabled, the radically underpriviledged, the psychotic, or to institute preventive measures for the social problems which produced those neurotics with whom we most often work. Thus the present developments are likely to actualize insights and ideas many of us have had for a very long time.

The problems with which community psychology attempts to cope are "purely" psychological. The less priviledged the group, the more their psychological problems are inseparably meshed with problems of social structure and environment. A "purely" psychological problem is one which, if solved, would enable the individual to handle all the rest of whatever he is up against. The assumption that he can do so applies only to high opportunity individuals who can move about freely and

change jobs, friends, and locale. Thus one can see that they have a psychological problem. The individual takes such a problem with him wherever he goes, and it is a function of the individual as such. For the individual who cannot make himself independent of his situation, the problems also are not so clearly divisible. Few of his problems are independent of his situation. What these people are up against must be worked with as an interconnected whole. The social context must be worked with along with the individual.

The survey was conducted by a group of psychotherapists. Why were psychotherapists concerned with this question? As yet, we know little about how to integrate the psychotherapist into the broader community programs. We ourselves have long said that psychotheraphy can't solve everything alone, but it is surely one necessary ingredient in a successful broader approach. If we don't find some place for the close, therapeutic type of personal relating in the plans of the community approaches, these purely structural community methods alone are quite likely to fail also.

Analogous problems also hold for other psychological specializations: in the long run, successful programs will need research methods, psychometric testing, developmental knowledge, etc. Yet, emphatically, these programs are *not* looking for (or thinking in terms of) these various areas of specialization as such. They are seeking psychologists.

In constructing our survey, many discussions were held with various agencies and individuals. The striking fact emerged that most often no answer exists for the question: "What should this psychologist for whom you are looking, do?" The reply regularly is: "What he considers necessary," or, "That's just what we want a psychologist to tell us," or, "We are sure our program will suffer, if there isn't a psychologist to help in the planning, and then to remain sensitive to needs that develop, which he would be the one to notice when there is still time to do something about them."

Thus there is no predefinition of the content of psychological knowledge wanted. Only the kind of ability, activity, and sensitivity is specified.

Requests have often come to APA headquarters for psychologists for certain positions. When these requests are unclassifiable in the terms of the Employment Bulletin, they cannot be found through listings. They are not recognizable (general, $10,000, State of New York). And, even if they were recognizable, the psychologists who might be challenged by these jobs are probably not even looking for a job!

SURVEY ON PSYCHOLOGISTS' AVAILABILITY FOR POSITIONS IN GOVERNMENT

Currently there is a great expansion in federal, state, and local public programs. Psychologists are being sought for positions on all levels. Many of these positions cannot be classified in the usual categories ("clinical," "counseling," "experimental," "research," etc.) because they don't require this or the psychological specialization. Rather, they require the psychologist's broad background in dealing with human problems and in devising research.

For the more usual functions (even in unusual settings) the federal and state civil service listings and the APA's monthly Employment Bulletin are adequate. However, such listings (in terms of location, salary range, and qualifications required) do not characterize the new, hard-to-define positions. Yet the inherent challenge and interest of these functions will attract some and not others. It has been impossible, so far, to make psychologists broadly aware of these opportunities, and to find out who are those who might be attracted by positions of this sort. If you are one (if any or all of the sample functions listed below might interest you), please return the survey, indicating geographical area and the minimum salary above which you would wish to hear more about such opportunities.

Sample Functions:

1. *Creates and Administrates Program:* A large city seeks a psychologist to define, plan, set up, and then direct an entire community mental health program, including preventive, crisis, and rehabilitative projects, as well as some subprojects to be supported by the federal poverty program. (Only broad goals are given; guidelines can be found in examples from many programs in other places.)

2. *Psychological Member of a Team:* A large state program just getting under way seeks a psychologist to help define and coordinate human relations aspects of the program, to bring various groups in the community together as necessary, and to devise structures for continued ways to deal with mental health problems. The whole program would then include dimensions he first perceives, defines, and plans for.

3. *Outside Consultant:* As part of a city's program, the psychologist visits schools, the police, welfare agencies, employment agencies, etc. He assists these inside their own setting to become more able to deal with mental health problems. Thus he might consult with teachers and discuss what they now do with disturbed children, aid them, as well as principals, and discuss what they now do with disturbed children, as well as help create a new structure in which more teachers perhaps with supervision, resources and liaison to the outside, can work with disturbed children. He may aid (and help set up new patterns for) many other agencies in the community.

4. *Inside Consultant:* A federal bureau seeks a psychologist to act as consultant to it, first to discover and define problems and then to carry out his own advice regarding them. Consultation would concern the department's specific activities, its staff relations, and its basic goals and functions.

5. *Supervision of Newly Trained and Semi-Professionals:* A state seeks a psychologist to devise and direct training and continuing supervision for several classes of less elaborately trained professionals and semi-professionals who would perform several community functions in a statewide network.

6. *Research Director for a Government Department:* Again the psychologist is asked first to define the areas and problems for research, evaluation, or innovation and then to direct the research.

7. *Creation and Evaluation of Many Programs:* A federal government department has funds for research and for community programs. The psychologist would define possible new programs, would then arrange for outside psychologists and agencies to plan and submit such programs, and would finally direct the screening and evaluation of what is submitted.

I might be interested in functions somewhat like samples:

1	2	3	4	5	6	7	All
☐	☐	☐	☐	☐	☐	☐	☐

My interest is:

STRONG	MODERATE	QUITE TENTATIVE
☐	☐	☐

Geographical areas:

LARGE CITY		SMALL CITY		RURAL	
☐	☐	☐	☐	☐	☐
ONLY	PREFER	ONLY	PREFER	ONLY	PREFER

EAST COAST		WEST COAST		EUROPE		OTHER FOREIGN	
☐	☐	☐	☐	☐	☐	☐	☐
ONLY	PREFER	ONLY	PREFER	ONLY	PREFER	ONLY	PREFER

Salary: I would like to receive more information about positions at or above

$9,000–$25,000.

This survey is conducted by Psychologists Interested in the Advancement of Psychotherapy, Section II, Division 12, The American Psychological Association.

To meet this problem, we devised seven new categories based on the sort of role a psychologist might play in a broader program (head, team member, consultant) and the sort of broad functions he might exercise (direct, train, research, evaluation of programs).

METHOD

A brief questionnaire, entitled "Survey on Psychologists Availability for Positions in Government," was sent to all 19,199 members and fellows of the APA listed in the 1965 *APA Directory*.

The questionnaire contained four sections. In the first section, seven new job functions or categories were described. The respondents were asked to indicate which functions they were interested in; they could check as many of the seven as they wished. These seven descriptions were an initial sample of the novel roles for the psychologist in the new programs. Of course, more effective role definitions will develop as precedents are set. But at this stage, some classification, however rough, is essential for making a beginning. The major question was: Do these seven rough categories differentiate at all, or would psychologists tend to be interested either in all or in none of these?

Second, the subjects were asked to indicate their overall degree of interest in the functions. The three choices presented were "strong," "moderate," or "quite tentative."

In the third section, the respondents were asked for their geographical preferences. In the fourth section they were asked for the salary level at which they would be interested in obtaining more information about such positions; a range of $9,000 to $25,000 inclusive was provided.

THE RESULTING LISTS

There were 2,649 usable questionnaires returned, while 7 completely blank questionnaires were also returned. Responses to the questions were coded and punched onto cards.

Although there had been no place indicated on the questionnaire for writing name and address, many of the respondents did write their name and usually the address. Often they included letters and vita. By checking addresses or postmarks against the 1965 *APA Directory*, it was possible to establish which of like-named individuals had responded, or to resolve any ambiguities in spelling. (Only eleven of the names could not be identified.) The names were also punched onto the cards, yielding a listing of 1,717 psychologists who had stated that they might be interested in one or more of the seven functions, degree of interests, locales, and minimum salary.

Although the original purpose had been to survey the interest in the new roles and to assess the adequacy of these seven categories, the large number of respondents who stated interest and name, has turned the survey into a personal request for further job information. The nature of their response has led us to work toward the creation of an apparatus to service these requests. As a first step toward such an apparatus, the original list has been broken down by job and geographic preference (see Table 1) to create 35 sublists of psychologists who might be interested in a specific job in a specific region.

Each respondent appears on at least one list (i.e., interested in only one function and one geographic area) or as many as all 35 lists (i.e., interested in all functions and no geographic preference). Other groupings and sublists are also

TABLE I

Job	Number Expressing Interest*	Per Cent Interest	Per Cent of Agreement*					
			2	3	4	5	6	7
1	890	52	67	61	56	60	53	61
2	797	46		65	61	66	50	54
3	1,142	67			56	69	38	48
4	1,017	59				58	61	62
5	948	55					46	52
6	739	43						70
7	964	56						

* 245 subjects checked the "all" choice, rather than any of the seven. The number (and the per cent agreement) for each category, and pair of categories, given above, includes the constant 245 respondents.

possible (e.g., by job and salary, by number of jobs interested in).

RESULTS

There are no significant differences between the 1,717 subjects who added their names and those 932 who did not. The following are the results for the 1,717 subjects included in the lists.

Table I presents, for each of the seven functions, the number of subjects expressing an interest, the percentage which this number represents, and finally, the *percentage of agreement* among the seven jobs. (This is the sum of the per cent interested in both, and the per cent not interested in either.)

There is considerable agreement among the seven functions without extreme overlap. The amount of agreement[2] ranges from 38 per cent to 70 per cent with a median of 60 per cent! The functions can be thought of as falling into two major groupings: Numbers 3 and 5 cluster together and Numbers 6, 7 and 4 cluster together, while Numbers 1 and 2 fall between. In Table II, the agreement matrix is rearranged. The ordering does not correlate with endorsement level ($p = .43$ between the two rank orders).

Table III shows the number of respondents for each salary level, at or above which they wish to be informed. A total of 512 respondents wish to hear about positions at $9,000–$12,000 (including 161 who began at $9,000). Another 585 respondents began at $13,000–$15,000. The range from $16,000 to $18,000 drew 296 respondents.

Table IV represents a breakdown of the sample

TABLE II. Rearranged Agreement Matrix

Job	3	5	2	1	4	7	6	Number Expressing Interest
3		69*	65	61	56	48	38	1,142
5	69		66	60	58	52	46	948
2	65	66		67	61	54	50	797
1	61	60	67		56	61	53	890
4	56	58	61	56		62	61	1,017
7	48	52	54	61			70	964
6	38	46	50	53	61	70		739

* Highest value in each row underlined.

TABLE III. Salaries at or Above Which Respondents Wish to be Informed of Positions

Salaries in $1,000s	9	10	11	12	13	14	15	16	17	18	19	20	21	22	23	24	25
Number of respondents	161	72	29	250	86	97	402	97	59	140	6	217	6	19	5	3	68
Subtotals			512			585			296			223			101		
Per cent		30				34			17			13			5		
	9	4	2	15	5	6	23	6	3	8	.03	13	0	1	0	0	4

TABLE IV

Degree of Interest	Group Size	Mean Number of Functions	Mean Minimum Salary (in Dollars)
Strong	790	4.06	14,668
Moderate	662	3.58	15,480
Quite tentative	170	3.24	16,100
Total	1,622	3.31	15,150

for the mean number of functions and the mean minimum salary that the respondents are interested in as a function of degree of interest. Ninety-five subjects did not indicate their degree of interest; for the remaining 1,622 subjects, there is a slight increase in the mean number of functions and a slight decrease in the mean salary, as the degree of interest increases.

Table V presents the geographical preferences; subjects could endorse more than one locale.

The findings indicate that while the seven categories did not do as well as might have been hoped, they do distinguish interest far better than just one description. Even if we were to eliminate only just one of those two categories which show the highest agreement, we would lose the information that roughly a third of those interested in one are not interested in the other. The other categories differ more greatly. While this in no sense establishes these categories as ultimately useful, they can stand as a first tentative scheme with which to conceptualize this field of new functions for psychologists.

The large number of psychologists interested and wishing to hear of such positions (in the vicinity of 10 per cent of APA members) is also a finding of some interest.

NOTES

1. The survey was conducted by P.I.A.P. (Psychologists Interested in the Advancement of Psychotherapy), Section II, Division 12. Analyses were conducted with the assistance of the computing facilities of the Division of Biometrics of the Illinois Institute for Juvenile Research.

2. 245 respondents checked the category "all," which was an alternative presented along with the seven separate functions. They thus indicated that the differentiations constituted by the categories were not particularly meaningful to them, since they viewed "all" as the most appropriate choice. These 245 are 14 per cent of the 1,717. They were counted as interested in each category, and they form part of the percentages of agreement reported in the table. Thus, our table somewhat understates the differentiating power of our categories, since it represents the 245 respondents who chose not to use the categories as having treated each two categories in the same way.

TABLE V. GEOGRAPHICAL PREFERENCES

	Only	Prefer	Total
Large City	209	807	1,016
Small City	22	605	627
Rural	2	102	104
East Coast	180	548	728
West Coast	132	600	732
Europe	25	514	539
Other Foreign	19	366	385

33. *The Psychologist as Expert Witness: A Case Report and Analysis of Personal Experiences Previously Reported in the* AMERICAN PSYCHOLOGIST

JACK ARBIT

THE complementary articles by Schofield (1956) and McCary (1956), the former a general discussion of the psychologist as an expert witness in courts of law, his interactions with attorneys in this situation, and the potential pitfalls to the psychologist, the latter a technical report of legal findings and opinions in a number of civil and criminal, state and federal court cases in which psychological testimony was involved, have presented an exellent introduction to the psychologist interested in the problems of testifying as an expert witness. In addition, McCary (1960), in the form of a hypothetical trial transcript formed from transcripts of three actual court cases, reports nearly the entire range of problems the psychologist as a witness may encounter.

Legalistically oriented reviews of court cases in which psychologists have appeared and a discussion of various state and federal policies and decisions regarding testimony, privileged communication, etc. may be found in Louisell (1955, 1957, 1958). These reviews, in the main, are concerned with *clinical* psychological testimony as opposed to the testimony of social psychologists in, for example, desegregation cases. The problems of these two groups of psychologists testifying as expert witnesses are similar only in part: in his critique of the thesis that expert psychological testimony had a marked bearing upon the desegregation verdict of the Supreme Court, Cahn (1954, 1955) does not even raise the question of the psychologist as an expert while this is a most common experience of the clinician in court.

The present note will concern itself with the clinical psychologist as a court witness as revealed in the personal experiences reported in the *American Psychologist* with a single listing of references to these "case histories" as well as to the legal references previously scattered unsystematically in this journal. This analysis will include a discussion of the author's recent court experience.

The particular case to be reported here concerned a petition for bankruptcy in a United States District Court (Northern District of Illinois, Eastern Division: In Bankruptcy No. 58 B 8226; Vacating order entered April 22, 1959). The individual in question, in 1958, borrowed money from a loan company at which time, and subsequently, he failed to indicate that as financial secretary of a union local he was responsible for a monetary shortage and was in the process of making restitution to a bonding company for this loss. Ten months after making the loan bankruptcy proceedings were instituted by this individual. Because of the omission noted above, the loan company filed a petition for the denial of discharge of debt. A hearing was held and a ruling made in favor of the loan company.

At this time the bankrupt petitioned for a rehearing of the loan company's objections on the basis that at the time of the loan the bankrupt lacked the mental capacity to prepare and execute a financial statement. In support of this argument to the Federal Court, a petition was filed and a decree entered in Probate Court declaring the bankrupt incompetent and a conservator was appointed to handle his financial affairs. On the basis of this additional evidence a new hearing of the bankruptcy petition was ordered.

At this juncture I was called into the case by the loan company with a request for a psychological evaluation of the bankrupt with particular reference to his sanity some 20 months earlier. I had no information about this individual other than the inferences I drew from a knowledge of the source and nature of the referral; in addition, I had at no time during the proceedings any of the usual case

Reprinted from *American Psychologist*, 1960, *15*, 721–724, by permission of the American Psychological Association and the author. Dr. Arbit is Assistant Professor of Neurology and Psychiatry, Northwestern University Medical School.

237

history material. The attorney for the bankrupt was present throughout the approximately six hours of testing, but remained unobtrusively in the background and appeared not to interfere with the test procedures. A report was submitted to the attorney for the loan company noting that at the time of testing the bankrupt showed signs of organic brain damage possibly due to a history of alcoholism and reacted in a manner frequently associated with schizophrenic disorders, for example, disturbed thought processes and a failure at reality testing. However, this appeared to be an individual who could make an adequate adjustment to the world on a simple level: he could perform simple work; engage in simple interpersonal relationships; and handle adequately his needs in terms of food, clothing, and shelter. I was then informed of the legal aspects of this case and requested to testify as to my findings in the upcoming court hearing.

The hearing was held and several lay witnesses testified as to their knowledge of the bankrupt's mental condition; in addition, the librarian of a hospital wherein the bankrupt had been hospitalized on several occasions with what appeared to be acute alcoholic episodes read excerpts of the physicians' notes into the record. Neurological examinations during these hospitalizations were "unremarkable." A psychiatrist then testified regarding his examination and finding that the bankrupt was mentally incompetent due to brain deterioration produced by an alcoholic condition. Cross-examination centered about the fact that if the bankrupt could handle his job, living requirements, medical and legal affairs, why is he incompetent when he borrows money from a loan company? Also, emphasis was placed upon the fact that the psychiatrist's evaluation was based almost solely upon what the bankrupt told him and the possibility that this might be somewhat biased considering the legal difficulties in which he was involved.

I was then called as a witness and immediately after my education and experience were noted the admissibility of my testimony as an expert was questioned by the bankrupt's attorney who emphasized my lack of a medical degree. The court ruled that as a psychologist I was competent to discuss the findings of psychological tests and thus could testify as an expert witness. An additional objection was then raised: by testifying without the bankrupt's consent I would be violating a confidential patient-doctor relationship. The court ruled that since I was not a physician I did not have a privileged relationship with the bankrupt and therefore could testify as to my examination. Cross-examination attempted to indicate that only a physician could testify as an expert concerning organic brain damage (the attorney used the phrase "organic brain *disease*") and that all schizophrenics were incompetent. Subsequently the psychiatrist was again called and testified that schizophrenia was like pregnancy—there were no degrees; and, although *he* did not find the bankrupt schizophrenic that if he were, as I had noted in my testimony, he would have a "split personality" and "these individuals are definitely mentally incompetent and are not responsible for their actions." Emphasizing the psychiatric testimony and the finding of mental incompetency in the Probate Court, the District Court ruled for the bankrupt allowing him discharge of his debts.

Although the case discussed here is concerned with bankruptcy proceedings (and I am not aware of a previous case of this nature in which a psychologist testified), there are many similarities with those instances already reported by psychologists. For example, Shoben (1950) was faced with the choice of either testifying or facing contempt of court charges because his argument that communications between himself and the defendant were privileged was rejected by the court. In the case reported here we also see this question arise, although in a somewhat different context, and a ruling similar to that in the Shoben report handed down. This question appears to be one which arises relatively infrequently but upon which there is some unanimity of opinion.

A more frequent occurrence is the objection raised to the psychologist testifying as an expert witness. McCary (1956) and Louisell (1955, 1957) discuss the legal precedents thoroughly. In the present case, as well as those reported by Frank (1956), Schofield (1956), Stopol (1957), Weitz (1957), and McCary (1960), the psychologist was allowed to testify as an expert. In one instance (May, 1956) the psychologist's testimony was excluded by the trial judge on the grounds that the psychologist was not a medical man, but a Court of Appeals reversed this decision. Individual differences do occur in these cases: for example, in Schofield's report the psychologist was allowed to cite specific factual observations from test behavior and responses, but could not interpret these data in terms of a statement as to sanity or psychosis. The case reported in which psychological testimony was accepted most readily (Frank, 1956) concerned testimony as to the extent of the organic and personality disturbance produced in an accident by establishing facts and their validity. At present it appears of somewhat greater concern that our licensing or certification bills should not hinder the

the defendant who had already been designated solely responsible.

Only in the case reported by Eisen (1953) was the psychologist barred from testifying as an expert witness, and since his testimony was then as a layman he could not report on the defendant's responses to psychological tests. Interestingly, the present case was conducted in Illinois as was Eisen's and considering that federal courts tend to adopt the rulings of the state in which they operate, the discrepancy in these two instances is quite sharply delineated.

It appears that in terms of measurement and evaluation based upon psychological tests, psychologists are accepted in the main as expert witnesses. This tends to be related to the acceptance of social psychological studies of the effect upon personality, as measured by various types of tests, of, for example, foreign languages taught in grade school and desegregation (Kendler, 1950). In regard to statements as to the implications for insanity or psychosis of these behavioral and test observations, there is some support for the view that psychologists are *not* allowed to testify. There was no objection in the present case however to the statement that the bankrupt's test responses were similar to those frequently obtained from schizophrenics.

McCary (1960) notes the possible use of the technique of derogating the psychologist by attacking his use of the title "doctor." Schofield indicates that this may be done either intentionally or in honest error through the attorney's own equating of the term doctor with physician. The author's experience is similar to that of Stopol in which there was no overt harassment but a subtle attack through the frequent interspersion of questions as to the psychologist's lack of a medical degree and inability to treat medical disorders some time after these facts had been well established.

McCary (1956) implies that certification or licensing of psychologists may solve the problems of the psychologist as an expert witness. This appears to be an oversimplification, for, as we have already noted, limited acceptance is already here. The difficulties encountered, probings, questionings, and the search for definitive and uncontradicted statements of fact once one is on the witness stand appear to be valid legal techniques for acceptability already obtained by the psychologist

in the courts or the opportunity of the psychologist to evaluate individuals involved with the law.

Although others do not report this circumstance, the somewhat less than ideal conditions surrounding my examination (the bankrupt's attorney was present) and evaluation of test results (due to unavailability of background and developmental information) may be expected on occasion and the psychologist is cautioned to take whatever action is deemed necessary to avoid an exceedingly difficult situation.

In the present attempt to accumulate cases and reports a number of difficulties arose. For example, only the articles by Schofield and McCary and the cases reported by May and Frank were abstracted in the *Psychological Abstracts;* the other case history reports had to be obtained through search of the "Comment" and its predecessor, the "Letters to the Editor" section in the *American Psychologist.* Other references were found in the "Notes and News" as incidental items of general information. Possibly the APA Committee on Relationships with Other Professions enlisting the aid of psychologists and lawyers interested in this area might attempt to accumulate references to the widely spread literature including, in addition to the case history reports of clinical and social psychologists and reviews published in the legal literature, such diverse items as Wolfle's (1947) testimony as to the fraudulence of certain mail order personality courses.[1] The psychologist's reports are extremely valuable for they frequently communicate a great deal more than the sometimes barren and cold legal opinions whose value derives solely from the fact that they *are* legal decisions.

Lastly, psychologists reporting experiences should take care to give reference to courts, dates, case number, etc., so that specific incidents may be traced to obtain additional information. If generally available the cost of transcripts may be noted for those interested in complete reports—this latter, possibly, for research purposes.

NOTES

1. To some extent this has already begun on the state level. A recent note in the *American Psychologist* (1960, *15*, 238) refers to a paper entitled "The Psychologist as a Witness in the California Court."

REFERENCES

CAHN, E. Jurisprudence. In R. B. McKay (Ed.), *1954 annual survey of American law.* New York: Oceana, 1954. Pp. 809–828.

CAHN, E. Jurisprudence. In R. B. McKay (Ed.), *1955 annual survey of American law.* New York: Oceana, 1955. Pp. 655–667.

EISEN, N. H. Testifying as an expert witness. *Amer. Psychologist*, 1953, *8*, 595–596.

FRANK, I. H. Psychological testimony in a courtroom. *Amer. Psychologist*, 1956, *11*, 50–51.

KENDLER, T. S. Contributions of the psychologist to constitutional law. *Amer. Psychologist*, 1950, *5*, 505–510.

LOUISELL, D. W. The psychologist in today's legal world. *Minn. law Rev.*, 1955, *39*, 235–272.

LOUISELL, D. W. The psychologist in today's legal world. Part II. *Minn. law Rev.*, 1957, *41*, 731–750. (A third report in this series is to be published.)

LOUISELL, D. W. Increasing importance of psychology to law. *Va. law Wkly.*, 1958, *18*(6).

McCARY, J. L. The psychologist as an expert witness in court. *Amer. Psychologist*, 1956, *11*, 8–13.

McCARY, J. L. A psychologist testifies in court. *Amer. Psychologist*, 1960, *15*, 53–57.

MAY, R. A psychologist as a legal witness. *Amer. Psychologist*, 1956, *11*, 50.

SCHOFIELD, W. Psychology, law, and the expert witness. *Amer. Psychologist*, 1956, *11*, 1–7.

SHOBEN, E. J., JR. Psychologists and legality: A case report. *Amer. Psychologist*, 1950, *5*, 496–498.

STOPOL, M. S. A recent court experience. *Amer. Psychologist*, 1957, *12*, 42–43.

WEITZ, R. D. An expert witness. *Amer. Psychologist*, 1957, *12*, 42.

WOLFLE, D. Psychological frauds. *Amer. Psychologist*, 1947, *2*, 27–28.

IV
INTERPROFESSIONAL RELATIONS AND COMMUNICATION

Clinical psychologists, except the minority in full-time private practice, constantly interact with members of other professions in the course of their work. Optimal functioning of the psychologist depends heavily on the nature of these interprofessional relationships and on the effectiveness of interprofessional communication.

To assist the psychologist in this important area, the American Psychological Association published in 1954 a little brochure, *Psychology and Its Relations with Other Professions.* The six fundamental principles that should guide the psychologist in his interprofessional dealings discussed in the brochure have been reprinted in this part.

The papers by Brody, Hunt, Hildreth, and Henry and his associates all deal with relationships with medicine and social work. (Hildreth and Henry *et al.* prepared their reports specifically for this book.) Members of these two disciplines, together with the clinical psychologist, compose the mental health "team" that is the basic working unit in many psychiatric hospitals and clinics.

Redmount, who is both a clinical psychologist and an attorney, suggests how the legal profession might profitably use the services of the psychologist. It is interesting to compare Redmount's paper with Arbit's paper in Part III, which notes how the psychologist-lawyer dyad has actually functioned.

The major avenue of communication between the psychologist and other members of the mental health team is the case conference, which Holzberg and his associates discuss.

34. *Basic Principles to Guide the Relationships between Psychology and Other Professions*

AMERICAN PSYCHOLOGICAL ASSOCIATION

THE foregoing considerations have led the Committee to the formulation of a series of basic principles which we believe will serve as useful guides to psychology in its relationships with *any* other profession and will also have an important bearing on psychologists' relations with colleagues in other scientific disciplines. Some of the principles have greater relevance to the academic situation, some to the work of the applied psychologist, and still others to the laboratory. Although certain of these principles are implicit in the previous discussion, we believe it useful to state each principle as explicitly as possible. And, because of the several distinctive roles played by psychologists in American society, it seems preferable to formulate certain of the basic principles with respect to these roles, e.g., teacher, researcher, administrator, or practitioner.

PRINCIPLE 1

Guided primarily by the criterion of social welfare, the American Psychological Association, as the official national organization of psychologists who function as researchers, teachers, practitioners, and administrators, accepts full responsibility for coordinating the development and functioning of the profession of psychology. As members of the Association, psychologists accept: (*a*) the responsibility for advancing basic knowledge concerning human behavior, (*b*) the responsibility for training qualified aspirants to professional competence, (*c*) the responsibility for establishing and maintaining standards of professional competence, and (*d*) the responsibility of formulating and maintaining high ethical standards.

Excerpted from *Psychology and Its Relations with Other Professions* (Washington, D.C.: The American Psychological Association, 1954), pp. 8–14, reprinted by permission of the American Psychological Association.

PRINCIPLE 2

Psychology is concerned with the application of the methods of science to the problems of human behavior. The profession assumes responsibility for encouraging research and facilitating the communication of research findings. Specifically, psychology accepts the obligation of:

a. promoting research by emphasizing its importance in the training of students, in awarding scholarships and fellowships, and in professional advancement;

b. developing sources of financial support for research in the behavorial sciences;

c. protecting freedom of investigation and fostering a social climate favorable to scientific enquiry;

d. fostering the highest ethical standards in the conduct of research;

e. sponsoring journals, professional meetings, and other means for the dissemination of the results of research; and

f. encouraging cooperation with investigators of other disciplines in the development of new knowledge about human behavior.

PRINCIPLE 3

As teachers, psychologists accept and share the ethics and ideals of the teaching professions. These include:

a. the freedom to teach in accordance with the dictates of one's conscience;

b. the self-imposed restriction to keep one's teaching activities within the bounds imposed by the teacher's limits of skills, knowledge, and competence;

c. the willingness to teach all that one knows to all qualified persons who seek to learn.

PRINCIPLE 4

As administrators of the professional activities of psychologists and/or other professional persons, psychologists accept and share the responsibilities and ethics of persons serving in an administrative capacity. These include:

a. primary loyalty to the over-all social function of the organization which he administers as contrasted to loyalties to the program of any subgroup within the organization;

b. the maximal utilization of the professional competences of all staff members in achieving the goals of the organization;

c. the maximal freedom of professional behavior of staff members consonant with the good functioning of the organization.

PRINCIPLE 5

As appliers of their knowledge, skills, and techniques, psychologists accept and share the responsibilities and ethics of the group of professions which deal with human advancement and welfare. With a primary concern for the welfare of the persons and institutions served, psychologists accept the responsibilities of:

a. developing new knowledge and techniques of practical value;

b. educating new members of the profession, not only in technical competences but also in a profound appreciation of social responsibilities;

c. sharing with related professions its research techniques and findings and its resources for training.

PRINCIPLE 5.1

The professional services rendered by psychologists vary greatly in their distinctiveness. Some are rarely carried out by nonpsychologists; others are shared with several other professional groups. Public welfare is advanced by the competent performance of socially useful services by a number of professions. Psychology believes it undesirable to attempt to control the practice of all psychological functions by restricting them to members of any single profession *except insofar as it can be clearly demonstrated that such restriction is necessary for the protection of the public.* Psychology, therefore, does not favor narrowly restrictive legislation, which provides that only psychologists (or teachers, or physicians, etc.) may engage in certain applications of psychological knowledge and techniques.

PRINCIPLE 5.2

In performing its applied functions, either alone or in association with other professions, psychology accepts the responsibility for adopting every feasible means to protect the public from the incompetent or unwise application of psychological knowledge and techniques.

Principle 5.21. Psychology accepts the responsibility for (a) establishing meaningful standards of professional competence, (b) designating to the public those members of the profession who have met these standards, and (c) effectively informing the public concerning the meaning of the established standards of competence.

Principle 5.22. Psychology accepts the responsibility for establishing and certifying standards of professional competence of its own members, and since some applications of psychology are shared with members of other professions, it believes that these other professions should also accept the responsibility of maintaining standards of professional competence of their own members with respect to the application of psychological knowledge and techniques. Psychology stands ready to cooperate with all other professional groups in devising means of protecting the public from charlatans and quacks in the human relations field.

(Psychology has accepted the responsibility for formulating a code of ethics adequate to protect the public and for enforcing this code among its members.)

Principle 5.23. In the interests of both the public and the client and in accordance with the requirements of good professional practice, the profession of psychology is obligated to seek legal recognition of the privileged nature of confidential communications with clients.

PRINCIPLE 5.3

In situations in which psychologists share their applied functions with members of other professions, or work in association with them, psychologists accept the obligation:

a. to abide by all applicable legal provisions surrounding the rendering of such professional service;

b. to know and take into account the traditions, mores, and practices of the professional group or groups with whom they work;

c. to collaborate fully with all members of the professional groups with whom a service function is shared.

PRINCIPLE 5.4

Since society endorses independent private practice of the professions, the profession of psychology regards it as appropriate for its members to choose this mode of practice, provided that they are properly qualified.[1]

Principle 5.41. Recognizing that independent private practice, whether in clinical, counseling, or industrial psychology, involves the assumption of grave professional responsibilities[2] requiring both high technical competence and mature judgment, the profession of psychology will support a member's decision to elect this mode of practice only if, in the judgment of his peers, he is qualified by training, experience, maturity and attitudes to hold himself forth to the public as a qualified psychologist.[3]

Principle 5.42. Since the practice of psychology in institutional settings or under qualified supervision or in team or group practice (whether supported by a community or by private fees) encourages collaborative decisions and provides for certain social controls, such practice may be appropriately engaged in by psychologists who do not yet meet the high qualifications expected of persons for independent practice.

Principle 5.43. Individuals electing to function independently, not as psychologists but in more limited roles where they do not assume the responsibilities for professional decisions, may also appropriately do so with lesser qualifications than are expected of those who hold themselves forth as qualified psychologists. Examples of such persons are those trained as teachers of remedial reading, speech correctionists, or specialists in a particular testing technique. Such individuals should confine their professional services to those functions for which they are well qualified by training and experience and refrain from holding themselves forth as psychologists.

Principle 5.44. The profession of psychology approves the practice of psychotherapy by psychologists only if it meet conditions of genuine collaboration with physicians most qualified to deal with the borderline problems which occur (e.g., differential diagnosis, intercurrent organic disease, psychosomatic problems). Such collaboration is not necessarily indicated in remedial teaching or in vocational and educational counseling.[4]

PRINCIPLE 6

As an autonomous profession, psychology cannot accept limitations upon the freedom of thought and action of its members other than limitations imposed by its social responsibility and by considerations of public welfare. The profession must resist moves from any source to establish nonfunctional restraints on the behavior of psychologists whether in the role of teacher, researcher, administrator, or practitioner.

PRINCIPLE 6.1

The profession of psychology will lend every feasible assistance to any responsible member subjected to undue limitations upon his opportunity to function as a responsible teacher, scientific investigator, administrator, or practitioner.

PRINCIPLE 6.2

Psychology as a profession will resist all attempts at restrictive legislation which promise to limit unduly or to abrogate the psychologist's opportunities to function as an independent professional person. At the same time, through its ethical code, the profession will demand that its members collaborate fully with members of related professions whenever such collaboration appears in the best interests of a client or of society.

PRINCIPLE 6.3

As a matter of public policy, psychology will cooperate with any responsible professional organization in combatting any unwarranted limitations on the professional functions of the members of that organization.

NOTES

1. See also Principle 6.2.
2. Such as the responsibility for: *a.* deciding what kinds of problems and which clients he will accept or reject; *b.* deciding on the amount and the nature of his collaboration with other psychologists and other professional persons; and *c.* evaluating the quality of his own professional activities.
3. The most tangible evidence of such endorsement by peers is possession of a diploma issued by the American Board of Examiners in Professional Psychology, a diploma issued only after an intensive evaluation of a psychologist's training, experience, reputation, and professional attitudes in addition to written and oral examinations. Other current symbols of achievement or status (e.g., the possession of an M.A. or Ph.D. degree, membership in the APA or its divisions, previous experience in private practice, and certificate or license of a state) do not guarantee the

degree of professional competence deemed necessary for fully independent practice.

Some psychologists not holding an ABEPP diploma may admittedly be fully competent to assume the responsibilities of independent practice. However, psychologists electing to enter independent private practice without a certifying diploma must do so without the assumption that their colleagues or their professional associations will agree with the propriety of their decision.

4. The substance of this principle was originally adopted by the APA Council of Representatives on September 8, 1949. It is, however, believed desirable that it be included here in the present context. The principle is also included in "Ethical Standards of Psychologists" (Principle 2.51-4, pp. 79-80).

35. *Interprofessional Relations, or Psychologists and Psychiatrists Are Human, Too, Only More So*

EUGENE B. BRODY

PROBLEMS of interprofessional relations have been more productive of furor than fact. The current intense concern with such problems is probably symptomatic of some professional self-consciousness on the part of both psychiatrists and psychologists, and it is my impression that the uneasiness is most marked in the latter. The *American Psychologist*, for example, is a unique journal, expressive of the strivings and self-appraisal of a new profession. There is nothing quite comparable to it in psychiatry. Clinical psychologists, by comparison with psychiatrists, are Young Turks. They come from an academic, liberal, in many instances reformist tradition. Psychiatrists receive their basic training in medical schools, in a highly structured orthodox atmosphere, and tend to lean upon the tradition of medicine. Graduate students in psychology are expected to be skeptical and questioning; medical students begin their training with the absorption of static anatomical knowledge which has undergone little change in years. The American Psychiatric Association itself is more than one hundred years old, and the *American Journal of Psychiatry* has a list of former editors on its masthead which begins with Amariah Brigham, MD, who founded the Journal in 1844.

These preliminary remarks are not intended to identify psychiatrists as wise, experienced, or gray-bearded. They are intended to indicate the presence of a conflict, in which psychiatry seems to represent the established order, and clinical psychology the force which seeks to change it. It is the thesis of this essay that much of the furor about interprofessional relations can be traced to conflicts with significant emotional components, and that much of the energy currently devoted to interprofessional aggression may be diverted to more

constructive purposes if these conflicts are better understood. The crucial problems to which we must eventually address ourselves are not those involving relationships between two organized groups of professional people or between rebels and defenders of the old order. They are rather the problems of how to improve our understanding of human behavior, how to help people who suffer from the behavior disorders, and how best to train workers who may contribute to the solutions of these problems, both through research and therapy.

PROFESSIONAL AND SOCIAL ROLES

Clinical psychologists who practice, as well as psychiatrists, are cloaked by society with the mantle of the healer. For a discussion of this general concept, see Parsons (6) and Jenkins (2). The healer's role, inherited from the witch doctor and the medicine-man, is one which the present-day practitioner does not earn by his own efforts. He receives it, even though he may not want it, as, for example, when he conceives of neurotic and psychotic disturbances purely as disorders of learning to be helped by re-education or counseling, and even though he does not use the term *sick* to describe those he tries to help. This role involves the assumption of certain responsibilities which, again, may be conferred upon the practitioner without his wishing to have them, and even without his conscious awareness. They stem from the attitude of the person who needs his services. The person, call him patient or client, who comes to a professionally labeled helper because of some psychological or emotional problem, assumes a special role as a solution to his problem. This role involves some withdrawal from social activity, the abandonment of certain defensive processes, and (with or without the person's deliberate decision) the assignment of certain ego and superego functions to the practitioner to whom he goes for help. These respon-

Reprinted from *American Psychologist*, 1956, *11*, 105-111, by permission of the American Psychological Association and the author. Dr. Brody is Professor of Psychiatry and Director, the Psychiatric Institute, University of Maryland.

sibilities are important constituents of the social role which is thrust upon the practitioner of psychology or medicine by virtue of the function he tries to perform, regardless of his private ideas or public utterances. This role may evoke in the practitioner behavior which tends to strengthen it, which tends to deny it, or which may be clearly indicative of conflict about it. *Intrapersonal conflict in this area is often reflected in interprofessional conflict.*

When the psychiatrist practices a type of "medicine" which involves almost exclusively the use of words, speaking and listening, he abandons the gadgetry, the work habits, and to a significant degree the attitudes which he acquired during his years of medical school and internship training. The resident reveals this when he expresses his pleasure at identifying a clue to the proper medical diagnosis which was missed by the internist or surgeon calling for consultation. The joking phrase, "it made me feel like a real doctor!" suggests the presence of hidden anxiety which may well activate other defensive processes, particularly when it comes to relations with members of a nonmedical profession who practice the same type of "medicine." In these relations his emphasis on the issue of medical responsibility, at times, seems to serve the function of reassuring himself that he is, indeed, a "real doctor."

While psychologists, in scholarly settings, were addressing themselves to academic problems, psychiatrists were in the field trying to apply what knowledge they had. Now, as clinical psychologists are aspiring to become practitioners, they find that the field which might have been uniquely their own has already been staked out by another group. Some of the emotion inspired by this situation was revealed in the explosive burst of laughter in response to a remark of David Reisman's, several months ago, when he spoke to the psychology colloquium at Yale. He said, "the psychologist is very impressive to other disciplines. You may not know that because here you also meet doctor's—MD's." This laughter suggests hostility and anxiety about status which may motivate various defensive behaviors. The clinical psychologist's need to separate himself from any medical connotation, in his effort to define his own unique and necessary role, is also suggestive of his problem in handling the healer's role. Role uneasiness is reflected in psychologists' rejection of the idea that the person to be helped may be considered as "sick," and his insistence, at least in the context of interprofessional discussions, that psychological helping procedures must not be considered comparable to medical treatment.

In terms of social tradition there is no doubt that the possession of an MD degree (regardless of competence) grants a certain security not given by the PhD as far as the treatment of patients is concerned. The practitioner without this degree (even though his training in psychotherapy may be superior) still seems, often, to need to defend himself against some inner feeling of inadequacy.

PROFESSIONAL TRAINING AND ROLES

If the goal of adequacy to conduct research and therapy in the behavior disorders is accepted as legitimate by psychologists and psychiatrists, it becomes clear that the nature of professional training is a significant topic for discussion. Certain differences in the character of the training leading to certification in psychiatry or in psychology are immediately apparent. The basic training of the MD begins with the cadaver, and ultimately encompasses the structure and function of the total organism. In the third and fourth or clinical years the student assumes partial responsibility for the ward, outpatient, and emergency room care of patients and is prepared for internship where he assumes major responsibilities. Three years of specialty training in psychiatry begin after one or more years of internship, and sometimes after one or more additional years of residency in pediatrics or medicine. Both internship and residency include 24-hour responsibilities, and in the latter instance, periodic administrative responsibility for the entire hospital or service, in contrast to the 8-hour day of the psychological trainee. The physician becomes eligible for the American Board examinations two years after the completion of his specialty training. By this time he is usually almost thirty years old and is clearly identified with the healing role.

Increasing numbers of psychiatrists are entering professional training in psychoanalysis, usually within five years after their second year of residency. In this respect it is important to note that with the incorporation of psychoanalytic principles into the best residency training programs the tradition of psychoanalysis may be assuming an importance almost equal to that of other aspects of medicine in the general orientation of the psychiatrist.

The aspiring clinical psychologist acquires the bulk of his training before he receives his doctoral degree. This permits him to complete his training at a considerably earlier age than the psychiatrist for whom specialty work is almost exclusively a postdoctoral affair. The graduate student in psychology lives in an atmosphere of research and skepticism, in which theories are constructed and abandoned, in contrast to that of the medical student, intern, and psychiatric resident who learn to apply already established knowledge and are reluctant to attack established theories, especially those espoused by respected figures in the field. The young psychologist's experience with research techniques and the literature of his own field is great. His experience with people and their problems and in the assumption of responsibility is slight.

It is immediately apparent that after PhD and even internship training clinical psychologists actually have many possible roles. They function as high level technocrats, advisors to figures in industry and government, specialists in the field of general human relations, marriage, advertising, education, *et al.* Psychiatrists, on the other hand, are identified with illness. The psychologist is potentially much more mobile and flexible in terms of the possible roles which he can assume. This may account for some unexpressed hostility on the part of psychiatrists who see psychologists functioning in what they considered to be the medical field, at the same time that they hold on to the other roles which they have been developing. So far, psychiatrists, taking the narrow medical role, have largely failed to participate in the broader fields of human relations. They have not set up consulting firms and only rarely do they have quasi-managerial roles in industry. This may be a result of their prolonged training which usually robs them of strong professional interests in other areas, as well as a result of the high rewards from functioning in their traditional manner. However, there are now indications of developing interest by psychiatrists in nonmedical and nontherapeutic fields of human relations, and we may ultimately see a situation in which psychologists feel that their proper activities and functions are being pre-empted by psychiatrists.

PROFESSIONAL TRAINING AND PSYCHOTHERAPY

Both psychologists and psychiatrists may function as psychotherapists. The integration of the role of psychological healer into the individual's personal economy poses many interesting problems. Ernst Simmel (8), many years ago, discussed this when he wrote of the "doctor game" as played by children. From the child's point of view the doctor is permitted to enjoy forbidden pleasures. He feels no shame, pays no heed to clothing, is allowed to hear and see everything, and knows all the mysteries. He may hurt without being hurt and

he exercises a kind of omnipotence over the body of the patient.

All of the elements seen so clearly in the play of children, are less obvious but present in the adult counselor or practitioner of psychology as well as medicine. It has long been established that sexual and aggressive elements of many varieties may play a part in determining the countertransference of the psychotherapist.[2] To this I add the assumption that *the therapist's attitudes toward his patients are in part a function of his relationship with his own profession*, i.e., *his professional identifications. They also reflect and determine his attitudes toward members of other professions who assume therapeutic roles.* If the practitioner is reasonably mature, and the basic problems revealed in the childhood doctor game have been resolved before he chose and entered his profession, what then is the influence of the two types of professional training, psychological or psychiatric, on his relationships with his patients, and with others who also see patients?

The temptation is strong, for the psychiatrist, forgetting the uneven quality of specialty training in his own field, to emphasize without preamble the inadequacies of professional training designed to produce psychologists who are also clinicians. It is also easy to conclude with inadequate evidence that certain ways of behaving with patients reflect intrapsychic conflicts activated in part during the course of professional training. Examples of possible conflicts involve the influence of the type of professional training on the development of an ingrained sense of responsibility for one's patients, and the issue of motivation to do research or therapy. The way in which these are handled by the individual practitioner may be particularly important in influencing his attitudes toward practitioners from another discipline who have markedly differing training, yet who try to achieve similar goals, with similar techniques, with similar patients.

It is not always prudent, of course, to describe the behavior of members of a group in terms which imply the presence of underlying defensive processes —especially when one is not a member of the group being described. Furthermore, one runs the risk of creating stereotypes which may have only occasional validity. Therefore, it should be emphasized that the formulation of an adequate theory, or theories of behavior—and of rational approaches to disturbances of human behavior—must draw upon the data and creative thinking of all professional groups concerned with the problem. It is this need which makes it particularly distressing to note the presence of interprofessional conflict reflected in a tendency by one discipline to ignore, if not to be overtly contemptuous of the contributions of others, and the presence of inadequacies in training on the part of both psychiatrists and psychologists which might be remedied by greater awareness of each other's more useful features.

Several years spent in a setting in which psychologists and psychiatrists work in close approximation and the opportunity to supervise such people in psychotherapy, have left me with some impressions about the attitudes of the various people concerned. These are noted, herewith, understanding the hazards involved, because they are relevant to the perception of the professional training of one's colleagues from the other discipline. Noteworthy is the observation that psychoanalytically trained psychiatrists regard similarly trained PhD's as psychoanalysts, not as psychologists, and generally do not question their psychotherapeutic ability. This is true, as well, for psychiatric residents who often express mixed feelings about clinical psychologists. Analytically trained or oriented psychiatrists, and this is gradually coming to include most of those who work in large teaching centers, apparently recognize the value of a type of supraordinate training which is not part of the residency program per se. This recognition has resulted in the infiltration of psychoanalytic principles into the field of psychiatry at large with a consequent blurring of the distinction between analyst and nonanalyst.

Residents tend to admire the theoretical sophistication of psychologists, but to resent what seems to them to be the omniscience expressed in test reports, and to cover their feelings of inferiority by emphasizing the relative immaturity and clinical naivete of the psychology trainees who work with them. Similarly, residents tend at times to over-emphasize the uniqueness and complexity of their own training, to regard most research by psychologists as basically sterile and far removed from the "realities" of life, and, depending upon who carries it out, to regard research activities as attacks upon their patients. During the current year two of the fourteen beginning residents on my service have PhD degrees in psychology and a third has virtually completed his PhD requirements. All have worked actively in both research and therapy before obtaining their MD degrees. This has created a mild cleavage in the resident group apparent at conferences where the superior theoretical knowledge of the PhD is evident. Their superiority does not, however, extend to work on the wards where they, like their other colleagues, must accustom themselves to simultaneously playing many roles for patients, families, staff members of various categories, and others who make up the therapeutic community. In psychotherapy the major criticism of their supervisors is that they tend to be "theory-bound" to a degree which occasionally makes them less effective than their more unsophisticated colleagues. The recent influx of applicants who were psychologists before entering medical school has also had some effect on the staff, one of whom wrote in the report of his evaluative interview: "F— should be a good resident if he can get over thinking like a psychologist."

This is an intriguing statement, because it reflects something which has never been clearly verbalized, but which often influences decisions and attitudes rationalized in other terms. What does a psychiatrist mean, when, after several years in a university setting, he says, "thinks like a psychologist"?

Psychiatrists often express the feeling that the education of the clinical psychologist is basically intellectual and theoretical in contrast to the situation in medical school, internship, and residency training in which the young physician is constantly steeped in "practical" clinical material. Similarly, many psychiatrists look askance at the limited therapeutic training of the young clinical psychologist who usually works only with a small number of patients. Questions are raised, both as to the possible countertransference distortion with such a small case load, when all the therapist's "eggs are in one basket" and when the psychologist's responsibility is always limited as it is in hospitals to the end of the working day, while 24-hour responsibility is carried by the psychiatric resident staff.

In spite of these divergent influences data obtained in supervision suggest a remarkable similarity in the general nature of the countertransference problems in the two groups: trainees and residents. The basic anxieties and conflicts stimulated in the therapeutic situation were similar. However, there were certain differences in the ways of handling the problems which occasionally seemed to be related to the therapist's professional training. At the risk of creating stereotypes, it was my impression that residents tended more to accept the omnipotent role conferred upon them by patients, to deal more with their unconscious aggression against patients by authoritarian activity, and to exhibit a greater degree of flexibility in crises than did the trainees. The latter tended to deal with their own threatening impulses more by excessive passivity, or by withdrawal into the role of scientific observer rather than participant, to intellectualize the process in more abstract theoretical terms, and to be more bound by predetermined therapeutic plans. There was some evidence suggesting that their medical school and internship experience had given the residents an opportunity to work through some of the more frightening and disturbing feelings evoked by aggressive, frightened, seductive, or disorganized patients. On the other hand the medical man traditionally trades on the transference instead of attempting to understand it, and in this respect previous training sometimes proved to be a handicap. The influence of early medical training upon the functioning of the psychotherapist has been discussed elsewhere. See Lewin (4); Fleiss (1).

COLLABORATIVE RESEARCH

Another area of conflict between psychiatrists and psychologists has been in the sphere of research where surface relations are often most cordial. Many of the problems here seem to be those common to any effort at interdisciplinary collaboration. See Redlich and Brody (7).

For the medically trained scientist research, other than gathering clinical data from his patients, is often a source of conscious conflict since he is usually able to earn far more if he practices his specialty alone. This is becoming true for some clinical psychologists as well. Unconscious conflict involving drives to gratify infantile curiosity and the wish for omniscience may be reflected in marked sensitivity to criticism about one's research, a high degree of emotional investment in it, and defensiveness in this apparently impersonal area.

All of these elements assume additional importance when, to the conflicting motivations of the individuals in a research group, are added the problems of different professional orientations, including differing value systems, status requirements, and work habits. The MD enjoys prestige in the eyes of society at large, but his fellow investigators usually see him in a different light. His early professional identifications are with physicians, not with academic scientists, and his basic allegiance is to his patients, not to investigation. Psychiatrists in contrast to psychologists usually do research in short spurts, interrupted by clinical and administrative duties. Their tendency to float in and out of a research project as tacit "expert" consultants, can be as annoying to investigative colleagues as the psychologist's omniscient Rorschach report can be to the psychiatrist struggling with the case.

It has been suggested that unconscious guilt and anxiety are more prominent in investigations of human behavior than in other fields. See Redlich and Brody (7). It follows that the individual researcher on behavior utilizes certain defensive operations to deal with his guilt and anxiety, that research by a group makes it impossible for the individual to utilize some of his previous defenses, and that conflicts are intensified when group members are from different fields. Behavior reflecting defensive needs may include, for example, ascribing great importance to one's own contribution and belittling the contribution of others; feeling misunderstood by colleagues; insistence on one's own methodological bias; emphasis, as noted above, on the uniqueness and complexity of one's own professional training; overt aggression directed downward in the hierarchy of a project; excessive passivity and need to placate authority figures in the project, and so forth. All of these have the ultimate effect of impairing the productivity of the research effort.

FUTURE PROSPECTS

As the human population has increased, so has the population of specialists in human relations. As these specialists explore new areas a certain degree of intergroup conflict is inevitable. Like other human beings they cannot be expected completely to abandon narcissistic considerations in the interest of an hypothetical common good. They can, however, be expected to engage in occasional examination of their own motives and behavior, with particular reference to their professional activities. Such examination may contribute to the solution of the numerous unanswered questions which clog the field.

Some of these questions pertaining most to the problems of psychotherapy and interprofessional relations are listed here in their crudest and most general forms. What are the best criteria for the selection of future psychotherapists for training? How is it possible effectively to train students so that they are adequate for both therapy and research? What are the major differences and similarities in training leading to the MD and PhD degrees in terms of their impact upon the student and his later functioning in the field of human behavior? Does it really make sense for the MD to have two courses of postgraduate training—the one leading to his professional degree, and the one leading to specialization? What are the major differences and similarities between those psychologists and psychiatrists who have had professional training in psychoanalysis? Between analytically trained psychologists and psychiatrists and those without such training? Should systematic attention be devoted to major curriculum changes or combinations—for example, Kubie's proposal (3) for a doctorate in medical psychology[3]; or an MD with a "major" in psychiatric medicine; or the limitation of predoctoral work in psychology to the traditional scholarly and research requirements with the clinical and therapeutic work coming after the PhD is earned; etc.? Is a doctoral degree of any kind a necessary part of the training of a psychotherapist? Should there be a special curriculum leading to the production of psychotherapists whose previous training might have been in nursing, social work, the ministry, etc.? Is doctoral training of any variety a possible handicap in the development of a psychotherapist? What are the mechanisms and results of the variously labeled psychotherapies? What are their common denominators and differences?

Under what conditions may they best be applied? What is the relationship between training for psychotherapeutic effectiveness, and for effectiveness in other fields of human relations? To what degree are principles applicable in psychotherapy also applicable in the other areas to which they are often applied? What are the current degrees of overlap and of differences in the functioning of psychologists and psychiatrists with respect to *nonpsychotherapeutic* activities?

The questions noted above are general and not all-inclusive. Most of them can be answered to some degree, but not definitively. They are all interrelated. Obviously, questions about professional training in the field of human behavior cannot be separated from basic questions about the nature of behavior. It seems equally apparent to the writer that no question about training, or the nature of psychotherapy, can be clearly separated from questions about the influence of personal psychoanalysis or of education in the psychoanalytic field, although the rapid permeation of psychoanalytic principles into residency training programs is making this less easy to define. Questions about training, research,

and "just what is it that I am doing, and is it really necessary," reflect a lack of complacency which should characterize any thoughtful psychologist or psychiatrist, and which should diminish the intensity of interprofessional warfare.

CONCLUSIONS

Psychologists and psychiatrists must perforce share common goals with respect to understanding and helping emotionally and intellectually disturbed people. The achievement of these goals is being hindered by interprofessional conflict which frequently reflects intrapsychic problems on the part of individual members of the professions. The issues of role definition and responsibility, motivation for research or therapy, the need to attack or defend an hypothetical "established order," and of professional training and professional identification are among those which contribute to the more obvious aspects of conflict. The most crucial focus for study may be the subject of professional training since attitudes, identifications, and role behavior established during the course of this training are important contributors to the intra- and interpersonal problems of the practitioner—whether reflected in his relationships with members of his own or other professions, or with his patients or clients.

NOTES

1. Eugene B. Brody, MA (psychology), MD, is a member of the Committee on Relations with Psychology of the American Psychiatric Association. This paper does not, however, represent the viewpoint of the Committee, but is the author's personal interpretation.
2. In the voluminous literature on countertransference see, for example, Nunberg (5).
3. Kubie's valuable discussion should be read, although it may not be found uniformly palatable by everyone concerned with the problem.

REFERENCES

1. Fliess, R. The autopsic encumbrance. *Int. J. Psychoanal.*, 1954, *35*, 8.
2. Jenkins, R. Understanding psychiatrists. *Amer. Psychologist*, 1954, *9*, 617–620.
3. Kubie, L. S. The pros and cons of a new profession: a doctorate in medical psychology. *Tex. Rep. Biol. Med.*, 1954, *12*, 692–737.
4. Lewin, B. D. Countertransference in the technique of medical practice. *Psychosom. Med.*, 1946, *13*, 3.
5. Nunberg, H. Psychological interrelations between physician and patient. *Psychoanal. Rev.*, 1938, *25*, 3.
6. Parsons, T. Illness and the role of the physician: a sociological perspective. *Amer. J. Orthopsychiat.*, 1951, *21*, 452–460.
7. Redlich, F. C., & Brody, E. B. Emotional problems of interdisciplinary research in psychiatry. *Psychiatry*, 1955, *18*, 233–239.
8. Simmel, E. The "doctor-game," illness, and the profession of medicine. *Int. J. Psychoanal.*, 1926, *7*, 470–483.

36. Psychology's Relations with Psychiatry: A Summary Report

JANE D. HILDRETH

FORMAL relations between psychology and psychiatry go back a number of years. On November 2, 1944, the then Council of Directors of the American Psychological Association (which will be referred to as APA throughout this paper) voted to create a Committee on Clinical Psychology "with the general purpose of clarifying the relationship between Psychiatry and Clinical Psychology and studying related problems" (APA, 1945, p. 701). The committee was appointed in January of 1945, with Laurance F. Shaffer as chairman. (The American Pyschiatric Association had appointed a parallel committee.)

In the first report of the APA committee, the following sentence appears: "Preliminary steps have shown that the major issue [professional relationships] is inseparable from two others, the area and functions of clinical psychology, and the qualifications of a clinical psychologist" (APA, 1945, p. 725). It is probably true that the same sentence could occur in a report written in 1966, a situation that implies a certain lack of progress. However, to make such an assumption would be a mistake, for a great deal of progress has been made, as the following brief history will indicate.

The emphasis here is on published reports and actions of the relevant associations, and only major ones will be discussed at any length. A list of references is included for any reader who might wish to delve deeper.

Records exist that indicate that the two relations committees have met together at least thirteen times over the past twenty years. There have been fourteen written reports from the APA committee, of which five were published (APA, Committee on Clinical Psychology, 1945, 1946, 1947; Committee on Relations with the American Psychiatric Associ-

ation, 1958, 1960). The committee's name has been changed twice, to the Committee on the Relation of Psychology to Psychiatry in 1947 and to the Committee on Relations with the American Psychiatric Association in 1958. The other APA's committee, appointed originally as the Committee on Clinical Psychology, was renamed the Committee on Relations with Psychology in 1954.

The 1946 report of the Committee on Clinical Psychology included fifteen principles agreed upon jointly at a meeting of the two relations committees in June 1946. The report was approved by the APA Council of Representatives in September 1946, and by the Council of the American Psychiatric Association in December 1946. What were some of these principles? (1) Unqualified endorsement to steps being taken by the APA leading toward the certification of clinical psychologists (the establishment of the American Board of Examiners in Professional Psychology). (2) Agreement that the team approach should be a basic concept in the training of both psychiatrists and psychologists. (3) Vigorous pursuit of research on better selection of candidates for training in psychiatry and psychology. (4) Depending upon the setting, no *essential* (emphasis added) relationship between professional and administrative responsibility. (5) Both fields jointly responsible for the extension of knowledge through research. (6) An exchange of articles in professional journals and of speakers at meetings of the two associations.

It is probably fair to say that underlying these somewhat bland principles (some of which were reiterated in the 1960 joint report of the two committees) were the emotionally laden problems in the practice of psychotherapy by psychologists and in legislative efforts to certify or license psychologists by state law. A related issue concerned proper patterns of collaboration, viewed as "consultation" by most psychologists, but as "supervision" by some psychiatrists.

The American Psychological Association res-

This article was prepared by Mrs. Hildreth at the editors' request. She is Administrative Associate with the American Psychological Association.

253

ponded in several ways to both the overt issues and the covert ones. ABEPP was established in 1947. Dael Wolfle's "Secretary's Desk" (1949) reports a conference held in June 1949 on certification, licensing, and interprofessional relations, to which representatives from the following organizations were invited: American Psychiatric Association, American Association of Psychiatric Social Workers, American Management Association, National Educational Association, National Vocational Guidance Association, Society for the Advancement of Management, and the American Medical Association. All but the AMA sent representatives. The group agreed that legislation is desirable to protect the public, that any legislation which is genuinely in the long term interest of one professional group will also benefit colleagues in related disciplines, and that drafting of psychology bills is a function of the American Psychological Association and state psychological associations, rather than of an interprofessional group.

In 1949, upon recommendation of the Committee on the Relation of Psychology to Psychiatry, the Council voted the following statement of policy, which was later incorporated in *Psychology and Its Relations with Other Professions* and in *Ethical Standards of Psychologists:* "We are opposed to the practice of psychotherapy (not to include remedial teaching, vocational and educational counseling) by clinical psychologists that does not meet conditions of genuine collaboration with physicians most qualified to deal with the borderline problems which occur (e.g., differential diagnosis, intercurrent organic disease, psychosomatic problems, etc.)" (Peak, 1949, p. 445).

In November 1951, the Council of the American Psychiatric Association adopted a resolution that included the following two pertinent paragraphs:

As a measure to protect the public from unqualified persons, an establishment of standards of competence in the psychological profession is regarded of great importance. The American Psychiatric Association fully supports the desirability of designating by legal certification those, who by education and experience, should have the privilege to be known as qualified psychologists. . . . The Association emphasizes that when clinical psychologists work with illness, whether such illness be manifested in physical or psychological symptoms or signs, it is essential that they work under the continuing direction of a licensed physician who is properly qualified to assume responsibility for the particular patient involved. In general, the physicians best qualified for this direction are psychiatrists[11] (American Psychiatric Association, 1951).

For many years, the American Medical Association was opposed to any kind of governmental (by which they meant state) certification or licensure of psychologists. Additionally, they held firm views on the medical nature of psychotherapy. In 1954 a Resolution on Relations of Medicine and Psychology was developed jointly by special committees of the American Medical Association, the American Psychoanalytic Association, and the American Psychiatric Association, the key sentence of which was the following: "Psychotherapy is a form of medical treatment and does not form the basis for a separate profession" (American Medical Association, 1954).

The situation changed, however, and in 1960, the AMA adopted a report of its Committee to Study the Relationships of Medicine with Allied Health Professions and Services. Its most relevant recommendation is the following:

The medical profession believes that the adoption of a position on governmental (state) regulation which would apply permanently to all health related sciences, professions and services is not in the present nor future interest of the public. In relationship to this general principle, the medical profession believes that:
(a) The extension of governmental licensure and/or certification for scientific, professional and technical health personnel is not indicated except when it is mutually agreed that such regulation is necessary in the public interest and such regulation is jointly developed and supported by the medical profession and the segments of medicine concerned and the group seeking statutory regulation.
(b) If instances do arise in which it is jointly agreed that it is necessary in the public interest that governmental (state) licensure and/or certification be developed for persons in activities directly involving the care of patients: (1) Such statutes must require acceptable educational standards as determined by individuals acknowledged as leaders in education and practice in the field; (2) such statutes relating to services which involve the diagnosis of treatment of nervous, mental or physical illnesses or disorders of individual patients should require such services to be performed under the direct supervision of or in genuine collaboration with a qualified physician (American Medical Association, 1960).

December 1960 saw the completion of the Final Report of the Joint Commission on Mental Illness and Health, with which most readers are familiar. In the summary of its recommendations, the following forward-looking statement appears:

In the absence of more specific and definitive scientific evidence of the causes of mental illnesses, psychiatry and the allied mental health professions should adopt and practice a broad, liberal philosophy of what constitutes and who can do treatment within the framework of their hospitals, clinics, or other professional service agencies, particularly in relation to persons with psychoses or severe personality or character disorders that incapacitate them for work, family life, and everyday activity (Joint Commission on Mental Illness and Health, 1961, pp. ix–x).

In May 1962, the American Psychiatric Association adopted as policy the report of the AMA mentioned earlier, and in 1964 they issued a position statement incorporating the AMA recommendations, Principles underlying Interdisciplinary Relations between the Professions of Psychiatry and Psychology (American Psychiatric Association, 1964). Many psychologists were critical of this position statement, feeling that there was too much emphasis on medical direction, the language couched too often in leader-helper terms, with psychologists in the role of helper. On the other hand, it was the view of many others, including our relations committee, that the statement contained a number of forward steps. Specifically, it recognized that the public interest may require licensure and/or certification of psychologists, it accepted "genuine collaboration" in lieu of "supervision," it agreed that collaboration might be with physicians other than psychiatrists, it accepts the fact that psychotherapy may often be carried out by persons with professional backgrounds other than psychiatry. In addition, it makes a statement regarding the care of children which makes no claim for the primacy of psychiatry, and in a concluding comment calls for the end of "petty squabbles," and collaboration between the two professions on problems related to manpower shortages in the mental health fields.

No summary of relations between psychiatry and psychology would be complete without mention of the so-called "moratorium." A detailed accounting appears in Fillmore H. Sanford's "Across the Secretary's Desk" of February 1955 (Sanford, 1955a), and only the highlights will be abstracted here.

At a meeting of the two relations committees in October 1954, a joint resolution was developed, for approval by both associations. It made three recommendations: a program of active exchange of viewpoints, including publications in each other's journals; a joint research program on patterns of collaboration; and a "moratorium on all legislative actions which would modify the relations between the two professions, except as such actions may be mutually agreed upon by our two associations." There was an additional recommendation that the associations agree to begin working toward mutually satisfactory certification procedures for psychologists. The Council of the American Psychiatric Association was meeting at the time, and the joint resolution was approved, with an expressed hope that the moratorium would extend for at least five years.

The joint proposal and the psychiatric invitation to action, along with a supporting statement from our committee, were sent out to members of the APA Board of Directors and Council of Representatives, to officers of state psychological associations, and to members of the Conference of State Psychological Associations (an APA organization then in existence made up of delegates from the state associations). All were asked to discuss the proposals with colleagues and to communicate reactions. No accurate count was made of the number of reams of mimeograph paper used in what was a massive exchange of views, *pro* and *con*, splitting about fifty-fifty. Communications were duplicated and circulated, in a monstrous feedback operation. The upshot of it all was easy agreement with the recommendations for continued interprofessional discussions and publications and for research on interprofessional relations.

The moratorium proposal, however, was a different matter. Opinions on it were so equally divided, and for equally cogent reasons, that it was not possible for the APA to adopt the proposal officially. One of the difficulties was that the AMA at that time was still opposed to legislation in any form, thus placing the psychiatrists in the position of supporting certification (meeting certain criteria) through the American Psychiatric Association, but opposing it as members of the AMA. It should be pointed out that the committees did go ahead and hammer out an agreement on a recommended form of certification legislation—an agreement that was adhered to by state associations seeking legislation. The New York law, for example, was passed in 1956, and copies of it were sent to the members of both APAs, with covering statements of endorsement from both committees.

In 1955, a joint research proposal was drawn up for an extended study of practices throughout the country that bore on interprofessional relations of psychiatry and psychology in the areas of research, training, and practice. The proposal was submitted during 1956 to several foundations, without success. Nevertheless, there has hardly been a meeting of the two committees that has not included discussion of the need for data, particularly on patterns of collaboration, and not just in private practice relationships. There is a great deal of collaborative research going on, for instance, between psychiatrists and psychologists—physiological as well as clinical—and there are cooperative training programs here and there. But sound data are lacking.

Toward the end of the fifties, relations between

the two professions went through a period of great strain. The Council of the American Psychiatric Association, in November 1957,

rescinded its earlier approval of legal certification of psychologists for several impelling reasons including unsatisfactory experience with certification bills in several states; a strong resolution from the Assembly of District Branches that such action be taken; lack of legal clarity about the implications of certification; and a consensus that such matters could be best handled by District Branches in the several states. Further, the Council reaffirmed the 1954 Resolution approved by APA [American Psychiatric Association], AMA, and the A. Psa. Assn. [American Psychoanalytic Association] on psychotherapy as a form of medical treatment and directed that it be republished. . . . (American Psychiatric Association, 1957).

In September 1958, the American Psychological Association's Council adopted as official policy a series of recommendations contained in the 1958 Annual Report of our relations committee (APA, 1958). This document, which contained fairly straightforward instructions to our own membership on matters of ethics, centralized review of legislative activities, and concern for the effects of existing laws, was looked upon by many psychiatrists as a "declaration of war." They were particularly sensitive to two statements: the announced intent to attempt to defeat amendments to basic science or medical practice acts that would restrict the role and practice of psychology, and the expressed willingness to join in the legal defense of any member engaged in professional practice who is charged with the practice of medicine in terms of psychotherapy. The psychiatrist's committee reported its dissatisfactions in December 1958 (*Newsletter*, American Psychiatric Association, 1958).

The situation improved in 1959, and a joint report resulted from the meeting of the two committees, a report that was published in both the *American Psychologist* and the *American Journal of Psychiatry*. "The members of both committees felt it essential to re-establish more effective communication in order to avoid a continued public quarrel that might eventually discredit both parent groups" (APA, 1960, p. 198). Meetings of the committees in recent years have been characterized typically as having been held in an atmosphere of "essential good will."

Currently, the two committees are more active than they have been in some time. At their meeting in October 1965, the committees agreed upon a series of topics which could profitably be discussed, at future meetings, with an eventual joint report in

mind. The topics included the following: administration and management of community mental health and mental retardation programs; professional standards with respect to working relationships (collaboration) of psychologists and psychiatrists with each other and with members of related professions; legislation; shortage of professional manpower in the mental health field and possible activities of psychology and psychiatry in helping to alleviate this shortage; training practices needed to prepare psychologists and psychiatrists for work in community mental health programs; and interprofessional collaboration in training students in psychology and psychiatry.

At their meeting in February 1966, the committees discussed the first four of the proposed agenda items listed in the previous paragraph, as well as reimbursement for services under prepaid medical insurance plans, and added three more topics for future discussions: ways and means of aiding the public in identifying professional competence; how to establish rewards and value systems to attract competent personnel to continued service in community mental health centers; and self-study of the functions of the two committees.

It seems clear that the committees can be kept busy for some time, and that the climate, at the national level, is favorable. On the other hand, a frequent problem over the years has been that the parent organizations have not always agreed with the recommendations of the committees, and there has been an equal lack of enthusiasm on the part of psychologists and psychiatrists at the local level toward some of the actions proposed by the committees. The committees, however, seem at the present time to be willing to keep trying. It is perhaps reassuring to report that *The New York Times* of May 10, 1966, quotes Dr. Howard P. Rome, President of the American Psychiatric Association, as urging psychiatrists to abandon the "invidious" conviction that they alone can understand and control the vagaries of human behavior.

An attempt has been made here to chronicle the ups and downs of relations between psychology and psychiatry on official levels, primarily on the basis of the work of the relations committees of the two relevant associations. They were handicapped in the earlier years by having to serve as reference committees on problems involving legislation to certify or license psychologists. Not until 1954 did the American Psychological Association have a Committee on Legislation. The psychiatric committee asked several times to be relieved of the responsibility for evaluating psychology bills. Complicating the picture always was the changing position of the American Medical Association. A temporary setback to the work of our committee, although not to the Association at large, was the creation in 1951 of an *ad hoc* Committee on Relations with the Medical Profession (changed to Other Professions in 1953), on the grounds that relations with the medical profession generally should be explored before developing specific policies toward psychiatry. Attempts at the state level to limit the practice of psychotherapy to physicians (so far without success) have been reflected at the national level in a hardening of the extreme positions taken by some psychologists and some psychiatrists, reflecting in turn on the work of the committees (Sanford, 1953, 1954, 1955b, 1955c; Cook, 1954).

Is a new day coming? The signs look good. The following four recommendations were presented to the Council of Representatives in September 1966 for adoption. They stem from the February 1966 meeting of the two relations committees.

1. Any agreements reached by the two committees on principles regarding legislation should be reported to the parent organizations, and recommended for approval and distribution to state and local groups, particularly those now working toward legislation.

2. Collaborative arrangements in the handling of clients should not be a matter of law but of mutually agreed-upon decisions based on the needs of the client, the competences of the participants, and the ethics of their professions.

3. There should be close collaboration among related professional groups in the development of legislation at the state level.

4. In legislation concerning the practice of psychology, adequate provision should be made to protect the legitimate pursuits of qualified members of other professions sharing activities performed by psychologists (such as social workers, physicians, the clergy, etc.).

REFERENCES

AMERICAN MEDICAL ASSOCIATION. Report of Committee on Mental Health. *Journal of the American Medical Association*, 1954, *156*(1), 72.

AMERICAN MEDICAL ASSOCIATION. *Final report of the committee to study the relationships of medicine with allied health professions and services.* Chicago: American Medical Association, 1960.

AMERICAN PSYCHIATRIC ASSOCIATION. *The A.P.A. Newsletter*, 1951, *4*(4), December 15.

AMERICAN PSYCHIATRIC ASSOCIATION. *The A.P.A. Newsletter*, 1957, *10*(4), December 15.

AMERICAN PSYCHIATRIC ASSOCIATION. *Principles underlying interdisciplinary relations between the profesions of psychiatry and psychology.* Washington, D.C.: American Psychiatric Association, 1964.

AMERICAN PSYCHOLOGICAL ASSOCIATION. Proceedings of the Fifty-Third Annual Meeting of the APA. *Psychological Bulletin*, 1945, *42*, 695–750.

AMERICAN PSYCHOLOGICAL ASSOCIATION, Committee on Clinical Psychology. Report of the Committee on Clinical Psychology. *Psychological Bulletin*, 1945, *42*, 724–725.

AMERICAN PSYCHOLOGICAL ASSOCIATION, Committee on Clinical Psychology. Report of the Committee on Clinical Psychology. *American Psychologist*, 1946, *1*, 520–522.

AMERICAN PSYCHOLOGICAL ASSOCIATION, Committee on Clinical Psychology. Report of the Committee on Clinical Psychology. *American Psychologist*, 1947, *2*, 499.

AMERICAN PSYCHOLOGICAL ASSOCIATION. *Psychology and its relations with other professions.* Washington, D.C.: American Psychological Association, 1954.

AMERICAN PSYCHOLOGICAL ASSOCIATION, Committee on Relations with Psychiatry. Committee on Relations with Psychiatry: 1958 Annual Report. *American Psychologist*, 1958, *13*, 761–763.

AMERICAN PSYCHOLOGICAL ASSOCIATION. Joint report on relations between psychology and psychiatry. *American Psychologist*, 1960, *15*, 198–200.

AMERICAN PSYCHOLOGICAL ASSOCIATION, Committee on Relations with the American Psychiatric Association. 1966 Annual Report. Mimeo.

COOK, S. W., & ZUCKER, H. The demise of the Greenberg Amendment. *American Psychologist*, 1954, *9*, 549–552.

JOINT COMMISSION ON MENTAL ILLNESS AND HEALTH. *Action for mental health.* New York: Basic Books, 1961.

PEAK, HELEN. Report of the Recording Secretary. Proceedings of the Fifty-Second Annual Business Meeting of the APA, Denver, Colo. *American Psychologist,* 1949, *4,* 443–485.

SANFORD, F. H. Across the Secretary's Desk: Relations with psychiatry. *American Psychologist,* 1953, *8,* 169–173.

SANFORD, F. H. Across the Secretary's Desk: Psychology, psychiatry and legislation in New York. *American Psychologist,* 1954, *9,* 160–164.

SANFORD, F. H. Across the Secretary's Desk: Relations with psychiatry. *American Psychologist,* 1955, *10,* 93–96. (a)

SANFORD, F. H. Across the Secretary's Desk: Psychology, psychiatry, and legislation. *American Psychologist,* 1955, *10,* 135–138. (b)

SANFORD, F. H. Across the Secretary's Desk: Relations with psychiatry: Bulletin 674. *American Psychologist,* 1955, *10,* 310. (c)

WOLFLE, D. Across the Secretary's Desk. *American Psychologist,* 1949, *4,* 364.

37. The American Psychological Association Committee on Relations with the Social Work Profession, 1950 to 1966: A Summary Report

WILLIAM E. HENRY, JAMES G. KELLY, ALFRED S. FRIEDMAN AND HOWARD E. MITCHELL

SOCIAL workers and psychologists have understood with some clarity the previously desperate aims and professional activities of each. Within the broad definition of society's commitments to human welfare these two groups have had nonoverlapping activities. Social work's dedication to welfare assistance and the provision of guidance for the psychologically and socially distressed seldom conflicted with or duplicated the psychologist's past focus upon testing for abilities and psychological deficits. Even during the upsurge of the team of psychiatrist, social worker, and psychologist, their functions remained distinct, becoming coordinated only at the point of the joint conclusion regarding the best interests of a patient.

The past ten to fifteen years have been characterized by altered foci of interest and activity within each of these two professions and by altered relations between them and to the related profession of psychiatry. Psychology, while continuing some of its assessment activities, has become very actively involved in direct therapeutic programs, earlier clearly the province of the psychiatrist and the

This report was written at the request of the editors especially for this book. The authors are or have been Chairmen of the APA Committee on Relations with the Social Work Profession during the period covered by the report. The chronology of chairmen is: Malcolm G. Preston (1950–52), Howard E. Mitchell (1952–54), Leonard S. Kogan (1954–56), Boyd McCandless (1956–57), Julius Seeman (1957–58), Howard E. Mitchell (1958–61), Alfred S. Friedman (1961–63), James G. Kelly (1963–65), William E. Henry (1965–). Dr. Henry is Professor of Psychology and Human Development and Chairman of the Committee on Human Development, University of Chicago. Dr. Kelly is Associate Professor of Psychology, University of Michigan. Dr. Friedman is Chief Psychologist and Director of Research at the Philadelphia Psychiatric Hospital. Dr. Mitchell is Director of the Human Resources Program, University of Pennsylvania.

social worker. Social work has added more elements of independent (as opposed to supervised agency setting) therapeutic work. Psychologists are becoming involved in divergent agencies and settings in other than testing roles, and social workers have joined the ranks of active research workers. Both professions, in their own ways, have sought increased professional autonomy.

It is perhaps not inappropriate to suggest that the establishment of committees on professional relations, by the American Psychological Association and the National Association of Social Workers, reflects to some degree their joint recognition of changes in professional identities. These changes have been occurring principally in those sectors where social work and psychology have begun to overlap, essentially the offering of service to the agency or private client.

INVITATION BY AAPSW TO DIVISION 12

In this connection it is relevant that the initial impetus to the formation of the committee came from the American Association of Psychiatric Social Workers and was made to Division 12 (Division of Clinical Psychology) of the APA. Division 12 designated persons "to explore the relationship between the two professional groups and the means of improving mutual interprofessional contributions."

FORMATION OF APA COMMITTEE

At the same time this correspondence between Division 12 and the AAPSW was forwarded to the Board of Directors of APA, with an expression of the view that the issue of joint professional discussions should probably be arranged on a broader base than was appropriate for a single division. The Council of Representatives of APA accepted both the invitation of the AAPSW and the recommendation of Division 12 and appointed a Committee on Relations with the Social Work Profession in 1950.

The early activities of this body were complicated by the organizational status of social work bodies. Divided at that time into seven organizations, of which the AAPSW was only one, these units were engaged in the task of considering their various tasks and responsibilities. It was the thought of the APA that the joint professional problems meriting discussion were broader than those of psychiatric social workers and broader than those of clinical psychologists, confounded by the observation that while psychiatric social workers were defined by their working in a psychiatric setting, clinical psychologists tended to work in a variety of settings. After some attempt to broaden the base of these discussions by developing relations with additional groups of social workers, some clarity was achieved by the amalgamation of social work units into the single National Association of Social Workers, Inc., in 1955.

The present joint committee on relations between NASW and APA named by each organization are now representative of the membership of the national associations and are broadly charged with review and formulation of recommendation for joint professional interests that include but clearly go beyond the direct interaction of psychiatric social work and clinical psychology.

During the first years since 1950, the activities of the committee were not exclusively involved with these changing organizational matters, but did actually undertake some special work, these included: studies of effectual and ineffectual relationships between clinical psychologists and psychiatric social workers in a variety of settings, consideration of the differing philosophies of service as related to professional training, negotiation with their parent bodies on several issues affecting both professions.

PHILADELPHIA CONFERENCE ON PROFESSIONAL INTERACTIONS

The consideration of actual studies of mutual relationships in work settings constituted the agenda of a joint meeting in Philadelphia organized by Mrs. Margaret Williams (NASW) and Dr. Howard Mitchell (APA), in 1961. This was based upon pairs of psychologists and social workers from 28 different agencies in the Philadelphia area

who met to deal with direct reports of mutual interactions in mental health clinics, mental hospitals, child guidance clinics, child residence centers, special schools, and family and children's community agencies. The import of this conference was not only its demonstration of a working model for considering this kind of interrelationship, but also demonstrated that participants reported that there was considerable harmony in these experiences. While some aspects of disharmony were reported, they appeared equally common between members of the same professions as they did between professions. Differentiation of roles appeared rather more clear with respect to intake and diagnosis than treatment. Flexibility of roles were considered desirable, though some anxiety was felt insofar as it appeared to make it difficult for each discipline to maintain a uniqueness. Interspersed through all of these considerations were the issues of the role of the psychiatrist as it influenced the psychologist–social worker interaction. Efforts to finance a national conference based on the Philadelphia Conference were unsuccessful. The Philadelphia Conference nonetheless convinced the joint committees that such exchanges of views and experiences were a valid means to examine interprofessional issues.

FURTHER ACTIVITIES DURING 1962–1964

During this period and up through 1963, the joint committee continued its concern with a report on these studies of interaction, conducted a discussion on the recommendations of the Joint Commission on Mental Health and organized a symposium for the 1963 APA meetings. Further activities of the committee during 1964 included an exchange of literature between the two groups on the backgrounds of each group, preparation of a critical review of empirical studies on interprofessional relations and the development of a working paper on the conceptual orientations of the two groups. Several direct activities related to on-going professional issues were also dealt with, including appearance before the NASW Regional Hearings on Private Practice and informal consultations on matters of legislation for marriage counselors, social workers, and psychologists.

CHANGED FOCUS SINCE 1964

Activities to this point might be said to have focused upon the practical relationships between these two groups in a variety of direct clinical settings and upon the joint concerns of these groups with the profession of psychiatry and with a variety of professional and legislative issues which arose outside of the committee. From 1964 on, a somewhat new focus has developed. This was an effort to identify some issue on the public scene which had impact upon the two professions, as opposed to exclusive concern with strictly interprofessional issues. Initial attention was given to the three types of changes affecting the professions: (1) evaluation of nontraditional and new roles for the two professions, (2) the evaluation of activities of persons with minimum professional training, and (3) the evaluation of the activities of the indigenous or nonprofessional worker who has received limited specialized training for a particular task. The joint committee considered the third activity, generally called the study of the nonprofessional, to represent the area of greatest mutual interest, as well as the one with the broadest implications for the total mental health and welfare services. A subgroup of the joint committee met and designed a plan for a two-phase conference on this topic. It is designed to analyze information on current projects which have attempted to train previously nontrained persons and then evaluate such training on the future outcome upon the occupational, social and personal lives of the nonprofessional. The plan for the conference provides for direct confrontation of professionals, trainers, nonprofessionals, and, in as many instances as possible, persons who have employed and supervised nonprofessionals. The latter group is included so as to develop guidelines for employing nonprofessionals in a variety of national programs. The joint committees have jointly applied, through the American Psychological Association, for funds for such a conference to be held during the 1966–67 year. These funds were awarded by the National Institute of Mental Health, and planning for the actual conference is now in process.

It is the feeling of the present joint committee, that the past year's experiment in interprofessional confrontation has been a profitable one, resulting not only in increased understanding of mutual interests and problems, but providing a base for the subsequent direct attack upon important social and welfare developments. While the concern with directly professional matters such as legislation, will clearly continue, the selection of common substantive issues will permit attention to the social problems to which these two professions are ultimately dedicated.

38. *Professional Interaction between Psychology and Medicine*

WILLIAM A. HUNT

THE explosive proliferation of scientific knowledge during the last twenty years brings an embarrassment of riches. With our information doubling in amount in a cycle which at present is probably no longer than every six years, it would seem that never before has science had such technological potential for the advancement of human welfare. At the same time, the necessity of coordinating this tremendous body of data and integrating it into professional practice so that its full possibilities may be realized and applied in the most efficient manner poses an almost overwhelming task for the human intellect.

Nowhere is this situation more apparent than in the field of medicine where new advances in chemistry, physics, physiology, genetics, the behavioral sciences, etc., offer radically new and promising approaches to the treatment of human illness. Yet medicine faces the gargantuan problem of understanding these new developments in all the fields of science, of grasping their implications for medicine, and of directing their application to patient care. Moreover, as medicine gradually steps up its goal from that of cure to the more difficult one of prevention, to the maintenance of health rather than its mere restoration, its reliance on its sister disciplines in science will increase, and its relations with them become increasingly complex.

As I compose this, R. S. Ledley and L. B. Lusted are writing in the January 19, 1962, issue of *Science* pointing out the promise of the new field of biomedical electronics; however, if this promise is to be realized, it will be necessary to provide not only adequate financing, but also more adequate cross-disciplinary communication and cross-disciplinary training. To our task of intellectual understanding we must then add the task of social organization, of blending the disparate disciplines involved into a harmonious and efficient working team directed toward the betterment of human health.

Nor can we place the burden of communication and understanding solely upon medicine. Each allied science supportive to the medical profession must bear its share. This task of understanding is a tripartite one. Many of these supportive disciplines are primarily scholarly and have come only lately to the professional field. The prestige and authority of scholarship they carry with them often covers their ignorance and inexperience in professional matters. A realistic and discerning self-perception is necessary since the public health effort is a truly cooperative one. Then there is the additional need of mutual understanding among the allied sciences themselves. However ignorant chemistry, physics, and the behavioral sciences may be of medicine, or medicine of them, it is safe to say that they are even more ignorant of each other and their present and potential roles in public health. There is a greater gap between the clinical psychologist and the clinical chemist than there is between either and the practicing physician. For this reason it is encouraging to see some of the allied sciences training at the Ph.D. level attempting to organize a council whose purpose would be to increase mutual understanding, extend the comprehension of their individual and mutual roles in the public health effort, and better their communication with medicine. For understand medicine they must, since as our health effort expands they are destined to spend more and more of their time and effort working with her in the public good.

I have deliberately referred to medicine as both a discipline and a profession, as these are two separate aspects of any science, and they must be kept distinct if we are to understand our problem of relationships. Under the disciplinary aspect I would include the content or body of knowledge specific to the science, the procedures involved in the increase and elaboration of this content (research and scholarly activities), and the means by which

Reprinted from *Pre-Med*, 1962, *2*, 18ff., by permission of *Pre-Med* and the author. Dr. Hunt is Professor of Psychology, Biological Sciences, and Education, Northwestern University.

this knowledge is passed on to others (teaching duties). Because libraries, laboratories, and classrooms so often exist in colleges and universities, it is easy to think of this aspect as "academic."

By professional I mean those activities and procedures by which the knowledge of the science is applied to the solution of some human problem, to the servicing of some human need. The study of reinforcement in the learning laboratory of the psychologist has led to the discovery of principles which may be applied to the classroom by the use of various types of automated teaching devices for programmed learning. Thus, Professor Skinner of Harvard has led us from the pigeon in the laboratory (where the pertinent principles were developed) to the child in the classroom (where the principles are applied). When Skinner is working in his laboratory, I would call him a scholar. When he is devising machines and applying them to actual classroom situations I would call him a professional man. The disciplinary and professional aspects overlap and they may exist in the same person or be relegated to specialized personnel. They often produce subspecialties just as clinical psychology developed from psychology and clinical chemistry from chemistry.

The professional aspects of a discipline involve not only its service procedures, but also those social and cultural conventions that govern and guide their use, i.e., the social control of the quality and right of practice through professional societies, accrediting boards, and legal restriction. It is in this professional area that the interaction between disciplines can become messy, for the problem of intellectual understanding involved in grasping the content of another discipline is a relatively calm type of interrelating compared to that involved in the working out of service or professional relations. Anyone may be accorded the privilege of having a bright idea, but trouble arises when you try to dictate who has the privilege of using it. At this point self-interest, prejudice, power politics, etc. all become involved and the emotion they bring with them is sadly disrupting to the peaceful interaction of rational minds.

It is in this step from the theoretical to the applied, from the laboratory to the operating room, from the scholar to the practitioner that most of our problems of interdisciplinary harmony arise. Sometimes the step is accomplished within a discipline as when clinical psychology with its service orientation split off from psychology; interestingly enough, it is further subdivided within itself as the research group within clinical psychology veers away from the service group. Sometimes the step is

interdisciplinary as when the advertising man may use psychological principles for application to salesmanship. When Skinner's findings on reinforcement were applied to automated teaching devices the technique rapidly expanded beyond the psychologist. Mathematicians, language teachers, etc. immediately began preparing programs in their specialties, engineers began producing novel and improved machines, and the electronic computer people introduced a new and challenging flexibility for the older machines by tying them into computer circuits for guidance. No one has challenged this diverse participation and no one seems likely to do so. Skinner himself is more apt to grumble about the intrusion of service demands on his time for scholarly activity. Basic science is a human asset, part of the public domain, and it is only when its application has economic implication or threatens injury to people that competitive restriction comes in.

Interdisciplinary rivalry is no new phenomenon, nor is it a stranger on the college campus. Human knowledge is a constantly developing creative phenomena, with its outlines blurring and its boundaries shifting with growth and progress so that no disciplinary domain can be accurately defined for long and transfer of title in perpetuity becomes impossible. Look at the current university problem of who should teach statistics. Does it "belong" to mathematics or may economics, psychology, and sociology, for instance, each teach their own peculiar and specific adaptations of it. Surely mathematics as content is part of our common heritage and belongs in the public domain. Anyone may learn and subsequently apply it to his problems. But there is some vested interest in its teaching. No one objects to economics or psychology developing a mathematics of its own suitable to its own research needs, but can it be taught by them independently of the mathematics department? Or does statistics as a derivative branch of mathematics belong to the basic mathematical domain, with all tribal rites of preservation and initiation into its mysteries inflexibly relegated by tribal law to those scholars formally defined and recognized as mathematicians by our society? Most of us in academe would consider such subtleties slightly absurd, but there are those that take them seriously.

Such interdisciplinary competition is not new to medicine. Where, as medicine does, you draw upon the practices of other disciplines you will necessarily attract some of their members as practitioners. Thus a psychiatry that bases its procedures on psychological principles inevitably encourages the practice of psychotherapy by psychologists; and a medicine that utilizes the diagnostic procedures of chemistry may expect to see clinical chemists developing in their own right. Where the social status and the professional pecking order are clearly defined in terms of primary responsibility for the basic knowledge and technological procedures involved, the assumption of the obligation for basic research, the length and quality of preparatory training, the cultural prestige of the discipline involved, etc., the problems that arise are minor. Medicine is clearly in control and the related professions accept this, albeit grudgingly and sometimes rebelliously.

Where differences in status are not clear and where the areas of competence are not easily delimited, as in dentistry for instance, friction will arise. Thus a clinical chemist trained at the Ph.D. level is sorely beset to understand why he cannot administer and subsequently report the findings of an analytic chemical test procedure without medical supervision, particularly since the technique may be the product of his own research effort and ingenuity and even bear his name. In turn the medical man often cannot comprehend what makes a "laboratory technician" want to act like a "doctor." As medicine extends its comprehensive approach to human welfare it will become increasingly involved with those established disciplines that train at the Ph.D. level, and problems of this sort will be increasingly important. Professional interaction here is further complicated by the fact that while the clinical chemist or the clinical psychologist may serve in a role subsidiary to that of the doctor in the medical setting, he comes to that role, rightly or wrongly, with the pride and independence engendered by his membership in a scientific discipline that in the university setting is accustomed to dealing with medicine on a basis of friendly equality.

This is no special plea either for or against the sciences allied to medicine—I have no desire to appear here as an advocate for medicine or for my own discipline of psychology for that matter. Let me call only for an impartial and fair discussion of the issues involved, for there are some very basic issues here. Their solution will require the wisdom of a Solomon, the patience of a Job, and the naive faith in human nature of a Boy Scout. The most pertinent problems would seem to revolve around professional training and competence, patient welfare, and social responsibility. They are difficult problems, but they are problems of fact, answerable by fact, and the scientific disciplines involved in time will uncover the facts to answer them.

If I may be allowed to risk the hostility of everyone else concerned, I should like to state my own opinion:

1. In some areas such as surgical or pharmaceutical interference in illness the data are clear and medical responsibility is obvious.

2. In other areas such as the execution of a laboratory analysis and the reporting of the results (exclusive of diagnosis?), as well as such matters as the use of psychological techniques in psychotherapy, the data are as yet fragmentary and inconclusive and primary responsibility cannot be determined at this time.

3. Where the issues have no clear solution at present, it would seem wise to me to accept the guidance and authority of medicine, provided it were administered maturely, fairly, and with dignity.

There are other problems, not as pertinent, but just as real, and possibly even more difficult of solution. These involve economic competition, social status, institutional perseverance, etc. They arouse the intense emotions associated with such motivational systems as the desire for personal gain and the threat to one's security or self-esteem. And they recognize no boundaries of caste or class. Sometimes the consequences are grim, but often they are petty and ridiculous, as when the interaction between two professions has all the formal ritual of the mating dance of the sand hill crane (but as a friend points out, this is better than approaching a colleague with an unsheathed knife, and in the case of the crane at least does result in some productive communication).

As an example of this pettiness let me point to my own semantic practices in this article. Earlier I have mentioned those disciplines, including psychology, that are "supportive" to medicine. A medical man might have used the more common term, "ancillary," but I am touchily aware of its dictionary implications of "subordinate" or "subservient." So I use "supportive." If organized medicine objects, pointing out that "supportive" implies "sustaining" and complaining that medicine has existed and can exist if necessary without any help from psychology, then I shall gracefully shift to "adjunctive," since the innocuous connotation of "contributing to" can be accepted with honor by all of us while we subsequently privately define the size of the contribution to suit our personal needs. Yet such problems of touchiness and undue sensitivity, however inappropriate and even comical at times, are still very real and very human and very much a part of the whole problem of professional relations.

Against this general background, let us now look at psychology as a specific discipline related to medicine. The basic fact that must be comprehended in understanding psychology is that it is primarily academic in its orientations. Despite the great increase in its applied or service functions since World War II, psychology as a profession still retains its academic flavor. The two scholarly pursuits of teaching and research, usually within an institution of higher learning, engage the majority of its members. This is natural since the Ph.D. degree, as its title (Doctor of Philosophy) implies, is essentially a scholarly degree and the training involved is focussed mainly on preparing the student for increasing the body of knowledge in the field through research and for passing it on to others through teaching. This concentration on academic matters is disturbing to many psychologists interested in the service aspects of their profession and occasionally rebellious voices are heard calling for a professional degree such as Doctor of Psychology with more attention paid to specialized professional training. So far, however, the universities have resisted such a step and the obvious and increasing needs for intensive professional training in special areas are being met through post-graduate educational programs.

It seems fair then to suggest that an exceedingly vital service that psychology renders to medicine is in this teaching function. Many a medical student had his first contact with the behavioral sciences of man in an introductory psychology class and his first contact with the experimental investigation of human behavior in a psychological laboratory. Many continued into courses in adjustment, abnormal, social, experimental, personality, or physiological psychology. Some even found time to major in the subject. It is an unusual year here at Northwestern University when at least one of the undergraduates doing independent study in our senior honors program does not go on to medical school. This pervasive teaching function, often overlooked because there are no obvious problems of professional relations here, may well constitute our most important relationship with medicine.

Another important relationship lies in the research area. I am not thinking here of basic psychological research that might have implications for medicine but rather of cooperative, interdisciplinary research where the clinical skills of the physician and his thorough grounding in medical science are supplemented by the research and statistical skills of the psychologist; for intensive training in experimental design and the statistical analysis of data are the major features of most Ph.D. programs in psychology. This research relationship has been a productive one over the years and remark-

ably free of inter-professional tensions. Both psychology and medicine have found it profitable and rewarding, and have pursued it generally in mutual harmony.

To the psychologist of course, the ways in which psychology might relate to medicine are innumerable. While the human engineer is not commonly consulted on the design of surgical and medical equipment, the social psychologist has been consulted on the design of the social climate within the hospital. Personnel psychologists are busy designing tests to aid in the selection of both hospital aides and medical students. Physiological and comparative psychologists render important assistance in the evaluation of new drugs. And, of course, psychologists do get sick and relate to medicine in this fashion! The area most up for discussion these days, however, is psychotherapy and here the relationship is stormy and disturbing. As is so often true in human controversy the issue generates more heat than light, more sound than fury, more straw men than actual opponents, but there are some very real issues here and they must be settled eventually for the public good.

The basic issues are those of professional competence and social responsibility as they concern patient welfare. There are additional issues of economic competition and social status, but these will play a minor role once the issue of what is best for the patient is settled.

Clinical psychology resulted from a coalescence of psychological skills and knowledge in the areas of diagnostic testing, research procedure, and behavioral change. I say behavioral change rather than therapy because the psychologist's basic interest is in the broad field of the control of manipulation of human behavior in general. When this knowledge of behavioral change is applied to the realm of mental hygiene it becomes therapy. It was inevitable that as this knowledge was applied to human problems some psychologists would follow it out of the laboratory and into practice, or, as a medical man might put it, out of psychology into medicine.

So long as psychiatry maintained its organic orientation there was little friction. The psychiatrist viewed the psychotherapeutic endeavors of the psychologist as complementary to his own, and the psychologist accepted the ultimate responsibility of the psychiatrist in the field of physical illness or disease. With the dominance of the dynamic orientation in psychiatry the situation changed. The psychiatrist adopted psychological procedures and found himself in competition with the psychologist, while the psychologist seeing the psychoses and neuroses put in the class of learned behavior patterns rather than organically determined disorders challenged the psychiatrist's responsibility for them. As I said in my 1954 Salmon Lectures, "Dynamic psychiatry has abandoned the physiological tradition of medicine and entered the field of psychology—and it has found psychology already there, and not happy about being dispossessed."

Actually the argument today is not about the practice of psychotherapy by psychologists, but about the psychologist's right to practice independently and without some kind of medical supervision. Many clinical psychologists would accept this, if supervision were defined as a collaborative relationship. Indeed it is the situation in which they presently exist, since truly independent private practice is not the common rule in clinical psychology. The psychologist no doubt would further qualify his agreement by saying that such supervision would extend only to his practice with the ill. The difficulty lies in defining both "supervision" and "ill."

Indeed, our basic ignorance of the field is the big stumbling block in any settlement of the professional issues involved. Professional competence and social responsibility could more easily be ascertained had we answers to two questions: what is

the etiology of the psychoses, neuroses, and character disorders; and what is psychotherapy? Without adequate knowledge of the fundamental determinants of mental disorder, and without being able to give any comprehensive and precise definition of exactly what is going on in psychotherapy, I do not see at present how we can arrive at any final determination of the best allocation of therapeutic functions in the interest of patient welfare. In the meantime, I would be willing to accept medical responsibility for the psychoses and severe neuroses with some form of medical supervision or collaboration when I was working with them. Unfortunately, not all my colleagues would agree.

These issues can be faced realistically in adult fashion by both professions and there are signs that some mature working agreement may be reached that will ease the current tensions. Meanwhile, we should not forget that psychotherapy is not all of clinical psychology, and that clinical psychology and psychiatry are not coextensive with psychology and medicine. The difficulty with psychotherapy should not blind us to those other areas in which psychology and medicine have cooperated with mutual benefit and to the clear benefit of the public. The tradition is too old and too fruitful to be abandoned.

39. *The Use of Psychologists in Legal Practice*

ROBERT S. REDMOUNT

THE creative practice of law is a sensitive and resourceful blend that combined prudence in its reliance upon tested and established rules and procedures, and enterprise in its use of newer views and procedures that may prove attractive and highly effective. In the practice of law, one gauges the promise of newer methods and techniques in terms of their probable or proven ability to protect and conserve the interests of clients, to create advantage for a client because of the appeal of their added skill and reliability, and to clarify and afford more reliability on matters of notable uncertainty. They may demonstrate their value to the attorney in counseling with his client in the law office or to the court in its consideration of some litigable issue.

The increasing range of systematic skills, techniques, and information about human behavior held by the psychologist, some well-established and recognized and others experimental in character, affords a fertile resource to be tapped by the creative attorney in his practice of law. Following are some possibilities, both tried and untried, that may benefit an attorney in his office practice and in the conduct of litigation.

DRAFTING WILLS

Mr. Elder Crotchety, a client of strong passion and conviction, wishes to draft a will containing substantial devises and legacies that are highly partisan and unexpected. He knows that his designing sons will not approve and can be expected to contest the will on grounds of mental incompetence or undue influence. He wants his attorney to make the will, and the issue of competency or capacity, as ironclad as possible against destruction in court. He advises his attorney to leave no stone

Reprinted from *The Practical Lawyer*, 1965, *11*, 23–38, by permission of *The Practical Lawyer* and the author. Dr. Redmount, trained both in psychology and the law, is Director of the Guidance Center, Hamden, Connecticut.

unturned in the exercise of effective preventive law procedures.

Attorney Sharp knows that mental incompetence and undue influence are legal concepts but that they assume some factual basis in judgments of human conduct. An attack on competency and capacity seeks to show poor operative intelligence and judgment, perhaps a lack of emotional stability verging on the abnormal, and possibly some distorted thinking and ideas.

CERTIFICATION OF MENTAL COMPETENCY

Gauged by professional standards and practices, among the most widely recognized and accepted individual psychological measures of intelligence (including within it denominators of alertness, comprehension, mental control, and social judgment) is the Wechsler Adult Intelligence Scale. The Rorschach Technique is a measure widely used to gauge emotional stability, and this, as well as the Thematic Apperception Test, are broadly used to assess distortion in, and the character of, thinking and ideas.

These assessment techniques have a history of decades of use in measuring mental and emotional capacities and dispositions in educational, military, medical, and other settings. Thousands of persons have been evaluated by these assessment techniques, which may be highly skillful and informative when they are utilized by competent and experienced psychologists.

Attorney Sharp might suggest to his client that, by taking a standard psychological examination in conjunction with the execution of his will, he may seek to certify his competency. Expert opinion may be offered and supported by measured facts and standards. The competence, relevancy, and probity of this timely expert certification may be strongly argued on the facts in a progressive court, albeit there is as yet a dearth of legal precedent and litigation on the procedure.

This evidence should be viewed as more probative than the later reconstruction and retroactive judgments of competency that are now utilized. The cost in time and expense is negligible where an estate has any substantial value.

DAMAGES IN ACCIDENT CASES

Mrs. Fairly Hirt was recently involved in an automobile accident involving the negligence of another driver. Mrs. Hirt claims that her head was injured in the accident, that she had headaches that have now subsided, but that she has suffered permanent brain injury affecting her capacity to work. She has memory lapses and has confusion and difficulty with mental control (e.g., in arithmetic problems) such as did not previously exist. She also claims that she wrenched her back and now has severe, intermittent low back pains and, as a consequence of the accident and injury, she suffers a perpetual nervous condition.

The defendant claims and seeks to prove that Mrs. Hirt was always an emotionally unstable person and given to passing aches and pains of minor intensity. Defendant also claims Mrs. Hirt simply has a poor memory and is poor in arithmetic. The defendant's position is that there is no brain injury.

Attorney Tortle, for the plaintiff, seeks to prove, not only brain damage and resultant consequences because of the accident and injury, but also an increase in anxiety and emotional disturbance. He also wishes to establish a degree of pain such as would indicate the need for very substantial compensation on the matter of pain, as well as upon the issues of mental and emotional injury.

EXAMINATIONS FOR BRAIN INJURY

Attorney Tortle observed, during a period of military hospitalization when on wartime duty, that psychologists were used to assess whether cortical functions had been impaired in a manner that had come to be recognized as characteristic of brain-injured persons. Psychological examinations, consisting of standardized and clinical tests of intellectual functioning, memory, perceptual-motor skills, and the like, were utilized as supportive evidence. The same or similar psychological examinations were used—and now, with the benefit of extensive clinical experience, continue to be used regularly— to suggest whether there might be evidence indicative of brain injury and to verify or anticipate the findings of neurologists on this issue.

EXAMINATIONS FOR EMOTIONAL DISORDER

It is also well-established practice for psychologists to conduct standard psychological examina-

tions of emotional disturbance and disorder, either as a part of, or independently from, psychiatric examinations on the matter. The Rorschach and Thematic Apperception Test techniques, along with other techniques and measures, are widely used to give evidence of emotional instability and of the patterns of conduct that may result, and evidence of changes in emotional status and the like.

MEASUREMENT OF PAIN

The measurement of pain is a somewhat more uncertain, and consequently not a standard, psychological procedure. However, techniques that have been subjected to experimental verification have been developed and have been used by psychologists for this purpose. Generally, the psychologist's clinical examinations of a person require perhaps the greater part of a day, and then some additional hours are needed to evaluate the data and to prepare a report.

COMPETENCE OF PSYCHOLOGIST TO TESTIFY

Attorney Tortle also has the benefit of favorable legal precedent to use the qualified psychologist and his proper examinations, not yet so much to assess pain, but more particularly to assess mental and emotional disturbance and abnormality. Psychologists in increasing numbers of cases have testified on such matters. The issue of the psychologist's competence to do so has been litigated in recent years consistently in the psychologist's favor.

The issue of the psychologist's competence and qualification to render expert testimony in the field of mental disturbances and disorders was thoroughly litigated in *Jenkins v. United States*, 307 F.2d 637 (D.C. Cir. 1962). The Court sat en banc to consider the issue raised by virtue of the fact that the psychologist's professional opinions were excluded in the case by the trial Court on grounds that the psychologist was incompetent to testify as an expert in the matter.

A brief as amicus curiae was submitted by the American Psychological Association. It argued that psychology, a learned profession with a considerable history and tradition, provides systematic training and occupational experience in the assessment of behavior and behavior disorders, that the profession of psychology is controlled and guided by ethical standards and certification practices, and that properly qualified psychologists are, indeed, expert in the field of mental disorder.

A brief as amicus curiae was also submitted by the American Psychiatric Association in opposition to this argument. This brief argued that mental disturbances and disorders are exclusively within the medical province, that psychiatrists are the only established medical experts on the matter, that psychological examinations and results are a part of the psychiatric examination to be evaluated by psychiatrists, but that they do not have independent standing and psychologists are not independent experts on the matter of mental disorder.

The Court, in a 7-2 opinion, upheld the view that psychologists are independent experts in matters relating to the existence and effects of mental disorder and that the failure to allow the opinion of qualified psychologists on this issue is reversible error.

This holding is in line with the strong preponderance of decisions on the matter. See *Hidden v. Mutual Life Ins. Co.*, 217 F.2d 818, 821 (4th Cir. 1954); *Watson v. State*, 273 S.W.2d 879 (Tex. Crim. 1954); *Carter v. Oklahoma*, 376 P.2d 351 (Okla. Crim. 1962); *People v. Hawthorne*, 293 Mich. 15, 291 N.W. 205 (1940) (dictum); *State v. Padilla*, 66 N.M. 189, 347 P.2d 312 (1959) (dictum).

While these holdings have mostly to do with criminal matters, where mental disturbance or disorder comes up in connection with the issue of insanity, the psychological issues and evaluations in mental disturbance or disorder in tort matters are very similar and sometimes identical.

TESTIMONIAL RELIABILITY

Attorney H. E. Wonders is interviewing a prospective witness in his office, on behalf of a client. The witness, Pete Soshur, asserts unequivocally that he saw Mr. Panicki, and no other, behind the wheel of the car that brushed the plaintiff, knocked him down, and then sped off. If true, then Attorney Wonders feels he has an airtight case against Mr. Panicki on the matter of accident liability.

But, what if Mr. Soshur is not accurate in his identification and ultimately is proved to be lacking in credibility? Attorney Wonder's interview with Mr. Soshur is not entirely reassuring on this matter. He feels, too, that, since the matter of liability may well rest on Mr. Soshur's credibility, the judge, as the only trier in the case, is going to be strongly influenced by impressions and evidence relating to Soshur's ability to make accurate identification.

TESTING ABILITY TO IDENTIFY OR ESTIMATE

The ability to make correct identifications and estimations of physical reality (as in gauging distance, speed, color, and size) is measurable by

psychologists using precise scientific procedures. While there are few widely used, standardized tests for these purposes, a psychologist can use brief, objective laboratory procedures to judge the reliability or consistency of a person's identification or estimation abilities, and he may compare one person's performance to that of others so as to get some judgment of relative capability.

Admittedly, at this point, this would require some creative interest and skill on the part of a psychologist, but these procedures can be developed for forensic purposes. The value of this kind of evidence is likely to be in the objective, scientific judgment procedure, with probative value in the findings.

There is little or no tradition for the legal use of such evidence, but it may well appeal to an attorney or a court as having value, at least as a check upon impressionistic judgments of credibility. It may appeal as an addition to courtroom examination techniques and findings that determine credibility mostly by inference from logical inconsistencies or from approximately related observational oversight.

The laboratory procedures involved, particularly once they are developed, can be brief and inexpensive. In such circumstances, Attorney Wonders might feel the expenditure involved would be well worthwhile if he had some greater assurance about witness Soshur's capabilities to make identification and, in addition, could present some objective evidence on this matter in court. The psychologist, being well-trained in precise experimental methods and in the assessment of behavior, would be quite competent to develop examining procedures and to make such appraisals.

TRADEMARK CASES

The Pepiscoke Bottling Company has fixed itself in public consciousness with its famous trademark "Pepsicoke 8" and the distinctive sign "P" enveloped by an 8.

A new competitor, the Pepticole Bottlers, Inc., has recently entered the market with its product "Pepticole ∞" and the distinctive sign "P" enveloped by the sideways 8.

Pepsicoke, fearing the damage to its markets and public name, claims a trademark infringement and brings action against Pepticole Bottlers. The attorney for Pepsicoke seeks to establish, as an important element in his case, that the trademarks "Pepsicoke 8" and "Pepticole ∞" are confused by the public, and that the public assumes that "Pepticole ∞" is really "Pepsicoke 8."

MEASUREMENT OF ASSOCIATIONS

The psychologist, as a trained experimenter on matters of human conduct, can develop brief, simple, timed-exposure association experiments and carefully designed inquiries to compare reactions to "Pepsicoke 8" and "Pepticole ∞." This scientific evidence, based on a substantial and representative consumer sample, is likely to be of considerable probative value and may create a strong impression.

Such scientific experimentation, though brief for individual subjects, may involve some time and cost because of the desirability of having a good sample of consumer reactions. However, sampling may vary in scope depending upon how virtually conclusive one requires or desires the experimental evidence to be. If the damages sought and the prospect of winning (with good evidence) are substantial, the time and expenditure for carefully conducted experiments relating to trademark infringements may be well-spent.

Precedent has existed for the use of psychologists and their skills in trademark litigation since the case of *Coca-Cola Co. v. Chero-Cola Co.*, 273 Fed. 755 (D.C. Cir. 1921). In this case, psychological tests and experiments were used and testimony regarding these was received, but the testimony was not placed in issue or commented upon.

DOMESTIC RELATIONS PROBLEMS

Cyrus D. Kingman, an old friend and client of Attorney Foster Corplaw, is involved in a domestic dispute with his wife, and they have decided to seek a divorce. Attorney Corplaw, who has been asked to handle the matter, feels rather uncomfortable about it. His law firm does not handle divorce cases as a general rule, but he would like to help his old friend, Cyrus Kingman. He has known Cyrus and Beth Kingman for a long time and would like to see them stay together.

He wonders if divorce is necessary and if there are possibilites for reconciliation. On the other hand, he does not want to advise the Kingmans to seek reconciliation if this is likely to prove a rather involved and fruitless process. He wonders, too, how to advise them concerning custody of their two children, if they should seek a divorce. He does not want to be unjust or insensitive to either spouse or to the needs of the children. He has some ideas of his own about the problems but knows that he does not have the degree of expert skill and knowledge that would be most penetrating in assessing the situation.

ADVICE ON MARITAL PROBLEMS

Problems of family relations and child development have long been a familiar area of study for psychologists. In recent years, an increasing number of clinically trained psychologists have provided services as family relations and child development specialists. Some psychologists provide services as marriage counselors. Their functions are diagnostic, providing assessments and recommendations. They are also corrective, providing counseling and therapeutic services.

Attorney Corplaw might enlist the brief consultation of a psychologist who has special skills and sensitivities for marital problems. Such a person might meet with the Kingmans and, in the process of interview and examination, develop reliable judgment about the problems of the marriage, the prospects for conciliation, and desirable adjustments in the event of divorce. The Kingmans' involvement with a psychologist for this purpose would be brief and comparatively inexpensive. Attorney Corplaw would have a firmer basis from which to make further recommendations and to take further action with the Kingmans.

FAMILY AFFAIRS

Jeremiah Harwork and his wife Jenny are thinking of retiring. Through industry and frugality over 35 years, they have built up a prosperous business and a tidy nest egg. Jeremiah would like to perpetuate the Harwork Company in the Harwork family, but he is not sure how to go about it.

He would like to turn the business over to his son, Buzzy, but he doubts that Buzzy has the stability and the wisdom to oversee the business properly. He also has a daughter, Dolores, who appears to be rather unstable. He is not sure whether he should make provision for her care and guardianship in any disposition he makes, or whether he can count on her to be self-sustaining and a source of strength in protecting and preserving the Harwork interests.

Mr. and Mrs. Harwork differ in their view of the problem. Mr. Harwork feels some sort of a trust arrangement is desirable or that the interests should be assigned to other reliable management within the Harwork family. Mrs. Harwork wishes to make an outright assignment of the interests to the children, since she is confident they are perfectly capable of managing their affairs prudently. The Harworks have never agreed in their assessment of their children.

Furthermore, Mrs. Harwork is fearful that her

husband really intends to convey the Harwork Company to a favorite brother of his, with the brother to offer assurances of a place for Buzzy and Dolores in the organization. Mrs. Harwork does not have confidence that her husband's brother would, as a practical matter, abide by any such understanding.

The Harworks have decided to place the matter in the hands of their trusted adviser, Attorney Solomon Pater, and they seek his advice as to the best course of action.

Attorney Pater, from his familiarity with the Harworks, is convinced that neither will be satisfied unless each can feel that the attorney is on his side and will be partial to his point of view. They both seek vindication, notably concerning their disparate views of the children, as much as they seek a solution. Neither is inclined toward a compromise or an experimental approach, since each is adamant in his need for full approval of his viewpoint.

ADVICE ON FAMILY RELATIONSHIPS

Attorney Pater is faced with a delicate situation involving many psychological factors. There is obviously hostility and suspicion between the Harworks where their children are concerned. It is perhaps desirable or necessary that the Harworks deal, at least briefly, with the psychological problem of their mutual feelings and their individual relationship with their children, as a basis for better understanding and agreement.

From an astute professional point of view, it would also be important to know how deep-seated and sustaining are Buzzy's limitations. How unstable and perhaps mentally ill is the daughter, Dolores? In fact, a clinically trained and experienced psychologist can be called upon to deal with such problems, to offer tactful assistance and clarification through conferences with the Harworks and evaluation of their children.

This becomes an instrument for the clarification of problems as an adjunct to effective legal consultation and services. The discharge of tensions and uncertainties of a psychological nature might well be worthwhile to the Harworks. Attorney Pater would be in a position to develop a legal solution to the Harworks' family business problems that would be acceptable.

STANDARDS OF CONDUCT

In a suit against T-Am Airlines and Jason Service, Mrs. Dora Fright alleges that she was assaulted in flight by Mr. Service, acting in his capacity as a steward for the airline, and that T-Am was negligent in hiring Service for a position as steward. She claims that she suffered physical and mental anguish when she was assaulted by Mr. Service, that she is now permanently fearful of flying and this seriously handicaps her because of the travel requirements in her business, and that she suffers, in consequence of the assault, a permanent nervous condition.

The stipulated facts are that Mrs. Fright was enplaned along with other passengers on a T-Am flight from Chicago to San Francisco. At a certain point in the flight, passengers were cautioned that they were about to experience a good deal of bumpiness and discomfort.

During this period of fairly severe bumpiness, Mrs. Fright became hysterical. She began to cry and to moan. Then she became more upset and started to shriek and threatened to run up the aisle. She panicked, shouted that the plane was going to crash and that she was going to die, and she threatened to jump out of the plane.

Mr. Service, the steward, observing Mrs. Fright was hysterical and in a state of panic, and that, on this account, other passengers, were becoming more upset and fearful, slapped Mrs. Fright in the face and told her very sternly to be quiet. Mrs. Fright, who was on the edge of her seat at the time, fell back into her seat sharply but without apparent injury, and her panic subsided. Shortly thereafter, the plane emerged from the area of turbulence, and the flight was continued and completed without further event.

Mr. Service and T-Am claim that Mr. Service's conduct was reasonable and proper under the circumstances, that he was rendering first aid, and that no assault is involved. Mrs. Fright argues that it was unnecessary for Mr. Service to strike her and this constituted a wanton act, that, had she been left alone, her momentary fears would have subsided, and that it was known and announced that the period of air turbulence would be brief.

A principal point in the litigation is whether Mr. Service did, in fact, act in the manner of a reasonable man and properly as a steward under the circumstances. The defendants risk considerable loss, in reputation and in monetary damages, should Mrs. Fright win her case or should there be a substantial settlement in her favor.

ATTITUDE AND BEHAVIOR SAMPLING

In view of the circumstances, Attorney Dilgent, for the defendants, desires to make the reasonable-man issue as airtight in his clients' favor as he possibly can. The services of a psychologist would be helpful in properly framing the issue and in conducting a brief systematic survey of opinion of a comparatively small, select sample of psychologists and psychiatrists familiar with hysterical conduct, of lay or random or average persons, and of stewards of T-Am and other airlines.

Courts and jury are still free to infer as they will about the proper expectation of a reasonable man, but carefully developed, systematic information on the matter, scientifically acquired by experts such as psychologists, is at least strong evidence.

The problem of legal admissibility of survey evidence would appear to rest more on the issue of proper and careful sample selection and sampling techniques (probity) than on the objection that evidence of this kind is hearsay (competency). It does not appear that survey techniques and information have been used as evidence relating to conduct of the reasonable man. They have been offered in evidence, however, on matters relating to trade practices. Some of the issues regarding the admissibility of survey evidence have been raised and litigated in *United States v. Aluminum Co. of America*, 35 F. Supp. 820 (S.D. N.Y. 1940) and *United States v. E. I. duPont de Nemours & Co.*, 177 F. Supp. 1 (N.D. Ill. 1959). See Licht, Christophersen, and Sammis, *Public Opinion Polls as Evidence in Unfair Competition Cases*, THE PRACTICAL LAWYER, Oct. 1956, p. 15.

Since this assessment is brief in scope and does not entail large or broad sample surveying, the expense in the acquisition of this information is not likely to be excessive or prohibitive for use in litigation. The positions of T-Am and Mr. Service may be substantially supported by such evidence.

COMPETENCY HEARINGS AND INSANITY PLEAS

The parents of Johnnie Malhom have retained Attorney David Goliath to defend their son against a charge of homicide. Johnnie, an excitable and sometimes morose young man, has killed his girl friend's father in a fit of rage.

CLINICAL EXAMINATION OF MENTAL STATUS

Attorney Goliath has decided upon insanity as his best line of defense. He already has a psychiatric expert witness who will testify to the insanity of his client. He may well be able to fortify his case if he also utilizes a clinical psychologist and the specialized examination conducted by this expert as further, independent evidence.

Clinical psychologists conduct standard psychological examinations, consisting of the Rorschach, Thematic Apperception Test, and other techniques to determine the nature and extent of mental and emotional disorders in individuals. Substantial precedent exists for the acceptance and use of such testimony where the issue of insanity arises in criminal litigation. The psychologist's role as an expert witness on this matter has been upheld against challenge. See *Jenkins v. United States*, 307 F.2d 637 (D.C. Cir. 1962); *Carter v. Oklahoma*, 376 P.2d 351 (Okla. Crim. 1962); *Watson v. State*, 273 S.W.2d 879 (Tex. Crim. 1954); *People v. Hawthorne*, 293 Mich. 15, 291 N.W. 205 (1940) (dictum); *State v. Padilla*, 66 N.M. 289, 347 P.2d 312 (1959) (dictum).

Attorney Goliath might create a stronger impression in behalf of his client if he were to utilize a range of expert opinion, perhaps consisting of the testimony of a psychiatrist, or two psychiatrists, and a clinical psychologist.

BEHAVIOR TENDENCIES

Mrs. Ruth Iluck has brought suit against the Double Stamp Department Store, claiming serious injury as a result of the defendant's negligence in permitting obstructions in passageways. Mrs. Iluck's attorney, Louis Dessein, expects the defendant to make a strong argument of the facts that Mrs. Iluck had a slight accident in the same store a year before, that she had an automobile accident three years previously, and that she had had other occasional accidental injuries. Defendants seek to avoid liability in part by establishing that Mrs. Iluck is accident prone.

The existence or clear nonexistence of specific behavior tendencies and character dispositions are difficult matters to measure. At best, they are inferred, usually from a heuristic combination of prior acts and behavior that seem to be encompassed by a certain kind of notion or judgment, e.g., that John Doe has the character disposition to be dishonest.

ASSESSMENT OF ACCIDENT PRONENESS

Psychologists, in their research use of a variety of personality measures, have sought to establish by psychological criteria the syndrome of accident proneness. Though findings are not conclusive as to the existence or measurement of such a syndrome, there is psychological evidence and opinion on the matter.

Attorney Dessein may effectively counter the Department Store's line of defense by presenting a psychologist as an expert witness to give evidence as to the scientific status, or lack of status, of the concept of accident proneness. He may have his client take a pertinent psychological examination of personality and, from expert testimony as to the results, perhaps establish that his client is not accident prone according to the best criteria available from scientific studies of the matter.

This evidence may be admissible, if only because it is based on systematic study of the issue and, to state the matter conservatively, is at least as valuable as the highly impressionistic data and judgments about behavior tendencies that are now permitted in testimony.

PERSONALITY INJURY IN PERSONAL RIGHTS AND CUSTODY CASES

Mrs. Adolph Prusse seeks to protect her daughter, eight-year-old Penny, from the influence of her ex-husband. She alleges his conduct is detrimental to the welfare of the child. She has petitioned to have visitation rights denied Penny's father on the ground that his sustained efforts to provide the child with sex education are immoral, unhealthy, and can cause permanent damage to her personality.

Mr. Prusse has made it a practice during Penny's authorized visits to him to show her pictures of nudes and to explain sexual relations to her. He has encouraged her nudity and has made it a point to have her see him nude when they arise in the morning and when he is in the bathroom. Mr. Prusse is adamant in his belief that such conduct is desirable and necessary so that Penny will have a full and accurate understanding of sex early in life. He argues that, as a result, she will benefit in that she will not be confused, hurt, or offended by sexual contact and experience when she becomes older.

STUDIES OF PERSONALITY DEVELOPMENT

Attorney Wright, counsel for Mrs. Prusse, is aware of a considerable body of psychological findings, knowledge, and opinion resulting from clinical and experimental investigations of child development. To support his client's position, he may call upon a qualified psychologist to provide expert testimony on professional information and opinion about the effects of different sex information practices, rendered at different ages, upon the personality development of a child.

Attorney Justin, representing Mr. Prusse in opposition to the petition, seeks to probe another factual issue in the case. To offset the effects of expert testimony, however limited, in favor of Mrs. Prusse, he might introduce psychological expert testimony of another sort. From a knowledgeable analysis of the existing body of psychological findings and opinion, he can present evidence showing the effect upon personality development when a child loses or is denied contact with a male parent.

Expert knowledge and testimony is unlikely to be conclusive. However, it may be sought and valued by the trial court as another and substantial course of information to aid in arriving at a difficult decision on a complicated and not altogether familiar matter.

BUSINESS ORGANIZATION AND MANAGEMENT

Mr. J. Small Tycoon, a man in his early sixties, has decided to retire from active management of his corporate business. At the same time, he wishes to retain substantial control and to be assured that the enterprise will continue to be well-managed and profitable. His stock holdings in the corporation represent a very substantial part of his wealth and he does not wish to see their value jeopardized. Mr. Tycoon meets with his attorney, Learned Wise, to seek his advice on some workable arrangements for the transfer of management and the granting of some minority control in the corporation to others who would carry on an active interest.

One possibility that has occurred to Mr. Tycoon is that he could vest some interest in, and give over managerial control to, some of his trusted long-time lieutenants. Mr. J. T. Figures, the comptroller, has an excellent grasp of the financial end of the business. He, perhaps, could be the new president, but he is a mild-mannered person who may have difficulty in being strong enough in the position to assert effective authority. Mr. Jonas Kitteridge is a whiz at technical development and knows how to get new products into production, but he lacks the breadth of knowledge or interest for overall company direction. Swifton Rockett, the marketing manager, is a dynamo at marketing, but he is likely to run a loose, one-man show.

Mr. Tycoon has kept a firm hand on the corporate wheel, enabling these and other rather different personalities to jell as a unit. He is afraid that if he transferred to each of the aforenamed managers a 10 per cent interest in the corporation and gave each top managerial responsibility, with one as the overall leader, much bickering, rivalry, and inefficiency would develop.

He wonders if there is some way to organize management so as to capitalize on the strengths of his men and, at the same time, contain their liabilities. Mr. Tycoon feels that, since Attorney Wise is not only corporate counsel but also secretary to the corporation, he might have some valuable suggestions as to how to combine the legal and business solutions to his client's retirement problem.

Mr. Tycoon has also been informally negotiating for the purchase of a successful smaller company in the same line of business. This company is run by a very capable, energetic younger man, Sylvester Bright, who appears to have the talent for making a success of corporate ventures. Mr. Tycoon is also considering Mr. Bright as the new president of the Tycoon Corporation, and this enters into his mind as he negotiates with Mr. Bright. However, he wonders if Mr. Bright would work well with Tycoon's trusted top lieutenants, whom he would like to retain. The question also arises of the kind of stock split that would be most desirable under such a management arrangement.

It is also possible that Mr. Bright's company could be merged with Mr. Tycoon's organization, or it could be retained as a wholly owned but independently managed subsidiary. Which arrangement would be most feasible would depend in part on the kind of personnel organization and working relationships that could be developed between the key personnel of the two companies.

PERSONNEL APPRAISAL

A function that is well-established and widely recognized for some psychologists is the psychological assessment of personnel and the resolution of management organization problems using professional evaluation techniques and insights. Mr. Wise might be particularly helpful to his client, Mr. Tycoon, if he were to suggest personnel appraisal and consultation with a competent psychologist on the complex human relations problems presented in Mr. Tycoon's alternatives for arranging his personal retirement. The expert information and assessment is an adjunct to the legal consultation. It can be both helpful and reassuring to client Tycoon and attorney Wise as a basis for designing and executing the specific legal arrangements that would best carry out Mr. Tycoon's intent.

STATISTICAL PROBABILITIES IN BEHAVIOR

Mr. Frank Devoir, a defendant in a serious automobile accident involving large damage claims, is accused of wantonly reckless driving, which appears as the initial cause of the accident. It is alleged that this defendant, travelling at a high rate of speed, flagrantly and with wanton disregard

ignored a stop sign and improperly entered a highway intersection. In consequence, the plaintiff, who had the right-of-way but was a short distance from the intersection, applied his brakes quickly, came to a sudden halt, and was severely damaged and permanently injured by another car that did not or could not stop and hit him from the rear.

Mr. Devoir seeks to mitigate, if not completely to avoid liability, by proving that it was virtually impossible for him to see the stopsign under the circumstances. Firstly, there was a black car some distance ahead consistently travelling in his lane and directly toward him, and this occupied his attention. Secondly, his attention was also drawn to the cars, including the plaintiff's, coming up quickly from the left, and he assumed they would slow down for him. Thirdly, he was travelling into a setting sun with a yellowish glow and could not readily see the yellow stopsign with this background and other distractions. Fourthly, he was initially travelling fast, but not at an improper rate of speed, and this gave him less than five seconds in which to see all the relevant elements, including the stopsign, and come to a stop.

PERCEPTUAL CAPABILITY

The defendant's argument here rests on a number of psychological assumptions and on the probabilities of certain behavior occurrences given certain circumstances. For instance, if a large background (sun and horizon) and a small object in front of it (stopsign) are of nearly the same (yellow) color, how many seconds will it take to see the small object from some distance away, with or without distractions? If a large moving object is directly in front, at what distance and in what length of time can an observer note a small stationary object (stopsign) in front of him? If a person is given five seconds to notice several objects varying in movement, color, and position, and perhaps importance, which will he observe and which will he omit? Since there is some variation among the reactions of different persons, the answers to each of these questions, pertinent to the defendant's case, may be expressed in terms of the statistical probability that a person would or would not perceive or act in a certain way.

The defendant's attorney might help his cause if he called a qualified psychologist to advise, and perhaps testify, as to the relevant scientific information in psychology that would throw light upon or answer the questions concerning the statistical probabilities or possibilities in personal conduct. Perception and perceptual capability is, and has been, a major area of experimentation for psychologists for many years. Many findings have been accumulated, and some may be .relevant to the problems and issues presented in the defendant's case.

THE PROFESSIONAL QUALIFICATIONS AND CHOICE OF A PSYCHOLOGIST

Psychology, though an older science, is an emergent profession. There are over 20,000 members of the American Psychological Association, an organization founded in 1892 and the only national organization representing the discipline of psychology.

Today, every state has a state psychological organization affiliated with the American Psychological Association. Fifty-three per cent of the states have certification or licensing laws relating to the practice of psychology before the public. Thirty-nine per cent of the states have nonstatutory regulatory bodies, usually associated with the state psychological organization.

Qualified psychologists may be distinguished not only by certification but also by their specialized interests and competences. The national organization has some 20 different divisions. Among professional practitioners there are, notably, clinical psychologists, industrial psychologists, experimental psychologists, marriage counselors and child development specialists, educational and school psychologists, counseling psychologists, and social psychologists. Some psychologists can develop and are proficient in varying combinations of skills and problems and are equipped to deal with a variety of the problems with which an attorney is concerned.

CONCLUSION

Psychologists, for the most part, have little practical experience with attorneys and with the legal context. Some have served as expert witnesses, and others may have been approached or consulted more informally by attorneys. There are differences in training, interest, attitude, and temperament among psychologists, as there are among attorneys. Likely, factors of personal adjustment, involving matters of attitude and temperament, between a particular attorney and psychologist will determine whether natural professional barriers and biases can be overcome, and whether the psychologist, his skills and his knowledge, can be successfully utilized by the attorney.

40. *Psychological Consultation and the Referral*

JEROME D. PAUKER[1]

CLINICAL psychologists, when they act in their diagnostic role, are considered by some of their colleagues in other professions to be, at the one extreme, charlatans, and, at the other extreme, the ultimate in psychodiagnostic prognostication. Most of the persons who make referrals to clinical psychologists fortunately take some more moderate, in-between view, but there is still wide variation in the evaluation of what the psychologist actually contributes to the diagnostic process. It is not the purpose of this paper to go into the reasons for this diversity of views. These views certainly do condition what will be asked of the psychologist and what will be expected of him. The way in which he responds to these requests and the extent to which he meets these expectations will, in turn, affect the attitudes which are held toward him.

For a long period in their relatively brief history, clinical psychologists have tried to provide answers to all questions put to them, and, though acting in good faith, have at times overextended themselves in attempting to fulfill the obligations which persons from other fields have hopefully placed upon them. The aspirations of clinical psychologists themselves have also tended to produce the same results, as clinical psychology has sought to find firm grounds on which to advance its professional value and status.

It is only relatively recently that clinical psychologists have made penetrating, often painful analyses of their diagnostic activities and have made clear what they consider their own diagnostic abilities and limitations to be. The result has been that many clinical psychologists are no longer willing to be passive recipients of requests for performance of their diagnostic duties, but now define the areas in which they have the most confidence and state the kinds of diagnostic questions for which they feel they have the most valid answers.

The following discussion is intended as a guide to the most appropriate and economical use of the psychological consultation. It is directed primarily to psychiatrists, but it is also offered to social workers, pediatricians, neurologists, and the members of any other professional discipline who might have reason to request the services of a clinical psychologist, but who might not be acquainted with what the psychologist is prepared to provide. It is written in an attempt to give the referring source an idea of what he may expect of the clinical psychologist and to indicate the kind and extent of referral information which the psychologist needs in order that he may function most effectively. It will present a very general introduction to the field of clinical psychology and will then review what is involved in a psychological evaluation with particular reference to the significance of the referral and with particular focus on the intellectual and personality evaluation.

Psychology in general is concerned with the description, the understanding, the prediction, and the control of human behavior.

Clinical psychology deals with the application of findings in the various areas of psychology to the description, understanding, prediction, and control of the behavior of the individual person.

The work of the clinical psychologist falls into 4 main categories: (1) psychodiagnostic evaluation; (2) research; (3) psychotherapy; and (4) teaching.

Which area or areas will be emphasized in the work of the clinical psychologist depends on the setting in which he is working and, perhaps more importantly, on his own interests, capabilities, and training.

In all of these areas, there is some overlap with other disciplines in content and approach. In the psychodiagnostic evaluation, for example, the interview is an important psychological method, though it is obviously not exclusively a technique of clinical psychology.

The *unique* contribution of psychology to diagnosis lies in the development of standardized tech-

Reprinted from the *Archives of General Psychiatry*, February, 1961, Volume 4, 182–190. Copyright 1961 by American Medical Association. Reprinted by permission of the American Medical Association and the author. Dr. Pauker is Associate Professor of Medical Psychology, University of Missouri School of Medicine.

niques for elicting and examining behavior. These techniques involve standard sets of stimuli, standard procedures for presentation of the stimuli, standard ways of organizing and scoring responses to the stimuli, and standards (norms) against which results may be compared. They are loosely and colloquially grouped under the heading of "psychological tests," although many psychological procedures do not meet the criteria for the definition of "test" and might better be termed "psychological methods."

The patient is tested on the assumption that his behavior in the test situations is indicative of his behavior in other, nontest situations. Tests do not, however, answer questions automatically. They are samples of behavior which have to be interpreted by the psychologist on the basis of what he knows about human behavior and psychological principles in general and what he knows about responses to the specifically administered stimuli which constitute the psychological tests and techniques.

The psychologist is, therefore, an integral part of the psychological evaluation. This is further evident in the patient's reaction to the general testing situation. The patient responds not only to the specific psychological materials, but also to the psychologist. The examiner's sex, age, race, and personality characteristics may all play a part in arousing a variety of attitudes and feelings within the patient, and may thereby contribute significantly to the amount, the form, and the content of the patient's productions.

The initial task of the psychologist is to select the proper evaluative techniques which are in keeping with (1) the nature of the problem; (2) the type of patient and his characteristics (physical and psychological); (3) the kinds of methods with which the psychologist is familiar and in which he has the most confidence (the latter will vary with time and with experience and with research results).

The character and direction of the generalizations which will be made will depend on many factors, among which are the following:

1. The reason for referral

2. The kinds of norms which are available

3. The clinical perceptiveness or sensitivity of the psychologist

4. The base rates for the behavior being discussed

5. The available history of the patient

6. The extent to which the responses to a battery of psychological methods fit together

7. The theoretical framework within which the psychologist orders his data.

THE REFERRAL

It would be uneconomical, besides being impossible, to attempt to explain *everything* about a patient's behavior, or to attempt to predict his every response in all types of situations. The referral problem provides a focus for the psychological investigation, so that consideration may be addressed to certain limited areas of interest. The more clearly the reason for referral is stated, the better able is the psychologist to apply himself quickly and efficiently to the problem and to provide meaningful and relevant information.

The generalizations and predictions which are made in psychological reports are not facts, but are statements about what *may* be going on and about what *may* be likely to happen. They do not answer questions in terms of what *is* true, but rather in terms of what is *most likely* to be true. When a question about a patient's behavior is presented to the psychologist, the referring person has already ruled out many possibilities and has narrowed down the direction in which possible answers may lie. Thus, for example, if help with a differential diagnosis between manic-depressive psychosis and schizophrenia is asked for, and if the presence of manic-depressive psychosis or character disorder is suggested on the basis of the psychological evaluation, then manic-depressive psychosis has a higher probability of being present than character disorder or any other possibility which the results of the psychological investigation might suggest. This kind of consideration becomes especially pertinent when one considers the generally accepted view that the same type of behavior may be determined in different persons by different antecedents. Also pertinent here is the fact that behavior usually has multiple determinants, i.e., that there are probably a number of factors which coincide and interact to result in one specific response or behavior sequence.

It is possible, therefore, to explain the same behavior in a number of ways. The more specific the referral questions are, the better are the chances that the information provided will be valid and of value.

The collection of the psychological protocols may take anywhere from one to several testing sessions, and the complete psychological evaluation may require as much as a day and a half to complete. It is usually a rather expensive procedure in terms of both time and money. A referral should *never* be made, therefore, unless it serves some definite purpose; the referring person should have some problem in the diagnosis, management, treatment, or other disposition of the patient which *requires* psychological consultation. It is a relatively rare case that will be referred merely because it is an "interesting" one.

There are some other, rather obvious conditions under which a referral should *not* be made for psychological evaluation. A patient's ability to respond to the psychological materials may be markedly impaired if he is in an acutely confused state, if he is receiving electroshock treatments, if he has just recently completed a series of EST, or if he has just been started on a high dose of a tranquilizing drug.

NORMS

The norms which are available vary widely from test to test in their adequacy and applicability. The norms available for use with intelligence tests are probably the most carefully compiled and the most complete. In gathering the normative population of 2,175 persons for the Wechsler Adult Intelligence Scale, for example, attention was paid to sex, age, education, occupation, geographic distribution, and urban vs. rural residence. The norms for projective techniques, on the other hand, are much less adequate and, when they are available, are liable to be applicable only to limited populations.

The norms which are available, their type, the range of their applicability, and the adequacy of the sample on which they are based play a part in determining the kind of statement which may be made and the certainty with which it is proferred. If, for example, a patient has a Wechsler Adult Intelligence Scale Full-Scale I.Q. of 100, it can be said with reasonable confidence that this patient's performance falls within the "average" classification of general intelligence, as measured by this scale and as compared with others of this patient's same age. If, however, a patient's M (movement) to C (color) ratio on the Rorschach is 3:2, there is no place at present where one can get the same kind of normative data. This does not mean that an M to C ratio is without value; it does mean that an I.Q. can be interpreted more simply and more easily than the M to C ratio, and that it is necessary to have more backing for a statement based on the latter than for one arising out of the former.

CLINICAL SENSITIVITY

Although the formal norms of standards for comparison may be lacking or incomplete in the case of certain psychological evaluative techniques,

the clinical psychologist will still use these data in making inferences about the patient. This does not mean that the generalizations have no basis in reality. Every clinician carries with him a set of more or less implicit norms based on the sensitivity of his perception and on the amount and extent of his experience. The latter includes his training, his contacts with people of all kinds, the number of times he has used psychological methods for evaluative purposes, and the insights into behavior which he has gained through personal interaction with his colleagues and through the writings of the recognized authorities in his profession.

BASE RATES

Many kinds of behavior and personal characteristics have a better chance of occurring in one population than in another. In a public hospital which collects its patients mainly from an indigent population, for example, there is likely to be a higher percentage of patients who will be called mental defectives than in a private and very expensive hospital. This is also likely to be the case with respect to diagnoses (schizophrenia vs. manicdepressive, for example) and with respect to suggested kinds of treatment (drug therapy vs. intensive psychotherapy, for example). While a certain amount of bias or "halo effect" enters into these and many other designations, it is also true that they are determined by a complex system of personal, social, and environmental factors. When the psychological data offer a choice between one or another interpretation, then the base rates in the referral population (when they are known) for the presence of the two possibilities may help to determine which of the two will be given more weight.

HISTORY OF THE PATIENT

Here, again, the psychological evaluation gains in relevance if it is set within the framework of a particular, personal, historical setting. There is the danger, of course, that the history may bias the psychologist, that the historical information may inadvertently form the basis for the evaluation rather than provide the data for more acute observations. For this reason, some clinical psychologists prefer to have as little information as possible about the patient until they have made a preliminary evaluation of the psychological data. Other psychologists, however, feel that knowing the patient's history from the start will not hinder an objective appraisal of the patient's responses to the test stimuli.

RESPONSE TO BATTERY

Any one response, or any one test, does not usually provide the answer to the question asked. Just as the final diagnostic formulation usually arises out of the contribution of the several members of the diagnostic team, so the psychological evaluation usually results from an assessment of the similarities, concordances, and differences in performance on a number of psychological methods. As an interpretation is found to hold over a number of different psychological situations, then it gains in validity. The importance of initial interpretations may also be *lessened* if they do not find support in other tests.

THEORETICAL FRAMEWORK

An interpretation from the psychological data may be expressed in many different ways depending on the particular theoretical persuasion of the psychologist. The important point is not so much the particular terms used in presenting the interpretation, but whether referral questions are answered in a manner which is enlightening and useful to the referring person.

INTELLECTUAL EVALUATION

An intellectual evaluation involves more than just an I.Q., although this may be included when appropriate as an estimate of where the patient stands in over-all intellectual functioning with respect to others of his age.

What is more important is *how* the person uses what he's got, and *what* may determine his particular applications of his abilities to the problems involved in getting through life.

What this entails is a kind of personality evaluation focused on the cognitive functions and psychomotor performances which are arbitrarily put together under the heading of "intelligence." It includes a qualitative examination of the person's responses, of his individual style, his idiosyncratic ways of responding, the gaps in his performance, the relative impairment of, or superiority in, certain functions.

We may attempt, therefore, to answer such questions as:

1. What are the person's intellectual assets?
2. What are his intellectual liabilities?
3. Is he functioning below his "potential" intellectual level?

4. How does he respond to success?
5. How well, and in what manner, does he tolerate failure?
6. Is there any deterioration?
7. How does anxiety affect his performance?
8. What is the differential effect of any mental illness?
9. What will the person bring to psychotherapy?
10. Does the intellectual functioning explain in any way the person's particular attack on his problem?

The reason for which the referral is being made must, therefore, be specified in order for the most pointed and efficient and useful information to result. If there is no clear reason for requesting an intellectual evaluation, then it should not be asked for.

Depending on the reason for the referral and the type of patient, the intellectual evaluation may be handled in a number of ways:

1. If the reason is to establish or rule out mental deficiency, then an I.Q. plus a brief statement as to its validity will be sufficient. This may be accomplished through a complete Wechsler Adult Intelligence Scale (WAIS), through a partial WAIS using subtests which have a known level of correlation with the total I.Q., through special performance or verbal tests if the patient cannot hear or see or speak or has some other disability, through alternate forms of the usually administered tests if practice effects from previous evaluations are suspected, and so forth.

2. It might be a matter of determining whether or not the patient has enough intelligence to function outside an institution. Mental defectives with the same I.Q. can vary quite a bit with respect to specific abilities and aptitudes, impulsivity, social judgment, etc. These factors may make one person a candidate for institutionalization and another person a likely bet for self-maintenance. It might require a battery of tests to answer the question.

3. If the question is asked whether the patient has a high enough level of intellectual functioning to benefit from an insight kind of psychotherapy, then this may not necessarily be answered in terms of any formal intelligence testing or I.Q., but may be assessed by the clinical psychologist from other techniques he may use. For example, the general level of intelligence may be estimated in certain ways from the manner in which the patient approaches the Rorschach. In addition, some very valuable aspects of intellectual functioning, such as concreteness, rigidity, and intellectualizing may be assessed in the process of personality evaluation.

4. If the purpose is to determine the extent to which the patient's intellectual level may be a factor in contributing to his behavior, then some

of the patient's strivings, disappointments, frustrations, aspirations, ambitions may be highlighted by a personality test.

5. A person may be having difficulty in getting through college and there may be some question about his intellectual ability. In such a case, depending on how well the person is known, a test of verbal intelligence might suffice, a broader evaluation of his functioning might be required, or perhaps only a battery of tests would give a clear picture of the social-psychological aspects of the patient's intellectual functioning.

6. If there is a question of intellectual deterioration, a Rorschach might be helpful in giving some indication of a previous level of functioning.

In all of the above 6 examples, the request *could* be worded simply as "intellectual evaluation" or "I.Q.," but then the real question behind the referral very easily might remain partly or completely unanswered.

There are occasions when a clinical psychologist will use tests of intelligence even though an intellectual evaluation may not have been specifically requested. For example, when there is a question of disturbed thought processes, it is sometimes possible to demonstrate the disturbance very clearly in the patient's responses to some of the intelligence test items which require abstraction or judgment or reasoning. In this case, as is the case with the other techniques which the clinical psychologist may employ, the usefulness of any particular approach depends on the psychologist's experience and ability.

PERSONALITY EVALUATION

A referral for psychological evaluation which asks for a personality evaluation and gives no further clarification would be akin to a referral to social service with a request which states merely "case work study" and no more, or a referral to psychiatry from general medicine with a request for a psychiatric evaluation or for a mental status. In the latter case there would be certain procedures which the psychiatrist could follow and a very decent understanding of the patient might be achieved, but whether or not the *specific* questions which the referring physician had in mind would be answered would not be known until after the psychiatrist had sent in his report. It would have been much more to the point and much more useful to the psychiatrist as a guide if, for example, the referring physician would have also written: "This man suffers from recurrent epigastric distress, but the medical examination is essentially negative. He

seems a bit tense and he is having some marital difficulties, I would like to know if there is some psychiatric difficulty which contributes to these symptoms."

Personality evaluation should be made with reference to specified problems in the understanding and management of the patient. It should be as clearly indicated as possible just what it was that prompted the referral for psychological consultation.

Again, as was noted in the case of the intellectual evaluation, the techniques of evaluation used by the psychologist will depend on the problem, the patient, and the preference of the psychologist. Broadly speaking, the psychological materials may be divided into 2 types: the objective and the projective. The objective tests are "objective" in that the test materials are clearly structured or clearly recognizable materials which are to be handled in clearly specified, limited ways. The Minnesota Multiphasic Personality Inventory (MMPI), for example, contains statements which are to be judged by the patient as being true or false as applied to himself. The projective tests are sometimes called "unstructured," because they do not involve the clearly defined and generally comprehendable stimuli which are found in the more structured objective tests. The term "projective" is not used here in the sense that projection as a defense mechanism is used. What it means here is that we organize, give meaning to, and describe our experience in accordance with our past experiences, associations, emotional involvements, conflict areas, modes of expression, etc. In this sense, a part of us is projected into everything we do. Projective techniques involve stimulus materials which are designed to allow the most play to this projection and to show it most clearly.

There are a tremendous number of tests of personality, both of the objective and of the projective type. There are no clinical psychologists who would claim to be able to use all of them. Every psychologist has his own repertoire of techniques which he has found to be the most helpful to him in offering leads to the psychological understanding of the patient. There is a certain amount of disagreement among clinical psychologists as to which tests give the most reliable and valid information, which techniques give rise to the most useful inferences, and which combination of techniques constitutes the best battery.

It *is* generally agreed, however, that the individual psychologist must use those techniques with which he is the most familiar and in which he has the most confidence. To do otherwise would be to lower his efficiency and reduce his value; in addition, insofar as he would be applying techniques which he could not honestly justify, he would be doing the patient a disservice, compromising his own standards, and acting in a manner contrary to the code of ethics set forth by the American Psychological Association.

With respect to this issue, there is a type of referral which almost every clinical pyschologist has come across at one time or another. This referral, aside from whatever else may be in it, may include in the statement of the information requested, the following cryptic note: "Projectives." It has also been found in the following form: "I would be interested in what the projectives show about this person," or, "How does he do on the Rorschach and the T.A.T.?"

This kind of request is inappropriate. The psychologist must himself take the responsibility for determining the manner in which he will conduct his evaluation and the techniques which he will use. From the many approaches available to him, he must choose those which he can in best conscience employ. His choice will be guided by his experience, his personal affinity to the kinds of approach involved in the various psychological methods, and his knowledge of the research with which these methods have been assessed. His selection of methods may not coincide with that of another psychologist, but this does not mean that their conclusions will be different. At this stage in the development of clinical psychology, the tools play a very subsidiary role to the skill in their application.

THE REPORT

The form of the psychological report will vary from place to place, but will usually include:

1. Some identifying data—e.g., age, race, sex, marital status, religion, education, occupation
2. A statement of the referral questions and their background
3. A listing of the psychological methods used
4. A description of the general behavior of the patient during the testing session
5. The evaluation

Most of the report will be devoted to answering the referral questions and to clarifying the answers. This clarification may be aided by the use of illustrative data from the test protocols when the data serve to establish an interpretation more fully or more succinctly. Raw data, however, will not as a rule be furnished in the report because interpretations are not often based on discrete, isolated bits of information.

The F+ per cent of the Rorschach method may be taken as an example. The F stands for "form," and the plus refers, broadly speaking, to the "goodness" of form. A response to the Rorschach may be scored F for the use of the form of the blot as a determinant of the response. It will, in addition, be scored either for good form (F+) indicating that there is some reasonable correlation between the shape of the blot and the form in real life of the object which the patient perceives in the blot, or for poor form (F—). The F+ per cent is arrived at by dividing the number of responses scored F+, by the sum of the number scored F+ and the number scored F—. The size of the F+ per cent is assumed to have meaning with respect to "reality contact" or "ego control" or "reality testing" or other concepts of a similar nature. The F+ per cent cannot, however, be given meaning in isolation. Its full significance depends on a number of other Rorschach factors among which are the following:

1. The total number of responses to the Rorschach blots.
2. The number of responses which are scored for form alone. An F+ per cent based on 5 form responses, for example, does not have the same significance as the same per cent based on 25 form responses.
3. The number of responses which are scored for other determinants (e.g., color, shading, vista, texture) and which also contain a form element of plus or minus gradation.
4. The number of "popular" responses (responses which appear frequently enough in a general population so that they may be specially designated).
5. The sequence in which the plus and minus responses appear and the cards which particularly elicit the poor form responses.
6. The general diagnostic classification of the patient being evaluated. A marginal F+ per cent in an hysterical setting may have a different significance from the same F+ per cent in an obsessive-compulsive setting.
7. The scoring system used. There are at least 6 Rorschach scoring systems in use, with wide differences among them in the manner in which the presence of form as a determinant is established and in the criteria for the judgment of good or poor form. In the Beck system, for example, tables of good and poor form responses are set up as guides to scoring and have at least a partial statistical basis, whereas the Klopfer system relies heavily on the experience and the subjective appraisal of the psychologist.

It should be obvious, then, that to list an F+ per cent in the report could easily be misleading, while to present the complete rationale for an interpretation would involve listing a good deal more of the data and would be awkward, bulky, boring, and unnecessary.

The purpose of the report is to attempt to

describe, explain, and predict the behavior of the patient in accordance with the referral problems; the presentation in the report of a justification for the evaluation would be out of place and distracting.

The main body of the report will be devoted to description and explanation. Prediction, when it enters, is likely to be offered in much more cautious terms than the rest of the report, and is more likely to be restricted to statements of a broad, prognostic nature than to be directed to specific behavioral events. The following statements, for example, might be found in a psychological report: "This patient will continue to display hostile acting-out-behavior," or, "The depression should return, in view of the nature of the patient's unresolved conflicts and his characteristic response to stress." In contrast to these 2 statements, the following 2 would be unlikely to be written: "This patient will kill his wife," or, "The patient will commit suicide." The former 2 statements may be made with a certain degree of confidence if the psychological techniques reveal consistent trends in the patient's reaction pattern. The occurrence of the events listed in the latter 2 statements depends on a variety of factors, both environmental and personal, and psychological methods do not include a wide enough sampling of behavior to be able ordinarily to justify such specificity in prediction. The phrase "given the right circumstances" could be added to such sentences, but then the statements would become ones which could be applied to everyone.

The report furnishes the referral source with what seems to be the most likely of the many inferences which the evaluative procedure has offered. The statements which are included do not all have the same likelihood of being true. Ideally, there should be an indication of which inferences hold the most water and which the least, but this hierarchy is not always clear. Sometimes, the psychological evaluation will appear to furnish all the answers with amazing accuracy. At other times it will seem that the report misses the boat entirely.

There is no reason to expect that the psycho-logical evaluation will always have the same value in the assessment of the patient. It is only one of many approaches to the understanding of the person, and its worth must be estimated anew for each patient as it is compared and correlated with the inferences based on psychiatric examination, social service review, and nursing service description. There may be widely differing views among the 4 approaches, and it is then the task of the diagnostic team to determine whether the 4 opinions present different but compatible facets of the patient's behavior, or whether one or more of the approaches has proven to be unfruitful in this particular case.

In both instances, there is much to be gained by an interchange of opinions and ideas. It is this kind of feedback that fosters refinements in technique, fresh insights into behavior and interpretation, and new leads for research.

SUMMARY

This paper discusses what may reasonably be expected of the clinical psychologist when he is asked for a psychological evaluation of a patient. Several points are emphasized: the kinds of questions which may most profitably be put to the clinical psychologist, the content of the referral, the kind of referral data which results in the most valid, useful, economical, and rapid evaluation, and the professional ethics and responsibilities of the clinical psychologist in his psychodiagnostic role. Much of the discussion centers about the intellectual and personality evaluations and the content of the psychological report.

NOTES

1. This guide draws heavily on the views and comments of the members of the psychology staffs at the Malcolm Bliss Mental Health Center and the Washington University School of Medicine, and on the writing of several persons who are listed at the end of the paper. The opinions presented here, however, are those of the writer and do not necessarily reflect the viewpoint of the reference sources.

REFERENCES

1. AMERICAN PSYCHOLOGICAL ASSOCIATION. Ethical Standards of Psychologists, Washington, D.C., American Psychological Association, 1953.
2. HARLOW, R. G., and SALSMAN, L. F. Toward the Effective Use of the Psychological Consultation, Am. J. Psychiat., 115, 228–231, 1958.
3. SCHAFER, R. Psychoanalytic Interpretation in Rorschach Testing, New York, Grune & Stratton, Inc., 1954.
4. WATSON, R. I. The Clinical Method in Psychology, New York, Harper & Brothers, 1951.

41. *Psychological Case Reporting at Psychiatric Staff Conferences*

JULES D. HOLZBERG, SALVATORE L. ALESSI
AND MURRAY WEXLER

WHATEVER the nature of the psychiatric setting in which the clinical psychologist functions, he will be expected to meet with his professional colleagues in psychiatry and social work in order to discuss cases with which all or some of these workers have had contact. It is this meeting, the clinical staff conference, that has been for so long one of the basic vehicles making for the "team" approach in psychiatric practice. If this "team" approach to an individual's problems has any intrinsic worth, then the importance of this conference cannot be overstressed. While the ostensible purpose of the meeting is to permit the various professional disciplines to contribute to the understanding of the case at hand, an equally important, but not often emphasized, purpose is to provide a medium for the mutual education of professional workers. The latter purpose is as important for the psychologist as it is for his professional colleagues.

While it is obvious that participation in the clinical staff conference is an important function for the psychologist, it is of interest that little attention has been given either in universities or in clinical settings to the process of psychological case reporting at staff conferences. A cursory review of the literature revealed little if any attempt to discuss this aspect of the psychologist's function in terms of techniques of reporting and in terms of problems involved in the psychologist's participation in the staff conference.

Two techniques of reporting are prevalent today in clinical practice: (1) the psychologist reads the

psychological report verbatim as it was written for the psychiatric record, or (2) the psychologist gives a generalized summary consisting entirely of interpretations. It is the feeling of the authors that neither of these two techniques satisfies the two purposes of the staff conference, i.e., clarification of the patient's status and mutual education. The first technique ignores the fact that the psychological report written for the psychiatric record may be oriented toward a goal that is distinctly different from that of a report presented at a case conference. Thus, a written psychological report may have been prepared to assist in differential diagnosis, whereas the case conference may be geared toward evaluating the most desirable therapy for the patient. In addition, the organization and style of a written psychological report does not lend itself readily to verbatim reading because of its formal character.

The second technique of reporting described above is one in which the psychologist presents abstractions regarding the patient's behavior. The abstractions may lie considerably removed from the concrete, and therefore practical, aspects of behavior in which the psychologist's professional colleagues are likely to be interested. This type of report frequently loses the individuality of the patient by dealing with broad and vague generalizations rather than with concrete data about the patient.

All psychological reporting at case conferences may not fall into these two discrete categories, and frequently a presentation may consist of both of these approaches; but the net result has often been that the colleagues of the psychologist begin to look upon his participation in the staff conference as a necessary evil, i.e., he should be there in order to give public demonstration of the "team" approach, but his reports fail to help in understanding the patient and in fostering mutual education.

The purpose of the present paper is to present a guide to more adequate psychological reporting at

Reprinted from *Journal of Consulting Psychology*, 1951, *15*, 425–429, by permission of the American Psychological Association and the authors. Dr. Holzberg is Director of Research, Connecticut Valley Hospital, Middletown; Dr. Alessi is Chief Psychologist, The Hartley-Salmon Child Guidance Clinic of Children's Services of Connecticut, Inc.; and Dr. Wexler is Professor of Psychiatry (Psychology), University of Southern California School of Medicine.

clinical case conferences which takes into consideration the limitations of the practices described above.

GUIDES FOR PSYCHOLOGICAL REPORTING

PREPARATION

As indicated above, the psychological report written for the psychiatric record is frequently not in a desirable form for presentation at case conferences. Consequently, the psychologist must prepare specifically for the case conference. When the patient has been seen by the psychologist weeks or possibly months before the conference, it is expecially important that the psychologist review the case and prepare an outline of the material that he will present. The frequent practice of reaching for the psychological documents a few minutes before the conference and attempting to ad-lib a report can only result in a very poor presentation.

Preparation is vital to the psychologist's participation at the staff conference. This preparation involves the development of an outline of the relevant material to be discussed. However, such an outline, once prepared, should not be used rigidly. It may be necessary to reduce the length of presentation because of limitations of time, or it may be important to focus more intensively on fewer factors. Here, there can be no substitute for the psychologist's utilizing good judgment in determining the use of any outline that he prepares.

Fequently, the psychologist looks upon the case conference as a burden and would prefer to devote his time to other psychological activities. This attitude is unfortunate in that the psychologist fails to recognize the importance of the case conference from the point of view of the patient, the psychologist, and psychology as a profession. The case conference should be accepted as an integral part of the total responsibility of the psychologist.

PERTINENCE

The psychological report prepared for the psychiatric record should contain as much detail as possible since what appears as a minor factor at the moment may take on greater significance at some future time. Consequently, it is not necessary to present at the case conference everything that appears in the formal psychological report.

A case conference usually has a specific goal in mind. A conference may be called in order to establish a nosological or etiological diagnosis, and here the psychologist should be concerned with contributing maximally to this goal. Another conference may be called to discuss the therapeutic possibilities for a given patient, and here the emphasis of the psychologist should be geared toward meeting this objective. Another type of conference may be concerned with the desirability of discharge of a patient from a mental hospital. This may require a different emphasis in the psychologist's presentation from either a diagnostic or therapeutic conference. A conference may be called with reference to the disposition of a court case. Here the psychologist should contribute material that has pertinence for the purpose of the conference. Thus, with the case conference concerned with specific problems, the psychologist is responsible for preparing his material so as to contribute maximally to the goal of the conference.

Here an objection may be raised by the psychologist who feels that what he may omit from his presentation may nevertheless be very vital for understanding the patient. This necessitates consideration of another aspect of the psychologist's participation at the staff conference. The role of the psychologist at the conference may be considered in two phases: (1) the formal report based on an outline prepared in advance of the conference which draws together data pertinent to the patient's particular problem being discussed; (2) the psychologist's participation in the discussion of the case subsequent to the presentation of the formal report. The second aspect of the psychologist's role in the case conference is often underemphasized in clinical practice. Frequently, the psychologist will look upon his role as merely that of presenting a formal report and then withdrawing from discussion in subsequent stages of the conference. At these latter stages the psychologist can introduce other material about the patient which at that particular moment becomes pertinent to the staff discussion. Parenthetically, it should be noted that at this stage of the discussion the psychologist should not feel himself confined to his test data. He should feel free to make contributions concerning the problem at hand even though his ideas are not derived from his tests.

In some settings, the other participants in the staff conference share responsibility for the psychologist's failure to accept the second phase of his role in the case conference. Thus, it has been observed that the psychiatrist frequently accepts the psychologist's role as simply that of preparing a formal report without encouraging his participation in the subsequent discussion.

The tendency of the psychologist to feel that his contribution is finished once he has delivered his formal report may have serious consequences for the patient. The psychiatrist, in attempting to integrate the psychologist's thinking into the total psychiatric picture, may misunderstand the psychologist's reasoning, resulting in distorted conclusions about the patient. For example, a psychologist reported at a staff conference that a patient was functioning in the defective range of intelligence. He reasoned that there was evidence to indicate that certain morbid processes were seriously disturbing intellectual activity and that the intellectual potential was in all probability considerably higher. The psychiatrist, in summarizing the case, overlooked the psychologist's evaluation. The former stated that because of the defective intelligence, there was little likelihood that the patient would benefit from psychotherapy. If the psychologist in this case had not further elaborated upon his interpretation of the patient's performance, a disservice might have resulted.

ORGANIZATION

The psychologist's report at the staff conference should be well organized and integrated. While this may appear to be an obvious principle requiring no special emphasis, it is a principle honored more often in the breach than in the observance. If the purpose of the conference is to answer a specific problem, the psychologist should arrive at his solution through a process of logical reasoning. In order to achieve this, the psychologist should not report on a test-by-test analysis, but should make a cross-test analysis of the pertinent psychological factors.

EVIDENCE

The inclusion of verbatim test material in the presentation of the psychological report is vital if the dual purpose of clarifying the patient's problems, and mutual education is to be served. If one of the purposes of the staff conference is to provide better understanding of a patient, then the goal is to present a rich and vibrant picture of the personality. If the psychologist compounds his conference reports with a series of psychological cliches and poorly deduced generalizations, then his auditors at the staff conference will soon begin to feel that tests are unable to discriminate between different personalities. As one moves from the test data and its specific interpretations to broad dynamic formulations, the patient, as a specific personality, begins to lose his identity. These remarks are not to be construed as opposed to the presentation of generalizations that are supported by specific and concrete data.

An additional reason for the inclusion of test data is to fulfill the second purpose of the staff conference, namely, mutual education. Perhaps nothing is more important in the process of mutual education than the sharing with other professional personnel of the thinking that went into the analysis of a given case, beginning with the original test data.

For example, the psychologist may report, without any preliminary attempt to build up or present the evidence, that the patient is "an orally sadistic individual." In capsule form, the psychologist is attempting to convey a motivational formulation, but it loses its richness because the specific ways in which the patient thinks and feels about this problem are absent.

For presentation at the staff conference, such a formulation will become meaningful and instructive to the other participants if the psychologist presents his data, and his ways of reasoning from his information. Instead of the generalization, "an orally sadistic individual," the following method of presentation is suggested. "The Rorschach data reveals several percepts which suggest that sadism is related to the oral zone. 'A crocodile snapping his jaws shut,' 'a man and woman arguing,' 'a snake poised to sink his fangs into his victim.' Other tests such as word association test and the Thematic Apperception Test offers evidence which further demonstrates the oral sadistic trends. To the word 'kiss,' the response is 'bite'; to the word 'talk,' the response is 'argue.' On one card of the Thematic Apperception Test (7 BM), the patient says, 'These are two politicians. The young one has just debated with his opponents. His words were so brilliant and *stinging* that he literally *destroyed* all opposition.' " The evidence that went into the conclusion "oral sadism" is presented. It gives the listener an opportunity to witness the patient's thinking. The interpretive job is by no means complete with the observation that the patient is orally sadistic. "Oral sadism" telescopes a great many ideas, and simply to attribute such traits to a patient does not convey much that is meaningful about him. Thus, the following is a continuation of the psychologist's description of the patient. "The data suggest (kiss—bite) that the erotic relationships seem to be colored by sadistic traits. Further, argumentation may be a vehicle through which these traits may be expressed. Words seem to have a magical significance and are used in an aggressive and destructive manner. The Thematic Apperception Test data concerning oral sadism and the psychological importance of language to the patient can be further illustrated by responses on the Wechsler-Bellevue. For example, to the word 'hara-kiri,' the patient says, 'This is an ancient and honored custom among the Japanese. It derives from an innate sense of honor to the Motherland and from a philosophy of Stoicism which only the oriental people have. It consists of driving a blade into the stomach and ripping out the viscera. I find a certain fascination in contemplating the scene.' " Such examples clarify and elaborate the psychologist's reasoning and make for a richness of reporting which will both hold the listener's interest and instruct at the same time. The Chinese proverb that one picture is worth a multitude of words is as true in psychology and psychiatry as it is in other areas of instruction.

Occasionally, the psychologist will offer objection to the idea that he should present evidence in substantiation of his interpretations and generalizations. He may consider this a reflection on his professional status and will correctly raise the question, "Do the other professional workers offer evidence when they are presenting cases?" The answer to this objection is twofold. (1) There is no inconsistency between presenting test data as evidence for one's thinking, and maintaining one's professional status. In reality, it is an earmark of a scientist carefully at work, who is determined to make no interpretations and generalizations without adequate evidence. (2) The failure of other professional groups such as psychiatrists and social workers to offer evidence to support their thinking should be as readily condemned as the psychologist's failure to do so. The psychiatrist who offers a diagnosis or therapeutic plan without any attempt to build up the evidence for his thinking carefully, and the social worker who gives a judgment regarding a family situation without presenting the underlying evidence, are engaging in unscientific practices that can only lead to failure to attain the purposes of the staff conference.

CONTENT

There is certain minimal information that should be incorporated into the psychologist's presentation of a case at staff conference. The following sequence is not meant to suggest the order of presentation at the staff conference, although for most cases this order should prove satisfactory.

1. Date of examination. This is important because a patient may have been last seen several weeks and possibly months before. Significant psychological changes may have occurred since the patient was seen. Knowledge on the part of the other staff members of when the psychologist saw the patient places the report in proper perspective.

2. Reason for referral. This defines the responsibility of the psychologist in terms of the type of psychological study he has performed. It may be stated with reasonable assurance that most clinical settings cannot afford to engage in extensive testing of patients but must confine testing to the exploration of specific problems that have been raised. Consequently, a given patient may not have been studied for a problem which suddenly emerges at the staff conference. A patient may have been seen by the psychologist in order to explore the personality of the patient to aid in defining therapeutic objectives, and the entire battery of psychological tests may have been directed toward this end. At the staff conference, however, a problem may arise concerning vocational rehabilitation which the psychologist had not explored with the patient. Thus, it is important at the outset of the report to structure carefully the reasons why the patient was referred for psychological study.

3. Behavioral observations. This aspect of the psychologist's report to the staff conference is frequently underemphasized for two reasons: (a) behavioral observations by the psychologist approach in content the mental status examination performed by the psychiatrist. The psychiatrist may therefore look upon the reporting of behavioral observations by the psychologist as an intrusion into his domain of study; (b) the psychologist may fail to recognize that the study of the patient's behavior while taking tests may be as important as the data procured from the tests themselves. It is the authors' contention that these two reasons for the psychologist's neglecting to report behavioral observations are totally invalid. If one views the administration of the psychological examination as an opportunity to observe the patient under standardized interview conditions, such observations should be an important supplement to the psychiatrist's observations derived from relatively unstandardized interviews. From the psychologist's point of view, the behavior of the patient defines the frame of reference within which the interpretation of test data can be made. If the psychologist is to be "patient-oriented" rather than "test-oriented," the reporting of behavioral observations is a vital part of his contribution at the staff conference. The patient's attitude toward the examiner, toward the pictures on the wall, or toward the challenge of being tested may be just as significant as his formal responses to a specific test.

4. Intelligence. Where an intelligence test has been given, a statement of the patient's present functioning level and his optimal capacity should be reported even if no further report on the intelligence test results will be made. This type of information, just as behavioral observations, is vital for structuring the frame of reference within which to understand the patient's performance on other tests.

5. The main report. The body of the report is concerned with the concrete evidence, the interpretations, and the generalizations. When previous psychological studies have been performed, these should be incorporated for comparison purposes.

6. Conclusions. The psychologist should complete his report, rendering his opinion regarding the problem for which the patient is being presented. It should be an integration of all that the psychologist has previously reported. However, the summary should not merely be a repetition. The psychologist's conclusions should be qualified in terms of the degree of certainty with which he offers his opinion. His conclusions may be tentative hypotheses, and then should be stated as such. On the other hand, the conclusions may be definitive and supported by voluminous evidence, in which case the psychologist should voice the certainty of his opinion. It must be emphasized that a conclusion regarding human behavior at our present state of knowledge permits varying degrees of assurance. It is no more a reflection on the psychologist to qualify his opinions than it is on his colleagues in other professions to qualify theirs.

MANNER

While it is not the authors' intention to urge a Dale Carnegie approach to psychological reporting at the staff conference, it must, however, be stressed that unless the psychologist is enthusiastic and interested in what he is presenting, there is not likely to be much enthusiasm or interest on the part of those that are listening. It is amazing to discover the number of psychologists reaching advanced stages of training in clinical psychology who are unable to meet with colleagues and to exchange thinking without experiencing feelings of severe threat and debilitating anxiety. The net result of these feelings is to prevent intelligent and effective participation in the case conference.

The use of technical psychological language does not make others accept the psychologist as a scientifically trained person. It should be stressed again that his status as a scientific worker will depend upon his ability to present evidence logically and convincingly in support of his interpretations and generalizations. The injudicious and unexplained use of such terms as "extratensive," "flexor," "deterioration ratio," "succorance need," etc., while ringing with scientific erudition, will only result in isolating the psychologist from his professional colleagues.

This paper has stressed that a concrete approach to the staff conference is most desirable. Concreteness can be emphasized most strongly when the psychologist comes to the staff conference prepared to present the actual test materials with which the patient has worked. Thus, presenting the Rorschach card on which the patient has given an unusual response, the TAT card which has produced a significant story, the human-form drawing which takes on special significance in the psychologist's analysis of test data, or the Wechsler-Bellevue subtest that delineates the special problem area in the study of the patient—these and any other concrete presentations of test material should make for a richness in psychological reporting that will not be equalled by the mere presentation of interpretations and generalizations.

CONCLUSION AND SUMMARY

This paper has attempted to focus the need for clinical psychologists to receive training in the proper techniques of reporting at psychiatric staff conferences. Principles have been enumerated which are considered appropriate for the presentation of psychological reports. While it is not the authors' intention to submit these principles as the last word on the problem, it is hoped that they may stimulate thinking about the psychologist's role and function at the staff conference, based on a recognition of its importance in his daily professional life.

V

INTERNATIONAL ASPECTS OF CLINICAL PSYCHOLOGY

As Henry David points out in the first article of this part, "Clinical psychology, in common with its sister sciences, knows no national boundaries." The developmental history and the pattern of role definition of clinical psychology in each country varies, sometimes markedly. The variability is a natural result of diverse local needs, resources, academic patterns, interprofessional relationships, etc. Although the United States has moved with more speed in the expansion of clinical psychology training programs and has by far the largest number of trained clinical psychologists of any country in the world, it is important to know the patterns of training and practices in other countries in order to maintain perspective.

We have included in this part articles that describe psychology in Canada, Great Britain, Israel, Germany, Austria, and the Soviet Union. David's lead article presents vignettes of clinical psychology in additional countries. Countries other than those represented are at various stages in the development of training programs and the utilization of clinical psychologists. Additional information concerning international aspects of clinical psychology can be found in the references at the end of each article in this part.

42. *Clinical Psychology Abroad*

HENRY P. DAVID

CLINICAL psychology, in common with its sister sciences, knows no national boundaries. Current journals, texts, and international congresses reflect steadily expanding horizons of scientific and professional interests that effectively transcend geographical, linguistic, and ideological barriers.

These very brief, nontechnical observations of clinical psychology abroad will be limited to some recent trends noted in the United Kingdom and Continental Europe, including the Soviet Union. The observations are based, in varying degree, on a cursory survey of recent publications, informal correspondence, and fleeting conversations during the Brussels International Congress and other travels abroad. No claims are made for complete accuracy or all-inclusiveness; a process of "selective perception" may be assumed, both here and in earlier comments (David, 1957; David & Von Bracken, 1957).

UNITED KINGDOM

Clinical psychology in Britain, as in the United States, is largely a postwar affair (Summerfield, 1958). Its recent growth has occurred predominantly within the context of the 1948 National Health Service. Qualifications, standards, and salaries were developed with the counsel of the British Psychological Society whose clinical representatives sat on the national and regional advisory bodies responsible for mental health. An interesting professional trend may be reflected in the 1957 founding of the (British) Association for Child Psychology and Psychiatry with its equal number of medical and nonmedical board members.

Beginning in 1946, a highly intensive one-year

Reprinted from *American Psychologist*, 1959, *14*, 601–604, by permission of the American Psychological Association and the author. The "Addendum" was prepared by Dr. David especially for this book. Dr. David is Associate Director, International Research Institute, American Institutes for Research, Washington, D.C.

graduate training program was inaugurated in the Psychology Department of the University of London Institute of Psychiatry at the Maudsley Hospital. The orientation of the department has been expressed by Eysenck (1949), who believes that a fully trained clinical psychologist should first complete a year's internship and then proceed to write an appropriate doctoral thesis. The approach is operational and methodological and leans heavily on statistical techniques. Although students are not trained in psychotherapy as such, they are encouraged to apply the techniques of experimental psychology both to the diagnostic investigation of the individual patient and to his treatment via therapy based on learning theory and other validated principles.

More qualitative studies are pursued at London's Tavistock Clinic, one of two institutions recognized for practicum training by the National Health Service. Although not university affiliated, the clinic provides training in child psychotherapy to qualified nonmedical psychologists, as does the Hempstead Child Therapy Centre under the supervision of Anna Freud. The British Rorschach Forum offers a platform for projective techniques.

A second university graduate program in clinical psychology is currently in the planning stage at Edinburgh. It may affiliate with the Department of Psychological Research at the Crichton Royal Hospital, the only other institution approved, at this time, for practicum training by the National Health Service. Similar programs are under consideration in at least two other British university centers, but are handicapped by the relatively small number of practicum vacancies for trainees.

WESTERN EUROPE

Visitors to the Continent have been impressed by the postwar surge of psychology. The academic and professional influence of clinical activities is beginning to be felt, even though training programs do not yet enjoy the broad support commonly attained in the United States. Interest in educational and industrial applications is growing, but psychotherapy is often considered the province of psychologically trained physicians.

In several countries university departments are still emancipating themselves from philosophy, and only a relatively few are in a position to foster clinical research or encourage doctoral theses in this area. Desirable opportunities for supervised internships or practicum training are at a premium and must usually be arranged on the student's initiative and at his own expense.

Most Continental European "clinical psychologists" are physicians with specialized postgraduate training. They are taught to administer and interpret projective techniques and are frequently the only ones permitted by law to do psychotherapy. A good prototype of the situation is the two-volume *Handbook of Clinical Psychology* published in Switzerland and edited by Stern (1954), a German trained psychiatrist practicing in France. Most of the multinational contributors are physicians, and the emphasis is entirely on diagnostic testing.

France, parent of the first intelligence test, is not so active at present in clinical psychology. Psychiatry is intimately associated with neurology, treatment is along classical lines, and there is less interest in dynamics. Insofar as can be ascertained, no university department offers a clinical degree, and most teaching, when not subsumed under philosophy, is done by psychiatrists. Professional problems are complicated by unqualified persons posing as psychotherapists.

German clinical psychology has made considerable postwar strides. Projective techniques are receiving attention, especially at the University of Freiburg. Impressionistic aspects and subjective sequential interpretation are emphasized, though there seems to be a strong trend toward greater objectivity. Tubingen, where Kretschmer and his associates have long been exploring personality and body types, offers one of the few European examples of an integrated multidisciplinary research program with opportunities for advanced study and degrees for psychologists in a medical setting.

Although much of *Dutch* psychology is still strongly dominated by philosophy, the Universities of Amsterdam and of Utrecht have for some time been among the most active European centers for the professional development of clinical and industrial psychology. *Belgium*, a most cordial host for the fifteenth International Congress, offers some opportunities in the clinical area. Its scientific tradition is closely allied with France.

Psychology in the Scandinavian countries has been greatly influenced by the quantitative approach. However, clinical psychologists are practicing in many *Danish* and *Norwegian* mental hospitals and clinics, and graduate training programs are in development at the Universities of Copenhagen and of Oslo. Emphasis is mostly on diagnostic testing and play therapy. There has also been progress in child psychotherapeutic training in *Sweden* and *Finland*. Psychiatry has a predominantly somatic and biological orientation, emphasizing genetic and physiological research.

Switzerland, the cradle of so many advances, presents a curious paradox. Clinical psychology has limited official standing in academic university programs and is often considered a medical specialty. Courses in projective techniques are taught in medical schools, frequently by psychologists who received their training in nonuniversity connected "institutes" or private seminars. Professional psychologists generally restrict their practice to vocational guidance and/or remedial work with difficult children; few hospitals have full-time psychologists on their staffs.

In *Austria*, university training in clinical methods is given mostly in Vienna and Innsbruck. *Italian* psychology still seems closely tied to philosophy and an organically oriented psychiatry. *Spain* and *Portugal* continue to follow a similar tradition.

EASTERN EUROPE

In recent years considerable attention has been focused on psychological trends in the *Soviet Union* and Eastern Europe (Mintz, 1958). The 1954 and the 1957 International Congresses provided unique opportunities for individual meetings, frequently resulting in the recognition that Soviet colleagues usually employ a different terminology, based on Pavlovian concepts of the physiology of higher nervous activities and the Marxist philosophy of dialectical materialism. No matter what their specific interests, however, most were also exceedingly well informed of psychological studies in other lands.

Soviet psychiatric textbooks emphasize physiological factors. While the possibility of psychogenic disorders is acknowledged, there is little discussion of childhood experiences or of family influences. Psychotherapy is mentioned, usually without description of techniques; major emphasis is on detailed surveys of drugs and chemotherapy. Although Freud was not unknown in the Soviet Union and a psychoanalytic society did exist in the early 1930's, psychoanalysis is presently considered unscientific, idealistic, and as leading to political reaction.

"Work in the field of pathological or clinical psychology is an essential part of Soviet psychology." So writes Luria (in Simon, 1957), Director of the Psychology Section of the Institute of Defectology of the RSFSR Academy of Educational Sciences in Moscow, which is especially concerned with research and the diagnosis and education of severely handicapped children. He adds that "the work of Soviet psychopathologists at the present time [1956] is mainly directed to the study of pathological change in the dynamics of the nervous processes which lie behind disturbances in psychic activity."

While it may be said that Soviet clinical psychology is predominantly experimental in orientation, it does not appear to be exclusively concerned with physiological mechanisms, but rather with psychophysical functioning—e.g., perceptual discrimination, conditioning, extinction, synthesis and analysis, and system formation.

Psychological tests have been severely criticized since 1931 and were condemned in a 1936 resolution of the Communist Party Central Committee as unscientific, detrimental to public education, and "in conflict with both dialectical materialism and with the practical experience of Soviet society."

Textbooks usually ignore objective, quantitatively scored tests or criticize them for failing to specify the processes resulting in a given performance; projective techniques are rarely mentioned. However, much of the work in industrial settings— e.g., the selection of Moscow subway employees— seems dependent on aptitude and other tests, even though these procedures may be described by different nomenclatures.

It may be pertinent that Piaget and his colleagues recently noted an apparent reconsideration of the qualitative use of psychological tests. Also, in May 1957 the *New York Times* reported that the Soviet Ministry of Education had requested copies of American intelligence tests as part of the new exchange program.

As observed by Razran (1958) Soviet psychology has had considerable impact on colleagues in Eastern European countries. In his view, the Pavlovian influence is strongest in *Rumania* and *Bulgaria*. There is little or no knowledge of current (1959) work in *Hungary*. *Czechoslovakia* continues its awareness of Western clinical techniques, with a good deal of research emanating from the Psychiatric Clinic of Charles University in Prague. Visitors to *Yugoslavia* report active group therapy programs in the mental hospitals and an interest in personality theory. Psychologists in the *German Democratic Republic* have developed a training program in clinical psychology at Humboldt University in East Berlin.

Of major importance perhaps was the publication in *Poland* of an article by Choynowski (1957), later excerpted in the *American Psychologist*. He appealed for a change in the official attitude toward psychology as an ideological, philosophical, or pedagogical science, based only on the physiology of central processes, and urged reconsideration of the 1936 resolution against testing methods. [Ed. Note: Choynowski subsequently became Head of the Psychometrical Laboratory of the Polish Academy of Science in Warsaw.]

CONCLUSION

It seems reasonable to conclude from this very limited bird's-eye view of European trends that clinical psychology, as a science and profession, is making significant strides abroad. American psychology has no monopoly on progress. It may well behoove us to look beyond our oceans and linguistic frontiers. International congresses, such as those sponsored by the International Union of Scientific Psychology, the growing interest of APA and of its divisions, the support of other affiliated or related groups, and perhaps the realities of the jet and space age augur well for International Psychology.

REFERENCES

CHOYNOWSKI, M. [On the awakening of Polish psychology. *Culture and Society*, 1957, 1, No. 1.] (Transl. by R. B. Zajonc. *Amer. Psychologist*, 1957, *12*, 730–733.)

DAVID, H. P. Clinical psychology in other lands. In D. Brower & L. E. Abt, *Progress in clinical psychology*. Vol. III. New York: Grune & Stratton, 1958.

DAVID, H. P., & VON BRACKEN, H. (Eds.). *Perspectives in personality theory*. New York: Basic Books, 1957. London: Tavistock, 1957. Bern: Hans Huber Verlag, 1958.

EYSENCK, H. J. Training in clinical psychology: An English point of view. *Amer. Psychologist*, 1949, *4*, 173–176.

MINTZ, A. Recent developments in psychology in the USSR. *Annu. Rev. Psychol.*, 1958, *9*, 453–504.

RAZRAN, G. Psychology in communist countries other than the USSR. *Amer. Psychologist*, 1958, *13*, 177–178.

SIMON, B. (Ed.) *Psychology in the Soviet Union*. Stanford, Calif.: Stanford Univer. Press, 1957.

STERN, E. (Ed.) *Die Tests in der klinischen Psychologie*. Zurich: Rascher Verlag, 1954. 2 vols.

SUMMERFIELD, A. Clinical psychology in Britain. *Amer. Psychologist*, 1958, *13*, 171–176.

ADDENDUM

Communication and exchange with colleagues abroad have continued to expand since the publication of this paper in 1959. The International Union of Scientific Psychology held its triennial Congress in Bonn in 1960 and in Washington in 1963. The Eighteenth International Congress is scheduled for August 1966 in Moscow. In between, the International Association of Applied Psychology met in Copenhagen in 1961 and in Ljubljana in 1964. The *Proceedings* of these meetings well reflect the advances of our science and profession, the increasing international cooperation, and the numerous efforts to facilitate communication. In contemplating the international scene, however, it is not always realized that more than half of the world's psychologists live and work in the United States, and that this percentage rises even more if only Ph.D.'s are counted. It should not surprise visitors that American psychology is perceived as a Goliath and that colleagues in other lands are sensitive about the attention given to their contributions.

Recent trends in clinical psychology in 58 countries outside the United States are cited in *International Resources in Clinical Psychology* (1964). For most nations the information given includes an introduction to the prevailing situation, opportunities for graduate university training and supervised practicum experience, professional roles, emerging trends and legislation, and relations with psychiatry. Nearly 90 correspondents contributed to this effort. A summary of graduate training abroad appears in the *Sourcebook for Training in Clinical Psychology* (1964); professional aspects are discussed in the *Handbook of Clinical Psychology* (1965).

A review of the current world scene leads to the conclusion that concepts of clinical psychology and professional practice differ from country to country. The model of an accredited doctoral level graduate training program with an approved internship enjoying massive government and private support, appears unique to the United States.

In reading about or visting other lands it is useful to note the varying approaches to professional practice and academic training. In many countries the term "clinical" has long been equated with "applied" psychology, where traditionally a Ph.D. degree has not been considered a prerequisite for advancement. Patterns of education differ and the stage at which professional practice begins varies widely. Doctoral requirements may be more or less systematized and of shorter or longer duration than in the United States. A degree may be granted in recognition of a truly scholarly contribution or awarded for a lesser effort when combined with many years of dedicated service. Equating doctorates obtained in one country with those given in another can be very perplexing. To facilitate better understanding of educational resources, the International Union of Scientific Psychology joined with the American Psychological Association in calling the 1962 Conference at La Napoule, France, on International Opportunities for Advanced Training and Research in Psychology. It is anticipated that the reports from approximately 80 countries will shortly become available (Ross, 1966).

Relatively few countries make statutory provisions for clinical psychology. Within the broad spectrum of services provided, diagnostic evaluation and psychometrics are universal tasks. Psychotherapy by psychologists, whether subrosa or officially sanctioned, is more prevalent outside Western Europe than within it. Similarly, relations with psychiatry tend to be less abrasive where institutional controls and stereotyped attitudes are not historically embedded in professional conduct. In the merging lands where resources are more limited, professional personnel tend to be characterized by the breadth of their activities rather than narrow specialization or traditional prerogatives (David, 1966).

Over the years American clinical psychology has grown extensively, becoming increasingly sophisticated in concepts and methodology. While rich in numbers and resources, it claims no monopoly on ideas. The conclusions of 1959 remain valid in 1966.

SELECTED REFERENCES

DAVID, H. P. *International resources in clinical psychology.* New York: McGraw-Hill, 1964.

DAVID, H. P. Graduate training abroad. In Blank, L., and David, H. P. (Eds.), *Sourcebook for training in clinical psychology.* New York: Springer, 1965.

DAVID, H. P. International trends in clinical psychology. In Wolman, B. B. (Ed.), *Handbook of clinical psychology.* New York: McGraw-Hill, 1965.

DAVID, H. P. *International trends in mental health.* New York: McGraw-Hill, 1966.

ROSS, S. (Ed.). *International opportunities for advanced training and research in psychology.* Washington, D.C.: American Psychological Association, 1966.

43. *Clinical Psychology Training in Canada*

C. M. MOONEY

THE following report on clinical psychology training in Canada is based upon replies to a general letter which I sent out on January 20th to heads of departments of psychology in some thirty-six Canadian colleges and universities.

GRADUATE TRAINING

Nine universities offer graduate training in clinical psychology. Here they are, showing degrees granted, training emphasis, and the centres providing supervised intern training.

Dalhousie University, Halifax, Nova Scotia, is the centre for clinical psychology training for Nova Scotia, Prince Edward Island, and Newfoundland. It offers the M.A. and the Ph.D., placing emphasis on experimental training. It grants a diploma in clinical psychology based on an internship program. Twenty students are presently taking the graduate course. Three clinical centres provide supervised intern training: The Nova Scotia Hospital, Dartmouth, N.S.; DVA Hospital, Camp Hill, Halifax; Hospital for Nervous and Mental Diseases, St. John's, Newfoundland.

Laval University, Quebec, P.Q., offers the licence and doctorate, equivalent to the M.A. and Ph.D., with emphasis on clinical method. Supervised intern training is given at St-Michel-Archange Hospital (mental hospital) and in unspecified departments of psychiatry in general hospitals.

University of Montreal, Montreal, P.Q., offers the licence and doctorate, equivalent to the M.A. and the Ph.D., with emphasis on clinical method. Intern training is provided at the Training Centre in Applied Psychology of the Institute of Psychology, and in unspecified outside clinics.

McGill University, Montreal, P.Q., offers a M.Sc. (applied) degree in clinical psychology, and

the Ph.D., with emphasis on research. Intern training is given at Montreal Children's Hospital, Queen Mary Veterans Hospital, Verdun Protestant Hospital, Allan Memorial Institute, Montreal General Hospital.

University of Ottawa, Ottawa, Ontario, offers the M.A. or the M.Ps. (comprising added courses plus practical training in lieu of thesis) and the Ph.D. (either clinical or child clinical), emphasizing the interdependence of clinical psychology with education. Intern training is given at the Guidance Centre, and the Child Guidance Centre, of the School of Psychology and Education, Royal Ottawa Sanatorium, and psychiatric units of Ottawa General and Ottawa Civic Hospitals.

University of Toronto, Toronto, Ontario, gives the M.A. and the Ph.D., emphasizing basic theory, method, and research. Supervised intern training is provided at Toronto Psychiatric Hospital; Ontario Hospital, New Toronto; Toronto General Hospital; Hospital for Sick Children; Sunnybrook Hospital; Thistletown Hospital (for disturbed children); Crippled Children's Treatment Centre, Institute of Child Study of the University; twelve of the Ontario Hospitals and Ontario Hospital Schools (for 4-month summer internships); and others.

Queen's University, Kingston, Ontario, offers the M.A., or the Diploma in Clinical Psychology (M.A. courses plus one year practicum and added courses sans research project), and the Ph.D., emphasizing applied experimental aspects. Supervised intern training is given at Kingston General Hospital, the Ontario Hospital, Kingston (for nervous and mental disorders), Kingston Rehabilitation Centre, and the Ontario Hospital, Smiths Falls (for the mentally defective).

University of Alberta, Edmonton, offers the M.A. as a general course, with special work in clinical, and it has made provision for a Ph.D. in clinical psychology that might be effective in 1964. Internships would then be available at the University Hospital, and at other unspecified guidance clinics, mental hospitals, rehabilitation centres, and research centres.

Reprinted from *Canadian Psychologist*, 1963, *4*, 74–86, by permission of the Canadian Psychological Association and the author. Dr. Mooney is Consultant in Psychology, Department of National Health and Welfare, Ottawa, Canada.

University of British Columbia, Vancouver, offers the M.A., with intern training provided at unspecified provincial mental hospitals, DVA and general hospitals.

While the following universities are not offering graduate training in clinical psychology, they see it as a likely future development: Memorial, Acadia, McMaster, York, Western, Waterloo, Assumption, Manitoba, Saskatchewan. These do not see it as likely in the foreseeable future: St. Francis Xavier, New Brunswick, Carleton.

THE GENERAL SITUATION

The introductory note was struck here, perhaps, by the Toronto spokesman: "The general situation of clinical psychology in Canada at this time is a mess."

Dalhousie reported thus: "In Nova Scotia there are 15 practising clinical psychologists, 3 with Ph.D., 11 with M.A., and one with B.A. Four of these are part-time. There are positions for six more. In Newfoundland there are three practising clinical psychologists; two are Ph.D. candidates (both part-time) and one an M.A. candidate. There are positions for two more. There are two practising clinical psychologists in P.E.I., one with M.A., and one an M.A. candidate. The psychologists work in mental hospitals, Community Mental Health Centres, Child Guidance Centres, and for the Department of Welfare."

From the *University of Montreal*, these comments: "Clinical psychology, as well as modern psychiatry, is relatively new in the province. The training of psychologists began at the University of Montreal in 1942. Although it has developed rapidly in this institution, it has never been able to cope with the growing demand for psychological services in the various hospitals and health organizations. McGill University has also trained psychologists; these graduates who received the degree of Master of Science in Applied Psychology represent a very small number of the population of psychologists working in the Province of Quebec. Laval University in Quebec City has also been providing training in psychotherapy. However, from all reports there have been only a handful of graduates from this school. Laval has founded (1962) a Department of Psychology which will yield graduates at the M.A. level starting from 1966. Therefore we can expect that there will be in the Province of Quebec a lack of clinical psychologists for several years to come. The Institute of Psychology of the University of Montreal, with a yearly enrolment of

over a hundred psychological students, still remains the main source of clinical psychologists. I would venture to say that there is great need for similar training centres in the province and, from all appearances, in Canada at large."

From *Queen's:* "In Ontario there appears to be a very serious shortage of trained clinical psychologists, mainly in the Ontario Health Service, to work in mental hospitals and child guidance clinics. There is also a large demand for post-graduate training facilities for clinical psychologists in the universities. At present, Queen's University receives many more applications for its graduate programmes in clinical psychology than can be handled with the present facilities."

Assumption University of Windsor: "Clinical psychology appears to be increasing in prestige. The demand for clinical psychologists exceeds the supply. One reason for this may be connected with the type of course work done in universities where the clinical aspect is played down."

University of Manitoba: "At the present time there are approximately twenty clinical psychologists in Manitoba. With respect to training and professional development, Manitoba is probably behind most of Canada."

The appropriate concluding remark comes from *Victoria College*, Victoria, B.C.: "The climate of clinical psychology in Victoria is excellent. Much better, for example, than in Vancouver, and many other areas of Canada. Our status and our relations with other professions is similar to that found in major centres in the U.S. We are recognized as expert witnesses in the courts, and have co-professional relations with psychiatrists."

RESPONSIBILITIES OF CLINICAL PSYCHOLOGISTS

Most respondents simply observed that the responsibilities generally assumed by clinical psychologists are the usual ones of psychodiagnosis, psychotherapy, research, and training. A few amplified this.

University of Montreal: "In psychiatric hospitals and in the psychiatric departments of general hospitals, the clinical psychologist usually works under the direction of a psychiatrist. His task ordinarily consists of testing and diagnosis and often includes psychotherapy (individual or group). The control of the psychiatrist over this work is more or less remote varying with the institutions. There are very few autonomous departments of psychology in these hospitals. There are also a few primarily psychological clinics, either privately operated or related to some provincial organizations, where the psychologist carries on professional activities in a fully independent way. As to research in clinical psychology, one could say that it is flourishing in university circles or in organizations directly affiliated to universities. Some research is going on, but probably less of it, in the various applied institutions. It should be finally noted that clinical psychologists working in these various departments are directly responsible for the supervision of the professional activities of the interns sent by the university and will also in some cases be called upon to give lectures on psychology to psychiatric interns and nurses."

The University of Western Ontario: "It varies greatly from setting to setting, but depends to a large extent, I think, on the amount of academic training which the psychologist has. My impression is that senior psychologists with the Ph.D. are more and more being encouraged to do research along with some psychotherapy. Persons with only the M.A. degree continue to do mostly, I think, personality appraisals, but they may be research assistants and do some group, if not individual, psychotherapy. Senior psychologists generally take part in training programs offered by the institutions in which they work. Another function which they may have is ward supervision when certain special programs such as "re-motivation" or "total-push" therapy are all in progress."

Memorial University of Newfoundland: "Psychologists in Newfoundland have always been given a free hand in assuming responsibilities. A certain amount of psychological testing is required, but psychologists have been encouraged to participate in individual and group therapy under psychiatric supervision. Research has been encouraged and psychologists have participated in many aspects of the psychiatric resident training program."

St. Francis Xavier University, Antigonish, N.S.: "The duties of the clinical psychologist include both psychodiagnosis and psychotherapy. The psychologist is not looked upon as a mere technician but participates in all aspects of the Clinic's work."

Acadia University, Wolfville, N.S.: "(We) in addition to our teaching duties, do part-time clinical work at the Fundy Mental Health Centre and are involved in psychological testing and diagnosis and in individual and family therapy."

Assumption University of Windsor: "Clinical psychologists in most places seem to be relegated to the role of diagnosticians and/or researchers. Few places give them opportunity or training in therapy. This seems reprehensible."

The University of Manitoba: "Increasingly the clinical psychologist is employed in settings where opportunities are provided for psychodiagnosis, psychotherapy, training and research. At the present time the single largest amount of time would be devoted to psychodiagnosis, though during the last three to four years there has been a distinct broadening of professional role."

Brandon College, Brandon, Manitoba: "From my observations at the .... Hospital, I am of the opinion that the psychologists employed ... are very restricted in function. They employ two people they designate as psychologists. One of these has completed a B.A., the other has completed a B.A. Honors General Course, and neither of them has had any graduate training in either psychology or clinical psychology. One of them has attended sessions in projective techniques and testing procedures on an observer basis since his academic record was inadequate to permit him to register for credit. The other one has had no training beyond the Honors level at the University of Manitoba. In terms of functions these two psychologists are engaged entirely in the job of administering and scoring tests. They do not participate in staff training or research or similar activities, and are not involved in actual psychotherapy. One other individual who holds a B.A. degree is in charge of research. His training included three courses in psychology during his B.A. work, and he has had three months in statistical seminar. The nature of his research is something I have not yet been able to determine. I do believe, however, that the superintendent of the hospital would be very cooperative and give a wider range of possible activities to a better trained psychologist than he now has on staff. There is the problem however that salaries at the hospital are much too low to attract anyone with advanced training."

University of Saskatchewan, Saskatoon, Sask.: "Clinical Psychologists here in the Province appear to aim in one of two directions. First, there are a number who devote their time to routine clinical activities. Second, there are those who engage in full-time research. For those who work clinically the main function is psychodiagnosis. A few clinicians are doing group psychotherapy and play therapy. Very little individual psychotherapy is practised."

University of Saskatchewan Regina Campus: "All psychologists employed in clinical work in the province are employees of the Psychiatric Services Branch and thus come under the classification laid out in the enclosed job specifications."

The University of British Columbia, Vancouver:

"In past years some of our students, after receiving the M.A., have been employed as Grade 1 psychologists in the Provincial mental health facilities. The level of qualifications for employment has generally increased in these settings and a few Ph.D.s are already to be found on their staffs. The Psychologists in these settings are usually employed in diagnostic work, but those who show a special talent for communicating with patients have been encouraged to participate and improve their skills in group psychotherapeutic techniques."

Victoria College: "In our practice, we receive both diagnostic and therapy referrals from the local psychiatrists and general practitioners and . . . have staff consultant status at the local hospitals, where we maintain offices approximately one half-day each week. Our department has four grants for research on clinical-related problems."

PROFESSIONAL LEGISLATION

Legislation providing for the certification and registration of qualified psychologists now exists in the provinces of Quebec, Ontario, Saskatchewan, and Alberta. The details of such legislation need not be set down here. The main purpose of the acts is to limit the use of the term "psychologist" to persons with specified academic and professional qualifications.

Nova Scotia respondents report that the Association of Psychologists of Nova Scotia was recently established and will offer non-statutory certification for clinical psychologists—the requirement being a doctoral degree in psychology, at least two years experience, one of which must be under satisfactory supervision, and the passing of an examination set by a Board of Examiners.

This from Quebec: To become a member of the Corporation of Psychologists of the Province of Quebec (incorporated in 1962), one must have at least a licentiate or master's degree recognized by the Council of the Corporation. There are now about 140 members, and the number is increasing regularly and rapidly.

In Ontario two hundred psychologists are now registered under the Psychologists Registration Act (1960). Registrants must possess a Ph.D. degree and a minimum amount of professional experience. The status of the new Diploma offered by Queen's University has not yet been determined. Provincial government employees or University staff members, if employed as Psychologists, do not need to be registered under the Act to use the term "Psychologist"—their employers determining what qualifications they will accept. But, unless registered, such psychologists cannot accept fees for outside professional psychological work.

The Saskatchewan Act respecting the Profession of Psychology (passed April 14, 1962) defines psychologists in terms of the Ph.D. and places restrictions on the unqualified use of the terms psychological, psychologist.

The Psychological Association of Manitoba is contemplating the certification of psychologists, possibly providing for two levels of practice, one requiring a doctor's degree, the other a master's degree. This is in rough draft and has a long way to go before being accepted by all interested groups. The experience of other provinces is being studied, and the resulting legislation might follow that in Saskatchewan and Alberta.

Psychologists in British Columbia have recently attempted to formulate a certification and licensing Bill; but the local association (Vancouver) would not support the level of qualification proposed. Most members (mostly M.A.s) felt that an M.A. plus four years of experience was equivalent to a Ph.D. and one year of experience. Accordingly, the proposed Bill has been sent back to Committee for further consideration, and it will remain there for a while before a new proposal appears. It is unlikely to be presented to the legislature for another year or more.

PROFESSIONAL RELATIONS WITH MEDICINE

Most remarks addressed to this topic were to the effect that relationships between psychologists and psychiatrists, and other medical colleagues, were amiable and reflected mutual respect.

Dalhousie observed that clinical psychologists are responsible to clinical or hospital directors who are usually psychiatrists. The knowledge, concepts, methods, immediate objectives and responsibilities of clinical psychologists and practising psychiatrists tend to be quite different. This calls for continuing efforts to clarify the distinctions and to convey to psychiatrists the variety and the nature of the independent contributions which clinical psychologists can make to mental health services.

Acadia reported that, on the local scene, relations with psychiatry are extremely good, as there is a tendency for the psychiatrists to recognize the competence of psychologists to make satisfactory assessments of personality dynamics and to participate in therapy except in cases where medication or electro-shock is indicated. The tendency is definitely towards the team approach and the increasing use of family therapy rather than individual, and of shorter rather than long-term treatment, thus making possible the treatment of greater numbers. There is also a tendency for the psychiatrist, and to some extent the psychologists, to act as consultants to various other agencies such as Children's Aid societies, the N.S. Sanatorium, the County hospitals, and the schools. From the beginning, the relations of the staffs of Mental Health Clinics with the medical profession have been cordial; and most patients are referred by local medical practitioners.

The University of Montreal reports that psychiatrists are becoming more aware of the important services that psychologists can provide. But they still tend to look on psychology as an ancillary discipline and seek to preserve control over the most important psychological activities such as diagnosis and therapy. Undeniably, however, considerable progress is being made, and the importance of clinical psychology as a profession should keep on increasing as the universities develop a greater number of competent psychologists.

Toronto reports that "Relationships with both psychiatry and medicine in Ontario are excellent. There are very few clinical psychologists in private practice. Salaries are disastrously low. Thus, clinical psychologists represent no threat to psychiatrists either in private practice or in salaried positions. Relationships are excellent."

From *Queen's* comes the observation that the Psychology Department there has always had a very close and cordial working relationship with the Department of Psychiatry, and with other local psychiatrists. Many research projects are carried on jointly.

The University of Western Ontario avers that relationships with psychiatry and medicine in that setting are cordial. Staff and students have been, on a number of occasions, involved in research projects at the Medical school; and they are always welcome in the local hospitals and clinics. Psychologists take part in teaching psychiatrists in training and at Westminster Hospital psychiatric trainees are accepted as interns in the psychology department.

Alberta comments that the relationship with psychiatry and medicine is constructive and cooperative; and that the prevailing psychiatric orientation does not place the emphasis on psychoanalysis.

Assumption University: The relationship between psychiatry and psychology seems to emphasize a type of "team work" system, highly commendable, with mutual respect for each other's position.

Saskatchewan reports that psychiatry remains somewhat ambivalent towards clinical psychology. Most psychiatrists encourage psychodiagnostics; however, there are a few who prefer the clinical psychologists to devote themselves to full-time research. This minority tends to feel that the psychologist's function should not include clinical activities. Psychologists who engage in research tend to be fiercely independent in choice of research topics and at times this situation has resulted in some criticism by psychiatrists (at times open hostility). The climate in which the clinical psychologist functions seems to depend in a large measure on the background of the psychiatrist who heads the clinic.

Manitoba remarks that the prevailing psychiatric orientation is analytic, with increasing interest in behaviouristic psychology. By and large the relationship between psychiatry and psychology is an amicable one and there is no reason to think that this will not continue. Institutes on psychotherapy (Ellis, Bettleheim), learning theory (Mowrer), and research (Harlow) have been held including groups from psychology, psychiatry, and social work.

British Columbia says that relationships with psychiatry there seem favourable and in some ways there is probably more schism within psychiatry in B.C. than between clinical psychology and psychiatry ... "(thus) we shall have to "ride two horses" and avoid showing undue favor to either. Our relation with both factions seem to be as good as they can be under the circumstances." A note from *Victoria College* states that relationships are better than the correspondent has ever known elsewhere. "Three of our local psychiatrists help us teach our advanced psychopathology course. Two of our local M.D.s are research associates on our staff and two others are consultants on a project in brain damage. Many local medics attend our behaviour colloquium series. We receive more referrals from medics than we are able to handle, etc. I have heard that this happy situation does not exist in Vancouver."

STATUS, STAFF AND PAY PROBLEMS

The comment of a senior Dean at St. Francis Xavier University summarizes the picture reported across Canada: "One difficulty I have noted is the availability of trained clinical psychologists in Canada. I am afraid that salary levels for psychologists in community mental health centres and other government-related agencies is too low to attract competent people, especially those who have a doctor's degree. If this continues, the lower status of the psychologist in a mental health setting will continue unless we have a good supply of people who have training comparable to that of the psychiatrist."

Dalhousie reports that psychologists there are trying to get the Provincial Government to adopt a realistic salary scale for clinical psychologists . . . that it is difficult to convince them either of the value and hence price-tag of Ph.D. trained people, or of the realities of the supply and demand situation. These three points are made: (1) There are insufficient numbers of clinical psychologists to meet current needs in the area; approximately eight could be placed now. (2) There is a need for greater emphasis on experimental training for clinical psychologists. (3) The frame of reference, orientation, concepts, and skills of the clinical psychologist are inadequately known by other disciplines with which they work.

The University of Montreal reports that the profession of clinical psychology is taking increasing importance in the eye of the public and of parallel professions. The number of clinical psychologists is growing and, most important, their professional qualifications are improving. There remains the problem of facilitating the relationship with psychiatry, of improving the standing of the profession among other psychiatric services, and of raising the salaries offered the clinical psychologist.

From the *University of Toronto:* "There are no strengths to speak of except good quality of training. There is no market here for the product at anything beyond the minimal M.A. level of training. So after training and a few years of experience, nearly all the good clinical psychologists leave to enter other fields (e.g., schools, industry, research and teaching, etc.) or else leave for other places (like Minnesota)."

The *University of Western Ontario* sees the major problem as a shortage of trained people at senior levels, due, in part at least, to inadequate salary schedules. Employers are accepting too many people with only the M.A. degree; and if these do not have adequate supervision they may fail to develop what potentialities they have. The Registration Act is having the effect that a number of persons who were content with the M.A. degree are now seeking advanced training.

Saskatchewan comments that psychology has been slow to emphasize to the psychiatric profession its contents and methods. The result is that many psychiatrists' understanding of psychology is somewhat less than that found in an introductory course. The minor emphasis given to psychology in many

psychiatric training programmes seems to insure that the psychiatrist's perception of the psychologist will not extend beyond the administration of intelligence tests.

Alberta observes that the Province needs more clinical psychologists; and that one of the weaknesses in clinical psychology in Canada is the lack of a model for the training of clinicians and of a statement of the objectives of the area of clinical psychology.

British Columbia notes that standards of qualification are improving and a notable change in the numbers coming to Vancouver seeking employment with Ph.D. qualifications. But the greatest difficulties arise in finding appropriately salaried jobs for such persons. Standards of pay in the Provincial services ($6500.00) are not what they should be to hold a Ph.D. trained person. The point is repeated by *Victoria College*—thus: "Aside from the shortage of competent psychologists in Canada, which can only remedied by better graduate training, a major problem is salaries. Academic salaries for psychologists are respectable, but those for institutional psychologists are insulting. For example, the national average for a clinical psychologist with a Ph.D. (about $6500.000) is at least $2500.00 less than the *starting* salary for clinical Ph.D. in the U.S. Veterans Administration. We badly need two doctorate clinicians in Victoria, but the salary our provincial government is willing to pay is less than half the amount paid for a comparable man in a comparable situation 80 miles away in Washington State. This is a job of education for the C.P.A.

CONCLUDING COMMENTS

With this, I have pretty well emptied the net and sorted the catch. The information is general, statistics are lacking, and the implications are difficult to assess. Adhering strictly to the role of reporter, I would venture only the following general observations:

Clinical psychologists are employed in a variety of settings in Canada—in mental hospitals, psychiatric units, mental health clinics, private practice, social service, and industry. Many, in association with doctors and psychiatrists, are engaged in research studies supported by Federal-Provincial health research grants devoted to the prevention and treatment of mental illness. Many others in the various treatment centres, are engaged in psychodiagnostic testing, staff training, group and milieu psychotherapy, rehabilitation counselling and training. Others have administrative responsibilities for the planning or direction of clinical training and research programs. A small but increasing number are becoming involved in advisory, research, and administrative roles in forensic clinics, alcohol treatment and drug addiction centres, and penal institutions. The creation of several new Canadian universities, and the expansion of existing ones, is drawing many experienced and senior clinical psychologists onto the staffs of psychology teaching and research departments.

Legislation providing for the certification and registration of qualified psychologists now exists in the provinces of Quebec, Ontario, Saskatchewan and Alberta, and similar enactments may be expected in the remaining provinces. The main purpose of such legislation is to limit the use of the term "psychologist" to persons with specified academic and professional qualifications. A difficulty in bringing about these enactments has been the uncertainty among psychologists concerning the minimum academic criteria to be specified. The tendency is to aim at the Ph.D. as an ultimate requirement, while making reasonable interim provision for those with the M.A.

This issue reflects practical difficulties of an almost circular nature, which are not unique to Canadian psychology but are intensified by the proximity of the United States. The salaries offered to Canadian psychologists, especially in clinical fields, are not predicated on high qualifications.

There is, moreover, a serious and continuing shortage of competent clinical psychologists, aggravated by the fact that the experienced and highly qualified can command more compatible salaries in the United States. In these circumstances it is difficult to hit on the best strategy of bringing good salaries and high qualifications into line, while meeting the need for at least minimally trained personnel; and, until this is accomplished, Canadian psychologists cannot assuredly enjoy professional parity with medical, psychiatric, and other scientific colleagues.

In sum, it may be said that graduate training in clinical psychology in Canada is not lightly undertaken in any of the universities, and where it is offered it is academically thorough and scientifically oriented. The pattern of such training varies widely from those departments which emphasize the acquisition of clinical skills to those where the emphasis is on clinical research. Working relationships with doctors, psychiatrists, social workers, and others are notably good by virtue of the sound training given clinical psychologists and by the fact that their competence is grounded in psychodiagnostic and research fields rather than in analysis and therapy. Professional working conditions are becoming more varied and attractive by virtue of the premium being placed upon high qualifications and the underwriting of professional standards under the new certification and registration regulations being adopted by the various provinces.

44. *Clinical Psychology in Britain*

ARTHUR SUMMERFIELD

THE course of professional development in other countries may often be examined with advantage, as was suggested in the article on "Clinical Psychology in Britain" (2) which appeared in the *American Psychologist* this last year. Since this earlier article was based on the situation as it was in 1954, it may be of interest to American psychologists to see the pattern of events traced more fully up to date.

Clinical psychology in Britain is a postwar development. It has depended upon the farsightedness of a number of psychologists who were at work during and before the war. But when the war ended few psychologists were working in this field. In essentials the development of clinical psychology has therefore been that of a new field of application rather than the expansion of one which was already well established on a smaller scale. It has differed markedly in these respects from occupational, industrial, and educational psychology.

Two other factors have been influential. Its development has occurred (*a*) in a time of increasing demand for applied psychologists of all kinds; and *b*) almost entirely within the context of the National Health Service, brought into being on July 5, 1948 by the National Health Service Acts of 1946 and 1947. These environmental factors have therefore to be taken into account.

THE NATIONAL HEALTH SERVICE

To see where the clinical psychologist fits in, some conception of the National Health Service as a whole is needed (cf. 1). In administrative structure it is extensively decentralized. The Treasury exercises overall financial control. There are two

Reprinted from *American Psychologist*, 1958, *13*, 171–176, by permission of the American Psychological Association and the author. The "Addendum" was prepared by Professor Summerfield especially for this book. Professor Summerfield was General Secretary (1954–59) and President (1963–64) of the British Psychological Society and now is Professor of Psychology, University of London at Birkbeck College.

central authorities, the Ministry of Health (for England and Wales) and the Department of Health for Scotland. Their primary functions are general supervision and coordination of the three distinct systems of which the service is composed: (*a*) the welfare health services, like maternity care and child welfare, administered by local government authorities (county and county borough councils); (*b*) the general practitioner services administered through specially established local executive councils; and (*c*) the hospital service. It is in the last of these that nearly all clinical psychologists are employed.

The hospital service covers hospitals of all kinds and the clinics attached to them: general hospitals, teaching hospitals associated with medical schools, specialized hospitals, mental hospitals, and hospitals for the mentally defective. The decentralized organization is primarily regional. Within regions, groups of hospitals are administered together—a group in some cases being a single large hospital, in others covering several hospitals differing in size and function. Mental hospitals may be grouped with hospitals of other kinds, but have tended not to be. The teaching hospital groups occupy a distinct position. They have a special form of administration (Board of Governors) directly responsible to the central authority and not subject to regional supervision. At the same time a principle which was fundamental to the establishment of the regions was that the hospital services within each should be associated with at least one medical school and teaching hospital. There are 14 regions in England and Wales, including 4 metropolitan regions for the Greater London area with its high concentration of teaching hospitals, and 5 in Scotland. The South-west Metropolitan Region includes the only teaching hospital group for psychiatry and neurosurgery—the Bethlem Royal and Maudsley Hospitals Group in association with the Institute of Psychiatry of the University of London.

Administration within each region is at the two levels of Regional Hospital Board and Hospital Management Committees. Service on either of these kinds of body is honorary. Their members are

TABLE 1. SALARY SCALES FOR CLINICAL PSYCHOLOGISTS IN THE NATIONAL HEALTH SERVICE, 1952–1957

Grade	PTA 10 (1952)			PTA 18 (1953)			PTA 27 (1954)			PTA 39 (1956)		
	Entry to Grade	Annual Increment(s)[a]	Limit of Scale	Entry to Grade	Annual Increment(s)[a]	Limit of Scale	Entry to Grade	Annual Increment(s)[a]	Limit of Scale	Entry to Grade	Annual Increment(s)[a]	Limit of Scale
Psychologist[b] "Entry Grade"	£380	£25 (4)	£480	£415	£25 (4)	£515	£415	£35 (1) £50 (1)	£500	£550	£25 (4)	£650[c]
"Basic Grade" (at age 25)	£530	£25 (6) £30 (3)	£770	£565	£25 (2) £30 (3)	£805	£575	£30 (8) £25 (1)	£850	£700[d]	£30 (8) £35 (1)	£975
Senior Psychologist	£810	£40 (9)	£1,170	£845	£40 (4) £35 (4) £25 (1)	£1,170	£875	£40 (3) £35 (6)	£1,205	£1,000	£40 (7) £45 (1) £50 (1)	£1,375
Top Grade Psychologist[e]	£1,300	£75 (4)	£1,600	£1,300	£75 (4)	£1,600	£1,335	£75 (4)	£1,635	£1,500	£75 (4)	£1,800

[a] The figure in brackets after each amount is the number of such annual increments.

[b] The description and conditions attaching to this grade have changed several times; the terms "Entry grade" and "Basic grade" are not official terms (see text).

[c] Amended from £550–£25 (3)–£625 (PTA 39) to £550–£25 (4)–£650 by PTA 52 (1957).

[d] Appointments below age 25 are now envisaged with abatement of the salary on entry to the grade by £30 for each year below 25.

[e] The figures shown for entry to the Top Grade are minimum salaries, actual salaries are subject to upward adjustment in individual cases; the four increments of £75 are, however, fixed.

drawn locally from academic, professional, business, and other walks of life, as well as from the medical profession. Each Regional Hospital Board is responsible for the general planning and supervision of hospital services in its region and for the allocation of finances to the Hospital Management Committee in charge of each hospital group. Between them, these bodies are responsible for appointments. Senior medical appointments are made by the Regional Hospital Board. All other appointments are made by Hospital Management Committees. Hospital Management Committees are therefore the "employing authorities" for clinical psychologists.

Notable as an exception to the general pattern of decentralization are the national arrangements on salaries, qualifications, and conditions of service. They apply to all kinds of staff: medical, technical, nursing, clerical, and so on. The machinery for negotiating them is based on that developed in the Civil Service. There are nine negotiating bodies—Whitley Councils—for different groups of staff, and an additional general one. The "management side" of each council is composed of representatives of the central departments (Ministry of Health and Department of Health for Scotland), the Regional Hospital Boards, and the Boards of Governors of the Teaching Hospital Groups. The Association of Hospital Management Committees now also has one seat on each council. It was not at first so represented, in spite of the position of Hospital Management Committees as employers of all except senior medical staff. The "staff side" consists of representatives of staff organizations, trade unions, and professional associations. Agreements negotiated in the councils are published as official circulars. Clinical psychologists come under "Professional and Technical Whitley Council A," as do other non-medical, graduate scientists, e.g. physicists and biochemists. Agreements concerning these professional groups are included in the "PTA" series of official circulars.

CLINICAL PSYCHOLOGY IN THE NATIONAL HEALTH SERVICE

The first PTA Circular, No. 10, on the qualifications, conditions of service and promotion, and salaries of full-time clinical psychologists in Health Service was issued on February 7, 1952. There have been four others, Nos. 18 (February 28, 1953), 27 (February 16, 1954), 39 (July 24, 1956), and 52 (September 11, 1957). Additional circulars have been concerned with part-time appointments.

Table 1 shows the progressive changes in salaries specified in the five main circulars. The table also shows that from the beginning three major grades of clinical psychologist have been distinguished, with a subdivision into two of the "Psychologist" Grade. (Table 2 is included for comparison. It gives the general level of salaries paid to academic staffs of British universities, including psychologists, in 1952 and 1957). Salaries apart, it is in relation to appointments in the Psychologist Grade that the terms of the successive circulars have principally differed. Conditions of appointment in the senior grades have hardly changed at all.

The *Top Grade for special posts* has throughout applied "to a psychologist occupying a post of exceptional responsibility"; establishment of Top Grade posts has required the sanction of the central authority (Minister of Health or Secretary of State for Scotland, as heads of the respective departments), which has in this matter the advice of a small committee of psychologists. Subject to the sanction of the central authority, employing bodies (Hospital Management Committees) have been enabled to fix salaries at or above the prescribed minima. All Top Grade appointments are considered individually. "Exceptional responsibilities" are not defined; they might therefore be, for example, in practice, research, supervision and training, or some combination of these.

The *Senior Psychologist Grade* has all along been for posts of greater than usual responsibility; duties

TABLE 2. Salary Levels of University Teachers in 1952 and 1957

Grade of Appointment	1952			1957[a]		
Assistant Lecturer	£400	£50 (2)	£500	£700	£50 (3)	£850
Lecturer	£500	£50 (12)	£1,100	£900	£50 (9) £75 (4)	£1,650
Senior Lecturer and Reader	Varying maxima up to £1,600			Varying maxima up to £2,150		
Professor	£1,600 upwards			£2,300 maxima up to £3,000		

[a] Wightman (3).

"might or might not include supervision of other psychologists" (permitting appointments to be made in this grade also to posts whose responsibilities were other than supervisory in nature). It has always been considered that the supervisor of psychologists entering the service should be a Senior Psychologist.

The *Psychologist Grade* is the grade to which basic qualifications and training and conditions of entry relate directly. On this account it has been, and continues to be, the subject of the principal changes. In one way or another, it has from the start been divided into two categories. For convenience these categories have been distinguished in Table 1 by the unofficial terms "entry" and "basic" divisions of the Psychologist Grade, since the official usage has varied. It has been a basic premise that a clinical psychologist in the basic Psychologist Grade might work on his own in an independent appointment.

From the outset the conception of the requirements for appointment in this grade, in addition to a basic education in general psychology, has been the combination of a training in clinical psychology with actual experience of work in clinical psychology in the National Health Service or elsewhere. This broad conception with its twofold emphasis on training and experience commands the general support of psychologists and continues to prevail. At the same time, the sense in which it does so depends upon the way in which training and experience are themselves conceived. The developments of the past ten years in this connection are evidently fundamental and are next considered.

ENTRY TO THE NATIONAL HEALTH SERVICE AS A CLINICAL PSYCHOLOGIST

The definitions, gradings, salaries and conditions of service set out in this agreement are for psychologists holding an honors degree in psychology of a University of England, Wales, Scotland or Ireland, or such other qualification as may be approved by the Minister of Health or the Secretary of State for Scotland.

The basic statement of qualifications took this form in 1952 (PTA Circular 10), as it continues to do. A psychologist so qualified but lacking previous experience in clinical psychology could be appointed in the entry grade. The emphasis was on "inservice" training as the approach to specific training in clinical psychology.

In considering this approach, it is relevant to take account of the conditions prevailing at the inception of the National Health Service to which

reference has been made earlier. It is also to be considered that honors degrees in psychology, while not involving specific training in any field of application, nevertheless represent a high level of specialization in the subject. A counterpart of this is the tradition in all disciplines that higher degrees are awarded for research. Thus the PhD is awarded on the basis of an original research thesis; there is no advanced course work and no written examination. The same tradition attaches to master's degrees, but their award is sometimes dependent, wholly or in part, upon written and practical examinations. Postgraduate (i.e. graduate) diplomas and certificates have been the form of qualification awarded by universities in connection with courses involving actual practice, as well as instruction in underlying principles and research methods. It is also an established tradition that a person needs to have completed a proving period "on the job" before he can be reckoned fully competent for work in an applied field, however extensive his formal academic qualifications. Longer or shorter probationary periods, graduate apprenticeships, or terms of inservice experience under supervision are therefore customary in widely differing fields, e.g. engineering and technology as well as medicine.

During the past ten years, clinical psychology has come to show the influence of all these approaches:

1. Two institutions within the National Health Service have specialized in the inservice training of clinical psychologists: the Tavistock Clinic in London and the Department of Psychological Research at the Crichton Royal Institution in Scotland. Students taking these courses have already been admitted to the entry grade of National Health Service clinical psychologists. Inservice training is not, however, limited to these institutions, but may be given in any hospital.

2. Beginning in 1946, training in clinical psychology for honors graduates in psychology was developed in the Psychology Department of the University of London Institute of Psychiatry at the Maudsley Hospital. The course, extending over one year, was officially recognized by the university in 1950, since when a diploma has been awarded (the University of London Academic Postgraduate Diploma in Psychology, Section D, Abnormal Psychology). Students taking this course have been full-time, fee paying university students.

3. The Bethlem Royal and Maudsley Teaching Hospitals Group is, as mentioned earlier, in the Southwest Metropolitan Region of the National Health Service. Advantage has recently been taken of this relation for trial of an arrangement whereby

three clinical psychologists admitted to the entry grade within the region each year are seconded for their first year to the Maudsley Hospital to take the university diploma, while in the pay of the National Health Service. On successful completion of the course, they remain in the entry grade for a further period (normally a year) during which they work under the supervision of Senior Psychologists in the region.

4. Arrangements are currently being made to start a postgraduate course in clinical psychology by the Psychology Department of Edinburgh University, with the collaboration of other university departments and the Regional Hospital Board. It is expected that the first students will be enrolled in October 1958.

These developments have so far been reflected in a number of modifications to official arrangements. It was envisaged in 1952 (PTA Circular 10) that an honors graduate entering the National Health Service as an Assistant Psychologist might be "eligible to enter the grade of Psychologist" after "at least one year of training in clinical psychology, either under a Senior Psychologist or at a recognized training course, plus other appropriate experience"; he might, however, spend up to four years in the grade. In 1954 (PTA Circular 27) the grade of Assistant Psychologist ceased to be distinguished as the entry grade. Instead, the Psychologist Grade was divided into two parts, of which the first three years were to be a probationary period leading to a proficiency bar. To pass the bar into the basic part of the Psychologist Grade, the probationer was required to "obtain a certificate of proficiency from the employing authority." If he did not do so at the end of three years, he was entitled to two further reviews at six-months intervals. The "employing authority" for a clinical psychologist, as has been explained, is a Hospital Management Committee. Psychologists were fully alive to the difficulties potential in this arrangement, and recommendations to the Ministry of Health were made on the point by the British Psychological Society. In 1956 (PTA Circular 39, currently operative), the requirement of a certificate of proficiency from the employing authority was deleted, and the probationary period conceived as follows:

Before taking up an independent post in the National Health Service a psychologist shall normally have attained the age of twenty-five years and shall have satisfied one of the following conditions:

(*i*) He shall have served for three years under supervision and to the satisfaction of the employing authority.

(*ii*) He shall have taken an approved course of postgraduate training in clinical psychology for one year full-time followed by one additional year of full-time service, under supervision and to the satisfaction of the employing authority.

(*iii*) He shall have taken an approved course of postgraduate training of at least two years full-time. It shall be at the discretion of the employing authority whether or not he shall be required to serve under supervision for a period of one year.

It is specified that supervision is to be by a Senior or Top Grade Clinical Psychologist. The period of service under Conditions *i* and *ii* may be extended by one year at the discretion of the employing authority. A clinical psychologist who qualifies in one of these ways for reduction of his period of probationary service also qualifies for a corresponding increase in his starting salary, e.g., if he qualifies under Alternative *ii* for a reduction of two years, he starts at a salary two points above the minimum, that is at £600 per annum.

The original conception of "inservice" training has therefore been undergoing modification. The consensus of opinion among psychologists is that in clinical psychology, as in other fields of applied psychology, full competence is best achieved through the combination of postgraduate academic training followed by work under supervision on the job, with this period so organised as to give experience of all the principal kinds of work carried out. This view is not confined to psychologists, but is the direction in which current developments are moving. It is also fully appreciated that the profession needs, in addition, to receive a continuous input of research experience. In fact it has. The most recent development is an explicit recognition of this need. A higher degree now qualifies an entrant to the National Health Service for a higher starting salary. The latest agreement (PTA Circular 52) specifies that one annual increment of salary may be added to the starting salary for each year of postgraduate study "in preparation for a higher degree or as a research student" up to three years. These increments do not apply to time spent in postgraduate training in clinical psychology, the allowances for which have been described above, nor is the length of probationary service affected. An entrant who possesses both postgraduate training in clinical psychology and research experience does, of course, qualify for increments of salary on both counts, up to a maximum starting salary of £615, and for a reduced period of probationary service in view of his training. The advantages of higher degrees and research experience are thus recognised, while emphasis on adequate training and professional experience is retained.

The foregoing is an account of changes in formal agreements. In examining them and the

TABLE 3. SALARY SCALES FOR CLINICAL PSYCHOLOGISTS IN THE NATIONAL HEALTH SERVICE, 1958–1966

Grade	PTA 59 (1958)			PTA 72 (1959)			PTA 87 (1961)			PTA 101 (1963)		
	Entry to Grade	Annual Incre-ments*	Limit of Scale	Entry to Grade	Annual Incre-ments*	Limit of Scale	Entry to Grade	Annual Incre-ments*	Limit of Scale	Entry to Grade	Annual Incre-ments*	Limit of Scale
Psychologist "Entry Grade"	£580	(4)	£680	£580	(4)	£680	£625	(4)	£730	£650	(4)	£760
"Basic Grade"	£735	(9)	£1,025	£735	(9)	£1,050	£790	(9)	£1,100	£820	(9)	£1,145
Senior Psychologist	£1,050	(9)	£1,445	£1,025	(8)	£1,425	£1,100	(8)	£1,500	£1,145	(8)	£1,560
Principal Psychologist‡	—	—	—	£1,425	(5)	£1,725	£1,495	(5)	£1,810	£1,555	(5)	£1,880
Top Grade Psychologist	£1,575	(4)	£1,890	£1,775	(4)	£2,100	£1,865	(4)	£2,205	£1,940	(4)	£2,295

Grade	PTA 112 (1964)			PTA 121 (1965)			PTA 126 (1966)		
	Entry to Grade	Annual Increments*	Limit of Scale	Entry to Grade	Annual Increments*	Limit of Scale	Entry to Grade	Annual Increments*	Limit of Scale
Psychologist "Entry Grade"	£730†	(5)	£880	£752†	(5)	£906	£854†	(5)	£1,097
"Basic Grade"	£930	(9)	£1,300	£958	(9)	£1,339	£1,154	(9)	£1,563
Senior Psychologist	£1,325	(8)	£1,750	£1,365	(8)	£1,803	£1,604	(8)	£2,127
Principal Psychologist‡	£1,825	(7)	£2,325	£1,880	(7)	£2,395	£2,168	(7)	£2,820
Top Grade Psychologist	£2,400	(4)	£2,750	£2,472	(4)	£2,833	£2,914	(4)	£3,338

* Only the numbers of annual increments are given because they have usually not been equal in amount.
† For new entrants with 1st or 2nd class honours degrees £780 (1964), £803 (1965) and £926 (1966), followed by *three* annual increments in each case.
‡ The grade of Principal Psychologist was introduced for the first time in 1958.

salary scales they contain, it is also relevant to take account of promotion into the higher grades. The following is one example. An able clinical psychologist, now between 35 and 40, was awarded a PhD in 1950; in 1951 he was appointed into the Senior Psychologist Grade; and in 1957 promoted into the Top Grade. There are also other recent and more numerous cases of well trained and able people under 30 who have been appointed into the Senior Psychologist Grade.

The past decade has therefore seen a rapid growth of clinical psychology in Britain from small beginnings. Throughout this time there has been no lack of interest on the part of psychologists. The expanding body of clinical psychologists has continued to be keenly aware of its own problems of training and professional service and has maintained its search for ways of improving its standard of proficiency. In 1945 a group of members working as professional psychologists in the field of mental health was formed in the British Psychological Society. This group, which has so far been known as the society's Committee of Professional Psychologists (Mental Health), had 77 members at the end of 1945, of whom the great majority were educational psychologists working with children. It now has some 400 members, of whom over 100 are members of an Adult Section, formed in 1951, for clinical psychologists working with adult patients in the National Health Service. Subcommittees of these groups, in collaboration with others of the society's committees, are actively concerned in the formulation of policies for improving standards of qualification and proficiency and extending training facilities in the universities and elsewhere.

Psychologists in Britain have been vigorous in shaping their professional status. Training facilities are being extended and efforts made to extend them further. Higher degrees are encouraged. The structure of the psychological service is flexible, and adjustments have been made in response to new demands. Effective channels of communication have been established between those concerned with training and practice in clinical psychology, between employers and employees in the National Health Service, and between the British Psychological Society and the Ministry of Health. The past ten years have been years of progressive development, development which there is every reason to suppose will continue and increase.

NOTES

1. I am indebted to the Chairman, the Secretary, and other members of the committee of the Adult Section of the Committee of Professional Psychologists (Mental Health) of the British Psychological Society, and to the President and the Deputy President of the society, for valuable comments and suggestions.

ADDENDUM

The main changes which have taken place since the foregoing article was written at the end of 1957 are five. (*i*) There is now a larger number of approved courses of post-graduate training. (*ii*)

TABLE 4. SALARY LEVELS OF UNIVERSITY TEACHERS IN BRITAIN, 1966*

Grade of Appointment	Lower Limit	Annual Increments	Upper Limit
Assistant Lecturer	£1,105		
		£75 (1)	
		£80 (2)	
			£1,340
Lecturer	£1,470		
		£90 (6)	
		£85 (2)	
		£90 (5)	
			£2,630
Senior Lecturer and Reader	Varying maxima up to		£3,415
Professor	£3,570	Maxima up to	£4,990

* As from 1st April, 1966.

Some of these courses now lead to the award of a Master's Degree. (*iii*) A new grade of 'Principal Psychologist' was introduced in 1958. (*iv*) Since 1964, possession of a good honours degree (1st or 2nd class honours) on entry to the 'entry grade' has been recognized by the award of a salary which is two steps above the minimum for less well qualified entrants. (*v*) Salaries, of course, have risen generally.

APPROVED COURSES

Arrangements which were on trial or under consideration in 1957 have since been developed and new courses have been started. The arrangement between the University of London Institute of Psychiatry (at the Bethlem Royal and Maudsley Hospitals) and the Southwest Metropolitan Region of the National Health Service, which was on trial in 1957, has provided a model which has now been followed in new arrangements elsewhere. The list below gives the seven approved courses of post-graduate training in clinical psychology and the three additional courses approved for psychologists working in the National Health Service with children only, at 1st January, 1966. The university degrees or diplomas that are awarded in connection with some of the courses are also shown in the list.

1. Institute of Psychiatry (University of London). Maudsley Hospital, London, S.E.5.

   Two-year course: Master's Degree.
   One-year course: Academic Postgraduate Diploma in Psychology (Section D, Abnormal Psychology).

2. The Tavistock Clinic (Adult Department), London, W.1.
   Two-year course.

3. The University of Liverpool.
   Two-year course: Diploma in Applied Psychology (Clinical).

4. The Queen's University of Belfast, Northern Ireland.
   Two-year course: Master's Degree.

5. The University of Glasgow and Crichton Royal Hospital, Dumfries, Scotland.
   Joint two-year course: Diploma in Clinical Psychology.

6. The University of Edinburgh and the South Eastern (Scotland) Regional Hospital Board.
   Joint two-year course: Diploma in Clinical Psychology.

7. The University of Newcastle-upon-Tyne and Newcastle Regional Hospital Board.
   Joint two-year course: Diploma in Clinical Psychology.

   For work in the National Health Service with children only:

8. Department of Psychology, University College (University of London), London, W.C.1.
   One-year course: Academic Postgraduate Diploma in Psychology (Section B, Educational Psychology).

9. London Child Guidance Training Centre, 48, Cosway Street, London, N.W.1.
   One-year course.

10. The Tavistock Clinic (Department for Parents and Children), 2, Beaumont Street, London, W.1.
    One-year course.

The grade of 'Principal Psychologist' was introduced in 1958 between the grades of 'Senior Psychologist' and the 'Top Grade for special posts'. Admission to the 'Top Grade' continues to be restricted to posts of exceptional responsibility, and the published scale continues to be a minimum scale in this case. The new grade has therefore extended opportunities for promotion above the Senior Psychologist level. A Principal Psychologist is defined as 'a psychologist with considerable responsibilities and duties greater than the Senior Grade and who normally is in charge of psychological services at an institution'. Table 3 shows the salary scale of Principal Psychologists in relation to the scales for other grades, and the changes in the scales from 1958 to 1966 (cf. Table 1); current salary levels of academic staffs, including psychologists, of British Universities are again given for comparison in Table 4 (cf. Table 2).

REFERENCES

1. ACTON SOCIETY TRUST. *Hospitals and the state.* London: Acton Society Trust, 1955–57. 4 vols.
2. MAHER, B. A. Clinical psychology in Britain: A laboratory for the American psychologist. *Amer. Psychologist*, 1957, *12*, 147–150.
3. WIGHTMAN, W. A. University salaries, 1957. *Universities Rev.*, 1957, *30*, 26–29.

45. Psychological Training Facilities in Austria and West Germany

GEORGE F. J. LEHNER

THE Fulbright Act, also known as Public Law 584—79th Congress, is one of the most extensive of the programs which provide opportunities for foreign study, lecturing, and research. To enable psychologists better to utilize the advantages of this program for pursuit of their interests in Austria and Germany, traditional meccas for psychological hegiras, the writer, while on a Fulbright Research Grant to the University of Vienna for 1952–1953, collected information from visits and a questionnaire sent to universities in Austria and West Germany concerning such questions as the following:

1. Psychological personnel and their fields of specialization for instruction and research.
2. Admission and residence requirements for American students, including requirements for the doctorate.
3. Special training facilities, such as in clinical, for the pursuit of an applied specialty.
4. Miscellaneous information of possible value to exchange professors and students.

The data obtained are summarized in Table 1, 2 and 3. Questionnaires were mailed to 19 universities, with all but 4 supplying the requested information. Data for these four schools here presented were obtained from their catalogues, and are consequently less complete than those obtained from the questionnaire.

Table 1 presents the data from the three major universities in Austria—Vienna, Graz, and Innsbruck. Table 2 presents a similar summary for the major universities in West Germany, and Table 3 presents the data for the four universities which did not complete the questionnaire.

No elaborate analysis of these data is intended, but a few observations may be of interest. The total psychological staff for the 15 schools completing

Reprinted from *American Psychologist*, 1955, *10*, 79–82, by permission of the American Psychological Association and the author. Dr. Lehner is Professor of Psychology, University of California at Los Angeles.

the questionnaire is 88, of which 74 are at West German universities, 14 at the three Austrian universities, or an average of 6 psychologists per university. The total number of PhD candidates at these 15 schools in 1953 was 209, with 142 at the 11 West German universities, 67 at the Austrian universities, or an average number of 14 students per school. The staff-student ratio when taking total students in relation to total staff comes to 2.3 students per professor for all the schools, or 1.9 students per professor for the West German universities and 4.8 students per professor for the Austrian universities (with the 50 students at Vienna accounting for this higher ratio).

The areas of specialization listed for the 17 schools (here two of the schools not completing the questionnaire are included on the basis of areas listed in their catalogue) include 40 designations. The areas, and the frequency with which they were listed by the schools, are as follows: diagnosis, theory of tests, and test methods—10; genetic and developmental—9; social—8; characterology—6; perception and educational—each 5; personality, industrial, general, abnormal, applied, dynamic and psychoanalysis, and anthropological—each 4; clinical measurement and statistics—each 3; experimental, "unconscious," gestalt, cognition, criminal, "types," graphology, comparative, and adolescence —each 2; and vocational, language, sensation, physiological, theoretical, methodology, history, memory, and learning—each 1.

Following are a few general observations which may be of interest to professors and students contemplating study abroad.

The psychology department, or *Psychologisches Institute* as it is generally known, is usually related more closely to the philosophy department than in the United States, with corresponding expectation that students acquire background in such areas as theory of knowledge, logic, epistomology, etc. Philosophy as a minor is often obligatory.

The Austrian and German universities (as is

TABLE 1. AUSTRIAN UNIVERSITIES

University	Faculty	Areas of Department Specialization	Admission Requirements for American Students	Credit Given for Studies in U.S.A.	Requirements Residence for the PhD	Minimum No. of Units Required Per Semester	Clinical Training Facilities	Areas of Clinical Training	U.S. Psychological Journals Available	No. of PhD Candidates in 1953	Miscellaneous
Vienna Liebigg. 5	Prof. H. Rohracher, Prof. F. Kainz, Prof. S. Klimpfinger, Dr. W. Toman, Dr. L. Bolterauer, Dr. E. Mittenecker, Dr. H. Rittinger	Experimental, Personality, Measurements, Test methods, Vocational, Language, Unconscious, Developmental	2 years of college Latin	1–2 semesters for BA, 3–4 semesters for MA	8 semesters	15	Psychiatric clinic	Some clinical	Major journals	50	6 U.S. students of psychology; 15 units of philosophy required
Graz Universitaets-platz 2	Prof. F. Weinhandl, Dr. K. Birgele, Dr. F. Eichinger, Dr. E. Ticho	Gestalt, Character, Tests & methods, Types, Sensation, Perception, Developmental, Industrial	2 years of college Latin	Depends on individual case	8 semesters	15	None	None	Major journals	14	Philosophy required
Innsbruck Schoepfstr. 41	Prof. Th. Erismann, Dr. I. Kohler, Dr. P. Scheffler	General, Cognition, Perception, Philosophical, Educational	2 years of college Latin required for PhD	Depends on individual case	8 semesters— at least 2 sem. at Innsbruck	15	Psychiatric clinic	Some clinical	Major journals	3	1 U.S. student of psychology; *Thorough* study of philosophy required

TABLE 2. WEST GERMAN UNIVERSITIES

University	Faculty	Areas of Department Specialization	Admission Requirements for American Students	Credit Given for Studies in U.S.A.	Requirements Residence for the PhD	Minimum No. of Units Required Per Semester	Clinical Training Facilities	Areas of Clinical Training	U.S. Psychological Journals Available	No. of PhD Candidates in 1953	Miscellaneous
Bonn Am Hof 1	Prof. E. Rothacker Prof. Fervers Dr. Thomae Dr. Roters 3 instructors	Methods & theory Anthropological Clinical Personality Perception Educational Social	2 years of college	No credit for BA Possibly 2–3 semesters for MA	8 semesters	No regulation	City Health Department Board of Education	Child guidance	Some journals	28	
Berlin Freie Universitaet Gelferstr. 36	Prof. O. Kroh Prof. M. Schorn Dr. H. Maertin Dr. K. S. Sodhi 5 instructors	Developmental Educational Characterology Applied Social Experimental Perception Psychoanalysis	2 years of college	Depends on individual case	8 semesters— at least 2 sem. at Berlin	4	Institute for Psychological Research Youth clinic	Clinical Child guidance	Some journals	12	1 U.S. student of psychology U.S. students may obtain scholarships
Hamburg Bornplatz 2	Prof. C. Bondy Dr. M. Eberhardt Dr. Fritz Roessel Mrs. A. Hardesty 3 instructors	Developmental Adolescence Social Personality Dynamic Abnormal Tests Diagnostic	2 years of college Latin required	Depends on individual case	8 semesters	4	Board of Civil Service Examinations Nurseries Psychiatric clinic for adolescents	Vocational Diagnostic Child therapy Social work	Major journals	6	1 U.S. student of psychology Foreign student advisor available
Muenchen Geschwister- Scholl-Platz 1	Prof. Ph. Lersch Prof. M. Keilhacker Prof. A. Vetter Prof. F. Seifert Prof. A. Huth 5 instructors	General Educational Personality Unconscious Applied Comparative History	2 years of college Latin required for PhD	Depends on individual case	8 semesters— at least 3 sem. at Munich	12	6-week internships at youth centers	Child guidance Adolescents	Some journals	9	Munich has a psychotherapeutic institute specializing in clinical psychology
Mainz Saarstrasse	Prof. A. Wellek Dr. G. Muehle Dr. W. Beck Dr. W. Muehlmann 3 instructors	Gestalt Characterology Diagnostic Social Developmental Anthropological Statistical	2 years in college Latin required for PhD	1–2 semesters for BA (or BS) 4–5 semesters for MA	8 semesters— at least 3 sem. at Mainz	10	Neurological clinic	Clinical	Some journals	13	U.S. students may find part-time employment as teaching assistants (Lektoren)

Institution	Staff	Admission	Credit	Duration		Practical training	Fields	Journals		Remarks
Heidelberg Hauptstr. 126	Prof. J. Rudert Prof. W. Hellpach Prof. W. Witte Dr. R. Kirchhoff Mrs. Loofs-Rassow	Developmental Social Industrial Characterology Graphology	2 years of college	Depends on individual case	6 semesters	12	Neurological clinic Psychiatric clinic	Neurology	Major journals	18	3 U.S. students of psychology
Kiel Neue Universitaet	Prof. K. Mierke Dr. H. Wegener Dr. B. Wittlich	General Comparative Adolescence Abnormal	2 years of college —	Depends on individual case	8 semesters	12	4-week internships in nurseries, prisons, psychiatric clinics, etc.	Counseling Adolescents Vocational	None	10	
Freiburg/Br. Bertoldstr. 17	Prof. R. Heiss Prof. H. Bender Prof. H. Biaesch 4 instructors	General Abnormal Theoretical Industrial Test methods Graphology	2 years of college (applicants with high school diploma only may be admitted on probation)	Credit given for up to four terms at a U.S. university or college	8 semesters	8	Some practicum seminars; clinical facilities rather limited	Clinical Counseling	Major journals	6	1 U.S. student of psychology
Tuebingen Muenzgasse 11	Prof. E. Kretschmer Prof. H. Wenke Prof. R. Kienzle Prof. G. Pfähler 4 instructors	Clinical Abnormal Types Educational Genetic Industrial	2 years of college Latin required for PhD	Depends on individual case	7 semesters	4	6-week internships at psychiatric clinic and other institutions	Clinical Neurology Children	Major journals	5	U.S. Library with many U.S. textbooks in the Amerika Haus of Tuebingen
Erlangen Schloss Zimmer 48	Prof. E. Lichtenstein Dr. W. Arnold Dr. M. Lindner Dr. Flick	Social Applied Developmental Psychoanalysis Criminal	2 years of college	Credits evaluated by State Board of Education	8 semesters—at least 2 sem. at Erlangen	4	6-week internships at psychiatric clinic, Juvenile Court, Dept. of Employment	Clinical Vocational Adolescents	Some journals	5	
Wuerzburg	Dr. W. Revers Dr. W. Schraml Dr. K. Strunz Dr. M. Zillig Prof. V. v. Gebsattel	Social Characterology Psychoanalysis Statistics Developmental Clinical	2 years of college Latin required for PhD	Credits evaluated by State Board of Education	8 semesters—at least 2 sem. at Wuerzburg	4	Child guidance clinic	Children	Some journals	30	
Koeln Meister-Ekkehartstr. 11	Prof. U. Undeutsch Dr. M. Krudewig	Characterology Diagnostic Theory of tests Methodology Criminal	2 years of college	Depends on individual case	8 semesters—at least 2 sem. at Koeln	4	Some practical training within the Institute	Educational Criminal	*Psychological Abstracts* only	?	1 U.S. student of psychology Possibility of scholarships for U.S. students after first semester

generally true of European universities) adhere to the principle of *Academische Lernfreiheit*, leaving the student free to formulate his own program of study and research. Formal course requirements or an organized course program as we know these are at a minimum. Simply put, the student is expected to acquire, by means he judges most appropriate, a thorough knowledge of his major subject, with one or two "minors" in certain cases. This freedom is also reflected in the absence of any examination system similar to ours. In some instances a student might face no examination until the completion of eight semesters' work for the PhD, while some require a preliminary examination after five semesters and some have examinations immediately preceding or following the presentation of the dissertation.

The universities here listed offer no academic degrees corresponding to our BA or BS. Successful completion of an academic education leads to the PhD or, for certain psychologists, the *Diplompsychologe*, a certification degree available from a few universities. This latter degree is somewhat ambiguous: at some universities it can be acquired after six semesters and corresponds, roughly, to our MA; while at other institutions the residence requirements, at least, correspond to those for the PhD,

which is usually eight semesters. The main difference between the PhD and the *Diplom* appears to involve a more pragmatic and "service" emphasis for the latter with a somewhat narrower range of academic preparation.

The concept of "clinical" psychology as we know it hardly exists in Austria and Germany, and the psychologist, in contradistinction to the psychiatrist, is "nonclinical," although he engages in diagnosis, counseling, guidance, and even therapy, in schools, clinics, and hospitals, in a manner that makes his performance often similar, though without the descriptive label, to that of the clinical psychologist here. Facilities for training in clinical psychology are very limited.

Admission requirements for an American student usually are two years of college to match the preparation of entering students from the German *Gymnasium* or the Austrian *Mittelschule*. Evaluation of such American preparation is usually liberal and flexible provided the student can demonstrate adequate knowledge. Application for admission should be addressed to the dean of the *Philesophische Fakultaet* or to the director of the psychological institute. In the tables presented the first name listed is that of the director, and the address is that of the psychological institute.

TABLE 3. WEST GERMAN UNIVERSITIES

(Incomplete information only was available on these universities)

University	Faculty	Areas of Department Specialization in Psychology	Miscellaneous
Frankfurt A.M. Mertonstr. 17	Prof. E. Rausch Prof. Bappert Prof. Block	Perception Memory Cognition Applied Anthropology	Training facilities rather limited—Institute is part of Department of Natural Science
Goettingen Hoher Weg 15	Prof. v. Allesch Prof. Wilde Prof. E. Meyer Prof. Hische	Developmental Learning Anthropology Social Tests	Degree of certified psychologist after 6 semesters
Marburg Universitaetstrasse 7	Prof. H. Dueker		Degree of certified psychologist after 6 semesters—International vacation courses— 189 foreign students at University in 1953
Muenster Rosenstr. 9	Prof. W. Metzger		Degree of certified psychologist after 7 semesters

46. *Some Notes on Psychology in Germany*

STANLEY ZUCKERMAN

BECAUSE Germany figured prominently in the development of psychology until the "blackout" of free scientific thinking and intellectual inquiry that came with the advent of the Nazi era, it is timely to comment on the state of segments of the profession nine years after the overthrow of Hitler. These notes have special reference to clinical psychology which the writer had occasion to observe from September through December 1953 while a U.S. Specialist under the auspices of the Department of State International Educational Exchange Program. Serving in a consulting role to a state Social Welfare Ministry in the northwestern (British) zone of Germany, the writer had opportunity to make some observations in most of the West German Republic (including such key cities as Berlin, Hamburg, Munich, Bremen, Frankfurt, Cologne, Essen and Dusseldorf) which may be of interest to psychologists in America.

THE STATUS OF PSYCHOLOGY

Psychologists are relatively few in number for the present population of Western Germany by comparison with the United States. Not only are psychologists a small group but they are, moreover, quite limited in influence. This situation stems partly from the fact that the German public is by no means as accepting of the profession and its practitioners as is the American public. It is hard to avoid the feeling that psychology in Germany today does not venture far from the university and does not come nearly as close to the life of the average citizen as in America. Even within the university, psychology does not have the popularity or recognition as on the campus here. Despite important scientific contributions of individual German psychologists in the past, psychology still appears

Reprinted from "Some Notes on Psychology in Germany, 1953," *Journal of Clinical Psychology*, 1954, *10*, 353–357, by permission of the *Journal of Clinical Psychology* and the author. Dr. Zuckerman is Assistant Vice-President, Carter, Berlind, and Weill, Inc., New York.

to be struggling to establish itself in the universities as a discipline independent of philosophy.

HOW PSYCHOLOGISTS ARE UTILIZED

In non-academic positions in the fields of "applied psychology," not very many psychologists are employed though conditions may be somewhat different in the southern portion of Germany in which the American influence is greater. Taking hospitals as an example, the writer found psychiatrists, some of whom had at least been exposed to psychology, doing clinical testing. In the psychiatric ward for children in one of the better large general hospitals in the Rhineland, the staff psychiatrists and nurses—the latter without formal training in psychology—were doing clinical testing using measures of intelligence as well as projective techniques. Without questioning their intent or sincerity, it was obvious that these people were working at tasks which would more effectively have been done by psychologically trained clinicians. One statewide hospital's psychiatric ward for children was not atypical in having a psychiatric staff, but no psychologist. Similarly, the mental hospitals employ few psychologists to date. The writer visited a mammoth institution which serves more than five thousand mentally ill, defective and welfare cases. Though some of the psychiatric staff had psychological training, the one-man Psychology Department averred that psychological services are not much more plentiful even in smaller hospitals.

Just as physical damage to the cities is impressive even after rapid reconstruction, one cannot be in Germany for any length of time without noticing the large number of physically handicapped persons as an aftermath of the war. While a relatively high proportion of the population receives some form of benefits for war injuries or losses, there is no large separate agency with its network of hospitals and out-patient clinics corresponding to our Veterans Administration and employing many trained clinical and counseling psychologists.

Psychological services are conspicuously absent from the German schools with the possible exception of the elementary and secondary schools of Bavaria in the southern part of the country. For example, in the State of Northrhine Westphalia, with a population of 16,000,000 and with some 1,600,000 youngsters in school, not one psychologist was employed in the educational systems in his specialty to serve this large number of pupils. Notwithstanding, some 25,000 youngsters out of this total group have been segregated into schools for the retarded (*Hilfsschulen*). None of these youngsters has been tested by a school psychologist or adequately evaluated psychologically by American standards. Cain has observed recently in this connection that the schools are not fully aware of the potential values and hence are "not really interested in psychological services."[2] Though teachers are highly trained they are generally academically oriented, especially at the secondary school level. They seem geared to stressing achievement presumably at the expense of a deeper understanding of the individual pupil and his problems. Although large classes and over-crowded schools may be slightly extenuating factors, much work remains to be done and German school systems need real encouragement to stimulate their utilizing psychological services.

One quite encouraging trend was noted in the field of out-patient clinical services. It was especially heartening to find child guidance clinics in the American pattern being established and functioning in the cities of Bremerhaven, Bremen and Berlin, among others. The team-principle of collaboration between psychiatrist, psychologist and psychiatric social worker appeared to be accepted and applied in these settings. As team members, though doing some therapeutic work, psychologists were recognized in these clinics for their diagnostic contributions derived from both projective and objective techniques.

Psychologists play a very minor role in the German judicial process. Those psychologists who do serve the courts are called in ordinarily on a consulting basis from one of the university-affiliated "Psychological Institutes" in the country —most often to appraise the reliability of testimony. Judicial personnel have been less interested up to now in the offender than in the offense committed; consequently psychologists have been looked to less for information on the personality problems and motivations of offenders than for an evaluation of the credibility of testimony. However, some of the psychologists who work with the courts are trying to do an educational job to show what

psychological data can contribute towards diagnosis and treatment of the delinquent. Moreover, enlightened jurists and penal administrators throughout the country are calling for increasing attention to the psychological understanding of offenders.

There are few psychologists serving in their specialty in prisons and correctional institutions despite the size of the delinquency problem. Although a couple of psychologists are prison directors in the Rhineland, there were no more than three psychologists doing clinical work in penal settings in the large area not under exclusive American supervision. Of these, two psychologists serve as members of the diagnostic team in the rather progressive correctional system of the city of Hamburg, and one psychologist is working in a maximum-security prison in the western sector of Berlin. Psychologists also are employed in a few of the correctional homes for problem children and younger offenders. However, they are a small group numerically. In the fledgling probation and parole services now developing in the country, as yet psychologists have played little part.

Concerning private practice, a certain amount is being done. The writer visited with several practitioners who were university trained at the equivalent of our Master's or Ph.D. level. Such private clinical work seemed to be done on a referral basis from courts, welfare agencies, or physicians. The private work of these individuals was in addition to their regular academic jobs, however. Overall, the extent of this private practice is quite limited.

As for other settings, psychological services to industry are far more limited than in the United States. Such personnel with backgrounds in clinical psychology as have been employed are not being used as consultants utilizing a broad range of techniques to evaluate and select key employees, nor as staff counselors. Rather, they seem to be used primarily as handwriting analysts. Data on this point are somewhat limited, however.

One of the main employers of non-academic psychologists at present is the network of Labor Offices in Germany. Universities excepted, the largest single group of psychologists in the state of Northrhine-Westphalia was working as testers and to a lesser extent as vocational counselors in the district Labor Offices.

In the early stages of the last war, quite a few psychologists were utilized by the Armed Forces in service and research roles. Since postwar Germany has no regular military establishment but only a modest "police force," the psychologists formerly so engaged have found employment instead in such other settings as Youth Offices, Labor Offices and the Psychological Institutes.

THE FUNCTIONING OF THE CLINICIAN

Clinical psychologists are functioning primarily as testers employing a variety of individual and group instruments. On examining these materials, a colleague from the United States is likely to get the impression that their objective measuring instruments are somewhat "behind the times" and not as well standardized as those with which we are accustomed to working. Generally, there seemed to be less attention paid to the availability of large-scale norms in tests used in the field. In addition, there appeared to be a greater element of subjectivity in the scoring and interpretation of objective tests. This point was discussed with several German psychologists who stressed the fact that they tend to concentrate more on the reactions of the individual to the test situation and on qualitative performance and less on the objective test data than do their American counterparts.

In appraising personality, psychologists there lean fairly heavily on instruments of a projective nature, mostly of European origin. Among these, the *Sceno* Test, which is similar to our World Test, figures prominently. Interestingly, the Rorschach technique though widely used does not appear to be quite as generally employed as it is here. It was not clear just what theoretical basis or frame-of-reference underlay the use of the projective devices there, but they seem to be used to quite an extent in an empirical way. In some settings such American tests as the Thematic Apperception Test and the Symonds' Picture Story, as well as recent theoretical texts may be found despite the cost of these materials due to the limited purchasing power of the *Deutschmark*. However, little interest was evident in clinical settings visited in the questionnaire approach to the evaluation of personality.

Establishing the intelligence level and evaluating intellectual functioning is another well-defined area of operation. To aid in this, standardized tests of German origin are used as well as translations of American instruments. A version of the original Stanford has been available for some time, and there is considerable interest in a project currently under way at Hamburg to standardize German versions of the Wechsler-Bellevue and the Wechsler Intelligence Scale for Children.

Among clinicians in Germany, graphology is an interest that is often in evidence. This probably can be traced to the fact that a couple of training centers focused especially on graphology. While generally more sympathetically disposed than psychologists here, occasional discussions indicated practitioners today regard the analysis of handwriting as a revealing though still-to-be-proven tool among methods for evaluating personality.

Psychologists also are doing some therapy in Germany. Intensive counseling or therapeutic work appears to be done primarily in the newly-developed child guidance clinics and also in private practice. In one or two of the training schools for delinquents the psychologists are engaged in counseling that is limited by the pressure of work loads. To the rather limited extent that psychotherapy is done in Germany, the question as to which discipline—psychiatry, psychology or psychiatric social work—should do it has not arisen to the extent that it has here. This is partly an outgrowth of the fact that German psychologists working in the clinical field see their role largely as that of diagnosticians. Moreover, because of the small number of psychologists in applied clinical work, they are neither a professional nor a financial threat to their psychiatric colleagues. Incidentally, the psychotherapeutic principles and methods employed were not too clear-cut: clinicians seemed to favor eclectic approaches ranging from extremes of the directive to the non-directive.

Psychologists employed in vocational settings are engaged in some counseling of a relatively brief nature directed at helping clients to establish vocational objectives besides testing intelligence and aptitudes. Again, the heavy load of cases to be served undoubtedly affects the batteries of tests employed and the pace and nature of the counseling process.

FINAL OBSERVATIONS AND CONCLUSIONS

German education above the eighth grade is highly selective and a much smaller proportion of the population attends full time school beyond that level. College training is rigorous. Instruction is characteristically thorough academically, but there is a lack of attention to the rounding out of training of the young psychologist by affording practical experiences in settings related to his field of specialization. Evidently the universities still operate largely on the assumption that theirs is the realm of theoretical psychology and that the preparation of students to serve in applied settings like child guidance centers, hospitals and clinics is less within their sphere. As a result, there are few internship opportunities affording supervised training coupled with actual experience. The Psychological Institute of the University of Hamburg stands out among centers of its type in Germany in offering that sort of training. Though only several other corresponding units elsewhere in the country were visited, the Institute at Hamburg directed by Professor Bondy seemed to resemble American graduate training centers in clinical psychology most closely in method and spirit.

Some general conclusions present themselves in reviewing the observations and experiences of three months in Germany. Despite the writer's own restricted ability to make contact with German colleagues because of a language barrier, he was impressed by the caliber of the people working in psychology at the professional and the graduate student level. They are intelligent and intensely interested in their work. They were clearly quite devoted to their field and by no means preoccupied with financial return which affords them less in actual standard of living though their income in *Deutschmarks* corresponds roughly to the dollar income of psychologists in comparable positions in America. Those German psychologists who have been to the United States or England through some exchange program seemed generally quite sensitive to professional trends current in the United States and in the United Kingdom. While these ideas have not been invariably adopted, quite a few of the exchangees have been active disciples of the approaches they had had opportunity to observe. Ironically, some exchangees were serving to re-introduce concepts of modern dynamic psychology into a country in which such thinking was effectively eradicated under Hitler.

It was especially encouraging to see the concept of the team approach implemented with a reasonable degree of success in at least a few of the child guidance clinics. Not only is the team approach important as a method of operation, but it assumes special importance for Germany as it marks a departure from the more stratified, authoritarian pattern that has been so characteristic of the country as a whole. The pattern of collaborative effort of a group of specialists each contributing in his particular way to the understanding and re-educative work with the individual is one which will probably take considerable time to establish broadly there.

It was also heartening to find a sensitivity for a need for soundly standardized tests in Germany. While American tests have been "adapted" for use, there was genuine recognition of the fact that something better than make-shift applications to the German population are needed. Even more significant than this attitude toward the techniques, was a reawakened interest in the individual coupled with a greater concern for his needs and his problems. This interest is by no means confined to psychologists, but is shared by forward-looking administrators in the welfare, social services, youth activities and correctional fields.

One especially rich and enlightening experience stemmed from participating in a training seminar for workers in the child guidance field conducted by a British psychiatrist and psychiatric social worker. The discussion of basic concepts that took place served to underscore the differences that remain in the thinking of trained German professionals and a "pick-up" Anglo-American team of clinicians. However, we felt that we derived interesting insights in the interchange of ideas with our German counterparts. It is to be hoped that further exchange of our colleagues with workers in Germany—to allow for even more intensive collaboration and cross-fertilization of ideas—will be possible in the future.

NOTES

1. The courtesies of two other recent U.S. Specialists, Prof. Gisela Konokpa of the University of Minnesota and Dean Leo F. Cain of the San Francisco State College, in commenting on the manuscript are gratefully acknowledged.

2. Cain, Leo F. Personal communications, March 19, 1954.

47. *Clinical Psychology in Israel*

JOEL SHANAN AND AVRAHAM A. WEISS

IN this paper the brief history of clinical psychology in Israel, as well as its present professional status, will be surveyed and some of its major problems concerning future development will be discussed.

The rapid growth of psychiatry in Israel since the establishment of statehood in 1948 was accompanied, from its very beginning, by a growing awareness of the actual and potential contribution of clinical psychology. Today, there is not a single public institution, whether hospital or outpatient department, in this country without a psychological service of some sort. The need for such services is steadily growing, particularly in view of the strong trend in present-day Israel psychiatry towards a psychotherapeutic orientation and in view of the growing emphasis on training and research in psychiatry, in which psychologists take an increasing share. These needs are only partly met because of the lack of young competently trained clinical psychologists due to the fact that only as late as 1957 was a department of psychology established in the major academic institution of the country, the Hebrew University.

In spite of the difficulties arising from the absence of academic training facilities in the field of clinical psychology, its contribution to psychiatry has developed slowly but steadily. The number of clinical psychologists has grown through the addition of Israelis returning from their studies abroad —mostly in the United States, Switzerland, France, and the U.K. During the last few years, immigration, too, has brought a few trained clinical psychologists into the country. Today, about one third of approximately 170 members of the Israel Psycho-

logical Association are clinical psychologists, organized in the section of Clinical Psychology. Two thirds of approximately 50–60 clinical psychologists hold Ph.D. degrees, the remainder, M.A. degrees. An M.A. degree and approved clinical internship are the minimum requirements for membership in the clinical section of the I.P.A. At the time of this report, first attempts are being made at establishing academic groundwork at the graduate level for later clinical training. Considering the limitations in space, supervisory facilities, and availability of training funds, it will take a number of years before the requirements for fully trained clinicians can be filled by locally educated individuals. One of the dangers here, as well as abroad, lies in the possibility and temptation to interrupt academic studies before the completion of the Ph.D. to take up jobs readily available as personnel needs in the field are growing continually at a considerable pace.

By and large clinical psychologists in Israel are employed in salaried positions. While some of them are involved in part-time private practice of diagnostic testing, consulting, and psychotherapy, only a negligibly small number are in full time private practice.

The majority of clinical psychologists—about two thirds—is employed in Government clinics and psychiatric hospitals. They are involved in diagnostic psychological testing, in psychotherapy including group psychotherapy and group work, in counseling and supervisory work. While basically most of them are psychoanalytically oriented, too few have been given an opportunity during the last decade to become fully trained lay analysts and members of the Israel Psychoanalytic Society. In view of the pressing service needs in the various government institutions, relatively little time is apportioned to clinical psychologists for research and in-job training. The remaining third of clinical psychologists work for the Worker's Sick Fund, Youth Aliya, the Army and for academic institutions such as University departments and the Hadassah-Hebrew University Hospital and the

Reprinted from *Israel Annals of Psychiatry*, 1961, *1*, 107–111, by permission of the *Israel Annals of Psychiatry* and Dr. Shanan. Dr. Shanan is Chief Psychologist and Senior Lecturer, Department of Psychiatry, Hadassa University Hospital, and Department of Psychology, The Hebrew University, Jerusalem, Israel. Dr. Weiss is Chief Psychologist and Senior Clinical Lecturer in Clinical Psychology, Talbieh Psychiatric Hospital, and Department of Neurology, Hebrew University-Hadassah Hospital, Jerusalem, Israel. The "Addendum" was prepared for this book.

"Talbieh" Psychiatric Hospital, affiliated to the Hadassah-Hebrew University Medical School. During the past few years, a growing interest has been observed on the part of the municipalities to integrate clinical psychologists gradually into the educational and health services. This may reflect a growing tendency on the part of educators to view the physical and intellectual development of the child in the light of his personality adjustment and his social adaptation. Some practical problems of teaching—particularly immigrant children—have drawn attention to the weaknesses of principles and methods which disregard the intimate relationship between development of thought processes and psychosexual development or personality function. The potential contribution of clinical psychology to the understanding of the process and methods of education may be seen in its emphasis on an approach to child behavior as a manifestation of a dynamic entity. An increasing impact of such trends is also felt in Government agencies dealing with education and educational research, personnel assessment, and vocational guidance.

With the establishment of the Department of Psychology in the Hebrew University and the even more recent inauguration of psychology departments at Bar Ilan University, Ramat Gan, and at the Tel-Aviv University, clinical psychologists are slowly becoming integrated into academic activity. There is a good number of signs justifying the hope that the status of clinical psychology in the universities of this country will be different from that in American and European universities. This seems indicated in view of the special research and service needs of this country, as well as the special and unique setting here, in which Israel's potential contribution to psychological research at large may be easily identified.

But even while working outside an academic framework, and under the pressure of service without appropriate funds and facilities, the research contribution of Israeli clinical psychologists is not negligible. It comprises about two thirds of all studies published by Israeli psychologists. Most of the studies are published abroad: in the United States, Switzerland, France, the UK, in South American journals, in Rumania, and in Yugoslavia.

Some of the work of clinical psychologists has been published in Israel medical and educational journals. Topics deal mostly with psychopathology, diagnostic testing, case studies and problems of psychotherapy. During the last five years, the number of fairly well controlled empirical studies, sometimes using quite sophisticated designs, has grown.

The time seems ripe now for experimental work proper in the field, for thorough and sophisticated multidisciplinary case studies, and last, but not least, for some serious efforts at obtaining broad normative information on the tests used and on the patient-populations to be evaluated.

All this requires funds and manpower in the field. For the latter there is now more hope than there was ten years ago. Regarding funds, it may be noted with some satisfaction that during the last five years a growing interest in clinical psychology in Israel has been shown on the part of foreign institutions such as NIMH, the Foundation Fund for Psychiatry and others as evidenced by research funds granted to Israeli clinical psychologists.

It is apparent that the function of the clinical psychologist within psychiatric settings is becoming more and more complex. This is reflected also in his position within the psychiatric team. The psychologist has become an integral part of such teams and participates in all phases of teamwork, be it diagnostic evaluation, therapy or research, and in many places shares responsibility for management with psychiatrists, social workers and other members of the team on an equal footing. In many instances, clinical psychologists serve as a convenient bridge in research between psychiatrists and other medical and nonmedical professions.

However, the developments which have been surveyed raise a number of questions for which solutions will have to be sought during the coming years. First and foremost, there is the problem of training. It is only natural that the recently established departments of psychology are still in search of a formula for adequate integration in their programs of those courses necessary for the development of attitudes and the acquisition of information basic for the prospective clinical psychologist. It will be one of the major tasks of the several university departments to find a *balance* of courses and seminars at *both* the undergraduate and, particularly, at the graduate levels, which will provide a broad basic education in the traditional fields of psychological theory and experimental methods—without which no modern clinician can do—and which will *at the same time* afford the student the opportunity to acquire the attitudes and information necessary for the absorption of specialized knowledge, skill and techniques, without which he could hardly start his internship in clinical psychology where his education is to be completed.

On the whole, it does not seem desirable at this point—particularly in view of the size of the country and its limited academic manpower in the field of psychology—to push in the direction of specialized degrees on the MA level (and certainly not at the BA level). On the other hand, the groundwork in terms of analysis of special theoretical issues and some didactic acquaintance with applied problems and techniques should be provided for. The final stage of specialization is to be placed in the period of clinical internship and in the field of interest developed in the doctoral dissertation. In other words, once the university has contributed its part, clinical training and experience within the clinic and hospital will have to carry the burden. In order to fulfil this task, a number of arrangements will have to be made in the training institutions: 1) to ensure an adequate amount and quality of supervision in diagnostic work and psychotherapy; 2) to provide some—however small—opportunity for the clinical intern to acquire a critically searching attitude by participation and training in clinical research; 3) it will also be necessary to provide opportunities for experience with patients of different types of pathology and of different age groups.

While this is not the place to discuss in detail the desiderata of a clinical training program, it should be obvious that the development and implementation of such a program will require recognition on the part of the training institutions that the psychological intern is primarily to be considered a student and not a professional worker on a low level of professional proficiency and a low level salary.

Experience abroad shows quite clearly that it is quality and amount of supervision and the opportunity to become deeply interested in the human and professional problems arising in clinical work which foster the good clinician and not the sheer quantity of Rorschachs administered, patients seen, or the number of hours spent as research assistant. It will be necessary to ensure close relationships between the training institutions and the university for which the student works on his degree, on the one hand, and between the Israel Psychological Association on the other hand, in order to set standards of clinical training from the start and to commit the training institutions to safeguarding these standards. In the course of time it will be an important responsibility of the university to provide opportunity for in-job training through summer courses and workshops and the like for those clinical psychologists who, due to their heavy service duties, did not have sufficient opportunity to keep up with scientific progress in the field. As in nearly all other countries, it will be the responsibility of the government to provide adequate funds to carry out training and research in the field of clinical psychology as an important branch of the scientific and professional effort to meet the community's growing needs and problems in the field of mental health.

The absorption of immigrants and their integration into the economy and culture of the country is clearly one of the major tasks of present-day Israel's polysegmental society. Widespread differences exist in this society in terms of educational background, value and work orientation, in techniques of socialization, and in the structure and function of family. Last but not least there exist considerable differences in dealing with the emotional aspects of life problems. In the process of absorbing immigrants problems of medical, psychological, and social pathology, as well as problems of education, of vocational adjustment, and of transition to democratic citizenship have been identified by those working day by day in close contact with immigrants. The pressure of service needs and the novelty of the problems imply the danger of an either oversimplified approach or the uncritical use of techniques and application of theories developed in different settings.

As other problems may certainly be expected to arise in the future course of the process of cultural change, clinical psychology along with other branches of psychology and other social and medical sciences will be faced with two major tasks:

1) to provide through creative, painstaking and stubborn research effort, the techniques and means to meet known problems in their new context in Israel, to identify new problems as such, and to find new ways of solving them.

2) to prepare clinical psychologists equipped with the specific skills, knowledge and attitudes required to extend the best possible service to all members of the community, whether in the hospital, clinic, or in educational–vocational field.

In the specific circumstances under which psychology has developed in Israel, there is a reasonable chance of avoiding such historic dichotomies as 'academic' vs. 'applied', 'experimental' vs. 'clinical', etc. There is a chance and a commitment to approach tasks of research, education, and service constructively. The process of cultural change provides settings for research which are quite unique for the investigation of such topics as individuation and socialization, the relationship between personality and culture, the problem of child development in cooperative settlements, and others. The question of the relative weight of cultural and social factors in the development and manifestations of psychopathology is another area for which the present Israel society may well serve as a natural laboratory. A well-planned utilization of these settings in multifaceted research, focused on the individual, yet amenable to generalization may well hold the promise for contributing to basic scientific issues beyond providing answers to the immediate needs of the community.

ADDENDUM

Since this survey was written, further and rather rapid developments have taken place. In the Department of Psychology of the Hebrew University, Jerusalem, a full two-year program in clinical psychology leading to a Master's degree was established. The program includes courses and seminars on theory, applied aspects and special seminars on research in clinical psychology as well as practicum units on diagnostic and therapeutic activities. Similar developments begin to take place at the Bar Ilan and Tel Aviv universities.

The number of clinical psychologists in Israel has increased by about 25 per cent as Israeli students, having completed their Ph.D. training, returned from abroad and some of our first students at the Hebrew University graduated.

The clinical section of the Psychological Association has developed an intensive program of internship and post-internship specialization, and is working now on licensing requirements.

Such Internship and Post-Internship program was implemented at the Department of Psychiatry of the Hebrew University–Hadassah Hospital. Some major universities in the US consider this program as equivalent to APA programs, and they allowed students to take their internship here in part fulfilment of their Ph.D. requirements.

Research in the field is expanding. The biannual reports of the Hebrew University on research in medicine and the social sciences may be viewed as an index reflecting the momentum clinical psychological research is gaining in the country.

Finally, large scale efforts are made by the Ministry of Education to introduce counseling psychologists into the educational system. A program for the promotion of counseling psychology has been initiated at the Hebrew University and the other universities, and enjoys Government support.

48. Soviet Mental Health Facilities and Psychology

HENRY P. DAVID AND TEMA S. DAVID

DURING the summer of 1960 we had a unique opportunity to visit mental health facilities in the Soviet Union and discuss practices and programs in that country.

We drove into the Soviet Union in our own car, crossing the Polish-Russian border at Brest, and proceeding via Minsk, Smolensk, Moscow, Kalinin, Novgorod, and Leningrad. Most of the time we were without official guide or interpreter, traveling a pre-arranged route, but free to go as we wished within cities. There were many opportunities to meet colleagues in the mental health professions, all of whom were gracious hosts and seemed as interested as we in exchanging information on common problems.

It has often been said that there are no experts on the Soviet Union, only degrees of ignorance. And so, our notes must be clearly labeled for what they are: impressions from a two week's whirlwind visit to a vast country so very different from our own that it becomes exceedingly difficult at times to make any sort of judgment.

While in Moscow, the State Committee for Cultural Relations with Foreign Countries arranged a trip to Kashenko Mental Hospital, one of the largest Soviet psychiatric centers, with 2,500 beds and a staff of 2,300. Of 160 physicians, 91 are qualified psychiatrists, most of them women. Patient care is in the hands of nurses; there are no psychiatric aides. Everything considered, the patient-staff ratio appeared more favorable at Kashenko than in New Jersey State hospitals (with whose facilities we are most familiar).

Admissions to Kashenko are about 10-12,000 per year, of whom approximately 90 per cent are readmissions. We were told that within a year's

Reprinted from Raymond A. Bauer (Ed.), *Some Views on Soviet Psychology* (Washington, D.C.: The American Psychological Association, 1962), 87–98, by permission of the American Psychological Association and the authors. Dr. David is Associate Director, International Research Institute, American Institutes for Research, Washington, D.C. Tema S. David is Mrs. Henry P. David.

time about 80 per cent of the patients go home, 1.7 per cent die, and 18.3 per cent remain in the hospital. As in New Jersey, emphasis is on early release with limited concern about the readmission rate.

In a sense, the mental hospital's setting was similar to that found in a general hospital. Patients were in pajamas and the staff in white. Doors were locked; instead of bars the curtained windows had special safety glass. The building was old and might well be considered substandard in New Jersey. However, the atmosphere was warm, cheerful, and homelike, with nurses and physicians obviously caring about the patients. Accommodations for children were especially attractive, including school rooms, a small zoo, and a garden tended by the patients.

The total hospital budget was about 40 million rubles, or about $10 million at the 1960 official rate and $4 million at the 1960 tourist rate. Per diem costs, at the tourist rate, are about $4.10, including $.80 for food. (New Jersey's per diem is $.83; the Veterans Administration per diem is $11.43.) Put another way, the cost of maintaining a patient in a Soviet mental hospital is about one and a half times the average income of Soviet workers. Patients are not required to participate in housekeeping chores or in the physical maintenance of the institution. All staff members, from director on down, receive a 15 per cent bonus for working with mental patients and 30 per cent if assigned to the children's unit. Nurses work on a 12 hours on and 48 hours off schedule, and enjoy an annual paid vacation of 36 working days (48 days on the children's service). Nursing is a coveted profession and there is no recruitment problem.

In Leningrad, we visited the Bekhterev Institute of Neurology and Psychiatry, a facility comparable to the National Institute of Mental Health Clinical Center in Bethesda. There are numerous in- and out-patient sections, with admission largely determined by teaching and research interests. Typical of the excellent staffing pattern is the 45-bed children's unit, with its chief physician and four full time assistants plus 12 nurses (five on each shift). Working hours, bonus pay, vacation schedule, etc., are identical with that noted in Moscow. There were an even number of boys and girls, ages seven to sixteen, and our hosts expressed surprise when told that in New Jersey we need about four times as many facilities for boys as for girls. Again, the atmosphere was warm and cheerful, and everyone we met seemed genuinely fond of the children.

In discussing Soviet mental health facilities with various hosts throughout our travels, we gained the impression that the overall picture is one of excellent care but limited resources to meet the country's needs. General hospitals have priority over mental hospitals. We were informed that for the 208 million Soviet population, there are currently about 130,000 beds and 4,500 psychiatrists, which is a rough ratio of about 1 psychiatrist per 28 patients. (For 175 million Americans there are about 750,000 state hospital beds and 3,000 psychiatrists, or 1 per 250 patients.) It may be more meaningful to note that the U.S.S.R. has more physicians than the United States, but only half the number of psychiatrists. We were told the number is rising. The largest Soviet mental hospital has 3,000 beds, and, as in New Jersey, current emphasis is on smaller units.

About 70 per cent of all psychiatrists are women, most of whom received six years of medical school training after graduating from high school, followed by two or three years as general physicians and a year's training in adult and child psychiatry. It was surprising to learn that the medical school curriculum apparently has no courses in psychological theory. The Soviet Ministry of Health is responsible for the hiring and training of all physicians; and personnel are assigned on the basis of regional needs and priorities. Beginning State salaries for professionals are about the same as those for skilled factory workers.

Within the facilities we visited, the basic orientation in psychiatry was organic. The view was widely expressed that the primary cause of most mental illness, especially schizophrenia, was probably organic and that, in time, research would provide the evidence. It was also postulated that organic changes may occur without psychotic components, which suggests that organicity may not be the sole basis for psychoses, and that environmental stresses function as a trigger mechanism. Neuroses are attributed largely to a faulty environment (school, family, etc.) and so the environment is changed. There appears to be less reluctance in the Soviet Union to hospitalize neurotic patients, but hospital authorities can refuse admission if they disagree with the diagnosis.

In discussing psychotherapy, we quickly learned that Freudian notions are still officially taboo; however, a type of brief, supportive "re-educational counselling" is employed in efforts to alleviate neurotic symptoms. While the possibility of psychogenic disorders is acknowledged, there are only infrequent attempts to delve into childhood experiences or family influences. Although Freud was not unknown in the Soviet Union, and a Psychoanalytic Society did exist in the 1930's, psychoanalysis is presently considered unscientific, non-experimental, idealistic, and a potential source of political reaction. While there seems to be general agreement that the problems explored by Freud are important, it is usually held that unconscious motivation should be considered in Pavlovian terms. Emphasis is focused on external influences and social environment, not on instinctual drives and anxieties. It should be noted, however, that Freud's volumes, in several translations and editions, are available in the Lenin Library and in psychological centers, and English-language publications are reviewed in Soviet journals. We were told that courses on psychotherapy are given to physicians in the main hospitals of each of the Soviet republics, and that pertinent books are received in training and research centers.

It should be recalled that Pavlov's views, pointing to a physiological rather than psychological basis of disorders, are particularly acceptable to Marxian materialism because they stress the physiological and rational (which fits the Marxian notion of man responsible for his behavior). Freud, on the other hand, emphasized the psychological and irrational. Soviet psychiatry thus endeavors to localize events in the brain, not in the mind. It is frequently held that behind every human action there is a definite physiological occurrence, effecting a state of excitation or inhibition in the brain. Therapy consists largely of drugs, insulin, sleep, and conservative use of electric shock. Pavlov, incidentally, was a Professor of Psychopharmacology before he obtained fame as a psychologist.

We saw little evidence of anything approaching a team concept. Qualified physicians seem plentiful in supply and they do all therapy. Clinical psychologists generally limit their activities to testing for organic involvement, and related research. There were no trained psychiatric social workers, in the American sense. We were told that there is less need for social workers in the institution since State agencies are responsible for housing, employment, rehabilitation, etc., and see to it that the individual's and the family's needs are met, both on hospitalization and on return of the patient. If a child is a ward of the State or placed in a special school, official agencies assume all responsibility.

The most recently established research section of the Bekhterev Institute is concerned with alcoholism, long a social phenomenon in Russian history. We were told that it has lessened somewhat since the Revolution, but there is no attempt to play down its severity. Although there is no Soviet counterpart of Alcoholics Anonymous, much interest was expressed in American efforts to cope with this common problem.

One of our objectives was to explore Soviet facilities for emotionally disturbed children. This term has no equivalent in Russian and it was difficult to convey to our hosts, psychiatrists or psychologists, just what we had in mind.[2] We only began to be understood when we indicated what some of our problems were in New Jersey and asked how similar cases might be approached in the Soviet Union. It appears that when little Ivan gets into trouble in school, the situation is handled by committee. There is a Mothers' Committee in school, a Tenants' Committee in the housing project, a Workers' Committee at the factory, etc. What is bothering Ivan is seemingly of less concern than how to stop him from bothering others and upsetting school routine. There is no organized system of child guidance clinics. A youngster who does not readily fit into an accepted social pattern is considered either an educational or medical problem. If educational, the school and the committees focus on "re-education," and teachers are expected to handle the problem. If considered medical, the child is referred to his local polyclinic where all of his medical records since birth are filed. (There is no choice of agency or physician.) A psychiatrist may then prescribe physical treatment, including drugs, or send the youngster to a hospital or boarding school. Unfortunately, we had no opportunity to explore the Soviet system of child rearing, the effects of crammed housing quarters, sexual mores, etc., all of which may have to be considered in attempts to understand little Ivan's emotional problem.

When we inquired about juvenile delinquency, we again made little progress until we discussed New Jersey problems and asked how similar children might be helped in the Soviet Union. It seems that juvenile delinquency is now reluctantly accepted as a fact of Soviet life, a by-product of increased industrialization and better times. But, there is an equal insistence that the problem is not as severe as in the West. It had been hoped that the Soviet system of collectives, Young Pioneers, Komsomols, etc., would keep youngsters well-organized and reduce the stimuli for delinquent behavior. Yet, one of the chief justifications for the educational reforms and the work-study program seems to be that it will discourage "hooliganism, stylism, and delinquency." Research on juvenile delinquents and their families has been initiated in the Pedagogical Institute, and appears to be directed both toward an understanding of the individual and toward an effort to learn how social group pressures can be employed more effectively. We were frequently told that horror comics and films are not permitted in the Soviet Union.

Assuming that, in fact, the U.S.S.R. does have a lower rate of juvenile delinquency than most other industrial countries, the real question may well be how much of this is due to up-bringing, as reflected in the individual character, and how much to contemporary conditions, such as organized social pressure or lack of stimuli, or both. There was general agreement that shifting family values and instabilities may be involved and that juvenile delinquency could provide a unique opportunity for cross-cultural research on a problem plaguing all societies. Later we learned that despite their interest there may be little hope of actually obtaining the cooperation of Soviet colleagues in social research. Such problems are considered the responsibility of society (the State and the Party), and not the province of psychology. Thus there is little social psychology in the traditional sense; those concerned with social issues tend to work not in psychology, but in the Academy of Philosophy and its subsection on Social History and Dialectical Materialism. The evaluation of group functions, the collective, and Soviet social experiments is considered the prerogative of the Communist Party.

During our stay in Moscow, Professor A. R. Luria escorted us on a brief tour through the very impressive Moscow University (where we later visited A. N. Sokolov's well-equipped laboratory) and also arranged an interview with the Head of the Section on Mental Retardation of the Institute of Defectology, one of eight institutes organized under the auspices of the Academy of Pedagogical Science. (Another is the Institute of Psychology, headed by Professor A. A. Smirnov, whom we also visited.) Professor A. N. Leontiev directs the Psychology Department of the Academy of Pedagogical Science. Professor Luria is a member of the Presidium of the Academy, teaches at Moscow University, and has a good deal to do with directing the work of the Institute for Defectology. He has described his experimental approach and theories in numerous publications over the past 40 years.

At the Institute of Defectology (center for the

scientific study of handicapped children), much emphasis is placed on hearing tests. We were told that approximately 30 per cent of allegedly mentally retarded children in fact suffer from deafness and are not actually retarded. Luria has observed that only one-half of one per cent of any age group falls into the defective category: "All other children can handle the curriculum." Those who cannot be rehabilitated or trained are institutionalized. (As in most States, there appears to be a shortage of beds.) During our visit to the Institute, we learned, among other things, that Soviet colleagues do not agree with our distinction between "educable" and "trainable" and that they, too, have difficulty differentiating between mentally retarded and schizophrenic children (although both handicaps are considered organic in origin). Schools for the retarded are headed by teachers trained in defectology; classes have about 12 to 15 students. There is a shortage of teachers and evening seminars have been developed to provide additional training. "Difficult" retarded children are considered medical problems and are housed in special institutions. Unfortunately, there was no opportunity to visit any of these centers.

Much has been said and written about Soviet psychology and its adherence to Pavlovian concepts of higher nervous activity and Marxist philosophy of dialectical materialism. On his 1960 visit to this country, Professor Luria defined Soviet psychology as the "science of voluntary behavior in man." Current research focuses on Pavlov's second signal system, involving aspects of physiology, conditioning, and speech in relation to problem solving. Much of the work done in Soviet psychological laboratories would be labelled physiological in the United States. However, "speech" is not regarded as purely motor or verbal; it includes culturally derived meanings and concepts. Although Russian psychology also emphasizes the importance of social interaction in man's historical development, we did not learn of any empirical studies in this field. As noted earlier, social psychology is usually considered the prerogative of the Party.

The Soviet Psychological Society has 1,800 members (compared to a membership of over 18,000 in the American Psychological Association). Basic undergraduate training requires about five years, with heavy emphasis on biological sciences, but little concern with statistics. A graduate student may work for several years in a university or institute laboratory, and after completing a thesis, attain the rank of Candidate, considered equivalent to a Ph.D. According to Professor Luria, about 250 Candidate degrees are awarded annually (100 in Moscow, 100 in Leningrad, and 50 elsewhere). A Doctor of Science degree may be awarded later for independent scientific research and is considered equivalent to our Associate Professor rank. We were told that 70 per cent of the graduate students read English and that major interest is in brain-neurological and educational-developmental areas. A Candidate receives about 2,500 rubles per month, or 250 dollars at the 1960 tourist rate and 625 dollars at the official rate.

The Institute of Psychology of the Academy of Pedagogical Science was established in 1912 and its current Director, Professor A. A. Smirnov, was one of the first students. It now has a staff of 118, including 72 scientific workers. There are laboratories in the traditional areas of experimental psychology plus growing interest in child development, teaching methods, and aspects of work. About 15 per cent of all Soviet graduate students in psychology are at the Institute. Current journals published by the American Psychological Association were on display in the Institute Library, and recently published American books were among new acquisitions listed on the bulletin board. Perusal of the catalog suggested an excellent collection of pre-1935 English-language publications, followed by a considerable gap until post-World War II editions. Freud's works were available in Russian, German, and English.

The Soviet psychological laboratories we visited were often located in old and cramped quarters reminiscent of our basement shops in American universities. They were, however, usually well-equipped, especially with conditioning and EEG recording apparatus. As Yvonne Brackbill later told us, about half of the human subjects are children, and there is frequently a waiting list of children whose parents want them to live for a while in pediatric research centers. Emphasis is on the experimental method, with an avowed goal of eventually applying research findings to practical field situations.

At the American Psychological Association 1960 Convention Roundtable, other visitors to the Soviet Union indicated their esteem for the work reported. Professor Neal Miller noted that the term "conditioning" is used synonymously with "learning" at all levels of complication, from classical conditioning to naturally learned responses, such as a rabbit eating a carrot thrust at him. It was also observed that despite the high level of Soviet mathematics, much psychological research is in the Helmholtzian tradition of replicating studies, using a minimum of statistics. A good deal of work is reported in the *Pavlov Journal of Higher Nervous*

Activity (authors are paid for articles), now available in English translation. Particularly noteworthy was the substantial financial support for researchers and their assistants, which permits long-term planning and provides cohesion for a productive group. Since the State is the sole employer and salary levels are fairly standard throughout the U.S.S.R., there apparently is little shopping for better positions once a satisfactory setting has been attained.

Soviet clinical psychology also follows a Pavlovian orientation, which means that major interest is usually focused on studies of pathological changes in the higher nervous processes believed to lie behind disturbances in psychic activities. Dean of Soviet clinical psychologists is Madame B. V. Zeigarnik, well-known in the United States for her earlier work with Lewin. She teaches psychopathology at the University of Moscow and heads the Clinical Psychology Laboratory at the Institute of Psychiatry, affiliated with the Academy of Medical Science. She was away while we were in Moscow, but we were told that her main interests are in evaluating pathological thinking and emotion in childhood schizophrenia. There are about 70 clinical psychologists in Soviet psychiatric centers. Many of them are concerned with "personality," which is considered to have a biological basis, with development depending on social environmental factors. Different types of temperament are believed to be products of different types of higher nervous activity, measured by physiological indices of brain processes.

Psychological tests were severely criticized in 1931, and condemned in a 1936 Communist Party resolution as unscientific, detrimental to public education, and "in conflict both with dialectical materialism and the practical experience of Soviet society." The I.Q. concept was rejected on the grounds that it allegedly reflects only innate intelligence and inherited abilities. We were told that one of the Russian objections to standard American tests is that "different children can achieve the same results in quite different ways." It is held that tests yield limited information about the process of problem solving considered so important for training.

There are indications that some form of psychological assessment is used. Yvonne Brackbill, for instance, was told on her visit to the Institute for Defectology that children suspected of mental retardation are asked to classify pictures, draw proper conclusions, match colors and forms, and describe a story shown in pictures. While there are no published norms, psychological examiners are expected to make clinical judgments on the basis of their experience.

Projective techniques are known and we were told that the Rorschach is used as a diagnostic aid in the evaluation of brain function. However, there is little interest in psychodynamics. As one Soviet psychologist put it, "We are not so much interested in probing man's depths as in understanding the heights he can attain."

Soviet colleagues asked many questions about our work in New Jersey and about psychological testing. We usually replied that the tests of 1960 were not those of 1936, and that considerable effort was continually going into research studies designed to improve reliability and validity of new devices helpful in education and industry, areas of general interest for the current Soviet seven-year plan. Many Soviet psychologists were exceedingly well-informed about American experimental studies. This is in part due to the journal, *Problems of Psychology*, which began publication in 1955. A recent issue reported on major psychological conferences held outside the Soviet Union, surveyed foreign literature received in Moscow's scientific libraries, and published an annotated bibliography of new acquisitions in psychology from abroad. An English language edition is published in Great Britain by Pergamon Press, under the sponsorship of the British Psychological Society.

Soviet mental health facilities and psychology are inevitably related to Soviet life. And, perhaps the outstanding fact of Soviet life is that it is planned. There appear to be fairly clear notions of desirable behavior, and a large network of institutional machinery has been created to attain these goals. Parent education, nursing schools, young pioneer programs, and other vast organizations that touch the varied life stages of most Soviet citizens have identical objectives and tend to operate on the same principles, supported by press, TV, and related mass media. It was especially interesting for us to observe the extent to which Soviet colleagues participate in this planning. For example, psychological research is instrumental to better pedagogical work, and psychologists in responsible positions in the Academy of Pedagogical Science play major roles in determining teaching methods.

As has been noted by visiting social scientists, another striking aspect of Soviet life is the uniformity throughout the whole society or collective. Norms are apparently generally accepted and there is much social pressure toward conformity. Thus any person can anticipate with some accuracy what others will notice and accept or reject. It may well be that this circumstance is at least partially responsible for the puritanism in Russian behavior and attitudes (especially toward sex) that was reported to us by several local observers. It should be added that the standards themselves, e.g. hard work, devotion to duty, cleanliness, orderliness, no public manifestations of sexual interest, are not considered uniquely Russian or communist; rather, it is held that such standards must be adhered to if one wishes to avoid public censure and maintain his standing as an accepted member of the collective.

Soviet colleagues believe that since an individual is so largely a product of his social environment, it is up to all those with some responsibility for his development to assure a correct social environment with the right stimuli to shape the right habits. In terms of Pavlovian learning theory, the right habits are continuously reinforced throughout life by the example of others and through group pressures. Thus in Soviet mental health practice, there is little interest in probing for psychodynamics or fostering insight. Rather, the Soviet approach seems intent on strengthening the positive, that is, those aspects of the person that are unimpaired, diverting a strong motive into constructive channels and main-

taining the social role of the collective, the State.

In reflecting on our trip, and comparing it with previous European travels in other years, it seemed to us that our Soviet experience in many ways was the most intellectually exhausting yet stimulating venture we have ever undertaken. No book or TV series can possibly portray the dynamism of Soviet life. It must be seen and personally experienced in all its paradoxical perplexities. We concluded that while there may be a gulf in our theoretical approaches, there is commonality in our empirical search for a better way to resolve human problems. Today, more than ever, there are impelling reasons for exchanging students, specialists, and tourists, and thus perhaps enhancing understanding between East and West.

NOTES

1. We wish to acknowledge the generous support of the Social Science Research Council, whose travel grant under-wrote a portion of our expenses, and the editorial encouragement of the New Jersey Welfare Reporter, in whose pages these comments first appeared.
2. The Russian term for "emotionally disturbed children" is "nervous children."

BIBLIOGRAPHY

BOGUSLAVSKY, G. W. Psychological research in Soviet education. *Science, 125*, 915–918, 1957. *Psychol. Abstr.*, 5833, 1957.

BONDARENKO, P. P. and RABINOVICH, M. KH. Scientific inference on the problems of the ideological struggle with contemporary Freudism. *Vop. Filos., 13*, 164–170, 1959. *Psychol. Abstr.*, 2383, 1960.

CAMMER, LEONARD M. Conditioning and psychiatric theory. *Amer. J. Orthopsychiat., 31*, 810–819, 1961.

CHAUNCEY, HENRY. Some notes on education and psychology in the Soviet Union. *Amer. Psychologist, 14*, 307–312, 1959.

DAVID, HENRY P. Report on Bonn and Moscow. *J. Proj. Techn., 25*, 282–286, 1961.

FEDOTOV, D. The Soviet view of psychoanalysis. *Monthly Review*, Dec. 1957.

FIELD, MARK. Approaches to mental illness in Soviet society: some comparisons and conjectures. *Soc. Prob., 7*, 277–297, 1960.

KERBIKOV, O. V. The teaching of psychiatry in the U.S.S.R. Geneva: *WHO Pub. Health Pap.*, No. 9, 159–167, 1961.

KLEIN, R. H. A visit to the P. P. Kashenko Mental Hospital. *World Ment. Health, 10*, 182–191, 1958, Mental Hospitals, 1958.

KLINE, NATHAN S. The organization of psychiatric care and psychiatric research in the U.S.S.R. *Annals, N.Y. Acad. of Sci., 81*, 149–224, 1960.

KLUMBNER, GEORGE M. Child psychiatry facilities in Moscow, Russia. *Amer. J. Psychiat., 116*, 1087–1090, 1960.

KUBIE, LAWRENCE S. Pavlov, Freud, & Soviet Psychiatry. *Behav. Sci., 4*, 29–34, 1959.

LEBEDINSKI, M. S. Psychotherapy in the Soviet Union. *Gp. Psychother., 13*, 170–172, 1960.

LURIA, A. R. Psychopathological research in the U.S.S.R. In Simon, B. (Ed.) *Psychology in the Soviet Union*, Stanford, Cal. Stanford Univ. Press, 279–287, 1957.

MURRAY, HENRY A., MAY, MARK A., and CANTRIL, HADLEY. Some glimpses of Soviet psychology. *Amer. Psychologist*, *14*, 303–307, 1959.

O'CONNOR, N. Russian psychology, 1959. *Bull. Brit. Psychol.*, 502, 1960.

O'CONNOR, N. (Ed.). Recent Soviet psychology. N.Y.: Pergamon Press, 1960.

PIAGET, JEAN. Some impressions of a visit to Soviet psychologists. *Newsletter, International Union of Scientific Psychology*, *1*, 13–16, 1956. *Amer. Psychologist*, *11*, 343–345, 1956.

POPOV, E. A. On the application of I. P. Pavlov's theory to the field of psychiatry. *Zh. Nerropat. Psikhiat.*, *57*, 673–680. 1957. *Psychol. Abstr.*, 2332, 1960.

RAZRAN, GREGORY. Recent Russian psychology: 1950–56. *Contemp. Psychol.*, *2*, 93–101, 1957.

RAZRAN, GREGORY. Psychology in Communist countries other than the U.S.S.R. *Amer. Psychologist*, *13*, 177–178, 1958.

RAZRAN, GREGORY. Soviet psychology and psychophysiology. *Beh. Sci.*, 1959, *4*, 35–48.

RAZRAN, GREGORY. The observable unconscious and the inferable conscious in current Soviet psychophysiology: interoceptive conditioning, semantic conditioning, and the orienting reflex. *Psychol. Rev.*, *68*, 81–147, 1961.

SIMON, BRIAN (Ed.). Psychology in the Soviet Union. Stanford, Cal.: Stanford Univ. Press, 1957.

SMIRNOV, A. A. The tasks of psychology in the light of the decisions of XXI Congress of the Communist Party of the Soviet Union. Vop. Psikhol., *5*(5), 7–28, 1959. *Psychol. Abstr.*, 6828, 1960.

TIZARD, JACK. Children in the U.S.S.R.: work on mental and physical handicaps. *Lancet*, No. 7060, Dec. 20, 1958.

WINN, RALPH B. (Ed.). Soviet psychology. NY: Philosophical Libr., 1961.

WINN, RALPH B. (Ed.). Psychotherapy in the Soviet Union. NY: Philosophical Libr., 1961.

WORTIS, JOSEPH. A psychiatric study tour of the U.S.S.R. *J. Ment. Sci.*, *107*, 119–156, 1961.

ZIFERSTEIN, ISIDORE. Dynamic psychotherapy in the Soviet Union. *Gp. Psychother.*, *14*, 221–233, 1961.

VI
GENERAL
INFORMATION

Of the many articles that might have been included in this part, we present "Ethical Standards of Psychologists" and "The Meaning of the ABEPP Diploma." Both of these articles have significantly advanced psychology as a profession and are important for the understanding of clinical psychology today.

The reader should also be aware of resource materials in the *American Psychologist*, which are revised annually: "APA-Approved Doctoral Programs in Clinical and in Counseling Psychology" (January issue), "Internships for Doctoral Training in Clinical Psychology Approved by the American Psychological Association" (October issue), and "Educational Facilities and Financial Assistance for Graduate Students in Psychology" (January issue). These resource articles are authored by Dr. Sherman Ross, who is Executive Secretary, Education and Training Board, American Psychological Association.

49. *Ethical Standards of Psychologists*

AMERICAN PSYCHOLOGICAL ASSOCIATION

THE psychologist believes in the dignity and worth of the individual human being. He is committed to increasing man's understanding of himself and others. While pursuing this endeavor, he protects the welfare of any person who may seek his service or of any subject, human or animal, that may be the object of his study. He does not use his professional position or relationships, nor does he knowingly permit his own services to be used by others, for purposes inconsistent with these values. While demanding for himself freedom of inquiry and communication, he accepts the responsibility this freedom confers: for competence where he claims it, for objectivity in the report of his findings, and for consideration of the best interests of his colleagues and of society.

SPECIFIC PRINCIPLES

PRINCIPLE 1. RESPONSIBILITY

The psychologist,[1] committed to increasing man's understanding of man, places high value on objectivity and integrity, and maintains the highest standards in the services he offers.

a. As a scientist, the psychologist believes that society will be best served when he investigates where his judgment indicates investigation is needed; he plans his research in such a way as to minimize the possibility that his findings will be misleading; and he publishes full reports of his work, never discarding without explanation data which may modify the interpretation of results.

b. As a teacher, the psychologist recognizes his primary obligation to help others acquire knowledge and skill, and to maintain high standards of scholarship.

c. As a practitioner, the psychologist knows that he bears a heavy social responsibility because his work may touch intimately the lives of others.

Reprinted from *American Psychologist*, 1963, *18*, 56–60, by permission of the American Psychological Association.

PRINCIPLE 2. COMPETENCE

The maintenance of high standards of professional competence is a responsibility shared by all psychologists, in the interest of the public and of the profession as a whole.

a. Psychologists discourage the practice of psychology by unqualified persons and assist the public in identifying psychologists competent to give dependable professional service. When a psychologist or a person identifying himself as a psychologist violates ethical standards, psychologists who know firsthand of such activities attempt to rectify the situation. When such a situation cannot be dealt with informally, it is called to the attention of the appropriate local, state, or national committee on professional ethics, standards, and practices.

b. The psychologist recognizes the boundaries of his competence and the limitations of his techniques and does not offer services or use techniques that fail to meet professional standards established in particular fields. The psychologist who engages in practice assists his client in obtaining professional help for all important aspects of his problem that fall outside the boundaries of his own competence. This principle requires, for example, that provision be made for the diagnosis and treatment of relevant medical problems and for referral to or consultation with other specialists.

c. The psychologist in clinical work recognizes that his effectiveness depends in good part upon his ability to maintain sound interpersonal relations, that temporary or more enduring aberrations in his own personality may interfere with this ability or distort his appraisals of others. There he refrains from undertaking any activity in which his personal problems are likely to result in inferior professional services or harm to a client; or, if he is already engaged in such an activity when he becomes aware of his personal problems, he seeks competent professional assistance to determine whether he should continue or terminate his services to his client.

PRINCIPLE 3. MORAL AND LEGAL STANDARDS

The psychologist in the practice of his profession shows sensible regard for the social codes and moral expectations of the community in which he works, recognizing that violations of accepted moral and legal standards on his part may involve his clients, students, or colleagues in damaging personal conflicts, and impugn his own name and the reputation of his profession.

PRINCIPLE 4. MISREPRESENTATION

The psychologist avoids misrepresentation of his own professional qualifications, affiliations, and purposes, and those of the institutions and organizations with which he is associated.

a. A psychologist does not claim either directly or by implication professional qualifications that differ from his actual qualifications, nor does he misrepresent his affiliation with any institution, organization, or individual, nor lead others to assume he has affiliations that he does not have. The psychologist is responsible for correcting others who misrepresent his professional qualifications or affiliations.
b. The psychologist does not misrepresent an institution or organization with which he is affiliated by ascribing to it characteristics that it does not have.
c. A psychologist does not use his affiliation with the American Psychological Association or its Divisions for purposes that are not consonant with the stated purposes of the Association.
d. A psychologist does not associate himself with or permit his name to be used in connection with any services or products in such a way as to misrepresent them, the degree of his responsibility for them, or the nature of his affiliation.

PRINCIPLE 5. PUBLIC STATEMENTS

Modesty, scientific caution, and due regard for the limits of present knowledge characterize all statements of psychologists who supply information to the public, either directly or indirectly.

a. Psychologists who interpret the science of psychology or the services of psychologists to clients or to the general public have an obligation to report fairly and accurately. Exaggeration, sensationalism, superficiality, and other kinds of misrepresentation are avoided.
b. When information about psychological procedures and techniques is given, care is taken to indicate that they should be used only by persons adequately trained in their use.
c. A psychologist who engages in radio or television activities does not participate in commercial announcements recommending purchase or use of a product.

PRINCIPLE 6. CONFIDENTIALITY

Safeguarding information about an individual that has been obtained by the psychologist in the course of his teaching, practice, or investigation is a primary obligation of the psychologist. Such information is not communicated to others unless certain important conditions are met.

a. Information received in confidence is revealed only after most careful deliberation and when there is clear and imminent danger to an individual or to society, and then only to appropriate professional workers or public authorities.
b. Information obtained in clinical or consulting relationships, or evaluative data concerning children, students, employees, and others are discussed only for professional purposes and only with persons clearly concerned with the case. Written and oral reports should present only data germane to the purposes of the evaluation; every effort should be made to avoid undue invasion of privacy.
c. Clinical and other case materials are used in classroom teaching and writing only when the identity of the persons involved is adequately disguised.
d. The confidentiality of professional communications about individuals is maintained. Only when the originator and other persons involved give their express permission is a confidential professional communication shown to the individual concerned. The psychologist is responsible for informing the client of the limits of the confidentiality.
e. Only after explicit permission has been granted is the identity of research subjects published. When data have been published without permission for identification, the psychologist assumes responsibility for adequately disguising their sources.
f. The psychologist makes provision for the maintenance of confidentiality in the preservation and ultimate disposition of confidential records.

PRINCIPLE 7. CLIENT WELFARE

The psychologist respects the integrity and protects the welfare of the person or group with whom he is working.

a. The psychologist in industry, education, and other situations in which conflicts of interest may arise among various parties, as between management and labor, or between the client and employer of the psychologist, defines for himself the nature and direction of his loyalties and responsibilities and keeps all parties concerned informed of these commitments.
b. When there is a conflict among professional workers, the psychologist is concerned primarily with the welfare of any client involved and only secondarily with the interest of his own professional group.
c. The psychologist attempts to terminate a clinical or consulting relationship when it is reasonably clear to the psychologist that the client is not benefiting from it.

d. The psychologist who asks that an individual reveal personal information in the course of interviewing, testing, or evaluation, or who allows such information to be divulged to him, does so only after making certain that the responsible person is fully aware of the purposes of the interview, testing, or evaluation and of the ways in which the information may be used.

e. In cases involving referral, the responsibility of the psychologist for the welfare of the client continues until this responsibility is assumed by the professional person to whom the client is referred or until the relationship with the psychologist making the referral has been terminated by mutual agreement. In situations where referral, consultation, or other changes in the conditions of the treatment are indicated and the client refuses referral, the psychologist carefully weighs the possible harm to the client, to himself, and to his profession that might ensue from continuing the relationship.

f. The psychologist who requires the taking of psychological tests for didactic, classification, or research purposes protects the examinees by insuring that the tests and test results are used in a professional manner.

g. When potentially disturbing subject matter is presented to students, it is discussed objectively, and efforts are made to handle constructively any difficulties that arise.

h. Care must be taken to insure an appropriate setting for clinical work to protect both client and psychologist from actual or imputed harm and the profession from censure.

PRINCIPLE 8. CLIENT RELATIONSHIP

The psychologist informs his prospective client of the important aspects of the potential relationship that might affect the client's decision to enter the relationship.

a. Aspects of the relationship likely to affect the client's decision include the recording of an interview, the use of interview material for training purposes, and observation of an interview by other persons.

b. When the client is not competent to evaluate the situation (as in the case of a child), the person responsible for the client is informed of the circumstances which may influence the relationship.

c. The psychologist does not normally enter into a professional relationship with members of his own family, intimate friends, close associates, or others whose welfare might be jeopardized by such a dual relationship.

PRINCIPLE 9. IMPERSONAL SERVICES

Psychological services for the purpose of diagnosis, treatment, or personalized advice are provided only in the context of a professional relationship, and are not given by means of public lectures or demonstrations, newspaper or magazine articles, radio or television programs, mail, or similar media.

a. The preparation of personnel reports and recommendations based on test data secured solely by mail is unethical unless such appraisals are an integral part of a continuing client relationship with a company, as a result of which the consulting psychologist has intimate knowledge of the client's personnel situation and can be assured thereby that his written appraisals will be adequate to the purpose and will be properly interpreted by the client. These reports must not be embellished with such detailed analyses of the subject's personality traits as would be appropriate only after intensive interviews with the subject. The reports must not make specific recommendations as to employment or placement of the subject which go beyond the psychologist's knowledge of the job requirements of the company. The reports must not purport to eliminate the company's need to carry on such other regular employment or personnel practices as appraisal of the work history, checking of references, past performance in the company.

PRINCIPLE 10. ANNOUNCEMENT OF SERVICES

A psychologist adheres to professional rather than commercial standards in making known his availability for professional services.

a. A psychologist does not directly solicit clients for individual diagnosis or therapy.

b. Individual listings in telephone directories are limited to name, highest relevant degree, certification status, address, and telephone number. They may also include identification in a few words of the psychologist's major areas of practice; for example, child therapy, personnel selection, industrial psychology. Agency listings are equally modest.

c. Announcements of individual private practice are limited to a simple statement of the name, highest relevant degree, certification or diplomate status, address, telephone number, office hours, and a brief explanation of the types of services rendered. Announcements of agencies may list names of staff members with their qualifications. They conform in other particulars with the same standards as individual announcements, making certain that the true nature of the organization is apparent.

d. A psychologist or agency announcing nonclinical professional services may use brochures that are descriptive of services rendered but not evaluative. They may be sent to professional persons, schools, business firms, government agencies, and other similar organizations.

e. The use in a brochure of "testimonials from satisfied users" is unacceptable. The offer of a free trial of services is unacceptable if it operates to misrepresent in any way the nature or the efficacy of the services rendered by the psychologist. Claims that a psychologist has unique skills or unique devices not available to others in the profession are made only if the special efficacy of these unique skills or devices has been demonstrated by scientifically acceptable evidence.

f. The psychologist must not encourage (nor, within his power, even allow) a client to have exaggerated ideas as to the efficacy of services rendered. Claims made to clients about the efficacy of his services must not go beyond those which the psychologist would be willing to subject to professional scrutiny through publishing his results and his claims in a professional journal.

PRINCIPLE 11. INTERPROFESSIONAL RELATIONS

A psychologist acts with integrity in regard to colleagues in psychology and in other professions.

a. A psychologist does not normally offer professional services to a person receiving psychological assistance from another professional worker except by agreement with the other worker or after the termination of the client's relationship with the other professional worker.

b. The welfare of clients and colleagues requires that psychologists in joint practice or corporate activities make an orderly and explicit arrangement regarding the conditions of their association and its possible termination. Psychologists who serve as employers of other psychologists have an obligation to make similar appropriate arrangements.

PRINCIPLE 12. REMUNERATION

Financial arrangements in professional practice are in accord with professional standards that safeguard the best interest of the client and the profession.

a. In establishing rates for professional services, the psychologist considers carefully both the ability of the client to meet the financial burden and the charges made by other professional persons engaged in comparable work. He is willing to contribute a portion of his services to work for which he receives little or no financial return.

b. No commission or rebate or any other form of remuneration is given or received for referral of clients for professional services.

c. The psychologist in clinical or counseling practice does not use his relationships with clients to promote, for personal gain or the profit of an agency, commercial enterprises of any kind.

d. A psychologist does not accept a private fee or any other form of remuneration for professional work with a person who is entitled to his services through an institution or agency. The policies of a particular agency may make explicit provision for private work with its clients by members of its staff, and in such instances the client must be fully apprised of all policies affecting him.

PRINCIPLE 13. TEST SECURITY

Psychological tests and other assessment devices, the value of which depends in part on the naivete of the subject, are not reproduced or described in popular publications in ways that might invalidate the techniques. Access to such devices is limited to persons with professional interest who will safeguard their use.

a. Sample items made up to resemble those of tests being discussed may be reproduced in popular articles and elsewhere, but scorable tests and actual test items are not reproduced except in professional publications.

b. The psychologist is responsible for the control of psychological tests and other devices and procedures used for instruction when their value might be damaged by revealing to the general public their specific contents or underlying principles.

PRINCIPLE 14. TEST INTERPRETATION

Test scores, like test materials, are released only to persons who are qualified to interpret and use them properly.

a. Materials for reporting test scores to parents, or which are designed for self-appraisal purposes in schools, social agencies, or industry are closely supervised by qualified psychologists or counselors with provisions for referring and counseling individuals when needed.

b. Test results or other assessment data used for evaluation or classification are communicated to employers, relatives, or other appropriate persons in such a manner as to guard against misinterpretation or misuse. In the usual case, an interpretation of the test result rather than the score is communicated.

c. When test results are communicated directly to parents and students, they are accompanied by adequate interpretive aids or advice.

PRINCIPLE 15. TEST PUBLICATION

Psychological tests are offered for commercial publication only to publishers who present their tests in a professional way and distribute them only to qualified users.

a. A test manual, technical handbook, or other suitable report on the test is provided which describes the method of constructing and standardizing the test, and summarizes the validation research.

b. The populations for which the test has been developed and the purposes for which it is recommended are stated in the manual. Limitations upon the test's dependability, and aspects of its validity on which research is lacking or incomplete, are clearly stated. In particular, the manual contains a warning regarding interpretations likely to be made which have not yet been substantiated by research.

c. The catalog and manual indicate the training or professional qualifications required for sound interpretation of the test.

d. The test manual and supporting documents take into account the principles enunciated in the *Technical Recommendations for Psychological Tests and Diagnostic Techniques*.

e. Test advertisements are factual and descriptive rather than emotional and persuasive.

PRINCIPLE 16. RESEARCH PRECAUTIONS

The psychologist assumes obligations for the welfare of his research subjects, both animal and human.

a. Only when a problem is of scientific significance and it is not practicable to investigate it in any other way is the psychologist justified in exposing research subjects, whether children or adults, to physical or emotional stress as part of an investigation.

b. When a reasonable possibility of injurious aftereffects exists, research is conducted only when the subjects or their responsible agents are fully informed of this possibility and agree to participate nevertheless.

c. The psychologist seriously considers the possibility of harmful aftereffects and avoids them, or removes them as soon as permitted by the design of the experiment.

d. A psychologist using animals in research adheres to the provisions of the Rules Regarding Animals, drawn up by the Committee on Precautions and Standards in Animal Experimentation and adopted by the American Psychological Association.

PRINCIPLE 17. PUBLICATION CREDIT

Credit is assigned to those who have contributed to a publication, in proportion to their contribution, and only to these.

a. Major contributions of a professional character, made by several persons to a common project, are recognized by joint authorship. The experimenter or author who has made the principal contribution to a publication is identified as the first listed.

b. Minor contributions of a professional character, extensive clerical or similar nonprofessional assistance, and other minor contributions are acknowledged in footnotes or in an introductory statement.

c. Acknowledgment through specific citations is made for unpublished as well as published material that has directly influenced the research or writing.

d. A psychologist who compiles and edits for publication the contributions of others publishes the symposium or report under the title of the committee or symposium, with his own name appearing as chairman or editor among those of the other contributors or committee members.

PRINCIPLE 18. RESPONSIBILITY TOWARD ORGANIZATION

A psychologist respects the rights and reputation of the institute or organization with which he is associated.

a. Materials prepared by a psychologist as a part of his regular work under specific direction of his organization are the property of that organization. Such materials are released for use or publication by a psychologist in accordance with policies of authorization, assignment of credit, and related matters which have been established by his organization.

b. Other material resulting incidentally from activity supported by any agency, and for which the psychologist rightly assumes individual responsibility, is published with disclaimer for any responsibility on the part of the supporting agency.

PRINCIPLE 19. PROMOTIONAL ACTIVITIES

The psychologist associated with the development or promotion of psychological devices, books, or other products offered for commercial sale is responsible for ensuring that such devices, books, or products are presented in a professional and factual way.

a. Claims regarding performance, benefits, or results are supported by scientifically acceptable evidence.

b. The psychologist does not use professional journals for the commercial exploitation of psychological products, and the psychologist-editor guards against such misuse.

c. The psychologist with a financial interest in the sale or use of a psychological product is sensitive to possible conflict of interest in his promotion of such products and avoids compromise of his professional responsibilities and objectives.

NOTES

1. A student of psychology who assumes the role of psychologist shall be considered a psychologist for the purpose of this code of ethics.

50. *The Meaning of the ABEPP Diploma*

NOBLE H. KELLEY, FILLMORE H. SANFORD
AND KENNETH E. CLARK

THE reorganization of the American Psychological Association in 1945 with the accompanying restatement of its purposes embarked the new APA on a program of professional as well as scientific endeavor. Already, emerging social needs for the services of professional psychologists were great and problems of creating a responsible profession were urgently in need of solution. As an essential step in fulfilling its purpose to advance psychology as a profession, the Policy and Planning Board in December 1945 recommended that the APA establish a procedure for the certification of its members who were qualified to perform professional services.

ABEPP: IN RETROSPECT AND NOW

As a first step in procedure, the Policy and Planning Board recommended to the Council of Representatives the adoption of an amendment to the Bylaws of the APA to establish an American Board of Examiners in Professional Psychology and further recommended that a Committee on the Board of Examiners be appointed to prepare further plans to present to Council in September 1946. Council approved this recommendation and the Board of Directors appointed this committee in April 1946. The proposed amendment to the Bylaws was approved by the APA membership in the summer of 1946 by a vote of 1,071 to 79.

IN RETROSPECT

In September 1946, the committee recommended and Council approved the creation of an independently incorporated American Board of Examiners

Reprinted from *American Psychologist*, 1961, *16*, 132–141, by permission of the American Psychological Association and the authors. Dr. Kelley is Research Professor of Psychology, Southern Illinois University; Dr. Sanford is Professor of Psychology, University of Texas; Dr. Clark is Dean, College of Arts and Science, University of Rochester.

in Professional Psychology. This recommended change from a board within the organizational structure of the APA to an independently incorporated board emerged from two important considerations. First was to provide legal protection to the APA and its financial structure. Secondly, it was recognized that a separate corporate body composed of competent and sincere persons with freedom and responsibility for independent action could best perform the task assigned. Whatever guidance or control is exerted by psychology as a whole must be effected through the wisdom and conscience of the members of the board. To establish an independently incorporated board involved repealing the amendment to the Bylaws, which was approved by the membership in 1947 by a vote of 1,663 to 30. Thus, by two general votes, the membership of the APA expressed itself overwhelmingly in favor of this professional undertaking.

ABEPP was incorporated on April 23, 1947, and nine members were elected to the Board of Trustees by the Council of Representatives. The newly elected board effected its formal organization and in July 1947 issued a general statement concerning certification and a first invitation to prospective candidates. By September 1947, 1,200 psychologists had requested certification forms.

The board considered that its first obligation was to the senior members in professional fields of psychology. The Bylaws of the newly incorporated ABEPP contained a "grandfather" provision which permitted waiver of the PhD requirement, its examination requirement, or both, if a candidate was judged qualified on the basis of training, professional work history, and satisfactory endorsement by colleagues. The determining date for "grandfather" status was the award of the baccalaureate degree on or before December 31, 1935. Final date for making application under this provision was December 31, 1949. 1,557 candidacies were received from senior members under the "grandfather" clause. Of these, 1,086 were certified with waiver of formal examinations and 30 were awarded the diploma by satisfactory performance on both written and oral examinations. About 85 % of these Diplomates held the doctoral degree. The last detailed report on the "grandfathers" who failed to attain certification appeared in the 1954 Annual Report of the Board of Trustees in the November 1954 *American Psychologist.*

In 1947 when ABEPP was incorporated, the total membership of the APA was only 4,600. In 1949 when the "grandfather" provision terminated, there were only about 1,400 Fellows of the Association. It was somewhat of a revelation to the original Board of Trustees that over one thousand of these psychologists met the standards for certification. It was evident that all of American psychology did not belong to the "ivory tower." A real and significant increasing trend in professional activities had existed over the years.

After the board had completed its thorough individual review of all candidacies active under the "grandfather" provision, it decided to make a final *block* review of all cases in which it had *not* voted to award the diploma with the waiver of the PhD and/or the examination requirement. This final review was made in January 1952. Three of the original Trustees, who retired from the board in September 1951, but who had participated from the beginning in the assessment and evaluation of "grandfather" candidacies, were invited to assist in this final review. Thus, the board continued to the end a deep concern for its obligations to the pioneers in professional psychology.

AND NOW

The work of ABEPP then moved into a new period, which was already underway, where both written and oral examinations were mandatory for the award of the diploma. The first written examinations were held in the fall of 1949 and the first oral examinations were conducted in Chicago in November 1950. Each year written examinations have been scheduled, usually in November, and oral examinations have been held annually in the spring following an evaluation of the performance of candidates on the written examinations. Decisions on the award of the diploma have been made at the Annual Meeting of the board ordinarily scheduled just prior to the APA Annual Convention.

Application for the diploma is voluntary and applications are invited from interested psychologists who meet the following requirements:

1. Membership in the American Psychological Association and/or Canadian Psychological Association.

2. A PhD degree in psychology from a college or university which, at the time the degree was awarded, met the existing standards of the American Psychological Association for doctoral training in the specialty of the applicant or the equivalent as judged by the board.

3. Five years of acceptable qualifying professional experience during which time the candidate shall have demonstrated superior performance. Four years of this experience shall be postdoctoral.

4. Presently engaged in professional work in the field of specialization.

Taking account of the many changes in professional psychology prior to, during, and following World War II, the board, during the first few years, did not deem it wise or fair to establish rigid policies with respect to training or the requirement of postdoctoral experience. As these situations changed, however, and as training programs became somewhat more systematic, the board adopted a graduated policy regarding postdoctoral experience. This policy provided a graduated increase from no postdoctoral experience to 2 years in 1951, to 3 years in 1953, and to 4 years of postdoctoral experience in 1955.

From the beginning, ABEPP has continued to award diplomas in three specialties: clinical psychology, counseling psychology, and industrial psychology. Early awards to psychologists in the specialty of counseling psychology were designated as "Counseling and Guidance." When the Division of Counseling and Guidance changed its name to the Division of Counseling Psychology, the board in 1955 changed the specialty title to "Counseling Psychology." In its procedures for identifying and evaluating psychologists at an advanced professional level, the board has held to the point of view that the traditions of psychology are the traditions of science. These traditions include disinterested scholarship, faithful reporting of observations, cautiousness in making interpretations from data, and a tolerance for alternative viewpoints. Further, the board has maintained the conviction that the psychological approach to all problems, including those encountered by the professional psychologist, is essentially investigative rather than dogmatic and that familiarity with and ability to understand and evaluate research are essential for personal professional development and for a high quality professional service to clients and patients. Other major aspects of the evaluation procedures are concerned with appraising the candidate's readiness and competence to undertake full responsibility for the welfare of the clients and patients he serves in his area of specialization.

As was true in the "grandfather" period, the board still evaluates the credentials of each applicant on each of the following criteria:

1. Adequacy and extent of basic training
2. Amount, breadth, and quality of professional experience
3. Evidence of special competence
4. Professional standing as a representative of psychology in the community

The credentials assembled, including letters of endorsement, must satisfy the board that the applicant meets appropriate professional standards for admission to candidacy and to further evaluation by examinations.

The first written examinations covered a period of 2 days; they have always included both objective and essay sections. Early examinations included a section on the basic fields of psychology. This was removed in 1953, mainly because the accreditation program of the APA had resulted in more uniform and systematic training for the PhD degree. In its place was included an objective examination covering psychological knowledge and principles basic to each of the three separate specialties. In 1955, the examination time was reduced from 2 days to 1. A candidate who fails this examination or any portion of it has the privilege of re-examination.

Each year the board reviews its written examination procedures and modifies the content of the examinations. Candidates taking the examinations and Diplomates administering them are invited to evaluate both the content and procedures. Periodically, selected Diplomates are invited to submit items and questions. A similar invitation is extended each year to the participating candidates. By this means, the board accumulates a reservoir of items from which selections can be made for future examinations.

The board has sought the opinions of its Diplomates on the appropriate categories or areas that should be included in the objective examination for each of the three specialties and the percentage of items that should be placed in each category. Responses to the essay portions of the written examination are evaluated independently by four Diplomates in the appropriate specialties. Ratings are assigned to assess the quality of the candidate's performance. Thus, the board continuously has benefited from the participation, assistance, and collective judgment of the profession in preparing a written examination that is appropriate for professional psychologists.

The oral examination presently includes the following three parts:

A. Diagnosis, appraisal, or evaluation (the definition of the problem faced by the professional psychologist)
B. Therapy, counseling, or constructive action (how to deal with the professional problem)

C. Organization and administrative problems of professional psychology (What are the conditions of acceptable and ethical professional practice?)

The first two parts deal with the major areas of professional practice. The third part deals with the psychologist's responsibility in client and professional relationships and his identification with professional psychology.

Each candidate is now examined by at least two separate committees. Each committee includes two Diplomates in the candidate's specialty, with a different member of the board (current or recent) serving as chairman of each committee. The oral examination involves a professional field situation in which the skills of the candidate in diagnosis, appraisal, or evaluation are directly observed by a Diplomate examiner. Prior to oral examination, a candidate is required to submit a recent sample of his professional work in therapy, counseling, or the making of recommendations to clients so that his examining committee can study his day-to-day work in these professional areas. At the end of each part of the oral examination, each member of the committee, including the chairman, makes an independent decision as to whether the candidate, in his judgment, meets the minimum standards for Diplomate status. Each examiner records comments supporting his decision. If the board member notes inconsistencies in the three judgments recorded, he calls for an immediate group discussion in which opinions, evaluations, and standards applied by each examiner are shared. An examiner, following this conference, may or may not change his decision.

In spite or because of the number of examiners who participate in the evaluation of each candidate, the board is aware that every examination may not meet its expectations for fairness or appropriateness in procedure or validity of judgments made. Against these possibilities the board attempts to protect the interests of the candidate in two ways: first, the final decision on the candidate is made by the board itself in physical meeting; second, each candidate is given the privilege of re-examination with a different committee of examiners.

As of May 31, 1960, 812 candidates had made application under the provision of mandatory examination. 125 of these have been received since July 31, 1959, the date of the last Annual Report. This is the largest number of new applications received in a given year since candidacy under the provision of mandatory examination was first activated in 1949. 348 candidates have been awarded the diploma by successful performance on examinations, 359 candidacies are in process, and 105 have been terminated. Of these 105, only 53 were terminated for failure twice on written or oral examinations. 52 were terminated under conditions where candidacy did not proceed to full examination privilege. Detailed information on the status of all candidacies appears in the Annual Reports of the board published in the *American Psychologist*. Of the 359 candidates in the process of evaluation, 134 appeared for oral examination in the spring of 1960.

The Board of Trustees of the corporation presently consists of 10 members who are elected by the board from a list of nominees approved by the Council of Representatives of the APA. Each of the three specialties is represented in the membership. There are five trustees from the specialty of clinical psychology, two from counseling psychology, and two from industrial psychology. These nine trustees are Diplomates. In addition, one trustee does not hold the diploma but is elected to serve as a representative of psychology in general. The non-Diplomate trustee is carefully selected to provide leadership by serving as President of the board. Term of office is for 4 years and no member, with the exception of the Secretary-Treasurer, may be elected for a succeeding term.

The board has had continuing concern for the meaning and value of its diploma not only to those who are willing to undertake its attainment but also to their colleagues in the APA. During the past year, ABEPP, by means of a questionnaire, sought the opinions of its Diplomates who have earned the award by successful performance on examination. The third part of this article presents the views of our responding Diplomates; the second part presents the definition of a Diplomate as seen by the oral examiners.

More detailed information on current operations of the board may be obtained by writing to the Executive Office (Carbondale, Illinois) for a copy of ABEPP's *Policies and Procedures*.

THE DEFINITION OF AN ABEPP DIPLOMATE AS SEEN BY THE EXAMINERS

Since 1950, approximately 810 ABEPP oral examiners have made pass or fail judgments about the professional competence of about as many applicants for the ABEPP diploma. This process—involving approximately 7,000 man-hours, many very uncomfortable, on the part of examiners and 3,000 man-hours, sometimes even more uncomfortable, on the part of candidates—had produced as of January 1, 1960 about three decisions by the

board to award the diploma for every two decisions —all very stressful—to deny it.

ABEPP examiners are making judgments about the professional competence of their colleagues, most generally their younger colleagues. And while they have sufficient confidence in their standards to do their assigned jobs, their confidence is by no means absolute. They continually try to check their operating standards against the reality that our science and our profession are truly and rapidly evolving.

Not only do the Trustees wish to check their standards against a changing reality, they want to communicate them for what they are worth *now*— to psychologists who are aspiring to the ABEPP diploma and to other psychologists who are training aspiring psychologists. With these considerations in mind, the Board of Trustees of ABEPP has attempted to communicate some information about this prevailing definition of what is a good professional psychologist, by putting together an article around some raw data which they thought could, without breaching either security or propriety, be released, and which they thought might serve as useful feedback from the board to the profession.

Each oral examiner, in each examination, records his evaluation of the candidate, and adds comments about the critical aspects of the candidate's performance. Anne Roe, Stanley Estes, Reign Bittner, and Edward Bordin, all members at the time of the ABEPP Board of Trustees, pored over these records from numerous past oral examinations, collecting and classifying all the comments made by all examiners in support of their evaluations. Data thus include comments about candidates who passed and candidates who failed.

This work led to a rich array of psychologists' judgments. As it turned out, it was mostly a negatively flavored richness since examiners consistently fail to justify highly positive evaluations. When the examiners see a performance of very high quality, their enjoyment of it seems to obliterate the necessity to write about it. It is also true, of course, that comments are recorded primarily about those aspects of performance which would suggest whether the candidates should pass or not; when no doubts existed, fewer comments would be written. By such an accent on the negative, perhaps we will be moving only toward a definition of what a good psychologist is not, but a look at these judgments may nonetheless tell something about professional standards in psychology.

No sampling of comments can do justice to the total list of remarks compiled, but perhaps the variety and nature of judgments can at least be illustrated. The following list was obtained by selecting every fifteenth comment from the entire list of items.[1]

FIELD SITUATION AND EXAMINATION ON DIAGNOSIS

He displays a degree of confidence which at times borders on exasperating smugness if not condescension. These attitudes at times become manifest also in his work with his patients.

He seemed immature and egocentric.

His approach to the client was literal, rigid, mechanical, and unimaginative.

Covered his uneasiness by flippancy.

No clear focus as to what she wished to learn from the patient.

Interview not well directed, many significant areas unapproached.

Has not fully thought through the entire problem of client relationships and subject support in the application of the technique in the work sample.

In a few instances failed to follow skillfully on significant leads during interview.

Question his judgment in using entire two hours for personality evaluation without minimal evaluation of formal thought processes.

He learned practically nothing about the patient, except a mass of unordered test data and a few items of personal history, such as date of birth.

A few misunderstandings of testing principles and findings.

Knowledge of appropriate instruments not adequate.

Candidate jumped to unwarranted conclusions about diagnosis and personality structure.

Rather incompetent in interpreting his data and in making a diagnostic evaluation.

Failed to define adequately the problem and to search out the more essential aspects of what might be wanted in the diagnostic situation.

Was a little "glib" in a couple of points in the examination and had to back up a little.

Report really does not tell the client what the results appear to show.

THERAPY EXAMINATION

One hundred hours with a psychotic patient, approached as "interesting" with few questions raised as to what is best for the patient, can be considered as rigid and lacking in sensitivity.

Weak on awareness of emotional factors and not skillful in dealing with them.

My feeling is that the candidate needs a good deal of training before he will be able to do therapy satisfactorily.

Not the *best* in therapy because limited in treatment of emotional or affect factors.

Industrial information limited.

Well qualified in the narrow field of test development, but is not qualified as a broadly equipped technician in the field of industrial psychology.

Case history was poorly organized and from the point of content was inadequate.

He was not able to formulate a theoretical frame of reference for his treatment program.

Candidate aware of probable nature of problems but indefinite in suggesting solutions.

Maybe he makes too much out of results on small numbers of cases—but he is not naive.

Takes all facts at face value.

RESEARCH EXAMINATION[2]

Candidate seemed not too well acquainted with design criteria, went off at tangent when specific design characteristic was approached.

No imagination re use of reference books on population statistics to check representativeness of obtained sample.

By own admission, he does not know statistics and could not handle detailed questions on the articles.

He showed knowledge of the five research articles assigned, but was unable clearly to assess the problems, procedures, and results.

I was not sure the candidate thoroughly understood the several studies discussed with him . . . his focus in the studies discussed did not seem to be sharp.

His criticisms of research were occasionally adequate, but not incisive, and did not seem to show extensive knowledge of the field.

Not too strong in theory.

Took critical points on research design and methodology rather lightly.

Describing his own research, he showed a similar lack of appreciation of problems involved. Poor conceptualization, formulation, and organization of the project.

I think the candidate is much better informed than one would judge on the basis of his answers. He seems quite circumlocutious and often failed to get back to the heart of a question—even when it was more of an opinion than an information question.

I give him the benefit of the doubt simply because I don't have the goods on him enough to fail him with confidence. He rambled on and on, tangentially and vaguely. I feel, however, that we did not seem to be able to interrupt him and keep him on track enough to formulate a surer judgment. I honestly don't know how much he knows about research.

ETHICS AND PROFESSIONAL RELATIONS

She sees ethical problems mostly in terms of protecting the client at all costs and regardless of other considerations. Cannot be pressed to give more than clichés.

He discussed ethical issues in a superficial way and showed very little thoughtfulness or sensitivity to the kinds of conflicting responsibilities usually encountered in clinical experience.

A little slow to answer the hypothetical question on ethics and a little slow to work through to the desired action in the real life situation.

Difficult to judge because he talked so much.

He has not thought through the ethical problems involved in selling a semiclinical type of service without validation data.

He is conscious also of referral needs, but not too good on the consultation concept.

His professional participation is apparently not high.

He was a bit vague and evasive. It was awfully hard to get him to state dilemmas of conflicting values, save in the professional aspects of things. He certainly is not a hair-splitter with his conscience . . . . I would not want to send a patient to him, not because I think he's unethical but because he's too unperceptive to see the issues and could do damage.

A prolonged study of the entire array of negative comments from which our sample was drawn could lead easily to the conclusion that it is *utterly impossible to be a good professional psychologist.* The fact remains, however, that 378 psychologists have been judged to meet the criteria with enough success to be awarded the ABEPP diploma. This fact, viewed in contiguity with the criteria suggested in the preceding sample of comments, may be taken to mean that the criteria apply only to the *ideal professional* psychologist—who may or may not exist. Perhaps we cannot hope that one psychologist can be a mature, integral human being, sensitive and deeply aware, highly skilled in the use of his professional tools, broadly educated—and still educable—in human affairs, artistically competent in professional practice while maintaining a scientific orientation both to the evolving knowledge in his field and to the assessment of his own performance, clearly demonstrating a keen awareness of the ethical issues involved in an intricate and unstructured professional role, and withal, joining with his fellows in scientific and professional organizations to confront general problems of common concern.

Yet we must establish this kind of image when we consider simultaneously the nature of the problems professional psychologists deal with, the state of our knowledge of human behavior, our historical allegiance to scientific and academic traditions, the youth of the psychological profession, and the fact that the control and guidance of professional practice must come from within the practitioner rather than from established and sensible social mechanisms that can protect the client from the incompetent, insensitive, and unethical person.

These factors prevent ABEPP from giving its diploma to any of variety of *partial* psychologists. We cannot approve of the skilled technician plying a frozen set of skills. We cannot approve the intuitive healer who scorns questions of logic, evidence, and demonstrability. We cannot approve the callow, inexperienced, and sometimes self-appointed practitioner who rushes into human affairs that may be beyond his depth and his ken. We cannot approve the scientist, however great his research creativity, who rushes into professional practice without the skills, the artistry, and the judgment required for handling concrete problems of behavior. We cannot approve the immature and the unaware, whatever the degree of intellectual brilliance. And we cannot approve the dullard, however proper his training and however extensive his alleged experience.

How seriously do the ABEPP examiners take the image of the ideal psychologist, the image that seems to underlie our array of comments? This is a very practical matter for anyone planning to take the examination or for any training institution which hopes its graduates will achieve ABEPP diplomas. While perhaps no candidate ever sailed through these examinations without disappointing some examiner on some occasion, and while many of the present negative comments were directed at successful candidates, the standards we infer here nonetheless do operate. No psychologist is awarded the diploma who is below a certain minimum on any of the operative criteria. It would be difficult to define or describe the precise minimum. But it is sufficiently high to give us the assurance that any psychologist who earns his ABEPP diploma through these examinations is, at least on the day of the examination, a human being of exceptional quality and a professional person of unquestionable competence.

In summary, then, we may draw certain inferences about the operating standards upon which the ABEPP diploma is awarded. First, there are qualifying requirements of training, experience, and endorsement. The ABEPP Diplomate must have received a PhD degree or its equivalent from a recognized institution giving graduate education in psychology. He must have accumulated qualifying experience, including experience under supervision. And his endorsers, preferably ABEPP Diplomates, must recommend him as a decent human being who demonstrates sound professional behavior in his chosen setting. On the written examination he must demonstrate knowledge of the language and content of the psychological culture and must show that he can write with reasonable literacy and intelligence on scientific and professional problems.

In the field and oral examinations on diagnosis, the candidate must demonstrate:

1. A sufficient freedom from personal deficits and urgencies to enable him to engage in a suitable relationship with the client
2. A properly developed skill at interviewing
3. Skill, knowledge, and judgment in using technical diagnostic tools
4. The ability to accumulate systematically the relevant diagnostic data and to organize, conceptualize, and express a meaningful interpretation of those data

With respect to treatment, the candidate must impress the examiners that he has:

1. The maturity, stability, integrity, and sensitivity to enable him to engage in an intricate and constructive relationship with a patient or client
2. A genuine and rounded competence, born of genuine and rounded experience, for the professional work he is doing
3. A possession and mastery of the professional skills involved in his work
4. The ability to formulate and articulate a meaningful plan for his work with the client or patient
5. A critical minded stance with respect to his own work
6. The ability to conceptualize in a meaningful way what he is doing and what he hopes to accomplish

In the examination on research, the candidate must demonstrate:

1. Enough basic knowledge of statistics and research design to enable him to read critically the research literature relevant to his line of work
2. Enough background and intelligence to enable him to understand, evaluate, and interpret the relevance of research literature

In the examination on ethics and professional relationships, the candidate must show:

1. An awareness of ethical issues involved in the practice of psychology
2. Mature attitudes with respect to relations with his colleagues in psychology and in other professions
3. An informed concern for the problems facing his profession as a whole
4. An interest in participating with his colleagues in the activities of psychological organizations

Here, then, is what we may regard with some certainty as the prevailing definition of a good professional psychologist. It will seem to many and perhaps to most psychologists a very sound definition, representing a creative amalgam of the best of the traditions of science and the traditions of professional service, and constituting a functionally significant image of which no psychologist, past or present, need be ashamed and in which many can and will take pride.

THE VIEWS OF RECENT DIPLOMATES OF ABEPP

A summary of the judgments of ABEPP examiners gives only a part of the picture of applying, taking written examinations, working in a diagnostic field situation, and taking oral examinations which ultimately leads to the award of the diploma or, alas, to the need to try again. Examiners are wise and sensitive critics, but they are critics, and the preceding report of their comments is enough to make the most confident candidate uneasy.

Let us look, instead, at the comments of those semiwilling candidates who subjected themselves to this critical scrutiny, and who were thereafter awarded diplomas.

Recent Diplomates of ABEPP all have been required to complete the process of application and examination described in earlier parts of this report. To the most recent 315 awardees, a questionnaire was sent in the fall of 1959 asking them to comment on effects of their having been boarded, to appraise the examination process, and to suggest ways in which operations could be improved. With no follow-up appeal, 269 questionnaires (85%) were returned by February 20, 1960. This response in itself attests to the strong identification with ABEPP that results from the award of the diploma.

We first asked our Diplomates if being boarded had provided advancement or other financial gains. Direct and immediate benefits of material gains of this sort were cited by 27%; others indicated some expectation of financial gain, or thought it likely that benefits they had received derived in part from their Diplomate status. Most respondents indicated that no direct or indirect material benefits came to them as a result of being boarded; many indicated that they had not expected any such benefits. Even the list of comments presented below suggests that ABEPP status is, at best, only slowly coming to have direct and immediate effects on salaries and professional rank.

Illustrations of the responses made by persons who had experienced material benefits are presented below:

Direct Benefits:

Was offered a fairly lucrative position with a psychiatrist in private practice. His eagerness—in-part—was attributed to the status of ABEPP. Also my position in this VA hospital was certainly enhanced, especially among other services.

Eligibility for position of Director of Psychological Center which I now occupy.

Five percent raise plus all expenses for ABEPP exams.

Appointment to the position of Chief Psychologist was in part dependent on ABEPP; we have however not succeeded—yet—in convincing Civil Service to recognize ABEPP in the same financial fashion Specialty Boards in Medicine are.

None, except on one occasion when it was possible to obtain a consulting position with the state where the *minimal* requirement was an ABEPP diploma.

Higher pay scale for my part-time teaching—little difficulty in getting another job and part-time teaching —other offers of jobs (all once I moved away from where I was when I took the exams).

Consultancies in several installations, providing (a) source of referral for private patients; (b) local prestige; (c) opportunity for me to share and learn.

Promotion to a top grade, with accompanying raise in salary; this grade specifically required possession of the ABEPP diploma.

Indirect Benefits:

I am an associate professor psychology in a large university. No financial reward has come directly from diplomate status. It does give our training program more public merit, and that satisfies me. It *may* be taken into account as *one* criterion for merit salary increase and promotions, i.e., I believe it will have some small effect among other factors.

No financial factors that I could pinpoint, though there is always the chance that these are influenced to some extent by the Diploma. Regarding "advancement" it is possible that the level of competence implied by the Diploma may have been one of the several factors that led to my having been considered favorably for my position in this department.

None has come as a direct result, so far as I know. I presume it *helped* me get a professorship and a VA consultantship.

No specific increments in income as a result. The Boards may have resulted in some additional referrals.

Possibly would not have been granted a promotion in faculty rank without the Diploma.

I have been contacted by at least two individuals offering me a position (ABEPP preferred).

Indefinite—if any, probably served to support small annual salary increments.

I don't know whether it's been the result, directly, of my obtaining the Diploma, but I have been promoted to Senior Psychologist, with a sizable pay increase.

None as yet. I did receive an unsolicited letter of commendation from the manager of the hospital where I am employed when the then current list of diplomates was called to his attention by routine dissemination.

Does being boarded have a favorable effect on professional status and prestige? Most Diplomates (69%) say yes. The way in which such affirmative responses are given is illustrated by the following sample responses:

Not being a "grandfather" appears to have status value.

It probably is a factor in my being considered as one of the more senior Clinical Psychologists in the area. It probably was important in my being appointed to the state association's Certification Board.

It's hard to assess, but I believe it has lent additional status or prestige.

Hard to say—certainly some positive effect on medical colleagues. Trouble is, if there *is* an influence, it's a silent or indirect one; the few people who make an overt display of being impressed are persons no one cares to impress anyway.

Considerable, I would say. One doesn't hear many negative comments so I can only report the positive things I hear. I am accorded considerable status as an "expert" by our staff. Possession of the diploma is certainly a factor.

Favorable effect on colleagues in psychology. I don't think colleagues in related disciplines have been influenced.

The Diplomate has very definitely been a status and prestige factor among colleagues. Psychologists realize what is involved but psychiatrists have a distorted notion, seeing it as exactly comparable to their Boards which are taken almost automatically—and of the same difficulty.

In this area, perhaps, there has been a noticeable increase in regard by colleagues. Some of my medical colleagues appear to have a higher status perception of the diploma than psychologists.

It has had a very definite favorable effect, in my estimation.

Considerable, since I am the first (?) and only Diplomate at my University.

I think favorable to a significant degree.

I feel that it has added to it slightly, since I have published very little and have little prestige via this route.

Very slight increase.

I don't know; probably some but nothing very striking.

This could only properly be evaluated by your asking among my colleagues. It is my impression that it has had some *minor* effect in raising prestige among a few psychologists and it has been of some interest to some physicians who seem to regard it as comparable to specialty boards in fields of their own profession. With none, however, does it seem to be regarded as a symbol warranting any significant alteration in prestige.

A little increase possibly.

Some, but how much or how little I cannot say.

This is intangible and subjective. There may be a bit of admiration and awe—but hard to evaluate.

We would expect some psychologists to express a more jaundiced view than this, and about one respondent in four has obliged. Most are reservations about the impact of being boarded; some are quite articulate in expressing the feeling that there are better bases than this for establishing status.

Very rare, but important to record, were such comments as the following:

Absolutely NONE!! It merely aroused the enmity of my colleagues who apparently have no attention [sic] of applying. It was not even acknowledged by the local psychological association, although it was the first one in the history of this group.

A preponderance (90%) of favorable responses was received to the third question, which was: "How do you feel now about having invested your time and money in going through the examination procedure?" Most Diplomates obtained a real personal satisfaction in the award of the diploma. They felt it was well worth the effort both from a personal standpoint, and as an important part of the development of the profession. A cross-section of responses given is presented here:

Rather than put it negatively by saying, "I've never regretted it," I would prefer to say that I have always been extremely gratified with my decision to take the exams.

Extremely valuable.

Very glad I did it.

Pleased.

It was worth the time, effort, and money, and I would do it again. The satisfaction of having successfully negotiated an added level of competence—attaining membership with the elite, so to speak—has repaid the investment.

I do have some degree of satisfaction.

Would do it again; makes me feel a little more secure to be approved of by authority figures, and to know I've passed the highest level of competence; feel the "idea" of board exams is a good one.

Wasted.

As a necessary requisite to becoming a professional psychologist, the exams had to be completed—but I have no strong affection for the procedure.

Well worth both time and money.

Glad that I did.

ABEPP has always expected that diplomas would be displayed. Are they? Seventy percent report they do, and almost 30% report that they do not display the diploma in a public place. Most of the latter indicate some reason why this is not appropriate, or indicate that the diploma hangs at home (home is considered a public place in this analysis only if there is indication that private practice occurs in the home).

An outpouring of comments, recommendations, criticisms, and commendations came in response to our questions about the way in which examinations were conducted. The Board of Trustees of ABEPP intends to devote a substantial amount of time to a review of these comments. Examining is an area of effort in which psychologists, if any group can, should be able to do an outstanding job. We should be able not only to conduct a useful social experiment with ABEPP's efforts to give professional status to selected psychologists, but also to provide a degree of technical sophistication in examining procedures which no other profession can do. We must also expect, of course, to have a more critical review of our procedures by the candidate group than other boards would encounter.

A detailed summary of comments by Diplomates about the examination procedures is not included in this report. Many of these relate to special circumstances in oral examinations; most are constructive and will be used in planning subsequent examinations. A few responses relate to problems of administration, or to practices in examination which no longer exist. The most serious objections to the examination procedures, even though made only by a modest number of respondents, concern the use of oral examiners who appear to the candidate to be biased, rigid, or less competent than he is; the diagnostic field situations are criticized for being somewhat tangential to the interests and capabilities of the candidate; the written examinations are considered to contain too much trivial or irrelevant or geographically distorted content. Yet most Diplomates feel that preparing for the examinations was worth the effort, that the entire process was reasonable and orderly, and that standards for passing are at about the right level. The Board of Trustees of ABEPP will use all suggestions in establishing future practices, and will use the responses to prepare a guide to prospective candidates, so that new candidates may capitalize on the recommendations of their predecessors for most appropriate procedures to use in preparing for the examinations.

It is clear from the reports we have from our recent Diplomates that the diploma is valued. Yet there are reservations. Perhaps most serious is that the ABEPP process "has not caught hold." This is the point made by those persons who count the number of "grandfathers" and the number of persons who have been boarded by examination. The record suggests that there are substantial numbers of qualified persons (especially in industrial and counseling psychology) who have not applied for the diploma. One reason for this is frequently cited by our Diplomates: that there are no "built-in" rewards, such as automatic salary increases, to being boarded in psychology, although there are such benefits associated with medical boards. Another factor is cost; as the number of candidates increases each year, some reductions may result, either in terms of greater amortization of the costs of preparing examinations and handling records, or in the lessened costs of travel associated with the exams. Yet the cost will never be appreciably lower than it now is, unless major revisions in the examination process are made.

Another important factor mentioned by many persons relates to the standards which ABEPP should set. This matter is related to the issue in the preceding paragraph. Even if all candidates had been passed during the past 10 years, the total number of Diplomates would not be increased substantially, since those who fail represent only a small proportion of the total number of persons presumed eligible for this status. Many of the persons in the relevant area of interest in psychology indicate that they consider that the diploma is not appropriate for them in terms of the work they are currently doing. Thus, presumably, they are not interested in doing the work which preparation for the examinations requires, or else are unwilling to pay the fees. Perhaps this group would be more interested if the diploma were easier to obtain.

If we lower standards however, ABEPP status changes: the use of the diploma to identify the fully qualified independent practitioner is lost. And it is clear from the comments in the preceding section that examiners would feel very strongly about any such lowering of requirements. More Diplomates who are replying to our questionnaire ask for an increase in standards than ask for reduction of standards.

Does our evidence suggest that the procedures of ABEPP and its total program may be considered successful? If we define success as indicated by the number of persons who consider the diploma essential, the answer is a qualified no. If we judge by the attitudes toward ABEPP of persons who have received the ABEPP diploma, the answer is a fairly strong yes. These Diplomates by and large are pleased to have received the diploma, are in the main content that the procedures used in examination are appropriate, and feel that the time and money they invested were well spent. How could we increase their feelings of satisfaction with the diploma: by having it produce more tangible and more immediate rewards for the recipient, and by having the diploma sought for by a substantially larger number of persons. The former goal requires the work of all psychologists, and perhaps especially of such persons as those in the APA Central Office, on the Board of Professional Affairs, or in related professional activities in state societies. The latter can be attained by the Diplomates themselves, whom we now advise to say to their well qualified colleagues: "Go thou and do likewise." It also requires, however, the achievement of ABEPP status to be perceived as an expected part of the work of professional psychologists in industry, government, hospitals, universities, and in private practice. And it might be a goal more readily achieved if graduate departments of psychology accepted some degree of responsibility for encouraging their PhDs to include "getting boarded" as a necessary and important step in their professional development.

NOTES

1. The original manuscript from which the list was drawn may be obtained by writing to Noble H. Kelley, Secretary and Treasurer of ABEPP, Southern Illinois University, Carbondale, Illinois. Items are grouped according to the areas in which the candidates were examined; most comments relate to the clinical specialty, but counseling and industrial areas are also represented.

2. Examination on research is now included in the written examination.

51. Certification, Licensing, and the Movement of Psychologists from State to State

NORMAN B. HENDERSON AND JANE D. HILDRETH

THE licensing or certification of psychologists, like the Pure Food and Drug Acts, exists to protect the consumer from dangerous or inferior commodities. Legislation for the protection of the public is not written to restrain trade nor to hamper the purveyor of quality goods. Thus, while psychologists should work for the kind of legislation which protects the public against unqualified psychological practice, they should restrain the individual psychologist only insofar as it is consistent with the goal of protecting the public. However, because states have sovereignty over these regulatory functions, psychologists will be needlessly limited in their movement and practice unless they continue vigilantly to compensate for the restricting aspects of sovereignty. An advantage of state sovereignty, on the other hand, is that it can allow for a variation in legislation which will lead to creative measures of control not possible in a monolithic Federal program. The American Psychological Association and the American Association of State Psychology Boards (AASPB) have been realistic in recognizing state control of licensing and certifying functions, and they are working toward uniformity in those aspects of legislation which will permit the free interstate movement of qualified psychologists.

STATUTORY AND NONSTATUTORY EXAMINING BOARDS

As an alternative to legislation creating certifying and licensing laws, some states have established nonstatutory certifying boards. These boards gen-

Reprinted from *American Psychologist*, 1965, *20*, 418–421, by permission of the American Psychological Association and the authors. The article has been amended so as to make the data current as of May 1966. Dr. Henderson is Associate Professor and Director, Navajo Rehabilitation Project, Northern Arizona University, Flagstaff, Arizona. Mrs. Hildreth is Administrative Associate, American Psychological Association.

erally are corporations which are set up under the egis of the psychological associations in states which do not have statutory controls. When laws creating statutory boards are passed, the nonstatutory boards are dissolved.

The number of states with statutory boards has increased steadily since the first legislation to certify psychologists was approved by the Connecticut Legislature in 1945. As of May 1966, there are 29 states and 4 Canadian provinces with statutory boards, and 17 states and the District of Columbia with nonstatutory boards.

For some psychologists, nonstatutory certification is seen to be as restrictive of movement as statutory licensing or certification. Although it does not have police power, the nonstatutory board has the power of moral and economic persuasion. Thus, psychologists face restrictive hurdles in commencing practice in 51 jurisdictions, and they are similarly restricted if they wish to transfer a practice to these jurisdictions. Already, in states comprising most of the population, a psychologist to be certified or licensed must meet statutory qualifications.

RECIPROCAL ENDORSEMENT

The laws creating statutory boards, and the constitutions and bylaws of the nonstatutory boards, reflect, as nearly as it was possible at the time of enaction, the intentions of the APA and the participating state psychological associations (see policy statements—APA, 1958; APA & CSPA, 1955). Naturally, in enacting any legislation, the sponsors of it face the possibility of opposition. Legislation sponsored by psychologists has been no exception. This is not the place for recapitulating incidents and forces opposing legislation for psychologists, and the compromises forced upon psychologists in passing legislation; but several statutes contain provisions strongly opposed by the state psychological associations and/or the APA.

All but two statutes, however, and all but four of the nonstatutory programs, include a provision for reciprocal endorsement (commonly referred to as reciprocity). Thus the laws and provisions do reflect, in this respect, the policy of the APA to place no barriers to the free movement of qualified psychologists from one state to another.

In moving into a number of states, in spite of the reciprocal endorsement provisions, a person, if he does not meet the maximum qualifications, may be required to take an examination. Furthermore, some of the boards make it no more difficult to be certified or licensed initially than to be certified or licensed under reciprocal endorsement provisions. In other words, it may be no more difficult to enter some states and obtain a license or certificate de novo than it is to enter another state via the process of reciprocal endorsement.

AMERICAN ASSOCIATION OF STATE PSYCHOLOGY BOARDS

The problems related to reciprocal endorsement, as the number of boards increased, led the Board of Professional Affairs of APA to sponsor a meeting of board representatives in Chicago in November 1959. By 1961, the AASPB was officially established. A primary purpose of AASPB is to facilitate communication among examining boards, not only to serve the public more effectively by maintaining adequate standards, but also to serve the individual psychologist by seeing to it that he is not needlessly restricted by examining board actions. The AASPB has developed an objective examination which may be used, on a voluntary basis, by any board as part of its examination procedures. There are plans for a uniform application blank, because the more uniform the standards and procedures, the less the restriction on movement of psychologists from state to state.

SOME REQUIREMENTS FOR CERTIFICATION AND LICENSURE

There is a fair degree of uniformity in standards at the present time, although there are marked exceptions. The two tables presented here will enable one, in most instances, to check his eligibility for certification or licensure in the various states. A "Yes" in the column headed "Reciprocity" means the presence of a provision. No table, however, can cover adequately the special conditions that hold for reciprocal endorsement. The only certain test of whether one meets the requirements is to apply

directly to the state board and wait for the decision.

Table 1 indicates for the states with statutory provisions the education and experience requirements, and whether an examination is required for certification or licensure. The columns do not cover grandfather provisions, nor do they cover requirements under reciprocal endorsement. A "No" in the examination column indicates that in the law the examining board is given some degree of discretionary power to waive the examination. The table also indicates whether reciprocal endorsement is permitted and whether one must be a resident in order to be certified or licensed.

A study of the laws indicates that with few exceptions the doctorate is required after the initial grandfathering; only one state (Maine) and one province (Alberta) permit certification at the professional level without a doctoral degree. More statutes require 1 year than 2 years of experience, but 2 or more years of experience are required in the majority of states. Some of the statutes (Colorado, Idaho, Louisiana, Minnesota, Nevada, New Mexico, Oregon, Virginia, Washington) require that the experience be postdoctoral. Several provinces and three states (Alabama, Arizona, Wyoming) do not require any experience; two states and one province require no experience at the subprofessional level.

An overwhelming majority of statutes requires an examination. Except for Arizona, all states have reciprocal endorsement provisions, but they vary in wording. Under certain circumstances two of the provincial statutes allow reciprocal endorsement; two others do not. An overwhelming majority of statutes says nothing about residence.

Table 2 lists the requirements for certification by nonstatutory boards. The variations in nonstatutory requirements and reciprocity are similar to the variations among the statutes. However, fewer nonstatutory than statutory boards require an examination.

Most of the laws cover the use of the title "Psychologist" and restrict the use of the title to those who hold themselves out to the public as psychologists and request a fee for their services. Likewise, the nonstatutory certificate is primarily a document which a professional psychologist uses to inform his clients that he meets the requirements established by his profession for entering into a contract to render psychological services. In so restricting applied psychological practice, both the statutory and nonstatutory boards have become arms for enforcing standards of psychological practice somewhere near the level of those set several years ago by the APA.

TABLE 1. Some Characteristics of Psychology Laws

State or province	Coverage	Education requirements	Experience requirements (years)	Examination mandatory	Reciprocity	Residence required
Alabama	Practice of psychologists	Doctoral	0	No	Yes	No
Arizona	Psychologist	Doctoral	0	No	No	No
Arkansas	Psychologist	Doctoral	1	No	Yes	No
	Psychological examiner	Master's	0	No	Yes	No
California	Psychologist	Doctoral	1	Yes	Yes	No
Colorado	Psychologist	Doctoral	2	Yes	Yes	Yes
Connecticut	Psychologist	Doctoral	1	No	Yes	Yes
Delaware	Psychologist	Doctoral	1	Yes	Yes	Yes
Florida	Psychologist	Doctoral	1	Yes	Yes	Yes
Georgia	Applied psychology	Doctoral	1	No	Yes	No
Idaho	Practice of psychology	Doctoral	2	No	Yes	No
Illinois	Psychologist	Doctoral	2	Yes	Yes	No
Kentucky	Practice of psychology	Doctoral	1	Yes	Yes	No
Louisiana	Psychologist	Doctoral	2	Yes	Yes	Yes
Maine	Certified psychologist	Doctoral or master's	1	Yes	Yes	Yes
Maryland	Psychologist	Doctoral	2	Yes	Yes	No
Michigan	Consulting psychologist	Doctoral	5	Yes	Yes	No
	Psychologist	Doctoral	1	No	Yes	No
	Psychological examiner or technician	Master's	1	No	Yes	No
Minnesota	Certified consulting psychologist	Doctoral	3	Yes	Yes	Yes
	Certified psychologist	Doctoral or master's	1	Yes	Yes	Yes
Mississippi	Psychologist	Doctoral	1	No	Yes	Yes
Nevada	Psychologist	Doctoral	1	Yes	Yes	No
New Hampshire	Psychologist	Doctoral	2	Yes	Yes	No
New Mexico	Psychologist	Doctoral	2	Yes	Yes	No
New York	Psychologist	Doctoral	2	Yes	Yes	No
Oklahoma	Practice of psychology	Doctoral	2	Yes	Yes	Yes
Oregon	Psychologist	Doctoral	2	Yes	Yes	No
Tennessee	Psychologist	Doctoral	1	Yes	Yes	No
	Psychological examiner	Master's	0	Yes	Yes	No
Utah	Psychologist	Doctoral	2	Yes	Yes	No
Virginia	Psychologist	Doctoral	2	Yes	Yes	No
Washington	Psychologist	Doctoral	1	Yes	Yes	No
Wyoming	Psychologist	Doctoral	0	Yes	Yes	Yes
Alberta	Psychologist	Master's	1	Yes	No	No
Ontario	Psychologist	Doctoral	1	Yes	No	No
Quebec	Psychologist Grade 1	Doctoral or master's	0	No	No	No
	Psychologist Grade 2	Doctoral	3	No	Yes	No
Saskatchewan	Registered psychologist	Doctoral	0	No	Yes	No

TABLE 2. Some Characteristics of Nonstatutory Psychology Provisions

State or province	Coverage	Education requirements	Experience requirements (years)	Examination mandatory	Reciprocity	Residence required
District of Columbia	Certified psychologist	Doctoral	3	Yes	Yes	Yes
Iowa	Certified psychologist	Doctoral	2	Yes	Yes	Yes
Kansas	Applied psychologist	Doctoral	2	No	Yes	No
		Master's	6	Yes	Yes	No
Massachusetts	Psychologist	Doctoral	1	No	Yes	No
Missouri	Psychologist	Doctoral	2	No	Yes	No
Montana	Psychologist	Doctoral	1	No	Yes	Yes
Nebraska	Psychologist	Doctoral	1	Yes	No	Yes
New Jersey	Psychologist	Doctoral	1	Yes	No	Yes
North Dakota	Clinical, counseling, or industrial psychologist	Doctoral	1	No	No	Yes
Ohio	Certified psychologist	Doctoral	1	No	Yes	No
Pennsylvania	Certified psychologist	Doctoral	5	Yes	Yes	No
Rhode Island	Certified psychologist	Doctoral	1	No	No	Yes
South Carolina	Certified psychologist	Doctoral	1	No	Yes	Yes
South Dakota	Psychologist specialist	Doctoral	2	No	?	Yes
	Psychologist	Master's	5	No	?	Yes
Texas	Psychologist	Doctoral	2	No	Yes	No
Vermont	Certified psychologist	Equiv. Co APA requirements for membership		No	Yes	Yes
West Virginia	Certified psychologist	Doctoral	1	No	Yes	No
		Master's	2	Yes	Yes	No
Wisconsin	Certified psychologist	Doctoral	1	No	Yes	Yes
		Master's	4	No	Yes	Yes

CONCLUSIONS

Obviously the setting of requirements for entering the practice of psychology has limited the "freedom" of many who would like to practice. It has ended the laissez faire epoch of applied psychology. It has demanded the filing of forms, sending for transcripts, and letters of recommendation. It has required taking examinations, often at long distances from home. It has involved bureaucrats and clerks in the processing of applications and in the enforcement of the laws. It has also demanded the services of hundreds of psychologists in creating examinations, developing examination forms, correcting written examinations, participating in oral examinations, and sitting on disciplinary tribunals. The psychologists enforcing the provisions have for the most part worked voluntarily or for token stipends. The conscious purpose of all this effort is to give the public at least minimum protection from the unqualified psychological practitioner.

REFERENCES

American Psychological Association, Committee on Relations with Psychiatry. Committee on Relations with Psychiatry: 1958 annual report. *American Psychologist*, 1958, *13*, 761–763.

American Psychological Association, Committee on Legislation, & Conference of State Psychological Associations, Committee on Legislation. Joint report of the APA and CSPA Committees on Legislation. *American Psychologist*, 1955, *10*, 727–756.

355

Brandon College, 298
Brannon, E. P., 227, 230
Brayfield, A., 210
Brenman, Margaret, 40, 48
Brigham, A., 247
Brill, A. A., 7, 18
British National Health Service,
    303–311
    See also Great Britain, United
    Kingdom
British Psychological Society, 307,
    310, 329
Britt, S. H., 15–16, 18
BRL Sorting Test, 39
Brodman, K., 172, 173
Brody, E. B., 251, 252
Bronner, Augusta F., 8–9, 12, 14,
    19, 26, 48
Brotemarkle, R. A., 7, 18
Brower, D., 293
Browne, C. G., 155, 160, 161
Buck, J. N., 14, 18
Buechley, R., 171, 173
Bulgaria, 293
Buros, O. K., 155, 161
Butler, J. M., 38, 48

Cahn, E., 237, 240
Cain, I. F., 318, 320
California College of Medicine,
    177
California Test of Personality, 157
Cammer, L. M., 330
Canada, 296–302
    certification of psychologists in,
    126
    psychology in (general picture),
    297
Canadian Psychological Associ-
    ation, 341
Cantril, H., 331
Caplan, G., 222–224, 226
Carleton University (Canada),
    297
Carnegie, D., 286
Case reports in industrial con-
    sultation, 202–204
Catharsis, 40–41, 43
Cattell Infant Scale, 157
Cattell, J. M., 4, 10, 18, 212–214
Cattell, R. B., 32, 48
Central record room, 139
Certification, 68–70, 86–87, 93,
    126, 254 ff., 350–353
    in Canada, 299, 302
    history of, 10
    related to psychologist as ex-
    pert witness, 238–239
Change, in psychotherapy, 43
Characterological approach, 24

Charcot, P., 5
Charles University (Czechoslo-
    vakia), 293
Chauncey, H., 330
Chemotherapy, 115, 292
Child clinical, 93, 108–109
Child guidance, 8, 12–13, 24, 40
    history of, 8, 13
Child guidance clinics, 213
    common-sense principles in,
    39–40
    in Germany, 318–319
Children, disturbed, in the Soviet
    Union, 327
    teaching of, in Israel, 322
Childrens Apperception Test, 157
Children's Clinic of the University
    of Colorado Medical
    Center, 198
Choynowski, M., 293
Civil rights movement, 104
Clancey, I., 167
Clark Committee Report, 101
Clark, J. H., 171, 173
Clark, K. E., 193
Classification of disorders, 31,
    115–116
Client-centered therapy, 25, 41–42
Client vs. patient status, 128–129
Clinical experience, 108
Clinical psychologist, definition
    of, 186
Clinical psychology, changing
    role in society, 7–8, 10–11,
    23–26, 87, 127, 132
    overview, 46–47
Clinical sensitivity in psycho-
    logical evaluation, 278
"Clinical vs. statistical" predic-
    tion controversy, 84
Clinician-teacher, professional-
    service role, 124–125
Clinics, psychological, 3, 7–8,
    11–13, 108
Cohen, J., 172–173
Colleague relationship between
    faculty and student, 120
Color Cube Test, 172
Columbia University, 177
    Teachers College, 133
Combs, A. W., 17–18
Commonwealth Fund, 167
Communication, 145–146
    skills in, 119
Community contacts in juvenile
    corrections, 196
Community mental health, 108,
    120–122
    concerns of, 120
    in Israel, 323–324

Community Mental Health Cen-
    ters Act of 1963, 207
Community mental health educa-
    tion, 187–188
Community as natural laboratory
    for study of man, 145
Community psychology, 103, 108,
    110, 210
Community resources, use of, 118
Competency of psychologists,
    early efforts to control, 10
Comprehensive community men-
    tal health centers, 207–211
Concept Formation Test, 156, 159
Concept of mental illness, 137
    See also Disease entity ap-
    proach to personality,
    Mental disease
Conditioning, 328, 330
Conference on the Professional
    Preparation of Clinical
    Psychologists (Chicago),
    88, 100–101, 103–112, 208
    conditions making for good
    clinical training, 107–108
    diversity in training, 112
    doctoral training models, 107,
    110–112
    professional-psychologist,
    111–112
    psychologist-psychothera-
    pist, 111
    research-clinician, 111
    scientist-professional, 111–
    112
    nature of good training, 108–
    110
    basic core, 108–109
    curriculum, 109
    psychotherapy training, 110
    research training, 109
    selection of students, 109
    self-awareness, 109
    sequence, 109
    problems confronting confer-
    ence, 103–104
    community psychology, 103
    identity as a profession, 103
    mental health needs, 103
    prevention services, 103
    social needs, 103
    professional preparation, 104–
    105
    doctoral training, 106–107
    postdoctoral education, 105–
    106
    subdoctoral graduate educa-
    tion, 105
    undergraduate   education,
    104–105